The Decline of
Constitutional Democracy
in Indonesia

The Decline of Constitutional Democracy in Indonesia

HERBERT FEITH
Professor of Politics
Monash University, Melbourne, Australia

Cornell University Press

Ithaca and London

First published 1962 by Cornell University Press.
Published in the United Kingdom by Cornell University Press Ltd.,
2-4 Brook Street, London W1Y 1AA.

Second printing 1964
Third printing 1968
Fourth printing 1973
Fifth printing 1978

PREPARED UNDER THE AUSPICES OF THE MODERN INDONESIA PROJECT,
SOUTHEAST ASIA PROGRAM, CORNELL UNIVERSITY

International Standard Book Number 0-8014-0126-7
Library of Congress Catalog Card Number 62-19171

PRINTED IN THE UNITED STATES OF AMERICA

For D.
who saw it all from the *kampongs* of Djakarta
and suffered

FOREWORD

DURING the past decade the study of the governments and politics of Southeast Asia has advanced significantly. Today, more and more of those who carry out these studies base them on extensive periods of rigorous research in the field, for which they are well equipped with respect to both knowledge of the area and its language and grounding in the discipline of political science. Because of the general paucity of relevant documentation—a problem which has in recent years become more acute consequent upon the increasing enfetterment of the press in most of the countries of Southeast Asia—such studies can be successful only when they can draw extensively upon interviews and informal discussions. The value of these sources is, of course, very much dependent upon the scholar's being fluent in the indigenous language, sensitive enough to local cultural values and attitudes to gain rapport with the people to whom he talks, and knowledgeable enough of the country's history and current situation to be able to ask the really significant questions. Such requirements may seem obvious, but it has been only in very recent years that they have been met by any respectable proportion of those foreign scholars doing research and writing on Southeast Asia. This book is one of the first to be written by this new generation of scholars; I believe it does honor to this group and augurs well for the quality of the work of its several members who are now completing their research and whose findings should be published during the next few years.

This is the first major study of the postrevolutionary political development of what is now the world's fifth most populous country. It describes and analyzes Indonesian government and politics from the Netherlands' acknowledgment of Indonesia's independence, at the end of 1949, until the overshadowment of parliamentary democracy by Guided Democracy, commencing in 1957. This has been a crucial and formative period. Not only is it intrinsically of importance; but clearly a knowledge of it is essential for an understanding of the present system of Guided Democracy.

Whether or not in modern Indonesia there exist the relevant cultural, social, and economic environment and the political circumstances appropriate for the effective functioning of constitutional democracy has for several years been a central question in the minds of those having a serious interest in the country's political development. And of course an essential complement to this question is an inquiry into the nature of the political processes and institutions incorporated into the rather special system of constitutional democracy attempted in Indonesia. In the course of his comprehensive account of Indonesia's modern political development, Dr. Feith gives major attention to these questions, his account constituting by far the fullest explanation yet to have appeared as to why the variants of constitutional democracy attempted in Indonesia did not function effectively and how it was that the way was opened for the introduction of Guided Democracy. In accomplishing this, he has described the relevant historical background and the social and economic factors which have most decisively influenced the country's political course. The running analysis which accompanies his account should be particularly welcome to those who have tried to understand the kaleidoscopic complexity of Indonesian politics.

In the course of four years of work in Indonesia, Herbert Feith gathered an impressive body of new data, which in itself constitutes an important contribution. The richness of his findings attests to his full fluency in the Indonesian language, his sensitive understanding of Indonesian culture, and the friendship and respect with which he has been regarded by Indonesians—qualities which made it possible for him to talk candidly to so many of them, a source of understanding without which this book could not have been written. Those who know Herbert Feith will be aware that his interest in Indonesia is not merely academic and that he has a profound personal affection for the country and its people. It might therefore be appropriate to mention that I believe his study constitutes a good example of the maxim that a scholar best serves such friendship through frankness of exposition and objectivity of appraisal.

The analysis which Dr. Feith has made of his materials evidences, I believe, a perceptiveness sharpened by substantial training in the social sciences and much serious thought as to the appropriateness of existing methodological approaches. He has endeavored to confront his data with a fresh eye, undertaking to shape his methodology to conform as much as possible to Indonesian realities and attempting to avoid the limitations of those aspects of the conceptual apparatus of political science which do not really fit—an approach shared by an encouraging number of other members of this new generation. In the course of his analysis he has developed several concepts whose applicability, I believe, transcends the Indonesian scene and should prove generally useful in analyzing political processes in other newly independent states of Asia and Africa.

GEORGE McT. KAHIN

Ithaca, New York
August 2, 1962

PREFACE

THIS is a book about Indonesian politics between December 1949 and March 1957. It begins as revolutionary warfare ends and the Netherlands government withdraws from its former colony. It ends as "guided democracy" is being ushered in.

Was this, then, a period of constitutional democracy? I have argued that it was, in a particular sense. The system of politics which operated in those years and finally broke down had six distinct features characteristic of constitutional democracy. Civilians played a dominant role. Parties were of very great importance. The contenders for power showed respect for "rules of the game" which were closely related to the existing constitution. Most members of the political elite had some sort of commitment to symbols connected with constitutional democracy. Civil liberties were rarely infringed. Finally, governments used coercion sparingly. This represented, at the very least, an attempt to maintain and develop constitutional democracy. The attempt was abandoned after 1957, and the political system was then transformed in far-reaching ways affecting each of the six features.

My aim here has been to tell the story of this attempt, presenting it in the setting of the month-to-month development of national politics. I have related it to the work of the seven cabinets of the period, their efforts to solve governmental problems and to maintain their own power and that of their regime. My concern has been particularly with the failure of the attempt, with why it was defeated and abandoned.

I have brought the story to an end on March 14, 1957, the day on which the second cabinet of Ali Sastroamidjojo resigned and martial law was proclaimed for the whole country. This was in a sense merely a halfway point in a process of political transformation which lasted from mid-1956 to mid-1958. There were to be two other major developments—the take-overs of Dutch enterprises in December 1957 and the regionalist rebellion beginning two months later—before the process was completed, before what may be called "guided democracy" came into operation. But the failure of constitutional democracy can be explained in terms of what had unfolded by March 1957. Thus it is only in an epilogue that I have discussed the take-overs of Dutch enterprises and the Sumatra-Sulawesi rebellion. It is also only there, and sketchily, that I have described "guided democracy" as a political system.

In many ways this is a premature study. It rests on virtually no historical perspective. That I have been bold enough to attempt it is a result in part of the encouragement of Professor George McT. Kahin of Cornell University and in part of the availability at Cornell of a rich store of primary source and monographic material on contemporary Indonesian society and politics. It also reflects my conviction that overseas studies of Indonesian problems should be accessible to Indonesians grappling practically with these problems. Nothing would please me more than to have this book interest Indonesians active in government or politics.

The book contains a host of judgments made on inadequate evidence. If I have not always admitted this in the body of the text, not emphasized again and again that my deductions from data are tentative and that the particular subject is one where further research is required, the reasons are aesthetic rather than scholarly. It goes without saying that this is only a preliminary effort at comprehension, preliminary in its tracing of the course of events, and preliminary in the conceptual tools applied to these events. I have attempted to present the story in a way that will make it useful for those who cannot accept the theoretical framework in which I have set it. For the rest I am relying on my critics to set the record straight. The significance of studies of this kind lies largely, after all, in the criticisms they call forth.

The book grew out of a doctoral dissertation presented to Cornell University's Department of Government in 1960. It also grew out of four years of work in Indonesia (June 1951–July 1953 and July 1954–August 1956) and two short visits made since (May to August 1957 and August to December 1961). Finally, it grew out of study I have been able to do as a Research Fellow of the Australian National University since October 1960.

The number of people to whom I am indebted for the opportunities, the trust, the encouragement, the co-operation, the intellectual stimulation, and the friendship which made my book possible is immense. My debt is particularly great to Professor Kahin, who contributed with profound generosity in all these ways. It was he who made it possible for me to study at Cornell University, who suggested this subject for my dissertation, and who as chairman of my Special Committee read each chapter carefully and critically as it was completed, offering numerous suggestions. It is he who established and has directed the Cornell Modern Indonesia Project, which has done so much to stimulate serious study of contemporary Indonesia and bring about co-operative effort by those engaged in such study. A great deal of whatever merit this book may have is a direct result of contact with Professor Kahin and the group of those who have been brought together by him and the Cornell Modern Indonesia Project.

My special thanks go to three other Cornell professors, to John M. Echols and G. William Skinner, who served as members of my Special Committee and as counselors and friends, and to Mrs. Claire Holt, who was always kind and ready with new ideas. Among those who were my fellow graduate students a very large number contributed to the discussion from which this book was born. Here I would like to express gratitude particularly to Hilman Adil, Benedict R. O'G. Anderson, Harsja W. Bachtiar, Ruth Bosma-McVey, I. N. Djajadiningrat, Tapi Omas Ihromi-Simatupang, J. E. Ismael, Kurnianingrat, Daniel S. Lev, Gerald S. Maryanov, David P. Mozingo, Mochtar Naim, Deliar Noer, Giok-Po Oey, Andrea Wilcox Palmer, David H. Penny, Donald H. Pond, Selosoemardjan, John R. W. Smail, Soelaeman Soemardi, Mary F. Somers, Rachmat Subur, John O. Sutter, Giok-Lan Tan, Iskandar Tedjasukmana, and Malcolm R. Willison.

Elsewhere in the United States and in Australia a number of people with specialist knowledge of Indonesian affairs have helped me greatly by their careful critical comments on some or all of the book in one or another draft. In this connection I would like to thank Professors Harry J. Benda, Clifford Geertz, Bruce Glassburner, Hans O. Schmitt, and Justus M. van der Kroef, as well as Messrs. Boyd R. Compton, Donald Hindley, M. A. Jaspan, J. A. C. Mackie, Alexander Shakow, and Kenneth D. Thomas.

Professor W. Macmahon Ball, head of the Department of Political Science at the University of Melbourne, deserves my lasting gratitude for first arousing my interest in Indonesia. I am indebted to Professor J. W. Davidson, of the Department of Pacific History at the Australian National University, for all the help that a kind and thoughtful head of department can give.

For the financial support that made it possible for me to prepare and write this book my gratitude goes to the University of Melbourne's Department of Political Science, which venturesomely paid return fares for my initial trip to Indonesia and then employed me as a Research Fellow between August 1953 and April 1954. It goes also to the Cornell Modern Indonesia Project, which provided me with fellowship funds during the academic year 1956–1957 (in Australia and Indonesia) and the academic year 1957–1958 (at Cornell), to the Rockefeller Foundation, which awarded me a fellowship for the two following academic years, and to my present employer, the Australian National University.

The book is, however, based primarily on what I learned in Indonesia. Here the scope of my indebtedness is even greater. It is impossible to list the large number of people whose friendship and help were involved in the learning process through which I went while in Indonesia. But I can and must say that I was able to collect materials for this study only as a result of the unfailing generosity and helpfulness of my superiors and colleagues at the Ministry of Information and their active support of the research I was doing alongside my office duties. It was those who at various times served as heads of the Information Ministry, notably Roeslan Abdulgani, R. M. Harjoto Judoatmodjo, Suwito Kusumowidagdo, Sumarno, the late Soetomo Djauhar Arifin, Jusuf Abdullah Puar, R. M. Darjanto, and Mr. Tedjo Soemarto, who made it possible for me to travel widely throughout Indonesia and to live in different parts of the archipelago. Such access as I obtained to political leaders was in large part a consequence of the trust which these men placed in me. At the same time, my colleagues, fellow employees of the Ministry, showered kindness upon me and led me into the world of the Indonesian political public.

In addition, I would like to thank all the many others in Indonesia who helped me to obtain information, sift it, and by it come closer to understanding. In particular I am grateful to the authorities of the Ministries of the Interior, Education, and Religious Affairs and to the heads and staff of the Central Electoral Committee. And I would like here to express gratitude also to the administrative officers and staff of the University of Indonesia and of the Institutes of Social Research and Economic and Social Research of the University's Faculties of Law and Economics.

Let me finally thank The Free Press for permission to quote from *The Religion of Java* by Clifford Geertz, the *American Anthropologist* for permission to quote from "Ritual and Social Change: A Javanese Example" by Clifford Geertz (LIX [1957], 32–54), and the Cornell Modern Indonesia Project for permission to quote from *Past and Future* by Mohammad Hatta and *The Office of President in Indonesia as Defined in the Three Constitutions in Theory and Practice* by A. K. Pringgodigdo.

Responsibility for the facts and interpretations which follow rests with me alone, as does responsibility for translations wherever I have provided an English text in quoting from an Indonesian or Dutch source.

HERBERT FEITH

Australian National University
Canberra, Australia
February 1962

One further word of appreciation. I am most grateful to Miss Evelyn Boyce of the Cornell University Press and Mrs. Susan Finch of the Cornell Modern Indonesia Project, both of whom have done a great deal more than their due to bring this book to publication. I am also indebted to Monash University, and particularly to Professor S. R. Davis and Miss Maureen Kelty, for financial and much other support at this final stage, and to Mr. Leigh Scott for preparing the index.

H. F.

September 1962

CONTENTS

MAPS

The Decline of
Constitutional Democracy
in Indonesia

Chapter I

Introduction: *The Heritage of Revolution*

SEVERAL recent theorists have emphasized the importance of the process by which a colonial dependency achieves independence. They argue that the pattern of subsequent political development is crucially affected by the character of this process, more than by the factors which are usually considered when the case is argued in terms of the question "Are they ready for independence?" [1]

INDEPENDENCE THROUGH REVOLUTION

In Indonesia the process was revolutionary. It was by violence, by a process of far-reaching disruption of old social relationships and substitution of new ones, that the Indonesian nation marshaled the strength to force the Netherlands to withdraw from the colony. If this was not a revolution in the same sense in which the word is used for the French, Russian, and Chinese revolutions, it certainly involved a deeper shattering of social foundations than occurred in the independence struggles of any other new nation of the postwar period—with the possible exception of Vietnam.

---

[1] See, for instance, David E. Apter, *The Gold Coast in Transition* (Princeton: Princeton University Press, 1955); S. N. Eisenstadt, "Sociological Aspects of Political Development in Underdeveloped Countries," *Economic Development and Cultural Change*, V, no. 4 (1955–1956), 289–307; and Eisenstadt, "Patterns of Political Leadership and Support," paper submitted to the International Conference on Representative Government and National Progress, Ibadan, Nigeria, 1959 (a paper of the Congress for Cultural Freedom, Paris).

Nor was this pattern of development accidental, a product of mis-understanding or of the fortuitous presence in the Dutch government and the government of the Indonesian Republic of persons with more than usually strong feelings of mutual hostility. There is no doubt that developments in the period of Japanese occupation of Indonesia were of major importance in contributing to the revolutionary character of the transition to independence. But in a sense which is probably even more important this had its roots in the nature of the colonial relation-ship between the two countries.

The Netherlands was more dependent on its colony than any other European colonial power in Asia. It had large investments there, an approximate 2,634 million guilders ($1,422 million) in 1940, earning an annual 191.5 million guilders ($103 million) in interest [2]—a large figure indeed in comparison with the Netherlands population of a little less than nine million. But its dependence cannot be measured in financial terms alone. If the colony was of importance to those in Hol-land whose income was larger because of it, it was of far greater im-portance to Netherlanders who actually lived there. And these were a large number of persons, 208,269 in 1930, the year of the last census.[3] (A probable majority of these were Eurasians of Dutch nationality. The inclusion is not inappropriate, however, at least as far as political atti-tudes are concerned, for the vast majority of Eurasians of Dutch legal status acted politically in support of the colonial tie.) The existence in the Indies of Netherlanders, "pure" and Eurasian, who were neither colonial administrators or technicians nor estate or commercial execu-tives, but "settlers," with their own local culture and cultural institu-tions, suggests parallels with a type of colonial relationship which was otherwise almost nonexistent in Asia—the type found in Southern and Eastern Africa and Algeria.

A third major dimension of Holland's dependence on its colony was the psychological one. The Indies were Holland's only colony of im-portance. With the Indies, Holland was the world's third or fourth colonial power; without them it would be a cold little country on the North Sea. Nor was this simply a jingoists' cause. So much of all that the Netherlands was proud of was in the Indies, so much of its science, its law, its religion, its education, and, of course, the colonial admin-istration in which it took so much pride. Under these circumstances,

---

[2] Sumitro Djojohadikusumo, *Persoalan Ekonomi di Indonesia* ("Economic Prob-lems in Indonesia"; Djakarta: Indira, 1953), pp. 8–9.

[3] *Statistical Pocketbook of Indonesia, 1941* (Batavia: Kolff, 1947), p. 8.

talk of a civilizing mission readily found adherents from among persons of a wide range of social and attitude groups. The paternalism of the post-1901 "Ethical Policy" was self-sustaining. The satisfying belief that the Indonesian wards had need of their guardians was for the most part genuine, and it extended to a large part of the Netherlands population.

It is against a background of economic, personal, and psychological interests of this magnitude that one must see the Netherlands' twentieth-century policies in the Indies. Unlike Britain in the case of India and Burma, and the United States in the case of the Philippines, the Netherlands simply did not accept the necessity of any cession of self-government to Indonesia in the foreseeable future. There were Dutch groups which favored development in the direction of self-government in the not too distant future. Their influence over policy was always sporadic, however, and was particularly slight in the 1930's.

But in Indonesia as elsewhere the socioeconomic contradictions of modern colonialism gave rise to a nationalist movement. By the beginning of this century the period of Indonesia's passive withdrawal in the face of the colonial impact was ending. In the first four decades of the century a small but growing group of Indonesians obtained secondary and higher Western education, partly to meet the needs of the government and the large foreign firms for cheap white-collar and technical personnel. With education there came a new spirit of self-awareness and self-help, a burgeoning of modern organizations of various kinds and, growing out of these, a nationalist political movement. At the same time Indonesians in Sumatra and to a lesser extent in Kalimantan (Borneo) and Sulawesi (Celebes), areas where indigenous entrepreneurship had long traditions which the Dutch had never broken, were adapting themselves to producing for an expanding world market. The rubber (in Sumatra) and copra (in Sulawesi) small-holder industries brought with them the rapid rise of a group of newly rich farmers and traders who also wanted modern education for their children. From this group, which provided much of the soil on which the Islamic reform movement grew in the same period, nationalism received a further body of recruits.[4]

[4] See George McT. Kahin, *Nationalism and Revolution in Indonesia* (Ithaca, N.Y.: Cornell University Press, 1952), pp. 18–100; W. F. Wertheim, *Indonesian Society in Transition* (The Hague: van Hoeve, 1956), pp. 95–116, 140–152; and Robert Van Niel, *The Emergence of the Modern Indonesian Elite* (Chicago: Quadrangle; The Hague: van Hoeve, 1960), pp. 46–72, 100–193.

The initial Dutch reaction to nationalism was mild. The early organizations and parties were subjected to a variety of restrictions, but they nevertheless could organize on a broad basis. The Sarekat Islam (Islamic Association), a militantly nationalist organization, led by merchants, persons of aristocratic origin, and others, many of them people with Western secondary education, was quickly successful in developing both urban and peasant support. By 1916 it had become a large organization, with some hundreds of thousands of members, and its branches functioned actively in many parts of Java, Sumatra, and Sulawesi. Moreover, it played an important part in organizing and uniting trade unions. For four years, between 1917 and 1921, Sarekat Islam was under the influence of Dutch and Indonesian Marxists. The year 1920 saw the birth of the Perserikatan Kommunist di India (Indies Communist Association).

The government's tolerance did not last, however. In the early 1920's, while Communists and anti-Communists fought for control of Sarekat Islam branches, the government intervened increasingly to prevent contact between the urban leaders of the organization and the peasantry. For this reason and others, many of the Sarekat Islam branches disappeared. When a section of the Communist leadership launched short-lived revolts in late 1926 (Batavia, Banten) and early 1927 (West Sumatra), the government panicked and resorted to sharp repression. Some 13,000 persons were arrested and 4,500 of these sentenced. Eight hundred and twenty-three went to Boven Digul, the political prisoners' camp in inland West New Guinea, where many of them remained till World War II intervened.[5] Communist activity was brought to a virtual end, to re-emerge as an important political factor only during the Revolution.

The center of anticolonialist politics now shifted to a third major current which was neither Communist nor specifically Islamic. In mid-1927 a group of students and recent graduates in Bandung, led by the young engineer Soekarno, established the Indonesian Nationalist Party (Partai Nasional Indonesia, PNI). The organization demanded complete independence. To achieve this it urged Indonesian self-reliance, nonco-operation with the Dutch authorities, and the boycotting of government employment.

[5] Kahin, *Nationalism and Revolution*, p. 86, and Van Niel, *op. cit.*, pp. 213–214, 231–236; also Harry J. Benda and Ruth T. McVey, *The Communist Uprisings of 1926–1927 in Indonesia: Key Documents* (Cornell Modern Indonesia Project, Translation Series; Ithaca, N.Y., 1960). For an account of conditions in Digul see S. Sjahrir, *Out of Exile* (New York: John Day, 1949).

The PNI's influence grew rapidly, and in consequence the government in 1929 arrested its leaders and ordered its dissolution. Soekarno was released in 1931, but he was arrested again in 1933 and this time exiled to far Flores. A similar fate befell a number of other prominent leaders, both of Soekarno's party and of other smaller ones. Hatta and Sjahrir, former leaders of the Indonesian Association in the Netherlands, who were later to emerge as leading champions of Western democratic values, spent the years from 1935 to 1942 in exile in Digul and Banda.

The 1930's were a time of polarization of feeling between the Dutch and Indonesian communities in the archipelago. The depression aggravated the already considerable economic competition between the two groups. As more and more Western-educated Indonesians turned from their earlier acceptance of tutelage to a radical and populistic nationalism, so fear grew in the Netherlands community of the Indies, and with it right-wing radicalism and quasi-Nazi organizations. Under Governor-General B. C. de Jonge (1931–1936), who believed that "we have ruled here for 300 years with the whip and the club and we shall still be doing it in another 300 years," [6] radical nationalism was severely repressed and trade unions were kept small and weak.

Moderate nationalist political organizations remained in existence, however. And aspirations of national uplift and eventual national independence were further nurtured as young Indonesians devoted their energies to teaching in small nongovernmental nationalist schools ("wild schools"), establishing co-operatives and social welfare institutions, running organizations for religious reform or cultural regeneration, leading discussion circles or scout groups, and editing dailies and weeklies in Indonesian (the Malay, sponsored and modernized by nationalists as a national language).

The same fears which made the Dutch government restrict and repress nationalist politics inhibited the development of representative government in the colony. In 1918 the government had agreed to the establishment of the Volksraad or People's Council, an advisory body whose membership would be partly nominated and partly elected, but indirectly and on the basis of a small and racially delineated franchise. In 1931 it agreed to admit a majority of Asians—Indonesians and "Foreign Orientals"—to the Council. But beyond this point there was no progress. The Council's wishes could always be overridden by the Governor-General. Most nationalists regarded the body with dis-

[6] Quoted in Sjahrir, *Out of Exile,* p. 112.

trust, and the more radical organizations forbade their members to participate in it.

Thus Indonesians obtained little experience of representative government. What political experience they did obtain under Dutch rule was in the politics of virtually permanent opposition. In the government service Indonesians had little opportunity to exercise leadership. Indeed, the Indonesian regents, bureaucratized aristocrats with territorial jurisdiction, had considerable power. But there were no Indonesian governors, only one Indonesian department head. Of the 3,039 higher-rank civil service positions in 1940, only 221 were held by Indonesians.[7] The armed forces were virtually closed to Indonesians till shortly before the Japanese attack, unless they were from specially privileged areas like Minahasa in North Sulawesi and Ambon in the Moluccas. Only a handful of Indonesians were allowed to rise above the rank of captain.

In 1936 the People's Council called for a conference to discuss plans for the development of Indonesia over a ten-year period toward self-government within the limits of the existing Dutch constitution. But the request was rejected by the Netherlands government. Even after the Nazi invasion of Holland in 1940, Indonesian nationalists were offered no more than a vague promise of reorganization in relations between the Netherlands and the Indies after the war.

Thus when the Japanese inflicted their quick defeat on the Dutch in early 1942 and moved in to occupy the archipelago, the most general reaction of Indonesian nationalism was one of applause.

The three and a half years of Japanese military occupation brought the most momentous changes; their catalytic effects were even greater. First came a large-scale turnover of government personnel. The Dutch were publicly humiliated and sent to camps; Japanese replaced them in the higher positions and Indonesians in the lower. Then came the change to a war economy. Export agriculture was unnecessary, and the estates were switched to production of rice. At the same time, regional autarchy was introduced and residencies, subdivisions of provinces, were forced to be self-sufficient. Forced labor recruitment, large-scale confiscations of food, and arbitrary beatings became regular practice.

In complete contrast to the Dutch, the Japanese sponsored political organization on a large scale.[8] Through a variety of semimilitary mass

[7] Kahin, *Nationalism and Revolution*, p. 34.

[8] See Harry J. Benda, *The Crescent and the Rising Sun* (The Hague: van Hoeve, 1958), pp. 103 ff.; Willard H. Elsbree, *Japan's Role in Southeast Asian Nationalist*

organizations, some specifically for young people and others not, some specifically for Moslems and others not, they spread a militant anti-Westernism through the entire population. At the same time they pressed popular leaders of the nationalist movement and of Moslem organizations into service in propaganda and labor recruitment. This did not, however, discredit these leaders; on the contrary, it greatly strengthened them, for they were given unprecedented access to the peasantry and allowed to foster nationalist aspirations among them. Japanese encouragement of the Indonesian language added further to the potential strength of nationalism.

But of greatest importance for the future was the Japanese policy of training Indonesian soldiers. Afraid of Allied landings and pressed by the Indonesian leaders' clamorings for arms and training, the Japanese agreed in late 1943 to the creation of small auxiliary forces under Japanese officers. By the time of the Japanese surrender some 62,000 Indonesians were trained in the Peta (Volunteer Army of Defenders of the Fatherland) and Heiho, the auxiliary corps established earlier. Two hundred and thirty thousand others had been drilled, disciplined, and indoctrinated (but armed only with bamboo spears) in several para-military youth organizations. The great majority of these were in Java,[9] and the rest in Sumatra and Bali.

In September 1944, when the Japanese were being forced to retreat from much of the South Pacific, they promised Indonesian independence "in the near future" and relaxed many of their earlier restrictions on the propagation of Indonesian nationalism. At the same time, they began to open high administrative posts to Indonesians, both to persons from the old aristocratic civil service and to some of the younger group of nationalist intellectuals. In March 1945 they allowed the establishment of an Investigating Committee for Indonesian Independence, with a membership representative of several of the main currents of the nationalist movement, and this committee worked on a draft constitution for the projected independent Indonesia.[10]

When the end of the war came on August 15, preparations for the

---

Movements (Cambridge, Mass.: Harvard University Press, 1953), pp. 76 ff.; M. A. Aziz, *Japan's Colonialism and Indonesia* (The Hague: Nijhoff, 1955), pp. 194 ff.; and Wertheim, *op. cit.*, pp. 152 ff.

[9] Aziz, *op. cit.*, p. 230; Guy J. Pauker, *The Role of the Military in Indonesia* (research memorandum; Santa Monica, Calif.: Rand Corporation, 1960), pp. 7–13.

[10] For verbatim reports of many of the meetings of the committee see Muhammad Yamin, ed., *Naskah Persiapan Undang-Undang Dasar 1945* ("Documents on the Preparation of the 1945 Constitution"; Djakarta: Jajasan Prapantja, 1959). For a full discussion see Benedict R. O'G. Anderson, *Some Aspects of Indonesian Poli-*

granting of Japanese-style independence were far advanced. But the new situation beckoned Indonesians to seize the initiative. Thus on August 17 Soekarno and Hatta, acting in conjunction with a group of youth leaders, proclaimed the Republic of Indonesia.

Within three weeks the new Republic, of which Soekarno became President and Hatta Vice-President, had a temporary constitution, an advisory Central National Committee of 135 men, a cabinet responsible to the President, and the support of virtually every group in Indonesian society, including the small anti-Japanese underground contact organizations. Before the end of September it had succeeded in obtaining large quantities of Japanese arms and in establishing a functioning administration in most parts of the country.[11]

Then came the Allied troops, first of all the British. They arrived in Java at a time of considerable violence, a time when Indonesians were using all means at their disposal to take what arms and local power the Japanese still held. When a short while later Dutch troops began to land under British cover, the situation became both chaotic and explosive. Toward the end of the year, as Dutch troops were landed in other parts of the country, widespread fighting developed—in most areas of Java and many parts of Sumatra and Bali.

Major political changes now developed inside the Republic. In October and November power shifted from the group of older nationalists who had sat on the Investigating Committee for Indonesian Independence to a young group under the influence of the underground leaders Sjahrir and Mr. Amir Sjarifuddin.[12] Constitutional pro-

---

tics under the Japanese Occupation: 1944–1945 (Cornell Modern Indonesia Project, Interim Reports Series; Ithaca, N.Y., 1961), pp. 16–42.

[11] For a fascinating discussion of the events of these few weeks see Anderson, *op. cit.*, pp. 65–126. The full-scale history of the Revolution is Kahin, *Nationalism and Revolution;* see also Charles Wolf, Jr., *The Indonesian Story* (New York: John Day, 1948); C. Smit, *De Indonesische Quaestie* (Leiden: Brill, 1952); and Alastair M. Taylor, *Indonesian Independence and the United Nations* (Ithaca, N.Y.: Cornell University Press, 1960).

[12] The title "Mr." (Meester) was and is used by graduates in law; the degree is comparable to that of Master of Laws. Engineering, Architecture, Agriculture, and Forestry graduates at approximately the same level use the title "Ir." (Ingenieur), and graduates in Economics, "Indology" (Netherlands Indies Studies), and Literature at this level are called "Drs." (Doctorandus). The title "Dr." is used by medical and dental graduates, occasionally by those with less than full university qualifications (who are strictly "Dokter" rather than "Doctor"), and also by holders of higher degrees in one of the other fields. When a person has a doctorate or holds a professorship, two or three titles may be used together, as in the case of the late Professor Mr. Dr. Supomo. These Dutch academic titles con-

cedures were completely overhauled, with the advisory Central National Committee being transformed into a legislative body and the presidential cabinet under Soekarno replaced by a parliamentary one under Sjahrir. At the same time the government called for the establishment of parties, and these quickly came into existence.

Soekarno, Hatta, and Sjahrir negotiated with the British and the Dutch, but they had no way to prevent the entry of large numbers of Dutch soldiers. In the course of 1946 the Netherlands established control over a number of cities and surrounding areas in Java and Sumatra, though the great majority of the people of these two islands continued to be governed by the Republic. Outside them the Dutch were more successful, being able to suppress most of the nationalist resistance and, with the help of Indonesian princely and aristocratic groups, to exercise governmental functions.

In Java and Sumatra, Republican military power—the power of the army and of numerous irregular bands recruited from former members of Japanese-sponsored mass organizations—remained great. But the Sjahrir government had made tremendous concessions, and political opposition to it was strong. This came to a head in the "July 3 affair" of 1946—an abortive attempt by the national-communist Tan Malaka and a politically heterogeneous group of associates to stage a *coup d'état*.[13]

Sjahrir's government, surviving the challenge, continued to negotiate with the Dutch.[14] At the end of November 1946, British pressure on the two parties resulted in the signing of the Linggadjati Agreement, by which the Netherlands agreed to recognize the Republic as the *de facto* authority in Java and Sumatra and to co-operate with it

---

tinue to be used by their holders, as do most religious titles, especially "K." (Kijaji, Islamic religious teacher) and "H." (Hadji, one who has made the pilgrimage to Mecca), the Protestant "Ds." (Domine, Reverend) and "Pt." (Pendeta, Reverend), and the Catholic "Pater" and "Pastoor." On the other hand, there is a marked disinclination among many holders of aristocratic titles to use them. Some, however, were used widely in our period, for instance, the Javanese "R." (Raden) and "R.M." (Raden Mas) and the Minangkabau "St." (Sutan).

[13] On the "July 3 affair" see Kahin, *Nationalism and Revolution*, pp. 147–195. See also *Putusan Mahkamah Tentara Agung Republik Indonesia di Djogjakarta tgl. 27 Mei 1948* ("Decision of the Military Supreme Court of the Republic of Indonesia at Jogjakarta, May 27, 1948"; Djakarta [?]: van Dorp, 1949), and Muhammad Yamin, *Sapta Dharma, Patriotisme Indonesia* ("The Seven Duties, Indonesian Patriotism"; Medan: Islamijah, 1950).

[14] See Idrus Nasir Djajadiningrat, *The Beginnings of the Indonesian-Dutch Negotiations and the Hoge Veluwe Talks* (Cornell Modern Indonesia Project, Monograph Series; Ithaca, N.Y., 1957).

toward the achievement by January 1949 of a sovereign federal Indonesia, to exist within a "heavy" Netherlands-Indonesian Union. But this agreement, which was strongly criticized on both sides, was little more than an agreement to agree. It provided few answers to immediate problems and frictions. Military clashes continued.

By July 1947 the Dutch had 150,000 soldiers in Indonesia. Then, charging the Republic with failure to comply with the Linggadjati Agreement, they launched a full-scale armed attack on parts of its territory. India and Australia lodged protests against this action with the United Nations Security Council, which, however, merely called for a cessation of hostilities and established a three-man Good Offices Committee to help toward a resolution of the conflict. The Dutch were permitted to retain the areas which they had been successful in wresting from the Republic; these included a number of important estate, mining, and surplus food-producing areas in Java and Sumatra. When in January 1948 the pressure of the United States chairman of the Good Offices Committee resulted in the signing of a second negotiated agreement, the Renville Agreement, the terms merely reflected the weaker military position of the Republic. By this time the Dutch had control of more than half of Java and most of the densely populated areas of Sumatra. There, as in Kalimantan and East Indonesia, they were establishing formally autonomous states, which, on the Dutch interpretation of the Linggadjati Agreement, would join with the Republic in the projected Indonesian federation.[15]

Meanwhile Sjahrir had left the prime ministership. Under his successor, Amir Sjarifuddin, the leader of the left wing of the Socialist Party whose right wing was led by Sjahrir, the PKI (Partai Komunis Indonesia, Indonesian Communist Party) and groups of similar outlook grew in power. In part this resulted from the bad economic conditions attendant on the Dutch blockade of Republican territory and the influx of large numbers of refugees from Dutch-held areas. After the signing of the Renville Agreement in January 1948, Amir's cabinet fell and was replaced by one led by Hatta, a cabinet composed mainly of ministers of the Moslem Masjumi and the nationalist PNI. Soon afterward there developed strong tensions between this cabinet and the Front Demokrasi Rakjat (People's Democratic Front), a pro-

---

[15] On the development of the Dutch-established federal states see A. Arthur Schiller, *The Formation of Federal Indonesia* (The Hague: van Hoeve, 1955). Cf. Kahin, *Nationalism and Revolution,* pp. 351 ff., and H. J. van Mook, *The Stakes of Democracy in South-East Asia* (London: Allen and Unwin, 1959), pp. 219 ff.

Communist coalition under Amir Sjarifuddin's leadership. As always, the opposition attacked the government for making too great concessions to the Dutch.

In August 1948 Musso, a leader of the Communists in the 1920's, returned dramatically from a long exile in Russia and quickly succeeded in merging the People's Democratic Front into an expanded Communist Party of which he assumed leadership. The situation came to a head on September 18 when a group of second-echelon Communist leaders at Madiun in East Java proclaimed a revolt against the Soekarno-Hatta government. The uprising lasted little more than a month, but bloody battles were fought before the Republican government suppressed it. Musso was killed in action; Amir Sjarifuddin and a number of other important leaders were subsequently executed. Indonesian communism suffered an important setback.[16]

In December 1948 the Dutch launched a second major attack on the Republic. With artillery and air support they quickly captured the Republic's capital, Jogjakarta in Central Java, and took most of its top leaders, including Soekarno and Hatta, to exile on the island of Bangka, off Sumatra. Further, they succeeded in establishing control over all the cities and larger towns in Java and almost all of those in Sumatra, though certainly not of the surrounding village areas or the road system. This was to be the knockout blow for the Republic. After a military victory, the Dutch hoped to establish a federal Indonesia on terms entirely their own.[17]

But the Dutch calculations, diplomatic, political, and military, were far wrong. The Security Council's reaction this time was very much stronger than it had been to the first "police action." In part this reflected a stronger reaction on the part of much of world opinion. In particular it reflected Asian reactions, as given political focus by the Inter-Asian Relations Conference on Indonesia, called by Nehru and held in New Delhi, January 20–23, 1949. But even more important was the change in the position of the United States, which now pressed actively for a pro-Indonesian resolution. This resulted in part from the new Asian emphasis in U.S. State Department thinking—the reap-

[16] Kahin, *Nationalism and Revolution*, pp. 256–303. See also Ruth T. McVey, *The Soviet View of the Indonesian Revolution* (Cornell Modern Indonesia Project, Interim Reports Series; Ithaca, N.Y., 1957), pp. 58–83.

[17] These were the terms of the act entitled Bewind Indonesia in Overgangstijd (Government of Indonesia during the Period of Transition), generally termed the "BIO Decree." See Kahin, *Nationalism and Revolution*, pp. 386–390, and Schiller, *op. cit.*, pp. 54–56.

praisal following major Communist victories in China—and in part also from a change in the department's attitude toward the Indonesian Republic, after the Republic had shown itself ready and able to suppress a Communist revolt.

Thus on January 28 the Security Council passed a U.S.-sponsored resolution ordering the Dutch to restore the Republican leaders to Jogjakarta and to co-operate with them in arranging elections for an Indonesian Constituent Assembly by October 1949 and for the transfer of sovereignty to a "United States of Indonesia" by July 1950. Moreover, it created field machinery, the UN Commission for Indonesia, with sufficient powers to resolve basic issues in the Dutch-Indonesian conflict. In this commission, as in its predecessor, the Good Offices Committee, the United States member held the balance of power (as between his Australian and Belgian fellow members, the nominees of Indonesia and Holland respectively). But by this time the U.S. role was very different from what it had been earlier.

In terms of intra-Indonesian politics too, the Dutch had been over-confident when they launched their attack. It was a severe blow to them when the cabinets of the two most populous of their federal states, East Indonesia and Pasundan, resigned in protest against the attack on the Republic. From this point on the hitherto rather puppet like federal states, and their organization the BFO (Bijeenkomst voor Federaal Overleg, Federal Consultative Assembly), moved closer and closer to a position of partnership with the Republic.

Moreover, early in the new year the military situation in Java and Sumatra had turned to the Republic's advantage. In the first months of 1949 its army and irregular formations were making an all-out effort. This not only made it virtually impossible for the Dutch to administer the territory they had newly acquired; it also created major new difficulties for them in areas from which Republican troops had withdrawn after the signing of the Renville Agreement and to which they now returned. The Dutch, ostensible victors, were beleaguered in all the territory they held. The December attack, desperate gamble that it was, had failed and run them aground.

The months between March and June saw a crucial turning of the tide. The vigor of Republican resistance and the effectiveness of scorched-earth policies resulted in major changes in the attitudes of the Dutch business groups in Indonesia. This, combined with strong U.S. Senate and administration pressure on The Hague (including the threat of suspension of Marshall Aid), finally persuaded Holland to change its policies basically. By May or June 1949, it had accepted the necessity of transferring complete sovereignty and transferring it to an Indonesia which, though federal in constitutional form, would be Republican in political reality.[18] It was difficult for the Dutch to resign themselves to this, but they had tried virtually every alternative course. And in this way they would at least get American support for the protection of their Indonesian investments.

The Roem–van Royen Agreement called for the transfer of power to be based on the results of a Round Table Conference at The Hague between the Republic, the BFO, and the Netherlands. In preparation for this conference the Republic and the BFO held extended meetings in July and August, at which most of the ground lines were drawn for the distribution of power in the new state. Formally the two bodies negotiated on a basis of equality, but with the removal of Dutch power in the offing, the political balance was heavily in favor of the Republic. In the new Republic of the United States of Indonesia (RUSI) the fifteen BFO states together would have 100 members in a House of Representatives of 150 and 30 members in a Senate of 32. But on the other hand the Republican army would form the core of the federation's army and no member state would have the right to separate military forces.[19] Informally it was agreed that President Soekarno of the Republic would be the head of the new state and that Hatta, Prime Minister of the Republic, would head its first cabinet.[20]

On August 1 the Republic and the Netherlands came to a cease-fire agreement. The Revolution, or this military phase of it, was virtually over. From August 23 to November 2 negotiations went on at the Round Table Conference at The Hague. There plans were finalized.

[18] See the text of the May 7 "Roem–van Royen Agreement" and the June 22 joint statement of the Netherlands, the BFO and the Republic, entitled "Meeting of Minds on the Holding of the Round Table Conference," in Ministry of Information, *Illustrations of the Revolution, 1945–50* (2d ed.; Djakarta: Ministry of Information, Republic of Indonesia, 1954), Appendix, pp. xliv–xlvi. On this period generally see T. B. Simatupang, *Laporan dari Banaran* ("A Report from Banaran"; Djakarta: Pembangunan, 1960).

[19] For the text of the agreement reached at these Inter-Indonesian conferences see Kementerian Penerangan (Ministry of Information), *Republik Indonesia, Daerah Istimewa Jogjakarta* ("The Special Territory of Jogjakarta of the Republic of Indonesia"; Djakarta: Kementerian Penerangan, 1953), pp. 310–320.

[20] *Keng Po* (Djakarta), July 19, 23, 25, 1949, and *Mimbar Indonesia* (Djakarta weekly: this is to be distinguished from the Djakarta daily established in 1952; all references here will be to the weekly unless otherwise specified), Aug. 6, 1949, quoted in John R. W. Smail, "The Formation of the Hatta R.U.S.I. Cabinet" (unpublished monograph, Cornell Modern Indonesia Project, 1958), pp. 14–15.

The Netherlands would "unconditionally and irrevocably [transfer] complete sovereignty over Indonesia" to the Republic of the United States of Indonesia.

Politically the transfer was not to be unconditional. Indeed, political conditions were the principal subject of discussions at The Hague. The outcome of the Round Table Conference was regarded as relatively favorable to Indonesia, more favorable at least than had been expected at the time of the Roem–van Royen talks in May when the Republic had agreed to participate in such a conference at The Hague. But conditions there were, and they were sharply resented in Indonesia.

In negotiations on the matter of a continuing special association between Holland and the new federation, the Indonesian delegations had a measure of success. It was agreed that the Netherlands-Indonesian Union to be formed would be "light," a mere consultative arrangement. Its Secretariat, its Court of Arbitration, and its projected biannual ministerial conferences would acquire political importance only as both goverements agreed to it. The Dutch crown as head of the Union would have no substantive powers, its role being defined with piety but vagueness as "effectuating the spirit of voluntary and lasting cooperation between the partners." [21] Reluctant as the Indonesian delegations were to agree to this arrangement of symbols, they regarded the formulation as a victory for themselves.

But on the other principal constitutional issue, West New Guinea (or West Irian), the conference ended in a victory for the Netherlands. It had proved impossible to break the deadlock between Dutch and Indonesians on this point. Perhaps the Dutch public could indeed not be pressed further with impunity; it is possible that a surrender of sovereignty over all the old colony would have involved the Dutch government in too great a risk of being disavowed by its parliament, or at least of not obtaining the two-thirds majority support in the First Chamber which was necessary to ratify the conference's results. Alternatively it may be that Holland would have come to terms with the two Indonesian delegations if the deadlock possibility had not been opened to it by the UN Commission for Indonesia (which mediated actively during the last weeks of the conference) and particularly by its United States and Australian members. Finally, the two Indo-

[21] See United Nations Commission for Indonesia, *Special Report to the Security Council on the Round Table Conference*, UN Security Council Document S/1417, Nov. 10, 1949, vol. II, p. 72. See also Taylor, *op. cit.*, pp. 230 ff.

nesian delegations agreed that "the status quo of the Residency of New Guinea shall be maintained with the stipulation that within a year from the date of transfer of sovereignty . . . the question of the political status of New Guinea be determined through negotiations" between RUSI and the Netherlands.[22]

In the military field also the Indonesian delegations had to cede prerogatives. The Netherlands would "attempt" to withdraw its 80,000 Royal Army (KL) troops from Indonesia within six months of the transfer of sovereignty. The 65,000-man (Royal Netherlands Indies Army (KNIL) would be dissolved, with RUSI accepting those of its Indonesian members who sought to serve in its armed forces. In addition, a Netherlands Military Mission of 600 men would be stationed in Indonesia to help train the RUSI forces.

But the most important Indonesian concessions were made in the fields of economics and finance. In the first place RUSI was to accept Netherlands Indies debts to the sum of 4,300 million Dutch guilders, of which 1,291 million guilders ($339 million) was external debt and thus to be repaid in foreign currency. This was in Indonesian eyes tantamount to paying for most of the four years of Netherlands military campaigns against the Republic. Moreover, the new state would be obliged to consult with the Netherlands in policy making in various financial fields in which Dutch interests were involved, in particular the exchange rate and the regulation of coinage and of the position of the central bank (private, Dutch). In addition, RUSI would extend a number of general guarantees to Dutch investors in Indonesia, acknowledging virtually all the rights, concessions, and licenses granted to private bodies by the Netherlands Indies government. Expropriation would be possible only on the basis of indemnification determined by mutual agreement or by a court of law, on the basis of the real value of the expropriated property.[23]

It was on this basis that Indonesia became free. Independence was achieved as a result of both fighting and negotiation. As most of the Indonesian leadership saw it, it came through a Revolution which was brought to a halt by a compromise solution. The effects of this course

[22] See Robert C. Bone, *The Dynamics of the Western New Guinea (Irian Barat) Problem* (Cornell Modern Indonesia Project, Interim Reports Series; Ithaca, N.Y., 1958), pp. 61, 56–73, and Taylor, *op. cit.*, pp. 235 ff.

[23] See Kahin, *Nationalism and Revolution*, pp. 438–445; Taylor, *op. cit.*, pp. 239–251, 479–481; and Hans O. Schmitt, "Some Monetary and Fiscal Consequences of Social Conflict in Indonesia, 1950–58" (doctoral dissertation, University of California, Berkeley, 1959), pp. 42–49.

were felt in every aspect of social, economic, and political life in the period 1949–1957.

Perhaps the most important effect of the revolutionary course was fast social change. Indonesian society in 1950 was vastly different from what it had been in 1942, because of the tumultuous changes wrought by the Japanese occupation and particularly the Revolution.

Dutch colonialism, in higher degree than most other forms, had based itself on the conservation and strengthening of traditional bases of authority. It was from this that the undeniable welfare effects of its agrarian policies flowed: there was no sudden disorganization of rural life in the Netherlands Indies, no large amount of absentee lordlordism. But the impact of the Western economy on the Indies, particularly its long and intensive impact on Java, had long undermined the older bases of authority. In Geertz's words, "The commercialization of Javanese agriculture had knocked most of the props from under traditional Javanese social organization." [24] Yet colonialism could permit no other basis, granted the basic imperialist motivation, "the wish to bring a people's products into the world economy, but not the people themselves, to have one's economic cake and eat it too, by producing 'capitalist' goods with 'pre-capitalist' workers on 'pre-capitalist' land." [25]

Thus local particularism was encouraged and respect urged for tradition and its bearers. At the national level, society was divided along racial caste lines and efforts were made to prevent the development of a common modern framework of country-wide social solidarity. The Indies afforded a striking illustration of what Eisenstadt calls the basic contradiction in colonial systems: "On the one hand attempts were made to establish broad modern administrative, political and economic settings, while on the other hand these changes were to be based on relatively unchanged sub-groups and on traditional attitudes and loyalties." [26]

With the collapse of the Dutch in the face of the Japanese armies, the colonial brace within which traditional relationships had been maintained was removed. Japanese military government operated through the same relationships at certain points, but at others it rode

[24] Clifford Geertz, "The Javanese Village," in G. William Skinner, ed., *Local, Ethnic and National Loyalties in Village Indonesia: A Symposium* (Yale University, Southeast Asia Studies, Cultural Reports Series; New Haven, Conn., 1959), p. 36.

[25] Clifford Geertz, *The Social Context of Economic Change: An Indonesian Case Study* (Cambridge, Mass.: Center for International Studies, M.I.T., 1956), p. 40.

[26] Eisenstadt, "Sociological Aspects of Political Development," p. 292.

over them roughshod. Moreover, the shock of the sudden transition, the extraordinarily arbitrary behavior of the Japanese, the runaway inflation, and the development of mass organizations and propaganda, all these disrupted the traditional organization of society.[27]

With the Japanese collapse the authority structure was shaken anew. A vacuum of power suddenly appeared, as it became clear that the Japanese occupants of virtually all important posts had abdicated authority. And the filling of the vacuum by Indonesians involved a complete restructuring of political and social relations.

Thus the Revolution was born. In the cities and towns power passed quickly to young Indonesian nationalists from the military and political organizations of the occupation period and to university and high school students. In many of the villages, especially in Java, there was a rapid turnover of officials, with power passing from the older traditionally and locally oriented heads to younger men more amenable to modern and nationalist ideas. The very openness of the situation, and the fact that most local and regional developments were beyond the control of the central leadership of the Revolution, meant that the scramble for power, between both groups and individuals, was intense. But at the same time nationalism provided new bases of social integration. The new parties, trade unions and peasant organizations which sprang up as part of the competition for power, served at the same time to establish new patterns of loyalty and authority. And the conditions of military and political warfare resulted in a powerful sense of collective solidarity which checked the divisive effects of active group competition.

These conditions, moreover, produced a significant closening of interclass and urban-rural ties. The guerrilla fighters, many of them townsmen, were proudly welcomed by the villagers. Between student soldiers, teachers, and propagandists on the one hand and villagers on the other, there developed an unprecedented degree of social solidarity. With all these changes came the rapid development of a new self-respect, a new dignity, collective and individual, which spread from the towns to many parts of the peasant population.[28]

The nationalist struggle brought forth enormous creative energy.

[27] Wertheim, *op. cit.*, pp. 152–157.

[28] These aspects of the Revolution are depicted in the work of the schools of literature and painting which are generally grouped together as Angkatan '45 (the 1945 Generation). For a sociological treatment by an active participant see Selosoemardjan, *Social Changes in Jogjakarta* (Ithaca, N.Y.: Cornell University Press, 1962). See also Kahin, *Nationalism and Revolution*, pp. 47–73, and Wertheim, *op. cit.*, pp. 157–163.

Individual achievement became the basis of prestige in many sectors of society—and there was a great deal of individu. l achievement. For the educated youth in particular, the challenges and opportunities were tremendous. It was they, persons under 30, who came to hold most of the positions of leadership in the army and bureaucracy. From the strenuous and intense life of some of this group there came an extraordinary artistic blossoming, particularly in the fields of poetry and painting. For these various reasons the Revolution was a peculiarly central personal experience for all those who were actively involved in it.

At the same time, the developments of 1945–1949 had an important leveling effect in society. The bargaining position of labor was considerably strengthened, partly as a result of government policy. In the villages, inflation wiped out much of the peasant debt, and outright repudiation of debts to Chinese moneylenders was widespread.[29] The government of the Republic made virtually no effort to collect its own land tax. In addition, there was a considerable transfer of wealth from urban white-collar groups to the richer peasants, as urban Republicans sold their belongings in order to be able to buy food.

Many of these changes, however, developed only in Java, or in Java and parts of Sumatra. In Kalimantan and East Indonesia, it must be recalled, the Dutch had been able to re-establish their power against relatively little organized resistance, and again with the assistance of traditional and aristocratic elements.

The difference is explained in good part by the different pattern of administration in these areas in the period of Japanese occupation. In Kalimantan and East Indonesia it was not the Japanese army, but the navy, which had held power, and it had accorded Indonesians few administrative opportunities and no militia-type training. There were, moreover, important differences in earlier historical conditioning. In an over-all sense one may say that the Dutch impact on society outside Java was superficial compared with its effect on the central island. In general the bearers of traditional social authority, including kinship heads and the heads of some hundreds of petty principalities, continued to command positive loyalties in large areas of society. There was not the same acute need as in Java for new bases of social organization and orientation.[30]

Whatever the explanation, it is important to note that fact—the

[29] Kahin, *Nationalism and Revolution,* pp. 473–475.
[30] Geertz, "The Javanese Village," pp. 34–41.

years of Revolution, exacting as they did an unprecedented sense of all-Indonesian social solidarity, saw the development at the same time of a political and administrative bifurcation on territorial lines. The intensity of nationalism in Kalimantan and East Indonesia was certainly great. But Dutch power there was for the moment established, and so nationalists had to keep within the narrow range of political activities permitted by the Dutch—or go to jail. Many did indeed go to jail, and others joined the groups of mountain guerrillas which operated in South Kalimantan, South Sulawesi, and Minahasa in North Sulawesi. But the great majority of nationalist political leaders in these areas co-operated with the Netherlands authorities to some degree, as civil servants or as parliamentary or cabinet officers of the BFO states.

Thus there was very little contact between nationalists in Kalimantan and East Indonesia and the Republican leadership in Java. But indeed it was not only from the BFO states in Kalimantan and East Indonesia that the Jogjakarta leaders were separated. Because of a careful Dutch blockade they were cut off also from their own administrations in Sumatra. Although Sumatra was a largely Republican island, its relationship to the Republic's capital was loose in the extreme. In matters of strategy, financing, and currency, the Sumatran Republican government set its own course.[31]

THE REVOLUTIONARY LEADERSHIP

If the period of revolution created a geographical multiplicity of patterns of politics and Administration, its divisive effects were felt equally at the level of the incipient nation's leadership. Not only did no single nationalist party lead the country through the critical last years of the achievement of independence. The long-standing divisions in the leadership grew in depth in the course of these years.

This fact was scarcely noticeable at the time of the transfer of sovereignty. The year 1949, and particularly the second half of the year, had seen the Soekarno-Hatta duumvirate dominate the political scene of the Republic, Hatta as chief negotiator and policy maker and Soekarno as chief architect of the revolutionary movement's integration. The two men were working closely together. Relations between them and the leaders of the BFO states had grown warmer than ever before. But this unity resulted in large part from the magnetic effect

[31] See George McT. Kahin, "Indonesia," in Kahin, ed., *Major Governments of Asia* (Ithaca, N.Y.: Cornell University Press, 1958), p. 514.

of imminent victory. With a Hatta-led government about to take power in all Indonesia, hostile groups had every incentive to sheathe their antagonisms. The antagonisms existed, however, and were deep.

The central leaders of the Republic were divided in some important aspects of outlook and perception not only from those who co-operated enthusiastically with Dutch authority, but also from the large group of nationalist-oriented persons who co-operated because of the necessity to have employment. Indeed, they were in some degree divided also from the nonco-operating nationalists in the BFO areas, from those involved in underground "shadow governments" in Dutch-held cities, and from the guerrillas and those in jail.

But of greater importance were the divisions within the central leadership of the Republic. These had important historical roots. The prewar nationalist movement had always been divided. From the very beginning there had been numerous nationalist parties, most of them small and some mutually hostile. There were divisions between those who permitted their members to be government servants and those who condemned all forms of co-operation with the colonial regime, between those who sought to establish mass-based organizations and those who concentrated on cadre formation, and between those who emphasized practical tasks of social and economic uplift and those who did not.

Communism was an important issue dividing the movement in the late 1910's and early 1920's. And, most important of all, acrimonious disagreements developed in the late 1920's and the 1930's between specifically Moslem organizations, which presented Islam as the proper basis for a free and regenerated Indonesia, and others who believed nationalism was itself the ideological key to cultural regeneration and who sought to have a secular or broadly theistic or pantheistic basis for the Indonesian state-to-be.

Three major attempts were made, in 1922, 1927, and 1938, to federate the various organizations and bring them into closer association with one another, but none had more than short-lived success. The story of nationalist political life in this period is in fact one of repeated splits.[32] None of the larger parties or federations succeeded

[32] See Roeslan Abdulgani, *Funksi Penerangan di Indonesia* ("The Function of Information Work in Indonesia"; Djakarta: Kementerian Penerangan, 1953), pp. 81–112. See also A. K. Pringgodigdo, *Sedjarah Pergerakan Rakjat Indonesia* ("History of the Indonesian People's Movement"; Djakarta: Pustaka Rakjat, 1950); L. M. Sitorus, *Sedjarah Pergerakan Kebangsaan Indonesia* ("History of the Indonesian Nationalist Movement"; Djakarta: Pustaka Rakjat, 1951); J. Th. Petrus

in establishing broadly based organization, such as might have offset the tendency for the leaders to regroup themselves in narrower clique-like formations in which relationships of trust and authority were sustained by face-to-face contact.

This instability of party organization resulted in part from the frequent jailings and exilings of leaders and in part from the fact that the parties had almost no rewards to distribute, being denied a significant place in the existing constitutional order. In part, too, it resulted from the nationalists' exposure to the pattern of political life in the Netherlands, with its multiplicity of small parties, and more particularly from the encouragement given to small parties by the proportional representation system which was operative in elections for the People's Council in the Indies. Finally, the multiplicity of small parties reflected the variety of value orientations prevailing in different ethnic and communal segments of the colony. But whatever the causes, it is a fact that the nationalist movement failed to develop the type of organizational cohesion and machinery for the settlement of conflicts which existed in the Indian Congress Party and the Philippine Nacionalista Party at the time.

The Japanese occupation undid some of the earlier bases of division in the nationalist leadership, but at the same time it created new ones. In the first place, little or no communication existed between nationalists in the three zones into which Indonesia was divided, the two army zones of Java and Sumatra (the latter for a time administered from Singapore) and the navy zone of Kalimantan and East Indonesia. Secondly, nationalists were treated differently in the different areas, repressed in the navy areas and to some extent in Sumatra, used as a tool in Java, and helped in their own endeavors to the extent that they were associated with the navy's liaison office in Djakarta (an office headed by men with a genuine sympathy for Indonesian nationalist aspirations). In Java, moreover, the Japanese used and aggravated divisions between the Islamic leaders on the one hand and on the other hand the main body of the co-operating nationalist leadership, including Soekarno and many of his associates from the prewar PNI and Hatta.[33] (In so doing they did increase cohesion within the Islamic

---

Blumberger, *De Nationalistische Beweging in Nederlandsch-Indie* (Haarlem: Tjeenk Willink, 1931); and J. M. Pluvier, *Overzicht van de Ontwikkeling der Nationalistische Beweging in Indonesië in de Jaren 1930 tot 1942* ("A Survey of the Development of the Nationalist Movement in Indonesia between 1930 and 1942"; The Hague: van Hoeve, 1953).

[33] See Benda, *The Crescent and the Rising Sun, passim.*

leadership itself, bringing together the Muhammadijah and Nahdatul Ulama, two large and theretofore mainly nonpolitical organizations with established village support.)

Most important of all, the Japanese occupation created a basis of division between collaborators, or "collaborators for selfish ends," and the leaders of the underground organizations. The latter did not harass the Japanese by guerrilla or sabotage activity, but their organizational networks were of importance (and might have been crucial had the expected Allied landings in Java taken place). As the Japanese collapse approached, they became less underground in character and gained influence among the leaders of many of the Japanese-established youth organizations. With the outbreak of Revolution, the underground leaders, particularly Sjahrir and Amir Sjarifuddin, became overtly anti-Japanese and made strong attacks on Indonesian leaders who had been the "running dogs" of the occupying power.[34]

The period of Revolution saw the development of even deeper cleavages in the leadership. Despite the intense sense of solidarity which nationalists then felt as they fought for independence, divisions within the elite were acute. For nine days of the first two weeks of the Republic's existence a single party, the Partai Nasional Indonesia, was in existence, at least on paper.[35] But then the state party idea was abandoned, because it was seen as redundant in view of the Central National Committee and its regional agencies, because it was thought imprudent to have governmental institutions appearing to bear the Japanese imprint, and because it was felt that the long-standing political divisions between the men at the head of the new party would prevent it from functioning effectively.

Thus in November 1945 a multiparty system began to be created. Sjahrir and Amir Sjarifuddin combined their followings in a new Socialist Party. Old members of Soekarno's PNI of the prewar period, and others, formed a new (third) Partai Nasional Indonesia. The representatives of almost all existing Moslem organizations combined to create the Masjumi (or rather re-create it, for a mass organization with the same name and partly similar leadership had functioned under the Japanese occupation).

[34] See S. Sjahrir, *Perdjoeangan Kita* ("Our Struggle"); Koetaradja: Ghazali Yunus, 1946). This was the widely distributed pamphlet in which the "running dogs" charge was made most vociferously. For a discussion of the important and long-lasting effects of this pamphlet see Kahin, *Nationalism and Revolution,* pp. 164–177.
[35] See Roeslan Abdulgani, *Funksi Penerangan di Indonesia,* pp. 115–119.

The number of parties established was great. But it was not, in fact, along party lines that the political leadership divided most sharply. The most important divisions transcended party lines. These were between negotiating governments and antinegotiating opposition groups. For four years from Sjahrir's assumption of the prime ministership in November 1945, Republican policy making was dominated by that group of the nationalist leadership, in particular Sjahrir and Hatta, in which the Dutch, and the Western powers generally, could be expected to place maximum trust. Soekarno was allied with this group, but he was not a leader of it. Opposition to the group came from a variety of sources.

Indeed, it was no easy task for Sjahrir, Hatta, and their associates to control the internal political situation—even with Soekarno's enormous help. It was they, particularly Sjahrir and Hatta, who were blamed for the long series of withdrawals to which the Republic was forced by increasing Dutch military power and the passivity of the rest of the world. And their enemies did not hesitate to use these opportunities to attempt to seize power from them.

The challenges came in the form of two major internal upheavals. In the "July 3 affair" of 1946 the supporters of the nationalist-communist Tan Malaka—and they included many of those who had worked with both the Japanese army and the Djakarta office of the Japanese navy came very close to succeeding in a *coup d'état* against the Sjahrir government. Their defeat was in part the result of President Soekarno's fear that the plotters meant to displace not only Sjahrir but Soekarno himself. In part it resulted from the strong support which pro-Communist (PKI) groups gave the government.

In the case of the second large upheaval, the Madiun affair, some elements of the situation were different. What began at Madiun was a revolt, not a palace coup. And it reflected a changing pattern of Cold War politics. But there were also elements of similarity, with merely a reversal of roles. This time the rebels were Stalinists while the Tan Malaka group, and the old-line nationalists, flocked enthusiastically to support the government's cause. Hatta was now Prime Minister in the place of Sjahrir. The government's negotiating policy was basically the same, however, and the principal opposition argument was given that the government was conceding too much to the Dutch.

Thus the policy of negotiating with the West, rational course that it was from the point of view of achieving independence as quickly as possible, was costly in terms of internal elite cohesion. If the Republic's leadership was united in 1949, this was partly a result of Soekarno-Hatta co-operation. But it was also a consequence of the suppression of the two major challenges—of the jailing of many of Tan Malaka's national-communist and old-line nationalist supporters (Mr. Subardjo, Mr. Iwa Kusumasumantri, Mr. Muhammad Yamin, and a number of others), of the withdrawal of others from the political area, of the killing of Tan Malaka himself in February 1949, and of the death in military action or by execution of a majority of the top PKI leaders. It was in a sense to a rump leadership group—one might say to the Hatta half of the nationalist leadership plus Soekarno—that all-Indonesian power came in December 1949.

It may be useful at this point to suggest analytical categories which throw light on the intraelite conflict developing in the period of the Revolution, particularly between supporters and opponents of government actions taken in negotiations with the Dutch. Changes in political alignments on this central issue were in good part simply changes in position as one group changed from being "in" power to being "out" or vice versa. But an important element of continuity existed, and one may find explanations of this, and in addition clues to political alignments in the period after the Revolution, as one looks at the roles of two skill groups.[36]

In broad terms, revolutionary leadership called for two types of skill. On the one hand there was an intense demand for people we shall call "administrators," men with administrative, legal, technical, and foreign language skills, such as are required for the running of a modern state. Such men, who normally had Western university or at least senior secondary education, were needed to take charge of the higher brackets of the government service (which had previously been manned almost entirely by Dutch personnel and, to a lesser extent, Japanese officers). They were needed for certain military tasks, particularly for central organization and strategy. And they were needed also for negotiations with the Dutch and the various Allied and UN mediator groups and for diplomatic and publicity activities overseas.

Equally necessary to the leadership of the Revolution, however, were men of skills of another type. The Revolution needed leaders with what may be called integrative skills, skills in cultural mediation, symbol manipulation, and mass organization. It needed leaders who could rally various sections of the population to full and active support of

[36] For a discussion of the concept of skill groups see Harold D. Lasswell, *Politics: Who Gets What, When, How* (New York: Meridian Books, 1958), pp. 97–112.

the struggle. These persons—we shall call them "solidarity makers"—might have higher Western education or only secondary or primary Western or Moslem education. They might exercise their leadership on the basis of traditional or charismatic authority or (most usually) a combination. They might be military figures—army leaders, guerrilla leaders in established organizations, or simply persons of local or regional power and arms. They might be political propagandists, or teachers, or religious leaders. Or they might be leaders and organizers of political parties, trade unions, or peasant associations.[37]

Between leaders possessing these two types of skills some important differences of interest and outlook existed. Each of the two skill groups had its own area of operation, and each obtained large status rewards. Indeed, the two types of skill were not mutually exclusive. There were many individual leaders who combined the two types. But this did not prevent conflict between the skill groups, between persons playing the roles of "administrators" and others playing the role of "solidarity makers." Granted the basic policy of all the revolutionary cabinets to negotiate with the Netherlands and attempt to persuade other countries (and particularly Western countries) to apply pressure on it, "administrators" in our broad sense of this term played the central role in government policy making. But governments relied on the "solidarity makers" too, for the outcome of negotiations would depend in large part on Indonesia's military and political strength. The task of maximizing elite cohesion was in large measure a matter of mediating conflicts between these two groups.

Indeed, such conflict was a constant feature of internal struggle in the Republic. It found manifold expression in civilian-military relations, in relations between the army's central command and its frequently highly autonomous regional commanders and between the army leadership and irregular guerrilla formations. It existed also be-

---

[37] This is one variation on a theme common to much of the literature on current non-Western politics. Eisenstadt speaks of the conflict between those who are concerned with administrative and instrumental ends and those who bear solidarity symbols. Lucian W. Pye speaks of administrators and agitators. Gerald S. Maryanov speaks of persons of technical and ideological orientation. See S. N. Eisenstadt, "Changes in Patterns of Stratification Attendant on Attainment of Political Independence," *Transactions of the Third World Congress of Sociology* (London: International Sociological Association, 1956); Lucian W. Pye, *The Spirit of Burmese Politics* (Cambridge, Mass.: Center for International Studies, M.I.T., 1959), pp. 48–54; and Gerald S. Maryanov, "The Establishment of Regional Government in the Republic of Indonesia" (doctoral dissertation, Indiana University, 1959), pp. 340–352.

tween different segments of the bureaucracy and within each of the main political parties, particularly the Masjumi and PNI. In every case the question to be decided was whether power and status should go to men with modern-type technical skills or to men with political qualifications, to those who were "capable" or those who were "acceptable." [38]

The fact that the Republic continued to function as a single political entity, despite the multifaceted conflict between the two skill groups, was in large measure due to the close co-operation between Soekarno and Hatta, themselves prototypical representatives of "solidarity making" and "administration" respectively. But one reason for this close co-operation was that it was co-operation on uneven terms, terms which were set by the current constellation of international forces and which greatly favored Hatta and the "administrators" associated with him. In the postindependence situation a new basis of co-operation between the two skill groups would have to be fashioned.

When independence came in December 1949, power passed into the hands of a segment of the nationalist leadership. The new power holders had been brought to their commanding positions by a variety of situational factors, many of them international, and this after a long period of turbulence in relations between different segments of the elite. Moreover, this was a group which possessed neither the long-established organizational machinery for the aggregation of claims, which its Indian counterpart possessed, nor the internal cohesion of its counterparts in the Bolshevik revolutions of Russia, China, or Vietnam.

INDONESIA AS A POLITICAL ENTITY

The difficulties which this situation presaged for the process of power consolidation become clear if one looks at the character of Indonesia as a political unit and examines the divisive forces growing from its geographical, economic, and sociocultural organization. Geography itself is not as divisive a factor as has often been thought. The archipelago character of the state is not a major barrier to political cohesion, because the calmness of the seas makes interinsular movement relatively easy, easier than inland travel in many of the mountainous parts of the country. Political power can fairly easily be exerted across the Indonesian seas and straits. As an archipelago state, moreover, Indonesia has rather clearly defined boundaries and thus

---

[38] See Selosoemardjan, "Bureaucratic Organization in a Time of Revolution," *Administrative Science Quarterly*, II (1957), 182–199.

few sources of border conflict with neighbors. On the other hand, there is important divisive potential in the fact that the country has several large cities, a number of them, like Medan and Makassar, situated so that their ties with the nearby rural areas are very much closer than those which bind them to the other large cities. Every other state of Southeast Asia is a one-city state.

A second category of divisive potentialities is the economic one. Here the principal fact is that Indonesia's export revenues since the Great Depression (which virtually killed the sugar export industry of East and Central Java) have come largely from estates, mines, and small-holder cash-crop areas outside Java. Thus throughout the period of this study Java was a net importer of goods, the "Outer Islands" a net exporting area. The discrepancy was in good part offset by the fact that Java supplied the other islands with certain foodstuffs, light manufactures, and teaching and other services. But there was nevertheless a basis of tension between net exporting and net importing areas, because of their conflicting interests as regards determination of the rate of exchange. To the extent that the exchange rate was unreal, that is, favoring importers and disfavoring exporters, this constituted a basis for resentment of the Java-based central government by the exporting Outer Islands, and thus a major centrifugal pressure.

Finally, Indonesian society in 1949 was beset with cleavages and obstacles to the attainment of consensus and legitimate authority as a result of ethnic and religious diversity, of the fact that loyalties and solidarity feelings attached to each of a large number of communal and quasi-communal groupings. Indonesia was a "plural society," a "mosaic society," a "multigroup society." In the first place, a sharp division existed, and was emphasized by Indonesian nationalism, between Indonesians (*bangsa Indonesia*) on the one hand and on the other hand Chinese, Arabs, Eurasians, and Europeans. These last four were separate communities, and most of their members were regarded, and regarded themselves, as being outside the group of Indonesians, whether they had Indonesian citizenship or not. Secondly, the community of Indonesians or *bangsa Indonesia* was itself divided into perhaps 366 traditionally self-aware ethnic groups [39] and included at least ten major groups with populations of over a million people, the

---

[39] This figure is given by M. A. Jaspan, "A Provisional List of Indonesian Ethnic Groups," *Sosiografi Indonesia* (Jogjakarta), I, no. 1 (1959), 75–90. The designation "group" refers in this list to the combined criteria of language, cultural area, and social structure. The figure 366 includes ethnic groups in West Irian.

Javanese, Sundanese, Malays, Minangkabaus, Toba Bataks, Buginese, and so on. In the case of several of these major groups the ethnic identification was strengthened by a particular set of religious loyalties. Indonesian nationalism played down this second category of divisions and served to diminish their political importance. But it could not undo them entirely.

The Chinese, Eurasian, European, and Arab communities functioned as aids to national solidarity by the very fact that they were so strongly "outgrouped." The Javanese or Buginese villager could readily be brought to understand the new idea that he was an Indonesian when this was explained to him in terms of not being a Chinese, European, or Arab (or Japanese). But by the same token the situation was pregnant with possibilities of scapegoatist and diversionary politics and with pressures toward discriminatory policies directed against both minority group citizens and residents of foreign nationality. Moreover, there was a source of threats to the legitimacy of governments in the fact that members of these communities, who performed integral functions within the economy, were virtually debarred from participation in legitimate politics and thus obliged to use bribery and other *sub rosa* techniques to protect and promote their interests.

Ethnic diversity within the *bangsa Indonesia* had more direct political effects. Loyalties attaching to ethnic groupings competed with the loyalties held by the state and national community throughout the period of this study. Furthermore, ties of common ethnic membership were frequently an important part of the cement of political groupings. Other things being equal, Javanese found it easier to work with other Javanese than with people of other groups, in politics as in other matters, and the same can be said for Achinese and Balinese and Minahasans.

Ethnic diversity was not in itself a cause of political cleavage, as was sometimes asserted. But it contributed to such cleavage where one ethnic group had strong traditions of hostility to another group, as in the case of the Toba Bataks and Karo Bataks of North Sumatra, and these served to aggravate resentments produced by current conflicts of interest. Combinations of the two types of conflict attitudes had explosive possibilities. However, the traditional attitudes themselves were scarcely ever determinative. Active hostility between traditionally inimical ethnic groups was found chiefly in urban areas, where there was economic, social, or sexual competition between the groups, and rarely in rural areas, where the purely traditional sentiments of ethnic hostility are stronger.[40]

In terms of its contribution to the ultimate danger of territorial disintegration ethnic diversity was perhaps not as important as outsiders usually thought. There were certainly groups in peripheral areas of the country whose sense of ethnic separateness contained the seeds of separatist politics. But these were small areas, which could only afford to challenge Indonesia's territorial integrity if their separatists obtained a large volume of foreign support. The very complications of Indonesia's ethnic composition reduced the ability of ethnic divisions to threaten territorial integrity. For in Indonesia, unlike such countries as Ceylon, Burma, and Thailand, there was no clear situation of one large majority group facing one or several minorities. To some extent a basis of political delineation existed between the ethnic Javanese, who were by far the largest single group, with perhaps 52 per cent of the country's total population,[41] and all other groups. But in 1949 there were no significant grievances between Javanese and non-Javanese. No attempt had been made to make Javanese the national language of Indonesia. Indeed, only a small number of the non-Javanese groups had a historical legacy of resentment of the Javanese; one has to go back to the fourteenth century empire of Majapahit for an example of an attempt to establish Javanese hegemony in the archipelago. And there was almost certainly more ethnic group conflict between different groups of non-Javanese than there was between Javanese and others.

Furthermore, the country's territorial integrity was bolstered by such factors as intermarriage and intermigration. Persons from different areas and ethnic groups had had secondary and university education together in Java for as long as these had existed for Indonesians. From such common educational experiences ethnic intermarriage had frequently followed. The presence of large numbers of Javanese in Sumatra and Sumatrans in Java had similar effects. Of course nationalism itself made a very important contribution to the country's terri-

[40] Skinner, ed., *Local, Ethnic and National Loyalties in Village Indonesia, passim.*
[41] This estimate was made on the basis of 1955 election statistics by M. A. Jaspan. See his "Leadership and Elite Groups in Indonesia: Aspects of an Unstable Social Symbiosis" (unpublished paper, Australian National University, 1961). The figure is 47.02 per cent according to the 1930 census. See Central Bureau of Statistics, *Statistical Pocketbook of Indonesia, 1941* (Batavia: Kolff, 1947), p. 9.

torial cohesion. Finally, there was the important fact that many of the divisive forces tended to cancel one another out. Thus the Medan area, as a major urban complex with little economic dependence on Djakarta and a large volume of estate products to export, generated powerful centrifugal tendencies. But these were largely offset by the great ethnic heterogeneity of this area and by the fact that the estates were owned by foreign companies, which could not afford to support movements hostile to Djakarta.

However, the problem of power consolidation was not only one of warding off threats to the country's territorial integrity. It was also a matter of attaining consensus on the ends of the state. The attainment of such consensus is an important task for any state, but it was particularly vital for Indonesia as a country whose government was to be unwilling, and perhaps unable, in the period of this study to use coercive power broadly.

Yet history had created in Indonesia a pattern of multiple "political cultures," of quasi-communal groups each of which was characterized by "a particular pattern of orientations to political action." [42] It is certainly true of the Indonesia of 1949 that a multiplicity of political cultures was in existence, in the sense that "large groups have fundamentally different 'cognitive maps' of politics and apply different norms to political action." [43] The entities to which particular "political cultures" corresponded were not usually simply ethnic groups, although one may perhaps speak of a Minahasan-Protestant political culture or an Ambonese-Protestant one. Far more important than these were what may be called the Javanese-aristocratic and Islamic-entrepreneurial political cultures. The roots of these lay in the differences of historical experience of different communities of the archipelago.

Historically three chief contrasts stand out. There were firstly the differences of traditional political organization. These were broadly between inland empires based on wet-rice agriculture (notably in the highly fertile volcanic basins of East and Central Java), coastal communities controlled by maritime commercial powers, and inland communities, mainly outside East and Central Java, where systems of

[42] The term "political culture" and this definition are taken from the work of Gabriel A. Almond. As Almond uses the term, it is not necessarily coincident with a particular political system or society or the same as the general culture. Almond asserts that an important characteristic of the political systems of preindustrial countries is their "mixed political cultures." See his "Comparative Political Systems," *Journal of Politics,* XVIII, no. 3 (Aug. 1956), 391–409.

[43] *Ibid.*

shifting cultivation were practiced and no large political units existed.[44]

In the second place, Islam penetrated different Indonesian communities to markedly different degrees. It came to command strong adherence in the coastal and commercial communities and subsequently spread inland into many of the areas of shifting cultivation. On the other hand, its impact was slight on inland East and Central Java, where rulers and ruled became nominal Moslems but continued in most of their earlier Hindu-animist beliefs and practices. And it left certain areas entirely unpenetrated and thus either Hindu as in Bali or animist as in Minahasa, Northern Tapanuli, Flores, and Timor, which subsequently became Christian areas.

Finally, Dutch rule was most uneven in its impact on different parts of the archipelago. It is only in Java, in certain parts of the Moluccas, and in a few port towns on the route to the Moluccas that the Dutch were the preponderant power from the seventeenth century onward and only in these areas that export crops were cultivated in any large quantities before the second half of the nineteenth century. Indeed, there are many areas outside Java which were not effectively incorporated in the Netherlands Indies until the early years of this century. In Java, by contrast, the Dutch impact was extremely intensive, especially in the nineteenth century. Javanese trade was virtually destroyed and the Javanese aristocracy bureaucratized. Java's population grew from an estimated 4.5 million in 1815 to 48.4 million in 1940. In many areas outside Java there was a period of intensive impact following the establishment of large estates and mines in the late nineteenth century and the early part of the twentieth century and the subsequent development of indigenous cash cropping. But there were other areas outside Java where the Dutch left relatively little impact on the existing organization of society.

In broad terms it may be said that these three contrasts of historical pattern have left two chief "political cultures" in Indonesia, the Javanese-aristocratic and the Islamic-entrepreneurial. The first of these, which is the political culture of the great majority of Javanese, was born of state organization in the wet-rice-agriculture-based inland empires of Java, of shallow Islamization, and of a long period of intensive Dutch impact, which produced enormous densities of population, a hollowing out of the structures of social integration, and an

[44] J. C. van Leur, *Indonesian Trade and Society* (The Hague and Bandung: van Hoeve, 1956), pp. 104 ff.; Wertheim, *op. cit.*, pp. 52–53.

incapacitation of entrepreneurship. The Islamic-entrepreneurial political culture is one whose adherents are far more dispersed and socially disparate. They include the *santris* of East and Central Java, members of distinct communities of thoroughly Islamic faith. And they also include most members of such ethnic groups as the Minangkabaus, the Achinese, the Bandjarese, and the Buginese, and smaller proportions of the members of numerous other ethnic groups. Historically this political culture is a product of the maritime commercial towns and states of coastal Sumatra, North Java, Kalimantan, and Sulawesi, of thorough Islamization, of a relatively slight Dutch impact, and of the revival of entrepreneurship in the present century.

Between these two political cultures as they existed in 1949 there were major differences of emphasis. It was not only that the one was contemptuous of economic pursuits and the other respectful, that the one was associated with support for a secular or broadly theistic or pantheistic state and the other with support for a state based on Islam. In addition, Javanese-aristocratic political culture involved a greater intensity of anti-Dutch sentiment than did Islamic-entrepreneurial and at the same time a less intense hostility to the Chinese. Javanese-aristocratic political culture tended toward nativism, while Islamic-entrepreneurial was generally more ready to accept and incorporate influences stemming from the modern West. But Javanese-aristocratic political culture was far more fully sympathetic to socialist ideas than Islamic-entrepreneurial. Needless to say, there were many individuals and groups whose political orientations reflected aspects of both these political cultures and many others whose orientations were markedly different from either of these two. But the contrast between the two main political cultures was sharp enough to presage serious difficulties for the process of maintaining consensus on the ends and proper procedures of government and politics.

THE TASKS AS PERCEIVED: NATION BUILDING AND ECONOMIC PROGRESS

What, then, were the values, the assumptions, and the images of the future with which the Indonesian leaders faced the postrevolutionary period? What were their goals and projections, what type of a society did they hope and expect to build? These are vastly complicated questions, and only the most impressionistic answers can be attempted here. But the attempt must be made lest it seem that the tasks faced by postrevolutionary governments were somehow "objective," lest the achievements of the postrevolutionary period be measured against the standard of goals and expectations interposed by outsiders.

It may be useful to distinguish immediately between various groups of Indonesian leaders. If one speaks of Hatta and the group of "administrators" who were associated with him in government leadership both before and after December 1949, their preoccupation was then almost entirely with the practical problems of the transition. They emphasized the need for legality and the maintenance of controls, the need for firm leadership and responsible politics, and the dangers of expecting too much from the new independence.[45] In part this was because of the enormous scope of the immediate problems before them. They had the problem of guerrilla restiveness on their hands and the danger that various groups of former freedom fighters would refuse to acknowledge their authority. They had to concern themselves with an economic and financial situation which was quickly to call for drastic surgery. A formidable problem of administrative reorganization was immediately upon them. And the federal structure on which the state was being founded was tumbling down even as it was being formally brought into existence.

But the Hatta group's view of the country's tasks was also related to the political position of the group and to factors of personal skill and orientation. All the members of the group had considerable technical skills relevant to the operation of a modern state. And these skills were an important factor in the claims of the group to continue to exercise power. Furthermore, most members of the group were men of a pragmatic turn of mind. This is particularly true of Hatta, but it is almost equally true of such nonparty men as Sultan Hamengku Buwono, Ir. Djuanda, and Professor Supomo, or indeed of such party leaders as Mr. Wilopo, Mr. Roem, and Dr. Leimena. These men did of course have their own images of the future, but they did not stress these in public pronouncements. Their approach to political leadership was characterized by an attitude of "Leave it to us. We know what has to be done." As government leaders they made little or no attempt to sketch middle-range goals which might have served to bridge the

---

[45] See, e.g., Sukardjo Wirjopranoto, "Pertanggung-djawab Atas Keamanan" ("Our Responsibility for the Maintenance of Security"), *Mimbar Indonesia,* Nov. 19, 1949, and Supomo, "Pertanggungan-djawab Pemerintah R.I.S." ("The Responsibilities of the RUSI Government"), *ibid.,* Dec. 27, 1949.

gap between their own current concern with immediate governmental problems and the utopian goals which had frequently been set forth as the cause for which the Revolution was fought.

As "administrators" were concerned with the immediate future, so "solidarity makers" tended to be concerned with images of a distant utopia. Political leaders of the "solidarity maker" group, including the President, made numerous statements about the Indonesia of the future, to which the Revolution was a bridge, the Indonesia of prosperity, justice, harmony, and strength. They repeated frequently and forcefully that this was the vision which had to be realized. But they too were little concerned about middle-range goals, or at least did not speak of them specifically. Thus there existed what might be called a bifurcation of attitudes toward the future. Virtually none of the leaders of 1949 were attempting to link long-term ends with short-term administrative programs, ideological appeals with the solution of practical problems. Soekarno fashioned symbols and reiterated the messianic demands and promises of the Revolution. Hatta made administrative policy and urged realism. The two approaches were neither fused nor bridged.

When one looks for the goals and perceptions which were shared by all the nationalist leadership, one comes first of all to what might be called the area of nation building. The creation of a nation—a people unified by ties of common language, common outlook, and common political participation, a people enthusiastically severing its outworn ties to local traditions and loyalties and achieving *kesadaran*, consciousness of the nation and of the world of modernity—this was probably the central goal which the nationalist leaders believed should and would be realized with the attainment of independence. Most of the Indonesian people were still asleep, cowed, passive, the nationalist leaders believed. But the Revolution had shown that they could and would respond quickly to the excitement of modern and national existence once the colonial shackles had fallen away.

For some leaders the first task was the destruction of ethnic barriers and the creation in society at large of the sort of all-Indonesian culture which already existed inside the nationalist movement. For others the first necessity was the creation of a "national will," the spreading throughout the archipelago of the same sense of common identification with the nation's political leadership which had prevailed in large sections of the population of the Jogjakarta-centered Republic. For others again the emphasis was on *élan* and enthusiasm, on excited responses to national leadership.

Nation building was perceived as a *noblesse oblige* responsibility of the leadership, but at the same time it was associated with emancipation. The people's horizons would be widened from above—by schooling, mass education, literacy work, and public information campaigns. But at the same time they would be given opportunities to better themselves. In this way they would be able to develop a "modern" and "national" style of life—as defined by the life style of the urban political leaders themselves.[46]

But national society after independence would not only be modern and free as colonialism had been conservative and restrictive. It would also be organically cohesive. Colonial society was depicted as a society where the economic interests of the few destroyed the values and ways of life of the many, a society where economic progress as defined by the large Dutch business houses had priority in the government's eyes over the physical and moral welfare of the people of the country. In Soedjatmoko's words, it was a "society without any organic coherence." [47] In general, Indonesian nationalists focused attention not on the paternalistic and (for Indonesians) antidevelopmental aspects of Dutch colonial practice, but on the social disruption which had followed from capitalist economic penetration despite the paternalism of the "Ethical Policy." Many of them took the "closed" village as their ideal political community. Almost all of them stressed that what was needed after independence was cohesion, integration, and solidarity—not "individualism" but "collectivism," not "liberalism" but "socialism." These words were not always used in the same sense as in the West. But it is significant that "individualism" and "liberalism" almost always had negative connotations while "collectivism" and "socialism" almost always had positive ones.[48] Capitalism was a particularly strong negative symbol, and a number of leaders based their

[46] On the "will to be modern" see Edward A. Shils, "Political Development in the New States," *Comparative Studies in Society and History*, II, no. 3 (April 1960), 265 ff.

[47] Soedjatmoko, "Point Four and Southeast Asia," *Indonesië*, IV (1950–1951), 6. See also Mohammad Hatta, *Past and Future* (Cornell Modern Indonesia Project, Translation Series; Ithaca, N.Y., 1960), p. 3.

[48] Thus even Hatta, in 1956, used "individualism" to convey the notion of selfishness and "collectivism" to mean social responsibility. See *Past and Future*, pp. 5–6. See also Roeslan Abdulgani, *Funksi Penerangan di Indonesia*, pp. 57, 61–62.

views of it on Marxist and Leninist critiques.[49] The Indonesian society of the postrevolutionary period would be in some sense socialistic, and its economy "based on the principle of family relationships." [50]

If the values and expectations of the nationalist leadership as regards the general area of "nation building" were relatively clear and widely shared, this was not the case with regard to the area of economic policy. Here there were important differences of viewpoint and image.

For many in the political elite, particularly "administrators" and men who saw power in terms of the possibility of solving governmental problems, the economic image of postrevolutionary society was one of planned economic development. The men of this group, of whom Hatta is representative, thought in terms of a rapid rise in material levels of living. They wanted to use foreign capital, and, in terms of practical politics at least, they were prepared to accept the economic settlement of the Round Table Conference. Thus they were prepared to allow the large Dutch firms to keep most of their very strong hold on plantation agriculture, exporting, importing, banking, shipping, aviation, and other sections of the economy.[51] Although they wanted to see the control and management of these various areas of economic life in Indonesian hands in the not too distant future, this goal was less important to them than maximization of production.

At the same time they did not demand or expect any dramatic leaps forward. Nor did they see economic progress as having primacy before social ideals. Most of them shared the extremely widespread view— enshrined in the national anthem among other places—that Indonesia is a rich country. Thus they believed that a rising standard of material welfare could be achieved without causing disruptions of the new nationalist style of life.

[49] On Marxism and the "national-Marxist amalgam" in Indonesian political thinking see Jeanne S. Mintz, "Marxism in Indonesia," in Frank N. Trager, ed., *Marxism in Southeast Asia* (Stanford: Stanford University Press, 1959), pp. 171–239. See also Saul Rose, *Socialism in Southern Asia* (London: Oxford University Press, 1959), pp. 145 ff.

[50] This is the phrase used in the various constitutions. See Wilopo and Widjojo Nitisastro, *The Socio-economic Basis of the Indonesian State: On the Interpretation of Paragraph 1, Article 38 of the Provisional Constitution of the Republic of Indonesia* (Cornell Modern Indonesia Project, Translation Series; Ithaca, N.Y., 1959).

[51] On the extent to which big Dutch capital dominated various sections of the economy at this time see John O. Sutter, *Indonesianisasi: Politics in a Changing Economy, 1940–1955* (Southeast Asia Program, Cornell University; Ithaca, N.Y., 1959), pp. 11–100, 619–637, 695–706.

On the other hand, there were Indonesian leaders—and here Soe-karno may be taken as representative—who did not place a high priority on the pursuit of economic progress. These men spoke frequently of *pembangunan*, literally "upbuilding," and the word was sometimes translated as "development" or "economic development." But it actually has rather different connotations, ones which are social and political, rather than economic. In fact their approach to power was characterized by a low degree of concern with problem solving in economic areas. Many of them were attracted by the idea of industrial power and its symbol of steel mills. But none of the group were drawn by the image of an industrialized society.[52] For the men of this group Indonesian village society was basically healthy. To the extent that they wanted to reform it, it was by removing foreign cultural elements and introducing national and "modern" consciousness. Basically "populists" in their response to the Western impact, they distinguished sharply—in a manner which suggests the psychoanalysts' "decomposition of ambivalence"—between things "modern" which they saw as good and things "Western" which they saw as bad. Hence they advanced different varieties of the *smörgåsbord* theory of modernization by selective borrowing.[53]

Many of the men of this group expected the postrevolutionary years to bring rising national welfare, but it was the nation's prestige and its sense of cultural identity which was the object of their principal concern. Although their point of view was not the dominant one at the end of 1949—because of the power and policy-making importance of Hatta at that time—it was probably representative of the views of a majority of the nationalist leadership as a whole.

[52] In the words of Soedjatmoko in 1954, economic progress "has failed to catch the imagination of the Indonesian people." Although party leaders "pay lip service to the idea of economic development, there is no evidence of any real concern on this issue." He speaks of the political leaders' "moral equivocation as to the virtues or disadvantages of economic advancement" and of "their rejection of the pattern of existence that will evolve with industrialism." See his *Economic Development as a Cultural Problem* (Cornell Modern Indonesia Project, Translation Series; Ithaca, N.Y., 1958), pp. 2, 11, 12.

[53] The term comes from Lucian W. Pye, "Community Development as a Part of Political Development," *Community Development Review*, no. 8 (March 1958), p. 18. For a stimulating presentation of this point of view by a PNI political theorist see S. Mangunsarkoro, *The Sociological and Cultural Fundamentals for the Educational System in Indonesia* (Djakarta: n.p., 1945). See also Benjamin Higgins, *Indonesia's Economic Stabilization and Development* (New York: Institute of Pacific Relations, 1957), pp. 115–120.

THE TASKS AS PERCEIVED: DEMOCRACY
AND CONSTITUTIONAL DEMOCRACY

What then were the prevailing values and images in the area of political institutions? How was democracy perceived, and how was it expected to be realized? Here again caution is required lest the Indonesian advocates of symbols and forms familiar in the West be regarded as seeing their country's problems in terms simply of Western images.

"Democracy" as a symbol was in almost universal favor. It was one of the Pantja Sila or Five Principles laid down by Soekarno in a celebrated speech of June 1945 and as such had become part of the official philosophy of the Republic.[54] In the constitutions and platforms of the fourteen parties included in the Information Ministry's *Kepartaian di Indonesia* ("The Party System of Indonesia") of 1950, the word is used frequently and almost always with unqualified approval. Qualifications were suggested only by two fairly small parties under the leadership of Javanese aristocrats, PIR (Persatuan Indonesia Raja, Greater Indonesian Union) and Parindra (Partai Indonesia Raja, Greater Indonesia Party). PIR declared itself in favor of a "democratic basis which accords with the condition and spirit of Indonesian society as it really is" and argued that a majority vote must not prevail against principles of humanity and decency,[55] and Parindra urged a regulated democracy (*demokrasi teratur*).[56] Similarly President Soekarno, speaking at the time of his installation as President of the Republic of the United States of Indonesia, argued that what was needed was "Eastern Democracy . . . Indonesian democracy . . . a democracy with leadership (demokratie met leiderschap)."[57] These were significant exceptions, but they were exceptions.

The great majority of parties were unreservedly for democracy, but the meanings which they read into this symbol were by no means identical with those which attach to the constitutional democracy of the

[54] See Soekarno, *The Birth of the Pantja Sila* (Djakarta: Ministry of Information, 1952). The principles may be translated as (Belief in) The One Deity (*Ketuhanan jang Maha Esa*), Nationality, Humanity, Democracy or People's Sovereignty, and Social Justice.

[55] Kementerian Penerangan, *Kepartaian di Indonesia* ("Political Parties in Indonesia"; Djakarta: Kementerian Penerangan, 1950), pp. 101–105.

[56] *Ibid.*, p. 121.

[57] *Amanat Presiden Pertama Republik Indonesia Serikat* ("Address by the First President of the United States of Indonesia"; Jogjakarta: Kementerian Penerangan, 1949), p. 7.

contemporary West, and even less with those of the small group of Anglo-Saxon democracies. In general, the parties wrote of democracy as "people's sovereignty," "peopleness" (*kerakjatan*), *vox populi, vox Dei,* and "government of the people, by the people, and for the people." There were several references to the need for democracy in the social and economic fields as well as the political, frequent affirmations of support for the equality of all citizens, denunciations of dictatorship, and declarations of support for such "basic rights of the people" as freedom of the press, freedom of assembly and demonstration, and freedom to strike. Moreover, the assumption was general that democracy implied parliament, parties, and elections. On the other hand, there was only one specific reference to majority rule and there were none to minority rights, the rights of individuals, or the institutionalized opposition. Only two parties associated democracy with law. Two other parties, the large PNI and the Catholic Party, declared their hostility to "liberalism."

Drawing on a wider range of contemporary views than the party platforms,[58] one can see a great deal of variety in the prevailing image of democracy. Among one group of leaders there was a tendency to define democracy in terms of traditional political and moral ideas. This sometimes led to mystical definitions like that of Soetardjo Kartohadikusumo of PIR who asserted that democracy was "the unity of God with his servant"[59] and President Soekarno's idea that "democracy is jointly formulating truth."[60] Occasionally the symbol of democracy was attached to ideas of leadership as a lofty calling and of the true leader as a warden of the state and a spiritually superior being.[61] And to many the symbol stood for a regeneration in modern form of the organically cohesive traditional community which had been disrupted by capitalist intrusions.[62]

Others, by contrast, saw democracy as freeing individual men from the shackles of ossified hierarchical traditions, affording them opportunities to develop their personalities, and rewarding them on the basis

[58] Many of these views have been brought to my attention by Professor George McT. Kahin, who was in Indonesia and in close touch with Indonesian political leaders in 1948–1949.

[59] Quoted in J. M. van der Kroef, *Indonesia in the Modern World,* II (Bandung: Masa Baru, 1956), 209–210.

[60] *Antara News Bulletin* (hereafter cited as *Antara*), Nov. 13, 1951.

[61] For a full discussion of Javanese views of leadership see Donald Fagg, "Authority and Social Structure: A Study of Javanese Bureaucracy" (doctoral dissertation, Harvard University, 1958), pp. 275 ff. and 378 ff.

[62] Cf. van der Kroef, *Indonesia in the Modern World,* II, 198 ff., 244 ff.

of talent and achievement. This view was characteristic of Sjahrir and the young men of higher Western education associated with him in the Revolution, and it was also the view of a whole tradition of literary figures, most prominently the novelist Takdir Alisjahbana and the poet Chaeril Anwar.[63] Some of the men with this image of democracy sought to establish its roots in indigenous social tradition. Thus they emphasized the egalitarian aspects of traditional village government and especially the idea of *musjawarah,* the notion that a leader should not act arbitrarily or impose his will, but rather make gentle suggestions of the path a community should follow, being careful always to consult all other participants fully and to take their views and feelings into consideration before delivering his syntheses-conclusions. Some of them argued further that the village had institutions through which protest could be channeled.[64]

In spite of all this variety, however, one can see an image of democracy shared by the great majority of political leaders and by the political public. It is an image with distinguishable present and future components. As far as the present was concerned, democracy was seen to mean primarily participation of the people in government and politics. Governments must consult the people and operate with their support, it was said. They must keep close to the people. The implication was that this popular participation and consent would be achieved at least in part through parliamentary institutions.[65] But parliamentary institutions were not seen as fulfilling representative functions. In fact, the idea of representation was almost entirely absent from Indonesian ideas of democracy. Parliamentary institutions were to serve the interests of the people. But the people were often seen as an undifferentiated mass, whose interests were overwhelmingly common rather than mutually antagonistic.[66] Divisions within the body

[63] See Achdiat K. Mihardja, ed., *Polemik Kebudajaan* ("Polemics about Culture"; Djakarta: Balai Pustaka, 1950).

[64] E.g., Hatta, *Past and Future,* p. 8. For a critical discussion of democratic claims made for traditional village society see van der Kroef, *Indonesia in the Modern World,* I (1954), 204 ff., and also II (1956), 204 ff.

[65] The prestige of these institutions was high, partly because they had been demanded repeatedly by the prewar nationalist movement. "A Parliament for Indonesia" had been a major nationalist slogan in the late 1930's. See Pluvier, *op. cit.,* pp. 138 ff.

[66] Lucian W. Pye writes: "To the extent that the national leaders of Southeast Asia seek to act as representatives of all their peoples and not as brokers aggregating specific interests, they perform in much the same manner as did the dominant leaders in traditional Southeast Asian societies. . . . Historically the rulers in the

of the people were accepted as legitimate where they were ideological. The Indonesian leaders, accepting the Dutch and other continental political systems as their models in this respect, saw ideological controversy as a proper and indeed essential part of modern democratic politics. As far as other types of division were concerned, however, they were thought to result not from differences of (legitimate) interest, but on the one hand from persisting ethnic and communal hostilities—in the eyes of many, a colonial vestige—and on the other hand from the selfishness of individuals and groups.

Moreover, there was little stress on parliamentary institutions having tyranny-preventing functions. Ideas of countervailing power, checks and balances, the need for a government of laws and not of men—all these had little or no part in the thinking of Indonesian theorists of democracy. Partly perhaps because of their close connection with government authority, these theorists concerned themselves little with tensions between authority and liberty. Only a few spoke in these years of the dangers of an indigenous authoritarianism or "fascism."

When Indonesian leaders spoke of democracy as a means, it was usually as a means of nation building, of educating the people to greater national and civic awareness and making them more dynamic and more active in the pursuit of their "real interests." As Hatta was to say later, "Political parties . . . arc a means of organizing public opinion in order that the people may learn to feel responsibility as citizens of the state and members of society." [67]

But democracy was not seen primarily as a means. More often it was seen as a basic principle, a new truth on which to build the state. It was as if "the people" had replaced God as the fount of state authority and parliamentary institutions and procedures were the ritual forms whereby the new deity's blessing was secured.

Above all, democracy was seen as a goal, an end to be achieved in the future. This was part of the "future orientation" which characterized the whole outlook of the nationalist leaders, part of their tendency to think in terms of an ideal future and of movement toward it rather than in terms of pragmatic reform of an existing situation. As victors in the Revolution and as subscribers to Marxist views of inevitable historical progress, the Indonesian leaders looked to the future with great

---

region were conceived of as embodying all the interests of their peoples." See "Southeast Asia" in Gabriel A. Almond and James S. Coleman, eds., *The Politics of the Developing Areas* (Princeton, N.J.: Princeton University Press, 1960), p. 124.
[67] *Past and Future*, p. 12.

confidence that their ideals would be realized. Resenting the colonial past intensely, they wanted to remake Indonesian society entirely, and believed that they could do so. To regulate the present therefore seemed relatively unimportant. What mattered was to see that the country was moving and moving fast in the right direction, toward realization of the national goals in the future. For many, in fact, the image of democracy was the image of these national goals. Democracy —not mere political democracy as in the West, but democracy extended to all spheres of life—was the good society of the future. It was the "just and prosperous society" for which the revolution had been fought. By implication, all actions which involved movement toward this goal were democratic.[68]

Thus the democracy so widely acclaimed had only very tenuous links with the Western-type constitutional system by which the state was to be governed in the years from 1949 onward. Sometimes democracy was an abstract symbol of future aspirations. At other times it was thought of as a legitimizing principle and an educational and nation-building force, and then it was usually linked with parliament and parties, cabinet responsibility, and elections. But it was only very rarely associated with such features of the constitutional system being adopted as individual rights, majority rule and minority rights, and the institutionalized opposition.

There was clearly no equivalent in Indonesia of the common commitment to a body of Western constitutional doctrine which characterized large parts of the political elite in contemporary India, Pakistan, and Ceylon. This fact may perhaps be explained by reference to the formally indirect nature of much of Dutch colonial rule, to the fact that government was exercised through traditional rulers as well as through Western-type institutions.[69] It is certainly connected with the fact that Indonesians had little experience of participation in constitutional politics in the prewar period and with the strong reaction against Dutch-brought liberal thought occasioned by the Japanese occupation and the Revolution.

Indeed, there were few Indonesians in 1949 who had specific ex-

---

[68] For a stimulating discussion of "democracy" and "democratization" in Indonesian political thought see Gerald S. Maryanov, *Decentralization in Indonesia as a Political Problem* (Cornell Modern Indonesia Project, Interim Reports Series; Ithaca, N.Y., 1958), pp. 17 ff.

[69] Pye, "Southeast Asia," in Almond and Coleman, eds., *The Politics of the Developing Areas*, p. 85. See also J. S. Furnivall, *Netherlands India: A Study of Plural Economy* (Cambridge, Eng.: Cambridge University Press, 1944), pp. 257–260.

pectations of how parliamentary institutions would work in fully independent Indonesia. There existed only a very blurred image of what the future might bring in this regard, an image with component elements drawn from Dutch parliamentary politics, the politics of the prewar Volksraad, the working of the Inner and Outer Parliaments of the period of revolution, and contemporary India. There was a general awareness that difficulties would arise—because of the large number of parties in existence, some thought, or, as others believed, because parliament would stand in the way of the strong government required. But there was no widely shared determination to surmount difficulties of this kind, certainly not plans for surmounting them. Perhaps the most common attitude was a neutral one of "wait and see."

Why then did the Indonesian leaders commit themselves to a Western-type constitutional democracy? What led them to adopt a constitutional system whose underlying principles were not part of the prevailing body of political values and perceptions?

These questions can be answered to some extent in severely practical terms: The Indonesian constitution of 1949 was written in the shadow of the Round Table Conference Agreement, at a time when it was expedient for Indonesia to adopt Western constitutional forms. Thus the United Nations Commission for Indonesia was able to report that "the Partners [to the Netherlands-Indonesian Union] undertake to base their form of government on democracy, to aim at an independent judiciary, and to recognize fundamental human rights and freedoms as enumerated in an appendix to the [Union] Statute." [70] Earlier, in November 1945, a Western-type parliamentary system had been established in somewhat similar circumstances. Its adoption had followed the rise of Sjahrir, who came to power partly because of the belief that the Republic would gain wider international acceptance if headed by a leader of an anti-Japanese underground organization. The November 1945 system succeeded the earlier system of the constitution of August 1945, which was modeled in part on the Chinese Organic Law of 1931 and departed in some important ways from Western democratic constitutions. [71]

[70] See UN Commission for Indonesia, *Special Report to the Security Council,* UN Security Council Document S/1417, Nov. 10, 1949, Article 45, p. 26.

[71] Under this constitution, whose preparation had begun in the last months of the Japanese occupation, the President as head of the executive was not responsible to the working parliament, but to a superparliament which was to assemble "at least once every five years." The constitution was originally employed (for nine days) in conjunction with a system of a single state party. On the 1945 constitution

A further practical consideration was that a parliamentary system was actually operating in the Republic of Indonesia in 1949. A parliament was in existence, and cabinets were expected to be responsible to it. Moreover, it was generally thought that the post-November 1945 constitutional system of the Republic, under which there had been close co-operation between cabinets and the Inner Parliament to which they were normally responsible, had functioned fairly well.[72]

Indeed, there was no other system of legitimacy symbols and constitutional arrangements on which consensus could have been achieved in the political elite at the time. Although it is true that there was no full commitment to Western constitutional democracy and certainly none to its underlying ideas, it is equally true that no other set of ideas about the proper forms and operations of government had widespread currency. Traditional ideas of authority varied considerably between different regions of Indonesia, and there was no body of theory linking these ideas with the functioning of the modern institutions already in existence. It would have been impossible to secure support for a return to the authoritarian constitution of 1945. Military rule was quite out of the question, being seen as incompatible with democracy.

Then too national self-respect demanded that a serious effort be made to operate Western-type democratic institutions, for this was the one way to show the Dutch that Indonesians could indeed govern themselves democratically. And had denial of this not been central to the colonial argument of the Dutch? In addition, it appeared in 1949 and 1950 that the "really Asian" nations were those practicing constitutional democracy. India and Burma, countries with the most appealing records of struggle against colonial domination, countries which had helped Indonesia in its fight for independence and which had served, as much as any country had, as models for Indonesian foreign policy—these were also the countries with a commitment to democracy on Western lines. This was a period when the prestige of Western democratic institutions in Asia was high. There was a liberal democratic tide, as there was to be an authoritarian tide in the late 1950's.

Finally, the attempt to operate Western democratic institutions accorded with the values of some of the men in power in 1949 and

---

see Yamin, ed., *Naskah Persiapan Undang-Undang Dasar 1945.* See also Anderson, *op. cit.,* p. 31.

[72] Cf. Kahin, ed., *Major Governments of Asia,* pp. 510–511.

with the interests of most of them. For men like Hatta, Natsir, Sjahrir, Sultan Hamengku Buwono, Wilopo, Djuanda, Leimena, Sjafruddin Prawiranegara, and Colonel Simatupang, who had drunk deeply of the traditions of European liberalism and socialism or drawn similar values from a modernist Islam, Western-type democracy was an important article of belief. These men believed public liberties and the rule of law to be of great importance, and many of them saw parliamentary institutions as necessary safeguards against a possible development of authoritarianism, fascism, or demagogue rule. It is true that they produced no doctrine to justify Western-type procedures in terms of the images of democracy which had general currency at the time. But this was not because they, as individuals, lacked a strong value commitment to the ideas which these procedures embodied. It was probably in part because their own liberal-socialist views were difficult to reconcile with the populist nationalism which dominated the thinking of most members of the political public.

Apart from men like these, there were many others then in power who supported Western forms of democracy without having a value commitment to them. For them such forms deserved support simply because they were *their* forms. If they were overthrown, from whatever side and with whatever substitute, it was likely that their influence would decline. Indeed, those who had been associated with Hatta were likely to lose from virtually every retreat from Western models in politics or economics or culture. Moreover, there were many outside the group of Hatta supporters with an interest in the existing system, for instance the parliamentarians, the leaders of parties which could exercise influence over government on the basis of their parliamentary representation, and various newspaper editors and journalists, judges, and university teachers.

Clearly, Indonesia's commitment to Western democratic institutions resulted from a great variety of factors. Several of these were accidental and transitory factors; some were not. Some of the group of leaders dominant in 1949 had a definite value commitment to constitutional democracy, and many more had commitments of interest. But it is a fact that many leaders and their followers took a neutral view of the whole matter. Thus, although the symbol of democracy enjoyed very great acclaim, constitutional democracy was accepted only tentatively by the greater part of the political public.

Chapter *II*

The Hatta Cabinet, December 1949– August 1950:

Transition and Unification

ON December 18, 1949, Ir. Soekarno, as the newly installed President of the Republic of the United States of Indonesia, announced the names of the *formateurs* who were to select the new state's first cabinet. They were Drs. Hatta, Ide Anak Agung Gde Agung, Sultan Hamengku Buwono IX of Jogjakarta, and Sultan Hamid II of West Borneo. Their instructions were to form a "national business cabinet of experts, with due regard to the desires of the parties." The four-man group had few decisions to make. On December 20 sixteen men were sworn in as the cabinet which seven days later was the formal recipient of sovereignty transferred by both the Netherlands and the Republic of Indonesia:

Ministry			*Party*
Prime Minister and Minister of Foreign Affairs	Drs. Mohammad Hatta	RI	Nonparty
Home Affairs	Ide Anak Agung Gde Agung	East Indonesia	Nonparty
Defense	Hamengku Buwono IX, Sultan of Jogjakarta	RI	Nonparty

Ministry			Party
Finance	Mr. Sjafruddin Pra- wiranegara	RI	Masjumi
Prosperity	Ir. Djuanda	RI	Nonparty
Education and Culture	Dr. Abu Hanifah	RI	Masjumi
Labor	Mr. Wilopo	RI	PNI
Justice	Prof. Mr. Dr. Supomo	RI	Nonparty
Communications and Public Works	Ir. Herling Laoh	RI	PNI
Information	Arnold Mononutu	East Indo- nesia	PNI
Health	Dr. Johannes Leimena	RI	Parkindo (Chris- tian Party)
Social Affairs	Mr. Kosasih Purwane- gara	Pasundan	Nonparty
Religious Affairs	K. H. Wachid Hasjim	RI	Masjumi
State	Hamid II, Sultan of Pontianak	Kalimantan Barat	Nonparty
State	Mr. Mohammad Roem [1]	RI	Masjumi
State	Dr. Suparmo	Madura	Nonparty

THE CABINET AND THE POLITICAL BALANCE IT REPRESENTED

As cabinet membership was in the Indonesia of this period a fairly reliable index of the relative position of various power groupings at a particular time, it is worth looking at the list in some detail. One immediately striking feature of the cabinet's composition is the predominant role of men of the Republic of Indonesia within it. Although relations between the Republic and the BFO or Federal Consultative Assembly had in the previous months been based on a formal assumption of equality, only five of the new ministers were men from the BFO states. Of these five, only one, Sultan Hamid II, came from the BFO "right wing" which had most constantly endorsed Dutch actions against the Republic. Only two of the five, Sultan Hamid and Anak Agung Gde Agung, were committed supporters of a federal

---

[1] On January 19, 1950, Mohammad Roem was appointed RUSI High Commissioner in The Hague and thereupon resigned from the cabinet. For the formal listing of the members of this cabinet and of all cabinets of our period see Kementerian Penerangan (Ministry of Information), *Kabinet-Kabinet Republik Indonesia* ("The Cabinets of the Republic of Indonesia"; 2d ed.; Djakarta: Kementerian Penerangan, 1957).

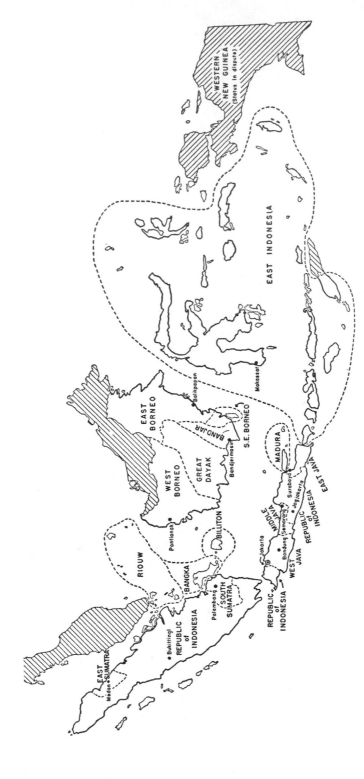

Map 1. Indonesia in December 1949. The state of Pasundan is designated here as West Java. (From George McTurnan Kahin, *Nationalism and Revolution in Indonesia*, Map 3; reproduced by permission, Cornell University Press.)

structure. For the rest, the cabinet was composed of men of the Republic of Indonesia.

This balance discloses an important political fact of the period, the already great weakness of the men of the Federal Consultative Assembly. As John Smail puts it in his perceptive monograph on the Hatta cabinet's formation:

[The Republican] preponderance was proof in advance of the coming triumph of unitarianism. The political atmosphere in the last half of 1949 which made this unbalanced cabinet seem logical—even those Federalists who had the most to fear from it acquiesced in its formation without public grumbling—was the atmosphere in which the unitarian movement flashed and grew in the early months of 1950.[2]

Indeed, the BFO had long been weak. A loose congeries of states without military forces or a common ideological position,[3] its only basis of independent power was its midway position between the Netherlands and the Republic of Indonesia. While the conflict between these two existed, it was able to exert influence by its freedom to throw support to either side. But when it became clear in mid-1949 that the Dutch government was reconciled to a virtually unconditional cession of sovereignty over Indonesia, this situation came to an end. Thenceforth the BFO's power declined rapidly.

Secondly, the Hatta cabinet's composition reflected the current dominance of Hatta in the politics of the Republic. In looking at this fact and searching for its roots, one comes quickly to most of the central political features of the period.

Within the RUSI cabinet the Prime Minister's position was indeed enormously strong. It was not that he towered over his colleagues in the way of leaders who choose men of markedly inferior ability as their associates and lieutenants. On the contrary, his ministers were men of a high order of both ability and prestige. His pre-eminence

---

[2] John R. W. Smail, "The Formation of the Hatta R.U.S.I. Cabinet" (unpublished monograph, Cornell Modern Indonesia Project, 1958), pp. 1–2. Smail follows the usage of the time in employing the term "Federalists" to refer to all those associated with the BFO states. I prefer to avoid this usage lest it give rise to the impression that the men of the Federal Consultative Assembly were all committed to a federal structure. This would be untrue of the state governments which were members of the Consultative Assembly. It would be even more untrue of the parliaments of their states.

[3] For a general discussion of the politics of the BFO states see George McT. Kahin, *Nationalism and Revolution in Indonesia* (Ithaca, N.Y.: Cornell University Press, 1952), pp. 351 ff.

was the result not of contrast between him and them, but rather of similarity. Almost all the eleven ministers from the Republic were "administrators," who shared Hatta's basic outlook on the country's needs, his concern for a practical grappling with immediate problems, for civil security, administrative efficiency, and carefully planned economic change. They too had a strong orientation toward using power to effect policy. In political style most of them were as pedestrian and lacking in circuses appeal as Hatta was. And most of them indeed had worked closely with him in the recent past.

But it is in the small role of the parties in the cabinet's formation that Hatta's dominance is seen most clearly. In the case of his previous cabinets, Hatta had emphasized the importance of the *zaken-kabinet* or business cabinet principle, the principle in Dutch constitutional practice whereby ministers are chosen for their individual technical competence rather than on the basis of party strengths.

In the case of the RUSI cabinet it was again a business cabinet that he wanted, rather than a coalition cabinet whose members were appointed as party representatives. And indeed he got almost exactly what he wanted, the opposition of various party leaders notwithstanding.[4] Of the eleven ministers from the Republic, four men belonged to no party. The other seven included four Masjumi members, two from the PNI, and one from the Parkindo (Partai Kristen Indonesia, Indonesian Christian Party). But only two or three of these seven can be regarded as in any important sense party representatives. They were not chosen on the basis of nomination by the executive councils of the respective parties. Moreover, a sizable number of candidates suggested by the leaders of the parties and rumored about in the press were bypassed. In Smail's words, "The party representation in the R.U.S.I. cabinet represents the party material that Hatta found he could use, not what the parties could obtain by measuring strengths against one another."[5]

One other sign of Hatta's position of dominance was the nature of his relationship with Soekarno. Soekarno had played a small public role throughout 1949, and this primarily in a ceremonial capacity. Exile in Bangka had isolated him from the military struggle which was of such key importance in setting the political trends of the first half

[4] See the statements of Mr. Ali Sastroamidjojo of the PNI in *Keng Po*, Nov. 16 and Dec. 10, 1949, and those of Dr. Sukiman and Mr. Samsuddin of the Masjumi in *Keng Po*, Nov. 28 and Dec. 7, 1949, quoted in Smail, "The Formation of the Hatta R.U.S.I. Cabinet," pp. 31–32.

[5] "The Formation of the Hatta R.U.S.I. Cabinet," p. 69.

of the year. And in the second half it was the development of the negotiations with the Dutch which was politically decisive; and this he had always left mainly to others.

The President's popularity at the end of 1949 was enormous. Townsmen and villagers, in the BFO areas as in the Republic, proudly hung his picture on their walls, and tumultuous crowds cheered him wherever he went. But in terms of power, his position was markedly inferior to that of Hatta. Lest the situation of later periods be falsely read into this one, it should be stressed here that political and personal relations between the two men were cordial at this time. The contrasts between them, in personality, ideas, and political style, were widely remarked upon, and many remembered their prewar political disagreements. But it was nevertheless customary to speak of Soekarno-Hatta as one political force. The two leaders had worked together in mutual loyalty for seven years, and their relationship to one another was seen chiefly in terms of the complementarity of their skills and roles, which fitted well with traditional ideas of the unity-in-duality of the cosmos.[6]

Why was Hatta's position so powerful? Firstly, no doubt, because of the successes he had achieved at the Round Table Conference. The Round Table Conference Agreement was certainly unpopular in Indonesia. In view of the fact that Holland had attacked the Republic just eleven months before, in a major military onslaught designed to destroy it, no treaty with the Dutch could have been popular. And the Round Table Conference Agreement did contain a number of provisions considered unpalatable. But the fact was that the Republic's position at the end of the conference was considerably more favorable than had been expected in May when Roem had committed the Republic to the "New Course" of negotiations which would end in a Round Table Conference. This was widely appreciated inside the Indonesian political elite, and to some extent also at the level of the political public. Inside the elite there was full appreciation of the central part Hatta had played at the Round Table Conference, of the enormous load of decision making he had carried there.[7]

[6] See J. M. van der Kroef, *Indonesia in the Modern World*, II (Bandung: Masa Baru, 1956), 138–157; and Moehammad Slamet, *Sekali Lagi Mengenai Kepribadian Bangsa Indonesia* ("Once More the Personality of the Indonesian Nation"; Social Research Centre, Padjadjaran State University, Occasional Paper no. 5; Bandung, 1960), pp. 17–18.

[7] See John Coast, *Recruit to Revolution* (London: Christophers, 1952), pp. 260, 269–271. See also Kahin, *Nationalism and Revolution*, pp. 433–435.

One aspect of the role of Hatta in the Round Table Conference deserves special attention: it was Hatta, more than any other Republican, who had inspired the trust, on the part of the BFO, the Dutch, and the Americans, which made the relatively favorable terms of the Round Table Agreement possible. To these various groups he was acceptable because of his generally moderate position, his legal orientation, his hostility toward unplanned change, and his long-held commitment to the protection of foreign investment in Indonesia. Nor would Hatta cease to play this role when the Hague Agreement had been concluded. On the contrary, the terms of the Round-Table-Conference-achieved independence, the continued presence of Dutch troops, and the state of administration and economic affairs at the time of the transfer of sovereignty implied a continued need for a man who had wide international and inter-Indonesian acceptability as well as high prestige in the Republic.

But Hatta's position of dominance within the Republic goes back beyond the Round Table Conference. It goes back to the two major happenings of the second half of 1948, the abortive Communist rebellion of September-October, the "Madiun affair," and the second Dutch attack on the Republic in December.

The crushing of the Madiun revolt meant the death of a major group of top Communist leaders; it meant the arrest, however short, of some 35,000 persons involved in the uprisings; and it meant that the organized power of the Communist Party within both the army and the irregular military formations was at an end.[8] Hatta, as both Prime Minister and Minister of Defense, had had a major personal role in the crushing of the revolt, and as a result of it an increased number of the high officers of the army were men of strong personal loyalty to him.

The chief significance of the Dutch attack for Hatta's position was that it put a virtual end to party political activity in the Republic. With no major towns under its control and its military forces dispersed into hundreds of guerrilla formations, the Republic had neither the leisure nor the surroundings for party politics. The one issue of internal political conflict which remained was how far the guerrilla leadership in Java and Sumatra was to lend its support to the top leaders of the Republic exiled in Bangka. This was a major conflict, with feelings of opposition to the policies of Soekarno and Hatta running high; for a time there was a real possibility that the Soekarno-

[8] On the rebellion generally see Kahin, *Nationalism and Revolution*, pp. 256–303.

Hatta leadership might be disavowed.[9] However, it was not a conflict between parties, but rather between different segments of the guerrilla government and different military formations, regular and irregular. Eventually in July 1949 it became clear that the "Bangka group" had succeeded in maintaining its leadership. It had succeeded partly because of the steady improvement in the Republic's negotiating position in relation to the Dutch, partly because of the great personal prestige of the Bangka leaders, and specifically because of the loyalty to them of a large group of the army leadership. From that point onward the Hatta government and the military leaders associated with it dominated the political scene.

It was only toward the end of 1949 that the parties began to be active again. But then they did not turn to issues; nor did they attempt to expand their influence at the level of cabinet politics. One of their principal concerns was organization.[10] They sought both to reestablish themselves in the old Republican areas and to move rapidly into the BFO areas as Dutch power was withdrawn, to establish footholds where virtually no party life existed, and to negotiate merger and affiliation arrangements with local parties where these did exist. And secondly they pressed to get government jobs for their members as the country's administrative structure was rebuilt. Here, indeed, the opportunities were immense, with hundreds of important bueaucratic positions to be filled, and tens of ambassadorial ones to boot.

But Hatta placed important restrictions on the parties' ability to secure themselves patronage and bureaucratic power. Thus where posts had great importance for policy or administrative efficiency, they

---

[9] See Kahin, *Nationalism and Revolution*, pp. 421 ff.; also T. B. Simatupang, *Laporan dari Banaran* ("A Report from Banaran"; Djakarta: Pembangunan, 1960). The veteran national-communist leader Tan Malaka used a guerrilla radio transmitter in the Kediri area to appeal for such a disavowal, and was thereupon killed by soldiers of Colonel Sungkono's First Division. See Muhammad Dimyati, *Sedjarah Perdjuangan Indonesia* ("A History of the Indonesian Struggle"; Djakarta: Widjaja, 1951), pp. 129–131. See also "Dimanakah Makam Tan Malaka, Bapak Republik dan Rakjat Indonesia?" ("Where Is the Grave of Tan Malaka, the Father of the Republic and of the Indonesian People?"), *Pembela Proklamasi* ("Defender of the Proclamation"), Sept. 3, 1955, and "Peringatan Sewindu Hilangnja Tan Malaka, 19 Februari 1949—19 Februari 1957" ("The Eighth Anniversary of the Disappearance of Tan Malaka, February 2, 1949"), *Bulletin Murba* ("Bulletin of the Murba Party"), Feb. 1957.

[10] For the Masjumi and the organizational problems discussed at its congress of Dec. 1949 see Deliar Noer, "Masjumi: Its Organization, Ideology and Political Role in Indonesia" (M.A. thesis, Cornell University, 1960). On the PNI at this time see Kementerian Penerangan, *Kepartaian di Indonesia* ("Political Parties in Indonesia"; Djakarta: Kementerian Penerangan, 1951), pp. 123–124.

were usually filled by men who measured up to Hatta's requirements, whether they were party men, or men of the currently influential Masjumi and PNI, or not. This was particularly true with regard to the appointment of the secretaries-general who would be the administrative heads of the RUSI ministries.

THE TRANSFER OF SOVEREIGNTY AND POWER

The practical problems of arranging the transfer of sovereignty taxed the full range of political resources at the disposal of Hatta and his associates. It was not until August 1, 1949, that the Netherlands and the Republic agreed to order a cease-fire. And then, with the Dutch army holding towns and the Republican army and irregulars in control of the greater part of the Java and Sumatra countryside, the truce was only partially maintained. September and early October saw a number of clashes. But tensions eased in the following two months, and there were numerous local transfers of military authority, in which Republican officers, acting as RUSI commanders, accepted responsibility from both Dutch and Republican irregular officers. The passions of warfare notwithstanding, the transfers were effected smoothly. It was a major feat of personal negotiation for the Republic's Coordinator of Security, Sultan Hamengku Buwono.

In certain areas, however, it was impossible for the Sultan to establish security. In a number of BFO regions such as South Sulawesi, South Kalimantan, and East Sumatra, where the anti-Dutch struggle had been fought by irregulars, some of these now refused to accept the authority of the Republican leadership.

Most difficult of all was the complex disorder of West Java. There a group of battalions of the Moslem military organization, Hizbullah, had exercised power in virtual independence of the Republic since early 1948, when the Jogjakarta government had withdrawn its more obedient troops from most of West Java in compliance with the Renville Agreement with the Dutch. In March 1948 this group had established itself as the Darul Islam (literally House of Islam), an autonomous organization with its own army, the Tentara Islam Indonesia (Islamic Army of Indonesia). And on August 7, 1949, its leader, S. M. Kartosuwirjo, had proclaimed the Negara Islam Indonesia (Islamic State of Indonesia).[11] The following months saw a considerable exten-

---

[11] See George McT. Kahin, "Indonesian Politics and Nationalism," in W. L. Holland, ed., *Asian Nationalism and the West* (New York: Macmillan, 1953), pp. 104–110; "Gangguan Keamanan di Indonesia" ("Security Disturbances in Indonesia";

sion of the power of this Moslem extremist organization, in West Java and into parts of western Central Java. Republican troops engaged its units in battle on several occasions, but were unable to check their expansion.

A second smaller group of West Java guerrillas who refused to acknowledge the authority of the Republic was the Lasjkar Rakjat Djawa Barat (West Java People's Brigade), an organization of Tan Malaka followers led by Chaerul Saleh, one of the youth leaders who had pressed Soekarno and Hatta to make the original independence proclamation of August 17, 1945. In mid-November 1949 this group, strong particularly in north coast areas of the province, denounced the Republic's leadership and proclaimed itself as the Tentara Rakjat (People's Army) to fight for independence free of the Round Table Conference terms.[12]

In addition to the Darul Islam, the Tentara Rakjat, and numerous smaller bands of former Republican guerrillas now unwilling to acknowledge the Republican leadership, West Java harbored several hundred armed men gathered in the force of the former KNIL captain of Dutch-Greek origin, R. P. P. Westerling. This force, the APRA (Angkatan Perang Ratu Adil, Army of the Messianic King), which asserted that its aim was to protect the state of Pasundan, included both former Republican guerrillas and dischargees and deserters from the KNIL, Dutchmen, Eurasians, Ambonese, and Minahasans. With the Republic militarily weak in West Java, the stage was set there for much of what would develop after sovereignty had been transferred, both the dramatic violence of 1950 and the long-festering terrorism of the following years.

Formal responsibility for preparing the transfer of sovereignty was borne by a National Preparatory Committee, a joint Republican-BFO agency originally foreseen at the mid-year Inter-Indonesian Confer-

---

II), *Mimbar Penerangan* ("Information Forum"; Kementerian Penerangan, Djakarta), June 1953, pp. 15–23; Sewaka, *Tjorat-Tjaret* ("Sketches"; n.p., 1955), pp. 165 ff.; and especially C. A. O. van Nieuwenhuijze, "The Darul Islam Movement in West Java," *Pacific Affairs*, XXIII (1950), 169–183.

[12] *Sin Po* (Djakarta), Nov. 17, 1949. See also the reply of Defense Minister Sultan Hamengku Buwono to the parliamentary question of Amelz on the arrest of Chaerul Saleh, in *Pertanjaan Anggota dan Djawaban Pemerintah* ("Members' Questions and Government Replies"; Djakarta: Sekretariat D.P.R.–R.I.S., 1950), I, 41–42 (from the Minister's statement to parliament on March 11, 1950). See, too, Kementerian Penerangan, *Republik Indonesia, Propinsi Djawa Barat* ("The West Java Province of the Republic of Indonesia"; Djakarta: Kementerian Penerangan, 1953), pp. 242–253.

ences and established on November 26. It was this body, headed by Mohammad Roem, which acted in lieu of the RUSI cabinet prior to the cabinet's formation. Its most important work by far was in the field of security for which the Sultan of Jogjakarta had assumed responsibility. In addition, the committee had a section to arrange for the transfer of administrative responsibility from the Dutch central bureaucracy of the "Interim Federal Government of Indonesia" to a skeleton RUSI bureaucracy and another to plan the procedural and ceremonial aspects of the transfer.

At the end of November the various states and territories began to vote ratification of the Round Table Conference agreements. In the case of the BFO states these votes were little more than formalities, but a good deal of attention was given to the ratification debate held by the Central National Committee (the "Outer Parliament") of the Republic. It was not that Republican ratification was in any serious doubt—for before the debate opened President Soekarno had already used his appointing power to increase support for the government, and it was clear that he could do this again if the need arose.[13] But whether the government could score a moral victory as well as a formal one was of major political importance. In these terms the outcome was reckoned by most to be a defeat, for the government in general and Hatta in particular. The number of members who arrived at the meeting was small; indeed, it was necessary that the Working Body (the "Inner Parliament") make the quorum requirement less rigorous. Then in the eight-day debate the government was attacked strongly for the agreement, with the attacks by no means confined to the PKI and the national-communist Partai Murba.[14]

Finally, on December 15 ratification was approved, by 236 votes to 62, with 31 abstentions. Opposition votes were cast by members of the two communist parties and of various smaller organizations related to one of these. The Indonesian Socialist Party and its sympathizers accounted for most of the abstentions.

On December 19 the Dutch parliament ratified the agreement, the lower house supporting it by 71 to 29 and the upper house by 34 to

---

[13] See *Antara*, Dec. 5, 1949. The President's power was based on Government Regulation 6 of 1946. For the text and elucidation of this regulation and a discussion of the circumstances which brought it into existence see Roeslan Abdulgani, *Funksi Penerangan di Indonesia* ("The Function of Information Work in Indonesia"; Djakarta: Kementerian Penerangan, 1953), pp. 97–98, 124–132. See also Kahin, *Nationalism and Revolution*, pp. 199–206.

[14] *Mimbar Indonesia*, Nov. 18, 26, Dec. 10, 17, 24, 1949.

15, one vote more than the two-thirds majority required. Now the way was clear for the final stages of the transfer. The RUSI President was elected, the cabinet was formed and sworn in, and the complicated ceremonials of transfer began. On December 27 ceremonies took place simultaneously at The Hague, where Hatta received sovereignty from Queen Juliana, at Djakarta, where Sultan Hamengku Buwono received it similarly from the Dutch High Commissioner Lovink, and at Jogjakarta, where Soekarno received it (transferred to RUSI from the Republic of Indonesia) from a newly installed Acting President of the Republic, Mr. Assaat.

One significant aspect of the transfer lies in the sharply contrasting reactions it evoked in different parts of the country. In Jogjakarta and other towns which had remained Republican for most of the period of Revolution the response was lukewarm. Here it was not felt that Indonesia was gaining independence. Indonesia had been independent for more than four years; this was at most a recognition of the fact. But in fact it was less than that, for the recognition did not go to the Republic which had given the blood of its best sons for independence. Instead it went to a compromise state, a state in which the revolutionary spirit of Indonesian patriotism would be diluted. As some Republicans saw it, it went to a restoration state, a state in which Dutch capital would again hold predominant power throughout the archipelago. Moreover, many in the Republican areas continued to doubt whether the transfer of sovereignty would be final. Seeing the continued presence of Dutch troops and remembering the Linggadjati and Renville agreements, each of which was to have brought peace and failed to, they adopted an attitude of agnostic and sometimes embittered withdrawal, an attitude of "wait and see." [15]

In the BFO states and territories the reaction to December 27 was entirely different. For the small group of people who supported the states the day was a sad one indeed, since most of them saw that these entities could not survive long once the Dutch had withdrawn their troops. But for the great majority of the populations of the states and territories whose sympathies lay with the nationalism of the Republic, it was a day of great joy and excitement. Now they would regain the independence which they had enjoyed briefly before the postwar Dutch reoccupation. Freedom would come, jails would be cleared, the

[15] For a discussion of these reactions see Jeanne S. Mintz, "Marxism in Indonesia," in Frank N. Trager, ed., *Marxism in Southeast Asia* (Stanford: Stanford University Press, 1959), pp. 216–217.

Dutch would depart, and at last Indonesians, they themselves, would have opportunities. The welcome which the people of Djakarta gave to President Soekarno when he arrived back there from Jogjakarta on December 28 was one of triumph in the highest degree.

In the world outside the creation of the new state was welcomed with pleasure and a measure of relief. Indeed, Indonesia's prestige was high. It came into existence as a nation which had earned its right to nationhood. In Asia there was rejoicing because of the Indonesian victory over colonialism. Asia had been watching the Indonesian struggle for years, with both admiration and concern. The plight of the Indonesian Republic after the second Dutch attack had led Nehru to call a conference of free Asian governments, the New Delhi Asian Relations Conference, of January 1949.

In the West opinion was more divided. Some feared a repetition of the insecurity which had followed the achievement of independence in Burma. But the feeling was widespread that the Indonesian nationalists had demonstrated high qualities of leadership, arousing the full support of their people and yet holding their ardor in check while negotiations were held. In every country the memory of the two Dutch attacks on the Republic was still fresh. The cause of the Republic had long drawn a warm response from those whose hearts went out to the underdog. More recently it had won the sympathy also of all whose hopes were pinned on the United Nations as a conciliator and preventer of aggression. In a sense Indonesia was, as India's Sir Benegal Rau was to say a little later, a "child of the United Nations." [16] Only in the Soviet bloc was there hostility toward the new state. In general, the Indonesian representatives who assumed diplomatic posts overseas in early 1950 were welcomed with sympathy and respect.[17]

THE DEMISE OF THE FEDERAL STATES

The peculiar set of circumstances which had brought about the Round Table Conference was of decisive importance for the role of the Hatta cabinet and gave it a dual character. On the one hand, the cabinet saw as its chief task the ordering of the complex administrative and military changes of the transition in such a way as to preserve and strengthen public security and legal norms. On the other hand, it

[16] Alastair M. Taylor, *Indonesian Independence and the United Nations* (Ithaca, N.Y.: Cornell University Press, 1960), p. 265. Sir Benegal was proposing Indonesia's admission to UN membership, Sept. 28, 1950.

[17] See Mohammad Roem, *Politik Indonesia, 1952* (Djakarta and Bukittinggi: Penjiaran Ilmu, 1952), pp. 10–11.

was itself an arm of a successful revolutionary movement which strove with all determination to extend its power to areas where it had theretofore been repressed. Within a few weeks of its assumption of power the Hatta cabinet came to face most of the problems inherent in this duality of roles.

In political substance RUSI represented a victory for Indonesian nationalism, but in legal form the Dutch had succeeded in imposing their will. One effect of this discrepancy was an enormous administrative confusion in the period immediately after the transfer of sovereignty.

In the BFO areas legal and administrative arrangements were characterized by an amazing variety of forms. Each and every one of the fifteen Dutch-established constitutional entities had its own peculiarities of structure and organization and its own particular basis for relations with Djakarta. The entities of highest constitutional status were the six "states"—East Indonesia, Pasundan (West Java), East Java, Madura, South Sumatra, and East Sumatra. The nine other units, which the RUSI constitution termed merely "separate constitutional entities" (*satuan kenegaraan jang tegak sendiri*) and which were usually referred to as territories (*daerahs*), were lower in status and were, on the earlier Dutch projection, at various stages of development to becoming "states" or parts of "states." They were the "special territory" (*daerah istimewa*) of West Kalimantan, the "territory" (*daerah*) of Bandjar, the four "neolands" Dajak Besar, Bangka, Billiton, and Riau, the two "federations" East Kalimantan and Southeast Kalimantan, and the "political entity" Central Java. In addition, there existed other quasi-autonomous units which had not participated in the BFO or the Round Table Conference. And then again there were subordinate units in some of these constitutional entities (notably in the state of East Indonesia), which had a degree of autonomy and direct access to Djakarta.[18]

What had hitherto given this whole ramshackle edifice cohesion was the presence of Dutch administrators, who had controlled both the (still predominantly powerful) central government in Djakarta and the lines of communication linking this government with the regional entities. But now these men were no longer in control. On administrative grounds alone it appeared that a major overhaul of governmental

---

[18] This legal structure is described with meticulous care (and a marvelous unconcern for political reality) in A. Arthur Schiller, *The Formation of Federal Indonesia* (The Hague: van Hoeve, 1955). See especially pp. 80–197.

relationships was necessary. And indeed this was foreseen in the RUSI constitution, which gave the federal authorities of RUSI wide powers to legislate concerning the area, the internal constitutional provisions, and the very existence of the member states and territories.[19]

Within the areas of the Republic of Indonesia the situation was more stable, and a considerable degree of governmental continuity prevailed. There was, however, a source of confusion in the fact that the Republic's legal area of competency as a member state of the federation was small compared with its actual power and prestige. Thus its officials tended to look to the RI government in Jogjakarta for instructions in areas of governmental activity which were formally the province of the RUSI government in Djakarta.

The chaos was greatest in those areas of Java and Sumatra where BFO areas bordered on territory of the Republic. Here the state boundaries—originally laid down in the 1948 Renville Agreement— were often irrelevant to the actual conduct of administration. In some formally Republican areas, areas occupied in the second "police action" of December 1948, Dutch officers continued to operate military government. In other areas, formally part of the state of Pasundan or the state of East Java, the Republic had long had "shadow" administrations. Frequently a condition of double administration prevailed, with no clear delineation of spheres of influence. Some of the confusion was alleviated by the fact that martial law prevailed throughout Java (not Madura) and Sumatra, placing ultimate governmental authority in the hands of RUSI army officers whose commands often extended across state boundaries. And certainly the administrative picture was simpler for the fact that the constitution was highly centralistic in its federal-state division of powers, giving the federal authorities competency not only in such matters as defense, foreign relations, and foreign trade, but also as regards police regulation and the appropriation of state-levied taxation. Nevertheless the new cabinet faced enormous problems of administrative regularization.

However, the most difficult problems before it were not administrative but political, and before long also military. With the transfer of sovereignty completed, large numbers of Republican guerrilla fighters

[19] See Articles 42 to 50. The constitution was published in Kementerian Peneranganan Republik Indonesia, *Perdjuangan di Konperensi Medja Bundar* ("The Struggle at the Round Table Conference"; Jogjakarta: Kementerian Penerangan, 1949), pp. 270–333. An English translation of the constitution may be found in United Nations Commission for Indonesia, *Special Report to the Security Council on the Round Table Conference*, UN Security Council Document S/1417, Nov. 10, 1949, vol. II.

came down from the mountains in triumph, ready to take an active part in the politics of the urban centers, most of them situated in BFO territory. They joined an important group of Republican political prisoners emerging from Dutch jails either before December 27 or soon afterward.[20] Welcoming them, often with particular vociferousness, was a third group important for an understanding of the new political situation, the group of those whose nationalist record had blotches to be erased.

At the same time, RUSI army units composed of old Republican soldiers moved in large numbers into the old BFO states. Here there continued to be a great many soldiers under Dutch command, 80,000 of the Royal Army (KL) and 65,000 of the Royal Netherlands Indies Army (KNIL).[21] Plans were in hand for the repatriation of the KL troops, but there had been only limited progress in the weeks before December 27 on the question of the terms on which KNIL troops would enter the RUSI armed forces. Most of the 65,000 therefore remained under Dutch command for some time.

It was in this setting that there developed the movement for abolition of the Dutch-established states. By the middle of January 1950 a crescendo of denunciations of the states and territories was coming from political parties and other organizations in almost every part of the country. First in one place and then in another, multiparty committees and fronts arose to urge a particular territorial entity to dissolve itself and merge into the Republic. In many cases this was coupled with a demand for the quick achievement of a unitary Republic of Indonesia extending over the whole country. In some areas of Java and Sumatra local heads within the administrative structure of one or other of the states declared that they would thenceforth be part of the Republic's administration. By the end of January various legislative councils within the Dutch-built structure, including those of East Java, Madura, and Central Java, had passed resolutions asking that they be incorporated in the Republic.

This already fast rising movement grew considerably stronger in consequence of a series of developments in West Java resulting from

[20] The Dutch had released 7,862 untried persons from their jails between August 10 and December 27, 1949, and another 4,589 convicted but amnestied persons between November 4 and December 27. Between December 27 and March 1, 1950, the RUSI cabinet amnestied and released another 4,414 convicted persons. See the March 11, 1950, statement of Minister of Justice Supomo in *Pertanjaan Anggota dan Djawaban Pemerintah*, I, 61–67.

[21] Taylor, *op. cit.*, p. 413.

the activities of Captain Westerling. On January 23 a Westerling force of some 800 fully armed men attacked the West Java capital of Bandung. Approximately 500 of them were members of Westerling's own APRA, the rest soldiers of the KL and KNIL. After sharp fighting, in which 79 members of the RUSI army and a sizable number of civilians were killed, the Westerling troops captured most key points in the city.[22] There were immediate negotiations in Djakarta between Hatta and the Dutch High Commissioner. As a result Major General Engels, commander of the KL garrison in Bandung, persuaded the Westerling units to leave the city. This they did on the afternoon of the same day.

A second phase of Westerling's coup developed on the following day, with Djakarta as its center. This time Westerling acted in close coordination with Sultan Hamid, the former BFO chairman who was then a minister without portfolio in the RUSI cabinet. On Hamid's instructions, Westerling's men were to attack the cabinet building that afternoon while the cabinet was in session. They were to kidnap all cabinet members, kill the Defense Minister, Sultan Hamengku Buwono, the Defense Ministry's Secretary-General Mr. Ali Budiardjo, and the Acting Chief of Staff of the Armed Forces, Colonel T. B. Simatupang, and shoot Hamid himself in the arm or leg. In consequence Hamid was to emerge as Defense Minister.[23]

The plot, which involved the one major assassination attempt of the seven-and-a-half-year period of this study, was in fact never executed. News of it reached the cabinet, which therefore stopped its meeting early. After some skirmishes with RUSI troops the Westerling units were driven out of the city. They became involved in several more engagements in the following three weeks. But failure and arrests were destroying their cohesion. On February 22 Westerling left the country in disguise, flying to Malaya in a Netherlands military plane. His following disintegrated quickly thereafter.

The Westerling affair was of major importance in accentuating Indo-

---

[22] See the January 24 communiqué of the RUSI Ministry of Defense in Kementerian Penerangan, *Republik Indonesia, Propinsi Djawa Barat*, pp. 270–273; Ministry of Foreign Affairs, Republic of Indonesia, *Subversive Activities in Indonesia: The Jungschlaeger and Schmidt Affair* (Djakarta: Government Printing Office, 1957), pp. 13–17; and Raymond ("Turk") Westerling, *Challenge to Terror* (London: Kimber, 1952).

[23] See Persadja (Persatuan Djaksa-Djaksa Seluruh Indonesia, All-Indonesian Public Prosecutors' Association), *Proces Peristiwa Sultan Hamid II* ("The Court Proceedings in the Case of Sultan Hamid II"; Djakarta: Fasco, 1955), *passim*. On April 8, 1953, the Supreme Court gave Hamid a ten-year sentence.

nesian mistrust of the Dutch. Some Dutch officers were clearly implicated in it, and others had shown what was regarded as an extraordinary inability to keep their own soldiers under control. Subsequently the Dutch authorities did co-operate with RUSI. But the damage was already done. RUSI army authorities stressed that the Dutch had done nothing about requests, repeatedly made of them in the months before the transfer of sovereignty, for action to be taken against Westerling.

Even more important, the Westerling coups produced a quick increase in activity directed against the BFO states. Initially there was no suspicion of Sultan Hamid's complicity in Westerling's activities. But parts of the government of Pasundan fell under immediate suspicion. On January 25 its Prime Minister Anwar Tjokroaminoto, its Communications Minister Suria Kartalegawa, and a number of its lower officials were arrested, and two days later the state's parliament passed a vote of no confidence in its cabinet and asked that the state should transfer its powers to RUSI. On January 30 the Pasundan head of state, R. A. A. Wiranatakusumah, resigned, and on February 10 the Hatta cabinet appointed Sewaka, currently the Republic's Governor for its areas of West Java, as RUSI Government Commissioner in charge of government in Pasundan.

Elsewhere, too, the movement against the BFO states and territories was gaining momentum. On January 27 the Sultan of Kutai, head of the sultanate council which was the most powerful body in East Kalimantan, announced his support for the unitary state. Soon thereafter the state of Madura requested and was granted a RUSI Government Commissioner, as the state of East Java and the "political entity" of Central Java had earlier. Similarly Djakarta acceded to the request of the representative council of the state of South Sumatra and placed this state under the authority of a RUSI administrator.

The clearest illustration of the political weakness of the Dutch-built states at this time came when the RUSI parliament assembled on February 15 and elections were held for parliamentary officers. In the Senate, where the BFO states had 30 of the 32 seats, a BFO leader, M. A. Pellaupessy, was elected speaker. On the other hand, in the House of Representatives, where the BFO states had 100 seats and the Republic of Indonesia the remaining 50, no BFO man was even nominated for the speakership or any of the three deputy speakerships or for the chairmanship of any of the parliamentary divisions (general committees) or sections (committees for particular areas of governmental business).[24] All these posts went to representatives from the Republic—and this notwithstanding the fact that a large number of the 100 BFO representatives had a record of pro-Republican sympathies and the further fact that a majority of the group had joined Republican-led parties.

Meanwhile rallies and demonstrations continued against most of the states and territories. The RUSI cabinet was giving no encouragement to this wave of nationalist protest, but at the same time it was afraid to be left too far behind the predominant popular current—if only because this might result in illegal actions against the BFO states. An over-all legal formula seemed to be in demand. Thus on March 8 the cabinet enacted an emergency law sanctioning the voluntary union of one state or territory with another.[25] The law stated that expression of a state's will for such a union was normally to be by plebiscite, or by the action of a specially convened session of the representative council where such a council was in existence, but that it could be by shorter procedures if the situation demanded this. The emergency law was immediately discussed and approved by both houses of parliament.

In the following three and a half weeks four states, eight territories, and three other constitutional units were merged into the Republic. In no case was this by plebiscite. In four instances, in the states of Pasundan, South Sumatra, East Java, and Madura, dissolution had been requested by an existing representative assembly, though not in sessions specially convened for that purpose.[26] In the other cases, demonstrations, rallies, and the like were taken as sufficient indication of popular will. In every case the RUSI House of Representatives had passed resolutions urging the merger.

By April 4 only four separate entities continued to exist within RUSI, the Republic of Indonesia, the states of East Indonesia and East Sumatra, and the special territory of West Kalimantan. A point had been reached where there were no longer any states left which could be toppled without serious resistance. This was the point at

[24] See Subakir, *Skets Parlementer* ("Parliamentary Sketches"; Djakarta: Pena, 1950), p. 12.

[25] *Lembaran Negara Republik Indonesia Serikat* ("RUSI State Documents"), Law no. 16, 1950. According to Articles 139 and 140 of the RUSI constitution the government was empowered to make emergency laws which were submitted to parliament after their enactment and continued to be valid unless rejected by parliament.

[26] See F. R. Böhtlingk, "De Nieuwe Eenheidsstaat," *Indonesië*, IV (1950–1951), 106 ff., for a discussion of legal aspects of the dissolution.

which a number of RUSI government leaders had hoped the situation would stabilize itself. They had foreseen from before December 27 that a number of states would rapidly disappear and had made no secret of this expectation.[27] But they had not wanted to see the federal form abandoned, or at least not until this could be done by a duly elected Constituent Assembly. This was the point of view of Prime Minister Hatta.

For a time in March it seemed possible that the movement against the Dutch-built states was slowing down. But this impression did not last long. On April 5 Sultan Hamid, head of the state of West Kalimantan, was arrested for his complicity in the Westerling activities of January. Demands for the dissolution of West Kalimantan quickly increased in volume, culminating in a general strike in Pontianak. On April 15 the RUSI House of Representatives voted for a merger of this special territory into the Republic. The RUSI government responded by placing the area under the authority of an administrator of its own.

It was in East Indonesia, however, that the fate of the federal establishment was finally sealed. East Indonesia was on all counts the most "real" of the BFO states. It was the oldest of the states, dating back to 1946, and the largest territorially (comprising Sulawesi, the Moluccas, and the Lesser Sundas from Bali to Timor). It included the two most important privileged areas of the old Netherlands Indies, Minahasa in North Sulawesi and Ambon in the Moluccas, areas with high literacy rates, large Protestant populations, and intensive Dutch cultural influence, areas which had long served as principal recruiting places for the KNIL and were therefore ambivalent in their responses to Indonesian nationalism. Moreover, the state included regions where traditional rule by the heads of petty principalities continued to have strong social roots. During the Japanese occupation, East Indonesia had been under a navy administration which had repressed nationalism and established no militias. In the years between 1946 and 1949 it had enjoyed greater effective autonomy than any other BFO state, and in 1950 it had a newly elected parliament.[28]

---

[27] See, for instance, the article by Minister of Justice Supomo, the chief Republican architect of the RUSI constitution, "Pertanggungan Djawab Pemerintah Indonesia" ("The Responsibility of the RUSI Government"), *Mimbar Indonesia*, Dec. 27, 1949.

[28] Schiller, *op. cit.*, pp. 165 ff. The elections had been based on direct voting in the case of Minahasa and the South Moluccas and on two-stage and three-stage procedures in the other regions.

Here too, however, the pressures for dissolution were strong. As against the two specially privileged regions of Minahasa and the South Moluccas, there were eleven other regions (corresponding roughly with particular ethnic groups) where there was no particular reason to fear Djakarta or the Javanese, or at least not more than one resented the current dominance in the East Indonesian state of Minahasans and Ambonese. Anti-"feudal" feeling was strong in a number of the regions of the state, not least in Bali and South Sulawesi, two areas whose traditional rulers played a particularly prominent part in the government of East Indonesia (alongside men from Minahasa and Ambon). Within the East Indonesian parliament there had long been many with a strong commitment to the cause of the Republic. Now, with the magnet of power in Indonesia as a whole in Republican hands, the influence of these men grew with great rapidity.

Militarily the KNIL maintained preponderance in East Indonesia. But Republican guerrilla units were active in several parts of the state, especially near the capital of Makassar. And when a Republican officer, Lieutenant Colonel A. J. Mokoginta, was placed in Makassar as a member of a three-man RUSI territorial command for East Indonesia, he brought with him a number of small Republican military units. Many of the newly arrived soldiers (who were mostly East Indonesians) worked actively for the downfall of the East Indonesian state.[29]

In the second half of March large demonstrations for the merging of East Indonesia into the Republic were held in various places in South Sulawesi. At the same time there were smaller counterdemonstrations in support of the East Indonesian state. The state government placed a ban on demonstrations, but was pressed to lift it a week later. On March 25, on the eve of a projected mass meeting in Makassar in support of the state, a hand grenade was thrown into the house of one of the leading organizers of the meeting, and a policeman was shot at.[30] The state authorities persuaded the organizers to call off the meeting.

For all this time tension had been mounting inside the KNIL units in South Sulawesi. KNIL officers had made a number of requests to Djakarta that the conversion of their units should proceed quickly. They had asked that those of their members who desired admission

[29] J. M. van der Kroef, "The South Moluccan Insurrection in Indonesia: A Preliminary Analysis," *University of Manila Journal of East Asiatic Studies*, I, no. 4 (1952), 7–10.

[30] See Mustafa Sulaiman, *Taufan Disekitar Negara Indonesia* ("The Indonesian State Caught in a Typhoon"; Djakarta: Widjaja, 1951), pp. 30–43.

to the RUSI armed forces be admitted rapidly (and without too much reorganization of units) and that the rest be discharged forthwith. Djakarta, aware of the advantages of doing neither, thereby keeping these soldiers politically neutralized, responded only slowly.[31]

Resentment within KNIL ranks rose sharply when it became known early in April that a large contingent of former Republican troops were being sent to Makassar. Upon hearing of this, a group of KNIL soldiers, some still in KNIL uniform, others officially or self-declared members of the RUSI armed forces, formed themselves into a Pasukan Bebas (Free Corps) under the leadership of Captain Andi Abdul Aziz.[32]

In the early morning of April 5 the force under Aziz attacked the RUSI military establishment in Makassar, arrested a number of its Republican officers, including Mokoginta, and occupied strategic points in the city. In a radio speech made on the same day Captain Aziz said that his action had been taken to prevent the landing of the expected RUSI troops from Java, and these were indeed prevented from landing. On April 5 also the East Indonesian cabinet of Ir. P. D. Diapari resigned, after its Prime Minister had stated that he regretted the action of Aziz.

On April 10 Hatta made a nationwide broadcast calling for a negotiated settlement of the Makassar conflict on the basis of what he described as the satisfactory results of a tripartite conference just concluded between representatives of RUSI, the Republic, and East Indonesia. He evidently hoped that the East Indonesian representatives would, on their return to Makassar, be able to persuade Aziz to surrender his power. But this did not happen. Two days later the RUSI government changed to a less conciliatory policy and ordered Aziz to consign his troops to their barracks, release all those whom he had arrested, and come personally to Djakarta within 48 hours. When April 14 came and Aziz had failed to appear, President Soekarno himself went on the air with a denunciation of Aziz as a rebel against the power of the RUSI government. A day later Aziz, responding to pressure from the East Indonesian President Soekawati, flew to

[31] Van der Kroef, "South Moluccan Insurrection," pp. 3–6.

[32] It became clear in the course of the trial of Captain Aziz in 1953 that he was urged to rebellion also by a number of political leaders, notably the East Indonesian Minister of Justice, Mr. Dr. Soumokil. See "Requisitoir Djaksa Tentara Terhadap Terdakwa Kapten Andi Aziz" ("Concluding Statement of the Military Prosecutor in the Case of Captain Andi Aziz"), in Kementerian Penerangan, *Laporan Pers Harian* ("Daily Press Report"), April 27, 1953.

Djakarta. There he was promptly arrested.[33] On April 18 RUSI troops landed near Makassar. They met little resistance, and on the following day the remainder of Aziz's troops surrendered to them.

With the collapse of the Aziz revolt the political position of the supporters of the East Indonesia state changed dramatically. In the first place, the military balance was entirely changed. Secondly, the moral position of the state was compromised. The relationship between Aziz's group and the leadership of the East Indonesian state, like Westerling's relationship with the heads of Pasundan, was ambiguous. But there was enough evidence of collaboration on the part of certain East Indonesian functionaries, notably the Justice Minister Soumokil, to produce a considerable widening of hostility to the state. Pro-Republican demonstrations were resumed on a large scale. On April 21, East Indonesia's President Soekawati announced that his state was prepared to become part of a unitary Indonesia if the Republic of Indonesia agreed equally to be absorbed in such a state.[34] May 9 saw the establishment of an East Indonesian "liquidation cabinet" under the Pro-Republican Ir. Putuhena.[35]

Faced with the impending collapse of the East Indonesian state, the Hatta cabinet came to the conclusion, around mid-April, that a unitary state had to be achieved quickly. There would simply not be time to wait for a Constituent Assembly to be elected and deliberate on a new constitution. The current political unrest, it was felt, could best be relieved by moving with maximum speed (the maximum consonant with legality and proper procedure) toward the establishment, or re-establishment, of a unitary state. This was the cause for which the cabinet leaders of the Republic of Indonesia had been pressing for some weeks. Once the Hatta cabinet had accepted its desirability, there remained only the matter of accomplishing the transition.

Even this, however, was by no means easy or uncontroversial. One course, advocated by the Republic's Minister for the Interior, the PNI leader Mr. Susanto Tirtoprodjo, was a dissolution of all the

[33] On April 8, 1953, he was sentenced by a military court to a term of 14 years (*Antara*, April 9, 1953).

[34] *Aneta News Bulletin* (hereafter cited as *Aneta*), April 21, 1950, quoted in Kahin, *Nationalism and Revolution*, p. 460.

[35] Mustafa Sulaiman, *op. cit.*, pp. 43 ff. See also Kementerian Penerangan, *Republik Indonesia, Propinsi Sulawesi* ("The Sulawesi Province of the Republic of Indonesia"); Djakarta: Kementerian Penerangan, 1953), pp. 161 ff.

remaining units into the Republic. Another, advocated by the East Indonesian President Soekawati, was the dissolution of all other units into RUSI, which would then "defederalize" itself. The RUSI government found itself caught between these two strongly held points of view.

Eventually, as a result of various conferences, a compromise was reached whereby RUSI and the Republic were to act jointly in the establishment of a new unitary "Republic of Indonesia." On May 5 after a three-day conference with Hatta, President Soekawati and the head of East Sumatra, Dr. T. Mansur, agreed to this formula, empowering Hatta to represent their states in the subsequent negotiations with the Republic which would set down the basis for the establishment of the new unitary state. Finally, on May 19, the Prime Ministers of RUSI and the Republic of Indonesia, Dr. M. Hatta and Dr. A. Halim, issued a Charter of Agreement: "We agree," its introduction declared, "to implement in co-operation and in the shortest possible time the formation of a Unitary State which shall be a materialization of the Republic of Indonesia based on the Proclamation of August 17, 1945." [36]

The next three months were a period of protracted negotiations on the new Republic's constitution. But they were also a period of continued sporadic fighting, notably in East Indonesia. In South Sulawesi large numbers of Republican guerrillas left their mountain strongholds after the defeat of the Aziz coup and began to challenge the political *status quo* of the towns. In some areas they were immediately successful; there the local aristocrats who had worked with the Dutch yielded their positions of power without serious resistance. Elsewhere, however, these did resist, using local KNIL garrisons for the purpose, and violence ensued. In Makassar itself there were two more major clashes in which KNIL troops were involved, on May 15 and August 5.

Meanwhile there had been a further KNIL-backed rebellion, this time in the South Moluccas, the KNIL recruiting ground par excellence. Here the initiative came from Mr. Dr. Soumokil, the former Justice Minister of East Indonesia who had been heavily involved in the Makassar coup of Aziz. On April 25 Soumokil, himself an Ambonese, proclaimed the "Republic of the South Moluccas"—with the support of the regional executive council of the area.

[36] Kementerian Penerangan, *Republik Indonesia, Daerah Istimewa Jogjakarta* ("The Special Territory of Jogjakarta of the Republic of Indonesia"; Djakarta: Kementerian Penerangan, 1953), p. 327.

Of all the KNIL-supported insurrections, this one undoubtedly enjoyed the greatest measure of local popular backing.[37] The demobilized KNIL soldiers who had returned home to spread fears of a Java-dominated, Islam-dominated, and Communist-dominated Republican Indonesia were in large part believed. It is hard to know how large a part of the South Moluccan population supported the separatist Republic. One factor working against the separatists' popularity was that very many South Moluccans had family members living in other parts of Indonesia. Another was the harsh military rule imposed by the Soumokil group during its months in power. But the genuineness of the rebels' support is not to be denied.

The RUSI cabinet's first reaction to the South Moluccas Republic was to send a mission to meet its leaders and discuss their grievances. Dr. Johannes Leimena, an Ambonese, a Christian Party leader, and RUSI's Minister of Health, was appointed as head of the mission and sailed to the Moluccas on a RUSI naval vessel. But the rebel leaders asked that they be first recognized as representatives of an independent state, and when this request was rejected, they refused to meet the members of the mission.[38] In June a further mission was sent, this time from a nongovernmental conference of South Moluccans resident in different parts of Indonesia. But the rebel leaders again refused to allow the would-be negotiators to proceed to Ambon. Meanwhile they appealed to the outside world, in particular to the Netherlands, the United States, Australia, and the United Nations Commission for Indonesia, for recognition and support.

Eventually the Hatta cabinet decided on military action. After a period of naval blockade 850 men were landed on the island of Buru on July 13. Bitter fighting ensued, with the RUSI troops making headway only slowly. Landings on the island of Amboina itself were begun on September 26. An appeal by the Netherlands Prime Minister that Djakarta should desist from military action against the rebel Moluccans was rejected by the Natsir cabinet, as was an offer of mediation offices made by the UN Commission for Indonesia. By mid-November organized military resistance on Amboina was overcome and the

[37] Cf. van der Kroef, "South Moluccan Insurrection," pp. 11 ff., and Guenther Decker, *Republik Maluku Selatan: Untersuchungen und Dokumente zum Selbstbestimmungsrecht der Ambonesen* (Goettingen: Schwartz, 1957); also J. C. Bouman *et al., The South Moluccas, Rebellious Province or Occupied State* (Leyden: Sythoff, 1960).

[38] See J. Leimena, *The Ambon Question: Facts and Appeal* (Djakarta: n.p., 1950), pp. 7–8 and *passim*.

greater part of the rebel leadership captured. On the larger and sparsely populated island of Ceram guerrilla fighting continued for several years, and small rebel bands remained at large there throughout the decade.

THE UNITARIST MOVEMENT: IMPETUS AND FUNCTIONS

At this point it becomes possible to draw some general conclusions about the politics of the movement which destroyed the federal Indonesian state. In the first place, it is clear that the movement had enormous popular support. The principal issue was a nationalist one. It was a matter not of unitary or federal constitutional forms, but of whether one was for the Republic which had fought for Indonesian independence and won it or for the states which the Dutch had built up in a divide and rule strategy against the Republic.

A second equally important aspect of the movement was the part it played in extending the Revolution to areas which had previously known it only briefly or not at all. The active protagonists of a unitary state fought not only for top-level political change, but for a radically new order in society. In a number of areas they destroyed the power of princely and aristocratic groups, and they weakened it wherever it existed. They brought political parties, trade unions, and other forms of modern organizational life with them wherever they went, and they dealt hard blows to local particularism.

In this light there is little point in discussing the view that abandonment of the federal basis violated the agreements reached at the Round Table Conference. It is not usually argued that the letter of these agreements was violated, for sovereignty had been transferred "unconditionally." Their spirit was indeed violated. But the point is barely relevant to a situation where revolutionary political reality was so rapidly outstripping legalities of every kind.

For the Republican leadership, the Round Table Conference Agreement was no sacrosanct document. It was merely the maximum political gain achievable in the current power situation. As the constellation of forces changed in the Republicans' favor, it would be possible, they believed, to bring their movement nearer to the achievement of its goals. Granted the character of these goals, namely, realization of the independence proclaimed on August 17, 1945, it is not surprising that many of the Republican leaders were little concerned to abide by the spirit of the Round Table Conference. Nor is it surprising that little importance was attached to the commitment to a federal structure which the Republic had repeatedly agreed to make in its negotiations with the Netherlands from the time of the 1946 Linggadjati Agreement onward.

Indeed, there was a minority of convinced advocates of a federal structure within the top Republican leadership, and Prime Minister Hatta appeared at times to be one of them. Writing in 1953 about 1950 developments, he said that "a federal system is in fact suitable for such a far-flung archipelago and might be expected to strengthen the feeling of unity." But then he went on to say that "the manner and timing of the move [to federalism] by the Netherlands Indies Government had aroused such antipathy towards ideas of federation" that the federal form had to be abandoned.[39] Only one or two relatively unimportant groups—one was the Sulawesi guerilla corps KRIS (Kebaktian Rakjat Indonesia Sulawesi)—then urged that the Dutch-built federal system be replaced by a federalism of another kind.[40]

To stress the importance of the nationalist and revolutionary aspects of the antifederalist movement is not, however, to say that it appealed to all groups in Indonesia, or to all in equal measure. Its appeal was undoubtedly greatest in Java. In Java, and most strikingly in Central and East Java, the Dutch-built states had virtually no social reality. Their boundaries corresponded to no ethnic entities, but simply to the limits to which the Dutch had been able to extend their military occupation. Moreover, the hold of nationalism was particularly strong in Java. As Geertz has pointed out, the Revolution generally had special importance for Javanese society, providing it with the basis for a long-overdue restructuring of social organization.[41]

In most areas outside Java the movement's appeal was not quite as intense and widespread, but it was great almost everywhere. Only in a

[39] Mohammad Hatta, "Indonesia's Foreign Policy," *Foreign Affairs,* XXXI (April 1953), 441 ff.

[40] The whole question of the desirability of federalism had been considered at some length in the debates of the Investigating Committee for Indonesian Independence during the last three months of the Japanese occupation. When the Constitutional Subcommittee of the Investigating Committee finally took a vote on the matter in July, the federalism advocated by the Ambonese Mr. J. Latuharhary lost out 2 to 16 against the unitarist position of the majority led by Soekarno. But it should be noted that the membership of the Investigating Committee was confined to Indonesian leaders currently resident in Java. See Muhammad Yamin, ed., *Naskah Persiapan Undang-Undang Dasar 1945* ("Documents on the Preparation of the 1945 Constitution"; Djakarta: Jajasan Prapantja, 1959), p. 259.

[41] "The Javanese Village," in G. William Skinner, ed., *Local, Ethnic and National Loyalties in Village Indonesia: A Symposium* (Yale University, Southeast Asia Studies, Cultural Reports Series; New Haven, Conn., 1959), pp. 34 ff.

few scattered areas was significant resistance offered to it. When an over-all view of this resistance is attempted, three main categories suggest themselves.

One major ingredient of resistance was the presence of KNIL troops, men who had fought for years against the revolutionary Republic and were apprehensive about their fate as either soldiers or dischargees in a predominantly Republican Indonesia. In some instances the fears of these men were fanned by Dutchmen aiming to damage the good name of independent Indonesia.[42] But the fears were real in the minds of the KNIL soldiers who harbored them.

A second basis for resistance was a distinctive cultural orientation of a particular kind, such as the Ambonese possessed. The point here is not that Ambonese culture was different from Javanese—it certainly was so, though no more than was, for instance, the culture of the strongly pro-Republican Toba Bataks—but rather that relatively few Ambonese shared in the all-Indonesian culture which had developed around the nationalist movement. In considerable measure this is traceable to the special position which Ambon, and with it Minahasa, enjoyed in the Netherlands Indies.

Thirdly, as we have seen, there was resistance from princely and aristocratic groups—notably in South Sulawesi and to some extent in other areas of East Indonesia, in West Kalimantan, and in East Sumatra.[43]

Significantly, generalized anti-Javanese feeling seems to have been of little importance. It was used in appeals by the leaders of the South Moluccas Republic, and on a small scale by Andi Aziz. But it was not very effective. Non-Javanese had always been well represented in the leadership of the Republic—its three Prime Ministers had all been Sumatrans. More important still, the government of the Republic had done nothing in the four years of its existence which any sizable group of people outside Java construed as favoring Java interests to the detriment of their own. Indeed, it had had little opportunity to do

[42] Ministry of Foreign Affairs, *Subversive Activities in Indonesia: The Jungschlager and Schmidt Affair, passim.*

[43] The state of East Sumatra survived the unitarist tide until August 1950 partly because it was supported by local sultan families, partly because a major group of local Malay commoners looked to the sultans to protect them against economically stronger ethnic groups of new arrivals in this ethnically heterogeneous area (principally Toba Bataks and also Minangkabaus and Achinese), and partly because it had a small security battalion of its own. See Kementerian Penerangan, *Republik Indonesia, Propinsi Sumatera Utara* ("The North Sumatra Province of the Republic of Indonesia"; Djakarta: Kementerian Penerangan, 1953), pp. 343 ff.

anything of this kind, for its effective authority outside Java had been weak, with the Dutch in control in so many major areas and with real power in the Republican-held areas being in the hands of the local revolutionary leadership rather than the Jogjakarta government. The Dutch had attempted to develop feelings of ethnic solidarity and suspicion of the Javanese. But, in the absence of concrete grievances, the attempt had backfired because it had been made by them. To place a high valuation on one's ethnic identity thus became tantamount to being pro-Dutch.

In 1950 nationalism was triumphant. Its power as a cohesive force binding the archipelago together was at its zenith. Thus the ethnic group feelings which came to be of major importance in subsequent years of the 1949–1957 period were of little importance. And this is true equally of the more general centrifugal pressures which were important from about 1954 onward and began to dominate politics in 1956. These were almost entirely absent in 1950.

Ironically, one consequence of the Dutch policy of creating the states and territories was to strengthen national territorial cohesion in the years immediately after their destruction. Those who had supported the BFO states became for the most part discredited and politically incapacitated minorities—rather than suppressed and restive majorities. The incapacitation removed one category of groups with an interest in centrifugalist politics. And it was to be a lasting incapacitation. Relatively few of the leaders of the BFO states were to return to positions of political prominence, at the national or the regional level. When regionalism became a political force in the period from 1954 onward, its leadership consisted almost entirely of old Republicans, rather than of former supporters of the BFO states.

One can isolate at least three main sources of initiative in furthering and organizing the movement against the federal states. In the first place, a number of Republican political parties were actively associated with it. Seeing a virtual vacuum of political organization in the BFO areas, the parties concentrated their energies heavily on these. There they were enthusiastically received, partly because many of those who were politically active there needed to clear their names of the taint of suspicion of collaboration with the Dutch. One way for these persons to do this was to associate themselves with a Republican political party. Another way was to be active in the movement to destroy the federal structure. Frequently it was possible to take the two steps at once.

But not all parties were equally active in their association with the unitarist movement. The PKI played almost no role in it, being weak and organizationally dispersed and at the same time opposed outright to the Soekarno-Hatta leadership of the state. The Masjumi, which organized actively in the BFO areas, was strongly unitarist in some areas, but cautiously so in many others. The party's congress of December 1949 had not made any demand for unification but rather declared that "plebiscites should be held as soon as possible to determine the status of the member states and territories." [44] Subsequently many of the Masjumi's central leaders became concerned about the tendency of the unitarist movement to outrun the RUSI government's capacity to control it and so to make more difficult what they saw as the country's primary needs, order, legality, and political stabilization.

In addition, their attitude related to a matter of party interest, the question of the timing of elections. If the unitary state were achieved without the need to hold elections for a new House of Representatives and Constituent Assembly,[45] there would no longer be any urgency about the holding of nationwide elections. The Masjumi, which expected, and was expected by most others, to gain an absolute majority or large plurality of votes in a general election, was opposed to a postponement. The demand of its December 1949 congress was for the "formation of the Constituent Assembly in the course of 1950." [10]

It was the nationalist parties and the national-communist Partai Murba which were most active in furthering and steering the movement against the states. Most prominent among these was the PNI. For the PNI, more than for parties like the PKI or Masjumi, nationalism was a central focus of value commitment. Thus PNI leaders saw the quick re-establishment of the Republic of August 17, 1945 as a concern of great intrinsic importance. And the party had additional cause to be active in the unitarist movement because of the fact that early elections would not, on current assumptions, have served its interests. They would certainly not have served the interests of the several smaller nationalist parties.

A second main source of initiative for the movement lay in the Re-

[44] Kementerian Penerangan, *Kepartaian di Indonesia,* 1951, p. 25.

[45] The RUSI constitution provided (Article 111) that a new House of Representatives should be elected within a year of the transfer of sovereignty. It also provided (Article 188) that the Constituent Assembly's membership should include the members of the newly elected House of Representatives and in addition a further equally sized group of members elected in the same way.

[46] Kementerian Penerangan, *Kepartaian di Indonesia,* 1951, p. 25.

publican units of the RUSI army and in the various more irregular guerrilla formations which had fought alongside the Republican army. The RUSI army leadership acted independently on a number of occasions, in sending ex-Republican troops into BFO areas where KNIL troops had theretofore been of decisive importance in the political balance. At the same time, regional army commanders in several areas, notably East Indonesia, took the initiative in encouraging opposition to the existing state governments and co-operated with irregular guerrilla groups as well as with political committees, fronts, and plebiscite movements in doing this. These developments gave rise to considerable conflict inside the RUSI cabinet, where the Sultan of Jogjakarta as Defense Minister supported the actions of the army leaders and regional commanders in the face of opposition not only from Interior Minister Anak Agung (and Minister without Portfolio Hamid, until April), but also from the Masjumi Finance Minister, Sjafruddin Prawiranegara, and the Prime Minister himself.

Thirdly and finally, initiative for the unitarist movement came from President Soekarno. The President was propelled by the same intense nationalist concerns as the leaders of the PNI. He was also happy to see politics lose some of the legal, diplomatic, and administrative cast which it had had in the second half of 1949. As politics became again characterized by "the overbrimming and blazing national spirit" which he saw as the mainspring of the movement to destroy the BFO territories,[47] so there developed more opportunities for the employment of Soekarno's own skills as an orator and manipulator of symbols. Thus the President actively encouraged groups working for mergers of their states into the Republic. He did this in the course of his travels in Indonesia and through some of the many regional delegations which came to the presidential palace.

The Hatta cabinet clearly had a most difficult course to steer. As a cabinet it was not a leader but a follower in the movement for unification. It worked to guide the movement so as to minimize disorder and maintain the state's good name internationally. But the movement outran the cabinet. Böhtlingk puts the point well:

The fact of the revolutionary background of the dissolution of the member territories . . . meant that the RUSI government was constantly placed before *faits accomplis*. However hard it strove to steer the revolution into

[47] Soekarno, *From Sabang to Merauke* (Speech on the Occasion of the Fifth Anniversary of Indonesia's Independence, August 17, 1950; Djakarta: Ministry of Information, 1950), p. 18.

legal channels, it was forced to confine itself to the legal confirmation of dissolutions which had already occurred in fact.[48]

Pressed hard by the various groups which channeled and furthered the movement against the federal states, the Hatta cabinet could marshal little countervailing power by which to contain the movement. The power resources which the Hatta leadership had had in the second half of 1949 were no longer there. The Dutch were well on their way out, and the BFO states were no longer an important power to reckon with. Thus Hatta found himself moving from a midway position between two main camps, where he was strong because of his acceptability to both camps, to a much weaker position on one side of a single Republican-dominated complex of power.

In the atmosphere of political drama and excitement produced by the unitarist movement, administrative programs lost the high priority which men of the Hatta group had wanted to see them accorded. Indeed, the implementation of a number of these programs had to be postponed for purely practical reasons. The movement inevitably favored the skill group of "solidarity makers" to the detriment of that of "administrators." Soekarno began to re-emerge from the weak and almost peripheral position to which he had been pushed by the developments of 1949. Hatta's power began to diminish.

THE HATTA CABINET: POLICIES AND POLITICS

The drama, turbulence, and movementlike character of the process by which the federal states were destroyed should not distract our attention for too long from the less spectacular developments of the time. The period of the Hatta cabinet was one of power consolidation as well as of political effervescence. It was a period of fast administrative action to regularize a confused and chaotic situation.

In the military field the tasks of consolidation were particularly formidable. The RUSI army was to be built with the Republican army as its core. But the Republican army itself was a heterogeneous and poorly integrated organization. Its origin, as we have noted, lay in the various auxiliary military forces and paramilitary youth organizations established by the Japanese.[49] With the outbreak of the Revolution

[48] *Op. cit.*, p. 109.

[49] Rudy Pirngadie, "The Problems of the Government and the Army in Indonesia" (unpublished manuscript, Harvard University Center for International Affairs, 1960), pp. 55–58; Guy J. Pauker, *The Role of the Military in Indonesia* (research memorandum; Santa Monica, Calif.: Rand Corporation, 1960), pp. 5–13, 36.

a large number of segments of these auxiliary forces and paramilitary organizations became part of the revolutionary army. But other local and regional segments became linked with irregular fighting formations established on a religious, political, or regional basis, such as the Islamic Hizbullah, the radical nationalist Barisan Banteng (Wild Buffalo Force), the socialist-communist Pesindo (Pemuda Sosialis Indonesia, Indonesian Socialist Youth), the KRIS (Kebaktian Rakjat Indonesia Sulawesi, Loyalty of the Indonesian People of Sulawesi), and the general fighting organization, Lasjkar Rakjat (People's Corps). Thus in the early years of the revolution some 500,000 men were linked in one or other military unit, but a majority of these were outside the army proper, and many even of those in the army served under highly autonomous commands.[50]

The cohesion of the Republic's military forces was somewhat improved as a result of the withdrawals and regrouping which followed the first Dutch attack in 1947, then again by the Hatta cabinet's rationalization policy of 1948, which involved the incorporation of numerous previously irregular units as well as large-scale demotions, and again by the Madiun affair in which the Communist-influenced armed units isolated themselves and were militarily crushed. Thus in the guerrilla campaigns which followed the second Dutch attack of December 1948, the Republic's fighting strength was for the most part composed of army members, and the army's central leadership was able to exercise a measure of control over most of its territorial units. On the other hand, however, the guerrilla situation meant that local army units attracted sizable numbers of villagers as "helpers."

The army which emerged after the cease-fire agreement to serve as the core for RUSI's military establishment was far more cohesive than the congeries of military groupings the Dutch had encountered in their early years of conflict with the Republic, but it was by no means a closely knit or well-disciplined force. Much of its organization was based on personal loyalties to local commanders, and clique and quasi-ideological conflicts made co-operation between units difficult. Moreover, the force had frayed edges; for, besides the 250,000 to 300,000 men whom the government recognized as soldiers, there were many

[50] The figure 500,000 is given in A. H. Nasution, *Tjatatan-Tjatatan Sekitar Politik Militer Indonesia* ("Notes on Indonesian Military Policy"; Djakarta: Pembimbing, 1955), pp. 311–313. See also A. H. Nasution, *Tentara Nasional Indonesia* ("The Indonesian National Army"), vol. I (Djakarta: Jajasan Pustaka Militer, 1956).

who had moved around the countryside with army units and thus considered themselves soldiers and were so considered by many of the company and brigade commanders, though not at army headquarters. And again most members of the revolutionary army were psychologically unprepared for peace, a peace which would require demobilization for many and a routinization of life for all.

The Hatta cabinet aimed to reshape this army radically. It sought to demobilize large numbers of former Republican troops, and it had to make possible the acceptance of all those of the 65,000 former KNIL soldiers who sought admission on RUSI's terms. At the same time the cabinet had to use the new army extensively to cope with law and order problems, and particularly to establish state authority in areas which were theretofore controlled by different groups of Republican irregulars.

Some of these tasks were performed successfully, others not. The problem of absorbing KNIL troops proved by no means easy—witness the role which KNIL groups played in the Westerling, Aziz, and South Moluccas "affairs." The political and psychological difficulties were great on both sides, but especially for the soldiers of the losing side, the KNIL. Very few KNIL officers were given command posts of significance, and RUSI's new military salary regulations placed former KNIL men on an equal footing with former Republican troops, who had previously lived on much lower pay and were usually less highly trained. However, by July 25, 1950, when the KNIL was formally dissolved, 26,000 of its members had been incorporated into the RUSI armed forces.[51]

The government had relatively little success in its efforts to demobilize men from the Republican component of the RUSI army. A considerable number of officers left the army to take white-collar posi-

---

[51] Another 18,750 officers and men had been demobilized in Indonesia, and 3,250 had left Indonesia for the Netherlands. The remaining 17,000 were given temporary status in the KL, the Dutch regular army, as of July 25. At the time it was expected that some 12,000 of these would be demobilized in Indonesia and another 5,000 would go to the Netherlands. In fact, the number that went to the Netherlands was greater, largely because of the course of the South Moluccas uprising which made it impossible for demobilized KNIL troops to return to the Ambon area and led many Ambonese to accept a Dutch government offer for them and their dependents to go to the Netherlands (Taylor, *op. cit.*, p. 413). In October there were 14,620 such persons in 56 accommodation centers in different parts of the Netherlands. See T. Wittermans, "Functional Aspects of 'Pela' among Ambonese Refugees," *Indonesië*, VII (1955), 214–230.

tions in the civil service or private business. But most soldiers lacked the formal education to do this and were reluctant to move, or return, to non-whitecollar positions. Many of them had the support of their commanders, particularly at the company level, for their efforts to stay within the army, and the government therefore found that it was faced by active nonco-operation from sections of the officer corps on this issue. Moreover, the government could not press its demobilization plans too hard lest this drive army members to join one of the bands of rebel guerrillas. Some tens of thousands of soldiers were absorbed by government development projects of various kinds established specifically for soldier rehabilitation. But the army nevertheless remained much larger than the government leaders had hoped. In November 1950 it was officially said to be 200,000 men strong—after the incorporation of the 26,000 former KNIL members and the allocation to reserve units of 80,000 Republican soldiers scheduled for demobilization.[52] As for the village young people who had followed army units around as auxiliaries, many of these were persuaded to return to their home areas. Most of the others went to the cities where they joined with other old fighters of various kinds to form a pool of men asking for army membership, educational opportunities, or at least some suitable employment. Some joined antigovernment guerrilla groups.

In the matter of military reorganization the government was far more effective. It brought about a major series of changes in territorial organization, establishing seven military districts (two in Sumatra, three in Java, and one each for Kalimantan and East Indonesia), each harboring a division of soldiers, and several separate formations of crack troops trained and stationed near the capital to be at the disposal of the central leaders of each of the services. This involved important personnel changes in divisional and regimental commands, changes which strengthened army cohesion and weakened the power of officers dependent on personal loyalty in particular localities. Moreover, it involved a tightening of command relationships. No longer were two or more units allowed to operate in a single area unless organizational and hierarchical relationships existed between them.

The maintenance of army discipline and good behavior was a constant problem in this period. Some army units carried out smuggling operations. Some commanders used their powers over civilian government to enrich themselves by irregular taxes and levies and through the acceptance of bribes. Wild behavior in the soldiery was fairly wide-

[52] Nasution, *Tjatatan-Tjatatan Sekitar Politik Militer*, pp. 314, 317, and *passim*.

spread. But misdemeanors were usually treated sternly by the military authorities, and their volume gradually declined.[53]

One of the most difficult problems the government faced was the one of rehabilitating the ex-guerrillas who were without army status. Many of these had been recruited to fighting through one of the quasi-ideological guerrilla organizations. Others had become attracted to units of the army without gaining acceptance as soldiers. And there were many who had done virtually no fighting but declared themselves to be ex-guerrillas and succeeded in gaining registration as such from a local military commander. Some of this large group entered the cities about the time of the transfer of sovereignty; some waited in the mountains to see how the situation developed. All were subject to attraction from guerrilla groups which proclaimed their determination to continue in defiance of the government, both from such more or less established organizations as the Darul Islam and the Tentara Rakjat (People's Army) and from smaller groups established on an *ad hoc* basis and without ideological pretensions, groups like the Barisan Sakit Hati (Legion of the Disappointed) and the Brigade Tjitarum (Tjitarum River Brigade) and others which were simply robber bands.

The Hatta cabinet made at least a big start with the task of rehabilitation. It accommodated large numbers of guerrillas in educational institutions of various kinds, many of them newly established. It set up a number of training centers to give short-term instruction in craft skills. It allowed many ex-fighters—perhaps, indeed, more than it knew—to enter the government service. And it made a beginning with a resettlement or transmigration program for ex-fighters.[54]

Inadequate as these measures were to deal with the problem in its entirety—and they were in a sense merely first steps—they did create a measure of confidence in the government's capacity to provide for ex-guerrillas. The good name which accrued to the government on

[53] For a catalogue of army misdemeanors in different parts of the country see the parliamentary address of I. A. Moeis (PNI) in *Perdjuangan PNI dalam Parleman* ("The Struggle of the PNI in Parliament"; Malang: Pembina Rakjat, 1950), pp. 65–69. See also *Pertanjaan Anggota dan Djawaban Pemerintah*, I, 35–49, II, 35–39.

[54] This program of the Ministry of Defense's National Reserve Corps (for former army members) and the subsequently established program of the Ministry of the Interior's Bureau for National Reconstruction (for those never accepted as army members) were to have taken 12,037 men and their families to South Sumatra, South Sulawesi, and South Kalimantan by the end of 1953. Another 14,548 families had been taken under the government general resettlement program. See Biro Pusat Statistik (Central Bureau of Statistics), *Statistik 1956* (Djakarta: Biro Pusat Statistik, 1956), p. 16.

their account was supplemented by the authority which it gained in the eyes of the revolutionary generation generally, as it became clear (especially with the victory of the unitarist movement) that independence was indeed real. Most important of all, the Hatta cabinet demonstrated power, notably by its successful reorganization of the army.

All these factors combined to add to the attractiveness of the government's offers of amnesty and rehabilitation to members of defiant guerrilla groups, both rebel organizations and robber bands. In addition, the army weakened the rebel and bandit groups by narrowing the area of their operation and in some cases taking military action against them. It captured Chaerul Saleh of the People's Army of West Java in March. It took small-scale military action against the Darul Islam in West Java in June, after an effort to negotiate with its leaders was rebuffed. By the end of the Hatta cabinet period there remained a number of areas where the government's authority was disputed— notably in West Java, South Sulawesi, and the Moluccas, but also in parts of East Java, Central Java, Sumatra, and Kalimantan. There were frequent raids on estates and occasional railway holdups. But the areas of insecurity had been narrowed down.

In the area of civil service reorganization also the cabinet saw the situation in terms of a need for fast but careful action. Inheriting the bureaucratic establishment of the Dutch-run "prefederal" government, with the center in Djakarta and operations extending through all the BFO states and territories, the cabinet sought to make this into an instrument suitable for its own purposes, to "nationalize" and "Republicanize" it, while at the same time maintaining discipline, organization, and routine-type incentives—and using the patronage possibilities for maximum political advantage. Later, when it became clear that the federal state would be dissolved, the Hatta cabinet, in co-operation with the Halim cabinet of the Republic of Indonesia, had to prepare the complete fusion of the RUSI and RI bureaucracies.

The difficulties of the transition were considerable. For several months after December 1949 RUSI ministers felt that they were not in full control of their ministries. Within the group of Republican civil servants who were fitted into the structure there was considerable resentment at the continuing influence of some 15,700 Dutch civil servants and of Indonesians of the BFO group.[55]

---

[55] The figure 15,700 is calculated from E. P. M. Tervooren, *Statenopvolging en de Financiële Verplichtingen van Indonesië* ("The Succession of States and Indonesia's Financial Obligations"; The Hague: Nijhoff, 1957), pp. 269–270.

On the other hand, the employees of the old prefederal government resented the influx of "Jogja" men who often went straight into the highest positions.[56] And many of them had special cause for resentment in the fact that their salaries were cut in a general overhaul of salary scales which put Republican and prefederal employees on an equal basis (and leveled off the steep ratio of highest to lowest salaries which had characterized the Dutch prefederal bureaucracy). There were to be tensions for several years between "non's" and "co's," between those with a clear record of nonco-operation with the Dutch authorities and those others who for reasons of choice or necessity had co-operated by working in a Dutch-built administration.

At another level the fusion produced a continuing problem of incentives. The administration of the revolutionary Republic had operated as part of a political movement. Moral incentives, appeals to powerful nationalist symbols, had obviated the necessity for incentives of a routine type. Now, however, these men had to work in an established bureaucratic structure with fellow employees who stood outside the ranks of the movement. In these circumstances it was hard to maintain incentives by moral appeals. At the same time routine-type organization and incentives were not readily accepted, and indeed many persons placed in responsible positions were reluctant to impose these, having themselves had little experience of them.

Finally, the fusion created a greatly enlarged bureaucracy whose size it was found impossible to reduce. Speaking on February 15, 1950, President Soekarno gave the approximate figures—180,000 federal civil servants and another 240,000 of the Republic of Indonesia—and expressed the hope that the total would be reduced from 420,000 to 220,000 in six months.[57] But on August 4 Hatta reported to parliament that because of the political difficulties which had arisen with the development of the unitarist movement, it had been found necessary to postpone reductions in civil service numbers until the reinauguration of the unitary state. The cabinet had established committees, but otherwise nothing had been accomplished.[58] In terms of the cabinet's policy objectives this was a major failure.

In the field of economics, the Hatta cabinet started from a point of

[56] For a list of top-echelon RUSI civil servants, with specifications concerning their Republican or prefederal origin, see *Almanak Indonesia, 1950* (Bandung: Pustaka Djaja, 1950), pp. 150–151.

[57] *Pidato Presiden pada Pembukaan Parlemen R.I.S.* ("The Speech of the President at the Opening of the RUSI Parliament"), pp. 25–26.

[58] *Pertanjaan Anggota dan Djawaban Pemerintah*, II, 23–24.

particularly great disadvantage. In 1949 the prefederal government had collected receipts totaling only 66.6 per cent of its gross expenditure and therefore accumulated a budget deficit of 1,304.8 million Dutch guilders.[59] The government of the Republic, in 1949 as in the previous years, had issued currency based on virtually no receipts. Thus when the two governments were fused, inflation was rampant. Nor was it expected that the budgetary position would improve in 1950. There would be very great demands for government spending in that year, for reconstruction work especially in scorched-earth areas, for military and security purposes, and for the maintenance of the large bureaucracy. And few easy ways of increasing government revenues were in sight (other than two projected overseas loans). In February 1950 it was estimated that the deficit for that year would need to be roughly 2,650 million guilders.[60]

Inflation and government deficits were closely related to other aspects of the economic picture. A large volume of smuggling, which resulted from exchange rate unreality—the black-market value of the U.S. dollar was 600 per cent or more of its official value for the entire first half of the year [61]—was robbing the country of both foreign exchange and an important source of government revenue. Hoarding and speculation were driving the price level further up. The heavy demand for imports, which resulted from the long period of blockade of Republican-held parts of the country, was posing a threat to foreign reserves. Moreover, strikes broke out in almost all the cities of the country and many of the estate areas in the months immediately after the transfer of sovereignty. The excitement of independence for workers in the BFO areas and the fact of new freedom to organize unions, coupled with the inflationary situation, produced strikes on an enormous scale among dock workers, various groups of factory workers, and estate workers on rubber, palm oil, and tobacco plantations.[62]

[59] The Java Bank, *Report for the Financial Year 1950–1951* (Djakarta, 1951), p. 44.

[60] *Pidato Presiden pada Pembukaan Parlemen R.I.S.*, pp. 22–25. Both guilders, the currency of the Netherlands Indies government, and rupiahs, the currency of the Republic, continued to be used in the first months after December 27, 1949, the official ratio between them being 1:1. The currency was unified on March 19, 1950. Thenceforth the rupiah was the only currency unit.

[61] The Java Bank, *Report for the Financial Year 1950–1951*, p. 38.

[62] The number of working days lost through strikes in 1950—a monthly average of 727,799 days or 18 days in a month for each of 41,017 striking workers—represents an all-time maximum for Indonesia. See The Java Bank, *Report for the*

Initially the cabinet took no drastic steps. By emergency law it continued the company tax at the rate of 40 per cent of net profits. At the same time it planned a number of other revenue-raising devices and negotiated with the United States and the Netherlands for economic aid.[63] Sultan Hamengku Buwono devoted much effort to the attempt to crack down on the smuggling trade. Meanwhile the cabinet took steps to speed up the restoration of past production, particularly on estates in areas where there had been revolutionary upheaval. The political difficulties notwithstanding, it restored a considerable number of estates to their alien proprietors.[64] In facing the labor situation it initially made an emergency law extending the Republic of Indonesia's legislation for a 40-hour week and a 7-hour day to the whole country. Later it frequently exhorted workers to consider the welfare of the general community before going on strike. On several occasions a military governor banned a strike or arrested union leaders, but in general the cabinet's policy was to promote conciliation without applying undue pressure on unions.

In March, however, it was thought that drastic measures were necessary. On March 13 the government introduced an exchange certificate system, in effect a form of devaluation, which changed the 1:1 ratio between Dutch and Indonesian guilders to one of 1:3 as far as export, import, and certain other transactions were concerned. This was in a sense a complement to the Dutch government's moves in September 1949 when the pound sterling had been devalued; the value of Indonesian currency had then been readjusted with reference to the

---

Financial Year 1951–1952 (Djakarta, 1952), p. 128. See also the subsequent annual reports of the Java Bank (later the Bank Indonesia).

[63] On Feb. 8 the Export Import Bank extended Indonesia a loan of $100 million (advances payable over a 20-year period commencing after five years with a 3½ per cent interest rate), but actual disbursement of funds (mainly for transport and communications equipment and also for a cement plant and electrification) did not begin until 1952. RUSI negotiators discussed a proposed loan from the Netherlands government on several occasions, but the loan was not actually extended until Jan. 26, 1951. It was then for 280 million guilders ($73.7 million) at 3½ per cent. Indonesia did, however, receive Marshall Aid goods worth $40 million in 1950, mainly textiles and rice, on the basis of requests made by the Netherlands Indies government in 1949. See Raymond E. Stannard, "The Role of American Aid in Indonesian-American Relations" (M.A. thesis, Cornell University, 1957), pp. 1–5 and 25 ff.

[64] See John O. Sutter, *Indonesianisasi: Politics in a Changing Economy, 1940–1955* (Southeast Asia Program, Cornell University; Ithaca, N.Y., 1959), pp. 695–701.

dollar area, but not with respect to Dutch currency. The certificate system was calculated to stimulate exports. But the danger was that the inflation resulting from the discouragement of imports might get out of hand before the measure could take effect.

To prevent this from happening, a "monetary purge" was announced on March 19. All currency notes of 2.50 guilders and above were literally to be cut in half, one half to be exchanged for new currency notes, the other half for government bonds. In addition, all bank deposits in excess of 400 guilders were to be halved, one half being taken by the government as a compulsory loan. This drastic and regressive measure caused personal suffering remembered for many years.

The question of the effectiveness of these two measures remains controversial.[65] They appear to have contributed to the subsequent upswing in exports and export production, and they may have slowed down the inflationary trend in some degree. Certainly Indonesia gained from the fact that it was no longer possible for Netherlanders to convert Indonesian money into Dutch money at a fictitious rate. On the other hand, the measures produced a liquidity crisis which required the government in May to enact emergency legislation for the issuing of new currency. Although some 1,600 million guilders had been taken out of circulation in the purge, the money supply had again reached the February 1950 level by September.[66]

By the end of the Hatta cabinet period the economic crisis had passed. But this was principally because of the onset of the Korean War with its immediate and dramatic effects on the prices of Indonesia's exports, notably rubber.[67] By August or so the position of Indonesia's foreign reserves was reasonably good. Prices had become much steadier, and the black-market value of foreign currency had fallen markedly. Production and export figures for 1950 show improvements over 1949 in almost all products. Nevertheless, the actual budget deficit for 1950 was no less than Rp. 1,736 million.[68] And very little had been done to lessen the government's burden of overhead expenditures.

Reviewing the Hatta cabinet's actions in these various areas of administrative policy—the army and soldier rehabilitation, civil service unification, and the general field of economics—one is impressed

[65] For a critique see Hans O. Schmitt, "Some Monetary and Fiscal Consequences of Social Conflict in Indonesia, 1950–58" (doctoral dissertation, University of California, Berkeley, 1959), pp. 51–74.

[66] The Java Bank, *Report for the Financial Year 1950–1951*, p. 29.

[67] *Ibid.*, p. 91.   [68] *Ibid.*, p. 44.

by the seriousness and resolution with which declared policies were pursued. If some later cabinets were to adopt an attitude of casualness to their stated objectives in the field of problem-solving policy, this was not the case with the Hatta RUSI cabinet. The cabinet started from the view that Indonesia's problems were great and that major efforts were required to achieve even the preliminary adjustments which were needed before Indonesia could set foot on the road to prosperity and welfare.

Indeed, the cabinet's operations reflected an outlook distinctly its own. In the matter of the unitarist movement, its prime concern was for legality and order. Similarly, in tackling the problems of army reorganization and guerrilla rehabilitation, its emphasis was on discipline and efficiency—not on either maintaining or rewarding revolutionary ardor. In the field of finances it was tough and austere.

The same general orientation was apparent in its handling of foreign relations. Foreign policy was low on the cabinet's scale of priorities. To the extent that it had a foreign policy it was one of pro-Western neutralism. Thus it sent ambassadors to all major Western and uncommitted governments, but no diplomatic representatives to any Communist power.[69] Besides seeking Western economic aid—the $100 million Export-Import Bank loan and the loan sought for and subsequently granted from the Netherlands—it negotiated an unpublicized agreement to receive U.S. military assistance on a small scale, in the form of police equipment worth approximately $5 million.[70] In Asia its closest relations were with India, with Soekarno going to India on a state visit in January and February 1950 and Nehru returning the visit in June.

But the most notable feature of the Hatta cabinet's foreign policy was its modest unassertive character. It involved no attempt to act out hero roles on the international stage, no effort to use foreign policy to fashion domestic solidarity. It was almost as if revolutionary nationalism had been decreed out of existence. Thus the cabinet made numerous endeavors to develop good relations with the Netherlands and did nothing to excite mass enthusiasm on the issue of West Irian. As the cabinet leaders saw it, good relations with the Netherlands would not only facilitate internal reconstruction, but also make it

[69] The RUSI government did, however, recognize the People's Republic of China and initiated measures for diplomatic relations with it. A Communist Chinese ambassador presented his credentials to President Soekarno on August 14, 1950. In return, Indonesia sent a chargé d'affaires who arrived in Peking on January 14, 1951.

[70] See Stannard, *op. cit.*, pp. 5–6.

possible to persuade the Dutch to leave West Irian by the end of the one-year period referred to in the Round Table Conference Agreement.

The Hatta cabinet's ability to pursue policies of austerity, matter-of-factness, and defiance of nationalist feeling—and to pursue them with a considerable degree of effectiveness—was rooted in political resources of various kinds. At the formal level, the cabinet was not responsible to parliament. According to the RUSI constitution—which as we have seen was made as a temporary constitution—parliament was unable to force the resignation of the cabinet or any minister. Informally, a number of other factors came into play. First, there was the great personal prestige of several of the cabinet's members, notably Hatta, but also the Sultan of Jogjakarta and several others in lesser measure. Even more important was the high degree of support which the cabinet received from the central leadership of the army and most of the key territorial commanders in the provinces. Co-operation between Hatta and the army leaders made it possible for his cabinet to be more successful than any other cabinet of our period (with the possible exception of the cabinet of Natsir) in using the army as an instrument of policy. Moreover, President Soekarno gave his full support to the cabinet for most of its actions. His speeches of this period placed considerable emphasis on the need for order, austerity, and hard work.

But the political efficacy of the Hatta cabinet was also a result of the abundance of material and prestige resources over which the cabinet acquired disposal rights by virtue of the transfer of sovereignty. By becoming heir to the Netherlands Indies government, RUSI acquired a large quantity of material assets—not only administrative offices, but also a number of large state enterprises (particularly in the production of tin, rubber, palm oil, and salt), all university colleges, and most schools. It acquired not only office buildings, but also cars, trucks, and buses and, not least important, large numbers of government houses. There was then a considerable quantity of rewards to distribute, in the form of both prestigeful roles and material perquisites. Moreover, diplomatic establishments had to be created and staffed, and overseas offers of scholarship and travel opportunities gave the government a further area for discretionary distribution of much-sought favors.

Finally, a number of business opportunities opened up for Indonesians as a direct consequence of the attainment of full sovereignty. Some of these were provided by the government itself. Thus Minister for Prosperity Djuanda announced a policy in April 1950 whereby the government would provide protection to Indonesian importers, by giving credits and reserving certain categories of goods for Indonesian firms.[71] More important, however, were other openings that were not created by the government but nevertheless functioned to alleviate the pressure of political claims under which it labored. Thus some Indonesians arranged to take over the firms of the Dutch and Eurasian small businessmen who were planning to leave the country. Most important was the category of those Indonesians, mainly politically influential persons, who were sought out by Dutch, American, British, and Chinese firms, usually large corporations, and offered posts as partners, representatives, agents, staff members, or simply "fixers."

But opposition to the Hatta cabinet's policies was considerable, especially from long-time Republicans, who were now a dominant section of the political public, and it rose over the eight-month period of the cabinet's existence. PKI and Murba representatives hammered hard and effectively on the theme of the continuing power of foreign capital and the comprador character of the Hatta "Round Table Conference" cabinet. Republicans of many political persuasions complained of the continued presence of Dutch soldiers—the last of the KL troops were to leave Indonesia only in June 1951—and of the fact that Dutch nationals continued to be employed in high places within the government service. Many protested vigorously that the cabinet was distributing positions exclusively on the basis of education and administrative experience and forgetting those who had sacrificed most in the cause of the Revolution. There was a widespread feeling that the Hatta cabinet was not providing the country with real leadership.

For the most part these criticisms drew their power from the inchoate general disappointment with independence, an independence which so many who had actively participated in the revolution found humdrum and uninspiring. They represented protest against the readiness of the leaders of the revolutionary movement to allow the movement to lose its momentum and its *mystique* and integrative capacity. They expressed a sense of resentment against the cabinet's concern for order and legality, which seemed to lead it to turn its back to the spirit of the Revolution, and hence to resemble a restored Dutch regime.

The power of criticism of the Hatta cabinet was all the greater because the waning of the movementlike character of politics resulted in a weakening of the sense of identification which the members of

[71] Sutter, *op. cit.*, pp. 1017–1019.

the movement had felt with the leadership, a feeling of increasing alienation from the centers of power. About individual ministers or secretaries-general of ministries the remark was often made, "He was one of us in the Jogja days, even though he was a high official of the government. Now he is caught up in all this Dutch-made formality and scarcely deigns to speak to his old friends."

But there were also more directly political factors which lent importance to criticisms of the Hatta government. As we saw earlier, the withdrawal of Dutch power and the decline of the BFO states resulted in a great change in Hatta's political situation. From being at the strategic center, as the moderate Republican trusted by the Netherlands and the BFO alike, he was pushed to one side, to the role of leader of the consolidationist forces within the Republican-dominated scene of political action.

On this Republican-dominated scene radical nationalism now came to play a role of great importance. We have seen how this was fostered by the entry of large numbers of former guerrilla fighters into the cities and by the release of Republican political prisoners from Dutch jails and how the upsurge of nationalist feeling in the BFO states quickly challenged the existence of these states. Similarly we saw how radical nationalist feeling in the army led it to play an active and independent role in support of the unitarist movement. And we noticed a widespread expansion of labor organizations, which followed and in turn promoted waves of strikes.

The threat which radical nationalism posed to the Hatta cabinet's position becomes particularly clear as one looks at the situation in party politics. Hatta's position throughout 1949 had been based on solid Masjumi-PNI support. In the first half of 1950 this changed quickly. On the unificationist issue the PNI was a leading champion of speed and advocated the dissolution of RUSI as well as its BFO member states into the Republic of Indonesia. The Masjumi, particularly its central leadership, supported the cautious policy of the Hatta cabinet at almost every stage.

On foreign policy too, contradictory policies between the two parties were evident. On April 3, Ir. Sakirman, parliamentary leader of the Communist-line Partai Sosialis, submitted a motion urging the government to "enter into diplomatic relations with the Democratic Republic of Vietnam." It soon became clear that the motion would have PNI support and that the government was opposed to its passage. On June 2, as voting was about to take place on the Sakirman motion, the Masjumi leader Natsir submitted what he described as a counter-motion, urging the government to "investigate what RUSI could do in a concrete way to promote the achievement of a settlement satisfactory to the national ideals of the people of Vietnam." This motion was clearly acceptable to the cabinet. On the following day it was accepted by the House of Representatives by 49 votes to 38—with the Masjumi and PNI voting on opposite sides.[72]

However, the clearest indication of the tendency of the two main parties to grow estranged came at the PNI's congress held in Jogjakarta, May 1 to 5. This was a notably radical congress. Its final resolutions included a call for "the establishment of an anticapitalist bloc," [73] interpreted by some as meaning co-operation with the Communist Party and the national-communist Partai Murba. As the new party chairman the congress elected Sidik Djojosukarto, a radical nationalist who had become acting chairman of the party in August 1949. Sidik had then displaced Mr. Soejono Hadinoto, who left the active chairmanship of the party when he departed for The Hague to participate in the Round Table Conference. Soejono, a Hatta associate, was not elected to any executive position at the May 1950 congress. Nor was any other leader of this general outlook elected.[74]

The victors at the PNI congress included those most capable of articulating the revolutionary mood, the inchoate general radicalism of those who tended to be critical of all stabilizing government. Also victors were the group of PNI leaders who had worked with the Japanese and had been eclipsed for most of the period of Revolution as a result of the domestic and international factors which had brought men like Sjahrir and Hatta to the fore. The congress result meant that the party would thenceforth be more reluctant to support the Hatta cabinet and that it would be more careful about the terms on which it co-operated with the Masjumi in the future.

One final aspect of the rising power of radical nationalism in the Hatta cabinet period was the change which it brought about in relations between Soekarno and Hatta. In much of its work the Hatta

[72] For a discussion of the two motions in terms of the parliamentary tactics used by their protagonists see Subakir, *op. cit.*, pp. 35–47.

[73] For the list of the resolutions of the congress see Kementerian Penerangan, *Kepartaian di Indonesia*, 1951, pp. 117–121.

[74] For lists of the membership of the party councils elected at the 1948 and 1950 congresses see Kementerian Penerangan, *Kepartaian dan Parlementaria di Indonesia* ("Political Parties and Parliamentary Affairs in Indonesia"; Djakarta: Kementerian Penerangan, 1954), pp. 23–24.

cabinet enjoyed the fullest support of the President. But Soekarno was by no means merely a propagandist for the cabinet. On the contrary, he made an effort to dissociate himself from some of the unpopular policies of the cabinet, in particular those doing violence to nationalist feeling. And he found an issue to make peculiarly his own in the matter of the struggle to gain the incorporation of West Irian. Thus Soekarno was not overshadowed by Hatta in 1950 as he had been for much of 1949. His power was increasing, and the fact became evident in his growing independence of action.[75] Hatta by contrast had been losing his power position rapidly.

In December 1949 it had seemed that governmental leadership and political leadership were largely coterminous. By August 1950 government and politics stood ranged in open opposition to one another. There had been a quick decline in the unity of the political elite and in the power of the government over the political forces in society.

MAKING A CONSTITUTION FOR THE UNITARY STATE

By early May 1950 it had become a principal task of the Hatta cabinet to prepare for the establishment of a unitary Republic, and thus its own resignation. In the following three months political interest centered on the matter of how the transition would be accomplished and, more particularly, on the matter of the content of the constitution on which it would be based.

The most important decisions on these two matters were made in May in negotiations between Hatta (representing the RUSI government and also the governments of East Indonesia and East Sumatra) and the Republic of Indonesia's Prime Minister Abdul Halim. In the Charter of Agreement which these two signed on May 19 it was stated that the new "Republic of Indonesia" would be established as quickly as possible by RUSI and the existing (member-state) Republic of Indonesia jointly. Setting down a series of basic features for the constitution of the new Republic, the charter went on to state that the actual provisions of the constitution would be deliberated upon by a joint RUSI-RI committee. This committee would report its findings to the two governments concerned, who would submit them to their respective parliaments (in the Republic's case the Working Body or

---

[75] Some Indonesian observers see significance in the fact that the Hatta cabinet of 1949–1950 was the first cabinet which did not hold its meetings in the President's palace.

Inner Parliament only). If the two parliaments were in agreement, the President would formally inaugurate the new unitary state in a joint meeting of the two houses of the RUSI parliament. Thenceforth the governments of RUSI and the Republic would be dissolved, and the President would take steps to have a new cabinet formed.[76]

Immediately after May 19 the Committee for the Preparation of the Constitution of the Unitary State was established. It was a fourteen-man committee, with seven members appointed by each of the governments concerned. Its chairmanship was held jointly by the RUSI Justice Minister, Professor Supomo, then a nonparty man, and the Republic's Deputy Prime Minister Abdul Hakim, of the Masjumi. This committee deliberated for almost two months, with frequent reporting back by committee members to the governments by whom they had been appointed and to their parties. Finally, in July it was possible for the committee to agree on a draft constitution, which the two governments accepted in slightly modified form on July 20. Then the draft was presented by the two to their respective parliaments, which, however, were denied the right to amend. Thus it was possible to have the constitution ratified by the two bodies by August 14.[77]

The May 19 Charter of Agreement provided for a unicameral legislature and for a parliamentary cabinet. Further, it established that President Soekarno would be President of the new state. The constitution would be temporary; thus there would be no change from the provisions in the 1949 constitution whereby a Constituent Assembly was to be elected to make a permanent constitution. However, the May 19 agreement also envisaged a Council for the Revision of the Constitution, which could come into existence without the holding of elections. In addition, the agreement set forth a number of ideas bearing on the directive principles or ideological clauses to be included in the new constitution.

Within the framework of these basic decisions there remained a great deal to be argued out. One important issue was the composition of the new unicameral parliament. The May 19 agreement had specified that the membership of this body would include the 150 members of the RUSI House of Representatives, the 46 members of the Republic's Working Body, and others to be appointed by the President after

[76] Kementerian Penerangan, *Republik Indonesia, Daerah Istimewa Jogjakarta,* pp. 326–327.

[77] See R. Supomo, *Undang-Undang Dasar Republik Indonesia* ("The Constitution of the Republic of Indonesia"); 8th ptg., Djakarta: Noordhoff-Kolff, 1958), pp. 4–17.

fuller discussion by the joint RUSI-RI committee. Subsequently the
RUSI members of the joint committee pressed for the inclusion also
of the 32 members of the RUSI Senate. The Republic was initially opposed to this suggestion, but finally agreed to it when it was coupled
with the inclusion of the 13 members of the Republic's Supreme Advisory Council and with the further provisions that the Republic of
Indonesia would appoint 19 members to act in the place of the 21
Pasundan representatives within the RUSI House of Representatives
whose credentials were in dispute.[78] The joint committee then agreed
that there would be no need for additional members appointed by
the President.[79]

Thus the initial composition [80] of the unitary state's House of Representatives would be as follows:

(1) Members from the RUSI House of Representatives
  (a) representing the Republic of Indonesia   50
  (b) representing the states and territories of RUSI
       other than the Republic of Indonesia and the
       state of Pasundan   79
  (c) additional members appointed by the Republic
       of Indonesia for the state of Pasundan   19

[78] See Mustafa Sulaiman, *op. cit.*, pp. 125 ff. The Supreme Advisory Council of
the Republic, established under the 1945 constitution, was a body of middle-aged
and elderly persons which was occasionally asked for advice by the President or
the cabinet on questions of general policy. Pasundan's representation within the
RUSI House of Representatives had been controversial for many months. On Feb.
16, 1950, the day after the opening of parliament, the interim chairman read out
a letter from Sewaka, the RUSI State Commissioner for the state of Pasundan,
who had been appointed six days earlier, in which he urged parliament not to
accept the credentials of the 21 members who had been selected by this state,
which was now "frozen," and instead submitted an alternative list of 21 names.
The compromise reached was to allow the 21 members already sitting to continue
to do so, but deprive them of speaking and voting rights. See Subakir, *op. cit.*,
pp. 9–12, and Miriam S. Budiardjo, "Evolution towards Parliamentary Government in Indonesia: Parties and Parliament" (M.A. thesis, Georgetown University,
1955), p. 118.

[79] It was stipulated that the minority groups of Indonesia citizens of Chinese,
European, and Arab descent would be represented by nine, six, and three members respectively, as under the 1949 constitution, and that these numbers would
be made up by government appointment where necessary; but in actual practice
it was clear that no appointment would be required.

[80] The table is taken from A. K. Pringgodigdo, *The Office of President in Indonesia as Defined in the Three Constitutions in Theory and Practice* (Cornell
Modern Indonesia Project, Translation Series; Ithaca, N.Y., 1957), p. 34. For lists
of the names of members according to the body from which they came to the 1950
House of Representatives see Kementerian Penerangan, *Kepartaian dan Parlementaria di Indonesia*, 1954, pp. 626–635.

(2) Members from the RUSI Senate	29 [81]
(3) Members from the Working Body of the Central National Committee of the Republic of Indonesia	46
(4) Members from the Supreme Advisory Council of the Republic of Indonesia	13
Total	236

Probably the thorniest of the issues which the RUSI-RI committee had to face was that of determining the relationship between parliament and cabinet. The RUSI cabinet, as we have seen, was not responsible to parliament. The Republic's cabinet was responsible to its legislative assembly, this on the basis not of the Republic's written constitution of August 1945, but of a convention dating back to November 1945. However, the convention also provided that the President could at times of emergency install a presidential cabinet not based on party strengths in parliament. The issue for the constitution makers of 1950 was whether or not to include an escape clause which would make such emergency actions possible under the new unitary state also.

Public discussions of this matter focused on the general question "Is our parliamentarism sufficiently mature to allow us to dispense with an escape clause?" But the heart of the matter lay elsewhere. The real issue at stake was the role of Mohammad Hatta. Hatta was the man who had been appointed in 1948 to form a presidential cabinet when it had seemed impossible to form a cabinet on the basis of party strengths in parliament.[82] And, as it was known that President Soekarno himself had a strong disinclination to take over control of the day-to-day affairs of government, it was Hatta who was expected to step in if such a situation arose again and an escape clause were in existence.

In the discussions of the joint committee the RUSI position was pro-Hatta. It favored an escape clause. Moreover, it opposed the suggestion that the office of Vice-President (which existed in the Republic but not in RUSI) should exist in the new unitary state; this in its view was an attempt to kick Hatta upstairs. But the RUSI position, which was also the position of most leaders of the Masjumi, lost

[81] Of the original 32 Senators three did not become members of the new House of Representatives.

[82] On the status of Hatta's two presidential cabinets see Pringgodigdo, *The Office of President*, pp. 16–17.

out in both instances. The final decision was to uphold the position of the Republic of Indonesia—which was also the position of the PNI and, significantly, of the Indonesian Socialist Party.[83] Thus the two governments agreed to reintroduce the vice-presidency and include no escape clause which would make a nonparliamentary cabinet possible. It was a decision which was to have important consequences in later years.[84]

In one respect the cabinet was given enormous power: the constitution prepared by the joint committee provided, as the RUSI constitution had, for the possibility of emergency laws which could be made by the government alone and would be valid until such time as they were specifically countermanded by parliament. In other respects, however, the new constitution was tilted in parliament's favor. Parliament was placed in the position of being able to force the resignation of a cabinet or of individual ministers. On the other hand, the power of the cabinet to dissolve parliament was less clearly specified. It waᶜ said in Article 84 of the constitution that "the President has the right to dissolve the House of Representatives," but also, in the next sentence, that "the Presidential Decree announcing such dissolution shall also order the election of the new House of Representatives within 30 days." [85] Thus it appeared, at least to one major school of constitutional interpretation, that dissolution was possible only in situations where it was feasible to elect a new House within 30 days.[86]

---

[83] The Socialist position was partly influenced by the hope that, with Hatta unavailable, Sjahrir would be able to return to the prime ministership. The Socialist Party's role in this matter was an important one because of the influence of the party within the cabinet of the Republic of Indonesia and may indeed have been determining. Certainly it was a role which Hatta and a number of Masjumi leaders continued to hold against the Socialists in subsequent years.

[84] On October 14, 1950, the parliament of the unitary Republic voted to recommend Hatta for appointment as Vice-President. Hatta obtained 113 votes, the prewar nationalist leader Ki Hadjar Dewantoro (now supported by the PKI) obtained 19, and several others were supported by one or two members. See Dewan Perwakilan Rakjat ("People's Representative Council"), *Risalah Perundingan* ("Report of Proceedings"), 1950–1951, V, 1880–1887.

[85] *The Provisional Constitution of the Republic of Indonesia* (Djakarta: Kementerian Penerangan, 1951 [?]). Unless otherwise specified, all translations quoted in the present discussion are taken from this official translation.

[86] See, for instance, Soenarko, *Susunan Negara Kita* ("The Structure of Our State"), II (Amsterdam: Djambatan, 1951), 29–35. Logemann maintained that dissolution would be constitutional only when both an electoral law and a voters' registry were in existence. See J. H. A. Logemann, *Het Staatsrecht van Indonesië* ("The Constitutional Law of Indonesia"; s'Gravenhage and Bandung: van Hoeve, 1954), p. 105.

On the matter of the powers of the President the RUSI-RI joint committee, in line with its proparliamentary bias, sought a narrow definition. Thus Article 83 reads:

(1) The President and the Vice-President are inviolable.
(2) The Ministers shall be responsible for the entire policy of the Government. . . .

And in Article 85 it is stated:

All decrees of the President, including those concerning his authority over the Armed Forces of the Republic of Indonesia, shall be countersigned by the Ministers concerned, except for the provisions in the fourth paragraph of article 45 [concerning the appointment of the first Vice-President by the President, upon the recommendations submitted by the House of Representatives] and the fourth paragraph of article 51 [concerning the appointment of cabinet formateurs and of ministers in accordance with the recommendation of the formateurs].

Pringgodigdo therefore maintains, with wide support from other constitutional authorities, that the constitution placed the President in a figurehead position, giving him no prerogative rights other than in the two situations mentioned above.[87] On the other hand, the President's position and that of the Vice-President were strengthened by the fact that no means was provided for their replacement prior to the promulgation of a constitution drafted by an elected Constituent Assembly.[88]

As for the Constituent Assembly, it was provided that this would be elected by free and secret ballot, its membership to be determined on the basis of one representative for every 150,000 residents of Indonesian citizenship. Unlike the 1949 constitution, there was no specification regarding any time within which the elections were to be held. The support of a two-thirds majority of the members of the Constituent Assembly present would be required in order to approve a new permanent constitution.

The selection of directive principles for the constitution was from

[87] *The Office of President*, pp. 42–43 and *passim*.
[88] In addition, Kahin has argued that the great expansion of the powers of the presidency which developed in actual practice was aided by ambiguity in the wording of the 1950 constitution. There was certainly considerable ambiguity, for instance, concerning the President's vote as regards dissolution of parliament and his role as "Supreme Commander of the Armed Forces." See George McT. Kahin, "Indonesia," in Kahin, ed., *Major Governments of Asia* (Ithaca, N.Y.: Cornell University Press, 1958), pp. 542–545.

both the 1945 and 1949 constitutions.[89] The charter of rights in the 1949 constitution (drawn up largely on the basis of the UN's Universal Declaration of Human Rights of 1948) was maintained in its entirety. In addition, the framers included a slightly re-edited version of a right safeguarded in the 1949 constitution of the Republic: "Every citizen according to his ability has the right to work worthy of a human being" (Article 28). They also preferred the 1945 constitution's phrasing on the matter of religion: "The State is founded on the One Deity [*Negara berdasar atas Ketuhanan jang Maha Esa*].[90] The State guarantees the freedom of every resident to profess his own religion and to worship according to his religion and belief."

On economic matters the new constitution also took much from the constitution of 1949, but one central article came from the 1945 document:

The national economy shall be organized as a common endeavor on the basis of the principle of family relationships.[91] Branches of production of importance to the State and which vitally affect the life of the people, shall be controlled by the State. Land and water and the natural riches contained therein shall be controlled by the State and exploited for the greatest benefit of the people.

An additional important formulation was new: "Property is a social function" (Article 26). Abstract and hortatory as these principles may be, they were regarded as highly important, a fact which reflects the concern with goals rather than institutions in Indonesian thinking about democracy and perhaps also the idea that directive principles might at some later stage provide a political rationale for side-stepping structural clauses of the constitution.

In addition to the literal contents of the new constitution the joint committee considered a number of related issues. As a result of these

[89] For article-by-article comparisons of the three constitutions see Muhammad Yamin, *Proklamasi dan Konstitusi Republik Indonesia* ("The Proclamation and Constitution of the Republic of Indonesia") (2d ptg.; Djakarta and Amsterdam: Djambatan, 1952), pp. 199–200 and *passim*, and A. K. Pringgodigdo, *Tiga Undang-Undang Dasar* ("Three Constitutions"; Djakarta: Pembangunan, 1954).

[90] Article 43. Here the translation is my own. The official translation reads: "The State is founded on the belief in the Divine Omnipotence."

[91] Article 38. Here too I hesitate to accept the official translation which reads: "The national economy shall be organized on a cooperative basis." See Wilopo and Widjojo Nitisastro, *The Socio-economic Basis of the Indonesian State: On the Interpretation of Paragraph 1, Article 38 of the Provisional Constitution of the Republic of Indonesia* (Cornell Modern Indonesia Project, Translation Series; Ithaca, N.Y., 1959).

discussions it was decided that Djakarta would be the new state's capital—rather than Jogjakarta for which the representatives of the Republic of Indonesia had argued. On the matter of provincial boundaries the settlement finally agreed on was one which paid little heed to regional or ethnic group feeling. On August 15 ten provinces were established by RUSI government regulations, three in Java (East, Central, and West), three in Sumatra (North, Central, and South), and one each for Kalimantan, Sulawesi, the Moluccas, and the Lesser Sundas. At the same time it was agreed that the Municipality of Greater Djakarta and the Special Territory of Jogjakarta would have an independent status equivalent to that of provinces. This was to remain the arrangement of province boundaries until November 1956.

Late in July the final draft of the constitution was presented to the RUSI parliament and the Republic's Working Body. In both bodies there were a host of criticisms of the draft and strong protests at the action of the governments which denied them the right to amend it. Party support had been organized, however, and the government argued persuasively that the new unitary state had to be in existence by the fifth anniversary of the proclamation of independence on August 17, 1945. Thus the two parliaments ratified the draft constitution with large majorities. The vote was 90 to 18 in the RUSI House of Representatives, unanimous in the RUSI Senate, and 31 to 2 (with 7 abstentions) in the Republic's Working Body.

On August 17 a new "Republic of Indonesia" was in existence. In formal terms the new state was a successor to RUSI. Its constitution was enacted as an amendment of the 1949 RUSI constitution—following the required procedure for amendment on the basis of a two-thirds majority in each of the houses of parliament. Politically, however, the new state represented a triumph for the nationalism of the Revolution. Its very name, as well as the date on which its inauguration was celebrated, signified the moral victory of the Republic of Indonesia proclaimed five years earlier.

Chapter III

The Elements of Politics

WITH the resignation of the Hatta cabinet and the ushering in of the unitary state the period of transition to independence was over. It is true that the power of the new regime was not firmly established in all parts of the country, and the balance of power within the political elite was by no means a firmly established one. But the problems of consolidation were no longer immediate. They had become complex sociopolitical problems of a long-term character. Nationalism no longer had immediate tasks or visible targets to the extent that this had hitherto been the case—although the West Irian issue remained. Political life had reached a point of "normality," a point where most elements of the process of postrevolutionary politics had begun to come into play. These elements will now be examined.

LEADERSHIP IN ITS SOCIAL SETTING

Throughout the period of this study, political power was in the hands of leaders who had been prominent or at least active in the struggle for independence. Not all of those who had been prominent in this struggle were correspondingly influential in the 1949–1957 period—the military leaders were one notable exception. But only very few of those who had stood aside from the revolutionary struggle were in the ranks of the politically powerful in these subsequent years.

Those who were prominent in the period of Revolution and those who attained leading roles in the 1949–1957 period may therefore be regarded as broadly a single group. The social, educational, and occupational origins of the civilian members of this group have been investigated by Malcolm R. Willison and Soelaeman Soemardi, on the basis of biographical information for the cabinet ministers of the 1945–1955 period, the members of the 1950–1956 parliament, and the holders of senior civil service positions in 1954.[1] From these studies it becomes clear that a principal characteristic of the group was possession of Western education. Thus Soelaeman Soemardi found that 83 per cent of his group of cabinet ministers, 59 per cent of his parliamentarian group, and 100 per cent of his group of senior civil servants had obtained a university or senior high school education. He also found that 94 per cent of the ministers (irrespective of their level of education), 91 per cent of the parliamentarians, and all the civil servants had been educated in Western, as distinct from Islamic, schools and universities.

A slight majority of the cabinet members whose background was investigated in the Willison study were persons who had at one time or another been employees of the Netherlands Indies government. However, only a small handful had worked in the general administrative corps, the Binnenlands Bestuur, or *pangreh pradja,* charged with over-all territorial administration. Most had worked as government doctors, engineers, and teachers or in an administrative capacity within one of the technical services. Those who had not been in the government service, or had left it, had worked mainly as journalists or teachers in private schools (usually run by religious and cultural organizations related to the nationalist movement) or as independent professionals, lawyers, doctors, engineers, or architects. A small group had worked as full-time employees of religious, cultural, or political organizations. Only three ministers were recorded as having operated business enterprises of their own other than newspapers and professional firms.

In terms of class origins, the group which became the political elite in our period was composed of a large number of aristocratic persons, in particular persons from the lower rungs of the various artistocracies.[2] The parents of these people had mostly been members of the Nether-

[1] Malcolm R. Willison, "Leaders of Revolution: The Social Origins of the Republican Cabinet Members in Indonesia, 1945–55" (M.A. thesis, Cornell University, 1958); Soelaeman Soemardi, "Some Aspects of the Social Origins of the Indonesian Political Decision-Makers," in *Transactions of the Third World Congress of Sociology* (London: International Sociological Association, 1956), III, 338–348.

[2] A slight majority of Willison's group of ministers were persons with some kind of aristocratic title. But only a very small number were from the very high families. Many men of the princely and high aristocratic families were among that small group of persons of higher Western education who held aloof from nationalism.

lands Indies government service; in some cases they had held office under one of the sultans and radjas through whom the Dutch ruled in certain areas. The group also contained a smaller group of children of commoners, many of them businessmen. But the role of the group as revolutionary leaders and rulers of independent Indonesia cannot be understood in terms of the interests of the classes from which its members were recruited. More important is the fact that these were persons who had had Western education and that they had been leaders of nationalist organizations, in most cases since the time of their early youth.

Another fact of great importance is that this was a group of men with few property ties. It is true that many of them were absentee owners of small plots of riceland, and some had family connections with the small indigenous Indonesian business class, the rubber producers and traders of Sumatra or the batik manufacturers of Java. Moreover, a considerable number had developed business associations as a direct result of their political importance. Some had become shareholders and board members of new firms, particularly in the importing field. Others had relatives who had been placed in high positions in foreign corporations. All these types of ties affected the political role of the group. But they were of secondary importance. They did not make these elite members behave as the representatives of a propertied class, because the basis of their power continued to be political—rooted in their ties to bureaucratic organizations, civil and military, and political parties—rather than economic.

The elite's power was directly political in derivation—this is a central fact of politics in our period. It must be seen in relation to the overwhelming power of government in Indonesia. The functions of government had long been extremely wide in the Netherlands Indies and had become more so in the period of the "Ethical Policy" in the first quarter of this century. The extent of its impact on the village was characterized by the saying that "a villager cannot scratch his head unless a district officer gives him permission and an expert shows him how to do it." [3] In the period immediately prior to the war in the Pacific the government itself had employed a majority of Indonesians of Western education, with small numbers of others being employed by either the large Dutch and other Western enterprises in plantation agriculture, mining, and commerce or the Dutch or German missionary

---

[3] J. S. Furnivall, *Netherlands India* (Cambridge, Eng.: Cambridge University Press, 1944), p. 389, also pp. 257–261.

establishments. The second major source of employment for Indonesians of Western education—taken here to mean education above the primary school level—was the nationalist movement and the various organizations related to it, in particular the Indonesian-language press, the religious, social, and educational agencies of the modernist Islamic organization Muhammadijah, and the schools of the modernist cultural-nationalist educational association Taman Siswa.

With the Revolution and the achievement of independence the role of government became even more dominant. It remained by far the most important employer of persons of modern education. It is true that Indonesians of modern education were employed by Western firms on a much larger scale than before the war and that some had found work as entrepreneurs, managers, or clerks in newly established Indonesian firms. But on the other hand there had been a vast increase in the number of Indonesians of modern education employed in the armed services. Moreover, the number of civilian government servants had grown very rapidly. And many of the nationalist-related religious, cultural, and educational organizations, which had operated as nongovernmental bodies before the war, had lost their leadership and personnel to government agencies.

A further factor heightening the importance of government was its power to influence social mobility. It was now government which bestowed almost all prestigeful social roles—with the important exception of those obtained through political parties and their associated organizations and the partial exception of those which came from educational attainments or wealth.

This was related to the image of government which prevailed in the political public. To be a government servant in 1950 was not only a matter of high prestige, as it had been all the century. It was seen as being literally in the service of the nation, as being part of the spearhead of national progress. The socialist content of Indonesial political ideology was important here, but of greatest importance was nationalism itself. Government had long been the great provider and protector. Now it was also the great leader. To be employed as its servant, civil or military, was to share in this leadership role. It was to be close to the sacred symbols of nation and nationality.[4] Only one role could be more honorable, that of the political leader.

[4] For a theoretical discussion of the transfer of the quality of sacredness from its traditional bearers to the bearers of the "charisma of nationality" see Edward A. Shils, 'The Concentration and Dispersion of Charisma and Their Bearing on

But the most important aspect of the dominant role of government
was the fact that few centers of power existed outside it—again with
the exception of the political parties. In the first place, there was no
bourgeoisie such as developed in the West and Japan, in the sense of
a business class with the resources for wielding major influence over
the general course of government. The largest chunks of economic
power were in the hands of the oligopolistic Western firms, mainly
Dutch, which dominated estate agriculture, the oil industry, stevedoring, shipping, aviation, modern-type banking, and exporting and
played an important role also in importing, the internal distributive
trade, manufacturing, and insurance. For the most part these were
very large organizations, having something of a "state within a state"
character, and the fact that governments saw themselves as needing
them, especially for their foreign exchange earnings, gave them considerable bargaining power. But this was more than outweighed by
the political disadvantages which followed from their foreignness.
Thus not only were they unable to press demands upon the government publicly; in addition, it was extremely difficult for the government to take overt action from which these firms stood to gain and
any Indonesian groups to lose. Most of the same limitations applied
to the Chinese enterprises, large and small, which controlled a great
part of the country's internal trade—moneylending, road transportation, rice milling, and small-scale manufacturing—and operated also
in the fields of importing, exporting, and plantation agriculture.[5] Members of the Chinese business community were denied a legitimate political role even where they regarded Indonesia as their home and expected to become Indonesian citizens.[6]

As for Indonesian business, it had been limited in the prewar period
to small trade, certain corners of manufacturing, like batik stamping

Economic Policy in Under-developed Countries," *World Politics*, XI, no. 1 (Oct.
1958), 1–19.

[5] Victor Purcell, *The Chinese in South East Asia* (London: Royal Institute of
International Affairs, 1951), pp. 534–546.

[6] Under a provision of the Round Table Conference Agreement, Dutch subjects
born in Indonesia of Chinese parents were to choose before December 27, 1951,
between Indonesian, Chinese (Chinese People's Republic), and Dutch citizenship.
Those who took no action would become Indonesian citizens on that date. This
passive system of acquiring citizenship applied also to persons of Arab and Indian
origin, but not to persons of European origin who could become Indonesian citizens
only by active option. See Donald E. Willmott, *The National Status of the Chinese
in Indonesia, 1900–1958* (rev. ed.; Cornell Modern Indonesia Project, Monograph
Series; Ithaca, N.Y., 1961), pp. 29–30, 115–116.

and the production of clove-flavored cigarettes, and the commercial growing of such crops as rubber, copra, and to a smaller extent tobacco and fruit and vegetables. In the postwar period a new business group had begun to develop on the basis of substantial credits and other support from Indonesian governments. But neither the "old" business class nor the "newcomers" could exercise much influence on governments beyond the eliciting of immediate favors. The group of prewar businessmen were handicapped because most of them had had no secondary schooling and hence did not share in the modern urban culture of the nationalist movement. Those businessmen who had built up large operations were far more dependent on government than influential over it, for, being unable to count on neutral rule application in government banks and licensing and foreign exchange offices, they had to cultivate political and bureaucratic friendships. As for the members of the "new" business group, they were dependent on bureaucratic favor in considerably higher degree.

Landlords were affected by the same cultural disability as members of the "old" business group, since they were a group of petty owners, a large proportion of them resident rather than absentee. In 1957 there were only 19,285 holdings of more than 5 hectares of wet rice land in Java and only 567 holdings of more than 20 hectares.[7] Moreover, none of these 567 appear to have been very large. Altogether property was a weak platform from which to influence political life.[8]

If business had little power independent of the government, the same is certainly true of labor. Labor unions were indeed powerful in 1950 and growing rapidly in membership and volume of activity. They were very much more powerful vis-à-vis employers than their miniscule predecessors of the period before the war. But this change was chiefly a reflection of independence itself. For most large-scale employers of labor were foreign and thus in a much weaker position generally in 1950 than in 1940. The power which the unions could

[7] Departemen Agraria (Department of Agrarian Affairs), *Daftar Rata-Rata Luas Tanah Sawah tiap-tiap Pemilik Sawah dalam Propinsi, tahun 1957* ("The Average Size of Wet Rice Holdings by Provinces in 1957"; Djakarta, 1960), quoted in Donald Hindley, "The Communist Party of Indonesia, 1951–1961: A Decade of the Aidit Leadership" (doctoral dissertation, Australian National University, 1961), p. 4.

[8] On the concept of "weak property" see Karl A. Wittfogel, *Oriental Despotism* (New Haven, Conn.: Yale University Press, 1957), pp. 4, 228 ff. See also Fred W. Riggs's discussion of the "dependency syndrome" in his "Prismatic Society and Financial Administration," *Administrative Science Quarterly*, V, no. 1 (June 1960), 16 ff.

sway in 1950 resulted in large measure from the sympathy of Indonesian governments for them. In the second place, it resulted from the intermeshing of parties in labor organizations. Most unions were run, at least at the higher levels, by white-collar persons who had been sent by their parties to work in the trade union field. Most of them too were heavily supported by party finances. Hence their strength depended almost entirely on governmental sympathy and party calculations.

Working-class class consciousness was very low—because of the small number of large industrial establishments, the close ties of urban and estate workers to their original village homes, the low levels of industrial skills, and the omnipresence of underemployment. And, lacking class consciousness, the great mass of workers considered themselves of too low status to be politically active. There were, of course, individuals who overcame these traditional inhibitions, usually through association with a party like the PKI or Partai Murba. But both of these served as ladders of social mobility, and workers who became fully "aware" members of these parties were usually transformed into white-collar functionaries of considerable prestige and into spokesmen for parties rather than class or interest groups. The PKI and Partai Murba must be considered as representing class interests to some extent, both the interests of the working class and those of a middle-level status group of craftsmen, primary school teachers, and low-level officials. Both parties, however, acted more frequently in their own directly political interests as parties than they did as representatives of socioeconomic classes.

Apart from labor unions, large numbers of modern-type voluntary organizations were in existence—women's organizations, youth organizations, student organizations, veterans' associations, and religious, cultural, educational, scouting, and sporting bodies. In fact, the proliferation of organizations of this kind was one of the most remarkable aspects of the social change wrought by the Revolution, in urban areas and a great many rural areas as well. But the organizations of this period, unlike their prewar predecessors, were mostly dependent on the government. Most of the nongovernmental schools, a large number of mosques, the Red Cross, and various dancing, music, and sporting groups were subsidized by government agencies. An even larger number were subordinated affiliates of political parties. Only a small number did not depend directly on the government or a particular party, and these were mostly without wide influence. Some were foreign-controlled, or seen as such, and therefore allowed to participate in Indonesian public life only under sufferance; this is true of some Christian churches and sects, some Dutch- and Chinese-owned newspapers, and organizations such as the Rotarians, Freemasons, and theosophists. Others, such as the more cosmopolitan student organizations, were seen as associations of selfish people who met to enjoy themselves in complete unconcern for the great tasks facing the country.

Finally, there remained traditional power centers in certain parts of the country—radjas in the Lesser Sunda Islands and Sulawesi, old-style Islamic leaders like Daud Beureueh in Atjeh. Some of these leaders associated themselves with parties, but none of them won significant influence through this channel. On the whole, they remained outside the power complex of government and parties. Not being assimilated to the modern urban culture of the nationalist movement, they could participate only sporadically in all-Indonesian politics. Their influence was slight throughout the period of this study.

Government, then, was central to social power. Political parties were its only major competitors. But in fact the relationship was one less of competition than of interpenetration. Power being widely dispersed within the bureaucracy (its civilian portion and to some extent its military part too) and within most of the parties as well, there was a thorough intermeshing of power relationships between the two spheres. By and large political leaders did not draw their power from class-delineated groupings. And they drew little of it from organized interests. Instead it came from control over segments of the army and civil service and from the support of parties and sections of parties. Not least important, it came from amorphous sections of the political public (and to a lesser extent the society at large) to which they were linked by informal personal ties.

Hence the actually implemented decisions of government resulted in part from the pressures of parties—pressures coming through party representatives inside the bureaucracy as often as through the formally responsible cabinet minister—and in smaller part from purely intra-bureaucratic pressures. They were rarely a response to pressure from a class or an organized interest.

In fact, the most important unit of influence was a political-*cum*-personal clique, a group of leaders with personal followings and personal ties to one another. Such a group normally straddled parties and the bureaucracy. It often controlled a small party or a faction of a larger one, and it bade actively to obtain and keep positions of leverage within the bureaucracy. At the same time it articulated a wide range of interests on behalf of all those who chose to accept its leadership and protection, party members, civil servants, and others with personal ties of any sort to the members of the clique. Almost all the country's principal political leaders were leaders of informal cliques of this kind.

THE POLITICAL ELITE AND THE POLITICAL PUBLIC

The central importance of government and the absence of major countervailing power outside it, the wide dispersion of power within the government bureaucracy and the parties, and the diffuse and personal nature of interest representation—these together justify the use of an elite model in the analysis of the politics of this period. In speaking of the Indonesian elite in this study we will be referring to the group of men who exercised greatest political power.[9] More specifically we shall define the elite as those 200 to 500 persons, mainly Djakarta residents, who contributed actively to the decision making which produced political crises or ended them.

This elite model, it will be noted, makes no reference to the institutional bases of power. It assumes an unstructured situation in which most political groups have a share of both institutional leverage and noninstitutional loyalties and support. The model focuses on the role of individuals in the political process, viewing them as participants in a leader-followers unit. And it sees the distribution of power outside the elite as resembling a series of concentric circles, with power diminishing as one's political distance from the elite increases.

For our purposes we shall use the image of a set of three concentric circles. The political elite constitutes the inside circle. The middle circle, consisting of men of lesser political influence, will be designated the political public. It will include all those who saw themselves as capable of taking action which could affect national government or politics. Finally, there is the outer circle, the group of the least influential, which we shall call the mass or those outside the political public.

The composition of the political elite is fairly clear from the foregoing discussion of the studies of Willison and Soelaeman Soemardi, although these studies were of formal office-bearers rather than wielders of power and although military leaders were not included in either of the two samples. By far the greatest number of members of the

[9] See Harold D. Lasswell, *Politics: Who Gets What, When, How* (New York: Meridian Books, 1958), pp. 13–27.

elite were professionally either bureaucrats (secretaries-general of ministries, divisional heads, army commanders, and officers of the General Staff) or politicians (cabinet ministers, parliamentarians, or full-time employees of parties or their affiliated organizations). A small number were practicing lawyers, doctors, professors, teachers, and newspaper editors. And a smaller number still had business as their primary occupation. Most of them had had Western-type higher secondary education, and a sizable minority held university degrees.

The group as a whole was steeped in the all-Indonesian modern urban culture which had grown up around the nationalist movement, and its members were correspondingly less closely allied to the cultures of their respective ethnic groups. Many members of the elite had contracted interethnic marriages and pointed to them with pride. In fact, the political elite had a considerable cultural homogeneity of its own. Its members had a fairly strong sense of constituting a single group, all political divisions notwithstanding—and this is particularly true of the year 1950. As a result of common schooling, common participation in nationalist political organizations, and particularly common residence in the Jogjakarta of the years of Revolution, most members of the elite knew one another rather well. They were in general at comparably high rungs of the social ladder—partly because political power as such brought a high degree of social status with it. They lived in houses of similar location, size, and style, used cars of similar make and age (usually with a low number on the license plate), and interspersed their spoken Indonesian with about the same number of Dutch words. They often met socially—at presidential or diplomatic receptions and at private parties. And it was not rare for members of their families to marry across party lines.

The political public may be defined as consisting of persons of a middle range of political effectiveness, persons outside the political elite who nevertheless saw themselves as capable of taking action which could affect national government or politics. This is the group of the politically aware, those who have mentally stepped out of their traditional society and into a modern subsociety and have come to translate the resulting new attitudes and perceptions into political opinions.[10] It is the politically focusing segment of what Deutsch has called the mobilized section of the population, the group of those who

---

[10] For a discussion of having opinions as a crucial point in modernization see Daniel Lerner, *The Passing of Traditional Society: The Modernization of the Middle East* (Glencoe, Ill.: Free Press, 1958), pp. 50–52, 69–75.

communicate frequently with others outside their own family, village, and district, whether by traveling, by letter writing, or, most frequently, by exposure to the mass media—newspapers, magazines, radio, and films.[11] Mobilization in this sense is a manifestation of overall transformation of a traditional society, and it correlates with urban residence, nonagricultural occupations, modern commodity tastes, relatively high social status, completed primary education, membership of nonascriptive associations, and, in the Indonesian case, active involvement in the Revolution. What determines it, however, is not any of these, but the state of mind which requires a man to communicate with persons other than those to whom he is tied within his traditional society. In the case of the political public, in the sense of the present definition, the determining characteristic is the mobilized man's state of mind when it finds a political focus. Involved are the possession of political opinions and the inclination to translate private feelings into positions on wider public issues.

In the Indonesia of 1950 most members of the political public so defined lived in cities and towns. But there were also many who lived in *ketjamatan* or subdistrict centers too small to be called towns. Others lived on estates. And still others were village dwellers—teachers, village officials, and some peasant farmers who grew cash crops for a wide market. Moreover, large portions of the populations of the cities and towns were outside the political public. Within the urban *kampongs*, the slumlike enclaves of village within the cities, large numbers of laborers, of underemployed petty traders, and of domestic servants continued to be below the threshold of political awareness.

A very high proportion of members of the political public as here defined were persons of relatively high social status, persons in white-collar occupations and their status equivalents, village officials, religious functionaries, labor leaders, middle-size traders, and revolutionary veterans. It is fairly certain that most of the 420,000 civil servants—President Soekarno's figure in February 1950—had the characteristic

[11] Karl W. Deutsch, *Natonalism and Social Communication* (New York: Technology Press of M.I.T. and Wiley, 1953), pp. 100–104, 240. Cf. Gabriel A. Almond, "Introduction: A Functional Approach to Comparative Politics," and James S. Coleman, "Conclusion: The Political Systems of the Developing Areas," in Almond and Coleman, eds., *The Politics of the Developing Areas* (Princeton, N.J.: Princeton University Press, 1960), pp. 50–51, 535. See also Edward A. Shils, "Political Development in the New States," *Comparative Studies in Society and History*, II, no. 3 (April 1960), 265 ff.

attitude to politics. And the same applies to most white-collar employees of foreign enterprises. Political awareness and status tended
to go together, with political awareness making men eager for status
advancement and opening doors to it and with status contributing
greatly to the capacity for political participation. Indeed, there was a
reflection here of the traditional two-class division of Indonesian societies, in which one class corresponded to the sphere of the state
and the other to the sphere of the village. But the status line was not
always the crucial one as far as membership of the political public was
concerned. On the one hand, not every civil service clerk in a subdistrict office had the characteristic political awareness. On the other
hand, there were scattered tradesmen, laborers, and cash-crop farmers
whose social status was lower than that of any such clerk, but who
were sufficiently politically aware to warrant inclusion in the category.

Membership of the political public approximated fairly closely to
the group of those who shared in the modern, urban-centered all-
Indonesian culture which had grown up around the nationalist movement. Most members of the public shared a diluted form of the culture
of the political elite and were correspondingly a step outside the culture of their own ethnic groups. But the political public also included
a large number of persons who were alienated from the nationalist
movement—on the one hand most citizens of Chinese, Eurasian, and
Arab origin and on the other most of the ethnic Indonesians who had
co-operated actively with the Dutch in the period of the Revolution.

The majority of the political public were members of modern nonascriptive associations—parties, trade unions, modern-type religious
organizations, veterans' leagues, cultural, educational, and sporting
bodies, and so on. Moreover in 1950, unlike the period of rapid expansion of party membership in the years before the 1955 elections, there
were not many members of associations of this kind who were not also
endowed with the attitudes characteristic of the political public.

But probably the clearest indication of membership of the political
public in the present sense was regular newspaper reading. Indonesian newspapers were expensive—Rp. 0.50 per copy in 1950—and
their content was almost wholly political. Those who read them regularly were persons who felt that political happenings concerned them.
At the end of 1950 the total circulation of newspapers was 499,150, with
the 67 Indonesian-language dailies accounting for 338,300 copies, the
11 Dutch-language dailies for 87,200 copies, and the 15 Chinese-

language ones for 73,650 copies.[12] Thus, estimating that Indonesian-language newspapers were read at least once a week by an average number of three citizens per copy—newspaper sharing between family members and neighbors constituted the multiplier factor here, but there was also a divisor factor, namely, the inclination of many to read several papers regularly—and estimating further that the average issue of a Dutch or Chinese daily found one regular reader who was an Indonesian citizen, one comes to the conclusion that between a million and a million and a half persons of Indonesian citizenship were reading newspapers once a week or more frequently. This was roughly the size of the political public in the sense in which we are using the term—but the size of the public grew rapidly in the period under study.[13]

Most of the nationally significant political action of the period of our study took place within the political public. When national politicians spoke or wrote, this public normally constituted the intended audience. Such was patently not the case in the elections of 1955. And, throughout the period, efforts were made by parties and other groups within the political public to rally sections of the masses outside this public to strengthen their own positions. It was done most effectively by the PKI through organization and through social welfare activities in the villages and urban *kampongs*. It was achieved in a more sporadic way through oratorical appeals and the projection of personal authority by individual political leaders with the gift of being able to cross the "communication gap" between the modern subsociety of the political public and the various traditional subsocieties.[14] President Soekarno had and used this gift to a far greater extent than any other political figure, but it was also used by such men as Sidik Djojosukarto of the PNI and Natsir and Isa Anshary of the Masjumi and by others in their

[12] Jajasan Lembaga Pers dan Pendapat Umum (Press and Public Opinion Institute), *Almanak Pers Indonesia, 1954–1955* ("Indonesian Press Almanac, 1954–1955"; Djakarta: J.L.P.P.U., 1955), p. 36. This volume also includes useful information on the composition of the newspaper-reading population. On the social composition of those who read one particular Djakarta daily see "Laporan Sementara: Readership Survey Harian Pedoman" ("Provisional Report on a Readership Survey of the Daily Pedoman"), *Warta dan Massa* ("News and the Masses," periodical of the Press and Public Opinion Institute, Djakarta), June 1957, pp. 2–29.

[13] By the end of 1956 the total circulation of newspapers had risen to 933,810. See Biro Pusat Statistik (Central Bureau of Statistics), *Statistical Pocketbook of Indonesia, 1957* (Djakarta: Biro Pusat Statistik, 1957), p. 29.

[14] The term "communication gap" is from Almond, in Almond and Coleman, eds., *The Politics of the Developing Areas*, p. 51.

own home areas. These activities were, however, peripheral to the main course of politics.

"ADMINISTRATORS" AND "SOLIDARITY MAKERS"

As the heuristic constructs of political elite, political public, and mass are to be used to clarify the vertical dimension of Indonesian politics, so the concepts on "administrator" and "solidarity maker" may serve to throw light on the horizontal dimension, on the determinants of power and influence within each vertical segment (or, in the earlier figure, each concentric circle). In discussing the revolutionary period we saw how the country's situation created conflict between "administrators," in the sense of leaders with the administrative, technical, legal, and foreign-language skills required to run the distinctively modern apparatus of a modern state, and "solidarity makers," leaders skilled as mediators between groups at different levels of modernity and political effectiveness, as mass organizers, and as manipulators of integrative symbols. In discussing the period of the Hatta cabinet we used the same concepts to throw light on the struggle between the RUSI government, with its attempt to concentrate on administrative policy making, and the various groups leading the unitarist movement, with their primary emphasis on the achievement of nationalist solidarity and the maintenance in government and politics of a sense of momentum. And in our discussion of the values and perceptions of the nationalist leadership in 1949 we saw how the two skill groups corresponded to characteristic views of the tasks the country faced.

In the situation after the victory of the unitarist movement the two skill groups represented alternative ways of seeking power within the politico-bureaucratic sphere in which the major conflicts of society were resolved. Thus "administrators" competed for power on the basis of their technical skills and of the status which they had acquired on account of their technical skills and accomplishments. They claimed leadership positions for themselves, in both the bureaucracy, civil and military, and the political parties, on the grounds of the idea, which colonialism had fostered as part of its own rationalization, that the educated had a right to govern.[15] In addition, they claimed that social prestige should be accorded on a similar basis, that is, to those who (on top of a clean nationalist record) had academic qualifications,

[15] Coleman in Almond and Coleman, eds., *The Politics of the Developing Areas,* p. 548.

professional skills, and an acquaintance with the intellectual culture of the world. "Solidarity makers," on the other hand, competed on the basis of their mass appeal and of the status they had acquired as a result. Thus they claimed leadership positions, again both in the bureaucracy and in parties, on the grounds that they were close to the people and understood their wishes. And they emphasized that the proper determinants of prestige were not formal qualifications, but true (political) leadership and service to the nation and the people.[16]

Most of those whose leadership during the Revolution had been based on "administrator" skills, on their performance in bureaucratic, military, or diplomatic work requiring modern-state-type skills, came to be engaged in similar work in the postrevolutionary period. But in the case of those who had become leaders on the basis of "solidarity maker" skills, as regional army leaders, guerrilla leaders, political propagandists, and religious leaders, the transition to peace was more difficult. Some of them changed roles to become "administrators." (The important distinction is one of skill roles rather than the simple possession of skills, and clearly there were many nationalist leaders who could be "administrators" or "solidarity makers" as either role was required by a particular situation.) Others found "solidarity making" roles in the nation-building and legitimizing activities of the Ministries of Information, Religious Affairs, and Education. But, partly because government was under the preponderant influence of "administrators" in the early postrevolutionary years, these roles were few and did not carry great status.

Increasingly, therefore, the skills of the "solidarity makers" were used for particular parties rather than the government or the nationalist movement as such. They continued to assuage men's thirst for a *mystique* and sense of momentum in public affairs, but did so now through ideological themes of a mutually antagonistic character.

Thus the conflict between "administrators" and "solidarity makers" was sometimes one between different groups of government leaders stressing different and conflicting aspects of government activity. At other times it was a conflict within government parties, usually involving antagonism between "administrator"-controlled factions advancing pragmatic arguments in support of government policies and "solidarity maker"-led factions opposing these policies in the name of

[16] For a discussion of education and organizational leadership as rival determinants of social prestige see W. F. Wertheim, *Indonesian Society in Transition* (The Hague: van Hoeve, 1956), pp. 160–166.

nationalist ideology or the ideology of a particular party. And at other times again it was a direct conflict between an "administrator"-led government and a "solidarity maker"-led opposition (or in later years between a "solidarity maker"-led government and an "administrator"-led opposition).

The importance of the skill-group factor in establishing the lines of political conflict followed largely from the absence of alternative foci of political struggle. Power competition inside the elite was intense at this time. The existing power balance was not accepted as in any way permanent, and important forces were at work to change it— principally, perhaps, the fact that the Republic no longer needed to be led by men acceptable to the Western world. In 1950, moreover, unlike earlier years, there existed no external enemy to foster domestic solidarity. And the power contest inside the political elite was all the more sharply competitive because, as is usual in newly independent states and after a revolution, power was a centrally important determinant of social prestige.[17] There was, then, a great amount of conflict between segments of the political elite—despite the elite's cultural homogeneity and the extensive social intercourse between its members.

But no rigidly fixed foci for this conflict existed. There were no antagonistic classes or organized interests around which the segments of the political elite might be grouped. Nor had parties as such acquired cohesion, or a powerful hold over the cliques and factions which existed within them. And, with the partial exception of the army and the *pamong pradja*, the Interior Ministry's corps of general territorial administrators, there were no cohesive institutional structures to set the pattern of alignment for intraelite conflict. Thus the principal unit of political competition was the virtually free-floating clique, an informal group of leaders with personal followings and personal ties to one another.[18]

What determined the actions of these politico-bureaucratic cliques more than anything else was the effort of their leaders to gain positions of power for themselves. (This was not because followers were heavily dependent on leaders—for indeed the followers' bargaining power was

[17] S. N. Eisenstadt, "Changes in Patterns of Stratification Attendant on the Attainment of Political Independence," *Transactions of the Third World Congress of Sociology* (London: International Sociological Association, 1956), III, 32–41.

[18] On the clique as a unit in the political process of non-Western societies generally see Lucian W. Pye, *The Policy Implications of Social Change in Non-Western Societies* (Cambridge, Mass.: Center for International Studies, M.I.T., 1957), pp. 20–21.

usually considerable in these cliques—but rather because the followers' ends of status, income, and protection could be realized only as the leaders acquired power positions.) And the claims used by individual leaders of the cliques in competing for positions were based principally on skill of either the "administrator" or the "solidarity maker" type. Thus the leaders of a clique were almost invariably either all "administrators" or all "solidarity makers," although the clique following was not usually homogeneous in this sense. One could expect, therefore, that the skill-group factor would remain useful for the analysis of politics to the extent that cliques remained largely free-floating, that is, so long as there were no conflicting class groupings or organized interests to determine alignments and so long as the major parties and the institutional agencies of the state continued to lack cohesion.

But the prominence of skill-group conflict resulted also from a second major factor, from conflict between the requirements of two areas of government activity, what may be called the areas of problem solving and maintenance of support. The problem-solving area was characteristically that of the "administrators." Government to them was the solving of practical problems by the application of the appropriate technical skills. And it was they who were responsible for making and implementing policy for material reconstruction and the maintenance and stimulation of economic activity, for financial stability and the efficient functioning of administration. All of these, it should be noted, were activities which paralleled what the colonial government had done.

But political support for governments engaged in these various activities was not a matter to be taken for granted. In this respect Indonesian governments of our period had tasks vastly different from those of their colonial predecessors. They were committed, as we have seen, to nation building, to the creation of a modern national system of solidarity. And they were committed to govern in a "democratic" way, which implied that they should use coercion sparingly. Indeed, they lacked the means to impose their will by a broad use of coercive powers; for they operated in a situation of postrevolutionary social ferment and had a military and police establishment which was neither completely cohesive nor completely obedient.

For these governments, therefore, maintenance of support was a complex task requiring much effort. It involved efforts to develop and maintain cohesion and loyalty in the bureaucracy, particularly the army, the police, and the *pamong pradja* corps. In addition, it involved maintaining support from parties and other organized groups. The distribution of rewards was one important aspect of this. Finally, it involved activities which would maintain the legitimacy both of the state as such and of particular governments in the eyes of the political public at large (and to some extent in the eyes of the mass of the population).

It was in the way in which problem-solving action was related to support-maintaining activities that "administrators" and "solidarity makers" came into conflict most clearly. The whole emphasis of the "administrators" was on problem solving, and hence they saw maintenance of support as a secondary matter. To the extent that they concerned themselves with it they placed considerable emphasis on improving the effectiveness of the army and the bureaucracy as instruments of control. In addition, they distributed rewards, in the form of civil service promotions, business opportunities, overseas trips, and so on, though with care lest this should violate administrative norms. As for legitimacy, they expected this to be maintained in part through the honoring of nationalist symbols. Further, they expected it to follow from constitutional democracy. Judicial institutions would be strengthened. General acceptance would be gained for the idea that government should be by rules. More specifically the idea was to be spread that those who came to power as a result of party and parliamentary processes had a moral right to govern.

But for many both inside and outside the political public this was not sufficient to legitimize the state. For most of those who had been caught up by the nationalist Revolution, and for others with traditional expectations of what government should do and should be, the new Indonesian state had to be meaningful and inspiring if it was to be legitimate at all. In the words of Donald Fagg, writing about a town in East Java, "The egalitarian undermining of the traditional status structure has left a sense of vacuum in the seats of power, a felt need for guidance and leadership." [19] The state was expected to provide positive and authoritative leadership. To honor nationalist symbols would not be enough; they or their equivalent would have to be central to the activities of the state. As for government by rules, this would be permissible only to the extent that it did not mean a sacrifice of the spirit of government for the letter, to the extent that the rules did

[19] "Authority and Social Structure: A Study in Javanese Bureaucracy" (doctoral dissertation, Harvard University, 1958), p. 106.

not attenuate the spirit of the Revolution, the spirit of unity, the spirit of freedom.

Attitudes of this kind were a widespread feature of Indonesian political life in the postrevolutionary situation. "Solidarity makers" expressed them. And "solidarity makers," if given a free hand, were potentially capable of assuaging the thirst they represented. By fashioning symbols and enacting ritual, they could conceivably endow the state with positive meaning for those who craved it. But for them to have a free rein would mean that they would have preponderant power over the problem-solving areas of government activity as well as the areas of legitimation. It would in fact involve the predominance of a "solidarity maker" view of what government should be and do.

The "solidarity makers" had few shared ideas about the problem-solving areas of government activity. But they shared an inclination to take these areas for granted. What was important for them was not governing as a set of activities but government as an image. As they saw it, the all-important thing was that government should be truly of "the people," and when they spoke of "the people" it was not as differentiated groups with particular sets of interests, but rather as an amorphous mass characterized by a set of value orientations. The "solidarity makers" were in fact principally concerned that government should serve as a fount of values. It must not be *zakelijk* (businesslike), impersonal, remote, soulless, or unloving. It must have meaning.[20] The meaning might be provided in traditional, nationalist, Islamic, or Communist terms—here the "solidarity makers" were sharply at odds with one another—but in any event the polity should be organically cohesive. But this was clearly incompatible with the emphasis of "administrators" on law, rules, and the efficient operation of agencies concerned to solve particular problems.

Looking at the political public in terms of the "administrator"–"solidarity maker" contrast, one sees that each of these had a constituency. This was not principally because interests of one type were represented by "administrators" and interests of another type by "solidarity makers." Indeed, groups and individuals with interests to press could often choose between working through an "administrator"-led clique or a "solidarity maker"-led one. What determined the division into skill-group constituencies was a matter of values rather than interests. However, the division was not between men seeking con-

[20] Edward A. Shils, "The Intellectuals in the Political Development of the New States," *World Politics*, XII, no. 3 (April 1960), pp. 338–342.

trasting value goals through political activity, but rather between those on the one hand who had firmly held values and sought to advance them through political activity and those on the other hand who were politically active for the sake of the activity itself and its meaning for their personal integration. It was a division between those for whom the instrumental aspects of politics were important and those who were primarily concerned with its expressive and symbolic aspects.[21]

The principal factor here was the existence of a large group of men, the constituency of the "solidarity makers" within the political public, who had been shaken in their commitment to traditional values as a result of disruptive social change, but had not as yet found the security of an alternative set of values. This was primarily a group of former revolutionaries, and thus its members had considerable prestige, as well as influence over others outside the political public. Most of them were men of only primary or junior secondary education, men who had known little before 1942 of the life style of urban white-collar Indonesia. The Japanese occupation and Revolution had torn these men from their moorings in a still predominantly traditional society and thrown them unprepared into modern life. While they had participated in the nationalist Revolution, the Revolution had provided them with values and sources of authority for these. Moreover, it had provided them with amply clear enemies, the Dutch. Hence a rationale existed for the anxiety they felt as men uncertain of where they belonged in society. And a target was available for the aggression built up by their involvement in intensified status competition and political conflict. But now with the Revolution over, they were faced with a host of new problems. For many of them, particularly those with few formal scholastic attainments, it was difficult to obtain suitable employment; although not left unemployed, these men suffered considerable status frustration in their new places of employment. Moreover, aggravating the status frustration of some of the group was the sense of anguish of all its members as the changing situation deprived them of their hold on the nationalist and revolutionary symbols which had theretofore given their lives meaning.

Most of them sought to cope with this anguish through political involvement. It was in political authority and political leadership that

---

[21] For a theoretical discussion of expressive politics and its role in non-Western politics see Pye, *The Policy Implications of Social Change,* pp. 39–41. Cf. Myron Weiner, *Party Politics in India* (Princeton, N.J.: Princeton University Press, 1957), pp. 234–237 and *passim.*

they had perceived sacredness in the period of Revolution, and it was here that they sought to find it now. Thus both the state as such and partisan ideological movements were expected to provide symbols to which they could defer, with which they could identify, and which would provide them with standards to adhere to in their personal and social behavior.

For this group of newly modernized persons, more than for most men, politics served to establish and maintain a certain order in the self. Hence they were concerned with the ideal, the symbolic, and the ritual aspects of politics and were disinclined to relate these to realizable goals and the means of attaining them. This does not mean that they were passive in the face of opportunities to advance personal and group interests through political action. But such actions as they took to advance their own interests were seen as something of which to be ashamed. For them no connection existed between politics as affirmation of the ideal and politics as the advancement of one's interests—except the connection between holiness and profanity. Oriented to political values in this expressive way, they were frequently highly unrealistic in their political expectations, responded enthusiastically to panacea formulas and scapegoatist claims, and were ready recruits when it came to symbolic acts of radicalism and rejection of compromise.[22]

All those whose political participation was not primarily expressive in character may be said to have formed the constituency of the "administrators" within the political public. These were on the whole men with relatively high status and rather more advanced formal education who had grown up in the white-collar life style, whether in urban or rural areas. A large number of them had been actively involved in the Revolution. But because of their previous experience of modern living—and because they usually found prestige-bearing employment —it was relatively easy for them to adjust to a more routine-bound urban life once the Revolution was over. In addition, the constituency included most of the small minority of Indonesians who had been actively pro-Dutch in the Revolution—some higher members of aristocracies, some Ambonese and Minahasans, and a large part of the Indonesian citizens of Chinese and European or Eurasian origin. And it included a large group of persons who had been at least partly sympathetic to the revolutionaries, but had not been drawn actively into their ranks—either because they had been too old (or too young),

[22] Cf. J. M. van der Kroef, *Indonesia in the Modern World*, II (Bandung: Masa Baru, 1956), 244 ff.

because they had had business interests to pursue, because they had not wanted to leave cities where their families lived, or simply because there had been no effective resistance to the Dutch in their area.

One part of this constituency consisted of those who were seriously alienated from the political process, politically aware persons who nevertheless felt virtually powerless to affect national political affairs. These men, most of whom had been identified with the Dutch in the period of the Revolution, now regarded themselves as excluded from public life, and they became cynical or apathetic toward political struggle. Although their sympathies went strongly to "administrator" groups within the political elite, they did little to support these groups, except perhaps financially.

It was from the other part of this constituency, those who were neither politically alienated nor expressive in their political participation, that the "administrators" obtained most of their support. The characteristic feature of this group was its relatively detached approach to political struggles. Most members of the group were members of political parties—of the Socialist Party, the Masjumi, the PNI, or one of the Christian parties—and some were active members. But they were hostile to extremist political sentiment and irredeemable promises. They tended to see themselves as citizens and as members of particular status groups, particular professional or occupational groups and particular ethnic and religious groups, rather than as adherents to any of the current ideologies or members of the national movement as such.

The members of this group were primarily instrumental in their political participation; they saw it as a means to certain ends, which for them were prior to the political participation itself. And they reflected a view of interests as legitimate and possibly consonant with one's values. Looking at particular governments, the members of the group tended to assess achievement rather than to orient themselves to an image on the basis of affirmation about their own ideological identity. In fact, they were fairly broad in the application of their critical faculties to political situations. Characterized by "general, diffuse, intelligent interest in public issues" and a "basic identification with the political order," they formed a group such as Eisenstadt sees as crucial to the successful functioning of representative government.[23]

[23] S. N. Eisenstadt, "Patterns of Political Leadership and Support," paper submitted to the International Conference on Representative Government and National Progress, Ibadan, Nigeria, 1959, pp. 314. Cf. Shils's discussion of "civility" in his "Political Development in the New States," pp. 265 ff.

To the extent that they were influential, they could provide a background of consensus for the contending parties and a public for which the parties would compete. Moreover, they could sustain the independence and regulatory role of the press and other media of communication.[24]

In 1950 the influence of this generally interested group was not great. The fact that the "administrators" were preponderantly powerful resulted less from the importance of their constituency within the political public than from what remained of the Hatta-built system of "administrator" control of top army and civil government posts. But the future of relations between "administrators" and "solidarity makers" would depend in large part on the constituency balance within the political public. It would depend on whether or not, as the post-revolutionary period wore on, the generally interested group would grow in influence at the expense of the group of those whose political participation was expressive.

THE POLITICAL PARTIES

With this theoretical sketch before us, let us now go on to look at the formal units of political activity, the parties. By August 1950 party political activity had recovered from its lull of 1949 and large numbers of parties were in existence. In the newly constituted parliament of 236 members no less than 22 parties, organizations, and parliamentary associations were represented. Perhaps as many as 20 parties wielded significant power nationally, and others were able to achieve public recognition, and sometimes a measure of patronage, by means of bluffing techniques.

The multiparty pattern of the prewar nationalist movement had re-emerged in November 1945, when the new Republic's government had formally called for the establishment of parties. Influenced by the model of the Netherlands and other continental countries with multiparty systems, the leaders of the Republic did not expect or hope for a system of only two parties. When the revolutionary KNIP (Komite Nasional Indonesia Pusat, Central National Committee of Indonesia or Outer Parliament) was given a legislative role and subsequently expanded and reconstructed, this was done on a system whereby President Soekarno, in consultation with Vice-President Hatta and the cabinet, estimated party strengths and asked party leaders to name

[24] See Almond in Almond and Coleman, eds., *The Politics of the Developing Areas*, p. 48.

representatives up to a number which he specified. The stated aim was
to provide direct representation to all significant groups in Indonesian
society, much as under a proportional representation voting system.
The effect was to encourage the existence of a large number of parties
and to provide the executives of the parties with a strong position.
Nine parties and four other political organizations were represented in
the cabinets of the Republic in the revolutionary period, and many
others had representation in the KNIP.

In 1950 the multiplicity of parties was recognized and further encouraged by the way in which membership of parliamentary committees and various government-established committees was determined, for this was often on the basis of one representative from each
of a large number of parties, more or less regardless of their size and
importance. Under an August 1950 regulation of the (member-state)
Republic of Indonesia, a somewhat similar method was provided for
determining the composition of interim legislative councils to be
established in provinces, regencies (*kabupatens*), and municipalities
in Java and Sumatra.[25]

The shape of the party system in 1950 was little different from what
had developed in the revolutionary period. But parties now had some
important new functions. The parties originally established in the Republic of Indonesia had spread rapidly in the RUSI period into the
federal states and territories and were joined by many of those previously active in the politics of these states. In this way they helped
to break down the political and psychological barriers which divided
"non's" from "co's," those who had not co-operated with the Dutch in
the revolutionary period from those who had. And they provided the
"co's" with a means of clearing their names.

Even more important, parties now had important patronage functions which they had not had before December 1949. In effect the
parties obliged the government to distribute its store of material and
status rewards largely through them. Thus even under the Hatta
cabinet coveted government posts, business opportunities, overseas
trips, houses, and cars tended to go chiefly to those with party connections. At a lower level party membership was usually an advantage
for ex-guerrillas looking for white-collar employment or educational
opportunities. Parties were a principal channel of access to the bureaucracy.

To be a party member was to be modern, politically conscious—an

[25] Government Regulation 39, 1950.

alert citizen aware of the importance of nationality. And to be an office-bearer of a party was to be a man of prestige, for political distinction had become probably the most important source of status in society as a whole. It was, furthermore, a step toward greater prestige, both the prestige of being a higher-echelon party leader and that of holding a high office of state to which one had come through nomination by one's party. In a society whose social demarcations had been blurred, where large numbers of men had "a sense that the old barriers are down, that feats of mobility are possible and extremely desirable," [26] parties were a principal means by which one's status ambitions could be realized.

Through party membership, moreover, or more frequently through membership of a party faction, an individual could often obtain protection, the redressing of grievances, and the informal adjudication of disputes by party leaders. Frequently, too, he could obtain assistance of a social welfare kind from fellow party members. Finally, party membership was usually personally meaningful. Party ideology and the authority of a particular party leader served to stabilize one's personal values and sense of identity, and party activity enabled some to rid themselves of anxiety and an oppressive sense of normlessness. For a large number of old revolutionaries party membership was a way of continuing to participate in the "movement" and the "struggle" which had given meaning and purpose to their lives between 1945 and 1949.

Almost all civil servants, including the top heads and including judges and public prosecutors, were party members. Only army and police members were forbidden membership in parties. When a prominent person was not formally a member of a party, it was common for him to be labeled on the basis of his personal associations and general outlook. Thus a parliamentarian or senior civil servant might be described as "officially nonparty, but in fact PNI."

How far party membership and activity extended outside the political public is more difficult to say. Enormous claims of over-all membership were made. Thus the PNI claimed to have 1,466,783 members on March 1, 1950, and the Masjumi went as far as claiming "approximately 10,000,000" members at the end of that year.[27] In 1951 the

---

[26] Clifford Geertz, *The Religion of Java* (Glencoe, Ill.: Free Press, 1960), p. 361.

[27] Kementerian Penerangan (Ministry of Information), *Kepartaian di Indonesia* ("Political Parties in Indonesia"; Djakarta: Kementerian Penerangan, 1951), pp. 124, 14.

Christian Party, Parkindo, claimed 320,000 members, and the National People's Party (Partai Rakjat Nasional, PRN) 2,000,000.[28] But these figures were usually treated with derision by all except those who announced them. They were part of the game of political bluff; this resulted also in party conferences to which one attempted to attract delegates from as large as possible a number of branches, real or fictitious. Indeed, bluff was the order of the day; with a multiparty system officially sanctioned and with party strengths unable to be measured in anything like an objective manner, tiny parties could arise and maintain the claim to have popular support merely by vociferous assertions to this effect.

The main concern of parties was with the political struggle in Djakarta. Where they operated outside the capital, they tended to concentrate their efforts on areas of high national-level political effectiveness, on cities, residency and *kabupaten* (regency) towns, and the detraditionalized areas of estate and small-holder production for the world market. But there were also many other areas, especially in East and Central Java, where party and party-related organizational activity had spread from small towns to surrounding villages. Here developed what Geertz has called the *aliran* pattern, whereby each major party was the center of an interrelated set of voluntary organizations— women's, youth, veterans', labor, peasant, religious, educational, cultural, and sporting organizations—with the whole complex forming an *aliran* or political stream. Whereas any *aliran*'s associational activity was greatest in the small towns, and particularly among the white-collar persons in these towns, parallel forms of activity had come into existence in a number of nearby village areas. Thus villagers were coming to accept urban political leadership, and village-level social and religious divisions were viewed more and more in ideological terms. This activity had as yet little or no importance for the course of national politics, since the organizational ties binding parties and their affiliated organizations as between the capital and the villages were still extremely loose. Its importance lay chiefly in the fact that it provided disorganized and formless segments of rural society with a new basis of social integration, transcending local ties and giving modern form to the orientations of traditional subcultures. In Geertz's words, "The intensity with which the Javanese peasantry has fastened on to political and quasi-political organizations . . . is an index of

[28] *Ibid.*, pp. 89, 194.

the degree to which new social structures are needed in the reconstruction of vigorous village life." [29]

Party organization was in general very poorly developed. The leaders and organizational heads of parties had usually only the vaguest idea of the size of their own membership. Thus in 1951 it was possible for Mr. Jusuf Wibisono of the Masjumi to write: "Based on the number of its branches, the membership of the Masjumi is estimated at 13 million, but only 600,000 persons are registered with the Secretariat of the Party Executive Council, and only 400,000 have been given membership cards." [30]

The situation was similar in the case of most of the other parties. Dues, though stipulated in the constitution of virtually all parties, were rarely collected except in the higher echelons—though an exception should be made here in the case of the Communist Party. There was probably no party whose financing was based mainly on membership dues. Such funds as were required for congresses, party periodical organs, or the salaries of the full-time party workers were raised mainly from a small number of large personal contributions, made in many cases from funds obtained as a result of bureaucratic power and connections.

Almost all the parties lacked cohesion. Intraparty divisions were of great importance and were openly admitted in the case of most parties, though not of the Communists (except briefly in 1950) or the Socialists. In fact, much of the energy of party leaders was spent in internal political struggle.

At first sight it would seem that parties were dominated by their top leaders, by the small group of men having close personal acquaintance with one another and influence at the highest levels of the government. However, there was active competition between these leaders for the allegiance of followers. It was not so much that party leaders were afraid that their members would desert them if not given sufficient rewards, for changes in party membership were fairly rare. But shifts from one faction or clique to another were a much easier matter,

[29] "The Javanese Village," in G. William Skinner, ed., *Local, Ethnic and National Loyalties in Village Indonesia: A Symposium* (Yale University, Southeast Asia Studies, Cultural Reports Series; New Haven, Conn., 1959), p. 37. See also Geertz, *The Social Context of Economic Change: An Indonesian Case Study* (Cambridge, Mass.: Center for International Studies, M.I.T., 1956), pp. 135 ff.

[30] Jusuf Wibisono, "Masjumi di Masa Datang" ("The Future of the Masjumi"), in Panitia Muktamar Masjumi ke-5 (Committee for the Fifth Convention of the Masjumi), *Indonesia Dalam Pembangunan* ("Indonesia Building"; Djakarta: Alvaco, 1951), p. 22.

and thus faction and clique leaders had to be vigilant lest their followers be won over to support of their rivals. Great as was the status of the leader, he was expected to be effective in advancing the interests and values for which he stood. If he failed in this, much of his following would leave him.

There was a reflection here of a major pattern of leadership prevailing in Indonesian society as a whole, that of *bapakism*, literally "fatherism." Where this pattern prevails, the *bapak* or leader is assured of very great respect from his *anak buah*, his followers or literally his children, often also of great affection, and of loyalty and support for whatever action he may take. But at the same time he has diffuse and far-reaching responsibilities for their protection and welfare and must take full account of their wishes whenever these are strongly felt. If he does not discharge these responsibilities adequately, it is thought proper that his followers should switch loyalties quickly.[31]

Finally, the importance of clique division should not be construed to mean that the parties' ideological positions had only a formal significance. In the case of some small parties the primary function of ideologies was indeed to serve as a cover for manipulative politics. But on the whole ideologies were important because of their meaning for party members. When party leaders presented ideological formulations—formulations based on nationalism, Marxism, Islam, Christianity, or some combination of these—they provided their members and supporters with modern patterns of values and perceptions in a form related to the values and perceptions of their traditional societies. Granted that values and cognitive patterns were in flux and in conflict with one another and that political belief was centrally important to their stabilization, there had to be great stress on political goals and on their explicit and sometimes schematic formulation. At the same time ideology served to rationalize one party's antagonism toward another, in the face of traditional and nationalistic restraints on open hostility.[32]

Certain of the more important parties will now be examined to determine the situation in which they found themselves at the time of the reinauguration of the unitary state in August 1950. (In Table 1 are given data on the representation of the various parties in parliament.)

[31] See Selosoemardjan, *Social Changes in Jogjakarta* (Ithaca, N.Y.: Cornell University Press, 1962), pp. 138–139; Fagg, *op. cit.*, pp. 275 ff.; and Boyd R. Compton, "Bhineka Tunggal Ika," *Report of the Institute of Current World Affairs* (New York), July 28, 1956.

[32] Josef A. Mestenhauser, "Ideologies in Conflict in Indonesia, 1945–1955" (doctoral dissertation, University of Minnesota, 1960), *passim.*

Table 1. Parties and parliamentary representation, March 1951 [*]

	Members from the Republic of Indonesia [†]	Members from BFO states other than Pasundan [‡]	Members from Pasundan [§]	Total
Masjumi	23	23	3	49
PNI	11	23	2	36
PIR	3	14	—	17
PSI	12	5	—	17
PKI	10	—	3	13
Democratic Fraction	—	13	—	13
PRN	5	5	—	10
Catholic	2	6	1	9
Parindra	5	2	1	8
Labor Party	4	2	1	7
PSII	4	—	1	5
Parkindo (Christian Party)	3	1	1	5
Murba	3	—	1	4
Labor Front (Front Buruh) [‖]	3	—	1	4
People's Sovereignty Fraction (Fraksi Kedaulatan Rakjat) [‖]	4	—	—	4
SKI	—	3	—	3
Peasant Group (Golongan Tani) [‖]	2	—	—	2
Members of no fraction	13	9	4	26
Total membership	107	106	19	232

[*] Adapted from a chart in Miriam S. Budiardjo, "Evolution toward Parliamentary Government in Indonesia: Parties and Parliament" (M.A. thesis, Georgetown University, 1955), p. 121. The figures refer to parliamentary fractions (*fraksi*), that is, parliamentary groupings composed of both members of the corresponding party and others who chose to become formally associated with them for parliamentary purposes.

[†] These include persons chosen to make up the 50-man group of Republic of Indonesia representatives in the RUSI House of Representatives, the 2-man group of representatives of the Republic from the RUSI Senate, members of the 46-member Badan Pekerdja or Inner Parliament of the Republic who were incorporated in the parliament of the unitary state in August 1950, and members of the 13-man Dewan Pertimbangan Agung or Supreme Advisory Council of the Republic who were incorporated at the same time.

[‡] These include members of the 100-man group representing the various BFO states in the RUSI House of Representatives and members of the 30-man group representing these states in the RUSI Senate. Excluded, however, are the 21 members who were to represent the state of Pasundan, a state which had been "frozen"

The discussion will begin with three parties which were not then of first importance in themselves, but played a major role in setting the issues on which political competition centered. These are the Indonesian Socialist Party, the Partai Murba or Party of the Proletariat, and the Indonesian Communist Party.

The Indonesian Socialist Party

The Partai Sosialis Indonesia, or PSI, headed by the former Prime Minister Sjahrir, was a small and fairly cohesive party dominated by intellectuals whose thinking was usually described as Western and was in fact closely related to the Western democratic socialist tradition. At the same time it was a party of "administrators" in our sense. Its leadership and much of its support came from a group of persons, most of them young, who had risen to prominence in the Revolution because they commanded skills needed for the running of a modern state.

The party had been formed in February 1948 when Sjahrir and a group of men around him left the Socialist Party, in which Sjahrir and Amir Sjarifuddin had shared leadership and which had become more and more dominated by Sjarifuddin and his Communist associates.[33] Most of those who joined the new party were people who had come to work with Sjahrir in the Japanese occupation or in the early years of the Revolution, but some were old members of the small Club Pendidikan Nasional Indonesia (National Indonesian Education Club or New PNI) which Hatta and Sjahrir had led in the early 1930's. The PSI did not have representation in the Hatta RUSI cabinet, although a number of the members of this cabinet were regarded as being among its sympathizers. In the Halim cabinet of the (member-state) Republic of Indonesia, three of its members held portfolios, and a number of other ministers, including Dr. Halim himself, were PSI sympathizers.

When it adopted ideological positions, and this was fairly infre-

---

[33] Kahin, *Nationalism and Revolution in Indonesia* (Ithaca, N.Y.: Cornell University Press, 1952), pp. 259, 319–320.

---

and placed under the authority of a RUSI Government Commissioner before the opening of the RUSI parliament.

§ These members were appointed as members of the RUSI parliament by the government of the Republic of Indonesia after the state of Pasundan had been incorporated into the Republic of Indonesia in March 1950.

|| Members of these three fractions, all of them inclined to vote with the PKI (and occasionally with the Partai Murba where these two parties took different positions), joined to form the Progressive Fraction in February 1952.

quently, the PSI spoke of its objective of socialism, using Marxist language. But at other times its leaders stressed that they saw Marxism as a method of social analysis rather than a guide to action. And in fact their policy orientation contained less of Marxism than of Fabianism. Its emphasis was on modernization, economic development, and rational planning and organization.

With the stress on things economic went strong opposition to what the party's leaders saw as impractical idealism, to radical and utopian slogans which bore no relation to existing realities in the country. The party leaders opposed extreme nationalism and antiforeign feeling, castigating them as legacies of Japanese rule. They believed that foreign capital would be needed for a considerable time to come. At the same time they were frequently critical of the Hatta cabinet during its term of office, arguing that its foreign policy was too timid and too much under American influence and that its caution in home affairs made impossible an effective harnessing of the dynamic energies of the revolutionary youth to the cause of building up the country.

In 1950 the PSI was not devoting itself to intensive organizational work as was the Masjumi and the PNI, although it was building up some labor union support.[34] The party leaders argued that more could be achieved by a small cadre party, a party of well-trained and well-disciplined political workers. Its greatest source of strength was its position in the higher echelons of the bureaucracy. Its influence at the level of departmental and divisional heads in the capital was second only to that of the PNI. Within the top leadership of the army it could count on more sympathy than any other party. It had wide influence in the press in many parts of the country. And, although its leadership consisted of persons who had been active partisans of the revolutionary Republic, it enjoyed considerable sympathy from the nonrevolutionary sections of the political public, including some influential members of the Chinese and Indo-European minorities and of the Minahasan and Ambonese ethnic groups.

One further source of PSI influence was the brains-trust function which the party fulfilled within the political elite generally. The PSI's way of perceiving the current condition of Indonesia and its policy

[34] At the time of the first congress of the party in February 1952 it claimed only 3,049 full members and 14,480 candidate members. See Saul Rose, *Socialism in Southern Asia* (London: Oxford University Press, 1959), p. 155. See also L. M. Sitoroes, "Laporan Organisasi dari Pebruari 1950 sampai 12 Pebruari 1952" ("Report on Organization, February 1950 to February 12, 1952"), *Suara Sosialis* ("Socialist Voice"; PSI periodical, Djakarta), vol. VI, no. 2 (April 15, 1952).

recommendations had widespread currency outside the party itself, both in the bureaucracy and army and within leadership groups of several of the other parties, in particular the Masjumi and to a lesser extent the PNI. On the other hand, strong enmity toward the PSI existed in certain sections of these and other parties. This was partly a result of the attacks which Sjahrir had made in the early months of the Revolution on all who had worked with the Japanese authorities during the occupation. It was partly a consequence of the resentments Sjahrir had aroused by his policy of giving concessions to the Dutch in the negotiations of the early years of the Revolution. And it was related to the fact that he had been personally estranged from President Soekarno since late in 1948. Most important of all, it represented the reaction of adherents of a populistic nationalism against a group of cosmopolitan intellectuals who were "far removed from the people." [35]

The Partai Murba

The nationalist-communist Partai Murba, or Proletarian Party, may be said to have been the prototype of the party of "solidarity makers," as the Indonesian Socialist Party was prototypically a party of "administrators." Its leadership was dominated by men without higher education who had come into prominence as leaders of mass organizations and military formations in the Japanese occupation and the Revolution. Its appeals were directed particularly to those who sought expressive political participation, including unaccommodated ex-guerrillas, low-ranking white-collar workers, and, outside the political public, urban and estate workers.

The Murba leaders, followers of the former PKI and Comintern leader, Tan Malaka, had enjoyed great influence in the Republic in the early days of the Revolution, because of their role in bringing about the proclamation of independence and their strong opposition to all negotiations with the Netherlands and after September 1948 because of the eclipse of the PKI as a result of the Madiun revolt. The

[35] Western critics tended to brush this assertion aside, maintaining that those who made it frequently lived as well as the Socialist leaders they were criticizing, with as many Western luxuries in their homes and with domestic servants who were similarly subservient before their masters. What these critics failed to understand was that the Socialist leaders were under fire for the foreignness and radical modernity of their thinking and social behavior—their desire for personal privacy, their calculating, businesslike attitude to time, their directness of speech, and their disrespect for many existing status graduations—rather than for its lack of egalitarian content.

party itself had been formed in October 1948, just after the Madiun affair, by a merger of three parties of similar outlook.[36] After 1948, as before, the men who led the Murba party refused to participate in any cabinet. Their position was that they could not share responsibility for a policy of negotiation with the Dutch and, later, that they would not be associated with any government functioning on the basis of the Round Table Conference Agreement.

In 1950 Murba's demands were clear: the Round Table Conference Agreement should be abrogated, Dutch properties should be confiscated, and all vital enterprises, including plantations, mines, industries, and transportation facilities, should be nationalized and collectivized. On the basis of this position the party was able to make both a radical nationalist appeal and a radical socialist one. It claimed to be a Marxist-Leninist party, and it was said that some of its leaders hoped that it would one day be preferred by Moscow or Peking over the PKI. Moreover, its leadership was fairly cohesive and its organization was tighter than that of most other parties, bearing a somewhat conspiratorial character. The instructions which the party's leaders gave to their cadres, however, reflected much less of Marxism and Leninism than of an inchoate messianic radicalism. Indeed, Murba was the citadel par excellence of the currently widespread attitude of "oppositionism," the attitude of refusing to recognize the practical difficulties of governments.

Murba-PKI rivalry was bitter, in veterans', labor, and youth organizations. The struggle was between fairly well-matched protagonists, for if the PKI was organizationally stronger this was compensated by the greater nationalist appeal which Murba could exercise. In addition, Murba had numerous sympathizers in other parties, particularly in the PNI and the smaller nationalist parties, and among nonparty members of parliament. It also had close associations with antigovernment rebel groups, in particular with the "People's Army" and "Bamboo Spear" organizations in West Java.

The Indonesian Communist Party

The PKI, Partai Kommunis Indonesia, like the PSI and the Partai Murba, had clearer ideological positions and greater organizational cohesion than the general run of Indonesian parties. But it was a small party. It was still suffering from the effects of the Madiun affair, which

[36] Kahin, *Nationalism and Revolution*, pp. 313–319.

had resulted in the death of its principal leaders, had left the party in a position of semi-illegality, and had given it the stigma of having betrayed the Republic's unity in the face of an impending Dutch attack. There were virtually no PKI members in important positions in the bureaucracy. Thus the PKI was out of power in a far more complete sense than any other party, including the Partai Murba. Its leaders competed for power as "solidarity makers."

The PKI's stand on national issues centered on its opposition to the Round Table Conference Agreement, which, the party maintained, left Indonesia in a semicolonial state. In the party's view the Indonesian revolution had been brought to a halt in early 1948 (when the Amir Sjarifuddin government had given way to the Hatta government). Soekarno, Hatta, and all those associated with them were attacked, as lackeys of American imperialism and, in the second place, of Dutch imperialism. At the same time the party denounced these two leaders for collaborating with the Japanese in the period of occupation.

Mid-1950 was a time of internal upheaval in the PKI. The few surviving leaders of the party's top leadership of pre-Madiun days, men like Tan Ling Djie and Alimin Prawirodirdjo, were losing control to a younger group of leaders, most prominently D. N. Aidit, M. II. Lukman, Njoto, and Sudisman, who were to emerge in January 1951 in clear control of the party. From August 1950 onward this younger group published articles in the party's theoretical journal *Bintang Merah* ("Red Star"), criticizing the party's current strategies. In particular they demanded that the Communist-controlled Partai Sosialis should be dissolved and its members brought openly into the PKI itself. They also condemned efforts being made to co-operate with the Partai Murba. And they called for greater attention to party theory.[37]

While the factional struggle was going on, however, the party was active in the ranks of urban and estate labor where the departure of the Dutch had resulted in a rush to unionism and strikes. Whereas the PKI was by no means the only beneficiary of this development, its labor federation, SOBSI (the Central All-Indonesian Workers' Organization), did steal an early lead over other federations (being effectively challenged in this only by the labor federation of the Partai Murba).

[37] See Ruth T. McVey, *The Development of the Indonesian Communist Party and Its Relations with the Soviet Union and the Chinese People's Republic* (Cambridge, Mass.: Center for International Studies, M.I.T., 1954). See also Hindley, *op. cit.*, pp. 98–109.

Within the peasantry the party had relatively little organized following, but there were a number of important areas in Java and Sumatra where it had potential support on the basis of organizational work it had done in the 1945–1948 period and, much earlier, between 1914 and 1927. In addition, it enjoyed support from groups of peasants illegally occupying estate lands and state forests. And it had connections with ex-guerrilla groups actively engaged in dacoitry, particularly in East and Central Java.

The number of PKI members of university education or completed secondary education was very small indeed, and the party had almost no support among students. There is a pointer here to a significant strength of the nationalist regime of the immediate postrevolutionary period: as a regime which greatly valued men of higher education and had very few available for its use, it readily offered power and position to all of these.

How much support the party had from the 2,250,000 Chinese residents in Indonesia is very hard to say. Those persons, mainly workers and students in Chinese-language schools, whose pride in the successes of the Chinese Communist Party led them to open partisanship with Indonesian communism, were a small minority. But there was a very large group of Chinese who, feeling apprehensive about the likely future implications of Indonesian nationalist hostility toward their community, came to look to the Peking regime to protect them, and thus represented a source of potential support for the PKI.[38]

The Masjumi

The Masjumi, a heterogenous party, generally considered the country's largest in 1950, illustrates better than the PSI, the Partai Murba, or the PKI the organizational features described above as characteristic of Indonesian political parties of this period. A loosely knit organization, whose membership was in practice not clearly defined, it exacted little discipline from its members. Indeed, it was openly split by factional disagreements. It was different from other Indonesian parties in that it was a "party of indirect structure,"[39] having not only individual members, but also "corporate members," namely, eleven Moslem religious, social, and educational organizations, the most im-

[38] See Willmott, *The National Status of the Chinese in Indonesia, 1900–1958,* pp. 19 ff. and *passim.*

[39] See Maurice Duverger, *Political Parties: Their Organization and Activity in the Modern State* (London: Methuen; New York: Wiley, 1954), pp. 5–17.

portant of these being the modernist Muhammadijah and the more traditionally oriented Nahdatul Ulama.[40]

The Masjumi had been a leading government party since the early days of the Revolution. It had been strongly represented in the Hatta cabinets, both those of 1948 and 1949 and the RUSI cabinet. In the 1950 Halim cabinet of the Republic it had also played a major part. However, within the nationalist leadership as a whole its role was considerably smaller than one might have expected in view of its claim to be the only party for Moslems in a country approximately 85 per cent of whose citizens were nominally Moslem. Within the nationalist leadership and in the middle and higher levels of the civil service, the number of devoted practicing Moslems, or *santri*, who supported the Masjumi as a specifically Islamic party was much smaller (and much smaller in relation to the proportions in the country generally) than the number of the more nominal adherents of Islam. This reflects the fact that relatively few members of the *santri* community had obtained higher Western education, and it also reflects the secularizing effects of this education on those who had obtained it.

In Islam the Masjumi had the basis of a political ideology, but it lacked a set of policies to which all groups within the party could be committed. Those who controlled the central leadership, "administrators" in the main and men with higher Western education, saw the party's task as being "a stabilizing and consolidating factor" in political life.[41] They supported administrative and economic policies such as the Hatta cabinet had been attempting to implement and favored a vigorous anticommunism. But they disagreed on many more specific aspects of policy. Moreover, there were potential challengers to their leadership position, groups and factions led by "solidarity makers," former leaders of Moslem guerrilla formations, and men of traditional religious authority in particular regions.

The fact that a group of men of higher Western education controlled the party's central leadership is rooted in the power of Islamic modernism in Indonesia. The Islamic reform movement which had its origins in the teachings of Mohammad Abduh of Cairo had spread rapidly in Indonesia in the first four decades of the century. Abduh demanded a return to the Koran and Hadith free from traditional accretions, urging Moslems to interpret the Koran and Hadith in the

[40] For a full discussion see Deliar Noer, "Masjumi: Its Organization, Ideology and Political Role in Indonesia" (M.A. thesis, Cornell University, 1960).
[41] Kementerian Penerangan, *Kepartaian di Indonesia*, 1951, p. 14.

light of the requirements of the modern world. This body of ideas gained followers quickly in the Indonesian Moslem community, particularly among urban traders. Thus there arose a number of modern-oriented religious, social, and educational organizations which stressed the necessity for Moslems to adapt to the new situations created by the impact of the West and in particular to master science and technology.[42] It was modernist organizations of this type, notably the large Muhammadijah, which provided the basis of the strong position in the Masjumi of such top leaders as Dr. Sukiman Wirjosandjojo, the chairman of the party's legislative council, and Mohammad Natsir, chairman of its executive council. At the same time it is clear that these "administrator" leaders were favored by a number of propertied groups supporting the party, because these groups sought such government as would restrain, or at least control, the pace of social change.

However, the Masjumi included also groups with other religious viewpoints, groups which were in general disinclined to follow the leadership of men such as Natsir and Sukiman. Most important of these was the conservative Nahdatul Ulama (Religious Scholars League) led by Kijaji Hadji Wachid Hasjim, who had held the Religious Affairs portfolio in the Hatta RUSI cabinet. The Nahdatul Ulama had been established in 1926 as a traditionalist counter to the increasingly influential Muhammadijah. It stood opposed to too fast an accommodation of Moslem social regulation to the demands of modern life. At the same time it fended off many of the reformers' attacks on what they regarded as accretions to pure Moslem doctrine and practice. Thus it defended what was in fact the mainstream of Javanese Islam, an amalgam of Islamic beliefs with the earlier Hindu and pre-Hindu beliefs of Java.[43]

In addition, one can distinguish a third religious current, although far less clearly than the other two. This may be called the group of radical fundamentalists. Having its origins in the antitraditionalist "Protestant" movement of which the Muhammadijah was the main channel, this group represented another more militant, illiberal, and antisecularist current. One mentor of the group was Kijaji Ahmad Hassan of the Bandung-centered Persatuan Islam (Islamic Associa-

[42] Harry J. Benda, *The Crescent and the Rising Sun* (The Hague: van Hoeve, 1958), pp. 47–50. See also Clifford Geertz, *The Religion of Java*, pp. 123 ff.

[43] Geertz, *The Religion of Java*, pp. 148–161. See also Mochtar Naim, "The Nahdatul Ulama as a Political Party, 1952–55: An Inquiry into the Origins of Its Electoral Success" (M.A. thesis, McGill University, 1960).

tion). An important political figure of radical fundamentalist convictions was the West Java organizer and orator Kijaji Isa Anshary.

Factional divisions in the party did not, however, follow the lines of religious cleavage only. The group of "administrators" who led the party and who were all modernists by denominational persuasion were by no means cohesive as a political group. Oversimplifying what was in August 1950 still a fairly fluid situation, one may say that they were divided into two main factions, that of Mohammad Natsir and that of Dr. Sukiman. Natsir and Sukiman and their respective factional groupings shared many policy viewpoints, but Sukiman's support was generally among older persons in the party councils, particularly those who had been prominent in prewar political activity, whereas Natsir's associates were mainly young men in their thirties and early forties, who had risen to prominence in the Revolution. Sukiman drew support mainly from Javanese leaders and Natsir mainly from non-Javanese, particularly from Minangkabaus (although numerous exceptions could be cited in both cases). Again Sukiman had a measure of confidence from the predominantly Javanese Nahdatul Ulama leaders, who generally mistrusted Natsir, whereas Natsir on the other hand had good relations with the group of (mostly non-Javanese) "radical fundamentalists." Finally, the members of the Sukiman group had closer political-*cum*-personal relations with the PNI leaders and with President Soekarno than did the members of the Natsir group. The Natsir group's relations were more particularly with the Indonesian Socialist Party.

Thus in observing the groups comprising the leadership of the Masjumi, one should bear in mind the existence of at least two important lines of cleavage, one between groups of different religious orientation (where there is a close correspondence to the division between "administrator" and "solidarity maker" leadership) and another between cliquelike factions within the "administrator" leadership of the party. Both these two lines of cleavage were to come to the front of the political stage within two years of the mid-1950 period under discussion.

More than any other party, the Masjumi gained support from groups whose political posture reflected particular property relationships. In Java, Masjumi supporters were prominent in most of the older sectors of capitalist enterprise where Indonesians had been able to hold their own against Chinese, especially in such fields as the production and trading of batik cloth and cloves cigarettes, but also to some extent in other distributive trades. Supporters of the party were also numerous in the group of landowners in Java, petty landowners by international standards but locally powerful nevertheless. In the Outer Islands too the party was the main political representative of the indigenous trading groups, which here had not generally suffered as near-complete a demise in the colonial period as in Java. And outside Java, particularly in Sumatra and Kalimantan, it was supported by the important entrepreneurial group of small-holder growers of rubber.

The Masjumi's greatest source of strength was in the countryside. The Japanese had given Islamic leaders a head start in village-level political organization, especially in Java,[44] and on this basis the Masjumi had benefited greatly from the burgeoning of associational activity at the village and small-town level which characterized the Revolution and the immediate postrevolutionary period. In almost all areas it had the support of the local religious leaders, professional and semiprofessional, the *ulamas* and *kijajis* (religious teachers or scholars), *hadjis* (returned Mecca pilgrims), mosque officials, and religious functionaries of the village councils. The Masjumi's organized strength at the level of the village helps explain its emphasis in 1950 on the need for early elections.

In urban areas the Masjumi was somewhat weaker. There did exist, however, sizable groups of ex-guerrillas of strong Masjumi convictions, many of them now in the cities. And an important factor in the party's favor, in urban as in rural areas, was its controlling position within the Ministry of Religious Affairs. The fact that religion was officially recognized and sponsored and that the governmental body through which this sponsorship was exercised was dominated by a single party gave this party not a little prestige and power.

The PSII (Partai Sarekat Islam Indonesia, Islamic Association Party of Indonesia)

The PSII had split from the Masjumi in April 1947, proclaiming itself as the same party which, as Sarekat Islam and later as PSII, had been the most prominent of the prewar Moslem political organizations.[45] The leaders of this party were men who had risen to prominence in both the prewar period and the periods of Japanese occupation and

[44] Benda, *The Crescent and the Rising Sun,* pp. 150 ff.
[45] Kahin, *Nationalism and Revolution,* pp. 209–210, 312–313.

Revolution. Most of them had played "solidarity maker" roles during the Revolution. A number had been involved in Tan Malaka's abortive attempt on July 3, 1946, to unseat the Sjahrir cabinet by coup. Subsequently the group had left the Masjumi because of their opposition to the leaders then dominant, particularly the Natsir group. Since the split the PSII had consistently failed to co-operate with the Masjumi, despite the frequent statements of leaders of both parties that the differences between the two were minor. The party was not distinguished by a particular position on religious issues or by a particular view of current policy problems. Although it obtained the loyalty of local religious groups in certain of the areas where its prewar forerunner had been strong, its national strength was not comparable to that of the Masjumi.

The Indonesian Nationalist Party

The PNI, the second largest party in the country according to the common estimates of 1950, stands in strong contrast to the Masjumi in a number of respects. It was predominantly a city party in its power base as the Masjumi was predominantly a party of the towns and rural areas. Its leaders had arisen from the vestigial aristocracies, and particularly the aristocracy of Java. Few of them came from a commercial background. Unlike the Masjumi, it was a party strong in the civil service. Such links as it had with entrepreneurship were with the new businesses established as an outcrop of political and bureaucratic leadership. It was in fact the principal organization representing the "Javanese-aristocratic political culture" as the Masjumi was the principal representative of the "Islamic-entrepreneurial political culture."

But there were also considerable similarities between these two major parties. The PNI too was a loosely organized body. It lacked effective party discipline. It was handicapped by serious internal divisions. Like the Masjumi it was bound together by a set of ideological orientations whose cohesive power was inadequate in the face of clique fission.

PNI ideology was centered in the Revolution. It was the formulation par excellence of the mood of nationalist political messianism characteristic of the old revolutionary fighters. This formulation, which had yet to be given its final official form, was "Marhaenism" (usually translated "proletarian nationalism") or "Socionationalist Democracy." [46] It was a political creed stressing national unity and national culture and socialist or collectivist economics. It affirmed the importance of democratic rights and opposed dictatorship, but condemned liberalism and individualism, declaring them to be offshoots of capitalism. Based on an eclectic selection of ideas from Western and Asian nationalists, Western socialists, and traditional Indonesian social thought, Marhaenism reflected both the PNI's attachment to the symbols of the nationalist Revolution and the difficulties which the party faced in establishing a highest common factor of ideological orientations. As a party for which nationalism itself was central to value orientations, it was particularly difficult for the PNI to adapt itself to the postrevolutionary situation, which seemed to many of its members to call for new issues, new goals, and new patterns of political perception. [47]

In cultural and religious outlook the PNI represented "Javanism." Most of its leaders were Javanese and members of the social group of the *prijaji*, the Javanese aristocracy which had in large part remained little affected by Islam. [48] Combining a nominal adherence to Islam with contempt for Islamic orthodoxy, these Javanese aristocrats held syncretistic mystical beliefs which owe more to Hinduism than to any branch of Islam. Proud of traditional Javanese culture, they saw this as the basis for a new Indonesian civilization and looked to it to provide an alternative to cosmopolitan culture. [49] Hence, although opposed to Islamic influence in the state, they did not hold a secularist view of politics.

In the period immediately after the transfer of sovereignty, the PNI was the most strongly nationalistic of the major parties. As mentioned earlier, it played a major role in the movement for a unitary state. It strongly urged the quick withdrawal of all Dutch troops remaining in Indonesia. More than any other large party it took the side of the men from Jogjakarta as they came to take over and be fitted into the

[46] See Kementerian Penerangan, *Kepartaian di Indonesia* ("Political Parties in Indonesia"; Djakarta: Kementerian Penerangan, 1950), pp. 78–80, and also Party Council of the Partai Nasional Indonesia, *Manifesto of Marhaenism* (Djakarta, 1954 [?]).

[47] For a stimulating discussion see Josef A. Mestenhauser, *op. cit.*, pp. 217 ff.

[48] On the *prijaji* see Geertz, *The Religion of Java*, pp. 227 ff.; Selosoemardjan, *Social Changes in Jogjakarta*, pp. 118–121; and D. H. Burger, *Structural Changes in Javanese Society: The Supra-Village Sphere* (Cornell Modern Indonesia Project, Translation Series; Ithaca, N.Y., 1957).

[49] See, for instance, S. Mangunsarkoro, *The Sociological and Cultural Fundamentals for the Educational System in Indonesia* (Djakarta: [no publisher,] 1945).

former Dutch administrative structure. More than any other, it emphasized the importance of the national claim to West Irian. At the same time, however, it succeeded in attracting to itself large numbers of political leaders from the Dutch-built states.

The PNI was a major government party during the Revolution and was represented in each of the Hatta cabinets and also in the cabinet of Dr. Halim. It included many "administrators" in its leadership. But its most important role in the first half of 1950 had been one in which "solidarity makers" had taken the lead. Their leading position was confirmed when the May 1950 Congress of the party elected Sidik Djojosukarto as its chairman. This did not mean that the issue had been sealed, however. The PNI continued to function in a great variety of roles.

To describe internal divisions in the PNI is even more difficult than in the case of the Masjumi, for the factions in the PNI leadership did not correspond to constituent entities within the party. The lines of factional cleavage were a highly personal matter within a small group of leaders and thus more ephemeral than in the case of the Masjumi. Nevertheless, a distinct pattern was discernible, a pattern set as in the case of the Masjumi by the "administrator"—"solidarity maker" delineation on the one hand and on the other hand by a division between two cliquelike segments of the "administrator" skill group.

The "solidarity makers" in the PNI leadership were mostly led by Sidik Djojosukarto, a former "bush lawyer" and highly effective mass orator. Sidik's following was composed principally of PNI members without higher Western education, men who had come to political prominence in the Japanese occupation and the Revolution, frequently through leadership of mass organizations and guerrilla groups. The members of the group were extreme in both their nationalist and their socialist demands and strongly "oppositionist" in their attitude to governments, in much the same way as the leaders of the Partai Murba.

Among the "administrators" in the PNI leadership two main groups were distinguishable. One large group centered on the men of professional training who had been prominent in the prewar PNI founded by Ir. Soekarno in 1927, men such as Mr. Sartono, who was later chairman of the RUSI House of Representatives, and R. Suwirjo, who became mayor of Djakarta in 1950. The other faction or embryonic faction, considerably smaller, was led by men of similar training who were younger and had come into prominence later. Important figures in this group included Mr. Soejono Hadinoto, Sidik's predecessor as party chairman, and Mr. Wilopo, who was Labor Minister in the RUSI cabinet.

Between these two groups of "administrator" leaders there were no clear or fixed lines. But factors of background, outlook, and personal associations established a certain pattern of division. Most members of the older group had accepted fairly prominent positions under the Japanese, whereas this was not the case with many of the younger group. In the early years of the Revolution, and particularly in the period of Sjahrir's prime ministership, the men of the older group had been kept from political prominence. A number of them had given their support to the Tan Malaka 1946 attempt to overthrow the Sjahrir cabinet by coup. The younger group by contrast had no strong grievance against the Sjahrir camp. Whereas the older group included many close associates of President Soekarno, the younger stood much closer to Vice-President Hatta. In general, the older group was more radical in its nationalism and more concerned with the nation's prestige and cultural identity than the younger group and less intensely concerned with problem-solving policies in the administrative and economic fields. Thus it was more capable of working with the Sidik group in the party leadership and with "solidarity makers" generally. At the same time its members had reasonably good relations with the Sukiman group of the Masjumi (the group of older "administrators," mostly Javanese), whereas the members of the younger group had better relations with the Natsir faction (whose members were younger and most frequently non-Javanese).

The main basis of PNI support lay in the lower rungs of the Indonesian aristocracies. This was the group which had provided the greatest number of pupils of Dutch secondary schools before the war and the greatest number of civil servants. The party had considerable support at all levels of the government service, and particularly at the lower levels. Initially it had been more attractive to the employees of specialized departments of the government service—teachers, health and agricultural extension workers, information officers, and so on— than to the *bupatis* (regents) and district and subdistrict officers of the powerful *pamong pradja* corps who were frequently of higher aristocratic origin. But by 1950 it had secured at least the passive support of a sizable section of the *pamong pradja* as well, not only in Java but also in a number of other areas. In addition, it attracted a large number of white-collar workers in private employment. A large proportion of its active supporters were ex-revolutionaries of one category or another.

To a large number of Indonesians in small towns and villages, that is Indonesians without ties to *santri* Islam, the PNI was *the* party of the Revolution and the nationalist movement. It therefore had the support of many of those who, while not holding clear positions on political issues, nevertheless sought to gain prestige as patriots and responsible citizens by joining a political party. It had had considerable success in rural Indonesia in establishing itself as the heir of the prewar nationalist movement, in all except its specifically Islamic sections. Thus the local leaders not only of many of the short-lived political parties of the 1930's but also of the progressive nationalist Taman Siswa schools and of the prewar nationalist scout organizations were drawn mainly to the PNI. In addition, the party attracted support in Hindu Bali and in the predominantly Christian areas outside of Java (particularly Tapanuli in North Sumatra and Minahasa in North Sulawesi) because of its opposition to links between Islam and the state.

The Minor Nationalist Parties

The minor nationalist parties were generally similar to the PNI in ideological orientations, but most of them had no strong commitment to either ideological positions or policy concerns. Lacking the support of any strong interest group and commanding only the most perfunctory organization, they were little more than cliques of parliamentarians and their followers and owed their existence as parties to the tendencies toward party fragmentation described above. But although considered to have few long-term prospects, they were able in our period to play a role of considerable importance, not only in parliament but also in cabinets.

PIR (Partai Persatuan Indonesia Raja, Greater Indonesia Union Party), largest of the minor nationalist parties, was somewhat untypical of this group in that it commanded the partial support of a significant social group. The party had been formed in December 1948 in Jogjakarta by a combination of nonparty persons and PNI leaders who decried their party's criticisms of Hatta's policies in negotiating with the Dutch.[50] Led by a group of older leaders, many of them from the higher Javanese aristocracy, it had in 1950 the support of a con-

---

[50] Kahin, *Nationalism and Revolution*, pp. 324–326.

siderable number of *pamong pradja* leaders both in Java (*prijajis* antagonized by the radical nationalism of the PNI) and outside Java (persons of aristocratic connections who had worked in one of the BFO governments). Its large parliamentary delegation was comprised mainly of men from the BFO states. In its policy orientation PIR stood for restoration of rural stability on a traditional basis and for the strengthening of the *pamong pradja* system of administration.

Parindra (Partai Indonesia Raja, Greater Indonesia Party) was a splinter party formed in November 1949 by R. P. Soeroso, who had been a leader in the larger prewar party of the same name. It was led by men of the same aristocratic background as PIR, but had no general support. In its positions on ideology and policy it stood somewhere between PIR and PNI.

The *PNI-Merdeka* (Independent Indonesian Nationalist Party) or *PRN* (Partai Rakjat Nasional, National People's Party), as it was to rename itself in October 1950, also lacked organized support. It resulted from a split in the PNI which had developed in July 1950, partly in protest against the victory of the Sidik group at the party congress in May.[51] PNI leaders branded the new party as right wing and capitalistic, but its own ideological pronouncements did not deviate from the diffuse radical nationalism of the PNI. Its subsequent actions suggest that it was capable of adopting a variety of ideological and policy positions as clique interests required.

SKI (Serikat Kerakjatan Indonesia, Indonesian People's Association) had been established in South Kalimantan in 1946. Its declared political position resembled that of the PNI, and the behavior of its parliamentary representatives was generally "oppositionist."

The *Democratic Fraction* was a purely parliamentary grouping of former BFO leaders, mainly from East Indonesia. Its orientation was one of opposition to radical nationalism, and it frequently co-operated with PIR.

The *Partai Buruh* or Labor Party, established in December 1949 by a group of non-Communist leaders seceding from the Communist-dominated Partai Buruh Indonesia, was a rather more significant organization, because of a certain amount of support from organized labor. Formally espousing Marxism, it was nevertheless primarily a nationalist party. Within the party leadership there was conflict be-

[51] For an account of the development of the split see Kementerian Penerangan, *Kepartaian di Indonesia*, 1951, pp. 126–127.

tween one clique supporting "oppositionist" PNI and Murba positions and another supporting the positions of the PSI.

The Christian Parties

The two Christian political parties, *Parkindo* (Indonesian Christian Party) and *Partai Katholik* (Catholic Party of the Republic of Indonesia), were minor parties of a different type. They were "permanent minority parties," rather than "personality parties" as the minor nationalist parties were.[52] With a reliable basis of mass support, much of it concentrated in particular areas such as Protestant Minahasa, Ambon, and North Tapanuli and Catholic Flores, they clearly had a more certain political future than the minor nationalist parties. Although there were only some three million Protestants in Indonesia and something less than one million Catholics, the influence of the two parties was considerable. This was partly because of the disproportionately large number of Christians in the civil service, the army, business enterprise, and the universities and schools and partly because of the individual prestige of leaders such as Dr. J. Leimena and Mr. A. M. Tambunan of Parkindo and I. J. Kasimo of Partai Katholik. The main policies of these parties were directed toward the maintenance of the groups' sectional interests and of religious liberty. Both parties were dominated by "administrators," men with fairly strong policy concerns. Both were moderate in their approach to nationalism, Parkindo standing somewhat closer to PNI ideological emphases than the Catholic Party.

[52] See Duverger, *op. cit.*, pp. 290 ff.

Chapter IV

The Natsir Cabinet, September 1950– March 1951:

"Administrators" Thwarted

TIMES of cabinet crisis, when an old cabinet was in office with demissionary status and a new one was in the process of being formed, were of particular importance throughout the period of this study. Considerable attention will be given to them because of the light they throw both on the mechanics of politics and on the changing balance of power between different groups and parties.

It was a feature of politics in the Indonesia of 1949–1957 that cabinet posts were most eagerly sought. The prestige of a cabinet minister was extraordinarily high, despite the fact that his tenure was normally expected to be short. Indeed, only isolated individual leaders in politics, administration, or education were able to enjoy the degree of prestige which was the lot of each and every minister while he was in office. One aspect of this was the minister's easy visibility. In Djakarta it was only the President, the Vice-President, the mayor, and cabinet ministers who were entitled to fly the national flag on the front of their car. Only they and a handful of military officers had army guard posts outside their homes. Symbols of this kind had great importance in a society where prestige, respect, and deference were sought particularly eagerly, probably more so than income or power as such.

146

But ministerial posts brought more than prestige. They provided opportunities to help family members, to repay obligations to others, and to create new ones to oneself. They also provided important sources of income, a car, a house, furniture, and purchasing facilities —and in some cases business opportunities and "gifts."

Moreover, cabinet posts brought power. Cabinet members may have been in a weak position to affect the broad economic and social policies to which they were formally committed. But when their role is looked at without reference to considerations of long-term policy, it becomes clear that they were men of great influence. Particularly in the new and administratively fluid ministries but in some older ones too, ministers could play a virtuoso role, making important decisions without being closely checked by the cabinet as a whole, by the senior bureaucrats of their ministry, or by their respective parties. They could issue ministerial regulations on a wide range of subjects, some-times without anyone outside their ministries knowing that a particular regulation had been made or what it involved. They could exercise a broad degree of discretion as regards the distribution of funds and the flow of patronage. And they had considerable freedom in the matter of appointments and transfers. In all these ways they could help not only their parties but also their own group of friends, associates, and followers. Thus it mattered a great deal who the individual occupants of ministerial portfolios were.

Cabinet formation politics was therefore much more than a matter of devising acceptable compromises between parties on policies and interests. Party viewpoints were important, but factional positions were often more so. Group interests were always involved, but these were usually the interests of political groups, at least in the first in-stance. Economic, regional, and other sectional groupings, being largely diffuse and without organization, had few means of direct ac-cess. Policies were usually also a matter for serious bargaining. But the key variable was often the individual political leader and his posi-tion in a complex pattern of interlocking personal-political cliques. One measure of a *formateur*'s power was the extent to which he was able to bring together a cabinet by compromises on policies and in-terests rather than by compromises between personal cliques whose demands were often not capable of being translated into self-consistent policy.

THE FORMATION OF THE CABINET

The formation of the Natsir cabinet may be said to have begun immediately after the ceremonial reinauguration of the unitary state on August 17, 1950. In the following four days President Soekarno conducted hearings with the representatives of most of the parties, consulting each of them in turn on the matter of the composition and program of the new cabinet to be formed and in particular on the matter of who was to be named to form the cabinet. On August 21 Soekarno exercised his prerogative and announced that the *formateur*ship would be entrusted to Mohammad Natsir, chairman of the executive council of the Masjumi, the party with the largest parliamentary representation. With this decision and Natsir's acceptance of it on the following day, the politics of cabinet formation went into high gear.

The central problems Natsir faced were those of relations between his party and the PNI, the party with the second greatest parliamentary strength. His view was that the Masjumi, as the party of the *formateur* and intended Prime Minister, should have greater influence in the cabinet than any other party. Moreover, the Masjumi and various of its factions and constituent organizations were pressing him to make high demands. Natsir's position, as he put it to the PNI in the earlier stages of their negotiations, was that the Masjumi should have six seats in the new cabinet, the prime ministership, the three other major portfolios of the Interior, Finance, and Defense, and the less important Education and Religious Affairs portfolios and that the PNI should have the major portfolio of Foreign Affairs and the Information, Public Works, and Labor posts.[1]

At this the PNI balked. In particular it wanted the Interior and Education portfolios for itself—Interior because of its importance for appointments of governors, residents, and regents and Education because of fear of excessive Islamic influence on the government school system. There were disagreements also on individuals nominated for particular posts. On several occasions the situation approached deadlock, with the two parties' viewpoints still widely divergent. President Soekarno attempted personal intervention to bring the two parties together, but this too was unsuccessful. Natsir twice offered to return

[1] See Deliar Noer, "Masjumi: Its Organization, Ideology and Political Role in Indonesia" (M.A. thesis, Cornell University, 1960). See also *Perdjuangan P.N.I. dalam Parlemen* ("The Struggle of the PNI in Parliament"; Malang: Pembina Rakjat, 1950), pp. 14–21.

the *formateur*'s mandate to the President, but Soekarno's reply was in each case to urge him to try again.

On the second occasion Soekarno widened Natsir's terms of reference. He instructed him to form a cabinet which was "not tied too much to the parties." In effect this meant that Natsir could form a cabinet with certain of the characteristics of a *zaken kabinet* or business cabinet, a cabinet with more nonparty ministers and one whose party-affiliated members were not necessarily the nominees of their respective parties. With this possibility in view, Natsir began afresh. He again negotiated intensively with the PNI and on September 3 came close to reaching agreement with it.

Then, however, the army entered the picture. It appears that Sultan Hamengku Buwono, still holding the Defense portfolio (although with demissionary status), wrote a personal letter to Natsir saying that several high officers of the army objected to Natsir's candidate Defense Minister, the Masjumi's Abdul Hakim.[2] Hakim had been Deputy Prime Minister in the Halim cabinet, and the PNI had approved his candidacy for the Defense portfolio. But Natsir, whose relations with the army high command were good, took heed of the letter. This meant reopening negotiations on various posts with the PNI, and the PNI, long suspicious of the army leadership, grew less co-operative.

It was at this point that the *formateur* set out on the novel course of action which led to the Natsir cabinet in the form in which it subsequently assumed office. He decided to confront the PNI with the possibility that he would "go it alone," that he would form a cabinet based on the Masjumi and the smaller parties and including a number of prominent nonparty persons, leaving the PNI to join the PKI and Partai Murba in the opposition. This decision set off heated opposition inside the Masjumi, with the Sukiman group and the Nahdatul Ulama leaders asserting that to leave the PNI outside the government would court serious parliamentary and bureaucratic obstruction and at the same time drive the PNI in the direction of the Communists. The PNI leaders, seeing the depth of the Masjumi division on the issue, were apparently confident that Natsir would not dare go ahead with his plan and therefore refused to make the concessions which Natsir had hoped this new alternative plan would wring from them. When several of the PNI leaders with whom Natsir had been negotiating left Djakarta, the gauntlet had been thrown down. Natsir, never a man for

[2] *Perdjuangan P.N.I. dalam Parlemen* (speech of Manai Sophian in parliament), pp. 16–17.

indecision,[3] took it up. On September 6 he reported to the President that he had formed a cabinet in which the PNI would not have representation. The composition of the cabinet as then announced was as follows:

Ministry		*Party*
Prime Minister	Mohammad Natsir	Masjumi
Deputy Prime Minister	Sultan Hamengku Buwono IX	Nonparty
Foreign Affairs	Mr. Mohammad Roem	Masjumi
Interior	Mr. Assaat	Nonparty
Defense (ad interim)	Dr. Abdul Halim	Nonparty
Justice	Mr. Wongsonegoro	PIR
Information	M. A. Pellaupessy	Democratic Fraction
Finance	Mr. Sjafruddin Prawiranegara	Masjumi
Agriculture	Mr. Tandiono Manu	PSI
Trade and Industry	Dr. Sumitro Djojohadikusumo	PSI
Communications	Ir. Djuanda	Nonparty
Public Works and Power	Prof. H. Johannes	PIR
Labor	R. P. Suroso	Parindra
Social Affairs	F. S. Harjadi	Catholic
Education	Dr. Bahder Djohan	Nonparty
Religious Affairs	K. H. Wachid Hasjim	Masjumi
Health	Dr. Johannes Leimena	Parkindo
State	Harsono Tjokroaminoto [4]	PSII

This list includes the names of a great many men who had held posts in earlier cabinets. Six of the new ministers had been members of the RUSI cabinet. Two others, Halim and Manu, had held key portfolios in the cabinet of the member-state Republic of Indonesia. Another, Natsir himself, had been one of the three *formateurs* of this cabinet. And a fourth, Assaat, had served as Acting President of the member-state Republic, having previously been chairman of the revolutionary Working Body or Inner Parliament.

All these men, who between them held most of the important portfolios, had worked closely with Hatta. With the exception of the Nahdatul Ulama leader Wachid Hasjim, they were all "administrators" in our sense of the word. The list as a whole reflects the fact that Natsir was successful in his effort to find men of ability, experience, and prestige, who would be in a position to stand up to many of the

[3] For an excellent personality sketch of Natsir see "Tjiptoning," *Apa dan Siapa* ("What and Who"; Jogjakarta: Kedaulatan Rakjat, 1951), pp. 33 ff.

[4] Harsono resigned from the cabinet as of Dec. 31, 1950.

pressures which parties, factions, and cliques would apply on them. Almost all the group shared the general approach to policy which was characteristic of the Prime Minister, who was in turn closely akin to both Hatta and Sjahrir in his policy ideas. And, at least among the occupants of the major portfolios, the intensity of orientation to policy was high. By the same token the group had a fairly high degree of internal cohesion.

In party terms the list was significant chiefly for the fact that the PSI obtained great influence. The party obtained one important portfolio in its own name, in that Dr. Sumitro Djojohadikusumo, the 32-year-old economist and former Economic Minister Plenipotentiary in Washington, moved into the Trade and Industry post. But more important was the fact that all of the five nonparty members of the cabinet had PSI sympathies in one or another degree. The Masjumi itself gained relatively few seats—four—and three of these went to Natsir group leaders. PIR, Parindra, and the Democratic Fraction, none of which had previously had cabinet-level representation, gained four seats among them. The Democrats' M. A. Pellaupessy, till recently chairman of the RUSI Senate, was the one man from the former BFO states who gained inclusion in the cabinet. The Labor Party was left out in the cold with the PNI. The PSII was included, but it was not accorded a portfolio; and it was to remain in the cabinet only for a little more than three months.

Reactions to the cabinet's composition were mixed. But they were one in describing Natsir's action as bold.[5] Not since Sjahrir's first cabinet of 1945–1946 had the PNI been unrepresented in a government. How would it now take this exclusion? Equally important, how would the Sukiman group of the Masjumi react? Within the political public, one widespread reaction was mild apprehension. The individual ministers whom Natsir had chosen were widely approved of, but many wondered whether he had not gone too far in placing a high priority on his own policy objectives to the detriment of national unity. The PNI after all was a party of great prestige, and it had grown in prominence in the previous months. Moreover, it had played a major role in bringing the unitary state into existence. Had the country's political leadership become so deeply divided, the critics asked, that

[5] "Extraordinarily bold" is the phrase used by St. Rais Alamsjah in his highly sympathetic biographical sketch of Natsir. See *10 Orang Indonesia Terbesar Sekarang* ("The Ten Leading Indonesians of Today"; Bukittinggi and Djakarta: Mutiara, 1952), p. 96.

it was necessary for this large segment to be excluded from office?

In the three rounds of parliamentary debates which followed the government's presentation of its program the cabinet was attacked on numerous grounds. In particular, PNI and PKI spokesmen and others hammered on the subject of the procedures whereby Natsir had formed the cabinet, although Natsir himself maintained that in this matter he was accountable not to parliament but to the President. They argued that he had in fact formed a business cabinet rather than a coalition cabinet based on the parties.[6] This, they said, was a violation of an unwritten agreement reached in the RUSI-Republic negotiations of May to August, and it weakened Indonesia's new traditions of parliamentarianism. In particular they stressed the fact that Natsir had yielded to army pressure. A significant aspect of the PNI charges is that they were extended to include President Soekarno. The party was not then as close to the President as it became soon afterward. Thus it was possible for at least two PNI leaders, Mr. Sunario, a member of the older Sartono-Suwirjo group in the party, and Manai Sophian, to criticize Soekarno's role.[7]

Parallel criticisms of Natsir were made by Masjumi leaders of the Sukiman group. Dr. Sukiman, speaking in parliament, said that the cabinet's composition reflected army pressure and that it was in fact a business cabinet and as such a violation of the President's instructions. Mr. Jusuf Wibisono, a close follower of Sukiman and a personal rival of Natsir, took a similar position, in an article in the weekly *Mimbar Indonesia.* When the confidence vote was taken in parliament on October 25, Jusuf Wibisono and another Masjumi leader, Mr. Burhanuddin Harahap, absented themselves.[8] Although Natsir had the backing of a majority of the Masjumi executive council for his actions, they resulted in a sharp aggravation of divisions in the party.

The parliamentary debates were long and in part acrimonious. The PNI, it seems, continued to hope for a change in the cabinet's composition. On October 25 it moved a motion calling on the President to name three *formateurs* for a new cabinet, one each from the Masjumi and PNI and one from another group. In reply the Natsir cabinet called for a vote of confidence and won it by a count of 118 to 73. Among

[6] The Ministry of Information's current designation was "parliamentary business cabinet." See *Kami Perkenalkan* ("We Introduce"; Djakarta: Kementerian Penerangan, 1951 [?], p. 8.

[7] *Perdjuangan P.N.I. dalam Parlemen,* pp. 14 ff. and 102.

[8] Noer, *op. cit.* See also "Kongres Masjumi Djuli jang akan datang" ("The Masjumi Congress Next July"), *Nasional* (Jogjakarta), May 23, 1952.

parties represented in the cabinet, the Christian Party Parkindo abstained and the PSII voted against the confidence motion. For the rest the opposition votes were cast by the PNI, the PKI and its sympathizers in various smaller parliamentary groups, and the Partai Murba. The only parliamentary group which was not included in the cabinet and yet supported it with its votes was the Independent PNI, soon to rename itself PRN or National People's Party. Despite the considerable margin of votes obtained by the government, the debate presaged bad cabinet-parliament relations.

In his various statements to parliament Natsir indicated that he was anxious to get away quickly from preoccupation with political issues. His statements all sounded a note of urgency.[9] Reorganization and rationalization of the army and civil service, fuller restoration of security in rebel and bandit-torn parts of the country, guerrilla rehabilitation, financial stability, stimulation of economic activity—all these were advanced as needs to which full attention should be given immediately. The one immediately political task which Natsir gave top priority was the holding of elections for the Constituent Assembly (which would serve also as a parliament). Indeed, he seems to have seen his cabinet as one which would hold Constituent Assembly elections sometime in 1951 and then resign.[10]

The actual course of developments, however, was very different. The Natsir cabinet remained in office until March 1951, but by that time there had been little progress toward elections. Parliament had not begun to discuss the elections bill which the cabinet had sent to it. On the other hand, the cabinet's period of seven months in office was one of repeated buffetings over other directly political issues, buffetings which greatly limited its ability to get on with the tasks of consolidation, reorganization, and developmental innovation it had set itself.

The parliamentary opposition challenged the cabinet first in November 1950 over an emergency law continuing a 300 per cent surtax

---

[9] *Membangun diantara Tumpukan Puing dan Pertumbuhan: Keterangan Pemerintah diutjapkan oleh Perdana Menteri Mohammad Natsir Dimuka Sidang "Dewan Perwakilan Rakjat Sementara" di Djakarta pada tanggal 10 Oktober 1950* ("Building Up Growth from a Pile of Rubble: Government Statement, Presented by Prime Minister Natsir before the Interim Parliament, October 10, 1950"; Djakarta: Kementerian Penerangan, 1950 [?]).

[10] When the cabinet's Justice Minister Wongsonegoro submitted an elections bill to parliament in early Feb. 1951, he expressed the hope that nationwide Constituent Assembly elections would begin in Aug. 1951 (*Antara*, Feb. 5, 1951).

on company profits. This surtax, which raised the effective company tax to 40 per cent, had originally been instituted by the postwar Netherlands Indies government, and the Hatta cabinet had extended it by emergency law for the year 1950.[11] Now the Natsir cabinet extended its operation for a further year, asserting that it would fetch Rp. 400 million and thus reduce the expected budget deficit by approximately one-third. A wide range of parliamentarians, including a number from government parties, objected to the emergency law, arguing that lack of differentiation between large and small companies was injuring newcomers and thus Indonesians as against foreigners. Although the Natsir cabinet was active in assisting the entry of Indonesian newcomers into business enterprises of various kinds and although the Korean War boom made it possible for the cabinet to act with considerable generosity in this respect, parliament remained dissatisfied. It was an early case of parliament's exerting pressure for policies of broader and more rapid Indonesianization of business activity. In this case, as in subsequent ones, the pressure sprang from the personal interests of a sizable number of parliamentarians, as well as from broader groups within the political public.[12]

Furthermore, there was considerable parliamentary resentment of the fact that the Natsir cabinet, like the Hatta cabinet before it, was making frequent use of its power to enact emergency legislation.[13] As the cabinet leaders saw it, this was made necessary both by the slowness of parliamentary procedure (and the need for firm and speedy government action to regulate a still turbulent social situation) and by the inability of most parliamentarians to understand the technical aspects of much of the needed legislation. In the eyes of a great many parliamentarians, the latter argument flowed from an arrogant "we know best" attitude which hid partisan interests behind a veil of technical argument, in a way altogether too reminiscent of the posture of the Dutch.

When the nonparty parliamentarian Mrs. Rasuna Said moved a motion asking for the withdrawal of the turnover tax law, she at-

---

[11] John O. Sutter, *Indonesianisasi: Politics in a Changing Economy, 1940–1955* (Southeast Asia Program, Cornell University; Ithaca, N.Y., 1959), pp. 1004–1005.

[12] For a survey from official records of the business interests of members of the 1950–1956 parliament see *ibid.*, pp. 1311–1312.

[13] For a general discussion of the use of emergency laws (between 1949 and 1955) see Miriam S. Budiardjo, "Evolution towards Parliamentary Government in Indonesia: Parties and Parliament" (M.A. thesis, Georgetown University, 1955), pp. 129 ff.

tracted considerable support from M.P.'s of the government parties, and it seemed for a time that her motion would receive enough votes to oblige the cabinet to resign. The motion, however, had not been submitted for voting when the Natsir cabinet resigned over other issues in March 1951.

CRISIS OVER WEST IRIAN

More significantly, the cabinet was confronted from the very beginning of its term of office with major political challenges arising from the issue of West Irian or West New Guinea. Earlier in 1950 there had been various unsuccessful conferences with the Dutch on the matter of sovereignty over this piece of territory whose status had been left in dispute by the Round Table Conference. A March meeting of the ministerial council of the Netherlands-Indonesian Union had established a six-man Joint Committee on New Guinea (Irian), on which each of the parties had equal representation. Subsequently the Joint Committee had met a number of times and traveled in West Irian. But the deadlock between the points of view had proved unbreakable, and in early August the Joint Committee had published two separate reports, in effect briefs for each side.[14]

From the Indonesian point of view it was of great importance that the issue of West Irian should be settled in Indonesia's favor by December 27, 1950, the end of the twelve-month period for which the preservation of Dutch authority in West Irian was specifically agreed on at the Round Table Conference. By the time of the Natsir cabinet's accession to office, however, there was strong feeling in the Netherlands for "not giving the Indonesians another inch." The great majority of the 55,900 Dutch civilians who arrived in the Netherlands from Indonesia in the course of 1950,[15] as well as a good many of the

---

[14] See Secretariat of the Netherlands-Indonesian Union, *Report of the Committee New Guinea (Irian), 1950* (Secretariat N.I.U., 1950). For subsequent statements of the arguments of each of the parties see Ministry of Foreign Affairs, Republic of Indonesia, *The Future of West Irian* (Djakarta, 1954 [?] and *Western New Guinea and the Netherlands* (The Hague: Netherlands Government Printing Office, 1954). For general discussion of the whole West Irian problem consult Robert C. Bone, Jr., *The Dynamics of the Western New Guinea (Irian Barat) Problem* (Cornell Modern Indonesia Project, Interim Reports Series; Ithaca, N.Y., 1958); Justus M. van der Kroef, *The West New Guinea Dispute* (New York: Institute of Pacific Relations, 1958); and F. J. F. M. Duynstee, *Nieuw Guinea als Schakel tussen Nederland en Indonesië* (Amsterdam: De Bezige Bij, 1961). The terms "Irian" and "West Irian" will here be used synonymously as they are in Indonesia.

[15] The figure 55,900 comes from J. H. Kraak *et al.*, *De Repatrieering uit Indonesië: Een Onderzoek naar de Integratie van de Gerepatrieerden uit Indonesië*

soldiers, were bitter about Indonesian nationalism, and their influence on Dutch public opinion was considerable. To many Dutchmen the quick liquidation of the federal structure of Indonesia seemed an act of perfidy. Sympathy for the "Republic of the South Moluccas" was widespread, and many pointed to Indonesia's continuing banditry and high level of strike activity as evidence of the government's inability to put its own house in order. It is true that a large group of Dutchmen resident in Indonesia and of business firms with extensive interests there were pressing the Dutch government to give up West Irian. And the Hatta cabinet had had encouraging indications along these lines from certain Dutch ministers, particularly at the March meeting of the ministerial council of the Union.[16] But Sydney Gruson of the *New York Times* wrote, also in March, that

the Dutch have not been acting like people who expect to be out of New Guinea by the end of the year. . . . The Dutch administration of the island has been steadily built up in the last few months. Garrison forces have been strengthened and commercial undertakings financed from the Netherlands have been started.[17]

Developments since March had not helped those in the Dutch government who favored a cession of the disputed territory.

Moreover, there was little in the United States position in relation to the West New Guinea issue to encourage the hope which existed in some Indonesian breasts that American pressure might force the Netherlands to relinquish its possession. The United States was still feeling the effects of Dutch resentment at the American role in the Indonesian developments of 1949 and felt disinclined to take any action which might turn Dutch nationalism into anti-American channels.

---

in de Nederlandse Samenleving ("Repatriation from Indonesia: An Investigation of the Integration of Repatriates from Indonesia in the Netherlands Community"; The Hague [?]: n.p., 1958), pp. 123–127. Net immigration into the Netherlands from Indonesia in the year 1950 was 46,700. The number of civilians of Netherlands citizenship who were in Indonesia at the time of the transfer of sovereignty may be estimated to have been 215,000, of whom perhaps 80 per cent were Indo-Europeans. Paul W. van der Veur has calculated that approximately 35,000 (31,500 of them Indo-Europeans) had taken Indonesian citizenship by the end of 1951. See Paul W. van der Veur, "Eurasian Dilemma in Indonesia," *Journal of Asian Studies*, XX, no. 1 (Nov. 1960), 56–59. See also Kraak *et al.*, *op. cit.*, and *Biro Pusat Statistik* (Central Bureau of Statistics), *Statistical Pocketbook of Indonesia, 1960* (Djakarta: Biro Pusat Statistik, 1961), pp. 14–15, for data on which the 215,000 estimate is based.

[16] See Duynstee, *op. cit.*, p. 189.
[17] *New York Times*, March 6, 1950.

Hence it maintained its position of "neutrality" on the issue, in effect supporting the *status quo* position. Such pressure as was being exerted on the Dutch by other countries came principally from Australia— and it was pressure for them to continue to rule their New Guinea territory. The conservative Liberal Party–Country Party coalition under Prime Minister R. G. Menzies, which had come into office in Canberra in December 1949, had since then waged an exceedingly active diplomatic campaign in favor of the *status quo* in the territory.[18]

In Indonesian domestic political affairs West Irian had become an increasingly prominent object of concern in the middle months of 1950. It was taken up actively by many of the same groups which had been the most vigorous promoters of the unitarist movement. By the time of the Natsir cabinet's accession to office a (nongovernmental) Badan Perdjoangan Irian (Irian Struggle Body) was functioning with "consulates" in many parts of the country, and numerous committees and fronts were active in statement warfare in favor of the Irian claim. For President Soekarno, Irian had become a central political concern. He talked of it wherever he went on tours of different parts of Indonesia.[19] He emphasized the importance of the issue particularly strongly, and with a significant implied threat, in his Independence Day address on August 17:

This is not a trifling question; this is a major issue. . . . This is a national task for us which cannot be evaded: Because we have pledged that we will fight till the end of time as long as one part of our Country—however small that part may be—is not yet free! We still hope that West Irian will be returned to us within this year. We still observe the provision in the R.T.C. agreements that the question of West Irian shall be settled peaceably within this year. After this year, neither of the parties will be bound by the R.T.C. provision. . . . If a settlement by negotiation cannot be arrived at within this year, a major conflict will arise on the issue of who will be in power in that island from then onward. For, once again I declare: We will not stop fighting, we will continue fighting, we will keep on fighting whatever may come, until West Irian has been returned to our fold.[20]

[18] See J. A. C. Mackie, "Australia and Indonesia," in Gordon Greenwood and Norman D. Harper, eds., *Australia in World Affairs, 1955–1960* (Melbourne: Cheshire, in press).

[19] On August 17, 1951, he was to declare: "Some people have described me as an 'agitator over the Irian question.' I shall inscribe that on my breast in letters of gold." *President Soekarno's Message to the Nation on the Sixth Anniversary of Indonesian Independence* (Djakarta: Ministry of Information, 1951), p. 9.

[20] *From Sabang to Merauke* (Djakarta: Kementerian Penerangan, 1950), p. 24. It should be noted that "fighting" here is a translation of the Indonesian word *berdjoang*, which is more usually translated as "struggling."

This was the situation which the Natsir cabinet confronted as it assumed office. A claim unlikely to have early realization was being asserted with increasing vehemence. Leadership for the assertions was coming from President Soekarno, but the responses and echoes emanated principally from parties excluded from the Natsir cabinet, especially from the PNI. President Soekarno had for some time been setting his own tone for pronouncements on the Irian issue and acting in independence of the cabinet. And he had repeatedly promised his audiences that Irian would be in Indonesian hands before the sun rose on the year 1951.

Irian was in a sense the same kind of cause that unification had been earlier. It was directly related to the central values of nationalism. It was something on which nearly everyone agreed (indeed, more so than on unification). It enabled issues to be focused in terms of Indonesians versus enemies of Indonesia, thus rallying all-Indonesian solidarity. It provided a central leadership role for "solidarity makers." And it helped to absorb some of the restless energies of former revolutionaries who wanted to be active participants still in a political movement (and who threatened to give their support to antigovernmental organizations if the government did not offer them outlets).

But, like the unification issue, the Irian issue was also in an important sense divisive. Its divisive effects within the political elite were in fact a central aspect of the issue. Indeed, all groups in Indonesian politics were committed to the "national claim," and all favored the inclusion of Irian in the Republic by December 27. But there were important differences between groups in the intensity of their commitment and the political reasoning which lay behind it. For Soekarno and other "solidarity makers" whose nationalist convictions provided them with their most strongly held values, the Irian claim was intrinsically of great importance. At the same time it served to provide them with a cause in which they were peculiarly well placed to provide leadership. For the "administrators" who dominated the Natsir cabinet and who tended to place less value on the symbols of national unity and national identity, the intrinsic importance of the claim was not as great. But the current temper of nationalism demanded that they espouse a vigorous "me too"-ism. Their response to this demand found its rationalization in their belief that only after the Irian issue was settled would it be possible to proceed with the practical administrative and economic tasks they regarded as all-important.

Closely connected with this difference of political motivation was a difference, indeed a conflict, between two possible strategies in relation to realizing the claim. The Natsir cabinet, like the Hatta cabinet before it, sought to work quietly and along conventional diplomatic channels. This was in part because the members of the cabinet believed that the best chances of success lay along this road. In part too they preferred this strategy because they feared the domestic consequences of the alternative of intensive domestic agitation, particularly the consequences in the event that the Dutch continued to hold on to the disputed area after December 27. In effect the Natsir cabinet staked its hope on Dutch moderation and good sense—and on the possibility of American pressure on the Netherlands. The leaders of the cabinet believed that the best they could do to prepare for the forthcoming negotiations on the Irian question was to press ahead with their general domestic programs, to establish more secure conditions of life in Indonesia and thus show that Indonesian governments had the will and the capacity to meet their international obligations and protect the foreigners living on their soil.

The second strategy was the one of "organizing power" domestically. This was the strategy of President Soekarno and his principal lieutenant on Irian affairs, the historian, poet, and Murba-sympathizing non-party parliamentarian Mr. Muhammad Yamin. It was the strategy of exciting mass feeling and threatening to let this get out of hand. Soekarno explained the line of thought underlying it in an address to the Indonesian Press Association in January 1951. The *Antara* news agency reported him as saying that it had been his conviction since 1927 "that the will of the people which had been given leadership had to be fashioned into power to balance the power of the adversary. . . . No class or group in power ever voluntarily surrenders its position." [21]

The Natsir cabinet had not been in power long before the conflict between the two strategies came to the fore. On September 20 parliament voted unanimously in favor of the formation of a parliamentary mission to travel overseas to expound Indonesia's case on West Irian. The government gave its blessing to the project, and six days later its nine members were chosen, with all major parties gaining representation. The Masjumi's cautious Dr. Sukiman was elected chairman of the delegation, and the position of delegation spokesman went to the fiery Mr. Muhammad Yamin (who had stated earlier in the year

[21] *Antara*, Jan. 16, 1951.

that he favored the inclusion of British Borneo, Portuguese Timor, and Australian New Guinea in Indonesian territory [22]). On October 27 the delegation left for overseas, with the Netherlands its first destination. On arrival in the Netherlands, Yamin shocked his Dutch hosts by stating that "if the Irian question is not settled before December 27 it will be difficult to safeguard the security of Dutch interests in Indonesia." [23]

The parliamentary delegation stayed in the Netherlands for over two weeks, but Yamin's initial remark continued to handicap its efforts to present Indonesia's case persuasively. In fact, the delegation was able to do little to lessen the existing hostility. Natsir, noting this, called the delegation home and thus prevented it from continuing its scheduled journey to several other countries.

Meanwhile pressures on the cabinet had been building up as a result of calls for action against the Dutch. Anti-Dutch feeling had risen in consequence of a telegram sent by the Netherlands Prime Minister, Willem Drees, on October 4, to protest against the Republic's military action against the "Republic of the South Moluccas." [24] Later in October there had been reports of political arrests in Irian. Throughout this time mass rallies in different parts of Indonesia were putting forth ever more radical resolutions, demanding that Irian be liberated. On November 5 the Bandung branch of the PNI called for the severing of all relations with the Dutch in the event that they failed to accede to Indonesia's demand by December 27.[25]

The most important of the demands for tough action came from Sutomo, then chairman of the small Partai Rakjat Indonesia (Indonesian People's Party) and previously a prominent leader of the revolutionary youth in the November 1945 Battle of Surabaja against the British. "Bung Tomo" stated on November 9 that his party would press for an economic boycott of the Dutch if they continued to refuse to yield in Irian after December 27. He added that nine other organizations had agreed to discuss his plan further with him. Sutomo's plan

[22] *Antara*, Feb. 1, 1950. Yamin did not make the statement in any official capacity. It is sharply at odds with the position taken by every Indonesian government of our period.

[23] *Antara*, Oct. 31, 1950. On the Dutch reaction see the summary of Dr. Sukiman's report to parliament on the delegation's work in the Netherlands (*ibid.*, Dec. 5, 1950).

[24] J. Leimena, *The Ambon Question: Facts and Appeal* (Djakarta: n.p., 1950), pp. 9, 30–36.

[25] *Antara*, Nov. 6, 1950.

was condemned by the Masjumi, the PSI, and Vice-President Hatta. The PKI did not comment, but its large trade union federation SOBSI joined in the condemnation of the Sutomo proposal.[26] The PNI's chairman, Sidik, stated that his party could agree to a boycott in principle, but only to a real boycott, not to property seizures or other chaotic or extreme actions.[27] On November 28 the cabinet issued a statement, the first of several of the kind, saying that it would not tolerate any intimidation or boycott and would take the necessary steps against such undemocratic actions. Nevertheless, the Sutomo statement had considerably aggravated the fears and apprehensions of the Dutch and Eurasian population of Indonesia.[28]

At the end of November there were various rumors of possible compromises on Irian's status, and on December 3 Hatta stated that Indonesia could succeed in its claim only if it was prepared to give concessions. But clearly the Natsir cabinet would not be able to go far in compromising with the Dutch on the issue. Its hands were tied by the way in which the Irian claim had been presented to Indonesians, especially by President Soekarno, as an all-or-nothing, colonialism-or-freedom proposition. Moreover, Indonesia had previously

[26] PKI actions in the Irian crisis were an important focus for disagreement between the two factions then battling for power in the party. The older Alimin–Tan Ling Djie faction, which had been in control up to that time, took a relatively hostile stand on the Irian claim, in line with its strong opposition to Soekarno, Hatta, and Natsir as instruments of American imperialism (and in line with the anti-Indonesian position then taken on Irian by the Communist Party of the Netherlands). The younger Aidit-Lukman-Njoto group was opposed to the party's taking too strong a negative position on a popular nationalist claim. On Dec. 2, 1950, the Central Committee issued an extraordinary statement asserting the party's hope for a Republic of Irian which would be free from the Round Table Conference agreements and tied in a Two-State League to the Republic of Indonesia which was not as yet free from these agreements. On Dec. 8 the Alimin group leader and parliamentarian Ngadiman Hardjosubroto defended this statement. Then on Dec. 12 the Central Committee issued a statement signed by Sudisman, one of the Aidit group, in which it declared that the Dec. 2 statement had not been issued by the Central Committee at all. It added that it was investigating the connection between "sabotage elements within the party, in particular the remains of anarchist and social-democratic elements" and the issuing of the Dec. 2 statement with the use of a false Central Committee stamp. On Dec. 25 the Central Committee announced that Ngadiman Hardjosubroto was no longer in parliament as a representative of the PKI, and on Jan. 7 the Central Committee announced the names of its new Politbureau in which Aidit, Lukman, Njoto, and Sudisman held four of the five seats (and Alimin the fifth).

[27] *Antara*, Dec. 4, 1950.

[28] See, for instance, the letter to Prime Minister Drees of the Netherlands by the Algemene Middenstands Bond (General League of Middle-Class Persons) in Indonesia (*Antara*, Nov. 28, 1950).

rejected several compromise suggestions, including one under which sovereignty would be exercised by the Netherlands-Indonesian Union and *de facto* administration by the Netherlands.

On December 4 the long-awaited conference between the two countries began in the Netherlands.[29] Initially the Indonesian delegation, headed by Foreign Minister Roem, attempted to persuade the Netherlands to accept a plan whereby Indonesian sovereignty over Irian would be agreed to by December 27 and actually transferred "in the middle of 1951" after a further conference to deal with the protection of Dutch interests in the territory. But this proposal was quickly rejected.

On December 11 the Indonesian delegation submitted a seven-point Oral Note which included further concessions. In the event of the transfer of sovereignty over Irian, the Indonesian government would, the Note stated, give preferential treatment to Dutch economic interests, would employ Dutch persons in administration, would allow the immigration of Dutch nationals, and would guarantee freedom of religion, at the same time aiding the humanitarian work of religious missions.[30] But the Netherlands was not prepared to change its position in response to these promises.

The Dutch delegation for its part made two conciliatory offers of another kind. It suggested first that the Irian population might "in due course" decide their own future "through a plebiscite under the joint supervision of Indonesia and the Netherlands." With this it coupled a proposal for a New Guinea Council to be established forthwith, which would be composed of equal numbers of Dutch and Indonesian representatives and would decide administrative policy, with sovereignty remaining vested with the Netherlands. When these two suggestions were rejected by Indonesia, the Dutch delegation on December 26 offered the proposal which had been discussed earlier in the year, whereby sovereignty would rest with the Netherlands-Indonesian Union, the Netherlands retaining responsibility for *de facto* administration. This was a very conciliatory proposal in terms of current Dutch domestic politics, so conciliatory, in fact, that it eventually resulted in the disavowal of Foreign Minister Dirk Stikker by his own Liberal party, which was a principal factor causing the fall of

[29] For accounts of the conference see "Irian Crisis in Indonesian-Dutch Relations," *Indonesian Review* (Ministry of Information periodical, Djakarta), I, no. 1 (Jan. 1951), 41–48. See also Bone, *The Dynamics of the Western New Guinea Problem*, pp. 90–97, and Duynstee, *op. cit.*, pp. 192–198.

[30] See Bone, *The Dynamics of the Western New Guinea Problems*, pp. 92–93.

the cabinet of January 24.[31] But domestic pressures on the Indonesian delegation were no less powerful, and thus it felt obliged to reject the proposal. Soon thereafter, on December 27, the conference broke up, in what Roem called "a complete deadlock."

Reactions in Indonesia were less dramatic than had been expected. The one-hour sit-down strike which the Irian Struggle Body was to have organized was not held. There were no boycotts and no violence. In Makassar, where the local leadership of the Irian Struggle Body had broken with the Djakarta leadership, there was a one-day general strike on December 28. But otherwise there were no reactions except denunciations of the Dutch, the Americans, and the government and calls for repudiation of the Netherlands-Indonesian Union and the Round Table Conference Agreement.

Within the top councils of the government, the weeks immediately before and after December 27 were a time of acute tensions. Natsir was determined to prevent too great a deterioration of relations with the Netherlands and insisted that he and the cabinet should have the last say on this matter. Soekarno, on the other hand, was most reluctant to see December 27 come and go without any indication that his earlier threats had been more than bluff. The issue came to a head at a cabinet meeting held at the presidential palace immediately after the return of the negotiating party from the Netherlands. There the President put forward his view that the Round Table Conference Agreement should be abrogated unilaterally and that pressure of various kinds should be put on Dutch business in Indonesia.[32] Natsir opposed this view, and when the matter was put to the vote, the great majority of cabinet members sided with Natsir, causing the President not a little humiliation.

It was January 15 before the President spoke publicly again on the Irian issue. Then he declared he was obliged to confine himself to what could be said by a head of state in a parliamentary system. He added pointedly, however, that he also had sworn allegiance to the constitution which stated that Indonesia consisted of all the former Netherlands Indies, including West Irian.[33] The cabinet had followed up its diplomatic defeat by a significant political victory. But the vic-

[31] Duynstee, *op. cit.*, pp. 198–203.
[32] Louis Fischer quotes the President as saying (in 1958), "In 1950 I urged the confiscation of Dutch properties, but Prime Minister Natsir and his Cabinet were opposed" (*The Story of Indonesia* [New York: Harper, 1959], p. 300). But I have found no confirmation of the truth of this statement.
[33] *Antara*, Jan. 16, 1951.

tory had been gained at the cost of incurring the strongest displeasure of the President, displeasure directed in particular against Prime Minister Natsir and against the civilian and military heads of the Ministry of Defense.

In parliament, there was widespread agreement that the Netherlands-Indonesian Union, which had acquired little reality in the year it had been in existence, should be liquidated. And some kind of revision of the Round Table Conference agreements was called for by all groups of parliamentarians (except those, like the PKI and Murba members, who demanded outright abrogation of the agreements). There were, however, differences of emphasis between the viewpoints of government-supporting and opposition parties.

These differences came to the fore when two motions were placed before the House on January 4. One motion of five government-supporting parties was moved by Mr. Djody Gondokusumo of the PRN or National People's Party. It urged the government:

(1) to be prepared to conduct further negotiations with the Netherlands on the basis of the transfer of Indonesian sovereignty over West Irian;
(2) to give the Netherlands at most two months to answer the Indonesian demand as in (1) above; and
(3) to abrogate the Union Statute and review the results of the Round Table Conference and other agreements with the Netherlands with a view to abrogating all agreements which are damaging to Indonesia if there is no Dutch answer, or no satisfactory Dutch answer, within the time stipulated above.

A slightly stronger motion was that of Rahendra Kusnan, signed by PNI and PSII members. Kusnan urged the government:

(1) to continue to demand the immediate incorporation of West Irian into the territory of the Republic of Indonesia, on the basis of its having the same status as other areas of Indonesia;
(2) to abolish the Indonesian-Dutch Union; and
(3) to review the other results of the Round Table Conference within three months with a view to obtaining their abrogation.[34]

On January 10 the cabinet declared that it could not accept the Kusnan motion, but that there was little difference between its own standpoint and that incorporated in the Djody motion. It stated that it would negotiate with the Netherlands only on the basis of the transfer of sovereignty over Irian. And it said it would appoint a Spe-

[34] *Pedoman* (Djakarta), Jan. 5, 1951.

cial State Commission to examine the Round Table Conference agreements with a view to seeing how they could be brought into line with the new situation created by the failure of the Irian negotiations.

Thereupon Djody withdrew his motion. On the same day a vote was taken on the Kusnan PNI-PSII motion. The government parties were unable to muster anything like full cohesion—the PSI was among the government parties abstaining from the vote—but they managed to defeat the motion, by the narrow margin of 66 to 63. On January 23 the cabinet announced the membership of the Special States Commission, which would re-examine the Round Table Conference accords, a commission to be headed by the former (RUSI) Justice Minister, Professor Supomo. By this time the immediate crisis had passed.

THE NATSIR CABINET'S FALL

But this did not mean that the Natsir cabinet's position had been secured. It was in fact extremely weak in the face of groups seeking its downfall and as much obliged as ever to concentrate its energies on the task of political survival—to the detriment of the policy concerns which its members were anxious to further.

The principal issue on which the cabinet's weakness was demonstrated from January to March 1951 concerned the composition of the regional legislative (and executive) councils established in Java and Sumatra in the months following the reinauguration of the unitary states. The Halim cabinet of the member-state Republic of Indonesia had on August 15, 1950, issued a regulation, which the Natsir cabinet subsequently took over (for Java and Sumatra), establishing an interim basis for the election of legislative councils at the provincial, *kabupaten* (regency), and municipal levels. This regulation (Government Regulation 39 of 1950) was based on the Halim cabinet's anticipation that it would be some time before general elections based on individual suffrage could be held at these levels. It provided for a system of election based on organizations which could demonstrate their established existence at the subdistrict level. Thus the members of a *kabupaten* legislative council would be elected by an electoral college, which would be composed of representatives from every established organization in every subdistrict. (The organizations could be political parties, or they could be labor, peasant, women's, youth, religious, or social organizations. But to be considered established, they had to exist in at least three regencies of the province concerned, and they had to have been organized at the subdistrict level as of June 30,

1950.) The members of a provincial council would be elected in turn by an elèctoral college composed of members of all regency and municipal councils in the province. Voting would be on a proportional representation basis.

It was provided, moreover, that each legislative council established would elect an executive council from its own membership on a proportional representation basis. The executive council would work with the centrally appointed "head of the region"—who was concurrently a Governor, *bupati* (regent), or mayor in the *pamong pradja* corps—with regard to all governmental affairs over which the central government had empowered, or would empower, the region to act autonomously. With regard to these areas of government the executive council would have as chairman the Governor, *bupati*, or mayor (in his capacity of "head of the region") and would be responsible to the legislative council. A large area of other governmental powers would continue to be in the hands of the central government and exercised through either the *pamong pradja* corps (thus the governors, *bupatis*, and mayors acting as representatives of the government) or the regional and local representatives of the various ministries.[35]

The man who had borne responsibility for the making of Government Regulation 39 on the election of the regional legislative councils was the Halim cabinet's Interior Minister, Mr. Susanto Tirtoprodjo, a leader of the PNI (and associate of the older Sartono-Suwirjo group). But the first few months of implementation of the regulation showed that it favored the Masjumi. The number of organizations of various sorts affiliated to the Masjumi was considerably greater in virtually every area where the regulation went into effect than the number affiliated to any other party. Thus the Masjumi was coming quickly in the months of October, November, and December 1950 to a position of near-dominance in regional legislatures. For instance, in the West Java legislative council elected on November 30 the Masjumi and its associated organizations obtained 34 of the 57 seats.

On December 15 a parliamentary motion was tabled asking the government to revoke Regulation 39 and "freeze" the councils established on the basis of it. The list of signatures on the motion was headed by the PNI's S. Hadikusumo and included representatives of two other

[35] See Gerald S. Maryanov, *Decentralization in Indonesia: Legislative Aspects* (Cornell Modern Indonesia Project, Interim Reports Series; Ithaca, N.Y., 1957), *passim.* See also John D. Legge, *Problems of Regional Autonomy in Contemporary Indonesia* (Cornell Modern Indonesia Project, Interim Reports Series; Ithaca, N.Y.; 1957), pp. 4 ff., 20 ff.

opposition parties, the Labor Party and the PSII. More dangerously for the cabinet, it also included representatives of three government parties, PIR, Parindra, and the Protestant Party, Parkindo. In the following month demands were made by party branches and multiparty committees in different parts of Java and Sumatra that the controversial regulation be revoked.

When the government came to present its case against the Hadikusumo motion in January, it declared itself in agreement with many criticisms of Regulation 39, but added that merely to dissolve the great number of councils which had already been established on the basis of it would be to produce chaos and confusion. Critics of the regulation should, the government maintained, support the early holding of general elections for the regional assemblies.

On January 22, only twelve days after the Natsir cabinet had narrowly survived the test of the Kusnan motion, the Hadikusumo motion was put. PIR, Parindra, and Parkindo voted with the opposition, and several other government and government-supporting parties, including the PSI, abstained. The result was a defeat for the government by the large margin of 70 to 48.

This immediately put the cabinet into a most difficult position. Minister of the Interior Assaat, who had previously stated that the motion was unacceptable to him, offered his resignation to the cabinet on the following day. But the cabinet, maintaining that it shared Assaat's position on the issue of the Hadikusumo motion, refused to accept the resignation. It was not, however, prepared to resign as a cabinet. Its political position was strengthened by statements of PIR and Parindra leaders asserting that their parties' support of the Hadikusumo motion did not mean that they favored the immediate dissolution of the councils, but only that they wanted the councils to be abolished as and when new ones were created on a different basis.[36] On January 27 Natsir told parliament that a clear conflict consisted between cabinet and parliament on the issue of the Hadikusumo motion. In effect he challenged parliament to choose between yielding on the matter of the regional councils and moving a direct motion of no confidence in the cabinet.[37]

The issue was left unresolved when parliament began a six-week recess on February 3. In the breathing spell which this gave him Natsir

[36] "The Resignation of the Natsir Cabinet," *Indonesian Affairs* (Ministry of Information periodical, Djakarta), vol. I, no. 3 (March 1951).
[37] Noer, *op. cit.*

began to negotiate with the PNI, with a view to including its ministers in his cabinet. Dr. Halim, the cabinet's Defense Minister ad interim, had resigned on health grounds in December; its minister without portfolio, Harsono Tjokroaminoto, had also resigned, because of PSII opposition to the cabinet. This, Natsir felt, gave him an opportunity to negotiate a major reshuffle to strengthen the cabinet. But the Masjumi-PNI discussions on a reshuffle came to nothing, for, while Natsir and his associates wanted to carry on with essentially the same team and the same policy approach, the PNI wanted major changes of both personnel and program. A completely new cabinet was also the demand of some important sections of the Masjumi and especially the Sukiman group. Thus Jusuf Wibisono publicly urged Natsir to resign, adding that he was "not afraid to be expelled from his party because of the many criticisms he launched." [38]

The Prime Minister continued to maintain that he wanted an express statement from parliament on its position in relation to the Hadikusumo motion. But the supporters of the motion did not want to accept either of Natsir's alternatives. They did not want a reopening of the issue of the regional councils and argued that to discuss again an issue on which parliament had passed a resolution would be to weaken the nascent parliamentary tradition. At the same time they asserted that advancing a no-confidence motion would serve merely to sharpen existing differences between the PNI and Masjumi.

The matter came to a head on March 20. On that day parliament was to discuss the Prime Minister's statement of January 27 on the Hadikusumo motion. But no quorum could be mustered. The PNI, PSI, Labor Party, PKI, and Partai Murba and a considerable number of nonparty members all boycotted the session. On the same day PIR stated that it was no longer prepared to support the Natsir cabinet and that it had asked its two ministers, Wongsonegoro of Justice and Johannes of Public Works, to resign. At this point the cabinet decided that it could no longer continue in office. On March 21, after just six and a half months in office, Natsir returned his mandate to the President.

It is not easy to discern the pattern of causes which led to the Natsir cabinet's fall. Clearly the PNI was strong in its determination to pull the cabinet down; it could only gain from a change, being virtually certain to gain inclusion, if not the leading role, in a successor cabinet. But PNI initiative alone was not enough. There had to be

[38] *Abadi* (Djakarta), March 5, 1951, cited in Noer, *op. cit.*

also a considerable amount of defection from the side of the small parties represented in the cabinet.

On the whole, these parties were disfavored by the election system established under Regulation 39. The system helped parties with many associated organizations affiliated or related to them, and of these most of the small parties had few or none at all. In addition, several of these parties, particularly PIR and Parindra, were thought to favor delays in the establishment of regional legislative councils, on the grounds that these councils would weaken the influence of the *pamong pradja* corps whose interests these parties represented. Moreover, several of the small parties in the Natsir cabinet were thought to be apprehensive about the enthusiasm with which the leaders of the cabinet pushed toward an early holding of general elections, elections for a Constituent Assembly which would choose a working parliament from its membership. General elections were expected to be greatly in the Masjumi's interest. And they were expected to disfavor almost all the small parties, which, it was generally agreed, were heavily overrepresented in the existing parliament.

In addition, there was dissatisfaction among the small parties with several of the policies which the cabinet had been attempting to implement and in particular with the intensity of its leading members in their commitment to these policies. Fiscal rigidity was of especial importance here. Sjafruddin Prawiranegara, as Finance Minister, held the purse strings with all the tightness which his Puritan moral seriousness demanded.[39] Thus, while unpopular taxes like the Netherlands Indies company tax were continued, patronage was in general distributed without generosity, and this despite the enormous expansion of revenues which followed from the Korean War boom in prices for Indonesian exports. Funds were used for a variety of new economic projects, but rarely for directly political purposes.

In effect Sjafruddin was attempting to continue the policy of consistent rejection of patronage requests which he had practiced in the period of the Hatta cabinet, and then with the full support of Prime Minister Hatta. But this policy, which had been highly unpopular in the political elite in the Hatta cabinet period, aroused even greater hostility now, both because of the Korean War boom and because there was no man of the prestige of Hatta to champion it. At the same

[39] Sjafruddin's view of his role as Finance Minister is seen clearly in the hard-hitting pamphlet which he wrote shortly after he left office, *Indonesia Dipersimpangan Djalan* ("Indonesia at the Crossroads"; Djakarta: Hidup, 1951).

time Sjafruddin drew widespread hostility toward himself by the fact that he left great power to Dutch high officials in his ministry, including power to deal with requests for funds for other ministries.[40]

Further, one should consider the fact that short-lived cabinets had become an Indonesian tradition. In the revolutionary Republic there had been six cabinets in less than two and a half years (before Hatta emerged in January 1948 to give the situation a degree of stability). In the two BFO states where parliamentary cabinets had been in existence the rate of turnover had been similarly high: eight cabinets in slightly more than three and a half years in East Indonesia and five cabinets in less than two years in Pasundan.[41] There was, then, nothing extraordinary in a cabinet's being toppled after six and a half months in office. The small parties of concern here had good reason to expect that they would gain inclusion in the cabinet succeeding Natsir's. In actual fact none of them failed to gain seats in the Sukiman cabinet, and PIR, which had played a major role in Natsir's overthrow, obtained three portfolios, including the important one of Defense. The same person might not again be minister on behalf of his party, but this tended to be seen by party leaders as a positive rather than a negative factor. Certainly the feeling of "let another man have a turn at being minister—these things ought to be shared fairly" was of considerable importance within several of the parties under discussion.

But it would be a mistake to wind up this brief discussion of Natsir's fall without reference to the role of the President. We have seen that Soekarno's attitude toward Natsir changed markedly between September and December. The reasons for this are not entirely clear, but it seems that the degree to which Natsir adopted policies and political

[40] In the government service as a whole the number of Dutch citizens had been falling fast, and their power faster. Many of the Dutch civil servants whom the Indonesian government had agreed to keep on its payroll for up to two years after the transfer of sovereignty actually left the country well before December 1951. In June 1952 the total number of foreigners employed as government servants was 7,111, of whom a very high percentage were Dutch. See *Keterangan dan Djawaban Pemerintah atas Program Kabinet Wilopo* ("The Government Statement of the Wilopo Cabinet and Replies to Parliamentary Questions"; Djakarta: Kementerian Penerangan, 1952), p. 178; also E. P. M. Tervooren, *Statenopvolging en de Financiële Verplichtingen van Indonesië* ("The Succession of States and Indonesia's Financial Obligations"; The Hague: Nijhoff, 1957), pp. 269–270.

[41] See Kementerian Penerangan (Ministry of Information), *Republik Indonesia, Propinsi Sulawesi* ("The Sulawesi Province of the Republic of Indonesia"; Djakarta: Kementerian Penerangan, 1953), pp. 124, 136–137, 158–159, and 171, for lists of the membership of the East Indonesian cabinets.

positions akin to those of Sjahrir and Hatta was much greater than Soekarno had expected. Certainly Natsir tried persistently to confine Soekarno within the bounds of the figurehead President's role, a role to which Soekarno had never resigned himself. Meanwhile the President's power was continuing to grow, as it had been throughout 1950. His nadir year of 1949 was receding into the past. And the new post-revolutionary situation made it possible for him to play a "solidarity maker" role without the encumbrances that he had had to bear in the years of the Revolution as a result of his alliance with the Sjahrir-Hatta forces, whose leadership had then been called for by the logic of the international situation.

Hence Soekarno was growing in power in the last months of 1950 and at the same time developing closer relationships with "solidarity maker" groups in the camp of the opposition parties. In particular his affinities with the PNI, which had not been very close in the previous two years, were growing. With Sidik Djojosukarto, a distant relative, he had excellent relations. Thus when the Soekarno-Natsir showdown over Irian came and Soekarno was forced to yield, he began to use his influence actively in support of PNI endeavors to bring the cabinet down.

If Natsir had had to rely on his parliamentary support only, it is likely that his cabinet would have been toppled as soon as the Prime Minister came into sharp conflict with the President. However, Natsir could bring countervailing power to bear in the form of support from the leadership of the army. Natsir, like Hatta before him, worked in close co-operation with the men who dominated the army leadership in this period, men such as the Acting Chief of Staff of the Armed Forces, Colonel T. B. Simatupang, and the Chief of Staff of the Army, Colonel A. H. Nasution. These men led an "administrator" group within the officer corps and were committed to policies of rationalization and routinization in the army which paralleled the policies that Hatta and Natsir sought to implement in the polity generally. Therefore a basis of interest existed for a relationship of mutual support between the cabinet and the army leaders. This was reinforced by a number of factors of personal and clique politics. And it was reinforced for this particular situation by the existence of anti-Soekarno feelings within the army leadership.[42]

---

[42] These feelings had grown strong in the period of the President's exile in Bangka in early 1949. They had been kept alive by efforts the President had made in 1950 to support members and former members of "Student Army" units, which were

Thus in the months of January, February, and March 1951 Prime Minister Natsir obtained considerable support from the army leaders in his covert struggle with the President. It was an early manifestation of what was to become a characteristic situation of the politics of our period, the situation where the two chief extraparliamentary centers of power, the President and the army, were pulling the contenders in the cabinet-parliament arena in opposite directions. But, whether because of the army leaders' disinclination to use their influence too openly—perhaps the result of internal army division—or because of a reluctance on Natsir's part to allow them to enter too far into civilian and constitutional politics, army support was not forthcoming on a scale sufficient to counterbalance the pressures exerted by the President.

At this point it may be useful to look briefly at what the Natsir government was able to achieve. In general, it continued the work of the Hatta cabinet. It was able to achieve considerable further successes in restoring order. Thanks in part to good cabinet-army relations a number of rebel-bandit groups of old guerrillas were driven out of their jungle fastnesses in Sumatra and Java. The cabinet established peace in much of South Sulawesi by virtue of the agreements which it reached in January and March 1951 with the guerrilla leader Kahar Muzakar. And it cleared Ambon of the "Republic of the South Moluccas." In dealing with the Darul Islam it was less effective. Its efforts to establish a peaceful settlement were rebuffed when the Darul Islam leader Kartosuwirjo refused to negotiate with Natsir's envoy Wali Alfatah and asked that a delegation of top-level rank be sent to confer with him.[43] Subsequently there was further military action, but no important successes were registered.

In a major arms roundup in November 1950 the Natsir cabinet succeeded in getting back many of the thousands of weapons which had long been in unauthorised hands. Army discipline continued to improve. At the same time considerable attention was devoted to the prob-

then in process of being dissolved, to gain admission into the army on favorable terms. And they were given vigorous and frequently irreverent expression by the Djakarta daily *Indonesia Raya,* which was known to reflect the views of an important section of the army leadership. In February 1951 this paper drew the President's anger upon itself by printing what purported to be a letter to the editor, blaming Soekarno for the death of many Indonesians in the Japanese occupation. See *Antara,* Feb. 28, 1951.

[43] Kementerian Penerangan, *Republik Indonesia, Propinsi Djawa Barat* ("The West Java Province of the Republic of Indonesia"; Djakarta: Kementerian Penerangan, 1953), pp. 212–242.

lem of reabsorbing former army members and guerrillas into civilian society, a number of new sources of employment being created with government credits.

As far as the economy was concerned, Natsir operated under favorable conditions, thanks largely to the Korean War boom in raw materials prices, which produced high export earnings and large sums in export duties during the whole of the cabinet's term of office.[44] With rubber earnings up to 2.60 Straits dollars per pound, the foreign exchange situation became buoyant, making it possible for the government to liberalize the import system and to supply credit generously to Indonesian entrepreneurs in trade and small industry.

The cabinet concentrated a good deal of attention on the field of credit, aiming not only to stimulate economic activity, but also to increase government and "national" control of the economy by lessening the power of the seven large banks which had hitherto held almost exclusive dominance. In this first major effort at "Indonesianization" of a part of the economy, they reorganized the Bank Negara Indonesia, which had been the fiscal agent of the government of the revolutionary Republic, transforming this bank into an agency to assist Indonesians to enter importing and making it the first Indonesian-owned foreign exchange bank. Furthermore, they reorganized the Bank Rakjat Indonesia (Indonesian People's Bank), which had provided village credit in the Dutch period and had 101 branches in early 1950.[45] This was now to support new business activity in internal trade and manufacturing, principally in small towns where there were no branches of the large foreign banks. Meanwhile the Co-operatives Service was taking over much of the village credit field in which the BRI had been active. In addition, the cabinet established a new government credit institution, the Bank Industri Negara (State Industrial Bank), to contribute to long-term financing of reconstruction and development.[46] Schmitt writes:

With the organization or reorganization of the Bank Rakjat (Indonesia), the Bank Industri (Negara), and the Bank Negara (Indonesia), the government had attempted to launch a massive financial assault upon the positions of the vested interests represented broadly by the customers of the seven foreign commercial banks.[47]

[44] The Java Bank, *Report for the Financial Year 1950–1951* (Djakarta, 1951), p. 91.

[45] Sutter, *op. cit.*, p. 984.   [46] *Ibid.*, pp. 958 ff.

[47] "Some Monetary and Fiscal Consequences of Social Conflict in Indonesia, 1950–58" (doctoral dissertation, University of California, Berkeley, 1959), p. 69.

Under the Natsir cabinet plans for industrial development were set down in much greater detail than before. An Economic Urgency Program (sometimes called the Sumitro Plan) laid down guidelines by which the government would control the establishment of new enterprises. It provided for the promotion of small industries in rural areas in such fields as leatherware, umbrella making, brick- and tile-making, and ceramics. In addition, medium- and large-scale industries were to be established—printing plants, rubber remilling plants, a cement plant, a tile factory, and some other units on a short-term plan and, as long-term projects, a caustic soda factory, a fertilizer plant, an aluminium plant, a paper factory, spinning and knitting mills, and several other plants.[48] The cabinet also commissioned an American firm, the J. C. White Engineering Corporation, to make a resources survey of the country, and prepared the establishment of a National Planning Bureau.

From the beginning of its period of office the cabinet was faced with labor unrest, arising in part from continuing inflation.[49] In September 1950 it settled a strike of some 700,000 Communist-led plantation workers by establishing a minimum plantation wage. But subsequently there were many smaller strikes, in a large range of enterprises. In most cases these were fairly well organized actions, much more so than those of the Hatta cabinet period had been, and leadership for them came principally from PKI-controlled unions. In some areas military commanders reacted by issuing strike bans, but there remained a major problem of strikes for the central government to tackle.

On February 13, 1951, the cabinet decreed a temporary ban on all strikes and lockouts in "vital" economic enterprises and provided that all disputes be brought before a ministerial Committee for Settlement. "Vital" enterprises would include all public communications and transport facilities, private railways, harbor enterprises, the oil industry, hospitals, dispensaries, state printing offices, electricity and gas, the principal banks, and all establishments of the Ministry of

---

[48] See "The Industrialization of Indonesia," *Indonesian Review*, I, no. 3 (April–June 1951), 185–189; also Sutter, *op. cit.*, pp. 772 ff.

[49] On the development of the labor movement at this stage see I. Tedjasukmana, *The Political Character of the Indonesian Trade Union Movement* (Cornell Modern Indonesia Project, Monograph Series, Ithaca, N.Y., 1959), pp. 25 ff. See also John E. Moes, "Trade Unionism in Indonesia," *Far Eastern Survey*, XXVIII, no. 2 (Feb. 1959), 17–24, and J. M. van der Kroef, "Indonesia's Labor Movement: Its Development and Prospects," *United Asia*, V, no. 4 (Aug. 1953), 223–231.

Defense. In all these enterprises the Committee for Settlement would have powers of compulsory arbitration. In nonvital enterprises, strikes would be allowed, but not while negotiations by the Committee for Settlement or one of its subsidiary organs were in progress. This measure, issued by the Ministry of Defense on the basis of the "State of War and Siege" regulations, was widely criticized as violating a basic constitutional right. Many who were opposed to the cabinet leaders' political alliance with the current leadership of the army condemned the ban as presaging a threat of militarism. But it was effective in achieving its immediate purpose.[50]

On the other hand, the Natsir cabinet was not effective in carrying out its stated plans to cut down the size of the civil service. Nor was it able to have a budget approved, for it fell just as its draft budget was to be discussed by parliament.[51]

In the field of foreign relations the cabinet's policies were almost as unspectacular as those of the Hatta cabinet. Like its predecessor, the cabinet was more inclined to evade foreign policy issues than to seek them. It faced a basically similar situation in that, like the Hatta cabinet, it was subjected to pressures to support U.S. policies in Korea and the rest of the Far East, pressures which ran strongly counter to the dominant "a plague on both your houses" and "no foreign armies in Asia" view of the Indonesian political public. The Natsir cabinet, like the Hatta cabinet again, was rather strongly pro-Western in its Cold War orientation. But it was bound by the terms of an already well established consensus on the *politik bebas* or "independent foreign policy" to refrain from any action which would appear to range Indonesia on the side of either of the two blocs.

Thus the cabinet's characteristic foreign policy position was one of warding off U.S. pressures and cautiously selecting from a range of U.S. offers of aid. In October 1950 the cabinet rejected an offer of American military aid made by the visiting State Department–Defense Department mission of John Melby. It did in the same month sign an economic and technical assistance agreement with the United States, but on the whole it used little aid funds. Later in 1950 at the Baguio conference in the Philippines, Indonesia helped to defeat the pur-

[50] See "Democracy, Strikes and Production," *Indonesian Affairs*, Vol. I, no. 2 (Feb. 1951), and Moes, *op. cit.*, p. 21.

[51] The draft was for 1950 as well as 1951 and was contained in a Financial Note which Finance Minister Sjafruddin submitted to parliament on February 8, 1951. For a full summary of the Financial Note see "The Proposed Budgets for 1950 and 1951," *Indonesian Review*, I, no. 4 (July–Sept. 1951), 315–323.

poses for which President Quirino had called this conference by its repeated declarations that it would not be party to any pro-Western or anti-Communist bloc.

The cabinet did, however, act positively on the world stage in the course of the UN debates on the Korean War. Indonesia had been admitted to the international organization on September 27 (as a result of Indian and Australian sponsorship), and its representatives played an active part with those of India in the conciliation efforts made at the time of the entry of the Chinese forces into the Korean War. Significantly its general foreign policy position was more anti-Chinese than that of India, as evidenced by the fact that it sent only a chargé d'affaires and a fairly junior man to be its first diplomatic representative in Peking. When it came to voting on the U.S.-sponsored resolution branding China an aggressor, Indonesia abstained, whereas India and Burma cast negative ballots.

In the very short time it had been in office the Natsir cabinet pursued its policy goals intently and with some success. It moved the country several steps along the road to civil security, administrative routinization, increased production, and planned economic growth. That it failed was clear from the fact of the very short time it had in office: it had failed to build itself a basis of political support.

Chapter V

The Sukiman Cabinet, April 1951–February 1952:

The Slowing of Momentum

WITH the resignation of the Natsir government on March 21, 1951, elite politics went again into the excitement of a period of cabinet formation. For five days the President conducted hearings with the representatives of the parties, and then on March 26 he announced that he had asked Mr. Sartono, a PNI leader and chairman of parliament, to form "a national coalition cabinet on a broad basis."

Sartono worked for 28 days without success. In attempting to establish a cabinet based on the PNI and the Masjumi he encountered many of the difficulties which Natsir had faced seven months earlier, as well as some new ones. The two parties were now committed to opposing stands on the matter of the turnover tax, the regional councils based on Regulation 39, and the complex of problems surrounding Indonesian-Dutch relations and the West Irian issue. On this last series of matters in particular they were markedly divided from one another, with the PNI wanting a unilateral abrogation of the Netherlands-Indonesian Union and some other parts of the Round Table Conference agreements and the Masjumi wanting all cancellations of agreement to be made on the basis of bilateral accord.

But probably the most important cause of Sartono's difficulties was the matter of the distribution of seats, in particular the post of Prime Minister. Sartono did not want the prime ministership for himself;

indeed, he did not want to be a member of the cabinet at all. But he did want the PNI to obtain the top cabinet post, and he pressed the Masjumi to accept the appointment of Mr. Susanto Tirtoprodjo, a member of the "Sartono-Suwirjo group" of the PNI and currently governor of the Lesser Sunda Islands. The Masjumi on the other hand argued that, as the *formateur* had agreed that his cabinet would follow the general line of policy which had been set forth and implemented by the Natsir cabinet, Natsir himself should again be Prime Minister.

Throughout the period of Sartono's negotiations for a PNI-Masjumi-based cabinet there was speculation on the possibility of a cabinet's being formed on the basis of the PNI and the smaller nationalist parties, with the support of the PKI and the exclusion of the Masjumi. The PKI, under Aidit and the other vigorous young men who had taken over its leadership in January, pressed for a cabinet on this basis. Thus on March 27 the inaugural meeting was held of what was soon to become the BPP (Badan Permusjawaratan Partai-Partai, Consultative Body of Parties), a confederative association of the PKI and ten other political parties, including the PSII and the Sumatran Islamic party Perti (Pergerakan Tarbijah Islamijah, Islamic Educational Movement), the Partai Murba, the Labor Party, Parindra, and PRN. These eleven were loosely joined together as of March 31 on the basis of a broadly nationalist Common Program which called for a "truly independent foreign policy," freedom from the Round Table Conference Agreement, the quick return of West Irian to Indonesia, the lifting of the "State of War and Siege" and of limitations on the freedom to strike, faster freeing of political prisoners, elections, nationalization of vital industries, industrialization, and a "just distribution of land to the peasants." [1]

For a while Sartono considered the possibility of a cabinet based on the PNI and the BPP parties. Indeed, it looked for a brief time as if the PNI might itself become a member of the BPP. But neither possibility eventuated, and most of Sartono's time was spent in efforts to bridge the PNI-Masjumi cleavage. Here, however, the familiar deadlock remained. The policy conflict on relations with the Netherlands still loomed large, and with it a conflict over the Foreign Affairs portfolio, which each of the two main parties wanted for itself. More important still, neither of the two main parties would budge from its

---

[1] For the text see *Bintang Merah* ("Red Star"; PKI theoretical journal, Djakarta), VII, nos. 6–7 (March 15–April 1, 1951), 168.

claim to the prime ministership. On April 18 Sartono went to the President to report failure.

On the same day Soekarno announced the names of two new *formateurs,* the PNI's chairman Sidik Djojosukarto and the chairman of the Masjumi's party council, or legislative body, Dr. Sukiman Wirjosandjojo. The two men were given five days in which to form a "coalition cabinet on a broad national basis," and then a further three-day extension. By this time a variety of face-saving compromise proposals had been discussed as ways of bridging the gap between the main parties on such issues as abrogation of the Netherlands-Indonesian Union, the Hadikusumo motion on the regional councils, and the company surtax. There remained, however, the formidable problems of allocation of seats.

Sukiman conceded early that the PNI should have a position of equality with the Masjumi in the cabinet to be formed—a major concession in the light of earlier assumptions on the relative strengths of the two parties outside parliament. The two parties would, it was agreed, have an equal number of portfolios. But the Masjumi *formateur* continued to insist that the prime ministership stay in Masjumi hands. To this the PNI could not agree. However, on April 23 the PNI suggested that the cabinet leadership should be in the hands of a third party. And on the following day it went further to concede that it would accept a Masjumi Prime Minister as long as he was not Natsir. Sukiman took up the latter offer.

From this point on, the division inside the Masjumi came rapidly to dominate developments. Earlier the Natsir-led Masjumi executive had endorsed Sukiman's acceptance of the *formateur*-ship only on the condition that he should return the mandate if his five-day attempt did not prove successful.[2] He had, however, accepted the extension of time which the President had offered to him and Sidik. Now, it seemed to the Natsir group of the party, he was allowing himself to be used to split the Masjumi. This feeling became all the stronger when Sukiman agreed to the request of the President that he, Dr. Sukiman, accept the prime ministership. For several days there existed the same high tension between Natsir and Sukiman supporters which had existed at the time of the Natsir cabinet's formation. Only a few hours before the *formateurs* took their completed cabinet list to the President the Masjumi executive body (led by Natsir) issued a statement

[2] Deliar Noer, "Masjumi: Its Organization, Ideology and Political Role in Indonesia" (M.A. thesis, Cornell University, 1960).

to the effect that Sukiman's actions as *formateur* were not valid as actions taken on behalf of the Masjumi.[3] When the new cabinet list was finally made public on April 26, no member of the Natsir group of the Masjumi was included.

THE SUKIMAN CABINET AND ITS EARLY PROBLEMS

The composition of the cabinet as first announced was as follows:

Ministry		Party
Prime Minister	Dr. Sukiman Wirjosandjojo	Masjumi
Deputy Prime Minister	Suwirjo	PNI
Foreign Affairs	Mr. Achmad Subardjo	Masjumi
Interior	Mr. Iskaq Tjokroadisurjo	PNI
Defense	Sumitro Kolopaking [4]	PIR
Justice	Mr. Muhammad Yamin [5]	Nonparty
Information	Arnold Mononutu	PNI
Finance	Mr. Jusuf Wibisono	Masjumi
Agriculture	Ir. Suwarto	Catholic
Trade and Industry (Economic Affairs)	Mr. Sujono Hadinoto [6]	PNI
Communications	Ir. Djuanda	Nonparty
Public Works and Power	Ir. Ukar Bratakusumah	PNI
Labor	I. Tedjasukmana	Labor
Social Affairs	Dr. Samsuddin	Masjumi
Education	Mr. Wongsonegoro	PIR
Religious Affairs	K. H. Wachid Hasjim	Masjumi
Health	Dr. Johannes Leimena	Parkindo
General Affairs	M. A. Pellaupessy	Democratic Fraction
Personnel Affairs	R. P. Suroso	Parindra
Agrarian Affairs	——————— [7]	

[3] *Ibid.* See also Mochtar Naim, "The Nahdatul Ulama as a Political Party, 1952–55: An Enquiry into the Origins of Its Electoral Success" (M.A. thesis, McGill University, 1960), pp. 14–15.

[4] Sumitro Kolopaking was, however, never installed. On May 4 he declared that he had changed his mind and would not accept the appointment as minister. On May 9 Sewaka of PIR was installed in the post.

[5] Mr. Yamin resigned on June 14, 1951. He was replaced on that date by M. A. Pellaupessy, who served as Justice Minister ad interim (as well as Minister for General Affairs) until November 20, when Mr. Muhammad Nasrun (nonparty) assumed the Justice portfolio.

[6] Mr. Sujono resigned on July 16. Three days later he was replaced by Mr. Wilopo of the PNI.

[7] This empty slot was finally filled on November 20, 1951, with the appointment of PIR's Mr. Gondokusumo, who, however, died on March 6, 1952.

This list contrasted with that of the Natsir cabinet in a number of ways. First of all, there was relatively little continuity of personnel. Only six of the members of the Natsir cabinet were included in that of Sukiman, three of them with different portfolios and none of them with major posts. Of the men who had given the Natsir cabinet its characteristic stamp there remained only the "veterans," Djuanda and Leimena.[8] All the rest, Natsir himself, the Sultan of Jogjakarta, Roem, Assaat, Sjafruddin, and Sumitro, were not included. Few of the members of the Sukiman cabinet had been active associates of Hatta, and fewer had close ties to the younger group of "administrators" who looked to Sjahrir for leadership.

A number of those in the most important positions in the new government were older men who had been prominent figures in the prewar nationalist movement and in the Japanese period and had been eclipsed in the period of Revolution. Dr. Sukiman himself does not quite fit this "older generation" pattern, in that his degree of prominence in the Japanese period was not great and that he was a powerful member of the first Hatta cabinet of 1948–1949. But he, like several others in the team which he now headed, was a man who had come to prominence in the prewar period and had been a strong opponent of Sjahrir and the group of his younger associates who had assumed power in the first years of the Revolution. Deputy Prime Minister Suwirjo and Interior Minister Iskaq, both of whom had been leaders of Soekarno's PNI of 1927, are excellent illustrations of the "older generation" pattern. The same is true of the highly colorful Subardjo and Yamin, both of them important leaders in Tan Malaka's abortive coup of July 3, 1946 (in which Sukiman was peripherally involved). Subardjo, who had a long history in prewar politics in the Netherlands, France, Russia, Japan, and Indonesia, was a top adviser in the Foreign Ministry before he entered the cabinet. He was a personal friend of Dr. Sukiman and had been a member of the Masjumi since 1948. But he had not been active or prominent in the party.

A majority of the members of the Sukiman cabinet were men whose prominence had been achieved through "administrator" roles rather than "solidarity maker" ones, but the "administrator" influence was considerably less in this cabinet than in its predecessor. Men such as Suwirjo, Iskaq, Subardjo, and Yamin owed their position at least as

[8] These two had held cabinet portfolios far more frequently than any other individual. Each of them had been a minister in unbroken continuity since the formation of the second Sjahrir cabinet in March 1946.

much to directly political skills of the "solidarity maker" type as to their understanding of technical, legal, or administrative aspects of modern statecraft. Moreover, their scale of governmental priorities was one on which the implementation of problem-solving policies in the fields of administration and economic affairs was of less importance than nation building, specifically the effective use of nationalist symbols to maintain the active support of all old revolutionaries.

Potentially there were considerable advantages in this addition of "solidarity making" to "administrative" skills. It could and did alleviate some of the sources of the political weakness which had plagued the Natsir cabinet. But to offset these advantages, the cabinet was much weaker in internal cohesion than either of its two predecessors. Its members were tied to one another by few loyalties other than those directly related to the cabinet's survival. Indeed, the cabinet was without a distinct and distinctive political coloration of its own. Furthermore, and perhaps even more important, it included a good number of men who were without intense personal commitments to problem-solving policies of any kind, men whose primary orientation was to political power as such. Here too there was a strong contrast with both the Hatta and Natsir cabinets.

In party terms the principal characteristic of the cabinet was that it had a Masjumi-PNI core. The Masjumi ministers were all followers or associates of Sukiman, although Wachid Hasjim, the Minister of Religious Affairs, had his base of power in the Nahdatul Ulama. As for the PNI ministers, four of them may be classified with the Sartono-Suwirjo group of the party. The same minor nationalist parties which had participated in the Natsir cabinet were again represented in this, the PIR strengthened and gaining the major portfolio of Defense. In addition, the Labor Party now gained inclusion, whereas the PSII did not. The Partai Murba, like the PKI, was not represented, but it was sometimes said that Yamin was an "undercover" Murba representative, and some maintained that this was true also of Subardjo. The Socialist Party was not included.

Press and parliamentary reactions to the cabinet were generally unenthusiastic. The Djakarta daily *Merdeka*, subsequently one of the cabinet's strongest supporters, commented on April 27 that many of the new ministers had yet to prove their ability. It added that leadership of the cabinet was in the hands of men not hitherto known as strong personalities.[9] Other newspapers, particularly PSI-sympathizing

[9] Quoted in *Aneta*, April 27, 1951.

ones, said that the cabinet's formation had been "forced" by the personal intervention of the President. There was much criticism too of the cabinet's size. Whereas there had been many suggestions in the course of the cabinet crisis that the number of ministries should be reduced, Sukiman and Sidik had instead created three new portfolios, Personnel Affairs, Agrarian Affairs, and General Affairs. Charges of "cow trading"—the Indonesian idiom chooses the cow in preference to the horse—were numerous.[10]

The Natsir group of the Masjumi was strongly critical of the Sukiman cabinet's composition. But on May 19 the party's executive body, on which Natsir and his supporters had preponderant influence, decided to "give the cabinet an opportunity to implement its program." [11] From this time there was no doubt that the cabinet would gain parliamentary backing without undue difficulty. The real problems it faced were internal. The Sukiman cabinet had been formed in considerable haste and with relatively little prior consultation on the basis on which conflicts of orientation and interest within its membership would be settled. Thus a large number of these conflicts came to the fore even before the parliament on June 15, 1951, gave the cabinet a 119 to 30 vote for an "opportunity to work." [12]

One of the first signs of open division in the cabinet came over the matter of the regional councils. On May 10 the PNI Interior Minister, Iskaq, ordered that the existing councils cease their activity. This aroused so stormy a Masjumi reaction that the minister was obliged to revoke his instruction two days later. The compromise eventually reached was that the regional legislative and executive councils already in existence would continue to function until they had been replaced by councils established on the basis of a new regulation. This new regulation would provide for representation of political parties only, not of labor, youth, social, religious, and other organizations. Meanwhile there would be no more setting up of councils on the basis of Regulation 39.[13]

[10] See, for instance, Sjafruddin Prawiranegara, *Indonesia Dipersimpangan Djalan* ("Indonesia at the Crossroads"; Djakarta: Hidup, 1951), p. 4.

[11] Noer, *op. cit.*

[12] It was Dr. Sukiman who had asked for a vote in these terms rather than a direct vote of confidence. It was thought that certain parties, like the PSI, which were not included in the cabinet, could be induced to support it if the request was made in these modified terms. The "opportunity to work" subsequently became a parliamentary convention.

[13] See *Keterangan Pemerintah atas Program Kabinet Sukiman* ("Government Statement on the Program of the Sukiman Cabinet"; Djakarta: Kementerian Pene-

Masjumi-PNI conflict came to the fore again in June after Iskaq had named PNI members as governors for West Java and Sulawesi (and succeeded in getting cabinet approval for them). In West Java, his nominee, Sanusi Hardjadinata, had not been among the candidates proposed by the regional legislature (which had been formed on the basis of Regulation 39 and had a Masjumi majority). In Sulawesi there was a negative response chiefly because Iskaq's candidate, Sudiro, was Javanese. Inside the Masjumi there was alarm about a further extension of the already great power of the PNI in the *pamong pradja* structure.[14] Before long a motion of censure of Iskaq had been tabled, by a PRN member from Sulawesi. The PNI threatened to withdraw from the cabinet if this was passed. It was not, nor was it defeated. The result was inconclusive because when the motion was put on September 5 the parliamentarians of the Masjumi, PRN, and PSI left the chamber, thus making it impossible to achieve a quorum. In practical terms it was a victory for Iskaq. But morally both he and the cabinet were losers.

Other evidence of cabinet dissension came on an issue of foreign policy. Commenting on the UN General Assembly's decision to place an embargo on the shipment of strategic war materials to China, Foreign Minister Subardjo declared on May 7 that Indonesia would "sell to the Devil if this would serve the people's interest." Press reactions to Subardjo's statement were favorable.[15] But the cabinet soon

rangan, 1951). See also "The Programme of the Sukiman Cabinet," *Indonesian Review,* I, no. 4 (July–Sept. 1951), 264. By this time councils established on this basis existed at the level of regencies and regency-level municipalities in all Java and in certain regencies of South, Central, and North Sumatra. Provincial councils had been established on the basis of Regulation 39 in Central and West Java.

[14] At the time of the Sanusi and Sudiro appointments there were already PNI governors in South Sumatra (Dr. Mohammad Isa) and the Lesser Sunda Islands (Mr. Susanto Tirtoprodjo) and PNI-sympathizing governors in East Java (Samadikun) and Kalimantan (Dr. Murdjani). Only two governors, Abdul Hakim of North Sumatra and Roeslan Moeljohardjo of Central Sumatra, were Masjumi men. In addition, a Masjumi man, Sjamsuridzal, was given the governor-status post of mayor in Djakarta in June 1951.

[15] See, for instance, *Merdeka* (Djakarta), May 15, 1951, quoted in George McT. Kahin, "Indonesian Politics and Nationalism," in W. L. Holland, ed., *Asian Nationalism and the West* (New York: Macmillan, 1953), p. 177. For three months before this time the Indonesian government had held discussions with the Chinese Embassy with a view to arriving at a barter agreement whereby Indonesia would get rice for rubber. In addition, there was suspicion in Djakarta that the U.S. motive in introducing the embargo motion was to place itself in a single-buyer position in relation to countries producing raw materials, and thus push down the prices of these materials. In actual fact rubber prices fell markedly after the passage of the embargo resolution.

felt pressure to disavow it. Subardjo himself did this indirectly on May 16, and the Sukiman cabinet subsequently abided by the embargo, as did the three cabinets which succeeded it.

The other important zigzag of policy came over a decision of the Justice Minister, Yamin, to release a group of 950 political prisoners. The jails were at this time filled by some 17,000 persons,[16] mainly men arrested by the army in the Hatta and Natsir cabinet periods for involvement in, or suspected collaboration with, rebel-bandit groups. Many of these were men against whom no specific charge had been made, and Yamin favored a policy of large-scale pardons. On June 7 he took what was to be the first step of this policy. He released 950 men, a number of them persons of political prominence like Chaerul Saleh, the Murba-sympathizing ex-leader of the People's Army in West Java.

Yamin had selected persons with whom he had a political affinity. He had listed individuals, rather than setting down categories of prisoners and leaving the specification of individuals to judicial agencies. And he had acted without consulting the leaders of the army, although the army, acting under the State of War and Siege regulations, had been responsible for arresting the men concerned. Yamin maintained that he had cleared his actions with Dr. Sukiman, but this was denied by the Prime Minister. In any event it was not long before angry reactions came from the side of the army leadership.

Within a few days the army leaders had acted on their own initiative to rearrest the 950 men. They succeeded in finding most of them, including Chaerul Saleh; the rest had taken to the mountains. At the same time there was strong army pressure on the cabinet for the Justice Minister to be disavowed and dropped. And there were intimidating movements of soldiers outside Yamin's residence.

On June 14 Yamin resigned from the cabinet. The next day the Prime Minister stated that the procedure followed in compiling the list of detainees to be released had been incorrect and that some of those on the list should not, in the government's view, be allowed their freedom.[17] Both Sukiman and the Defense Minister, Sewaka, denied that there had been a difference of opinion between the government and the armed forces. But the damage to the cabinet's prestige had been done.

By June 15, when the Sukiman cabinet received the support of parliament for an "opportunity to work," it had become clear that this

[16] See statement of Muhammad Yamin, *Aneta*, June 6, 1951.
[17] "The Programme of the Sukiman Cabinet," *Indonesian Review*, I, no. 4 (July–Sept. 1951), 268.

was a very different sort of government from that of Natsir, in terms of the group and clique network of elite politics, despite the fact that the two Prime Ministers belonged to the same party. It was apparent from the very beginning of the cabinet's existence that it had the personal support of President Soekarno, in much fuller measure than the Natsir cabinet had had it, even in its first months of office. Both of the *formateurs* were old friends of the President, and they had leaned heavily on his authority in forming the cabinet. Gradually in the first two months of the Sukiman cabinet's term a second principal aspect of contrast had come to the fore, as it became clear that this cabinet, unlike the Natsir cabinet, lacked positive support from the leadership of the army.

These contrasts had their reflections in the cabinet's policy approach and political style, but here generalizations come less easily. The new cabinet's policy approach was certainly not the familiar one of Hatta and Natsir, but what exactly it was, was not readily discernible. Like Natsir, Sukiman emphasized the great importance of a quick restoration of security and of increases in production. Like Natsir he promised early nationwide elections for a Constituent Assembly and pursuance of an independent foreign policy. On the matter of the future of the Netherlands-Indonesian Union, he announced a policy which was basically the same as that of the Natsir cabinet (and that of the Masjumi rather than the PNI). The new cabinet would study the recommendations of the Special State Commission established by the Natsir cabinet and then prepare for a conference with the Netherlands at which, it was averred, the Union would be replaced by ordinary bilateral agreements.

The differences of policy approach were apparent on other issues. The Sukiman cabinet spoke of security disturbances in tones of greater toughness than had its predecessor. Civil security was the No. 1 point of its stated program, whereas it had been only in third place on the seven-point program of Natsir. "Early elections" had been demoted from No. 1 to the No. 3 position. In financial policies the cabinet had begun to show itself less strict than its predecessor and more generous to the civil service. It had announced that the controversial company surtax would be lifted as of October 1, 1951,[18] and had given bonuses of from Rp. 125 ($11) to Rp. 200 ($17.50) to all civil servants on

[18] See John O. Sutter, *Indonesianisasi: Politics in a Changing Economy, 1940–1955* (Southeast Asia Program, Cornell University; Ithaca, N.Y., 1959), pp. 1004–1007.

the occasion of the Moslem fast-breaking feast of Lebaran. Subsequently it provided all civil servants with monthly allocations of rice. In its style of operation the Sukiman cabinet had demonstrated a certain sense of the dramatic which had rarely been in evidence in the operations of either the Hatta or the Natsir cabinet. Thus the new Finance Minister, Jusuf Wibisono, had used hist first press conference to announce that the Java Bank, the Dutch-run bank of circulation and citadel of Dutch financial power in Indonesia, would be nationalized.[19]

If these various aspects of the contrast between the Sukiman cabinet and its predecessors seem to form no clear pattern, this indeed was the impression formed by observers at the time. In part it was explained in terms of the all too evident disunity in the cabinet's ranks. And in part the explanation was that this new cabinet was indeed *sui generis*.

THE ANTI-COMMUNIST RAID OF AUGUST 1951

One thing which had not become clear by mid-June was that this would be an actively anti-Communist cabinet. The Hatta and Natsir cabinets had been decidedly anti-Communist in outlook. But they had not attempted to drive the PKI into semi-illegality. Nor were there to be attempts of this kind in the next six years. Yet this is what Sukiman tried to do, notably by his mass arrests of August 1951.

In the months of June and July and early August 1951 a number of developments had occurred to alarm the Sukiman government. Numerous strikes had broken out in defiance of the antistrike military regulation of February 13. Workers in a number of industries, including industries specified as "vital," were demanding that they too should, like civil servants, be given Lebaran bonuses. In addition, there had been a marked increase in organized theft of cargoes by dock workers, and here, as in the case of the new strikes, the greatest amount of activity was where unions were under PKI influence. The security situation had in general been improving in the first half of 1951. But there remained some major areas of rebel-bandit activity in West Java—areas of the Darul Islam and of remnants of the "People's Army," of Westerling's APRA (Army of the Messianic King), and of a host of smaller groups—and some minor areas of East and Central Java. In Central

---

[19] For a full discussion see Hans O. Schmitt, "Some Monetary and Fiscal Consequences of Social Conflict in Indonesia, 1950–58" (doctoral dissertation, University of California, Berkeley, 1959), pp. 89–90.

Java rebel-bandits reportedly connected with the PKI controlled a small tract of territory on the slopes of the Merapi and Merbabu mountains.

The general sense of alarm rose sharply in early August. On August 1 a hand grenade was thrown at a fair in the West Java town of Bogor, injuring 80 persons. On August 3 a Chinese-owned daily in Surabaja, *Java Post*, published a sensational article, subsequently reprinted and quoted elsewhere, in which it claimed that recent arrests of large numbers of persons in the Banjuwangi area of East Java had led the state organs to discover "a foreign-inspired illegal organization" attempting to overthrow the Indonesian government and replace it by a Soviet government. The paper went on to assert that the organization was co-operating with the PKI and mobilizing the energies of Chinese inhabitants of Indonesia.[20] On August 5 an armed gang bearing hammer and sickle symbols attacked a police post at Djakarta's port of Tandjong Priok, and there was shooting for a period of twelve hours, in which a number of policemen were killed and wounded. The PKI immediately denied that it had been involved and called on its supporters to be vigilant in the face of provocation.[21]

On August 7 the cabinet met with the chief public prosecutor and the head of the police, and after the meeting Information Minister Mononutu told the press that "it is the duty of the government to suppress rigorously any antinational movement or action which might impair the government's authority or tend to disturb security. . . . All government authorities have been ordered to act with the utmost severity, within the bounds of existing laws and ordinances." He added that "in my opinion there certainly is a connection between the disturbances in East and West Java." [22] In the following eight days there were arrests in East Java and West Java and arrests and large movements of tanks and armored cars in East Sumatra. The atmosphere in Djakarta was tense. There was dismay about the fact that PKI groups were planning to boycott the government-sponsored Independence Day celebrations on August 17; this was seen as a poignant and painful symbolization of the nation's lack of unity. And there was talk in some quarters of the possibility of another Madiun affair.

On August 16 a large number of prominent persons were arrested. The government announced that it had discovered evidence that the Bogor and Tandjong Priok affairs were related to a wider plot to

[20] Quoted in *Aneta*, Aug. 6, 1951.
[21] *Harian Rakjat* (Djakarta), Aug. 7, 1951.　　　[22] *Aneta*, Aug. 8, 1951.

overthrow the government by *coup d'état*. To prevent this it was con-
ducting a program of large-scale searches and arrests, which were not,
however, according to the government's statement, directed against
any particular ideology or political current. In Djakarta sixteen members of parliament were taken from their beds in the early hours of the
morning. Most of them were either PKI members or members of one
of the small parliamentary fractions which consistently worked with
the PKI. Two Murba parliamentarians and one from the Labor Party
(the party of the current Labor Minister, Tedjasukmana) were arrested for one day, as was the then PRN parliamentarian Abdullah
Aidit, father of D. N. Aidit of the PKI. In addition, a large number of
other persons were arrested in the capital, including labor leaders,
journalists, leaders of the Chinese community, and many of the
leaders of the PKI, but not Aidit, Lukman, Njoto, or Alimin. (Alimin
sought and found sanctuary within the Chinese Embassy.[23])

Outside Djakarta there were security sweeps in a number of towns,
large and small, in Java and Sumatra. Some Masjumi members were
arrested (including, in Bandung, the "radical fundamentalist" and
strongly anti-Communist Masjumi parliamentarian Isa Anshary), the
presumed explanation being that they were suspected of having associations with Darul Islam. But apparently the greatest number of
those arrested were either Chinese or supporters of the PKI. There
were also a number of searches of PKI offices and confiscations of
Communist literature. The arrests continued until the end of the
month. When the Prime Minister reported on them to parliament on
October 29, he gave the number of persons arrested since mid-August
as approximately 15,000.[24]

Initial reactions to the cabinet's drastic action were favorable. It
had cleared the air, and most of the Djakarta press was prepared to

---

[23] *Aneta*, Aug. 16, 1951, and Aug. 1951 *passim*. See also Donald Hindley, "The
Communist Party of Indonesia, 1951–1961: A Decade of the Aidit Leadership"
(doctoral dissertation, Australian National University, 1961), pp. 490–491.

[24] *Antara*, Oct. 29, 1951. For Communist comment see the statement of the
central committee of the PKI, "Tindakan Fasis merugikan Bangsa dan Tanah Air"
("Fascist Actions Harm the Nation and Motherland"), *Bintang Merah*, VII, no. 12–
13 (Aug.–Sept. 1951), 1–3; Iman, "Razzia Agustus, Suatu Bagian dari Rentjana
Pengluasan Perang Amerika" ("The August Raid, a Part of the American Plan to
Expand the War"), *ibid.*, pp. 5–9; S. Utarjo, "Tentang Razzia jang Bertentangan
dengan Hukum dan Keadilan" ("On the Illegal and Unjust Raid"), *Bintang
Merah*, VII, no. 14–15 (Oct.–Nov. 1951), 1–8; and M. H. Lukman, "Beladjar dari
Razzia Agustus" ("Learning from the August Raid"), *Bintang Merah*, VIII, no. 1
(Aug. 1952), 11–19.

believe that there had been fire somewhere under the numerous ill-explained columns of smoke.[25] But within a week a number of doubts gained currency. In the first place, it became known that the raid had completely surprised the great majority of members of the cabinet. Dr. Sukiman had previously asked the cabinet for, and been granted, power to deal with subversion in an emergency manner if this should prove necessary. But most cabinet members had had no idea then that Sukiman wanted to conduct an anti-Communist raid. The plan for the raid had been drawn up by consultation between Dr. Sukiman, one or two other cabinet members, and the chief public prosecutor, Suprapto. The President had, it appeared, indicated that he had no objections. But otherwise there had been no consultation. At the same time it became clear that the choice of persons to be arrested had been made hastily, with a high degree of discretion being left to local authorities, especially *bupatis*, to arrest whomever they considered dangerous to security in their areas. Finally, there was growing impatience at the fact that the government had given no evidence of the existence of the plot it claimed to have forestalled. More and more persons were inclined to believe that Sukiman had acted out of panic and in response to American pressure.

These suspicions remained even after the government had presented its case in parliament. The Prime Minister, speaking on an interpellation of the PSI member Tan Po Goan, found himself in a highly embarrassing position. He initially attempted a defense of the legality of his actions. But the chief public prosecutor had not succeeded in establishing a case for the arrests on any ordinary statutory basis. Furthermore, the army leaders, who had not been consulted when the arrests were planned and strongly resented this fact, refused to support the *post factum* bringing of the arrests into the legal framework of the State of War and Siege.[26]

Thus Dr. Sukiman was obliged to defend himself on purely political grounds. He argued that emergency conditions justified the use of a general warrant for arrests. Then he went on to detail the evidence he had received through the security agencies in early August of dangerous movements of various subversive groups. One Darul Islam unit under the Dutch captain Bosch had been trying to establish links

[25] See the editorials of *Abadi, Pedoman, Indonesia Raya, Merdeka, Java Bode* (Djakarta), and *Waspada* (Medan) in *Aneta*, Aug. 19, 1951.

[26] A. H. Nasution, *Tjatatan-Tjatatan Sekitar Politik Militer Indonesia* ("Notes on Indonesian Military Policy"; Djakarta: Pembimbing, 1955), p. 171.

with gangs in Djakarta, he said. The People's Army had a plan to assassinate cabinet ministers. The old Westerling organization APRA had developed contacts with left-wing political parties. An underground movement of left-wingers financed by a foreign power existed in Djakarta. Finally, news had been received of a planned attempt to kill the President and the Vice-President on their way to West Java mountain resorts.[27] On various of these matters the Prime Minister claimed to have documentary evidence. But he announced no plans for trials of any of those arrested. In fact, there had been a steady trickle of releases of arrested men—though not of Communists—from the latter part of August onward.

But Dr. Sukiman succeeded in rallying parliamentary support for his actions. On November 1 parliament voted on a PSI motion criticizing the government for the raid and, with the two major parties supporting the Prime Minister's action, the motion was lost 91 to 21. There was no strong hostility from the Natsir group of the Masjumi on the issue of the anti-Communist raid, and the PNI too was generally in support, partly because of its disinclination to see the cabinet fall.

As a result of the vote, the PKI was virtually isolated. The attempts it had made earlier in the year to draw closer to the PNI, the smaller nationalist parties, and the smaller Moslem parties had ended in failure. Moreover, its organizational strength and its influence in labor unions was set back markedly. It functioned almost like an underground party for the rest of the period of the Sukiman cabinet. Only in 1953 was it again able to achieve an over-all power position equivalent to the one it had had before August 1951.

There remains the interesting question of why the mass arrest action was taken. In retrospect most Indonesian political leaders believe that no threat of a Communist coup existed in August 1951. One widespread view is that Dr. Sukiman and chief public prosecutor Suprapto drew the logical conclusions from such intelligence materials as had been brought to their attention, but that they had been given inadequate and misleading reports by intelligence agencies, which operated at a low level of efficiency and with too great an addiction to cloak-and-dagger stories. Another widely held view is that Sukiman simply panicked. But neither of these two lines of explanation explains why Sukiman should have acted so secretively in relation to most of the members of his cabinet.

The remaining part of the explanation would seem to lie in the fact

[27] *Antara,* Oct. 29, 1951.

of Dr. Sukiman's strongly anti-communist outlook and to a lesser extent in his lack of strong concern for public liberties. Unlike Hatta and Natsir he worried little about the possibility that he might set unhealthy precedents for the country's development as a constitutional democracy.

Thus one may hypothesize that Sukiman, looking at the situation of early August 1951 and reading reports of links between PKI activity and the activity of the rebel and bandit groups in the mountains, saw an opportunity to deal a major blow to an archenemy, and took it. The fact that Sukiman had a close working relationship with the U.S. ambassador, H. Merle Cochran, cannot have been without importance, particularly as Cochran had come to have a very active interest in Indonesian politics and was zealous, in this year of the Korean War and of McCarthyite power in the United States, to woo Indonesia to a position of more active anticommunism.

TOWARD A PRO-AMERICAN FOREIGN POLICY

Along with its dramatic actions against the local Communists the Sukiman cabinet took a parallel series of steps in the field of foreign relations. In the first place, it placed a number of obstacles in the path of attempts by the Communist Chinese Embassy to play an active role on the Indonesian scene. There had been Indonesian concern throughout 1951 about the large and growing size of the Chinese diplomatic establishment in Djakarta and the influence it had acquired in Indonesia's large Chinese community. And the Indonesian government had become apprehensive about a series of Chinese Embassy actions which violated diplomatic courtesy. Thus the first Chinese consulate had been opened before express approval had been granted by the Indonesian government, and a military attaché had been added to the embassy's staff without prior Indonesian agreement.[28] The Indonesian government had turned down a Chinese request for permission to establish certain other consular offices in particular towns outside the capital.

In July 1951 relations with China became an issue of first-rank importance in Indonesia. On July 22 sixteen persons arriving from China to work in various Chinese consulates in Indonesia were refused permission to enter the country. In reply to a Chinese protest, the secretary-general of the Indonesian Foreign Ministry declared that the refusal

[28] "Violations of Diplomatic Courtesy," *Indonesian Review*, I, no. 4 (July–Sept. 1951), 277–278.

was a response to a Chinese breach of diplomatic courtesy. The sixteen Chinese officials had been given Indonesian visas, the secretary-general admitted. But their names had not been submitted to the Indonesian government for its approval until their ship was a day's sailing distance away from Djakarta. Thus the refusal would stand.[29]

Most of the Indonesian press gave full support to the government. At the same time it gave play to reports that the Indonesian chargé d'affaires in Peking, Ishak Madhi, had been discourteously treated and severely restricted in his movements. And it reiterated charges against the Chinese ambassador in Djakarta, Wang Jen-shu, who had written books accusing Soekarno and Hatta of being traitors to the Indonesian people.[30] Relations continued to be tense for three months, with the Chinese Embassy expressing extreme displeasure at the August raids. October 1 celebrations (of the second anniversary of the Chinese People's Republic) were forbidden by the Indonesian authorities. Later in October there were reports, greeted very favorably by the Indonesian press, that the government was studying the possibility of restricting the movements of foreign (read Chinese) representatives in Indonesia.[31]

But most of the Sukiman government's foreign policy attentions were focused on relations with the United States. And it was here that its actions stirred the two great controversies which eventually led to its downfall.

The first of these political storms developed over Indonesia's signing of the Japanese peace treaty. Initially it was not clear that the government would send representatives to the U.S.-prepared Japanese Peace Treaty Conference at San Francisco or sign the treaty. In July 1951 the Foreign Ministry's secretary-general stated that whether Indonesia participated or not would depend on the final form of the draft

[29] The semigovernmental publication *Indonesian Review* quoted reports to the effect that the average age of the 16 would-be officials was 19. It added that "many people have been wondering whether these persons described as consular officials are not just propagandists" (*ibid.*, p. 278). According to one report this was the third time that China had sent diplomatic and consular representatives to Indonesia without giving prior notice to the Indonesian government (*Aneta*, July 26, 1951).

[30] Wang had worked as a Communist organizer in East Sumatra until expelled from Indonesia by the Dutch during the course of the Revolution (Ruth T. McVey, *The Development of the Indonesian Communist Party and Its Relations with the Soviet Union and the Chinese People's Republic* [Cambridge, Mass.: Center for International Studies, M.I.T., 1954], pp. 66–67).

[31] See *Aneta*, Oct. 13, 15, 16, 21, 1951.

treaty. Meanwhile, he declared, Indonesia was negotiating with other Asian countries with a view to achieving a common standpoint on the issues raised by the projected agreement. On August 4 the Indonesian ambassador to Washington, Mr. Ali Sastroamidjojo, submitted a note with suggestions on the treaty to the U.S. Secretary of State. The note included a general request that Indonesia should obtain "fair and reasonable reparations" and urged that plebiscites be held before territories were detached from Japan (presumably the Ryukyu and Bonin Islands and perhaps also Formosa and the Pescadores). It requested, further, that an opportunity be provided at the San Francisco conference for attending countries to discuss the final text of the treaty and that the Chinese People's Republic and the U.S.S.R. be supported if they expressed the desire to participate in preparing the treaty.[32]

Indonesia was not given U.S. assurances on any of these points other than a general assurance on the matter of reparations. But the cabinet nevertheless decided on August 24 to send Foreign Minister Subardjo to San Francisco. It did so without committing itself to sign the treaty. Whether it signed or not would, it was said, depend on developments in the course of the conference.

Meanwhile Indonesian leaders were increasingly vocal on the issue. Most of the press and most of those parliamentarians and others who spoke out on the planned treaty expressed hostility or at least suspicion. Criticisms were made along many lines; but common to them all was the view that the draft was a purely American product and that for Indonesia to sign it would be to move away from its independent foreign policy and to align itself with the American-led bloc of states in opposition to the Communist bloc. Many critics pointed to the close connection which existed between the treaty and American plans for a separate military agreement with Japan (and others with the Philippines and Australia and New Zealand). For Indonesia to sign the treaty, these men warned, would be to yield a further step under American pressure, a further step toward Indonesia's incorporation in an American military bloc. When it became known that neither India nor Burma would send delegations to the conference, the argument was presented that for Indonesia to send a delegation would be to break decisively with the really independent and uncommitted states of Asia—and to desert friends who had rendered great help when Indonesia was fighting for its freedom. Indonesia's relations with

[32] *Aneta,* Aug. 4, 1951.

Japan were an Asian matter, it was strongly maintained, one best settled by bilateral arrangements between these two powers.

Those who favored Indonesia's signing the treaty mostly preferred to take a stand on practical rather than ideological grounds. The treaty had its defects, these men admitted, but it would go through anyway, and it would be to Indonesia's advantage to sign it and thus establish a basis on which later to negotiate reparation and fishing zone agreements with Japan. But on a matter so close to the central core of nationalist ideology it was impossible to argue for long on nonideological grounds. Thus the supporters of the treaty averred that signing it would not mean abandoning the independent policy. One had to distinguish, they maintained, between a "neutral" and an "independent" policy. An independent policy was a matter of judging each new international situation on its own merits and without yielding to the pressure of others. Such a policy could not be "static." Finally, there was a third series of arguments. Some supporters of the treaty said directly that a third power in Asia was in practice impossible to achieve, that Indonesia was geographically and strategically in the Anglo-American sphere, and that it needed foreign help to protect it against the threat of communism, domestic and international.[33] Sometimes this was coupled with the argument that an alliance with the United States was Indonesia's only hope of realizing its claim to West Irian in the near future. But this third group of arguments was rarely presented in public discussion.

The cabinet could decide its policy on the treaty only after long debate within the leadership of the two large parties. The Masjumi's large party council (of which Dr. Sukiman was chairman) met continuously from September 4 to September 6, and a major tussle of strength developed between the group of Sukiman and Jusuf Wibisono who supported the signing of the treaty and the group of Natsir, Roem, and Sjafruddin who stood opposed. The Sukiman group finally won on a 17 to 14 vote with 2 abstentions.[34] In the PNI the exact line-up of forces inside the party is not clear, though it is known that several prominent leaders associated with the older Sartono-Suwirjo group of the party, including Ali Sastromidjojo, who was currently ambassador to Washington, championed the signing of the treaty. In any event the final PNI decision taken by the party executive on September 7 was

[33] Dr. Sukiman himself took roughly this point of view. See *Suara Masjumi* (Masjumi periodical, Djakarta), Oct. 1951, quoted in Noer, *op. cit.*
[34] For a full discussion of this debate see Noer, *op. cit.*

to oppose the signing. Thus when the cabinet finally voted on the instructions to be sent to Subardjo in San Francisco its two main parties were on opposite sides. The decision to sign, taken on the evening of September 7, a few hours before the actual signing was to take place, was reached by a 10 to 6 vote. The Masjumi, PIR, Catholic, and Democratic ministers and the nonparty minister Djuanda supported the signing. The PNI ministers and the minister of the Labor Party were opposed.[35]

For several days it was thought that the Masjumi-PNI split might bring about the fall of the government. This was one interpretation of a statement of the PNI's chairman Sidik to the effect that his party would oppose parliamentary ratification of the treaty. But Sidik soon made it clear that he was opposed to seeing the cabinet fall on this issue. Subsequently, on September 30, the PNI's large party council upheld the Sidik position. Although the party would continue to oppose ratification, it would not support any parliamentary move for an early debate on the treaty. With this, the matter was disposed of. If a challenge to the Sukiman cabinet had existed—and it almost certainly had, particularly when the Prime Minister came so close to being disavowed by his own party—it had passed. The Japanese peace treaty was never ratified by the Indonesian parliament.

One aspect of the Sukiman cabinet's victory on the issue was the skill and energy which Subardjo had displayed in diplomacy related to the treaty. He and the Philippine negotiators had succeeded in persuading the United States to include in it a provision for bilateral reparations agreements between Japan and countries it had occupied. Then he had elicited a verbal promise of such a treaty from Japanese Prime Minister Yoshida, speaking from the floor of the conference. Subsequently he had held discussions with Yoshida, and these resulted in informal agreement on some of the items to be covered in the projected bilateral agreement.[36]

[35] *Antara*, Sept. 8, 1951.

[36] *Aneta*, Sept. 13, 1951. Negotiations for a bilateral treaty were begun in Tokyo in Dec. 1951 by an Indonesian delegation headed by Communications Minister Djuanda. But it was soon found that agreement on the major issues would be difficult to reach. Indonesia came in the course of the talks to agree to the principle that reparations payments should be scaled to Japan's ability to pay. But there remained great differences between the parties on the matter of the amount, the forms, and the timing of the reparations payments. The Indonesian delegation returned home in January, with full agreement having been reached only on the zoning of fisheries. See Sajoeti Melik, "Perdjandjian Bilateral dengan Djepang" ("The Bilateral Treaty with Japan"), *Mimbar Indonesia*, Jan. 26, 1952. A new

Before leaving the United States, Subardjo had discussed a $50 million loan with Secretary of State Acheson and apparently succeeded in having Indonesia placed in a special category of countries which were eligible to receive U.S. economic and technical assistance despite the fact that they were engaged in trade with Communist bloc countries.[37] The Foreign Minister capped off his overseas tour with a surprise visit to Australia, where he was warmly welcomed by government leaders, held discussions on the West Irian question with them, and succeeded in evoking an unusually favorable reaction from the press. Indonesia had reached a high-water mark in its relations with the (non-Dutch) West.[38]

However, if it was hoped that this would result in an early settlement of the Irian issue in Indonesia's favor, the hope was quickly destroyed. In August the Sukiman cabinet had sent Professor Supomo, the chairman of the Natsir cabinet's Special State Commission on the Netherlands-Indonesian Union, to conduct informal negotiations in the Netherlands on both the Irian question and the proposed abrogation of the Union. But Supomo was kept waiting till December before formal talks were begun. Meanwhile Dutch-Indonesian antagonisms were fanned high by a series of other developments. In early November the Dutch government had submitted to its parliament a proposal to write "Netherlands New Guinea" into the clause of its constitution which defined the territory of the kingdom. Then on December 7 Indonesian authorities in Djakarta's harbor of Tandjong Priok had seized arms from two Dutch merchantmen, arms which were being taken to West Irian. There had been protests and counterprotests at the governmental level and from radically nationalist Indonesian political leaders a number of demands for tough action against the Dutch. Indeed, the political atmosphere in Indonesia was similar

---

series of reparations talks was held late in 1953, but this produced no more than agreement on the salvaging by the Japanese government of vessels sunk in Indonesian waters during the war. Only in March 1958 did the Indonesian parliament ratify a full settlement of the matter. Japan then agreed to pay $223 million in goods over a 12-year period, and $400 million in private economic co-operation projects approved by the two governments, and to cancel Indonesian trade debts amounting to $177 million. See Willard A. Hanna, *Bung Karno's Indonesia* (New York: American Universities Field Staff, 1960), Pt. xxi, pp. 1–4.

[37] *Abadi*, quoted in *Aneta*, Sept. 23, 1951.

[38] Shortly after Mr. Subardjo's return home, Dr. Sukiman declined for a second time an invitation from Burma's Prime Minister Nu to attend a projected Nehru-Nu-Sukiman meeting in New Delhi. He accepted "in principle," but asked for a postponement (*Antara*, Oct. 3, 21; *Aneta*, Oct. 9, 12, 1951).

to what it had been when the Irian issue had been hot in the last months of 1950. The negotiations remained deadlocked.

Moreover, the Indonesian government's effectiveness in treating with the Dutch was lessened by its own disunity. While in late 1950 there had been division between the President and the (Natsir) cabinet, there was now division inside the (Sukiman) cabinet between its PNI and Masjumi components. Whereas the Masjumi was prepared to accept deadlock on the issue of Irian and go on to conclude an agreement on the matter of abrogation of the Union (on which the two governments were close to agreement), the PNI insisted that the two matters should be regarded as interwoven and inseparable. In February, Professor Supomo presented the Dutch with a final compromise proposal for Irian, a proposal for Indonesian-Dutch "joint responsibility" for the area, with administrative co-operation "on a practical level" and with the problem of sovereignty to continue to be discussed.[39] But the Netherlands government reacted coolly, making it clear informally that it could not accept the proposal. It had not yet replied to the proposal formally when on February 23 the Sukiman cabinet resigned and called the Supomo mission to come home.

THE ISSUE OF MUTUAL SECURITY AID

It was on the second major controversy arising from the Sukiman cabinet's pro-Western position in foreign policy that the cabinet was obliged to step down. This controversy stemmed from the Foreign Minister's acceptance of U.S. aid on the terms of the Mutual Security Act of 1951. Under this act responsibility for all United States military, economic, and technical assistance was vested in a single person, the Director for Mutual Security. In President Truman's words, "The change in emphasis of the economic aid program—from recovery to defense support—intensified the need for co-ordination between the Economic Cooperation Administration and the Department of Defense." [40]

The act required that all nations wishing to continue to receive any sort of U.S. assistance should declare themselves committed to certain

[39] See *Pedoman,* March 7, 1952, and Robert C. Bone, Jr., *The Dynamics of the Western New Guinea (Irian Barat) Problem* (Cornell Modern Indonesia Project, Interim Reports Series; Ithaca, N.Y., 1958), p. 115; also F. J. F. M. Duynstee, *Nieuw Guinea als Schakel tussen Nederland en Indonesië* (Amsterdam: Bezige Bij, 1961), pp. 206–208.

[40] *First Report to Congress on the Implementation of the Mutual Security Act of 1951.* Dec. 1, 1951.

agreements, somewhat different from those they had already entered. Economic and technical aid would be given to a state under Section 511b of the act if the giving of this aid would

strengthen the security of the United States and further world security, provided that the receiving State has committed itself to co-operate in the furthering of international understanding and goodwill and the promotion of world security, and to take steps as agreed upon for the abolition of international tensions.[41]

If on the other hand a state wished to receive military as well as economic and technical assistance, it was obliged, under Section 511a of the act, to commit itself to the following:

(1) To take joint steps to further international understanding, goodwill and security;
(2) To take steps as agreed upon for the abolition of international tensions;
(3) Fulfill the military obligations which it has already accepted in bilateral or multilateral treaties of which the United States is a partner;
(4) Make a full contribution, consistent with its political and economic capacity, its population, natural resources, facilities and general economic situation, to the development and maintenance of its own defenses and to the defensive strength of the free world;
(5) Take the necessary steps to develop its own defensive strength;
(6) Take reasonable measures to ensure the most effective use of the economic and military aid provided by the United States.

In a note to U.S. Ambassador Merle Cochran the Indonesian Foreign Minister, Subardjo, on January 5, 1952, committed Indonesia to acceptance of Mutual Security aid on the basis of Section 511a of the act, it being made clear that his note had the force of an international agreement. He did, however, or so it appears, insist on two modifications of the conditions laid down in the act.[42] The third of the points in Section 511a fell away entirely (not a very important change), and the words "and military" were omitted from point 6. Significantly— and for the Sukiman cabinet characteristically—this important step was taken without cabinet discussion. Ambassador Cochran's note of January 4 asked for a reply by January 8, thus giving the cabinet little time, though enough for a cabinet meeting to be called for the purpose. But this was not done. Prime Minister Sukiman was informed

---

[41] *Ibid.*
[42] Opposition critics suggested that these changes were in fact not made in the original.

of Subardjo's decision, as were several other cabinet members. It is probable that President Soekarno knew of it. Certainly, however, the Minister of Defense, Sewaka, was not informed. And, still more important politically, neither were any members of the armed forces high command.

It was not until a month later that the agreement became public knowledge. On February 4 the ministers of PIR, roused by the report of Defense Minister Sewaka on approaches made to him on the matter by U.S. officials, asked for a cabinet discussion. The following day the news was broken in the Djakarta daily *Abadi,* the voice of the Natsir group of Masjumi. On February 7 *Indonesia Raya,* often called the paper of the army command, headlined a rumor that the defense section of parliament would bring in an interpellation on the matter. Public interest was mounting rapidly.

On the following day, February 8, the cabinet discussed the issue for the first time. Objection was taken particularly to the conditions laid down in point 4 of Section 511a of the Mutual Security Act, and Subardjo was instructed to do his best to persuade the U.S. ambassador to accept a *post factum* change on this point. He was to try to have the point omitted altogether, or, if this proved impossible, to have the words "and the defensive strength of the free world" left out or, if this was also unacceptable, to obtain a statement that the United States accepted Indonesia's interpretation of the words "free world."

It was eleven days before the U.S. ambassador's reply to these requests was received, and these days were critical for the Sukiman cabinet. Those sections of the press which had long been attacking the cabinet now said that it was about to collapse and urged that it be replaced by a "business cabinet" to carry on till general elections were held.[43] Their case against Subardjo and the Sukiman cabinet received a more strongly favorable response than ever before.

The immediate circumstances of the case were the most obvious grounds for criticism. The rapid passing on February 14 of a parliamentary motion of Mr. Sunario (PNI) to the effect that all foreign treaties had to be ratified by parliament reflected the state of feeling against "secret diplomacy."[44] The fact that Subardjo and Cochran had tried to conceal their agreement, combined with the lack of a

[43] *Pedoman,* Feb. 11, 1952. *Pedoman* had close links with the Socialist Party. See also *Indonesia Raya* and *Abadi.*

[44] This motion, sponsored by the Foreign Affairs section of parliament, called for the strict interpretation of Articles 120 and 121 of the constitution. The government accepted the interpretation as set forth by Sunarjo.

clear explanation even when it had become a crucial issue, produced the strongest of suspicions.[45]

But more important in explaining the resentment which was felt was the general Indonesian attitude toward the United States and particularly toward U.S. attempts to bring Indonesia into fuller alignment with the U.S.-led bloc of states. The signing of the M.S.A. agreement, coming as it did on top of the signing of the San Francisco treaty (and coming as the action of a cabinet which had inaugurated repression of the PKI), seemed to strike at the very roots of the independent foreign policy. And this policy had become a cardinal symbol and central ideological tenet of the nation.[46]

In one sense the "independent (foreign) policy" was less than a policy—merely the agglomeration of the ideas of all groups of the political elite about foreign policy generally. Such was the prestige value of the term "independent policy" that, like "democracy" or "progress," it was applied by all groups to their own varying concepts of policy.

It was indeed given a variety of meanings. For some groups it meant an isolationist independence of the two world blocs, while others emphasized that independence was necessarily a relative thing not to be considered except in relation to Indonesia's concrete national interests. For some it meant a commitment to neutrality in the event of world war, while others merely emphasized not being committed in advance to either bloc, preferring to defer all mention of what would happen in this event. Advocates of closer alignment with the

[45] According to the *New York Times* of Feb. 25, 1952, the State Department's communication to Cochran had suggested that an economic agreement under Section 511b of the act would suffice for Indonesia, but the ambassador had asked the State Department to reconsider this advice, undertaking instead to induce Subardjo to accept the terms of Section 511a. This same source has it also that Cochran refused to allow the chief of the M.S.A. mission in Indonesia to participate in drafting the agreement, even declining to see him for a period of three weeks. See Kahin, "Indonesian Politics and Nationalism," in Holland, ed., *op. cit.*, p. 193. It would appear that Subardjo had never been told of the possibility that Indonesia could receive aid under Section 511b.

[46] For discussions of the policy in these earlier years of the postrevolutionary period see Mohammad Hatta, "Indonesia's Foreign Policy," *Foreign Affairs*, XXXI (April 1953), 441–452, and Kahin, "Indonesian Politics and Nationalism," in Holland, ed., *op. cit.*, pp. 169–178. See also Mohammad Roem, *Politik Indonesia 1952* ("Indonesian Policy, 1952"; Djakarta: Penjiaran Ilmu, 1952); *Tindjauan Politik dan Ekonomi Kita pada Dewasa ini* ("A Review of Our Politics and Economics at the Present Time"; Djakarta: Kementerian Penerangan, 1951); and "The Historical and Philosophical Background of Our Independent Policy," *Indonesian Affairs*, vol. I, no. 7 (July 1951).

United States found it useful to use the term, arguing that an independent policy was one which took Indonesia's internal requirements seriously. Communists used the term to mean the same as an "anti-imperialist" policy. No one was against the independent foreign policy, not at any rate in public. It was aptly said that it was a sort of ideological prism through which all practical policies had to be refracted.

Nevertheless, there was, at least within the main body of the nationalist movement, a commonly accepted core of meaning, which gave the term a certain precision and made it more than merely a prestige word. Practically all nationalists agreed that it was a policy of optimal independence of outside countries, that it was based on Indonesia's national interests, which included world peace, and on the desire for maximum opportunity for Indonesians to shape their society as they themselves wanted to, to prevent Indonesia from becoming either another power's political or cultural appendage or an ideological battlefield. A considerable majority of these nationalists agreed this involved working for a degree of independence of the two power blocs that permitted good relations with both and established a position from which third-party moves to promote conciliation would be possible. They added that such a degree of independence would eliminate the possibility of either bloc's having to fear that Indonesia would be used aggressively against it by the other. For quite a number of them the policy involved working for an independent Asian or Asian-Arab bloc which could ultimately perhaps hold a balance of power in world politics.

It is in the light of this type of thinking that the resentment of the Subardjo-Cochran agreement is to be understood. It is not clear how far Indonesia would have been committed to U.S. policies by the agreement if it had not later been superseded. But the symbolism of it, the insistence that Indonesia should make a formal ideological surrender by putting its signature to a statement of the ideas of the U.S. Congress about the nature of the world struggle—this was utterly irksome.

The supporters of the agreement argued that it was merely an executive step, that it did not involve a policy change.[47] They pointed to the fact that since the little-publicized Constabulary Agreement of August 1950 Indonesia had been receiving small amounts of military equipment—vehicles, radio sets, small arms, and so on—for its police

[47] *Keng Po,* Feb. 12, 1952.

force,[48] and they went on to argue that the Subardjo-Cochran agreement was an organizational arrangement for continuation of this, not a political step toward greater dependence on America. Others argued that it was necessary for Indonesia to accept aid under Section 511a of the act, rather than 511b, because this would enable it to buy arms and equipment which had been unprocurable in the United States or Europe except in exchange for political guarantees.[49] All these groups held that Indonesia's need for U.S. military supplies was greater than that of countries like India, Pakistan, or Burma, which had accepted aid under Section 511b only because they were either receiving military equipment through the British Commonwealth or had arms factories of their own. Less publicly some supporters of the agreement argued that Indonesia did indeed need to ally itself with the United States militarily for protection against Communist power.

As against these groups, the great majority who opposed the agreement recalled the fact that the Natsir government had refused U.S. military aid when this was offered by the Melby mission of the Departments of State and Defense in October 1950. They drew attention to a note which Ambassador Cochran had sent to the government on January 22, 1952, asking for a guarantee, which the cabinet did not give, that controls would be placed on Indonesian exports to countries of the Soviet bloc. Many of them argued that for internal security and political stability it was better to do without overseas equipment if the cost of obtaining it was a further strengthening of those groups in Indonesia which alleged that the Revolution had been betrayed by compromise with foreign powers. National unity, they said, required that the Cold War be kept out. If Indonesia was to continue to yield to American endeavors to include it in an anti-Communist bloc, there would soon be, they insisted, a point of no return as far as any independent foreign policy was concerned.

On February 12 came a major blow to the cabinet. The Masjumi executive, following its chairman Natsir, decided that "the Masjumi is unable to be responsible for the signing of the agreement concern-

[48] See *Third Semi-annual Report to Congress on the M.D.A.P.*, House Document no. 179, June 25, 1951.

[49] E.g., Jusuf Wibisono in *Mimbar Indonesia*, April 19, 1952. According to Kahin ("Indonesian Politics and Nationalism," in Holland, ed., *op. cit.*, p. 193), Indonesia desired some help in purchasing additional small arms during 1952. This was to be done outside M.S.A. or other U.S. government agencies but would have required some help in obtaining priorities.

ing Mutual Security Agency aid which has taken place." [50] This was followed four days later by a decision of the PNI executive to the effect that "the cabinet should return its mandate to the President in order to overcome the present difficulties." [51] It was a somewhat ambiguous statement, for there was no indication of when the PNI would want the mandate to be returned, and this was interpreted in the light of earlier statements by PNI leaders to the effect that a cabinet crisis should be avoided while negotiations were going on with the Netherlands about the future of Irian and the Netherlands-Indonesian Union.

For some days the issue was held in abeyance. The parties were known to be at variance on whether the cabinet should take a decision on the Subardjo-Cochran agreement. The small parties wanted a cabinet vote on the issue, but both the Masjumi and the PNI were against it, partly because of fear that this would further add to their own internal divisions and partly because they expected such a vote to complicate the task of forming a new cabinet.

On February 19 came Ambassador Cochran's reply to the requests the cabinet had made of his government at its meeting of February 8. The State Department, it read, was not prepared to agree to a *post factum* omission of the fourth point of the agreement which Subardjo had signed. But it had agreed that this point should be interpreted as follows:

Make a full contribution, consistent with its political and economic capacity, *as determined by the Indonesian Government* and with its population, natural resources, facilities and general economic situation, to the development and maintenance of its own defenses and to the defensive strength of the *free and sovereign countries.* [My italics.]

The answer strengthened the cabinet's position slightly. But it had come too late. It was clear that a preponderance of power was now with those who wanted to see Sukiman fall. On February 21 the cabinet passed a motion disapproving Subardjo's handling of the matter, whereupon the Foreign Minister, in accordance with his letter to the cabinet on February 11, resigned. Even this, however, was not enough. Prime Minister Sukiman had shared responsibility with Subardjo for

[50] Jusuf Wibisono in *Mimbar Indonesia,* April 19, 1952. Jusuf stated that the decision of the executive council was not the Masjumi's final decision as it still had to be approved by the larger party council or legislative council (headed by Dr. Sukiman). However, as no meeting of the legislative council was held to review the executive's decision, the latter was binding on the Masjumi ministers.

[51] *Antara,* Feb. 17, 1952.

the agreement, and so had several other cabinet members; their abandonment of Subardjo was therefore regarded as unprincipled.[52] In any case it was clear that the cabinet could not execute policy with a bearing on Mutual Security aid. It faced the prospect of having to give a full explanation of its actions in reply to a parliamentary interpellation on the matter, which was to be debated on February 25.

There seemed only one way out of the situation. On February 23 the cabinet decided unanimously to return its mandate to the President. It did so, it stated, "to improve the political atmosphere so that the difficulties which have arisen from the signing of the Mutual Security Agreement may be able to be overcome." It had not taken any attitude or decision on the agreement itself. A government broadcast of the same day stated that "the resignation of the cabinet should not be construed as meaning that the State would shirk its obligations arising from an agreement with a foreign country."[53]

In retrospect it is clear that the M.S.A. crisis was only one of the major causes of the Sukiman cabinet's fall. The fact that it fell when it did was due to the way in which its actions on the matter of U.S. aid had violated the ideological consensus on foreign policy prevailing in the political public. But pressures against the cabinet had been building up for many months.

On a number of issues with which the cabinet had attempted to deal, uncompromisable or near-uncompromisable differences of policy had developed between the Masjumi and the PNI—with the result that the cabinet had to resort to inaction to avert threats to its continued existence. It has been shown how this happened in the case of the San Francisco treaty. Also noticed was how the conflicting positions of the two main parties of the cabinet made negotiation with the Netherlands difficult for the Supomo mission. Furthermore, there was still deadlock between the parties on the matter of the regional legislative councils: it was clear from at least November 1951 onward that the two main parties could not agree on a basis on which interim regional councils could be established as an alternative to the basis laid down in the old Regulation 39 of 1950.[54] These paralyzing intracabinet cleavages were pointed to by opponents of the cabinet as evidence

[52] *Abadi,* Feb. 13, 1952; statement by Mr. Djody Gondokusumo in *Indonesia Raya,* Feb. 23, 1952.

[53] *Indonesian Affairs,* vol. II, no. 1 (Feb.–March 1952).

[54] See Sajuti Melik, "Pemandangan Dalam Negeri" ("Views on the Home Situation"), *Mimbar Indonesia,* Nov. 10, 1951.

of the need for a government established on a completely new basis. And many in the government parties were convinced that there was no other way out of the existing frustrations.

In the case of this cabinet too, as in the case of its predecessor, the "time for someone else to have a turn at being minister" factor was operative. This was rarely given direct expression in public statements, but there were a number of predictions of the early fall of the cabinet long before the M.S.A. crisis began. In December, Mr. Tadjuddin Noor, the chairman of the PIR parliamentary fraction, declared that the "cabinet may fall in March if there is no decrease in the price of commodities or if it fails to give economic support to national enterprises." The *Antara* report continues: "He added that in March the cabinet would be ten months old and thus had enjoyed much opportunity to work. If it falls, it cannot be said that people like cabinet crises." [55] Surely, Tadjuddin seemed to be saying, one could not be thought irresponsible for wanting a cabinet change after ten months. His party was one of those with a high turnover of individuals included in the various successive cabinets.

The Socialist Party, as a group with a clear interest in seeing the cabinet fall, had been campaigning since late 1951 for early elections and for the idea that Indonesia should be governed by a "business cabinet" until elections had been held. It had been working actively with the Natsir group of the Masjumi and also with individuals and groups in the PNI which sympathized with Sjahrir and Natsir positions. Its influence within the press, both in Djakarta and in regional centers, was brought to bear particularly in the last three weeks of the cabinet's life.[56] But before that Socialist-influenced newspapers had been hammering effectively on a number of anti-Sukiman themes. They had stressed the divisions inside the cabinet, its readiness to resort to horse-trading compromises, and its consequent inability to provide the country with inspiring leadership. They had attacked the government for its shortcomings with regard to the first point of its program, the restoration of security. They had attacked it for encouraging an inflow of large cars and other luxury commodities, while doing nothing to keep down the price of rice (which in fact rose unusually

[55] *Antara*, Dec. 10, 1951.

[56] On Feb. 25. 1952, two days after the cabinet's fall, *Abadi*, which usually spoke for the Natsir group of the Masjumi, said editorially that "directly or indirectly the press helped to throw out the old cabinet." On the same day *Pedoman*, which usually reflected the PSI position rather closely, ran a cartoon headed "A Victory for the Press."

steeply in the preharvest months of December 1951 to February 1952).[57] And they had criticized it for its tendency to yield before American pressure, thus compromising the independent foreign policy. For a great part of the political public, these were most effective appeals.

But if opinion within the political public and factional pressures inside the main government parties were two main elements of the power which brought down the cabinet, the leadership of the army was a third. There is some doubt whether army pressure for the cabinet to resign was exerted directly at the time of the M.S.A. crisis. But members of the political elite were given the clear impression that the army leaders would be pleased to see Sukiman step down. This was certainly a major factor in bringing the cabinet to admit defeat.

THE CABINET AND THE LEADERS OF THE ARMY

At this point it would be well to review the history of relations between the Sukiman cabinet and the army. We have referred to a number of instances where co-operation between these two was conspicuously lacking. We have seen how the army reacted to Justice Minister Yamin's action in releasing political prisoners without the army leaders' approval. We saw too how the army leaders refused to assist the Prime Minister when he sought to invoke the State of War and Siege regulations as a legal cover for the August mass arrests. In the case of these arrests, as with the earlier releases, the cabinet had not consulted the army leaders, and the same pattern repeated itself over the matter of the agreement on Mutual Security aid.

Nor were these the only signs of conflict. In August 1951 Defense Minister Sewaka told Parliament that he was not prepared to assume responsibility for his ministry's 1951 budget since this had been prepared by his predecessor.[58] The statement was interpreted as a sign of conflict on budgetary matters between him and the armed forces leaders. On December 7 an army battalion located at Kudus, Central Java, mutinied and began an attempt to establish itself as a Central Java section of Darul Islam. The reaction of the territorial commander for Central Java was to do everything to capture the mutineers, and he engaged some of them in fighting. Then on December 12—if one is to believe the report of the Semarang daily *Suara Merdeka* (whose

[57] The Java Bank, *Report for the Financial Year 1951–1952* (Djakarta, 1952), pp. 74–76.
[58] *Aneta*, Aug. 7, 1951.

editor was jailed for publishing it)—Prime Minister Sukiman sent a
cable to one of the battalion commanders who was pursuing the
mutineers, asking him to desist from any harsh action against them.[59]
In a press interview given in Jogjakarta near the area of the mutiny
in early February, Defense Minister Sewaka denied rumors that there
was a rift between him and the army's Chief of Staff, Colonel Nasution.
But he added: "The army in particular must realize that besides strong
and firm measures one must not forget justice and humanity or offend
religious sentiment." [60]

To understand these antagonisms between the Sukiman cabinet and
the army, one needs to remember not only the frequent conflicts between the civilian government and the army during the Revolution,
but also the very great political and governmental role which the
army had played in the period of Revolution. For many Indonesians,
particularly village dwellers, the army *was* the Republic in this period.
Particular army commanders were treated with respect and awe by the
inhabitants of their areas of command, and often with great affection.
At the same time they came to feel a strong sense of obligation to act
as guardians and defenders of these local people.

With the cessation of hostilities and the transfer of sovereignty much
of this had to change. The army had to be reduced in size, it had to
accept a working relationship with former soldiers of the KNIL, and
its members had to adjust themselves to a new situation of routinization and boredom. Furthermore, it had to accept a radical reduction of
its power and prestige. If constitutional democracy was to be the
state's form of government—and the army leaders supported this, or
at least accepted it without public grumbling—then civilians would
sway predominant power in government affairs at all levels and hold
an exclusive right on political activity. Regional commanders would
be deprived of their formal claims to the actual control of government
activity (this would be partly so while the State of War and Siege
regulations applied, and all the more so once they were lifted in particular areas), and official obstacles would be placed in the way of
their claims to represent the interests of the people in their area of
command. Large numbers of army officers would fall in the prestige
scale of their communities in relation to civilians of comparable rank.

Clearly it was a political task of major proportions to induce the
army to accept this change in its status. The Hatta and Natsir cabinets

[59] *Antara*, Dec. 18, 1951; *Aneta*, Dec. 19, 1951.
[60] See Sewaka, *Tjorat-Tjaret* ("Sketches"; n.p., 1955), p. 309.

had worked at the task with considerable success, co-operating as they did with the "administrator" group of army leaders, men like Colonels T. B. Simatupang and A. H. Nasution. By the time these two cabinets had completed their work the army was not only a far more cohesive and well-disciplined force, but also several steps further removed than in 1949 from participation in government and politics.

It is important to understand, however, that this was not a simple surrender of power on the army's part, but rather a conditional arrangement. The army leaders who worked closely with the cabinets of Hatta and Natsir did not do so to create a nonpolitical army in the Western sense. Such a goal would have been impossible of realization, and they would have had no interest in its realization. Their endeavor was rather to reorganize the ramshackle forces in such a way that the political pressure which army officers would inevitably seek to apply would be brought to bear centrally at the level of the cabinet, rather than diffusely at a variety of regional levels. Their aim was to build a strong, cohesive army with high professional standards and a good name in the community generally. To do this they believed they should withdraw their subordinate officers from political and governmental participation at regional and local levels and thus remove them from temptations of corruption and officiousness and free them for more intensive military training.

But the army leaders were not committed to doctrines of civilian supremacy. Several of them continued to speak of the army as a guardian of the state and the people, implying that they might subsequently claim the role of saving the state or the people from the civilian politicians. They stressed that the army was and would remain a political body, that it was composed of nationalists who had joined the force from political conviction, not to earn a living, and could not therefore be stripped of political influence. In effect, they insisted that the assistance they had given to civilian governments in withdrawing their subordinates from politics at the regional and local levels implied a *quid pro quo*. That *quid pro quo* was a great amount of influence for themselves as the army's central leaders in all such affairs of cabinet politics as affected the army's interests and tasks.

The terms of this informal reciprocal arrangement were adhered to in the period of the Hatta and Natsir cabinets. Army leaders then frequently attended cabinet meetings and had great influence on decisions affecting the army. Moreover, their interests were well served by the Sultan of Jogjakarta, a civilian who had played an active military role in the Revolution and was highly respected in the army. But in addition to pressing army interests in the cabinet, the Sultan pressed civilian viewpoints on the army. Thus he was responsible for much of the success achieved in restraining antipolitician feeling in the army. Cabinet-army frictions existed in this period, notably over army arrests of West Java Masjumi members suspected of supporting the Darul Islam [61] and over Natsir's decision (of which the army was not told) to send the Masjumi leader, Wali Alfatah, as an envoy to Kartosuwirjo of the Darul Islam. But they were not of great importance.

With the formation of the Sukiman cabinet a new situation developed in cabinet-army relations. At the time of the cabinet's formation the army leaders asked that the Sultan be given the portfolio of Defense, and the post was offered to him. But the Sultan declined, apparently because of dissatisfaction with the political character of the projected cabinet. When Sewaka of PIR was given the post, the army leaders felt slighted and resentful.

Sewaka, hitherto the Governor of West Java, was a man of the older generation—he was 56 whereas Nasution was 33 and Simatupang 31 —and, unlike every previous Defense Minister since 1945, he was not a first-ranking political figure. Thus relations between him and the army leaders were strained from the beginning. It was not that the army leaders regarded Sewaka as a politician put above them to keep them in order, but rather that they had wanted a minister who would actively assist them in the work of army reorganization and generally in promoting army interests as they saw them. When they found that Sewaka was not particularly interested in this and that he sought to establish his own contacts with officer factions hostile to their leadership, the sense of strain developed into a sharp feeling of resentment. It was stimulated further when they found that Prime Minister Sukiman was prepared to ignore them repeatedly in making decisions which they saw as directly related to their own sphere of activity.

Consequently the army leaders tended more and more to act without consulting any cabinet members. There was a marked decline in close contacts between the top leaders of the army on the one hand and the Defense Minister and the rest of the cabinet on the other. The army leaders tended to see the cabinet as a group of incompetent and reckless old men who did not know that to arouse the anger of

[61] See *Pertanjaan Anggota dan Djawaban Pemerintah* ("Members' Questions and Government Replies"; Djakarta: D.P.R.–R.I.S., 1950), I, 47. See also *Aneta*, Jan. 15, 23, 1951.

the army was to play with fire. The members of the cabinet looked at the Simatupang-Nasution group of army leaders as merely one faction in army politics and a faction which chose to be the military arm of the cabinet leaders' political rivals, the Natsir-Sjahrir-sympathizing younger generation of politicians.

Conflict between the army leadership and the cabinet developed particularly over the matter of the army's work in restoring security in rebel-torn areas. On the question of how the campaign against the Darul Islam was to be fought there had been cabinet-army friction long before the Sukiman cabinet took office. In general terms the issue was that the army insisted that it should have a free hand in pressing a military solution, whereas political party leaders, and especially Masjumi leaders, argued that a political and religious approach was necessary to win away the rebels' popular support. This issue was often most sharply focused on the role of Masjumi branches in the areas of conflict. Masjumi leaders in Djakarta argued that these branches offered the strongly Moslem population there a real alternative to supporting the Darul Islam, whereas army leaders tended to see the branches as harboring Darul Islam sympathizers and agents. Masjumi leaders, and often the leaders of other parties as well, protested whenever large numbers of persons in the areas of fighting were arrested. Army leaders resented every attempt of political leaders to intervene and particularly all attempts to negotiate with the Darul Islam.[62]

The Sukiman cabinet was in fact more disposed to seek a tough military solution to the Darul Islam problem than the Natsir cabinet had been. This was its announced policy, and its actions were substantially in accordance with it. Nevertheless, much of the same pattern of army-cabinet conflict continued to exist, and it was now aggravated by lack of close personal liaison between the army leaders and the cabinet. A further aggravating factor was the fact that government and army efforts to diminish the proportions of the rebel-bandit problem were failing.

Reviewing the situation from the time of the transfer of sovereignty,

---

[62] For the army view see Nasution, *Tjatatan-Tjatatan Sekitar Politik Militer*, pp. 160, 180, and *passim*. For one Masjumi view see M. Natsir, *Djangan Ditempuh Djalan Buntu* ("Let Us Not Walk down a Blind Alley"; Djakarta: Hikmah, 1952), *passim*. For a theoretical discussion of the difficulties of civilian control over the military in situations of "intrastate war" (which call for the merging of political and military roles on both sides) see Samuel P. Huntington, "Politics, Violence and the Military: Some Preliminary Hypotheses," paper presented before the American Political Science Association, New York, 1960.

one finds a fairly steady diminution of rebel and bandit power for a period of some eighteen months. The year 1950 saw a general strengthening of the government's military authority and the defeat of the three rebellions in which KNIL soldiers were involved, the Westerling, Aziz, and "Republic of the South Moluccas" revolts. The first half of 1951 saw a diminution of the power of the various bands of old Republican guerrillas still outside the government's control. It saw the negotiation of an agreement with Kahar Muzakar, the powerful leader of Republican guerrillas in South Sulawesi, as well as the effective suppression of a sizable wave of banditry by PKI-connected groups and others in several areas of East Java.[63]

Thus by the middle of 1951 the over-all situation had improved greatly. Secure conditions prevailed throughout Sumatra. There were still isolated mountain bands at large in parts of South Kalimantan (the group of Ibnu Hadjar), parts of Ceram (remnants of the "Republic of the South Moluccas"), and parts of East and Central Java (PKI-oriented groups and some ordinary robber bands). But nowhere outside West Java were there groups actively harassing the government on a significant scale. Even in West Java some successes had apparently been registered in restricting the area of rebel and no-man's-land territory.

But from the middle of 1951 the over-all trend turned against the government. The most important single development contributing to this change was in South Sulawesi, where for a year there had been negotiations interspersed with fighting between the government and the Republican guerrilla leader Kahar Muzakar. In July 1950 Kahar, theretofore recognized as a lieutenant colonel in the RUSI army, had cut his ties with the army, because its East Indonesian commander, Colonel Kawilarang, had refused to accept the en masse incorporation of Kahar's followers and recognize them as a separate brigade. In the following months Kahar's more than 20,000 men had operated as irregular guerrillas, controlling sizable areas of the mountainous southwestern peninsula of Sulawesi and apparently enjoying a significant amount of popular support.[64]

[63] See Kementerian Penerangan (Ministry of Information), *Republik Indonesia, Propinsi Djawa Timur* ("The East Java Province of the Republic of Indonesia"; Djakarta: Kementerian Penerangan, 1953).

[64] Prime Minister Natsir, speaking in October 1950, stated that "there are not 10,000 guerrillas in South Sulawesi but a multiple of this number" ("A Review of Indonesia's Reconstruction," *Indonesian Review*, I, no. 1 [Jan. 1951], 62). On the degree of popular support enjoyed by Kahar and his group see K. Tobing,

In October 1950 the Natsir cabinet had sent a mission to negotiate with Kahar, and by January 1951 both sides were moving toward a settlement. On March 24 Kahar's units were given official status as part of the National Reserve Corps, with the understanding that their members would subsequently be divided into two groups, those who would be accepted into the army and those who would be demobilized. On August 7 it was agreed that four battalions of Kahar's men, 4,000 in all, would be sworn in as members of the army on August 17, the anniversary of the proclamation of independence. Kahar Muzakar himself would be given the rank of acting lieutenant colonel and a degree of command authority over his four guerrilla battalions, and he would be an adviser to the government agency concerned with rehabilitating those of his followers whom the army would not accept.[65] Thus it seemed that the vexing problem would at last be solved.

On August 17, 1951, everything was ready in the city square of Makassar for the ceremonial incorporation of Kahar's four battalions into the army of the Republic. Iskaq, the Interior Minister of the Sukiman cabinet, flew to Makassar for the occasion, and thousands of Makassar people came out to join in the double celebration. But Kahar and his 4,000 men were not there. Instead they chose this day to leave Makassar for their old mountain hide-outs, where their comrades had remained. And they took with them trucks, weapons, ammunition, 4,500 military uniforms, and Rp. 1.8 million in cash. An announcement from them declared that the army command had failed to implement promises it had made to them, notably the promise that arrested followers of Kahar would be released and that "reactionary staff officers" of the East Indonesia command (centered in Makassar) would be transferred elsewhere.[66]

On August 29 Prime Minister Sukiman broadcast to the rebellious battalions, serving notice that they would be given five days in which to report to the authorities, after which time drastic action would be taken against them. Kahar's men remained loyal to him, however. Subsequent military measures achieved a degree of success, but by

---

Sulawesi Selatan ("South Sulawesi"; Djakarta: Lembaran Minggu, n.d. [1952?]), pp. 14 ff. A full account of the complicated negotiations from 1950 onward is contained in Kementerian Penerangan, *Republik Indonesia, Propinsi Sulawesi* ("The Sulawesi Province of the Republic of Indonesia"; Djakarta: Kementerian Penerangan, 1953), pp. 334 ff.

[65] Kementerian Penerangan, *Republik Indonesia, Propinsi Sulawesi,* p. 345.

[66] *Aneta,* Aug. 17, 1951; "Kahar Muzakar," *Hikmah* (Djakarta Masjumi-sympathizing weekly), Sept. 27, 1951.

the time the Sukiman cabinet fell the Kahar group had entrenched itself rather securely in a number of areas in particularly rugged mountain terrain. On January 20, 1952, Kahar Muzakar had written to the Darul Islam leader Kartosuwirjo, accepting an appointment as Sulawesi commander of Kartosuwirjo's Islamic Army of Indonesia.[67]

Kahar Muzakar's move to outright hostility toward the government was a major defeat for the Sukiman cabinet. The mutiny of the one battalion in Kudus, Central Java, in December 1951 was also a serious blow, for a significant proportion of the deserting troops swelled the ranks of the Darul Islam in western Central Java. In West Java itself the Darul Islam grew more active in the second half of 1951. The causes of this reversal of the earlier favorable trend in the establishment of security are by no means easily discovered. The problem calls for analysis in sociological and military terms as well as political ones, and it is probable that no major part of the explanation is to be found in particular policies of the Sukiman cabinet or of the army in the period of this cabinet. But certainly the fact of failure produced reciprocal recriminations between the cabinet and the army. These recriminations were an important factor worsening the already bad relations between the two.

THE RELATIONSHIP WITH PRESIDENT SOEKARNO

If the Sukiman cabinet was weakened by its strained relations with the army, it was partly compensated for this by the particularly favorable relationship which existed between it and President Soekarno. Indeed, only the powerful backing which the cabinet received from the President made it possible for the cabinet leaders to pay as little attention as they did to the wishes of the army high command.

We have noticed the important role which the President played in the formation of the cabinet. Both of the *formateurs* were long-time associates of the President, and most of the principal figures in the cabinet, men such as Suwirjo, Iskaq, and Subardjo, had likewise long been tied to Soekarno as associates or disciples. The personal back-

---

[67] See *Keng Po*, May 5, 1952, for the contents of documents released by the army containing correspondence between Kahar Muzakar and Kartosuwirjo. Cf. Tobing, *op. cit.*, p. 78. See also the evidence presented at the trial of Achmad Buchari, a leader of the Masjumi youth organization, who was convicted on Nov. 16, 1953, on a charge of aiding the Darul Islam, in Kementerian Penerangan, *Sekitar Pemeriksaan Perkara-Perkara Affandi Ridhwan dan Achmad Buchari* ("On the Trials of Affandi Ridhwan and Achmad Buchari"; Djakarta: Kementerian Penerangan, 1954).

ground existed for relationships of mutual trust and co-operation, and such relationships developed.

In notable contrast with the practice of its predecessor, this cabinet gave the President a free hand to act according to his own view of his position, the view that he was not only a constitutional president, but also a revolutionary leader of the Indonesian people. Budget allocations for the presidential establishment were increased in this period. Soekarno was left wide scope to plan the speech-making tours in various parts of Indonesia which had become one of the most important features of his role. Far fewer restraints were placed on him than earlier as to the political content of his speeches.

Moreover, the Sukiman cabinet acceded to the President's suggestions with regard to a number of matters of government business, particularly appointments. Thus the President vetoed the proposal of PIR and the Prime Minister that the vacant portfolio of Agrarian Affairs be filled by Sutardjo Kartohadikusumo, a PIR leader who had fallen out with Soekarno some time earlier. Similarly he pressed the Sukiman cabinet successfully to include Yamin as a member of the Supomo mission negotiating with the Netherlands.

The President for his part gave active support to the cabinet's efforts to keep itself in office, and here his role was of the greatest importance. Backing the cabinet as he appears to have done on such issues as the anti-Communist raid and the Mutual Security aid commitment, he was able to apply pressure on critical or wavering members of the government parties to keep them from disavowing the cabinet. For some political leaders Soekarno's inner authority was so great that they would accept political suggestions from him as instructions to be followed regardless of the probable cost. Other leaders obeyed because they calculated that Soekarno's personal power was great and to all appearances rising, that he was likely to be the central figure of politics for years to come, and that it would therefore be imprudent to offend him.

Further, the President assisted the Sukiman cabinet by his speeches. He did not criticize the cabinet either directly or indirectly—except perhaps on the occasion when he condemned the Indonesian leaders who "forgot to move the masses for the settlement of the Irian question and thought that the question could be solved simply over the discussion table." [68] And his speeches struck many of the same notes as did those of the leaders of the cabinet. The correspondence was by no

[68] *Antara*, Dec. 12, 1951.

means complete, but it covered a number of ideological areas where it might, in retrospect, seem surprising that the President did not steer a different course.

Throughout the Sukiman cabinet period the President placed great stress on urging the Indonesian people to work harder. Hard work, production, discipline, order, peace—the President dwelt on this set of themes with greater force and consistency than ever before.[69] He did not abandon his earlier emphasis on national unity and the claim to West Irian. But he now began to place equal stress on other symbols which had hitherto been far more characteristic of Hatta than of him. Thus he condemned those whom he called "politics-crazy" and declared that people could not live by eating flags.[70] He argued against those who urged the outright liquidation of the Round Table Conference Agreement. He decried excessive advocacy of nationalization, arguing that Indonesia lacked the necessary means and the necessary skilled personnel. At the same time he defended the cabinet's policy of encouraging expansion of foreign investment.[71] He also castigated those who "are playing strikes." [72] He made a number of anti-Communist speeches—"Do not sell your national soul for a dish of international lentils"—and warned the Chinese Communists that "if a social revolution starts in this country it will immediately become a racial revolution." [73] And he chose his Independence Day message to warn against engaging lightly in the creation of cabinet crises. No previous cabinet of the postrevolutionary period had had this degree of presidential support for its policies.

One interesting aspect of the President's role in this period is the way in which the Sukiman cabinet justified it to parliament. As a result of committee discussions in 1951 of budgetary allocations made for the President and Vice-President, the nonspecialized committees of parliament submitted various questions on the constitutional position of the presidency and a number of criticisms of Soekarno's perception of his role. Various members criticized the President for intervening to an unjustified extent in the conduct of state affairs. Particular reference was made to speeches in which the President had advanced views at variance with those of the cabinet currently in office or had

---

[69] See for instance, *President Soekarno's Message to the Nation on the Sixth Anniversary of Indonesian Independence, August 17, 1951* (Djakarta: Ministry of Information, 1951), pp. 16 ff.

[70] *Antara,* Nov. 10, 1951, July 30, 1951.

[71] *Aneta,* July 9, 1951; *Antara,* Sept. 10, 1951.   [72] *Antara,* Nov. 10, 1951.

[73] *Ibid.; Aneta,* Aug. 20, 1951.

criticized the political parties in a way said to endanger the prestige of democracy. One committee's report stated that

in more than one instance . . . the nature of the speeches was not in keeping with the dignity of the position of a Head of State, and, moreover, certain ill-judged comments made in these speeches could adversely affect the development of negotiations with other governments, as for example, the discussions with Holland recently [December 1950] on West Irian.[74]

In replying to these various parliamentary criticisms Dr. Sukiman enunciated what was in fact a new doctrine of the presidency:

The scope of the functions of the President and Vice-President at the moment cannot, in the opinion of the government, be defined solely on the narrow basis of purely constitutional considerations. Various other factors, notably those deriving from the actual conditions applying in this current period of transition, must also be taken into account. . . . Thus the President and the Vice-President are not, as would be contended on the basis of a strictly constitutional viewpoint, merely personal symbols of the state, but are national leaders having the fullest confidence of the people. . . . The government . . . maintains that there has been no violation of the fundamental principles of parliamentary government as expressed in the letter and the spirit of the constitution, since the cabinet remains answerable to parliament for all actions of the President and the Vice-President. The question of whether the cabinet agrees or disagrees with actions of the President and the Vice-President is an internal matter between the cabinet and the President and Vice-President themselves.[75]

With the propounding of this interpretation by the Prime Minister the President's constitutional power was greatly expanded. Mr. A. K. Pringgodigdo, the constitutional authority, commented on the government reply in these terms:

The scope of action in respect of which the President is inviolable is extended. . . . [and] now taken to apply to all activities of the President and the Vice-President having any bearing on state affairs. . . . Considered politically, the government statement affirms that the Head of State remains unconditionally in office, whilst the activities of the President and the Vice-President could possibly bring about the resignation of a cabinet.[76]

By this statement of Dr. Sukiman the political power which President Soekarno had regained for himself since 1949 (and especially since the

[74] See A. K. Pringgodigdo, *The Office of President in Indonesia as Defined in the Three Constitutions in Theory and Practice* (Cornell Modern Indonesia Project, Translation Series; Ithaca, N.Y., 1957), p. 49.
[75] *Ibid.*, pp. 43–45.   [76] *Ibid.*, pp. 43–45, 49.

August 1950 constitutional decision barring Hatta from a return to the prime ministership) and which he was consolidating during the period of the Sukiman cabinet was to some extent formalized.

PROBLEM-SOLVING POLICY AND INTEGRATIVE LEADERSHIP

In attempting to come to conclusions about the Sukiman cabinet, one notices the many contrasts between this cabinet and its predecessor, the cabinet of Natsir. Natsir's had been a cabinet based on one of the two main parties and thus had faced its greatest challenge at the hands of a parliamentary opposition. Sukiman's, as a cabinet in which the two main parties shared power, was threatened chiefly by internal division. Natsir's cabinet had been one of "administrators" and of the generation of younger politicians; opposition to it had come principally from older-generation persons, both "administrators" and "solidarity makers." The latter were the very groups which supported the Sukiman cabinet most strongly. Further, the Natsir cabinet had cooperated closely with the current army leadership and enjoyed its backing, while coming increasingly into conflict with the President. On the other hand, the Sukiman cabinet, whose relations with the army were persistently marred by friction, was favored by President Soekarno and given his political support.

There were, however, great similarities in the positions of the two cabinets. Both accepted what was basically an "administrator" view of the country's problems. Both had to devote a great part of their energies to maintaining themselves against a constantly threatening array of opposition forces and "oppositionist" sentiment, against the inclination of various groups to impose ideological demands on them. Both found themselves in a position where antiforeign feeling could be used against them—anti-Dutch feeling in the case of the Natsir cabinet, anti-American feeling in the case of the cabinet of Sukiman. The Sukiman cabinet, like the Natsir cabinet, was kept so busy with immediate problems pertaining to its continuation in office that it neglected many of the governmental tasks it thought important. But, like the Natsir cabinet too, it was a beneficiary of the Korean War boom and able, partly because of this, to register certain policy achievements contributing to social stability.

The Sukiman cabinet saw a turning of the tide in the theretofore effective campaigns of governments to weaken the power of rebel and bandit groups. But the cabinet was successful in its handling of certain other aspects of the restoration of law and order. The serious problem of cargo thefts in the large ports was largely overcome in the period of the Sukiman cabinet. The period brought a further general improvement in army organization and discipline. And it witnessed a development toward the situation reached in the middle of 1952 in which the army was prepared to surrender most of its State of War and Siege powers to civilian authorities (in all except the areas of conflict with rebel groups).

In the economic area the Sukiman cabinet pursued many of the same policies as the Natsir cabinet. The "Sumitro Plan" was taken over, small industries and co-operatives were given considerable attention, and large sums of money went into various of the regional development projects which the Hatta and Natsir cabinets (and preceding governments, Dutch and Indonesian) had planned. The Sukiman cabinet acted on the view that foreign capital was an important need of the country. At the same time it carried further the efforts of its predecessors in promoting the gradual "Indonesianization" of a number of areas of business activity, notably importing. By the time the Sukiman cabinet's successor took office in April 1952 the number of Indonesian importers—members of the "Benteng group," which had exclusive rights to import certain categories of goods and whose members were almost invariably ethnic Indonesians—was 741. It had been 250 at the end of 1950 and an estimated 100 at the time of the transfer of sovereignty.[77]

But there were significant differences of emphasis between the economic policies of this cabinet and those of its predecessor, particularly with regard to importing and budgetary allocations. The Sukiman cabinet's Minister of Finance, Jusuf Wibisono (of the Masjumi), was a man of fairly intense policy commitments, but he was not as strict in his control of disbursements as Natsir's Finance Minister, Sjafruddin Prawiranegara. Favored by a continuing high level of export earnings and seeing that a fairly generous distribution of rewards would help to keep the politically divided cabinet together, Jusuf initiated an informal arrangement whereby government banks gave credit to firms whose directors were from particular government parties.[78] The cabinet sent a delegation of 24 members to the UN General

[77] Sutter, *op. cit.*, pp. 1017, 1021.

[78] On this arrangement, which was continued by Jusuf's successors, see the statement of the head of the Finance Ministry's monetary section, *Suluh Indonesia* (Djakarta), Feb. 20, 1957.

Assembly meeting of 1951 whereas the Natsir cabinet had sent a delegation of five. It showed particular concern for civil servants, giving them Lebaran bonuses and allocations of rice. And the system of working with provisional budgets was continued, with a high degree of *ad hoc* improvisation in the whole financial structure of the government.

The Sukiman cabinet was able to register some important achievements in the field of labor. Following upon its repressive action against the Communists in August 1951, it introduced a new emergency law on labor disputes in September. This law, which replaced the February 1951 decree banning strikes in "vital industries," established a system of government labor mediation, with compulsory arbitration of disputes by the Labor Ministry where mediation efforts had failed and with a three-week "cooling off period" required before any strike action could be taken in any industry.[79] This more flexible series of provisions, in conjunction with the fact that Communist influence in labor unions was significantly set back by the mass arrests of August, resulted in a marked decline in the level of strike activity. As 1951 was a year when fewer working days were lost through strikes than in 1950, so 1952 was to show a further improvement over 1951.[80]

In the area of foreign policy the cabinet was initially successful. It carried on an active foreign policy, and for a time it appeared to be effective both in achieving the goals of its anti-Communist leaders and in raising Indonesia's prestige overseas. But finally it was foreign policy which precipitated the government's downfall, and thus most of its foreign policy achievements came to nothing.

The Sukiman cabinet, like the cabinets of Hatta and Natsir, was remarkably successful in its policies for the advancement of education and training. Dutch colonial policies had left Indonesia with only tiny numbers of persons with the skills required for the operation of a modern state,[81] and there was a strongly felt need for rapid increases in the number of such persons. Moreover, the Revolution had created a powerful drive for expanded opportunity, in both the rural and the

[79] For a discussion of the emergency law by the man chiefly responsible for its enactment and initial implementation see I. Tedjasukmana, *The Political Character of the Indonesian Trade Union Movement* (Cornell Modern Indonesia Project, Monograph Series; Ithaca, N.Y., 1959), pp. 113–114.

[80] Bank Indonesia, *Report for the Year 1954–1955* (Djakarta, 1955), p. 159.

[81] On the very small numbers of Indonesians given higher education in the prewar period see George McT. Kahin, *Nationalism and Revolution in Indonesia* (Ithaca, N.Y.: Cornell University Press, 1952), pp. 31–36.

urban population, and education was a principal ladder to occupational and thus social advancement. Finally, educational facilities served in many cases to absorb former revolutionaries for whom no other acceptable forms of civilian rehabilitation could be found.

Thus the first years after December 1949 were a period of very rapid educational expansion. One set of statistics has it that 5,609,485 children were attending primary schools in 1951–1952, as compared with 4,977,304 in 1950–1951 and 2,021,990 in 1939–1940.[82] Other statistics give a somewhat different picture,[83] but it is clear that primary school attendance was rising by an annual 10 per cent or so for several years of this early postrevolutionary period, with secondary school numbers rising at the rate of 15 to 20 per cent per year and university numbers even more rapidly.

At the same time numerous training programs were started for those already employed. Every government agency developed training facilities for its personnel. Every large firm, foreign as well as Indonesian, was obliged to train Indonesians in technical and managerial skills. Great numbers of men and women were given training overseas, either at Indonesian government expense or under one or another of the overseas fellowship programs sponsored by the United States, the United Nations, or the Colombo Plan.

The existence of this wide range of educational opportunities helped considerably to buttress the stability of the postrevolutionary regime. At the same time it contributed to the sustaining of hope that the just and prosperous society for which the Revolution had been fought was indeed in the process of realization.

In other ways, however, this hope had been dwindling for some time. Indeed, the Sukiman cabinet period was one in which feelings of disillusionment with the fruits of independence, feelings which had been widely prevalent since 1950, were expressed with great frequency. For some in the newspaper-reading public the focus of criticism was lack of achievement with regard to problem-solving policy. These persons deplored the failure of cabinets to make rapid progress with their self-set policies of re-establishing security, stabilizing the administration, and reorganizing the economy with a view to expansion

[82] *Statistik Pendidikan dan Pengadjaran tahun 1953–1954* ("Educational Statistics, 1953–1954; Djakarta: Kementerian P.P. dan K., 1954), p. 7.

[83] Biro Pusat Statistik (Central Bureau of Statistics), *Statistical Pocketbook of Indonesia, 1957* (Djakarta: Biro Pusat Statistik, 1957), pp. 20–26; also Appendix to Presidential Message, in *Hope and Facts* (Djakarta: Ministry of Information, 1952), p. 25.

and development. They decried the continued chaos in many areas of rebel and bandit activity, the persistence of confusion and inefficiency in the government service, the facts of inflation, repeated strikes, and bottlenecks of distribution. In general, they were inclined to blame these shortcomings on "politics." Their criticisms reflect the discrepancy which existed between the situation as they saw it and their own "administrator" view of the tasks of government. These same criticisms were occasionally echoed by persons who were themselves prominent in the leadership of the cabinets. Thus Sjafruddin Prawiranegara in his pamphlet of June 1951 ended a discussion of various aspects of administration and economic management by declaring that the country was in "a process of decline in all fields, which is only temporarily hidden by the pseudo-welfare of high export prices." [84]

Far more important, however, was the criticism of those who expected government and politics to be inspiring, to be able to create the same moral tension and sense of purpose which had existed for them during the struggle for independence and which had transformed the material sufferings of that struggle into badges of heroism. For persons like these the dominant features of political life in the Indonesia of 1951–1952 were lassitude, self-seeking, and division. In the government service they saw laziness, corruption, and clique infighting and, if they were themselves civil servants, a lack of meaningful work. In the political elite they saw more cliques and factions and in addition luxury, social climbing, and cocktail-party affectation. In the economy and social life they saw the continued prominence of the large Dutch firms and their personnel. And to many of them it appeared that the leaders of the Indonesian Revolution were adapting themselves to terms of economic and social existence set by these foreign firms rather than forcing the firms to accept the fact of Indonesian sovereignty in wholehearted fashion. Everywhere they saw a growing gulf between the leaders who had been raised to prominence in the Revolution and their followers, whose devotion and active support had made possible the success of the Revolution, but who were now neglected and forgotten. Wherever they turned they saw honor and position being distributed in ways which did not accord with the values of the Revolution. As Colonel Nasution put it, "Patriots and traitors are mixing about with one another." [85]

[84] *Indonesia Dipersimpangan Djalan*, p. 31.

[85] "Semangat 17 Agustus" ("The Spirit of August 17"), *Mimbar Indonesia*, Aug. 17, 1951.

Resentments of this kind had exceedingly wide currency. They were most characteristic of those sections of the political public whose members participated in politics expressively, having no firm basis for personal values outside politics. But they were by no means limited to these sections. In fact, they found expression everywhere, in the daily press, in weeklies and student monthlies, and at conferences of intellectuals and cultural leaders.[86] Everywhere the complaint was about the decline in the spirit of the Revolution, the spirit of Jogjakarta, the spirit of the days of the guerrilla struggle against the Dutch. Often it was accompanied by expressions of cynicism and disgust about the existing situation. Sometimes the sense of grievance was focused on a particular target—"the politicians" and their newly acquired business interests, the President and the pomp at his palace, or the "leaders who governed by grace of the Round Table Conference Agreement." Often too it had no particular focus.

The upsetting aspect of this seemingly omnipresent decline in revolutionary *élan* was its affect on personal integration. "On all sides," said President Soekarno, "we see our people drifting, rudderless, suffering from confusion and dullness of the spirit." [87] Those whose personal values and sense of identity had found their source and center in participation in the nationalist Revolution were now compelled (unless they found a similar source in partisan political ideologies) to make painful psychological adjustments. When they complained of lassitude and a decline in revolutionary spirit in the society as a whole, they were often describing their own inner anguish.

Normlessness and "moral crisis" were constantly spoken of in urban society.[88] On the one hand, moral demands of many different and mutually contradictory kinds were being made, as a result of the great

[86] See, for instance, *Abadi,* Dec. 31, 1951, and *Mimbar Indonesia,* Dec. 8, 15, 1951, and 1951–1952 *passim* (articles by Sugardo) and March 15, 1952 (articles by Pramoedya Ananta Toer). See also *Gadjah Mada* (Jogjakarta students' monthly), 1951–1952 *passim* and especially the brilliant cartoons of Soebantardjo. For some views of artists see *Indonesia, Madjallah Kebudajaan* ("Indonesia, a Cultural Periodical"), Jan.–Feb. 1952 (issue on Second Cultural Congress). See too *Symposion tentang Kesulitan-Kesulitan Zaman Peralihan Sekarang* ("A Symposium on the Difficulties of the Present Period of Transition"; Djakarta: Balai Pustaka, 1953), especially the remarks of Sjahrir (pp. 13 ff.) and Mohammad Said (pp. 103 ff.).

[87] *President Soekarno's Message . . . on the Sixth Anniversary of Indonesian Independence,* p. 15.

[88] Indeed, the words "moral crisis" (*krisis achlak*) were used so much that one cartoonist depicted an applicant for a radio announcer's position in the pose of merely repeating this phrase! See *Pedoman Radio* ("Radio Guide"), May 4, 1952.

speed of political and social change in the previous decade. On the other hand, there was something of a hiatus in sanctions for morality: the revolutionary morality was losing its relevance, and there were as yet few firmly established new social institutions to provide sanctions for the regulation of behavior.

Clearly, then, this was a period when political leaders were expected to provide new integrative equivalents of the revolutionary struggle. Inspiring leadership was in demand, and one central question of politics was whether consolidation-and-routinization-minded cabinets like that of Sukiman (or of Natsir) could provide it. What appeared to be necessary was a government which had long-range vision, an ability to fashion meaningful symbols, and authority based on the values of the Revolution and which at the same time was able to link its symbols of the greatness of the future to the practical, complicated, and divisive tasks of the present.

In these respects the Sukiman cabinet was largely unsuccessful. Born in an atmosphere of particularly bitter factional infighting, containing among its membership relatively few men of high prestige, showing the marks of internal division early in its period of office, and demonstrating no herolike intensity of concern for the achievements of its goals, it was not perceived as affording leadership that inspired. Nor did it champion long-range policies capable of firing the imagination of the political public. These shortcomings were only partly compensated by the cabinet's ability to work in close co-operation with President Soekarno.

Chapter VI

The Wilopo Cabinet, April 1952–June 1953:

The Breakthrough Which Failed

WHEN the Sukiman cabinet resigned, there arose a hopeful sense of anticipation, anticipation of something which could set a new course. On the one hand, there was hope for firmer and more effective government, for a government which would do what governments had been doing in the previous years but faster and better and with greater power to overcome resistance. On the other hand, there was hope for a cabinet which could provide inspiring leadership, which could make the humdrum tasks of developing the country seem appealing to the many who had shown themselves capable of idealistic devotion to a cause in the past and could, it was thought, be similarly capable if a great cause were presented to them in the future. On both these counts a cabinet was wanted which would stand above the bickerings of parties and their factions.

A CABINET OF HOPE

But it was by no means easy to see how such a cabinet could be formed. There were many in the political elite who were thought to possess the necessary personal qualities. But tensions between the parties, especially between the two largest parties, which almost certainly would have to be included in any new cabinet, were prominently in the foreground. Moreover, the number of outstanding issues on which the Masjumi and the PNI were committed to opposed positions had grown.

There was the issue of relations with the Netherlands: Was Indonesia to negotiate on the matter of the abrogation of the Netherlands-Indonesian Union if Holland insisted that this matter be separated from the issue of sovereignty in West Irian? The PNI said "No," the Masjumi "Yes." Again there was the matter of the Japanese peace treaty: the Masjumi was committed to ratification of Subardjo's signature to the treaty, the PNI was equally committed to opposing a parliamentary endorsement. And the old issue of the regional councils remained. The compromise on which the Sukiman cabinet had been based—that the existing councils based on Regulation 39 would continue to function until a new regulation for a new set of interim legislative councils had been made—had broken down in practice. The two main parties had been unable to agree on provisions for a new regulation. Now the Masjumi was demanding that further efforts be directed toward general suffrage elections, for both national and regional assemblies, while the PNI quietly sought to postpone such general elections.

The existence of these various divisions between the main parties and the demonstrated difficulty of operating a cabinet based on only one of them were put forward by PSI supporters and some others as evidence of the need for a business cabinet. The argument had been advanced before, but never so persistently; it was to be advanced again at every subsequent cabinet crisis of our period. Such a cabinet, it was argued, would bring men of high technical competence to office. It would minimize the effects of bitterness between parties and prevent the tension from increasing. It would eschew ideological postures and get on with the job to be done. It would be internally cohesive, and it would move rapidly toward nationwide elections.

In the eyes of those who opposed the Socialist Party's influence this was unpersuasive. Jusuf Wibisono, of the Sukiman group of the Masjumi, opposed the idea of a business cabinet as extraparliamentary and unworkable. Dr. Sukiman Wirjosandjojo stated that he thought a coalition cabinet better able to ensure political stability, and the PNI chairman, Sidik Djojosukarto, who had been co-*formateur* of Dr. Sukiman's coalition cabinet, took a similar stand.[1] The argument of these men gained strength when it appeared during the President's "hearings" that practically none of the parties were prepared to limit

[1] *Merdeka*, Feb. 2, 1952; *Abadi*, Feb. 25, 1952.

its own power by foregoing the right to exercise control over any ministers it might have in a cabinet.

In the early stages of the cabinet crisis the issue between a coalition and a business cabinet was presented as one of principle. But the two types were clearly more important as political symbols than as legal categories. The call for a business cabinet was made by groups which wanted a cabinet like Natsir's. Those who were against it and argued for a coalition cabinet desired primarily to have a cabinet like Sukiman's. The argument for internal cohesion and technical competence was a political argument of the younger-generation politicians against their older and Soekarno-allied opponents, both "administrators" and "solidarity makers."

On March 1 President Soekarno announced the names of two *formateurs*, Sidik Djojosukarto of the PNI and Prawoto Mangkusasmito of the Masjumi. The President did not specify that a coalition or business cabinet should be formed, asking the two leaders simply to form "a strong cabinet with sufficient parliamentary backing." Then it became clear that the question of a coalition or a business cabinet was one of degree. For a *formateur* it was a matter not of establishing a particular, legally defined, relationship between a cabinet and the parties, but rather of obtaining maximum cabinet unity and convincing the parties to be content with making suggestions to their ministers instead of absolute demands that forced a cabinet to choose between inaction and internal collapse.

Sidik and Prawoto worked for nineteen days, but their efforts ended in failure. The two men were divided not only by membership in different parties, but also by membership in interparty cliques. Sidik, whom we have classified here as a leading member of the radical nationalist group of the PNI, had close associations with President Soekarno. To some extent he spoke also for the older Sartono-Suwirjo group of his party, the group rooted in the PNI of 1927. And he had been able to co-operate with Dr. Sukiman in the formation of the Sukiman cabinet. But he was hostile to the Natsir group of the Masjumi, and Prawoto was a Natsir man.

The two *formateurs* were able to reach agreement on a cabinet program. But they could not escape deadlock over candidates for particular portfolios. The prime ministership was not the chief problem on this occasion. With elections expected to be held in the not too distant future, the Interior portfolio was now at least as eagerly sought as the prime ministership. The PNI was determined to maintain and further strengthen its position in the *pamong pradja* corps, while the Masjumi was determined to undo this influence—or at least to prevent a further development of the personnel policies of Iskaq. But the *formateurs* could not agree on the individual ministers who were to represent their respective parties. Sidik wanted such PNI leaders as Iskaq and Dr. A. K. Gani in the cabinet, but neither of these was acceptable to Prawoto. Prawoto wanted Roem as a Masjumi minister, but Sidik objected. Again Prawoto wanted to accept the army leadership's candidate for the Defense portfolio, the Sultan of Jogjakarta, but the Sultan was unacceptable to Sidik.

On March 19 the *formateurs* returned their mandate to President Soekarno, and on the same day the President appointed the PNI's Mr. Wilopo as *formateur*. Wilopo had been Labor Minister in the Hatta RUSI cabinet and Minister of Economic Affairs in the Sukiman cabinet. Sidik and Prawoto had considered him for the prime ministership and had agreed on him. He could thus build on much of what they had achieved.

It soon became clear that Wilopo's policy as a *formateur* was much closer to that of Prawoto than to that of his party chief, Sidik. Just as Prawoto had previously emphasized that a strong cabinet was possible only if individuals were selected for ministerial posts in accordance with a "specified composition" (whereas Sidik had rather emphasized party and parliamentary support), so Wilopo stressed what he called his "conception" of a cabinet. He was prepared to run the risk of uncertain party and parliamentary support rather than sacrifice the "conception" which would provide his cabinet with unity, teamwork, and a common policy orientation. He encountered a number of difficulties as it became clear that he selected men on the basis of a policy approach like that of Sjahrir and Natsir. Pressures of various sorts were brought to bear on him from the executive of his own party and from the President. But he made few concessions. On March 30 Wilopo submitted the names of his cabinet to the President:

Ministry		*Party*
Prime Minister	Mr. Wilopo	PNI
Deputy Prime Minister	Prawoto Mangkusasmito	Masjumi
Foreign Affairs	Mukarto Notowidigdo	PNI
Interior	Mr. Mohammad Roem	Masjumi
Defense	Sultan Hamengku Buwono IX	Independent
Justice	Mr. Lukman Wiriadinata	PSI
Information	Arnold Mononutu	PNI

Ministry		Party
Finance	Dr. Sumitro Djojohadikusumo	PSI
Agriculture	Mohammad Sardjan	Masjumi
Economic Affairs	Mr. Sumanang	PNI
Communications	Ir. Djuanda	Independent
Public Works	Ir. Suwarto	Catholic
Labor	I. Tedjasukmana	Labor
Social Affairs	Anwar Tjokroaminoto	PSII
Education	Dr. Bahder Djohan	Independent
Religious Affairs	K. H. Fakih Usman	Masjumi
Health	Dr. Johannes Leimena	Parkindo
Personnel Affairs	R. P. Suroso	Parindra

The list was not, however, given immediate endorsement. Instead the President said he would wait and would come to a decision after discussing the matter with Vice-President Hatta, who was then out of Djakarta. This step, unprecedented in Indonesia's constitutional history, led to considerable protest. Mr. A. M. Tambunan, of the Parkindo and first vice-chairman of parliament, argued strongly that it was unconstitutional, and papers like the pro-Socialist *Pedoman* did the same. On the other hand, men such as Jusuf Wibisono and the widely read commentator Sajuti Melik, defended the President's action. Not only did they point to the possible weakness of the cabinet that Wilopo had formed—the opposition of PIR and the Democratic Fraction; the ambiguous position of the Nahdatul Ulama, which, it seemed, would secede from the Masjumi, and of the PNI leadership, which had indicated that it was dissatisfied with a number of the men on the list; and personal factors such as the President's opposition to Wilopo's Foreign Affairs candidate, Mukarto Notowidigdo [2]— but in addition they argued that it was not necessary for Indonesia to follow Western constitutional precedents mechanically. Sajuti Melik strengthened his case by pointing to a statement of the President made several days earlier: "Our people's sovereignty . . . is not merely parliamentary democracy as in the West; that must be coupled with leadership." [3] Here again it appears that the political alignment was roughly between the forces grouped around the President and those grouped around the Socialists. The issue did not assume large

[2] Mukarto, then deputy representative to the United Nations, was objected to in a number of circles, particularly in the Foreign Ministry, because of his youth and relatively low diplomatic status.

[3] See *Mimbar Indonesia*, April 5, 1952, quoting from an address of the President to the students of a staff training course of the Information Ministry.

proportions, however, because after two days the President approved Wilopo's list.

The Wilopo cabinet resembled its predecessor, the Sukiman cabinet, in that it was based principally on the two main parties. But in most other respects it was different. First of all, it represented different factional groups of the two parties. None of the five Masjumi leaders who had sat in the Sukiman cabinet were included, and only two of the five PNI leaders. This was a cabinet of the "younger generation," whereas its predecessor was a cabinet of the "older generation." In political fact, therefore, the resemblance was greater with the Natsir cabinet—witness the important posts given to Roem, Sumitro, and Sultan Hamengku Buwono, all men who had also held major portfolios under Natsir. Potentially, however, this was a cabinet with considerably greater support than the Natsir cabinet, for it included the PNI.

Press reactions to the cabinet were favorable, more favorable than they had been to either of its two predecessors of the unitary state period. The Information Ministry's *Indonesian Affairs* commented that the cabinet "gives the impression [of being] of the 'younger' elements in Indonesian political life," adding that "for that reason many people feel that there is a hope of a 'new atmosphere' in political affairs." [4] The cabinet's composition was praised particularly by students and younger people of higher Western education and by many outside political parties who had hoped for a government above the petty bickerings of the parties. In addition, the reaction of Indonesians overseas was favorable.

In the matter of elections Wilopo took a position somewhere between the Masjumi and the PNI. He did not make any commitment, such as the Masjumi executive had sought in the formation discussions,[5] for Constituent Assembly elections within a year. But, by placing elections at the very top of his six-point program, he suggested that there would be fairly rapid action.

Concerning the regional councils, Wilopo accepted the Masjumi position entirely. All attention would be devoted to the establishment of elected councils. It was not clear whether the elections would take place before, after, or together with the Constituent Assembly elections, but regional council elections were included in the top point

[4] *Indonesian Affairs*, II, no. 1 (Feb.–March 1952), 6–7.
[5] Deliar Noer, "Masjumi: Its Organization, Ideology and Political Role in Indonesia" (M.A. thesis, Cornell University, 1960).

of the cabinet's program. Until elected councils were established, the councils already established on the basis of Regulation 39 would continue to function.

Foreign policy was placed last among the points of the cabinet's program and given little time in the Prime Minister's statements to parliament. Foreign policy, Wilopo said, would be determined by the requirements of the domestic situation. The government would reopen negotiations with the United States with a view to replacing the Subardjo-Cochran agreement with "another agreement with conditions which do not deviate from the framework of international co-operation in general and the spirit of the United Nations Charter in particular." [6] It would receive only economic and technical, not military, assistance.

The Prime Minister opposed suggestions of unilateral abrogation of the Netherlands-Indonesian Union, but said the government intended to resume the negotiations with the Netherlands on this and other related questions which were broken off in February. At the same time he announced that the cabinet had not yet made a decision on the matter of establishing diplomatic relations with the U.S.S.R. Indonesia and the Soviet Union had held preliminary negotiations on this matter in April 1950, but Indonesia had subsequently dragged its feet, largely as a result of Masjumi pressure. The issue had been brought to the fore again by Mukarto, who before leaving New York to be the cabinet's Foreign Minister had stated that he would see that an Indonesian Embassy was opened in Moscow.[7]

On the question of civil-military relations, the new Prime Minister stated that the greater part of the country had reached a stage where security could be maintained by the civil authorities. Therefore, he said, the government intended to begin lifting the state of siege imposed under the 1939 State of War and Siege (Martial Law) regulations. By the time of his second statement on June 3 this had been done for South Sumatra, and it was to be done for the rest of the country in July—with the provision that the milder State of War regulations (which gave military authorities a smaller range of emergency powers) would be effective in certain insecure areas. There had been considerable army hostility, especially in the regions, to earlier pro-

[6] *Keterangan dan Djawaban Pemerintah atas Program Kabinet Wilopo* ("The Government's Statement of the Policy of the Wilopo Cabinet and Its Replies to Parliamentary Criticism"; Djakarta: Kementerian Penerangan, 1952), p. 186.

[7] *Antara,* March 30, 1952.

posals for lifting the state of siege, although Colonels Simatupang
and Nasution supported it as a step toward higher military standards
and toward keeping the army from corruption and unpopularity.[8]
The Wilopo cabinet's action represented a successful assertion of
power, not so much by civilians over soldiers as by a combination of
cabinet and the central army leadership over officers with a regional
or local base of power. It was a combination reminiscent of the Natsir
cabinet period and one in which the Sultan of Jogjakarta again played
a major personal role.

The heavy emphasis of Wilopo's statements was, however, on the
economic situation and the situation of the government's finances.
With grim realism he outlined the situation of the country's economy,
which he described as being in "a decline of which one cannot yet see
the end." [9] He was speaking at just the time of the first major series
of falls in prices for Indonesia's exports, at a time when prices were
still falling from their earlier level of the Korean War boom. Explaining the importance of export duties as the largest source of state
revenue, he estimated that government receipts in 1952 were likely to
fall short of those of 1951 by Rp. 2,610 million. With previous commitments amounting to Rp. 3,800 million, the government would probably
face a deficit of Rp. 4,000 million, with revenues totaling less than
Rp. 9,000 million.[10] A balanced budget was an impossibility under these
circumstances, Wilopo said, but drastic cuts in government expenditure
and strict avoidance of waste were necessities. As far as possible the
cuts would not affect productive enterprises assisted by the government.

A number of demonstrative decisions such as the one not to implement the increases in salaries and allowances for ministers and departmental heads, which had been decided on by the Sukiman cabinet,
set the tone for a new austerity. Wilopo told parliament that his cabinet
would not reverse the decision of the Sukiman cabinet to raise the
basic salaries of civil servants by 20 per cent as of May 1. But it would
stop the recently introduced scheme of rice distribution for civil servants, and it would not give its employees Lebaran bonuses.

Having put forward his policy, Wilopo, on June 19, told parliament
that "the government will continue in its work—unless parliament

[8] A. H. Nasution, *Tjatatan-Tjatatan Sekitar Politik Militer Indonesia* ("Notes
on Indonesian Military Policy"; Djakarta: Pembimbing, 1955), pp. 171–172, also
pp. 159 ff.; Daniel S. Lev, "Aspects of the Regulation on the State of War and
Siege" (unpublished paper, Cornell Modern Indonesia Project, 1957)

[9] *Keterangan dan Djawaban Pemerintah atas Program Kabinet Wilopo*, p. 16.

[10] *Ibid.*, pp. 58–65.

thinks differently." Like his predecessor, he did not ask for a vote of confidence. A motion giving the cabinet "an opportunity to work" was passed on the same day by 125 votes to 5.[11]

CHANGING ALIGNMENTS: A NEW ROLE FOR THE NAHDATUL ULAMA

The formation of the Wilopo cabinet precipitated two highly important developments in the sphere of party politics. One of these was the secession of the Nahdatul Ulama from the Masjumi. The other was the turning of the Communist Party to a policy of lending support to the PNI and President Soekarno and seeking to associate itself with the symbols of the nationalist Revolution.

The Nahdatul Ulama had been established in East Java in 1926 as a religious organization which would oppose the modernism of the then fast-expanding Muhammadijah. Its leaders had initially engaged in sharp polemics with those of the Muhammadijah, but relations between the two organizations had become more cordial by 1942, when the Japanese began their occupation.[12] Relations improved further after 1943 when the two organizations were joined with several smaller Islamic associations in the Japanese-sponsored Islamic mass organization, Masjumi. When the Revolution came and a new Masjumi was formed, as a political party based on a large number of Islamic organizations of various kinds, the Muhammadijah and Nahdatul Ulama both participated in the party.

During the Revolution there was some rivalry between the two organizations. Most of the Masjumi's cabinet posts went to men of higher Western education whose connections were principally with the modernist Muhammadijah, and this fact was resented by the leaders of the Nahdatul Ulama. The rivalry did not assume very large proportions, however, largely because important roles existed which the NU leaders could play. They led the Islamic guerrilla organizations Hizbullah and Sabillilah.

But in the years after 1949 the problem presented itself anew. The Nahdatul Ulama leaders were men of great village-level influence. Much of the electoral support which the Masjumi expected would

[11] Only the Partai Murba and SKI were opposed, but the Progressive Fraction, PRN, PIR, the Democratic Fraction, a number of independents, and several individual members of the Masjumi abstained from voting. See Sajuti Melik in *Mimbar Indonesia*, June 28, 1952. A Progressive-Murba motion asking that a vote should be taken on the issue of confidence had been defeated immediately before.

[12] For a full discussion see Harry J. Benda, *The Crescent and the Rising Sun* (The Hague: van Hoeve, 1958), pp. 50–53 and *passim*.

come as a result of the activities of traditional Islamic leaders in the villages, many of whom, particularly in Java, were under the influence of the Nahdatul Ulama. But to keep the NU leaders within the Masjumi fold it would be necessary to provide them with rewards, and here a number of difficulties arose.

The Nahdatul Ulama leadership included virtually no one with modern-state-type skills.[13] The NU leaders were "solidarity makers," wielders of symbols, both traditional and nationalistic. They were not personally equipped to play important roles in a state organization such as the Hatta, Natsir, and Sukiman cabinets were operating. Although they shared in part these cabinets' goal of social and political stabilization—for their position rested in good measure on trading and petty landlord interests—they were opposed to various aspects of the three cabinets' policies on modernization and of their policies of moderation in relation to the Netherlands and Dutch interests.

In actual practice the NU had few positions of influence during these years. Its chairman, Kijaji Wachid Hasjim, was Minister of Religious Affairs in the Hatta, Natsir, and Sukiman cabinets, but none of its other leaders were able to obtain cabinet posts or to wield substantial power in other ways, either in the government or in the Masjumi party. The NU's lack of influence within the party was a cause of particularly sharp resentment. The Nahdatul Ulama leaders complained frequently about the decision of the party congress of December 1949 which changed the status of the Madjlis Sjuro or Religious Council of the party, depriving it of its legislative powers and making it a purely advisory body.[14] The NU had long held a position of pre-eminence within the Madjlis Sjuro, and in criticizing the change in the status of this council it was able to present it as a subordination of religion to politics. At the same time the NU leaders argued vociferously—all this still within the party—against the tendency of giving leadership positions to men without local or regional influence who had merely succeeded in exerting pressure in the capital.[15]

[13] For biographies of most of the top leaders of the Nahdatul Ulama see H. Abubakar, ed., *Sedjarah Hidup K. H. A. Wahid Hasjim* ("The Biography of K. H. A. Wahid Hasjim" [also written K. H. Wachid Hasjim]; Djakarta: Panitya Buku Peringatan Almarhum K. H. A. Wahid Hasjim [Committee for a Memorial Publication on the Late K. H. A. Wahid Hasjim], 1957).

[14] Abubakar, ed., *op. cit.*, p. 563.

[15] See Mochtar Naim, "The Nahdatul Ulama as a Political Party, 1952–55: An Enquiry into the Origins of Its Electoral Success" (M.A. thesis, McGill University, 1960).

It was against the Natsir group within the Masjumi leadership that the NU had its strongest resentments, and these grew in the period of the Sukiman cabinet. In this period Wachid Hasjim's policies as Minister of Religious Affairs came under parliamentary attack, particularly because of the minister's alleged mismanagement of shipping negotiations for the Mecca pilgrims of 1951.[16] The matter led to a personal disagreement between Wachid Hasjim on the one hand and Natsir and Sjafruddin on the other, and from that time it was clear that Natsir would endeavor in any future change of cabinet to block the reappointment of Wachid Hasjim as Religious Affairs Minister. Shortly thereafter the Nahdatul Ulama issued an instruction to its members to attempt to capture the leadership of the Masjumi organization at the subbranch or village level.

The conflict came to a head in the course of the cabinet crisis which followed Dr. Sukiman's resignation. Soon after the resignation Kijaji Hadji Abdul Wahab Chasbullah, a foundation member and highly venerated leader of the NU who was head of the Religious Council of the organization (and also a relative of Wachid Hasjim), was called to the presidential palace. Not long afterward he issued a statement calling for a coalition cabinet and declaring that the NU would review its affiliation with the Masjumi unless the Masjumi saw to it that Dr. Sukiman returned to the prime ministership in the new cabinet and K. H. Wachid Hasjim to the Religious Affairs portfolio.[17]

The Masjumi was divided as to what to do in the face of these demands, with Sukiman's followers tending to support them and Natsir's followers to be opposed. By the time that Wilopo assumed the *formateur*-ship it was clear that Sukiman would not be able to return to the prime ministership; but the question of Wachid Hasjim's portfolio remained, and the threat of NU disaffiliation continued to be made on this question. Eventually it was the actions of the NU leaders which solved the Masjumi's dilemma. When it became known that Kijaji Wahab had shown the current Masjumi-NU correspondence to the PNI *formateur,* many Masjumi leaders drew the conclusion that the NU did not in fact want to remain within the Masjumi and that a breach was therefore inevitable.[18] This conclusion strengthened the position of the Natsir group within the party councils. The Masjumi finally asked the *formateur* to choose the man he wanted as Religious Affairs Minister from a list which included the names of members of

---

[16] See *Antara*, Oct. 26, 27, 1951.

[17] *Abadi*, March 10, 1952, quoted in Noer, *op. cit.*   [18] Noer, *op. cit.*

both Nahdatul Ulama and Muhammadijah but not the name of Wachid Hasjim. Wilopo settled upon the Muhammadijah leader Fakih Usman.[19]

On April 6, two days after the Wilopo cabinet was installed, the central board of the Nahdatul Ulama decided that the organization would in principle disaffiliate from the Masjumi. Continued affiliation with the Masjumi, the board declared, would lead to the total neglect of the NU's principal duties in its own field, the field of religion. At the same time the NU urged, as it had done before, that the Masjumi transform itself into a federatively organized body.[20] Most political observers took this to mean that the NU would establish a political party of its own, and within several months they were proved to be right.

But it was difficult to evade the opprobrium which attached to those seen as breaking the solidarity of the Islamic community. Hence the transition was made by stages. In late April an NU congress decided by a vote of 61 to 9, with 7 abstentions—the opposition coming chiefly from delegates of Sumatran branches—to uphold the central board's disaffiliation decision.[21] On July 23 the NU sent out invitations to eighteen Islamic political parties and other organizations, calling upon them to join in the launching of a federative Liga Muslimin Indonesia (Indonesian Moslem League).[22] On July 31 all NU members still participating in Masjumi councils were withdrawn, and at the same time the NU set up a committee to consider whether it should establish a separate political organization. On August 30 the Liga Muslimin Indonesia was formally established as a federation of the Nahdatul Ulama, the PSII, the small Sumatra-centered Islamic party Perti (Pergerakan Tarbijah Islamijah, Islamic Educational Movement), and a tiny Islamic organization centered in Pare-Pare in Sulawesi. The NU leader K. H. Wachid Hasjim was elected as its first chairman. The Nahdatul Ulama itself dates its emergence as a political organization from the time of the establishment of the Liga.

The immediate effects of this series of developments on cabinet politics were not great. Seven members of the Masjumi's parliamentary delegation resigned to constitute themselves the NU parliamentary fraction, but this still left the Masjumi as the party with the largest

---

[19] For discussions of these developments see Noer, *op. cit.*, Mochtar Naim, *op. cit.*, and Abubakar, *op. cit.*, pp. 257–258.

[20] *Antara*, April 7, 1952.   [21] Abubakar, *op. cit.*, p. 564.

[22] Mochtar Naim, *op. cit.*

parliamentary representation. The earlier rumors that the forthcoming NU-based party might attract a number of prominent Masjumi leaders of the Sukiman group to itself [23] were not confirmed. Although the NU's disaffiliation strengthened the position of the Natsir group within the Masjumi, the Sukiman group remained within the party.

But there were long-term consequences of major importance. With the establishment of the NU and the Liga, the long-staked claim of the Masjumi to be the only party for Moslems became far less compelling. At the same time a major beginning had been made in preparing the ground for what many nationalists, and some Communists and Murba party leaders, had often hoped for, a cabinet without the Masjumi. And it was now much less likely that elections would issue in an overwhelming Masjumi victory such as most elite persons had theretofore expected (and very many continued to expect).

CHANGING ALIGNMENTS: THE COMMUNIST PARTY AND NATIONALISM

The PKI made a number of efforts in the second quarter of 1952 to develop a new relationship with nationalism and nationalist parties. As already noted, the Communist Party had stood in outright opposition to the Hatta, Natsir, and Sukiman cabinets. It had strongly and consistently attacked every one of these as reactionary governments and instruments of imperialism and sometimes as fascist. At the same time it had made little attempt to associate itself with the symbols of the nationalist Revolution. It is unlikely that it overestimated its strength so greatly as to have been preparing for an early uprising against the nationalist regime, as the Sukiman government alleged at the time of its mass arrests in August 1951. But the emphasis of its work was on weakening the economy and intensifying antigovernment feeling.

However, an important new strategy in relation to nationalism began to appear at the time of the formation of the Wilopo cabinet. Throughout the cabinet formation period the Communist Party was active in demanding that the BPP, the Consultative Body of Parties established after the fall of the Natsir cabinet, should be included in the new cabinet and, more vehemently, that the Masjumi should be excluded. But when it became clear that Wilopo would form a cabinet based on the PNI and Masjumi and including, from the BPP parties, only three men, all little amenable to Communist pressure, the PKI's central committee made an offer without precedent. It stated that it would support

[23] See, for instance, *Sin Po*, April 24, 1952.

Wilopo's cabinet as long as it was "progressive and national," even if the PKI was not included in it. In particular it stressed two demands relating to its own freedom of movement. One was for the freeing of all political prisoners, including those of the August raid, and the other was for the lifting of the State of War and Siege.[24] The terms on which it was now prepared to support a cabinet were clearly more minimal than in March 1951.

When the Wilopo cabinet had been formed, Ir. Sakirman, the PKI's parliamentary leader, declared that there were in the cabinet a number of individual men known as honest and sincere. From the point of view of the cabinet's program, he said, the PKI was unable to support it. But the cabinet had the opportunity to prove itself on other scores, and therefore his party would watch the practical steps of the government to judge whether it was honest and capable. At the same time the party took steps to assure the government of the conciliatoriness of its attitudes. On April 29 it deputized Sakirman as chairman of the Public Works Workers' Union to go to Central Java and persuade his union members there to accept difficult terms in order to end a current strike against the autonomous agencies of this province. Six days later the SOBSI-affiliated oil workers' union, Perbum, called off a threatened strike of 30,000 oil workers against two of the large foreign companies.

The party explained a number of aspects of its new position at the celebration of its thirty-second anniversary several days later. Speaking on this occasion, the first secretary of the party, D. N. Aidit, declared that it was the PKI's duty to "urge other parties—any who are prepared to and honest—to co-operate with the PKI in supporting a national united front and united fronts among various groups, workers, peasants, intellectuals, artists, women, young people, entrepreneurs, and so on."[25] In the same speech Aidit placed great stress on co-operation with the national entrepreneurs and the middle peasantry. The national entrepreneurs, he said, like the proletariat, were suffering under imperialism. The PKI was completely against their liquidation or the nationalization of their capital and set itself to defend the right of individual property.[26] Similarly the party sought the abolition

[24] *Harian Rakjat*, March 26, 1952.

[25] *Menempuh Djalan Rakjat* ("Walking the Road of the People"); Djakarta: Pembaruan, 1952), p. 9.

[26] A *Harian Rakjat* editorial of April 7, 1952, went so far as to justify a different scale of wage demands for workers in modern foreign-owned industries and those in small Indonesian-owned ones, on the grounds that the former could afford to

of large landlordism in order to create a free peasant community, a community of the middle peasantry, as an important condition for the development of a modern national economy.

At the same time Aidit set a new tone for party statements about the earlier cabinet by referring to it as the "Sukiman-Wibisono-Subardjo government," thereby emphasizing the Masjumi's strength in this cabinet and leaving unstated the fact that the PNI, the party of the national entrepreneurs by clear implication, shared responsibility in equal measure for its policies. Henceforth the PNI was to be wooed more actively than ever before, with the Communists making every effort to assure the nationalists that the National United Front alliance they sought involved no insistence on Communist hegemony. On July 24 Aidit stated directly that the PKI supported the Wilopo cabinet, adding that this was because it gave the party a better chance for political activities than other cabinets.

Under the new policy none of the earlier slogans were entirely put aside. Communist-led unions continued their strike activities in a number of places. But the emphasis in all the party's work and the work of its unions was on nationalist symbols and slogans. Even such government slogans as "national upbuilding" were accepted. The official party attitude toward President Soekarno changed entirely. No longer was he termed a collaborator with the Japanese. No longer was he classified with Hatta, Sjahrir, and Tan Malaka as a "false Marxist." No longer was his name associated with the policies of the Hatta, Natsir, and Sukiman cabinets.[27] Communists and those who took their cues from them ceased their condemnations of the pomp and luxury of his palaces and the large number of his cars. At meetings and rallies of the party his picture was displayed with those of Marx and Lenin. By contrast, there was no change in the attitude of the party toward Vice-President Hatta.

More vehemently than ever before the party emphasized the national claim to West Irian. Similarly it exploited every situation which could

---

pay more. It is not made clear in any of this discussion of the national entrepreneurs whether the term includes Chinese employers of labor. In Indonesia as in other parts of Southeast Asia, most Communist class analysis ignores the peculiar position of the Chinese minority.

[27] For two examples of such charges in the preceding year see Njoto, "Pemalsuan Marxisme" ("The Falsification of Marxism"), *Bintang Merah*, VII, no. 1–2 (Jan. 1–15, 1951), 16, and "Bahaja Fasisme dan Kerdjasama dengan Partai-Partai" ("The Fascist Danger and Co-operation with Other Parties"), *ibid.*, VII, no. 11 (June 15–July 1, 1951), 293.

be used to intensify hostility toward the Netherlands—such as the attempt made on May 21, 1952, by three followers of Westerling to assassinate the Indonesian military attaché in The Hague, Lieutenant Colonel Harjono. In addition, from its newly assumed vantage point of identification with the symbols of the nationalist regime, it campaigned effectively against the United States on the occasion of the visit of President Quirino of the Philippines in July.

The implications of this change of strategy were to become clear as the new policy worked itself out in the course of the next few years. It may be fruitful, however, to examine the causes of the change here, even if to do so entails arguing from evidence of a later period.

In the first place, the Communist Party of early 1952 was very much concerned for its own freedom of movement. The arrests of August 1951 had apparently crippled much of its organization. And it was clearly most anxious to emerge from the position of semi-illegality into which Sukiman had placed it. This it did, within a few months of the Wilopo cabinet's accession to office. By then large numbers of pro-Communists who had been arrested in the August 1951 raid had been released.

At the same time the party had been made conscious of its weakness. It was a very small party—with only 7,910 members in March 1952, according to statistics it published later—and, according to its own statements, it had little support among the peasantry. In the terms of Aidit's account of this period, given in October 1953, the PKI needed to gain time in order to expand its membership and therefore had to concentrate on co-operation with the national *bourgeoisie,* even to the extent of neglecting its work among the peasantry.[28]

Thirdly, it would appear that the party hoped by the new policy to use and widen the existing divisions between the Masjumi and the PNI. The policy of direct opposition to both the main parties of the nationalist regime had clearly brought disappointing results. At the same time it was evident that there were groups within the PNI which

[28] "Djalan ke Demokrasi Rakjat bagi Indonesia" ("The Road to People's Democracy for Indonesia"), *Bintang Merah,* IX, no. 9–10 (Sept.–Oct. 1953), 460–461, 464–465. On the importance of the August 1951 raid in bringing the party to adopt its new course see Sakirman, "Apa Arti Sokongan PKI kepada UUD 1945 dan Demokrasi Terpimpin" ("What Is the Meaning of PKI Support for the 1945 Constitution and Guided Democracy?"), *Bintang Merah,* XVI, no. 5–6 (May–June 1960), 213–214.

wanted co-operation with the PKI, or at least the power leverage which would result from the possibility of such co-operation.

A fourth factor was the party's good name. To regain this had been of vital importance in the party's thinking since its abortive Madiun revolt in 1948, when it had exposed itself to the charge of betraying the Republic's unity in the face of a probable imminent Dutch attack. The Aidit-Lukman-Njoto group of the party had fought the Tan Ling Djie–Alimin group on the issue of "liquidationism," that is, on the latter group's demand that the party should work within other parties to overcome the stigma of Madiun. But when the "liquidationist" group was defeated in January 1951, the victorious Aidit group was left with the task of finding an answer to the same problem. The new nationalist tactic was an attempt to achieve just this. But whereas the older foreign-trained leaders of the Tan Ling Djie–Alimin group had been concerned to prove the party's loyalty to democratic and parliamentary procedures, the group of Aidit, Lukman, and Njoto, all of them children of the Indonesian Revolution, emphasized rather its loyalty to nationalism.[29]

The new policy involved significant risks. If too much emphasis came to be placed on good relations with the PNI and other nationalist parties, there was a danger that the distinctiveness of the party and its strict theoretical orientation would become submerged. Thus it could conceivably lose its position as the major focus of the forces of social radicalism. There were to be warnings later of the danger of "rightist deviationism which exaggerates the importance of the national *bourgeoisie* and underestimates the importance of leadership of the working class and the worker-peasant alliance," the danger of "the party's losing its independence . . . [and] dissolving itself into the *bourgeoisie*." [30] Again there was the danger that the nationalists would achieve such strength as would enable them to turn against the Communists. But these risks seemed to be worth taking.

The new strategy was one for which no basis existed in contemporary Communist theory. It predated the later Soviet tendency to woo Asian neutralism. There was no comparable change in the policy of any other South or Southeast Asian Communist Party at the same

[29] See Donald Hindley, "The Communist Party of Indonesia, 1951–1961; A Decade of the Aidit Leadership" (doctoral dissertation, Australian National University, 1961), pp. 240–256, for a full discussion of efforts to create a favorable image of the party.

[30] "Djalan ke Demokrasi Rakjat bagi Indonesia," pp. 464–465.

time.[31] Furthermore, Soviet comment on Indonesia made at the time suggests that the PKI was leading Moscow rather than following. Soviet comment was moving in the direction of greater appreciation of the force of Asian nationalism and of the possibility that neutralism could work to its advantage, but this was not incorporated as a major part of its approach to Asian problems until some time in 1953.[32] The indications are that the party's new policy was the product of an empirical assessment of the domestic political situation made by a group of party leaders who were confident of having Russian trust and confident also, perhaps on the basis of communication and perhaps not, of being able to maintain it with the adoption of the new policy.

But why—and this is the more important and more difficult question —did the PNI agree to co-operation with the Communists? How did it happen that a party which was a main beneficiary of the regime established by the nationalist Revolution agreed to co-operate with a party pledged to the supplanting of this regime?

A good part of the answer lies in the hostility which several of the Wilopo cabinet's policies evoked inside the PNI. The policy of army reorganization on which the Sultan of Jogjakarta embarked as soon as he returned to the Ministry of Defense was one which strengthened the Simatupang-Nasution leadership and weakened the influence of PNI sympathizers in the officer corps. The cabinet's economic policies had a similar effect. The budget, credit, and importing policies which it initiated to deal with the post-Korean War slump situation placed the burden of retrenchment principally on the groups most closely associated with the PNI, on the new group of Indonesian importers and bankers, on civil servants, and, generally, on the white-collar people of the cities. Finally, there were many in the PNI leadership who were afraid of Wilopo's determined approach on the matter of early elections.

To many PNI leaders, therefore, the Wilopo cabinet appeared to be a cabinet established on the terms of the Masjumi (and the PSI). As these men's dissatisfaction with the cabinet grew, so also did their inclination to abandon co-operation with the Masjumi or at least use the possibility of co-operation with other parties, and particularly the PKI, as leverage to achieve better terms in the relationship with the

[31] *Keng Po* of Nov. 7, 1952, drew a comparison with the policy of the Iranian party toward the government of Mossadegh but this would appear to have been a case where immediate Russian interests were of much more importance, as compared with general revolutionary strategy, than in Indonesia.

[32] Information provided by Dr. Ruth T. McVey.

Masjumi. The power situation was such that the PNI held a balance position in relation to the Masjumi and the Communists. The terms of its co-operation with either of these parties would be favorable to the extent that it left open the possibility that it might co-operate with the other instead. Moreover, the PKI represented no immediate threat to the PNI. From its own statements and actions, it was clearly weak. On the other hand, the Masjumi was seen to be very strong.

Indeed, PNI leaders tended to be overawed by the power of political Islam. They had little realization, at this time, of the significance of the Nahdatul Ulama secession. They were alarmed by the continued strength and confidence of the Darul Islam, in their eyes the illegal wing of the Masjumi. And they saw a danger that the Moslem parties would attempt to change the state ideology, replacing the Pantja Sila with Islam. Islam therefore appeared as an immediate ideological challenge.

But perhaps the most important cause of the PNI's change to co-operation with the Communists lay in the increasing necessity for the party to speak the language of nationalist (and quasi-socialist) radicalism. Throughout the period after 1949 the PNI had stood uneasily between radicalism and consolidation, sometimes oscillating between the two postures, sometimes holding both at once. In party affairs the radical nationalist appeals of Sidik Djojosukarto and his group of "solidarity makers" had been dominant. In cabinet politics, on the other hand, the party's role had been one of supporting consolidation and planned economic change; and the party's cabinet representatives had been "administrators," mainly those of the Soekarno-linked Sartono-Suwirjo group, but also some of the younger Wilopo group.

In 1952, however, it became necessary to make a choice. The situation created by the post-Korean War slump made consolidation policies politically costly. And the determined and financially rigorous approach of the Wilopo cabinet to problem-solving policy created a strong basis for radical hostility to the cabinet. A contributory factor here was the fact that the Netherlands government was assuming a more strongly anti-Indonesian position in mid-1952 than previously and was more adamant in refusing to negotiate on the question of sovereignty over West Irian.[33] There was pressure on every party to speak and act in the terms of radical nationalism. For the PNI this took the form of pressure against the moderate politics of the two "administrator"

[33] See F. J. F. M. Duynstee, *Nieuw Guinea als Schakel tussen Nederland en Indonesië* (Amsterdam: Bezige Bij, 1961), pp. 208–212.

groups and in favor of the "solidarity maker" or "oppositionist" group of Sidik Djojosukarto. It was the latter group which was the forerunner of closer association with the Communists. Gradually in the course of 1952–1953 it succeeded in bringing the "administrator" group of Sartono and Suwirjo to support the new strategy and thus to oppose the Wilopo cabinet.

Finally, one must consider the important factor of the role of President Soekarno. The President's political viewpoint appears to have changed in 1952 in a manner almost exactly paralleling the change in the stand of the PNI. Thus there are clear signs of his opposition to the Wilopo cabinet, beginning at the time of its installation and growing and finding more and more public expression in the next six months. Whereas his speeches in the period of the Sukiman cabinet had emphasized the necessity of the people's working hard, there was little of this in what he said in the Wilopo period. Instead he now placed added stress on the need to complete the national Revolution. On November 10, 1952, he attacked "those who act as if the national Revolution were completed . . . who don't mention the words 'national Revolution' any more." At the same time he called for a tougher stand in the struggle for West Irian: "Let the history of our as yet incomplete national Revolution speak its own language." [34] On the Communist issue itself the change was specific. As late as May 20 the President had urged caution regarding the Communists' role as advocates of national unity, "lest one party not be sincere in its concern for national unity and cause another Madiun affair." [35] But this emphasis was not continued.

The President had certain personal reasons to feel antagonistic toward the Wilopo cabinet. The cabinet contained a number of the men with whom he had come into conflict in the period of the Natsir cabinet, and it indicated as soon as it had taken office that it would insist, as the Natsir cabinet had (and the Sukiman cabinet had not), on a sharp limitation of the President's prerogatives. The matter came to the fore at the very beginning of the Wilopo cabinet's period of office when the cabinet obliged the President to cancel arrangements made by him and the ex-Foreign Minister, Subardjo, for a presidential visit to Italy. The cabinet was to remain consistent in its attitude to-

[34] *Text of Speech of the President of the Republic of Indonesia on Heroes Day, November 10th, 1952, at Surabaja* (Djakarta: Ministry of Information, 1952).

[35] Quoted in Sajuti Melik, "Sekitar Pernjataan Bersama" ("Concerning the Joint Statement"), *Mimbar Indonesia*, May 31, 1952.

ward presidential powers. It limited the number of occasions on which the President was able to deliver speeches and reduced the budget allocations made for the Cabinet (Office) of the President.[36] And a number of its policies, especially those relating to the army, were as much of a threat to the President as to the PNI.

But probably the most important reason for Soekarno's reluctance to support the Wilopo cabinet was his unwillingness to set himself against the symbols of radical nationalism. He had done this in some measure in the life of the Sukiman cabinet, particularly in allowing his name to become associated with the cabinet's pro-American actions in foreign policy. But he did not like the role. He definitely did not want to play it in support of men he regarded as his political enemies.

To President Soekarno there was nothing frightening about a strategy which could be expected to strengthen the Communists. The President did not regard the PKI as radically different from other parties. And he did not believe it would be capable of an effective bid for state power in Indonesia in the near future. Remembering the successful use he had made of the slogan "Choose between Muso and Soekarno" in the Madiun affair of 1948, he was convinced that he could easily thwart any Communist effort to seize power in the foreseeable future. Of this the PNI leaders were also convinced. Thus the President's support made them confident that the dangers of the new strategy were not great.

They saw that dangers existed. The Madiun revolt remained in their minds as an example of Communist subservience to a foreign power—although, not being *santris* or fully committed Moslems, they remembered Madiun also for the cruelties which *santris* had inflicted on the revolters and for the Masjumi's success in making political capital out of the affair.[37] And most of them saw the possibility of Communist rule as an unhappy one. But the prospect was by no means as terrifying to them, the representatives of bureaucratic groups, as it was to Masjumi leaders, who were representatives of both independent business and organized religion. Furthermore, they did not expect it to be realized. Nor did they see themselves as playing a

---

[36] See "Pengeluaran untuk Presidenan" ("Expenses for the Presidency"), *Waktu* (Masjumi-sympathizing Medan weekly), Dec. 20, 1954.

[37] On the importance of this socioreligious pattern of cleavage within and between villages at the time of the Madiun revolt see Robert R. Jay, "*Santri* and *Abangan*: Religious Schism in Rural Central Java" (doctoral dissertation, Harvard University, 1957), pp. 201–204.

significant part in bringing it about. If communism was indeed the wave of the future, as some of them thought, then it would arrive in due course, more or less regardless of what they themselves did. But probably this would happen only in the distant future, if at all. Meanwhile there were definite and immediate advantages to be gained from an association with the Communists.

THE STORM IN THE ARMY

The "October 17 affair," which climaxed three months of deepening political crisis, was the most momentous development of the Wilopo cabinet period and sharply accentuated the incipient tendencies toward change in political alignments. It occupies a place of key importance in the history of parliamentary institutions in Indonesia and the attempt to confine political struggle to them. And it illumines a number of the key problems involved in the effort to create and maintain a unified structure of government in the context of archipelago geography and revolutionary history.

But if we are to understand the October 17 affair we must look first at a number of background factors, particularly those having their roots in the country's economic situation. "By the middle of 1952," Professor Higgins has written, "it was clear to the fiscal authorities in Indonesia that the country was facing a first-class financial crisis." [38] The price of Indonesia's main export product, rubber, which had been 2.60 Straits dollars per pound in February 1951 did not stop falling until it had reached 73 Straits-dollar cents at the end of September 1952.[39] The level of physical exports was fairly well maintained in 1952, but the receipts which accrued from them were alarmingly low. The country's general terms of trade index fell in 1952 to 77 per cent of its level in 1951.[40] Furthermore, the rice crop was disappointingly small; there had to be an increase in the already large expenditures on imported rice. The country faced a dangerously large unfavorable balance of payments, a rapid drain on gold and foreign exchange reserves, and sharp falls in government revenues.

Here, then, was a fiscal and economic problem with immediate polit-

[38] Benjamin Higgins, *Indonesia's Economic Stabilization and Development* (New York: Institute of Pacific Relations, 1957), p. 2.

[39] The Java Bank, *Report for the Financial Year 1952–1953* (Djakarta, 1953), p. 160. These figures are for No. 1 ribbed smoked sheets.

[40] Monetary Research Section, Ministry of Finance, "Economic Review of 1952 and Outlook for 1953," in *Ekonomi dan Keuangan Indonesia* ("Economics and Finance in Indonesia"), vol. VI, no. 3 (May 1953); The Java Bank, *Report for the Financial Year 1952–1953*, p. 105.

ical implications. The Korean War boom had simplified most problems of government and politics; it had tided the country over the difficulties of the situation which developed after the first rewards of independence had been distributed. It had made it possible for the government to meet rehabilitation expenses and initiate development activities, to expand educational facilities rapidly, to permit increases in the size of the civil service, to finance the entry of numerous Indonesians into business, and still to maintain, in 1951, a surplus budget of Rp. 1.3 billion.

Henceforth this would be impossible. The slump made it necessary for the government to make painful choices between alternative ways of allocating its truncated resources. It started with efforts to stimulate exports and domestic production. Soon, however, it had to do less popular things. In August it introduced a system of import restrictions. To raise government revenue and reduce the import demand, it placed 100 per cent surcharges on such items as watches, men's and women's clothing, stationery, and shoes and 200 per cent surcharges on toys, ice chests, car radios, and various jewelry items. Its next step was to oblige importers to submit a 40 per cent prepayment of the total value of their imports at the time of receiving an import license. On September 1 it established an allocation system for imports, with direct government controls over an importer's total expenditure of foreign exchange. The burden of these measures fell on middle- and upper-income consumers and particularly on importers. And, since the recently established national Indonesian firms were in general financially weak, the burden fell especially on them.[41]

Other measures placed the burden of the slump on the government service. The various austerity measures taken by the cabinet in its first months in office were followed on September 10 by a regulation radically restricting the use of motor vehicles by government officials and making use of them impossible outside office hours.[42] Government expenditure abroad, on delegations to international conferences and

[41] For a full discussion, including comparisons with the foreign trade policies of the earlier cabinets, see Hans O. Schmitt, "Some Monetary and Fiscal Consequences of Social Conflict in Indonesia, 1950–58" (doctoral dissertation, University of California, Berkeley, 1959).

[42] The words "For Service Use Only" were painted on all government cars except those of cabinet ministers and secretaries-general of ministries. Roeslan Abdulgani, secretary-general of the Ministry of Information, estimated on March 3, 1953, that the regulations would result in a saving of Rp. 131.8 million in their first year in Djakarta alone (*Funksi Penerangan di Indonesia* ["The Function of Information Work in Indonesia"; Djakarta: Kementerian Penerangan, 1953], p. 140).

on foreign missions, was subjected to economies. Furthermore, a "freeze" was imposed on the spending of various ministries and a new system introduced whereby expenditures above a certain minimum would require the approval of the budgetary control section of the Ministry of Finance.[43] Most important of all, plans were made for a reduction in the number of military and civil service personnel. According to Professor Higgins, who acted as a UN adviser to the Ministry of Finance at the time, it was expected in this ministry that the retrenchments of the 1953 budget would require the retirement of 60,000 civil servants, 60,000 soldiers, and 30,000 policemen.[44]

With regard to civil service personnel no action was taken—except for the issuing of a strongly worded instruction forbidding the acceptance of new employees other than those with special qualifications. But the government acted speedily to begin the retirement of soldiers.

Soldier demobilization had been effected on a considerable scale in 1950, but only a small number of those who wanted to stay in the army had been forced out. Since 1950 there had been virtually no demobilization, but reorganization schemes of various other kinds had been implemented. Numerous training schemes had been set in motion, some using personnel from the Netherlands Military Mission. The central army leadership had succeeded in reshuffling posts in such a way that most of the commanders both at the territorial level and at the regimental level one step lower were men transferred from elsewhere. In 1952 the central command still occasionally met obstruction when it sought to investigate the budgets of divisional and regimental commanders, but its power to impose its will on them was much greater than it had been.

This reorganization, however, had been highly unpopular in many sections of the army. Many *bapakist* local leaders, who had been given high rank in the Revolution in order to bring about the incorporation of their units in the army, had been demoted. Others had been transferred from areas where their influence was established. Others again had been separated from their troops, their *anak buah* ("children"), and thus deprived of their source of power. The new military tech-

[43] Higgins, *op. cit.*, p. 6.

[44] Higgins, *op. cit.*, p. 10. The 1953 budget was presented to parliament in Nov. 1952, along with the 1952 budget—the first time that an Indonesian budget was presented before it came into effect. Although allowing for a deficit of Rp. 1.8 billion, it called for a reduction in government outlays from Rp. 17.6 billion to Rp. 13.2 billion.

niques placed Japanese-trained officers at a disadvantage. The new training schemes penalized those without basic formal education. *Semangat,* the dynamic ardor which the Japanese had fomented and which had stood the Republic in such good stead in the Revolution, was now accorded less and less value. Charisma was ceding ground to bureaucracy. The "administrators" were gaining at the expense of the "solidarity makers"—and the "solidarity makers" did not like it.

But the "administrator" leaders of the army were not deterred by the hostility they had evoked. On the contrary, they were determined, now that they again had a Defense Minister sympathetic with their ideas, to press ahead further with their plans to professionalize the army. In particular they wanted the demobilization of many of the soldiers who could not meet minimal health and educational standards. They were concerned about the high average age of army members, which was then approximately 32.[45] And they argued that it would be necessary to transform the army into a "core" force if there was to be progress toward the establishment of compulsory military service (to which the government was formally committed).[46]

Hence a close correspondence existed between the budgetary pressures which the cabinet felt and the policy goals of the "administrator" leaders of the army. Therefore in mid-1952 the army leaders decided that a beginning should be made by the end of the year through the gradual retirement of 80,000 of their 200,000 men. Approximately 40,000 of these would be soldiers asking to leave or ready to be pensioned, but another 40,000—an earlier government figure had been 60,000—would be those unable to fulfill physical and health requirements and those of whom it could be proved that they possessed "unsoldierly characteristics." [47]

These plans called forth great disquiet among the soldiers to be discharged, despite the government's plans for generous financial assistance to such persons; for not only did military work bear high prestige, but also it would be extremely difficult for many old soldiers to find alternative employment. In addition, the demobilization plans

[45] It was 34 in 1954. See Nasution, *Tjatatan-Tjatatan Sekitar Politik Militer,* p. 203.

[46] See letter of Defense Minister Sewaka to Colonel Nasution, Dec. 22, 1951, in Dewan Perwakilan Rakjat (People's Representative Council), *Risalah Perundingan* ("Report of Proceedings"), Oct. 1, 1952.

[47] See Statement of the Minister of Defense in Dewan Perwakilan Rakjat, *Risalah Perundingan,* Oct. 1, 1952. See also Nasution, *Tjatatan-Tjatatan Sekitar Politik Militer,* pp. 203 ff., 262–295, 316 ff.

aroused the strong hostility of *bapakist* revolutionary leaders in the officer corps and of others opposed to the whole trend of profession-alization.

But the *bapakist* officers and their followers—they were frequently spoken of as the Peta group [48]—had considerable political resources. They had close personal and political connections with the PNI (par-ticularly its Sidik group) and several smaller "oppositionist" parties. Some of them had equally close links with President Soekarno. It was through these associations that the internal conflict in the army was projected into the political community at large.

President Soekarno had long been critical of the policies pursued in the army. Many of the personnel changes which the army leaders had effected in 1951 and the first half of 1952 had clearly lessened his influence within the army, and on at least one occasion in 1952 he had intervened against the army leaders' personnel policy by refusing to sign a decree. The President resented particularly the army leaders' decision to close down the Chandradimuka Military Academy at Bandung, a sort of ideological refresher school for army officers, where a number of his personal associates, men of the Peta group, occupied positions of leadership.

For some time before July 1952 the former head of the Chandradi-muka Academy, Colonel Bambang Supeno, an old Peta man and in-telligence officer from East Java and a distant relative of President Soekarno, had urged that Colonel Nasution be replaced. He had ap-proached the President to discuss this matter with him and had sub-sequently traveled in several parts of Indonesia collecting signatures of officers supporting Nasution's removal. To counteract this develop-ment Major General Simatupang called a meeting of territorial com-manders and other high officers at his home on July 12. At this meeting, at which Nasution was not present, Simatupang asked Bambang Supeno to give an account of his activities. Tempers were aroused, and before long Bambang Supeno walked out.

---

[48] This is in fact a somewhat misleading term, in view of the fact that many former Peta men, members of the Indonesian auxiliary army established by the Japanese, did adjust to the requirements of the reorganization and became its beneficiaries. However, the group of those who could not adjust defended their position in terms of the ideology of Peta, with its great stress on *semangat* (fighting spirit). Many of them had been strongly imbued with the Japanese "young officer group" view of the army as the soul of the nation. See Guy J. Pauker, *The Role of the Military in Indonesia* (research memorandum, Santa Monica, Calif.: Rand Corporation, 1960), pp. 20–23.

On the following day Supeno wrote a letter to the Defense Minister, the Prime Minister, and the Defense section of parliament, declaring he no longer had faith in his superiors because these had swerved from the original goals of the revolutionary struggle. In addition, he criticized a number of aspects of military policy, particularly personnel policy, educational policy, and the policy being pursued in relation to domestic insecurity. Four days later he was suspended from all duties by Colonel Nasution.

At the same time the Defense Minister, Sultan Hamengku Buwono, with Simatupang and Nasution, went personally to the President to discuss these matters with him. As a result of references to the President's own role in the Bambang Supeno affair, the conversation became heated, particularly between Soekarno and Simatupang, and the meeting finally ended without agreement being reached.

Meanwhile the matter had been taken up by the Defense section of parliament, and on July 28 parliament held the first of four secret plenary sessions, which were followed by seventeen public ones. Thus for ten weeks parliament gave much of its time and almost all its attention to a debate more acrimonious than any it had previously held, a debate in which criticism was directed against virtually every aspect, major and trivial, of the policies pursued by the army leaders and Wilopo's Minister of Defense.

A few days before the opening of the debate the Minister of Defense had submitted four bills on soldier demobilization, and although parliament decided to defer debating these formally, they were fully discussed in the context of the general debate. The critics of the army leadership argued that Indonesia could not in the near future fight anything but a guerrilla war. Therefore it needed an army close to the people. Revolutionary morale and close association with the people were what had given the army its victory over the Dutch; yet these were being sacrificed as a result of the "Westernizing" and "internationalizing" orientation of the army leaders. In addition, demobilization was dangerous. If the discharged men were not given treatment commensurate with their revolutionary services, this might well drive them to join rebel and bandit groups.

Similar opposition was expressed to the whole policy of army reorganization pursued since 1950. The critics opposed the Defense Ministry's demands for scholastic qualifications in new recruits. They condemned changes made in such matters as saluting, uniforms, and the method of marching, changes away from the Japanese forms which the revolutionary army had used. They attacked the way in which troop units had been shifted about and split as a result of the army leaders' attempts to establish a network of territorial commanders with their own approach to army organization. They cited case after case of celebrated revolutionary commanders whose services had been spurned. They declared that the 900-man Netherlands Military Mission had hoodwinked the army leaders and sabotaged the fight against the Darul Islam.[49] And they charged that old KNIL soldiers were being preferred to men who had served in the revolutionary TNI (Tentara Nasional Indonesia, Indonesian National Army).

As for Colonel Bambang Supeno, the parliamentary critics argued that his suspension was illegal, not having received the approval of the President. Giving President Soekarno's own interpretation of the ambiguous provisions of the 1950 constitution with regard to his powers as Commander in Chief of the Armed Forces, they argued that no officer of Supeno's rank could be suspended without the President's specific endorsement.[50]

Finally, the parliamentary critics charged that the army was being fashioned as a stronghold of the Socialist Party.[51] A number of high army officers and Defense Ministry officials were branded as PSI members or sympathizers. The Socialist press was said to be favored in bulk orders of newspapers for soldiers. Political articles written by Major General Simatupang were pointed to as suggesting Socialist partisanship in the Armed Forces Chief of Staff. A number of cases were adduced of actions taken by army leaders at times of cabinet crisis, actions which, it was said, favored the Socialist Party's interests. Almost all the many charges of corruption which were made were directed at members or sympathizers of the PSI. The attack culminated in the assertion that the whole reorganization program was aimed at strengthening the PSI's hold on the army, which it could then use for a *coup d'état*.

[49] The letters NMM were commonly said to stand for Nederlandsche Mata Mata (Dutch spies). Considerable evidence existed of the involvement of Dutch persons in Darul Islam activities. See Ministry of Foreign Affairs, Republic of Indonesia, *Subversive Activities in Indonesia: The Jungschlaeger and Schmidt Affair* (Djakarta: Government Printing Office, 1957), especially pp. 75 ff.

[50] See A. K. Pringgodigdo, *The Office of President in Indonesia as Defined in the Three Constitutions in Theory Practice* (Cornell Modern Indonesia Project, Translation Series; Ithaca, N.Y., 1957), pp. 27–29.

[51] See Kementerian Penerangan (Ministry of Information), *Ichtisar Parlemen* ("Parliamentary Chronicle"), Sept. 23, 1952 (speeches of Kobarsjih and Ir. Sakirman), and Oct. 14 (speech of Zainul Baharuddin).

The parliamentarians who contributed most actively to criticism of the army leaders' policies were from "solidarity maker" and "oppositionist" groups. In fact, a listing of them is virtually a listing of the "solidarity maker" elements in Indonesian political life at this time. The most prominent critic was Zainul Baharuddin, the nonparty chairman of the Defense section of parliament, who was a relative and close associate of the head of the armed forces' intelligence agency, Lieutenant Colonel Zulkifli Lubis. Among the others were leaders of the national-communist Partai Murba, of the Communist Party, and of the newly formed Progressive Fraction, which included supporters of both Murba and the Communist Party. Also prominent were such Moslem "solidarity makers" as Arudji Kartawinata of the PSII, Zainul Arifin of the new political party of the Nahdatul Ulama, and Isa Anshary of the Masjumi. Support came too from several minor nationalist parties, particularly PRN (the National People's Party), and, more importantly, from the Sidik group of the PNI. In the Djakarta press the group had its strongest support—and this amounted to a sustained campaign—from B. M. Diah's *Merdeka* (which had been the strongest supporter of the Sukiman cabinet in the Mutual Security aid crisis) and the new *Mimbar Indonesia* (daily), then edited by the Murba-sympathizing Muhammad Yamin.

It is difficult to say how far the multifarious charges were justified. There can be no doubt that the grievances which the members of the Defense section of parliament discovered on their tours of the provinces were real. When they pointed to the complaints of various neglected army units, when they listed the numbers of officers and men who wanted to resign because of dissatisfaction with their conditions and the atmosphere of their work, when they marshaled evidence of a thousand and one cases of injustice, due to rivalry between cliques or to sheer inefficiency, when they alleged that a gulf had developed between the army and the people in many areas—then their criticisms were valid. Indeed, Sultan Hamengku Buwono himself acknowledged many of them.

But if there was factual evidence for many of the charges, other charges and insinuations were sensational, vague, or unsubstantiated. By reading out anonymous letters and threats and using terms like "a certain colonel" and "a certain party" the parliamentary critics created an atmosphere similar to that "when someone at a market shouts 'pickpocket.'" [52] This reached a boomeranging degree of ab-

---

[52] "S.," *Sikap* (PSI weekly), Oct. 6, 1952.

surdity on October 6 when the PRN leader Bebasa Daeng Lalo called
the Sultan a-national and pro-Dutch. But in general the tactics were
politically effective. In such an atmosphere it was difficult to defend
the use of a military mission of Dutchmen and almost as difficult to
make out a case for a military pattern different from that of the
Republic in the period of Revolution. Government speakers appealed
time and again for objectivity and a businesslike approach and condemned the use of a scapegoat—but largely in vain. This was not
merely an argument about policies; it was a struggle for power.

Was the army indeed being made into a stronghold of the PSI? Certainly opponents of this party had been losing influence in the army.
And the party had undeniably benefited from a number of actions
taken by the army leadership and the Ministry of Defense in cabinet-
level politics. When political pressure was applied by the army in the
1950–1952 period, it was usually on matters directly related to the
army's own interests, for instance, in the selection of a Minister of
Defense. But it cannot be denied that the effect of such pressure was
a major strengthening of the PSI. In practice the candidates whom the
army leaders regarded as acceptable for the Defense portfolio, in the
first place the Sultan of Jogjakarta, were men of a fundamentally
similar outlook to that of the Socialists. In the same way the Socialist
Party gained from the army leaders' effective exertion of influence
against the attempt of the Sukiman cabinet to transfer Mr. Ali Budiardjo from the secretary-generalship of the ministry.

The army leadership was not, however, dominated by the PSI in
such a way that PSI interests would prevail over army interests. It
is true that both Major General Simatupang and Ali Budiardjo (who
was the major general's brother-in-law) were in some measure sympathizers of the Socialist Party, but this cannot be said of Colonel
Nasution, who had some dislike for this party, as well as most others,
and whose political orientation had the army as its center. Close co-
operation was possible between Nasution on the one hand and Simatupang on the other because they shared an approach to the building
up of a modern, cohesive, and powerful army. It would have been
impossible to achieve such co-operation on a basis which involved
control of the army by a civilian political group.[53]

The parliamentary attack came to a head as a result of a series of

[53] For a fuller discussion see Herbert Feith, *The Wilopo Cabinet, 1952–1953:
A Turning Point in Post-revolutionary Indonesia* (Cornell Modern Indonesia
Project, Monograph Series; Ithaca, N.Y., 1958), pp. 114–115.

motions. One motion moved by Zainul Baharuddin with Murba, Labor Party, and PRN cosignatories was submitted on September 23. It was an expression of "no confidence in the policy adopted by the Defense Minister to end the conflicts within the armed forces" and a call for a state defense law and other laws. Subsequently on October 10 the sponsors agreed to incorporate important modifications as suggested by the PKI parliamentary leader Sakirman. So modified, in what appeared to be an attempt to bring the PNI to its support, the motion called for "reformation and reorganization of the leadership of the Ministry of Defense and the Armed Forces," for a national defense law, and for "the establishment of a special parliamentary commission to investigate administrative and financial fraud in the Ministry of Defense and Armed Forces." [54]

Although this motion was not specifically directed against the Minister of Defense and was said by its proposers to be primarily against the "big three," Ali Budiardjo, Simatupang, and Nasution, the minister insisted that he would treat it as one of no confidence in himself. It soon appeared that the PSI, the Protestant Parkindo, and possibly also the Catholic Party would maintain solidarity with the Sultan and withdraw their own ministers if he resigned. As it was hardly conceivable that the cabinet could survive the resignation of four or five of its ministers, the Baharuddin motion soon came to be seen as an effort to bring down the cabinet.[55] This expectation worked in the Defense Minister's favor, for many who had criticized the army leaders did not want another cabinet crisis so soon. A number of prominent supporters of the cabinet now declared that it was unconstitutional for the legislature to make decisions on such matters as personnel policy and corruption. The Socialist Party was no longer politically isolated.

Within major sections of the army this later stage of the debate saw the development of very strong feeling against "politicians" and their parliament. Antipolitician feeling had always been strong in the army. Colonel Nasution was to write later of "the historic competition, dating back to the Jogja period, between parties and the army, a competition which is never spoken of, but is present in every action." [56] But in general the men of the central leadership of the army had attempted

[54] Kementerian Penerangan, *Ichtisar Parlemen*, Oct. 4, 1952.
[55] For specific suggestions that a cabinet crisis was not entirely undesirable see *Merdeka*, Sept. 18, Oct. 4, 1952.
[56] *Tjatatan-Tjatatan Sekitar Politik Militer*, p. 173.

to hold this feeling in check in the years after 1949. Now, however, they ceased to feel the need to restrain their subordinates in this way. Thus many army men, including men who were not otherwise supporters of Simatupang or Nasution, grew strongly resentful of the way in which army "dirty linen" was being aired in the parliamentary public. They were particularly angered by Zainul Baharuddin's use of parliamentary privilege to read out classified documents of the army.

The Socialist Party for its part attempted to associate itself with antipolitician feeling, both in the army and elsewhere. It made frequent attacks on parliament, stressing the numerical strength in it of men who had supported the Dutch-sponsored federal states. It castigated the parliamentarians for luxurious living, irresponsibility, and wasting time. In particular it condemned their disinclination to create an election law.[57]

On October 13 the government initiated what it hoped would be a concerted move of the parties supporting it to take the wind out of Zainul Baharuddin's sails. This took the form of a countermotion submitted by I. J. Kasimo of the Catholic Party with cosignatories from the Masjumi, the Labor Party, Parkindo, and Parindra. Efforts were made to have a PNI signatory as well, but after some hesitation the party's executive decided that none of its members could sign. The motion asked that the government should immediately establish a State Commission representing both parliament and the government, but with a majority of parliamentary representatives, to examine carefully and objectively all questions raised in the parliamentary debates and within three months present to the government concrete suggestions concerning "the possibility of improvements in the structure of the Defense Ministry and Armed Forces." Further, it called for a "hastening of the end of the Netherlands Military Mission's work" and asked that the State Commission be charged with reporting to the government within two months regarding concrete steps toward this end.

Within the PNI the demand was for a motion "stronger" than Kasimo's. Sidik had stated on October 9 that the PNI was "certainly not afraid of facing a cabinet crisis over this matter," and his position appeared to be stronger within the party on this issue than that of the supporters of Wilopo. Thus on October 14 the PNI, joining with the

[57] See, for instance, Sbs, "Politik Parlementer" ("Parliamentary Politics"), in *Sikap*, Aug. 11, 1952. See also Sindo, "Hendak kemana D.P.R. 'Sementara' ini?" ("Where Is This 'Temporary' Parliament Going?"), *ibid.*, Sept. 29, 1952.

PSII and Nahdatul Ulama, sponsored a motion of its own. This third motion, the Manai Sophian motion, was identical with the motion of Kasimo except that it included in the tasks of the State Commission the work of reporting on "the possibility of improvements in the leadership and organization of the Defense Ministry and Armed Forces." In political terms this meant the possibility of dismissals of the controversial top figures.

The last few days before the voting on the three motions were ones of intense political activity. On October 8 all secretaries-general of ministries met, reportedly to consider the threat to Ali Budiardjo's position. October 11 saw an extraordinary meeting in Djakarta of the seven territorial commanders, who thereafter remained in Djakarta awaiting developments. At the same time there were rumors of great restiveness in army units in and near Djakarta. From October 14 parliament was heavily posted with military guards. Party councils were conferring frequently. Zainul Baharuddin spoke on October 14 of the dangers of a military coup, citing recent happenings in Egypt and Thailand. *Nadjib-nadjiban* ("doing a Naguib") became part of Djakarta's political vocabulary.

By the evening of October 15, when the Defense Minister was to give his final reply to the criticisms made of him, tension was extremely high. Voting on the three motions was to take place that evening, immediately after the Defense Minister's reply. The Kasimo motion was accepted by the government at the last minute. The Baharuddin motion would, it was predicted, be defeated; no government party would support it. The crucial question was whether the Manai Sophian motion would win support. Hearing the minister's speech of reply, parliamentarians were surprised that there was no reference in it to the Sophian motion. They later found the reason: at a meeting of the PNI executive in the late afternoon Wilopo had succeeded in obtaining majority support for a proposal that the motion be withdrawn. This the Prime Minister had told to the Sultan, who then gave his speech anticipating that Sophian would announce the withdrawal immediately afterward.

But Sophian did not withdraw his motion. Instead the PNI parliamentary leader Hadikusumo asked that the vote be postponed until the next morning. Only later did it become known that President Soekarno had called Iskaq and Sunario to the palace on the evening of October 15 and applied pressure on these PNI leaders of the older Sartono-Suwirjo wing in support of Manai Sophian's motion. In a tightly balanced situation the President's voice had been decisive.

The voting took place on the morning of October 16. The Baharuddin motion was put to the vote first and was defeated by 80 votes to 39. Then the Manai Sophian motion was put and accepted 91 to 54. The Masjumi, PSI, Parindra, and the two Christian parties opposed it, while the Democratic Fraction and most members of the Labor Party abstained. All other parties and fractions, including the PNI, supported the motion.[58]

The vote created an impasse. The Minister of Defense was almost committed to resigning. He had made it clear that he would not accept any motion which was a priori in character and that he regarded attacks on the leadership of his ministry as attacks on himself. And the Sultan was known to be stubborn in such things. But clearly the problem was one in which the cabinet as a whole was involved. On the other hand, a resignation of the government was impossible; the situation was far too tense, for it was unlikely that the army leaders would remain silent. No one knew what would happen next.

On the morning of October 17 a surprise demonstration appeared in the streets of Djakarta. By eight o'clock a crowd of approximately 5,000 men, city and country laborers, had gathered outside parliament. There was no indication on its many well-painted banners and placards of who had organized the demonstration. But the demonstrators' demands were clear: "Dissolve Parliament," "Parliament Isn't a Coffee Shop," "Parliament for the Sake of Democracy, Not Democracy for Parliament's Sake," "The People Must Judge," "Purge the Corruptors," "Elections Immediately," "Use Section 84 of the Constitution,"[59] and so on. They soon broke into parliament, smashed some chairs, and wrecked the parliamentary cafeteria!

From there they moved around the city, attracting larger numbers, mainly the curious, to join them. After presenting a petition to Vice-President Hatta and after minor incidents in which several Dutch flags were pulled off their masts and torn up, the crowd, by now perhaps 30,000 strong, arrived in front of the Presidency. After some time the President came out and walked, among general cheering, to the fence where the demonstrators were standing. Then, in a masterly speech made from the Presidency steps, he both rebuked and soothed

[58] For a discussion of the pattern of alignments see Feith, *The Wilopo Cabinet,* pp. 120–123.

[59] This is the dissolution clause. It read: "The President shall have the right to dissolve Parliament. The President's declaration of dissolution shall at the same time be an order for the election of a new Parliament within 30 days."

them. There would be elections as soon as possible, he said. But meanwhile he could not simply dissolve parliament. To ask him to act thus was to ask him to become a dictator, to bring to nought what the people had fought so long and hard to win. In this way Soekarno sent the demonstrators home. They cheered him and went. Even if one admits that this was a hastily assembled group of people, it was an extraordinary demonstration of the President's authority.[60]

Some time after the demonstration was first seen a sudden burst of army activity took place. As the President was beginning his speech to the demonstrators, he saw before him two tanks, several armored cars, and four cannons, with some of the cannons and some of the machine guns on the armored cars trained on the Presidency. One army unit was inside the Presidency, and many more were outside. At 10:15 and 10:30, shortly after the President had concluded his address, two groups of senior officers, seventeen altogether and including five of the seven territorial commanders, arrived to see him.[61] Then for an hour and a half they conferred with the President, who called the Vice-President, the secretary of the President's cabinet, Mr. A. K. Pringgodigdo, Prime Minister Wilopo, and the acting chairman of parliament, Tambunan, to join in the discussions.

What transpired at this historic meeting was reported in a great variety of forms by different interested persons, becoming the subject of vehement controversy. But the general pattern of what was said is now clear. The officers wanted the President to dissolve parliament. Their principal spokesman, the Deputy Chief of Staff Lieutenant Colonel Sutoko, told Soekarno that the group saw the existing unrepresentative parliament as the root of the country's political instability and thus of the inability of the recent cabinets to continue in office long enough to implement their programs. Colonel M. Simbolon, the North Sumatra commander, spoke of the dangers of direct political interference in the placement policies of the army. Colonel A. E. Kawilarang of the crucial command of West Java, of which Djakarta was a part, spoke of the explosive state of feelings among his soldiers and of the danger of catastrophic consequences if the questions agitat-

[60] This account is based on the reports of the *Aneta* and *Antara* news agencies, and the description by Adi Negoro, *Pemilihan Umum dan Djiwa Masjarakat di Indonesia* ("Elections and the Spirit of the Community in Indonesia"; Djakarta: Bulan Bintang, 1953), on the government statement of Nov. 22, 1952, and on my personal observations.

[61] For a list of those present see *Pedoman*, Dec. 6, 1952, or Feith, *The Wilopo Cabinet*, pp. 124–125.

ing them were not settled or if there were further provocation of any kind.[62] All this, it was said, was evidence of the necessity for the President to break the deadlock by dissolving parliament. Sutoko presented the President with a statement drawn up by the officers after their meetings of October 16 and the early morning of October 17 which decided "to urge the Head of the State to dissolve the present temporary parliament and form a new parliament in the shortest possible time in a manner which takes the wishes of the people into consideration." [63]

But the officers meant to go further than this. Their statement urged also the "retiring of the elements in the present Parliament with tendencies such as described above"—spreading secrets of the armed forces, intentionally interpreting them destructively, and so on—and "the taking of steps against functionaries of the armed forces who have violated their duty to keep armed forces secrets." [64] This, however, was not officially admitted, the text of the statement appearing publicly only as the result of a "leak" to the newspaper *Merdeka* made more than a month later. Silence on this gave rise to a host of rumors to the effect that the officers had asked the President to assume dictatorial powers, that they had asked for the existing cabinet to be replaced by a triumvirate of Soekarno, Hatta, and the Sultan of Jogjakarta, that they had threatened the President, and so on.[65]

In any event it is clear that the President did not yield to the demands which were made of him. He would not endorse the army leaders' statement, nor would he commit himself on the question of the dissolution of parliament. This, he said, he would have to discuss with the cabinet. Having made this clear, he sent the officers away. When they had left the Presidency, Soekarno, Hatta, and Wilopo, in consultation with Tambunan, the acting chairman of parliament, urged the Consultative Committee of parliament to declare for a prolonged recess. This the committee did forthwith.

Meanwhile, however, army activity was increasing outside the Presidency. More and more soldiers came out on the streets of Djakarta.

[62] See Sutoko's press interview in *Antara*, Oct. 31, 1952, and *Indonesia Raya*, Oct. 31, 1952.

[63] For the full text see *Merdeka*, Nov. 24, 1952. The authenticity of this text was certified by Nasution. See the circular letter of the Biro Staf Umum Angkatan Darat (Bureau of the Army General Staff), *Pedoman*, Dec. 6, 1952.

[64] *Merdeka*, Nov. 24, 1952.

[65] See, for instance, *Merdeka*, Oct. 31, Nov. 1, 1952, and the statement of the Biro Informasi Staf Angkatan Perang (Information Bureau of the Armed Forces Staff), *Merdeka*, Dec. 5, 6, 1952.

At eleven o'clock telephone and telegraph communications, both internal and overseas, were stopped. Ship and airplane departures from Djakarta were delayed, and an eight to five curfew was imposed. All meetings of more than five persons were banned by order of the Djakarta city command. Six M.P.'s—including Sukiman, Yamin, and the PRN's Bebasa Daeng Lalo—were placed under arrest. Two dailies, *Merdeka* and *Berita Indonesia,* and two weeklies, *Mimbar Indonesia* and *Mingguan Merdeka,* were banned. The atmosphere was highly tense and remained so throughout October 18, with meetings of top army officers continuing.

But within three days almost all the army's emergency measures had been revoked. The arrested men were free, and the ban on publications had been lifted. Army activity in the streets of Djakarta had been reduced to the normal level. The stage was set for a new political battle.

What was the meaning of the events of October 17? Did they constitute an attempt to "do a Naguib"? Did the army leaders act out of anger and panic, or was there a clearly conceived plan of defending their positions by changing the whole balance of power? Did their desire for the dissolution of parliament spring from a wish to see the existing cabinet more capable of carrying out its policy? Or was their main aim to place the whole government in a position of dependence on themselves or perhaps to overthrow it? These questions continued to be debated vehemently for many months.

In the first place, it is clear that the demonstration was substantially an army-organized affair. It is true that feeling against parliament was high—the luxurious living of the M.P.'s, their business successes, and the connection between their role and the slowness of government action had made it easy for the PSI and other groups to make them targets for the inchoate general feeling of disappointment with the fruits of independence. But a number of those who took part in this rapidly and efficiently organized demonstration had traveled into the city in army trucks. Some, in fact, were identified as soldiers in civilian clothes. Furthermore, Colonel Mustopo, the eccentric head of the army dental service, actually stated in a press interview published on the morning of October 17 that he had organized the demonstration.[66] And the Deputy Chief of Staff, Sutoko, admitted that he

---

[66] Although Dr. Mustopo claimed to have taken the action on his own initiative, it is more likely that he was, as suggested by Sutomo (Bung Tomo), a former associate, "a small screw of a large machine." See *Merdeka,* Oct. 28, 1952.

had been told on the previous evening that a demonstration might take place.

A number of those who took part in the demonstration were either personal followers of Dr. Mustopo, a man whose influence in working-class Djakarta was considerable at the time, or members of ganglike *kampong* guard organizations with which he had associations. Some of those who took part are known to have done so for money. Moreover, certain parties appear to have been involved, notably the Socialist Party, the national-communist Partai Murba, and the PRI (Partai Rakjat Indonesia, Indonesian People's Party), the party of "Bung Tomo." But principal responsibility for the demonstration must be attributed to sections of the army leadership, including some high officers of the General Staff.

For an understanding of the purposes for which the army leaders enacted the drama of October 17 it is necessary to look at certain earlier developments inside the armed forces leadership. Despite some conflicting evidence, it may be regarded as established that Colonel Nasution was engaged, for several months before October 17, in working out plans for a type of military coup. It seems that his plans, to which the Minister of Defense and Major General Simatupang were opposed, involved using the Siliwangi Division, the West Java division commanded by Colonel Kawilarang, to effect a change which would make for a stronger government by giving greater power to President Soekarno, at the same time making him partly dependent on army support. Nasution had discussed much of this with President Soekarno and Vice-President Hatta some time before the October crisis, and he is reported to have received some encouragement from the former. In addition, several days before October 17, he had spoken about his plans to the Prime Minister.

Then an important disagreement developed between Soekarno and Nasution. The President would not approve a list submitted by Nasution of officers and politicians to be arrested at the time of the proposed coup. The changes demanded by Soekarno were resented particularly by a group of younger staff officers who had been supporting Nasution. The result was that by October 16 the initiative in planning the action had passed from Nasution to these younger men, in particular the Deputy Chiefs of Staff, Lieutenant Colonels Sutoko and Aziz Saleh, and the military police head, Lieutenant Colonel S. Parman. This group was not held together by any common political viewpoint other than the antipolitician ideology of the army, although some of its members had Socialist Party sympathies. What these men sought to do remains unclear, but there can be little doubt that there were some plans for a coup-type action.[67]

The larger group of army leaders who met on October 16 and again in the early morning of October 17 were faced with a situation at once exasperating and highly confused. They had been angered by the behavior of parliament and bewildered by the zigzags of PNI policy. Many were afraid of having their work undone, and some of losing their positions. Some too were seriously concerned lest army disunity should erupt in violence. This could be triggered, they believed, by the actions of the Black Dragon type of organization of the armed forces intelligence head, Lieutenant Colonel Lubis, an active leader of anti-Nasution elements in the army. Something had to be done—but what?

Relations between parliament and cabinet were at a deadlock. For the army leaders it was imperative that parliament should yield and not the cabinet; this pointed to dissolution. But dissolution was constitutionally dubious and in practice impossible without the approval of the President.[68] The President was the key to the situation, but his position on the central issues was unclear. On the one hand, he had shown that he shared the army leaders' hostility to parliament, but on the other hand his co-operation with Nasution had broken down, and he seemed to have supported the Sophian motion. The question which the officer group faced was: If action was to be taken, should it go only as far as was possible with the co-operation of the President, or should it be pressed further if need be?

[67] On October 15 the Djakarta English-language daily *Times of Indonesia*, edited by the editor of *Indonesia Raya* which had very close connections with the army leadership, published a version of the Djojobojo prophecy. In what were obvious references to Soekarno and the Sultan of Jogjakarta, the piece ended, "The Leader would soon pass from power and his place would be taken by a prince of the ancient land, Java."

[68] The statement of the 1950 constitution, "The President's declaration of dissolution shall at the same time be an order for the election of a new Parliament within 30 days," was interpreted by many as meaning that there could be no dissolution if it was technically impossible to hold elections within a 30-day period. According to a strict interpretation of the constitution the right of dissolution is vested not with the President as a matter of prerogative, but rather with the cabinet. See Pringgodigdo, *The Office of President in Indonesia*, pp. 26–27. However, President Soekarno had shown on previous occasions that he would not be bound to strict interpretations of his constitutional role. Moreover, some of the cabinet's legal advisers maintained that, by analogy with Dutch constitutional practice, a deadlock of this kind could be broken by a prerogative action of the head of state, in which he either dismissed the cabinet or dissolved parliament.

Action was particularly strongly urged at these meetings by the group of Sutoko and Aziz Saleh of the General Staff and S. Parman of the military police, and it appears that this group was supported by certain of the divisional commanders from the provinces, particularly Kawilarang of West Java. But the nature of the action which these men proposed is not clear. Nor is it clear what breadth of agreement was reached at the meetings. What is certain is that a number of the most important of the actions of October 17 were not the result of agreement by the larger officer group which met on October 16 and 17.

These actions in fact resulted from the independent initiative of a number of army elements. Thus most of the divisional commanders were taken completely by surprise by the occurrence of the demonstration—as indeed was the Defense Minister. Whatever the role of Dr. Mustopo in organizing the demonstration, he was certainly not acting as a disciplined member of a *Putsch* group. Even at the palace there were contrasts in the behavior of different members of the officer group. Some were defiant, others had tears in their eyes as they spoke. Similarly the burst of army activity, which had first appeared on the streets while the President was addressing the demonstrators, was the result of planning not by all the officers who later went to the Presidency, but by a smaller General Staff group co-operating with the Djakarta city commander, Lieutenant Colonel Taswin. It was this smaller group which cut communications, ordered the arrests, press bans, and curfew, and banned public meetings. The provocative decision to train cannons on the Presidency appears to have been taken by a single battalion commander.

The lack of co-ordination which characterized these developments goes far to explain why the officers were prepared to accept the President's rejection of their demands. It is a fact that certain groups within the army leadership wanted some sort of a coup, an assertion of military power which would radically change the power balance. But this group had only partial support from the army leaders who went to the President. The group as a whole had made a timing mistake by going to the President after he had addressed the demonstrators. And they had allowed the President's antagonism to be aroused by the guns which faced the palace. Thus when Soekarno stood firm against the demands which they brought to him, majority opinion within the group turned against the party which wanted to force the issue.[69]

[69] Perhaps, then, it is impossible to draw a sharp distinction between urging and intimidation in a situation like this—or in the similar situation of 1945 when Soe-

When this group presented its point of view again at the subsequent meetings later in the day and on October 18, it was clear that further action could be taken only if the army felt itself strong and united enough to take power into its own hands. This became clearer when Vice-President Hatta, who had previously encouraged the army leaders in their demand for the dissolution of parliament, was not prepared to become involved in an army action taken in defiance of the President. In addition, Bambang Supeno, Zulkifli Lubis, and their associates had by now had considerable success in organizing opposition to the army leaders, through use of the name of the President. And, as Simatupang stressed in these meetings, the army leaders had no clear conception of what they would do with full powers over civilian affairs once they had assumed them.[70]

It is not possible, therefore, to give a clear-cut answer to the question whether there was an attempt at *coup d'état*. There was an attempt to intimidate the President, but it was not pressed. Some important groups of the army leadership wanted action which would change the balance of power radically. But these groups did not have any carefully elaborated plans. And their influence within the leadership as a whole was not clearly predominant. One cannot say how far they would have tried to go in changing the constellation of power, or how far they would have been able to go in this way, if they had succeeded in forcing Soekarno to accept their will on October 17 or 18.

For some days after October 17 confusion and apprehension prevailed. On October 18 it was announced that the cabinet would continue in office, with consideration of the Manai Sophian motion postponed. There was no indication that Sultan Hamengku Buwono would resign. There would be no cabinet crisis, it seemed. As the army's emergency measures were undone one by one and the territorial commanders returned to their own commands, a reassuring uneventfulness came over the political scene. But the atmosphere remained strained. The press was unusually circumspect and unin-

---

karno was kidnapped by a group of youth leaders and pressed to proclaim independence forthwith. In one sense it is true that the officers went to the President "as children going to their father" (Sutoko, *Antara*, Oct. 31, 1952), and the Indonesian expectation is that a political *bapak* or father should do what his *anak buah* or children recommend if he sees that they feel very strongly on a particular matter.

[70] See T. B. Simatupang, *Pelopor dalam Perang, Pelopor dalam Damai* ("A Forerunner in War and Peace"; Djakarta: Jajasan Pustaka Militer, 1954), pp. 101–105, for a discussion of the practical case against military dictatorship.

formative. The numerous appeals of government and government-supporting leaders for moderation were evidence that the surface calm gave no proper cause for relief.[71] Meanwhile a tremendous variety of explanations of the events of October 17 were in circulation, and there were rumors of intense behind-the-scenes political activity both inside and outside the army. Members of the political public were bewildered and in many cases anxious, sensing that this was a situation in which new and unpredictable political forces were at work.

This sense of bewilderment was heightened when it became clear that the political battle of October 17 was shifting from Djakarta to the regions. Before long it appeared in one or another form in the center of every one of the seven military commands. Demonstrations like the one in Djakarta on October 17, with organizationally unidentified persons demanding the dissolution of parliament, appeared in Semarang on October 20, in Bandjarmasin, Kalimantan, on October 24, in Medan on October 27, and in Bandung on November 8. In the three other centers of military power there were happenings of much greater significance—bloodless coups to overthrow the local territorial commander.

The first of these coups was in the East Java division. East Java had long been the main stronghold of the "Peta group," of the sections of the army opposed to the politics of the Defense Ministry. However, the acting territorial commander there, Lieutenant Colonel Suwondho, who was in charge while Colonel Bambang Sugeng was on sick leave, was not a member of this group. When he returned to Surabaja from Djakarta on October 19, Suwondho found that a number of leading "Peta group" officers, including Colonel Bambang Supeno, Colonel Sungkono, Colonel Suhud, and Lieutenant Colonel Sapari, had arrived in East Java before him. These men had been encouraged by President Soekarno to rally opposition in East Java to the Djakarta leaders of the army, and in this they were quickly successful. Suwondho's position was weak, but on October 21 he struck back. In a strongly worded order of the day he attacked those members of the army who had been "screaming with the opportunists among the politicians, who had promised them positions." At the same time he appealed for army unity, stating that the alternative was "balkanization of the state." [72]

But Suwondho could not hold his position. Almost immediately after

---

[71] See the statements of Mohammad Natsir, *Aneta*, Oct. 18, 1952, Mohammad Roem, *Antara*, Oct. 18, 1952, and Wilopo, *Antara*, Oct. 22, 1952.

[72] *Aneta*, Oct. 22, 1952.

he had issued this statement, he was arrested by order of the Bambang Supeno supporters in the divisional headquarters. The General Staff in Djakarta sent Lieutenant Colonels Parman and Suprapto to Surabaja, armed with a mandate to take whatever action they thought necessary, but these men found they could do nothing but legitimize the power change which had taken place. On October 22 the divisional headquarters in Surabaja announced that Suwondho had been dismissed by the General Staff delegation from Djakarta, that the most senior regimental commander in East Java, Lieutenant Colonel R. Sudirman, had been declared acting territorial commander, and that he had revoked Suwondho's order of the day. Two days later Sudirman issued a long statement. He asserted that Suwondho's leadership of the division had become unacceptable because of his active participation in the undemocratic actions of October 17. He proclaimed as unjustifiable "firstly the acts of those armed forces functionaries who had used the powers of their offices to take action directed toward a dissolution of parliament and secondly the repressive measures which had been taken in close connection with these actions." Finally, he professed his loyalty to President Soekarno and expressed the hope that he, as Supreme Commander, would effect a settlement of the whole affair.[73]

Both the Minister of Defense and the Chief of Staff of the Army visited East Java in early November. But Sudirman maintained his position as acting territorial commander and made no concessions in his attitude to the army leaders in Djakarta. On the contrary, he made several public demands for punitive action against those who had been involved in the October 17 affair. It was clear that President Soekarno was supporting the Sudirman group. Faced with a political situation which was both complicated and highly dangerous—so much so that civil war was a seriously discussed possibility—the army leadership did nothing against Sudirman.

One consequence of this inaction was to encourage similar coups elsewhere. Thus on November 16 Colonel Gatot Subroto, territorial commander of East Indonesia with headquarters in Makassar, was arrested and displaced by his Chief of Staff, Lieutenant Colonel J. F. Warouw—in this case with the active co-operation of the PNI Governor of Sulawesi, Sudiro. The pattern was much as in East Java.

[73] *Aneta*, Oct. 26, 1952. See also the account of these developments in *Sumber* (Djakarta), Oct. 29, and in the statement of Sutoko, *Indonesia Raya*, Oct. 31, 1952.

There had been a visit from unofficial couriers of the President. The coup leaders justified themselves on the grounds that Gatot Subroto had been involved in the actions of October 17 (although in fact Gatot had not been among those who went to the Presidency on that day). Again the name of the President was used by the man usurping authority, and again the hope was expressed that the President would settle the whole army conflict.[74] An important difference lay in the fact that Warouw's statements were cast in stronger language than those of Sudirman. Warouw spoke of the events of October 17 as an attempt at *coup d'état* and as intimidation of the head of state and declared that he would be unprepared to meet Sultan Hamengku Buwono or Colonel Nasution on their planned visit to Makassar unless they carried a specific mandate from the President. Furthermore, there were signs that regionalist and anti-Javanese feeling had become associated with the affair, which many in the area saw as the ouster of a Javanese (Gatot Subroto) by a Sulawesian or Minahasan (Warouw).[75]

A week later a parallel situation developed in South Sumatra. Here the position of the "anti-October 17 group" in the army had just been strengthened by what President Soekarno had said in a five-day speaking tour of the area. Headed by the brigade commander Lieutenant Colonel Kretarto, this group finally acted on November 23, taking power out of the hands of the acting territorial commander, Lieutenant Colonel Kosasih. Kosasih was said to be unwilling to take a firm stand on the October 17 problem and unable to surmount the conflicts existing in the army under his command. In this case the government was able to find a solution which was acceptable to those who had made the coup and at the same time saved the government from the humiliation which it had suffered in East Java and East Indonesia. On November 24 it issued a statement condemning the Kretarto action, and the next day it reappointed the pensioned Colonel Bambang Utojo, a man of the "Peta group" who had been territorial commander of South Sumatra until September 1952.

There was indeed little that the cabinet or the central army leadership could do to assert their authority in the face of these challenges in the regions. Military action against East Java or East Indonesia was scarcely conceivable. There did exist the possibility of organizing

---

[74] One accusation which Warouw leveled against his superior, Gatot Subroto, was that the latter had told a group of officers that he would take orders only from the Vice-President and the Defense Minister (*Antara*, Nov. 18, 1952).

[75] See *Pedoman*, Nov. 18, 1952, and the denial by Warouw, *Antara*, Nov. 18, 1952.

countercoups against the usurping commanders, and this was considered. But it was rejected as also unlikely to succeed. It would be handicapped by disagreement within the cabinet and between the cabinet and the army leadership. And it would incur the active hostility of President Soekarno. Moreover, the fact that those who had usurped authority in East Java and East Indonesia had done so in the name of the President blurred the whole question of legitimacy. Thus a Djakarta-organized effort to subvert the power of Sudirman and Warouw would not be seen as simply an effort to restore legitimate authority. It would appear rather as an effort to pit the authority of Simatupang and Nasution, and perhaps of the Sultan and Wilopo, against the authority of Soekarno. The effect of such an effort would be to disrupt the hierarchical authority of the army further, and at lower levels. And it might prompt bloodshed. Although there were many in Djakarta, particularly in the central leadership of the army, who knew that their political lives depended on defeat of Sudirman and Warouw, there was no preparedness to take risks like this. The cohesion of the political elite was still sufficiently great that no group of its members wanted to reach for its ultimate weapons.

With the countenancing of the regional army coups, the political balance swung sharply to the advantage of the anti-October 17 forces. The army, now deeply divided, no longer constituted a counterweight to Soekarno, and thus the President and those associated with him held the political cards. The cabinet adopted a policy of slow and cautious adaptation to the new realities, the Wilopo *overkappingspolitiek* or "all under one roof policy."

Parliament reassembled on November 27. On December 5 the cabinet announced the first of a series of changes in the central army leadership. Nasution, Sutoko, and Parman were suspended. On December 16 Colonel Bambang Sugeng, the inactive commander of the East Java territory, generally regarded as the most moderate and technically skilled of the "Peta group" high officers, was appointed Acting Chief of Staff to replace Nasution.

But the Bambang Sugeng appointment immediately demonstrated the difficulty of a compromise solution. With the Sultan and Sugeng committed to widely different ways of tackling the problem of army disunity and with Sugeng in a politically stronger position, the Sultan had a choice of suffering humiliation or resigning.

The showdown came over the position of Warouw in the East Indonesia command. Late in December, Sugeng was in Makassar and there made a commitment to confirm Warouw as acting commander of the area.[76] The cabinet announced on January 1 that it upheld this decision, whereupon the Sultan resigned. The Deputy Prime Minister, Prawoto Mangkusasmito of the Masjumi, took over interim charge of the Defense portfolio, only to transfer it to Wilopo himself a few days later. Then on January 2, the same day that Warouw was ceremonially installed in Makassar as acting commander, the cabinet reversed its stand. In an attempt to prevent the threatened resignation of the two PSI ministers, it appointed another man, Colonel Sadikin, then divisional commander in Kalimantan and a man who had stayed neutral between the two main rival groups in the army, as East Indonesia commander. Presented with this *volte-face*, Bambang Sugeng immediately offered his resignation. But this was not accepted, and the Acting Chief of Staff remained at his post. Sadikin, it then became clear, was not prepared to go to East Indonesia. Warouw remained in charge of the East Indonesia command till 1956. The PSI ministers accepted the rebuff and remained in the cabinet.

For the political parties the two months following October 17 were full of intense activity, their press organs and central and branch committees frequently issuing statements on the changing situation. The first series of such statements concerned itself mainly with the question of dissolution of parliament. A number of minor organizations and a larger number of newspapers supported the dissolution and argued that elections should be held on the basis of emergency laws.[77] The great majority of parties opposed it and demanded that parliament should reassemble immediately.[78] These included not only the PKI,

[76] To install a person formally as the acting functionary in a particular military or civil post is a common technique in Indonesian governmental practice. It represents the first stage of a twofold process of legitimation. A person formally installed in an office on an acting basis has the opportunity to create for himself the support he needs to continue in that office. If he succeeds and maintains his superior's trust, he may be accorded full status. If he fails, he can easily be replaced. But in many cases he continues as the acting functionary for a period of many months or even years, exercising all the powers of the office but enjoying only some of its prestige, because the government prefers not to confer full authority on him.

[77] See the statement of Partai Kedaulatan Rakjat (People's Sovereignty Party), *Antara*, Oct. 22, and the editorials of *Indonesia Raya*, Oct. 25, *Indonesia Berdjoang* (Bandjarmasin), Oct. 21, and *Suara Rakjat* (Surabaja), Oct. 25, 1952.

[78] Up to Nov. 27, the time of the reassembling of parliament, 340 letters had been sent it by organizations and groups of organizations in support of its continued functioning. See Gusti Majur, "Pintu Pemilihan Umum" ("The Threshold of Elections"), *Mimbar Indonesia*, Dec. 20, 1952.

PNI, PSII, and PIR, but also the Masjumi. All without exception stated that they favored early elections.

After the coup in the territorial command of East Java the political issues became, more complicated. The Socialist papers, which now saw it as politically disadvantageous to advocate dissolution of parliament, concentrated on the case for government action against the usurper of military power in East Java, Lieutenant Colonel Sudirman. On this issue they were better able to win outside support, and a number of groups inside other parties, particularly the Masjumi and Christian parties, took their side. The opposition concentrated on the events of October 17. Their most commonly used technique was the joint statement signed by the representatives of a large number of parties and other organizations—trade unions, veterans', women's, and youth bodies, and so on—in a particular town or area.[79]

These joint statements were usually made as the result of joint PNI-PKI initiative. The local branches of the minor nationalist party PIR, the Moslem PSII, and the national-communist Murba were involved in almost every case, and some of the more moderately phrased statements were signed also by representatives of Masjumi and the Christian parties in the particular areas. All these statements supported the continued functioning of parliament until elections could be held, and some demanded that it should reassemble immediately. Several affirmed support for the President's speech to the demonstrators of October 17, and others used such terms as "fascist," *coup d'état*, and "dictatorship" in condemning the actions of the army leaders on that day. The most strongly worded denunciations of these actions came from different parts of East Java.

The events around October 17 therefore gave rise to two contrary trends in party alignments. Immediately after October 17 there existed a temporary alignment of PNI and Masjumi against the Socialist Party —inasmuch as the Sukiman group established a position of temporary ascendancy within the leadership of the Masjumi. There was sharp resentment in the Masjumi of the military police's arrest of Dr. Sukiman, and thus on October 29 the party executive voiced its disapproval of "the dissolution of Parliament at the present time in any way which is unconstitutional" and asked that parliament should reassemble

[79] See, for instance, the statements of 13 organizations at Jogjakarta, *Berita Indonesia* (Djakarta), Oct. 24; of 8 organizations at Bukittinggi, *Antara*, Oct. 31; of 15 organizations at Surakarta, *Antara*, Oct. 31; of 21 organizations at Semarang, *Aneta*, Nov. 3; of 43 organizations at Palembang, *Aneta*, Nov. 16; and of 15 organizations at Kutaradja, *Tegas* (Kutaradja daily), Nov. 17, 1952.

immediately.[80] For a time it seemed as if the groundwork was being laid for a renewal of co-operation between the older "administrator" leaders of the Masjumi and the PNI, and it was widely speculated that this co-operation could create the basis for a new cabinet like that of Sukiman. This was one interpretation placed on the demands made by Sartono of the PNI and a day later by Sukiman for the resignation of the Sultan.[81]

On the other hand, there was a much stronger tendency for the PNI to co-operate with the Communist Party and "oppositionist" groups and thereby to alienate the Masjumi and strengthen the hold in it of the PSI-oriented Natsir wing. The Communist Party was a strong and willing ally of the groups in the PNI which favored severe punishment of the army leaders of the pro-October 17 group, and its help was considerable in mobilizing the impressive demonstration of opinion represented by the many joint statements. In party terms the main beneficiary of PNI-PKI co-operation was the PNI. The shifts in army personnel worked clearly in this party's favor: the new Acting Chief of Staff, Bambang Sugeng, the reinstalled South Sumatra commander, Bambang Utojo, and a number of the leading men of the groups which had seized military power in East Java and East Indonesia were sympathizers of the PNI. The Communists asked no price in terms of army appointments; they hoped for no more than to see PSI influence in the army weakened and to strengthen their own association in the public mind with the PNI and President Soekarno.

Within the PNI the concern for an anti-October 17 solution united the Sidik group of radical nationalists with the older group of Sartono and Suwirjo and intensified their strength vis-à-vis the followers of Wilopo. Thus when the party held its sixth congress at Surabaja on December 6 to 11, the Prime Minister was criticized vigorously for his handling of the October 17 affair. In a particularly strongly worded pronouncement the congress resolved:

(1) to condemn the October 17 affair as a violation of democracy;
(2) to justify the efforts made in the provinces to prevent further violations of democracy;
(3) to urge the government to act faster toward a solution of the above

[80] *Abadi*, Oct. 30, 1952.
[81] Sartono, *Harian Umum* (Surabaja), Dec. 5; Sukiman, *Merdeka*, Dec. 6. See also the statement of Sukiman on Nov. 7, in which he denied that he sought the fall of the Wilopo cabinet, but added that if it fell it would have to be replaced by a presidential cabinet.

affair, it being understood that its efforts must be based on agreement between it and the President as Supreme Commander; and

(4) to urge all members of the party to remain alert in struggling for democracy.[82]

Wilopo had been all but disavowed by his own party. At the same time it became clear that the Masjumi continued to be a strong supporter of the cabinet. With the PNI so successful in turning the events of October 17 to its own advantage, Masjumi opinion had swung away from the anti-October 17 group again, and the Sukiman group lost its momentary ascendancy in the party. The over-all result was a major widening of the breach between the dominant leaders of the country's two main parties. With Masjumi-PNI co-operation thus undermined and the power of the Socialist-sympathizing groups generally greatly reduced, the cabinet was seriously weakened. It is only slight exaggeration to speak of it as existing in a "political oxygen tent" from October 17 to the time of its fall.[83] But the October 17 affair had strengthened its position with regard to one point of its policy, that of preparing elections.

TOWARD ELECTIONS

The country's first general elections had been promised and scheduled for a very long time. They were initially planned to be held as early as January 1946. But the circumstances of the Revolution did not permit the holding of more than regional (residency and regency) polls—except in certain of the Dutch-sponsored states, where, however, there appears to have been considerable official interference with the freedom of the ballot. In the period after December 1949 every cabinet made elections for a Constituent Assembly an important part of its program. The Hatta cabinet initially planned to conduct elections so that it would be an elected Constituent Assembly which would decide between a federal and a unitary state structure. But it was impelled to endorse unification brought about by more direct means, and little was done about elections.

The Natsir cabinet did introduce an elections bill in February 1951, a bill for elections on an indirect suffrage. The cabinet fell, however, before the bill had been discussed in parliament. Its successor, the Sukiman cabinet, organized four series of elections in selected

[82] *Aneta*, Dec. 10, 1952.

[83] Robert C. Bone, Jr., "The Future of Political Parties in Indonesia," *Far Eastern Survey*, vol. XXIII, no. 2 (Feb. 1954), 17.

areas, direct universal suffrage elections in Sangir-Talaud and Minahasa (both in North Sulawesi) in May and June 1951, indirect universal suffrage elections in the Special Territory of Jogjakarta in
August and October, and direct elections on a literacy franchise in
the town of Makassar in early February 1952.[84] At the same time it
agreed to support the bill which the Natsir government had submitted.
But on August 1, 1951, it was informed in a joint report from the subdivisions (nonspecialized committees) of parliament that this bill was
unacceptable, because parliament wanted a direct franchise. The Sukiman cabinet had submitted no further bill when it fell in February
1952.

When the Wilopo cabinet acceded to office, at a time when the
much-publicized Indian elections were nearing completion, there were
signs of a renewed emphasis on the importance of early elections.
In July the cabinet tabled a bill for the registration of voters. However, the subdivisions of parliament did not discuss this till September
and then replied with a statement of objections to some of its most
important features.

If one asks why parliament was so reluctant to deal promptly with
bills related to elections, a number of important political aspects of
this issue come to the fore. In the first place, many individual M.P.'s
owed their seats to circumstances and anomaly and realized clearly
that elections would unseat them. This group included not only independents and members of small parties and parliamentary fractions
with little or no mass backing, but also members of larger parties
who did not curry favor with their party leaders.

Of even greater importance was the fear of a major swing toward
the specifically Islamic parties. In the existing parliament these held
less than 25 per cent of the seats. This was in part because the *santris*
or fully committed Moslems were underrepresented in the leadership
of the Revolution. It also reflected the fact that it was aristocratic
elements, usually relatively weak in their Islamic loyalties, which had
occupied positions of greatest prominence in the Dutch-sponsored
states.

On the other hand, virtually all observers expected Islam to be the
strongest election symbol. The Islamic political leaders had long had
stronger connections with the villages than their non-Islamic rivals,
and these connections had been strengthened markedly during the
Japanese occupation. In regional elections held in a number of parts of

[84] See Feith, *The Wilopo Cabinet,* p. 95, and the references cited there.

Java in 1946 and in the closely watched election in the Special Territory of Jogjakarta in 1951, the Masjumi had gained absolute majorities of the vote or at least many more votes than any other contender.[85] Thus the Masjumi was generally expected to emerge as the strongest single party in national elections, and discussion of the likely outcome was chiefly about whether the Masjumi's plurality would be large enough to enable it to govern by itself and about which of the factions inside the Masjumi would have ascendancy after the elections. Among members of non-Islamic parties the fear was widespread that elections would mean the end of the state based on the Pantja Sila and its replacement by an Islamic State.[86] To a small number of persons of pragmatic orientation it seemed that this would mean merely a difference in the wording of the preamble to the constitution. But most saw the prospect as one of victory of one ideology over another. Some of these persons expressed fears that it would entail a major shift of power affecting the whole community, and especially the whole civil service.[87]

A third factor here was that an electoral system consistent with the provisions of the 1950 constitution would result in weaker representation for the areas outside Java (which were, in fact, considerably overrepresented in the existing parliament). And, fourthly, some important groups feared any further growth of political parties. Within the *pamong pradja* there was apprehension lest the social ferment of campaigning should disturb local patterns of power relations, and similar fears existed among the rulers of the 300 or so petty principalities which continued to exist, mainly outside Java and Sumatra. Many *pamong pradja* officials and many of the princely rulers—the two categories overlapped—had played a big part in the Dutch-sponsored federal states and thus had relatively strong representation in the parliament.

[85] See Feith, *The Wilopo Cabinet*, p. 95.

[86] A. R. Djokoprawiro, deputy leader of PIR in parliament, had declared that his party would work for the postponement of elections until the position of the supporters of the Pantja Sila was stronger. See *Sin Po*, April 19, 1952.

[87] According to Jusuf Wibisono of the Masjumi "the parties which are less strongly in favor of the early holding of parliamentary elections do not yet understand the ideals of the Islamic community, and specifically the Masjumi, in their bearing on the form of the Indonesian state" (*Nieuwsgier* [Djakarta], Aug. 28, 1952). Abikusno Tjikrosujoso, executive chairman of the Moslem PSII, had said he was convinced that the holding of elections would lead to "a very big shift in the political balance, which might harm the groups now occupying the leading position in the state" (*Indonesia Raya*, Sept. 4, 1952).

These factors go far to explain the reluctance of parliament to support moves toward early elections. In the case of the successive cabinets, which contributed to the delays in almost equal measure, there are also other factors to be considered, factors which bear on the whole problem of weak government in the postrevolutionary period.

In the first place, each of the cabinets of the 1949–1952 period had to face an enormous load of administrative tasks and a succession of immediately critical political issues. Such tasks as the holding of elections, which were not immediately pressing, were thus naturally pushed to the side of the governmental table.

In addition, whenever a seriously divisive issue arose and a cabinet took action upon it, it almost always fell. Thus its successors were warned against resolute action. The Natsir government fell on the issue of the composition of the regional councils; and such was the heat of party antagonism aroused on this question that successive cabinets were obliged to avoid taking any action on the matter. Deadlock at this point, particularly between the Masjumi and PNI, was an important cause of the long inaction of the central government in the whole matter of regional autonomy. The Sukiman government fell on the issue of acceptance of American aid on the terms of the Mutual Security Act. The Wilopo cabinet following it was obliged, as will be shown, to evade a number of foreign policy issues which, if acted upon, would have split the Masjumi-PNI coalition.

To bring in an election bill in this context was thought of as playing with dynamite. The fall of the Natsir cabinet, on the regional councils issue, was recalled. Any measure which bore on the future voting strengths of the parties could, it seemed, arouse divisions great enough to cost a cabinet its life. In fact, there were indications that the specific provisions of any electoral law would be controversial. Most important of all there was evidence that a number of parties, including some government parties, were afraid of early elections. To press vigorously for an election law in circumstances like these could easily produce an intensity of conflict between government parties which would give a cabinet no alternative but to resign. This was the situation which elections, it was hoped, would change. But meanwhile the situation existed.

Finally, these governments themselves feared some of the consequences of electioneering. Party and factional conflict at the Djakarta level was bitter. Was it wise to hold elections in an atmosphere like this, when campaigning could be expected to intensify the conflict and infuse it into many lower layers of society, at a time when the army, many of its cliques and groups subject to influences from different political parties, could not be relied upon to remain outside?[88] Would elections not lead to extremism of every sort? Would they not make the conflicts between supporters of the existing political order so bitter that its would-be heirs, the Communists and Darul Islam, and perhaps their foreign backers, would be able to involve themselves in these struggles? Hesitant on grounds like these, administratively over-burdened, politically weak, and faced by parliamentary hostility, governments relegated elections to a place of low priority.

It is clear, however, that most of the leaders of these cabinets wanted to hold elections. These men felt strongly that the existing parliament, based as it was on a compromise arrangement with the Dutch, did not symbolize popular sovereignty and therefore lacked authority. And most of them believed that elections would serve as a filter of political parties and thereby eliminate an important source of political unrest.[89]

Many of them, moreover, were sensitive to the repeated recommendations of foreign observers that elections should be held with maximum speed.[90] Some leaders accepted the overseas advice at its face value and believed that elections would indeed produce greater political stability. Others accepted it as a challenge to their pride in the democratic intentions of the Republic. Thus Sajuti Melik believed that elections would produce a worse parliament than the one then in existence, but advocated them nevertheless, because "indeed we are rather embarrassed, for our 'democratic state' has now been in existence seven and a half years, and still there have been no elections for parliament or Constituent Assembly."[91]

[88] The Armed Forces Chief of Staff wrote: "With the approach of elections the competition between political groups to widen their influence will be greater and sharper. The effort to ensure that the armed forces continue to act as a single united and disciplined organization standing outside this competition will be . . . more difficult" (T. B. Simatupang, "17 Agustus 1952 dan Persoalan-Persoalan Kemiliteran kita" ["August 17, 1952, and Our Military Problems"], *Mimbar Indonesia*, Aug. 17, 1952).

[89] Darsjaf Rahman, "Pemilihan Umum, untuk Ketenangan Politik dan Saringan Partai Politik" ("Elections for Political Peace and as a Filter of Political Parties"), *Mimbar Indonesia*, Feb. 9, 1952.

[90] These recommendations did not by any means come from Western sources only. They were made with great frequency by Indian journalists and commentators, particularly after the Indian elections had got under way at the end of 1951. See Phyllis Rolnick, "Indian Attitudes towards Indonesia, Fall 1950–Spring 1955" (unpublished paper, Cornell Modern Indonesia Project, 1959).

[91] *Pesat* (Jogjakarta weekly), March 8, 1953.

It was the October 17 affair which put an end to the cabinet-parliament "ping-pong" [92] and provided the momentum for a determined effort to move toward elections. After October 17 "early elections" was a political symbol to which all parties were obliged to accord respect. The demand that elections be held soon was included in virtually all the hundreds of statements and joint statements of political organizations in this period and in almost all political editorials. The advocates of the dissolution of parliament were most clearly in favor. Many of them proposed elections on the basis of an emergency law made by cabinet. However, their opponents, who advocated the continued functioning of parliament until elections could be held, were challenged to declare their support of early elections as determinedly, and did so.

For the Wilopo cabinet, faced with a political whirlwind and unable to do much more than keep a tenuous balance between the conflicting forces struggling for dominance, this situation provided a unique opportunity to recover lost prestige. On October 21 it took a formal decision to hasten the holding of elections for the Constituent Assembly, and by November 25 a newly drafted elections bill had been submitted to parliament. Two days later parliament reassembled and immediately began to discuss it.

In the following eighteen weeks the elections bill was debated in three readings and then clause by clause with a consideration of amendments. There were popular expositions of the idea of elections and of the particular bill under discussion in a variety of government and private magazines. At the same time a rush of booklets by lawyers, journalists, politicians, and government servants on the same subjects came from the publishing houses.[93] Parties began establishing special election committees and emphasizing elections as an occasion that demanded heightened party loyalty.

Efforts to delay or sidetrack the bill continued to be made, however. On the whole, the sections of the press which had supported the anti-October 17 groups were cool to the idea of elections, although

[92] This term is used derisively in Gusti Majur, *op. cit.*

[93] Rustam Sutan Palindih, *Rakjat Berdaulat dan Pemilihan Umum* ("The Sovereignty of the People and Elections"; Djakarta: Bulan Bintang, 1952); Sakirman, *Tentang Pemilihan Umum* ("Concerning Elections"; Djakarta: Pembaruan, 1952); Rachmady dan Husny Abbas, *Pemilihan Umum, Politis dan Technis* ("Elections, Political and Technical Aspects"; Djakarta: Endang, 1953). For an annotated list of the books and booklets on elections published after the bill became law see Adi Negoro, *op. cit.*, pp. 4–6.

their editorials mostly declared the contrary. These papers took the need to "settle the October 17 affair," that is, to punish the pro-October 17 groups, as their central slogan, as against "all attention to elections" which was the central slogan of the pro-October 17 groups. Thus *Merdeka* wrote that "there would not be anything fishy about the general elections, if they were not interpreted by some critical people as having been prompted by the October 17 affair." The same editorial outlined a number of difficulties with regard to elections, the possibility of interference by persons who took different stands on the October 17 affair, the bad economic conditions of the country, the lack of security in areas like West Java, and the apathy among the mass of the rural population.[94]

At the same time the PNI and PKI and several smaller nationalist groups co-operated with one another in sponsoring antigovernment motions on other issues, in such a way as might force the election issue off the center of the political stage.[95] The various efforts to delay passage of the elections bill reached a climax in early March, as parliament began the clause-by-clause stage of its discussion of the bill. No less than 200 amendments were tabled at this stage, and the debate proceeded very slowly, with a great deal of time being devoted to minor clauses. At the same time, however, press opposition to delaying tactics had reached a peak of intensity. The Medan daily *Waspada* wrote: "What seems like a majority of the honorable members are now acting as if they were intentionally sabotaging the bill so that their seats in parliament can be safe still longer."[96] Isa Anshary bluntly accused the PNI of being afraid of elections. Mohammad Natsir was indignant at a Communist-sponsored amendment for a census to precede the holding of elections. If passed, he said, this amendment would lead to a delay in elections of from one to two years.[97]

At this point the would-be delayers appear to have conceded defeat. The following weeks saw the introduction of various techniques to speed up debate on the bill. The government bill was passed on April 1 in an amended, but not too radically amended, form. It was a major political achievement for the cabinet.

As submitted to parliament on November 25, the elections bill was for universal suffrage elections for both a Constituent Assembly (elected, according to the interim constitution, on the basis of one

[94] Quoted in weekly press review of *Times of Indonesia*, Feb. 18, 1953.
[95] For a fuller discussion see Feith, *The Wilopo Cabinet*, pp. 149–150.
[96] *Waspada*, March 12, 1953.   [97] *Keng Po*, March 13, 1953.

member for every 150,000 residents, with appointees to represent Indonesian citizens of the Chinese, European, and Arab minority groups) and a parliament (elected similarly, but on the basis of one member for 300,000 residents, with similar provision for appointees). Literates would be able to vote either for the list of a party or organization or for one candidate within such a list; illiterates only for a list as such, by choosing a symbol marked on the ballot paper.

The basis of the government's bill was proportional representation. This was never publicly challenged.[98] The government proposed voting rights for everyone over eighteen, but on this its bill was finally modified by a Masjumi amendment which gave the suffrage also to persons under eighteen who were or had been married. Voting would be by direct ballot, the direct system being a part of the government bill and not challenged in parliament.[99]

The bill which became law on April 4 may be regarded as bearing the marks of ultrademocratic imagination, which promised to result in high expenses and administrative difficulties. But it provided for a workable system. Political factors apart, there was no reason why nationwide balloting could not be held within a year.[100]

But the political difficulties of moving on from creation of the law became clear even in the two months following the passage of the bill. The cabinet moved fairly rapidly to the task of appointing a Central Electoral Committee. According to its conception, this committee was to consist of one representative of each of the government parties. The independent M.P., Mr. Assaat, was to be chairman, and the Masjumi's

[98] In personal conversation I found several Indonesian leaders who believed a single member constituency system preferable. But these men also thought that it would be impossible for such a system to gain the approval of the existing parliament, dominated as it was by small parties which stood to gain from proportional representation.

[99] On the debates on the bill see Feith, *The Wilopo Cabinet*, pp. 152–155. For discussions of the law see Boyd R. Compton, "The Indonesian Election Law," *Far Eastern Survey*, vol. XXIII, nos. 4–5 (April, May 1954), and Herbert Feith, *The Indonesian Elections of 1955* (Cornell Modern Indonesia Project, Interim Reports Series; Ithaca, N.Y., 1957), pp. 1–5. The text of the law was published as a booklet of the Ministry of Information, *For the Election of Members of the Constituent Assembly and the House of Representatives* (Djakarta, 1953). Deeply influenced by Dutch constitutional and electoral practice, the bill also incorporated features which had been observed by electoral officers sent to Australia and India in 1951 and 1952. In addition, it reflected certain conclusions drawn from the trial elections held in Indonesia, particularly the elections in Minahasa and Jogjakarta.

[100] Minister of the Interior Roem stated in early March that elections would take place no later than ten months after the final passage of the bill (*Aneta*, March 27, 1953).

parliamentary leader, Mr. Burhanuddin Harahap, deputy chairman. The composition of the committee was decided upon at the cabinet's meeting on April 28. But no PNI member was named. Nor was the decision publicized. The PNI was clearly opposed to the cabinet's approach in the matter, and the result was that no committee had been formally established when the Wilopo cabinet resigned on June 2.

However, elections had been brought an important step closer by the passage of the bill, and party attention shifted increasingly to the village voter. One result was that party leaders spoke more and more in terms of broad ideological goals and less than ever in terms of issues and specific policies. By their ideological formulations they were able to articulate the value emphases of particular religious and ethnic communities. But this could not be done without increasing the volume of ideological conflict within society as a whole.

The new phase of political controversy was sparked by a speech of President Soekarno on January 27 at Amuntai in strongly Moslem South Kalimantan. Commenting on a banner which asked, "Indonesia a National State or an Islamic State?" President Soekarno is reported to have said:

The state we want is a national state consisting of all Indonesia. If we establish a state based on Islam, many areas whose population is not Islamic, such as the Moluccas, Bali, Flores, Timor, the Kai Islands, and Sulawesi, will secede. And West Irian, which has not yet become part of the territory of Indonesia, will not want to be part of the Republic.[101]

This speech was the cause of strong protest. The Masjumi leader Isa Anshary was the first to register objections. In a note to the government he declared the President's utterance to be undemocratic, unconstitutional, and in conflict with the ideology of Islam which is professed by the great majority of Indonesian citizens.[102] The Nahdatul Ulama, the Masjumi's youth organization GPII (Gerakan Pemuda Islam Indonesia, Islamic Youth Movement of Indonesia), the Front Muballigh Islam (Moslem Missionaries' Front) of North Sumatra, the Central Sumatra-centered Perti, and a number of other Moslem organizations also registered their disapproval.

The GPII stated that the President had exceeded his constitutional limitations, that his speech had sown seeds of separatism, and that it represented a taking of sides by the head of state with groups opposed

[101] *Antara*, Jan. 29, 1953.   [102] *Aneta*, Feb. 2, 1953.

to the ideology of Islam. The Nahdatul Ulama, in a similar declaration, expressed strong opposition to the idea that an Islamic government should be thought incapable of preserving national unity. The Front Muballigh Islam presented the view that although the Pantja Sila was not in conflict with Islam, it did not fulfill all the requirements of the Islamic teachings.[103]

A number of PNI leaders came to President Soekarno's defense.[104] They argued for the special preogatives of President Soekarno as a man who was a revolutionary leader and inspirer of his people as well as a constitutional head of state. Pointing to the strongly articulated fears of Indonesian Christians of what their lot would be in an Islamic State, they spoke of the danger to democracy of oppression by a majority. They singled out Isa Anshary and attacked him as a fanatic and an unscrupulous agitator. The radical PNI leader Sarmidi Mangunsarkoro referred to Anshary as a "new friend of the Darul Islam," and this charge was echoed by the Communist Party, which was then engaged in a campaign to link the Masjumi in the public mind with the Darul Islam. Thereupon Isa Anshary, repeating a demand for withdrawal of the President's Amuntai speech, said that this had helped the Darul Islam by shutting the door on the efforts of the Islamic community to realize its ends through parliamentary channels.

The bitter controversy was a source of considerable embarrassment to the "administrator" leaders of the Masjumi. These men saw Anshary's directness and his appeal to mass radicalism as a danger both to their own position in the party and to the party's relationships with other political organizations. Thus Natsir and Sukiman made statements which attempted to minimize the importance of the issue which had been raised. They contended that the disagreement resulted from a confusion of terms and that the matter was an internal one of the Moslem community and not to be discussed in exaggerated terms outside it.[105]

But the controversy raged on. It reached a second stage shortly after the elections bill had become law. At a rally in Djakarta on the occa-

---

[103] For a discussion of these reactions and of current views of what would constitute an Islamic State, see Boyd R. Compton, "President Sukarno and the Islamic State," *Newsletter of the Institute of Current World Affairs*, New York, March 8, 1952.

[104] *Sin Po*, March 11, 1953.

[105] See *Antara*, March 6, 1953, and *Aneta*, March 21, 1953, for Natsir's views and *Antara*, March 5, 1953, for Sukiman's.

sion of Mi'radj, the Prophet Mohammad's Ascension to Heaven, April 12, a number of leaders of Moslem political parties made challenging speeches centering on the hope of an Islamic electoral victory. The last and longest of the addresses, which was also the most uncompromising, was by Isa Anshary. Anshary came directly to the issues which the President's Amuntai speech had brought to the fore. "In Indonesia at the present time," he said, "there is a cold war between Islam on the one hand and on the other those who call themselves Islamic and aren't. The central question is whether the state is to be based on God's law or not." Let there be a demarcation line, Anshary said, between the Islamic and the non-Islamic groups, and let us be rid of those who are half and half. The Koran was totalitarian, he went on to say. The Islamic State, as established by Mohammad himself, ensured generous protection of the religious rights of Christians and Jews, but it gave no protection to *munafik* (hypocrite Moslems). An oblique reference made it clear that the speaker included the President among the latter. The heavy applause given to this speech of Isa Anshary stood in strong contrast to the cool and expressly unenthusiastic reception which President Soekarno received when he spoke at a large Mi'radj meeting at the presidential palace on the same evening.[106]

Anshary's show of strength produced a wave of reactions, however. At a mass meeting of the PNI in Bandung on April 19 four leaders of this party made election speeches. Isnaeni urged his listeners not to elect "double-dealers in religion." Gatot Mangkupradja challenged the voters to "choose between Isa Anshary and Bung Karno (Brother Soekarno). Anshary hit back by accusing Gatot of "political chicanery using the name of the head of state." It was, however, the Masjumi leader who came in for most criticism when the press voiced its fears of the consequences of immoderate electioneering.

As a result of these exchanges there was widespread apprehensiveness at the prospect of an election campaign in which all the contending parties would resort to unrestrained agitation. Observers noted that President Soekarno had found vehement support for his views on Islam in the state when he had traveled in Christian areas like Tapanuli and equally vehement opposition to them when he had spoken in such strongly Moslem areas as Atjeh. Many of them came to see that the infusion of rival ideologies into situations of communal cleavage

---

[106] These remarks on the atmosphere at the two meetings are based on my personal observations.

was bound to produce powerful social tensions. Some wrote of the possibility that civil war might break out if the parties were too extreme in their campaigning.[107] Large numbers of editorials echoed the words of the chairman of parliament, Sartono, that parties should not forget good manners in their pronouncements about one another.[108]

Although electioneering had barely begun, it had already sharpened divisions within the political elite. In effect it had exploded the compromise on the basis of which it had been possible to minimize ideological conflict in the period between 1945 and 1952. In the late stages of the Japanese occupation and the early months of the Revolution there had been open conflict between Moslems and secular or quasi-secular nationalists on the matter of the relationship between Islam and the state. But thereafter the Pantja Sila had been accepted, with its religious content in the principle of Ketuhanan jang Maha Esa (The One Deity). In the eyes of the secular nationalists this was a compromise; in the eyes of the Moslems it was a nationalist victory. However, the Moslems accepted the formulation without much active protest. Many of them asserted that they were accepting it only temporarily, until an elected Constituent Assembly began the work of fashioning a new constitution. But public criticism of the Pantja Sila by Moslem spokesmen was rare. For the most part it was accepted, along with the constitution, as a shared cluster of symbols of state to which all parties could give assent.

Now, with the onset of election campaigning, the consensus was destroyed. Moslems claimed that Soekarno had disrupted it by his increasingly frequent expositions of the Pantja Sila and his inclination to present these in a form which favored the partisan interests of the non-Moslem parties. On the other hand, PNI leaders defended the President as a man who was maintaining the unity of the country in the face of extremist pulls from the side of both the Islamic right and the Communist left. They placed the blame for the disruption of consensus entirely on the Moslems, especially Kijaji Isa Anshary. In any event the Pantja Sila "was no longer the umbrella under which political competition took place, but instead became part of the political

[107] E.g., Mohammad Ibnoe Sajoeti (Sajuti Melik), *Demokrasi Pantja Sila dan Perdjoangan Ideologis Didalamnja* ("The Democracy of the Pantja Sila and Ideological Struggle within It"; Jogjakarta and Djakarta: Pesat, 1953), p. 31 and *passim.*

[108] See, for instance, *Berita Indonesia,* April 23; *Harian Rakjat,* April 23; *Pemandangan* (Djakarta), April 24; and *Mimbar Indonesia* (daily), April 25, 1953.

competition and struggle itself." [109] It was a sign that the cohesion of the political elite had been severely undermined.

THE FALL OF THE CABINET

The first five months of 1953 were a period of more than usually evident social unrest. If the volume of dissatisfaction in politically participant society had not grown, there had certainly been a marked increase in readiness to give political expression to existing dissatisfaction. Some of it found expression through political parties, some of it through protest activities of a more direct, dramatic, and ephemeral kind.

Regionalist and ethnic protest was one way in which dissatisfaction was expressed, and such protest was becoming more frequent and widespread. Already in July 1952 the Djakarta press had reported the wide circulation of a letter which sought support for the establishment of a "state of Sumatra." [110] At the same time there had been reports of gang violence between Javanese and Sulawesi students studying at the Gadjah Mada University in Jogjakarta. [111]

Such manifestations became more common in the first months of 1953. Thus the reburial in April 1953 of the Toba Batak king, King Sisingamangaradja XII, killed by the Dutch in 1907, was made the occasion of challenging calls for Batak and Tapanuli solidarity. Among the Minangkabaus of West Sumatra regionalist and anti-Djakarta feeling was stirred at the same time in protest against the splitting up and disarming of several companies of the Minangkabau-manned "Pagarrugung Battalion," which had been stationed in West Java. Regionalism among the Sundanese of West Java had prompted the establishment in March of the federalist Pagujuban Daja Sunda (Sundanese Cultural Association), and similar sentiment in Sulawesi led to the launching of the Gerakan Pemuda Federal Republik Indosia (Federalist Youth Movement of the Republic of Indonesia) in Makassar in May. [112]

In all these areas anti-Djakarta resentment was expressed in the form of demands for more effective regional autonomy. In numerous parts of Sumatra and Sulawesi political leaders voiced disappointment at the

[109] Josef A. Mestenhauser, "Ideologies in Conflict in Indonesia, 1945–1955" (doctoral dissertation, University of Minnesota, 1960), p. 144.

[110] *Aneta*, July 15, 16, 1952.   [111] *Nieuwsgier*, Aug. 7, 1952.

[112] *Antara*, April 7; *Keng Po*, March 23; *Antara*, May 18, 1953.

smallness of budget allocations given to their area, in comparison with the particular area's record of fighting in the Revolution or its contribution to export earnings. On top of anti-Djakarta protests came ones directed against the ethnic Javanese, against the appointment of Javanese as high officials outside their own region, and against what were described as efforts to "Javanize Indonesian culture." [113] Various Djakarta political figures and newspapers warned of the dangers implicit in this rise of regionalist feeling,[114] and a number of high government officials in the capital were seriously concerned about the danger of separatist revolts.

Antiforeign protest, a second outlet for discontent, was also at a high level in this period. Where this protest was anti-Dutch, and most of it was, it should be seen in relation to the unconciliatory position taken by the Netherlands at this time on matters Indonesian. Thus in December 1952 the Dutch government arrested two prominent Indonesian students in the Netherlands suspected of being Communist sympathizers, Go Gien Tjwan, director of the *Antara* news agency in the Netherlands, and Sunito, chairman of the Perhimpunan Indonesia (Indonesian Association). Later in the same month the PKI leaders, Aidit and Njoto, who had arrived in Holland for a congress of the Communist Party of the Netherlands, were expelled from the country. And in April 1953 the Dutch government gave similar treatment to Chaerul Saleh, the former leader of the Murba-oriented People's Army in West Java, who was in Europe on a study assignment given him by the Wilopo cabinet when it released him from jail.

An analogous occasion for protest was the verdict of a Netherlands court in January in the case of the attempted assassination of the Indonesian military attaché at The Hague, Lieutenant Colonel Harjono, by Westerling supporters. The decision of the judge in this case was to give one of the accused a sentence of one year and declare the other

[113] See the statement of H. Darwisj Djambek, chairman of the Partai Islam Indonesia, with headquarters in Central Sumatra, *Aneta*, April 5, 1953. Such protests were made much more frequently than the newspaper record suggests; the fact that they did violence to nationalist feeling made pressmen loath to record them. For a full discussion of the development of regionalist attitudes in the postrevolutionary period see Gerald S. Maryanov, *Decentralization in Indonesia as a Political Problem* (Cornell Modern Indonesia Project, Interim Reports Series; Ithaca, N.Y., 1958), pp. 36 ff.

[114] See the statements of Otto Rondonuwu (Progressive Fraction), *Antara*, Jan. 25; of Sjahrir, *Keng Po*, March 18; of F. A. Pitoi (PIR), *ibid.*, March 19; of Jusuf Wibisono, *ibid.*, March 20, 1953. See also the editorials of *Sin Po*, Jan. 28, and *Siasat* (Djakarta weekly), March 8, 1958.

free.[115] In stark contrast was the January 30 decision of a court at Hollandia in West Irian, which gave jail sentences of up to 13 years to 43 Indonesians accused of infiltration into the uninhabited island of Gak, a part of West Irian.

The new Drees cabinet formed after the elections of June 1952 declared in September that it "sees no value in a resumption of discussions with Indonesia about the status of New Guinea." [116] This evoked numerous calls by Indonesian political leaders and editors for toughness against the Dutch. Thus on September 6, 1952, Mr. Djody Gondokusumo of the minor nationalist party PRN, who was then chairman of the Foreign Affairs section of parliament, stated that, in the event of failure of negotiations to secure the return of West Irian, Indonesia should employ force to this end—rather than to use what Djody saw as the other way open, that of asking for United States help. There were also frequent expressions of protest over reports that individual Dutchmen were involved in the bandit activity of the Darul Islam. Appeals for the government to take a firmly anti-Dutch stand came primarily from the side of the "oppositionist" parties and factions, sections of the PNI leadership, and the Communists, but some were made by representatives of almost every political group.

This protest activity can of course be accounted for in part by the Dutch actions which occasioned it. These actions, coming on top of a four-year revolutionary war and a situation where vast economic power in the country remained in foreign, mainly Dutch, hands, created a situation in which a high level of anti-Dutch sentiment could be expected. But this should not obscure the fact that anti-Dutch sentiment functioned both to express political discontent and to channel it off from possible domestic targets. Sjahrir stressed its role in "blinding the people to reality," [117] and Jusuf Wibisono discussed it in the context of a quotation from Karl Mannheim on scapegoatism.[118] This aspect helps to explain why there were relatively few manifestations of anti-Dutch feeling outside Java: discontent there could be channeled into resentment of Java.

It is not clear whether antiforeign feeling was more widely ex-

---

[115] Strong protests against this decision were made in the Dutch press at the time, e.g., *Het Vrije Volk*, Jan. 6, 1953; *Het Parool*, Jan. 7, 1953 (both Labor Party journals); and *De Volkskrant*, Jan. 7, 1953 (Catholic People's Party publication).

[116] Cited in Duynstee, *op. cit.*, p. 210.   [117] *Sikap*, Aug. 18, 1952.

[118] "Popularitet dan Tanggung-Djawab" ("Popularity and Responsibility"), *Mimbar Indonesia*, Aug. 17, 1952.

pressed in the Wilopo cabinet period than before. But it certainly remained at a high volume—and this despite the fact that the Wilopo
cabinet was more active in discouraging it than the Sukiman cabinet.
Part of the explanation for this lies undoubtedly in the increasingly
uncompromising attitude of Holland. But another part must be sought
in Indonesia itself, in the same factors which occasioned the wave
of regionalist protest, firstly, the social pressures creating discontent
and, secondly, the factors of political structure encouraging this discontent to find political expression. The social unrest was a product
of the general situation of revolutionary aftermath—social dislocation,
the rapid growth of white-collar life-style expectations, the existence of
a large group of uprooted ex-revolutionaries, many of them desiring
participation in a form of expressive politics, and so on. In addition,
it resulted from the high speed of ongoing social change—urbanization, new schools, literacy development, and the expansion of the mass
media. And there was a particular economic explanation for it in the
post-Korea fall in prices for Indonesia's exports. The fact that this
unrest now found open political expression more frequently than theretofore must be seen in relation to the weakness of the cabinet. Paralyzed by Masjumi-PNI antagonisms and virtually deprived of the army
as an instrument of political power, the Wilopo cabinet was poorly
equipped for the task of keeping protest activity within the bounds
of law.

The cabinet's weakness became evident over a series of acts of defiance of authority. Thus in April 1953 a group of Surabaja law students
smashed the offices of the Dutch-language daily *De Vrije Pers* after
this newspaper had stated editorially that the Dutch language remained a necessity for students of Indonesian law. The government
censured the students, but it took no legal action against them, and
the Minister of Information, Mononutu, declared that the incident
should serve as a warning to the foreign press not to regard Indonesian sensitivities lightly. Violence had been used earlier against the
premises of the Dutch-language *Malang Post* at Malang, the *Antara*
rooms at Semarang, and the offices of *Waspada* at Medan.

Other challenges to existing authority flowed more or less directly
from the October 17 affair. This was particularly true of the situation
in Sulawesi where the Warouw coup of November 16, 1952, had
fanned the flames of regional and ethnic feeling and seriously disrupted
hierarchical authority within the army. Thus in late December 1952
there were pitched battles between two battalions of government

troops at Pare-Pare. Two army officers were murdered in Makassar in January, and several others were kidnaped in the following months.[119] At the same time there were repeated reports of the persecution of Christians in Central Sulawesi, not only by Kahar Muzakar followers, but also by certain units of the government forces. In March the Djakarta weekly *Siasat* reported that several government agencies in South Sulawesi had begun to issue export licenses and to exact customs and taxes on their own authority. It added that the situation was gradually developing into one which could only be called warlordism.[120]

Also at this time the groups which had sponsored the regional army coups in the weeks after October 17 continued to challenge the cabinet on matters related to the developments of October and November. In the first four months of 1953 the army heads of East Java and East Indonesia made repeated demands, which were "leaked" to the press, for the dismissal and punishment of all those involved in what had happened in Djakarta on October 17. There was a widespread belief among the political elite that these demands were actively supported by the President. Moreover, they were coupled with threats. Thus on March 10, after the new Acting Chief of Staff of the Army, Bambang Sugeng, had decided to transfer the former acting commander of East Java, Suwondho, to Djakarta, Sudirman declared that the East Java army leadership "could not take it upon itself to guarantee the safety of Lieutenant Colonel Suwondho" if the latter went to Djakarta. Suwondho was then still under arrest. On the following day a report of an East Java army doctor was published to the effect that Suwondho was ill and thus could not go to Djakarta.

In reply the government made no attempt to assert its authority. Instead it decided on March 31 to transfer the secretary-general of the Ministry of Defense, Mr. Ali Budiardjo, to a position of deputy head of the National Planning Board and placed in his post ex-Colonel Hidajat, a man regarded as standing outside the division between the "pro-October 17" and "anti-October 17" groups in the army. Five days earlier an Indonesian and a Dutch delegation had begun discussions for the repatriation of the Netherlands Military Mission, which had come under such strong parliamentary fire in the pre-October 17 debates. In April an agreement was reached whereby the mission would be repatriated at the end of the year.[121]

[119] *Sumber*, April 15, 1953.   [120] *Siasat*, March 8, 1953.
[121] An exception was made for some 80 members of the naval arm of the mission, who would continue to work in Surabaja for some months longer. See

But the East Java command remained dissatisfied. At the same time its successes emboldened it. Thus on April 4 it wrote a letter to the government (with a copy to the Defense section of parliament), urging that "the investigation of the October 17 affair should at once be officially turned over to the Chief Public Prosecutor," further that "the government should take firm steps against those who are regarded as the instigators of the October 17 affair," and that the command "would not be responsible for the consequences if these things were not done by April 15." [122]

Again the cabinet gave concessions. Wilopo addressed a closed session of parliament on April 11, and thereafter more and more persons who were, or were thought to have been, involved in the activities of October 17 in Djakarta were called to *in camera* hearings at the chief public prosecutor's office. *Keng Po* reported that there would be transfers of 50 high- and middle-ranking officers in May.[123] These were steps to conciliate the East Java command, and they were condemned as such by the Masjumi and Socialist-sympathizing press.[124] But they too failed to satisfy the East Java leaders. Sudirman and his supporters were particularly concerned that the last of the earlier triumvirate, Armed Forces Chief of Staff Simatupang, should be taken out of his post. This demand was strongly supported by the President. But it was one to which Wilopo, with the cabinet behind him, had decided he would not accede.

On April 17 the Prime Minister, accompanied by the Defense Ministry's Secretary-General Hidajat and the Acting Chief of Staff of the Army, Bambang Sugeng, set off on a tour of four military districts. The climax of the trip came in East Java. Landing at Surabaja's airport on April 26, the delegation was not met by any of the East Java military leaders—but by a group of tanks! Going on to the headquarters of the East Java district in Malang, they found the headquarters offices empty.[125] Few greater indignities have been suffered by any Indonesian Prime Minister. Yet Wilopo felt he could do nothing in response.

Wilopo's last months in office saw also the first major eruption of a clique conflict which had been going on inside the air force, in particu-

---

Protokol Hasil Perundingan Penjelesaian Missi Militer Belanda ("Protocol of Results of the Negotiations for the Termination of the Netherlands Military Mission"; Ministry of Information, Djakarta, April 21, 1953).

[122] Quoted in *Keng Po*, April 15, 1953.   [123] *Keng Po*, April 15, 1953.

[124] See, for instance, *Haluan* (Padang), April 15; *Mimbar Umum* (Medan), April 16; *Mestika* (Medan), April 18; and *Sumber*, April 21, 1953.

[125] See *Pedoman*, April 29, 30, 1953.

lar between the Air Force Chief of Staff, Commodore Suryadarma, and the head of the educational division of the force, Vice-Commodore H. Sujono. In a letter of May 13 to the President, Vice-President, Defense Minister, and other high officers of the air force, Vice-Commodore Sujono declared that the Air Force Chief of Staff had abused his authority and should be investigated. Sujono was placed under house arrest by Suryadarma, whereupon some of his supporters in the air force submited *en bloc* resignations while others staged an aerial demonstration against the air force headquarters in Djakarta.[126]

This, then, is the background against which the party political developments of the last few months of the Wilopo cabinet period must be seen. The general social unrest of the period was finding outlets in protest politics of a type which undermined both government authority in general and the prestige of this particular cabinet, and the cabinet was able to do nothing about it—which fact in turn encouraged a further development of protest politics. Many members of the cabinet, aware of failure in their effort to master the sociopolitical situation, were demoralized.

On the parliamentary front April and May 1953 saw the development of a chain of crises each of which came close to being the cabinet's last. One such crisis resulted from a motion introduced by Otto Rondonuwu of the Progressive Fraction calling for the establishment of diplomatic relations with the U.S.S.R. by the end of the current year. As a corollary of the independent foreign policy in almost any of its many interpretations, this motion had general appeal. Its supporters buttressed their ideological arguments with practical ones of the advantages of trade with the U.S.S.R., arguments which were persuasive at a time when very low prices prevailed on the Western market for rubber and tin and when the United States and the United Kingdom were unco-operative in relation to proposals for price stabilization agreements. The PNI made it clear soon after the Rondonuwu motion was submitted on February 10 that it would support its passage. On the other hand, the Masjumi was opposed, arguing that a Soviet Embassy in Djakarta might play a Trojan horse role. For some time there was discussion of the possibility that the Masjumi would withdraw its ministers from the cabinet if the motion was passed. On April 9 it was passed, with support from four government parties, the PNI, the Parkindo, the Labor Party, and the PSII. But the Masjumi's parliamentary leader, Burhanuddin Harahap, declared that his party would

---

[126] See *Antara* and *Aneta,* May 13 to 31, 1953, *passim.*

consider withdrawing its ministers only if and when the cabinet decided to establish an embassy in Moscow.

At the same time the cabinet was under parliamentary fire on its
economic and financial policies. Even after its defeats over the October 17 affair, it persisted in its politically bold policies of placing the
balance of payments burden on the shoulders of importers, urban consumers of the upper- and middle-income groups, and the bureaucracy.
The budget it introduced in November 1952 was definitely pitched to
austerity. And its measures in the field of importing were particularly
controversial. On January 14, the Ministry of Economic Affairs announced that it would temporarily cease to accept new Indonesian
importers into the favored "Benteng group." Eight days later there followed a regulation of the Economic Affairs and Finance Ministers
revising and extending the import surcharge system. When this produced rapid rises in prices for the goods affected, the government
responded by increasing the required prepayment on applications for
foreign exchange from 40 per cent to 75 per cent. At the same time it
entered into a "gentleman's agreement" with the commercial banks to
observe credit ceilings for all importing, ceilings which would apply to national Indonesian importers as well as foreign firms.[127] These
measures were effective in undoing most of the earlier price rises, because they forced importers to sell their stocks cheaply in order to
get liquid working capital. But they antagonized the importers strongly,
especially the politically powerful group of national importers.

Thus in April and May parliament heard a long series of denunciations of the cabinet's importing policies by members of many parties.
On May 28 it voted unanimously for a motion sponsored by the Masjumi leader K. H. Tjikwan, protesting the Finance Minister's surcharge regulations and asking the cabinet to submit these regulations in the form of bills presented to parliament. It was an important
defeat for the cabinet, tempered only by the fact that a stronger motion
of Mohammad Sadak of PIR, which asked that the import surcharge
regulations be immediately frozen, was defeated by 58 votes to 27
on the same evening, with none of the government parties supporting
it. Economic and financial policy was therefore not an immediate
cause of the cabinet's fall as it had seemed it might be. But it was of

[127] "The Government Import Regulations," *Indonesian Affairs*, vol. III, no. 9–10
(Sept.–Oct. 1953). See also Monetary Research Section of the Ministry of Finance,
"Economic Review of 1952 and Outlook for 1953," *Ekonomi dan Keuangan In-
donesia* ("Economics and Finance in Indonesia"), vol. VI, no. 5 (May 1953).

importance in welding together the opposition which was eventually to overwhelm the cabinet.

The issue which finally precipitated the cabinet's fall developed from the existence of large numbers of peasant squatters on land leased to foreign estates in East Sumatra. Some of these persons, former estate workers and villagers from the surrounding areas, had begun to squat in the Japanese occupation; the Japanese authorities had urged them to grow foodstuffs, and they did so there, particularly on large areas of tobacco land lying fallow. Many others had come in the postrevolutionary period, mostly from the less fertile Tapanuli plateau, and were continuing to come in considerable numbers. By early 1953 there were approximately 62,000 families on the tobacco estates in the area alone.[128]

But the foreign lessees who had cultivated these lands before the war, and in many cases between 1946 and 1949, continued to have legal claims to them. Most of these came under the general guarantees accorded under the Round Table Conference Agreement of 1949. Moreover, the Indonesian governments of this period saw themselves as having an interest in the restoration of the lands to the foreign, mainly Dutch, companies which had leased them. This was partly because of their ability to earn badly needed foreign exchange. In addition, these governments believed that the request for return of these squatter-occupied lands in East Sumatra (and the other request from Royal Dutch Shell for return of its North Sumatran oil wells, then in the temporary charge of an Indonesian government board) was seen overseas as a test of their willingness and ability to protect the additional foreign investment which they sought to attract.

In July 1951 Iskaq Tjokroadisurjo of the PNI, as the Sukiman cabinet's Minister for the Interior, had settled on a compromise basis for a solution. He came to an agreement with the tobacco planters' organization, DPV (Deli Planters Vereniging), whereby the members of this organization would return 130,000 hectares of their 255,000 hectares of concession lands in exchange for a new 30-year lease for the remaining 125,000 hectares. The government would resettle the peasant families then squatting on the 125,000 hectares.

---

[128] Statement of Abdullah Jusuf, PNI parliamentarian, *Antara*, April 8, 1953. For general discussions of the whole problem see Karl J. Pelzer, "The Agrarian Conflict in East Sumatra," *Pacific Affairs*, XXX, no. 3 (June 1957), 151–159, and Clark E. Cunningham, *The Postwar Migration of the Toba-Bataks to East Sumatra* (Cultural Report Series, Southeast Asia Studies, Yale University; New Haven, Conn., 1958).

Little was done to implement the resettlement decision within the life of the Sukiman cabinet. But the Wilopo cabinet made a beginning. However, its efforts were challenged almost immediately as a result of what happened on March 16, 1953, in the subdistrict of Tandjong Morawa near Medan. On this date police tried forcible dislodgment of a group of peasants by plowing up their lands with tractors. The peasants, organized as demonstrators, replied by attempting to seize the policemen's weapons. The police started shooting, and five of the peasants, four of them Chinese and one Indonesian, were killed. Numerous arrests followed.[129]

The press outcry which followed the report of this incident led to the establishment of a number of committees of inquiry, both by particular parties and by parliament. Their investigations laid bare the explosiveness of the political and social background against which the Tandjong Morawa shooting must be seen.

Abdullah Jusuf, PNI member of parliament who was sent by his party to investigate the situation, concluded that the policy of the Governor of North Sumatra, Abdul Hakim, of the Masjumi, in allocating land to estates and peasants respectively was highly detrimental to the latter, who were given inferior land and inadequate compensation. Further, Abdullah Jusuf alleged that Hakim had received Rp. 600,000 from the DPV, officially as money to compensate the dislodged peasants, but in fact administered irregularly. Moreover, Hakim, who was governing without a legislative council, was, according to Jusuf, creating an atmosphere of fear by the extent to which he used secret police.[130]

Very different explanations were given by representatives of the Minister of the Interior and by the Masjumi members of the parliamentary commission which visited East Sumatra in late March and early April. These investigators emphasized the large role played by Chinese peasants in opposition to the government's land distribution program and connected this with the journey to Medan at the time of the Tandjong Morawa affair of a representative of the Chinese consul in Djakarta, a journey against which the Foreign Ministry had expressed objections. Further, they quoted the report of Sabiruddin, first commissioner of police in North Sumatra, to the effect that the

---

[129] For accounts of this incident see *Antara*, March 17; *Harian Rakjat*, March 17; *Keng Po*, March 21; and *Waktu*, May 2, 1953. See also statement of Minister of the Interior Roem, *Aneta*, April 10, 1953.

[130] *Antara*, April 8, 1953.

subsection committee of the PKI for Deli-Serdang was responsible for the incident which had occurred.[131]

The Tandjong Morawa shooting can be explained in part in terms of factors of party politics such as these. In East Sumatra at this time party competition was intense, not least so between different party-backed peasant organizations. The widespread opposition which existed to the strongly anti-Communist Governor was a factor of considerable importance, as was the PNI's concern to replace him with a candidate of its own. Communist organizational stiffening was important in explaining the vigor with which the peasants of Tandjong Morawa were prepared to defend their land. And the intensity of press and parliamentary concern resulted in part from the fact that powerful groups in the PNI had come to the point of wanting to force the cabinet to resign.

But the issue itself had explosive possibilities. The squatters naturally saw the government as acting in the interests of the estates, and the estates were in their eyes remaining representatives of the same foreign imperialism against which the Revolution had been fought. Thus the ground was fertile for peasant organizations which opposed the government's policies. For the PNI, then just establishing its peasant organization Petani (Persatuan Tani Nasional Indonesia) in North Sumatra, this was a crucial fact.

The Tandjong Morawa affair is a good illustration of the difficulties which the Wilopo cabinet and every other cabinet of our period faced in bringing power to bear where its policies involved deprivational consequences for particular groups and could be challenged as doing violence to nationalist goals. Weak in terms of party and army support, the cabinet was incapable of surmounting the challenges which small determined groups like the squatters of East Sumatra could advance. It was particularly weak in issues involving foreign enterprises. This was partly because of the power of the PKI and PNI labor and peasant organizations. It resulted also from the great weakness of foreign enterprises in all public aspects of politics. Perhaps more important still, it arose from the weakness of the propertied groups of Indonesians who had an interest in siding with foreign capital against unions and peasant organizations. The problem of squatting, not only on foreign-leased estate lands, but also on public lands in towns and forests in many parts of the country, continued to be a major obstacle to consistent problem-solving policies.

[131] See *Antara*, April 23, and *Pedoman*, April 28, 1953.

In the middle of May the government's land policy in East Sumatra was made the basis of a motion of no confidence in Minister of the Interior Roem. This was moved by the PKI-sympathizing representative of the SAKTI (Sarekat Tani Indonesia, Indonesian Peasants Association), Sidik Kertapati. Several days later it was modified, reportedly in an attempt to make it qualify for PNI support, and from then on it merely demanded that the process of transferring land to the DPV should be halted and all persons arrested in connection with the Tandjong Morawa developments released. However, after the parliamentary debates on the (modified) motion on May 21 and 22 it became clear that the Minister of the Interior still regarded the motion as one of no confidence and that the Masjumi supported him fully.

Would the PNI support the Sidik Kertapati motion? This was now the crucial question. At a meeting of representatives of the PNI and Masjumi on May 26, when a number of issues dividing the two parties were discussed, the PNI's attitude on the motion was still not known. However, by the time of the next meeting of Masjumi and PNI representatives on June 1, the situation had changed. By this time the PNI of North Sumatra had threatened to secede from the party if its parliamentary fraction did not support the motion. A majority of the PNI executive had decided that Roem would have to go if the cabinet was to be allowed to live on. But this was quite unacceptable, to the Prime Minister as well as to the Masjumi.

The PNI's final offer was on a quite different matter, the question of a replacement for the PNI Information Minister, Mononutu, who was soon to take up an appointment as ambassador to Peking. The PNI said that it would abstain when the Sidik Kertapati motion was put if the Masjumi agreed to forego its earlier veto of the PNI's candidate for the Information Ministry, Sarmidi Mangunsarkoro. But the Masjumi rejected this offer.

Thereupon the PNI party council decided to urge that the two main parties should together bring the cabinet to an end. On June 2, before a vote had been taken on the Sidik Kertapati motion, the cabinet decided to dissolve itself.

The Wilopo cabinet's fall can be traced in the first instance to the role of the PNI. PNI support for the cabinet had been unenthusiastic from the start. Already in the first months of the cabinet's term of office the party issued statements whose emphasis was strongly at variance with the policy approach of the cabinet. The army debates

and the October 17 affair brought the differences to the point of conflict. Then at the party congress in early December 1952 there was
a showdown.

This congress at Surabaja was an unusually stormy one. The October 17 dissensions had barely begun to subside. Through them the
long-standing dislike of the Socialist Party by a majority of the PNI
leaders had been newly set aflame. The feeling at the congress was
that the Wilopo cabinet was altogether too much influenced by the
PSI, particularly in its army and economic policies. Wilopo was subjected to vehement criticism for hesitating to take strong action against
the army leaders who had led the October 17 affair. The PNI Minister
for Economic Affairs, Sumanang, was attacked by almost every speaker
on economic policy for his announced policy of returning the North
Sumatran oil wells to Royal Dutch Shell.[132] All of the four PNI ministers were charged with indifference to party discipline.

One demand made frequently at the congress was that the PNI
ministers in the cabinet should do more to promote the party's interests.
This was urged particularly in relation to the forthcoming elections.
The ministers were instructed to use their influence to strengthen the
party and especially to overcome its poor financial situation.[133]

The party elections held at the congress resulted in a resounding
victory for Sidik Djojosukarto and the radical nationalist group in
the party. Thenceforth there was a protracted period of close co-
operation between the Sidik group and the older group of Sartono and
Suwirjo. In fact, it became common to speak of the "Sidik-Sartono

[132] These wells had been in Republican hands at the end of the period of armed
struggle in 1949. Thenceforth they operated under an Indonesian government
board on a temporary basis, producing at only 1 to 2 per cent of their prewar
annual rate (Higgins, *op. cit.*, p. 104). The Masjumi advocated their return to
Shell as the only way in which their production could be restored quickly. On
the other hand, there was strong feeling inside the PNI in favor of the alternative
course of nationalization. Both the Natsir and Sukiman cabinets had sought to
find a basis for returning the wells to the Anglo-Dutch company, but they had
taken no action. For a full discussion see Sutter, *Indonesianisasi: Politics in a
Changing Economy, 1940–1955* (Southeast Asia Program, Cornell University;
Ithaca, N.Y., 1959), pp. 819 ff.

[133] Among the members of the subcommittee established at the congress for the
purpose of collecting funds to defray the party's elections expenses were Mr. Iskaq
Tjokroadisurjo and Dr. Ong Eng Die. These two men had recently been appointed
to the directorship of the newly formed "PNI bank," the Bank Umum Nasional
(National General Bank), Iskaq as its board chairman and Ong as its executive
vice-chairman (Sutter, *op. cit.*, pp. 997–998). In the Ali Sastroamidjojo cabinet,
which followed upon that of Wilopo, Iskaq emerged as Minister of Economic
Affairs and Ong as Minister of Finance.

group" (or simply the "Sidik group," referring to the same persons) as one of only two major factions in the party.

The months following the congress saw little change in the cabinet's policies. Wilopo did give considerable concessions to the anti-October 17 group in his stand on the problems of the army. Sumanang ceased to press for the return of the North Sumatra oil wells to Shell (at the same time doing nothing about the PNI demand for their nationalization). But in economic and financial fields the cabinet continued and intensified its defiance of important interests allied or potentially allied with the PNI, firstly, national importers and, secondly, the whole upper- and middle-income groups of the cities. In the vital matter of advancing PNI interests through government influence, particularly in relation to the forthcoming elections, the PNI ministers continued to be unco-operative. While working resolutely for early elections— at a time when their party regarded itself as unprepared for these— they did next to nothing to strengthen the party's position in facing them. Sumanang appears to have been almost as quick to brush off requests for privileges when they came from the PNI as he was when they came from individual PNI businessmen.

By April 1953 if not earlier the PNI leaders were actively looking for a way to overthrow the cabinet. Their principal concern was to see to it that its successor was more to their liking. They did not want to see the formation of a Hatta-led presidential or business cabinet, such as was being canvassed by a number of Masjumi and PSI leaders. On the other hand, they stood to gain if the cabinet to succeed Wilopo's were another PNI-Masjumi coalition—for then they would see to it that the PNI portfolios were held by men who would take instructions from them. They would gain even more if it were a cabinet based on the PNI and smaller parties and excluding the Masjumi.

One central aspect of the Wilopo cabinet's fall was the fact that a cabinet of the latter type had become a distinct possibility. It was indeed unprecedented for the Masjumi, as the country's largest party and one most influential in the regional councils, to be excluded from a cabinet. But, on the other hand, Masjumi-PNI co-operation in a cabinet seemed to be fraught with greater difficulties than ever before. The Wilopo cabinet period had seen a decline in the influence of the Sukiman group within the Masjumi and a decline of the Wilopo group within the PNI. These tendencies could be expected to continue as the approach of elections made each party close its ranks and concern itself increasingly with its interests as a party.

Furthermore, the Wilopo period had seen the rise of parties and groups with an interest in a PNI-led cabinet which excluded the Masjumi. The Nahdatul Ulama had emerged as a political party. The PKI had grown in size and influence—and in conciliatoriness toward the PNI. And the pro-October 17 group within the army had sustained a crushing defeat, a defeat which greatly increased the power of "solidarity makers" in the army and at the same time lessened the influence of the army as a whole over cabinet politics, thus indirectly strengthening the influence of President Soekarno. One may therefore regard the Nahdatul Ulama, the PKI, the anti-October 17 group in the army, and President Soekarno as important agents along with the PNI of the process which brought the Wilopo period to an end.

The record of the Wilopo cabinet is one of notable achievements and instructive failures. When it returned its mandate on June 2, 1953, it had been in office for fourteen months, longer than any of its three predecessors of the postrevolutionary period. The hard work and ability of the individual ministers who composed the cabinet were generally recognized, as was the spirit of teamwork which characterized its operations. The cabinet's leaders were men with a concern for systematic planning, and they were bold in the range of governmental problems with which they attempted to grapple. Moreover, they had considerable success. Slight as was the Wilopo cabinet's respite from the recurring political crises which marked its term of office, it was nevertheless able to free itself in higher degree than any cabinet since Hatta's from pressure to apply *ad hoc* solutions to broad and basic problems.

The most significant achievements of the cabinet were in the economic field. The measures it took to meet the balance of payments crisis were highly successful. The stringency of its measures in the field of importing, combined with the fact of unexpected surpluses from the oil industry, made possible a marked improvement in the foreign reserves position. The cabinet was unable to prevent rises in the level of domestic prices, but it succeeded in confining these principally to luxury and semiluxury articles.

The cabinet had notable success too in the reorganization of government finances. The determination with which it pursued its austerity goals enabled it to persuade the separate ministries to accept severe budget cuts. Thus a detailed working budget for 1953 existed before the beginning of that year—a major achievement, despite the fact that parliamentary approval for the budget had yet to be given.

Furthermore, the cabinet greatly enhanced the effectiveness of the budget control machinery of the Finance Ministry.[134]

Within the government service the cabinet may be said to have "held the line" against pressures for expansion and greater political party influence. There was an increase in the size of the bureaucracy, but it was principally in such fields as teaching which were still under-staffed. Because the individual members of the Wilopo cabinet were as strongly loyal to one another as they were to their respective parties, the number of political appointments made in the civil service, or at least in its higher echelons, was small. Sparing use was made of spoils. At the same time corruption was kept at a fairly low level. The press was able to unearth only a small number of corruption cases in the whole of the fourteen-month period.

When all this has been said, the fact remains that the cabinet failed in terms of its own policy objectives. It attempted to implement its problem-solving policies even where this produced powerful hostile re-actions. It took little or no notice of the political warning lights. But it failed to muster the degree of political strength which could have made such boldness self-sustaining.

This was particularly clear in the case of its policies for the army. Here its efforts at reorganization were almost entirely self-defeating. Endeavoring to increase cohesion in the army, the cabinet in effect created sharper cleavage. Endeavoring to lessen political influence in the army, it stimulated a tightening of links between army factions and the factions of civilian politics. Attempting to strengthen the army's ability to unite the archipelago republic, it produced instead an in-tensification of tendencies to warlordism. Hoping to divert soldier energies into fields of reconstruction and development, it actually turned them to greater varieties of political activity and thereby added a new dimension to political instability.

As the role of politics in the army grew, the army's effectiveness against the rebels and bandits declined. In Sulawesi it was successful in the first few months of the cabinet's period in inducing a number of Kahar Muzakar's lieutenants to lay down their arms.[135] But there was a marked decline in the pace of army action after the coup which overthrew Colonel Gatot Subroto, and the second half of the Wilopo

[134] Higgins, *op. cit.*, pp. 6–7.
[135] Kementerian Penerangan, *Republik Indonesia, Propinsi Sulawesi* ("The Sula-wesi Province of the Republic of Indonesia"; Djakarta: Kementerian Penerangan, 1953), p. 351.

cabinet period saw the Kahar Muzakar group become further entrenched in its power on the island. The trends in the security picture in West Java gave more cause for hope. However, the Wilopo period saw no over-all advance in the efforts of the government to come to full control of its territory.

On the matter of foreign investment policy the cabinet had a similar record of failure. Its spokesmen repeatedly declared that efforts were to be made to attract the private foreign investor to the country. They made frequent promises that the cabinet would issue an explicit set of terms for the operation of foreign capital in Indonesia, a statement telling the investor what part of his profits he could transmit outside the country annually, what his obligations were to train Indonesian nationals, how long he would be secure against possible nationalization, and so on.[136] But no statement of this kind had been issued by the time the cabinet fell.

Of greater importance is the fact that the cabinet failed in its policies toward the foreign capital already invested in the country. Its weakness here was clearly demonstrated in the Tandjong Morawa affair, in which it was shown to be politically incapable of implementing its part of an agreement with foreign plantations. And if it failed by commission in the question of squatting on East Sumatran estates, it failed by omission in the matter of the North Sumatran oilwells. There the political hazards of taking the action on which the cabinet had decided were seen as too great. The damaged wells were not returned to Royal Dutch Shell, but continued in their uncertain status and very low rate of output.

The cabinet's political failure may be related in part to its exclusively "administrator" view of its tasks. Determined to demonstrate that it could succeed on the basis of effective performance, on the basis of what it was seen to be achieving rather than what it was seen to be, it acted no hero roles. In fact, its style of governing was peculiarly pedestrian and unspectacular. Nor did it provide hero roles for its followers. It certainly did not offer the type of leadership which would attract those who sought expressive participation in public life. Similarly it did not attempt to manipulate political unrest or to channel aggression to targets outside itself.

---

[136] See the statements of Information Minister Arnold Mononutu, *Antara*, July 3, 1952; Communications Minister Djuanda, *Antara*, Aug. 28, 1952; Prime Minister Wilopo, *Aneta*, Sept. 3, 1952; the official cabinet announcement of Feb. 27, 1953, *Antara*, Feb. 28, 1953; and the statement of Economic Affairs Minister Sumanang, *Antara*, March 28, 1953.

In terms of party politics, the roots of the cabinet's failure lay in the hostility which existed between the parties represented in it, particularly between the Masjumi and the PNI. As this hostility grew, the Wilopo group lost more and more of its influence inside the PNI and the cabinet's effective political support came to be limited to the Masjumi, the PSI, and the Christian parties. A new set of alignments developed, in which the PNI (and the PSII as another government party) co-operated with various parties outside the government, including the Nahdatul Ulama and the PKI and Murba.

This new party pattern was in one sense a sorting out and falling into place of the hitherto fluid constellation of political relationships. It put a temporary end to the pattern of the Natsir and Sukiman periods, in which factions and interparty cliques had been more important political units than parties or blocs of parties. But the principal cause of the realignment was a change in the over-all distribution of power, a decline in the influence of "administrator"-led groupings on the political stage as a whole and a rise in the power of "solidarity maker"-led groups. When the Wilopo cabinet took office, political conflict was still principally between factional groups of "administrator" leaders. It was between an interparty group of older "administrators" (Sukiman, Sartono, and the leaders of the PIR) and an interparty group of younger "administrators" (Natsir, Wilopo, and the PSI), with the "solidarity maker" parties and factions standing mainly on the side lines. By the time of the cabinet's demise, however, the conflict had become one between a cabinet of "administrators" and an opposition in which one group of "solidarity maker" elements had predominant influence.

Finally, the new pattern was a result of the basic power shift which came about after the October 17 affair. In consequence of the events of October, the "administrator" group of army leaders had had their base of power destroyed. The army, now deeply split, was no longer the counterpoise it had been earlier to the influence of President Soekarno.

Wilopo's defeat may be seen, then, as the outcome of two related trends. One was the growing estrangement between the Masjumi and its allies on the one hand and the PNI and its allies on the other. The second was the rising power of "solidarity makers," both in the parties and in the army.

Chapter VII

From Hatta to Wilopo:

Some Trends Unfold

IN the foregoing chapters we have discussed cabinets, policies, and issues. Our focus has been on parties and factions, on the army leadership and the President, and on the changing pattern of alignments between all these. Now to be considered are some more general aspects of the system of government and politics which existed in this three-and-a-half-year period—and in particular the attempt to operate constitutional democracy.

ADMINISTRATIVE AND ECONOMIC POLICIES

Between the four cabinets we have discussed there were great similarities. They were all cabinets composed predominantly of "administrators." On the whole, they were strongly oriented to policy, and all of them were concerned much more with solving practical problems than with effectuating ideological imperatives. Accepting an "administrator" definition of policy—it was basically a Hatta-Natsir-Sjahrir definition, which leaders like Sukiman and Suwirjo accepted with minor deviations of an *ad hoc* character—they concentrated their attention on normalization, the restoration of secure conditions, and the establishment of strong, unified and efficient government. In economic policy their first concern was to restore and increase production, to stimulate development, and to achieve and maintain fiscal stability. Their desire to restructure the economy was a matter of second priority.

In broad terms, all four cabinets may be said to have accepted the fact of the preponderant power of Westerners and Chinese in the economy. It is true that they established several new state enterprises [1] and that they devoted sizable sums of money to helping ethnic Indonesians enter certain business fields, particularly importing and to a lesser extent banking and bus transportation, which had previously been the virtually exclusive preserve of foreigners.[2] They imposed a variety of new regulations on the large foreign enterprises operating in the country and made it obligatory for these enterprises to give their Indonesian employees executive and managerial responsibilities. They acted directly to train Indonesians for economic leadership through various schemes. Their labor policies generally favored unions. The trend of their tax policies, in particular the fact that the peasantry was now scarcely taxed at all and that a large proportion of revenues came from foreign trade taxes, placed a considerable burden on the foreign-owned export industries. A similar effect was achieved by exchange rate unreality.[3] But there was no real challenge to the predominance of large Western enterprises, predominantly Dutch, in the estate economy, the oil industry, shipping, and exporting, and there was only a relatively small challenge to the position of the large Western firms in banking and importing. Nor was any major effort made to dislodge the Chinese from their very strong position in internal distributive trade, rural credit, and manufacturing. In the field of foreign trade, Indonesia kept to most of the patterns prevailing before 1949, selling raw materials in Western Europe, the United States, and Japan and buying industrial products there.

The cabinets had success with many of the administrative and economic policies they pursued. Whereas any attempt to make an assessment of the effectiveness of performance in these areas of policy must necessarily be highly tentative—if only because of the difficulties of choosing between the various possible standards of judgment—certain general observations may be made. The Indonesian governments maintained their authority with reasonable effectiveness during the difficult period of the transition to independence and to a unitary state. They unified and regularized the administration and made it

[1] John O. Sutter, *Indonesianisasi: Politics in a Changing Economy, 1940–1955* (Southeast Asia Program, Cornell University, 1959), pp. 786–790, 947–953.

[2] *Ibid.*, pp. 772 ff., 905 ff., 1016 ff.; Nan L. Amstutz, "The Rise of Indigenous Indonesian Importers, 1950–1955" (doctoral dissertation, Fletcher School, 1959).

[3] Douglas S. Paauw, "Financing Economic Development in Indonesia," *Economic Development and Cultural Change*, IV (Jan. 1956), 171–185.

a predominantly civilian affair (except in certain areas of disturbed security). They were able to restore internal communications facilities in many parts of the country. They eliminated armed bands from most areas—although important parts of West Java and South Sulawesi continued to be under rebel-bandit control. And they raised the level of soldier discipline. Furthermore, by giving support to the secretaries-general of ministries, they succeeded in establishing and maintaining a fairly high degree of respect for the norms of neutral and rule-bound administration. And they enabled their judicial agencies to enjoy a position of authority and considerable autonomy. Corruption was kept to a fairly low level.

In economic areas too they registered a number of successes. They managed to assuage the thirst for imported consumer goods in the areas where the blockaded revolutionary Republic had held power. They slowed down inflation and in 1952 and 1953 kept prices fairly stable. By providing credit to rural small industry, developing cooperatives, and improving villagers' agricultural techniques, they capitalized on the increased interest of peasants in technical innovations and succeeded in stimulating economic activity in many rural areas. They raised the over-all level of production, for both export and home consumption.[4] They were particularly effective in increasing rice production, which rose by 23.2 per cent between 1950 and 1953.[5] Furthermore, as we have seen, they greatly expanded educational and training facilities.

But they failed signally in their efforts to cope with some of the basic problems of reorganization demanded by their plans for longer-term policy. Their failures here are brought out with particular poignancy in the record of the Wilopo cabinet. However, the frustration which this cabinet experienced in its attempts to set a basis for planned development was different only in form and degree from similar frustrations experienced by its predecessors.

The pattern is clearly visible in the efforts of cabinets in three areas, their efforts to reorganize and rationalize the army, to reduce the size of the bureaucracy, and to come to terms with foreign capital. The Hatta, Natsir, and Sukiman cabinets succeeded in effecting a

[4] Biro Pusat Statistik (Central Bureau of Statistics), *Statistical Pocketbook of Indonesia, 1957* (Djakarta: Biro Pusat Statistik, 1957), pp. 51, 66, 78, 93.

[5] *Ibid.*, p. 51. For a discussion see Douglas S. Paauw, "The High Cost of Political Instability in Indonesia, 1957–58" in B. H. M. Vlekke, ed., *Indonesia's Struggle, 1957–58* (The Hague: Netherlands Institute of International Affairs, 1959), pp. 33–35.

measure of rationalization and reorganization in the army, but in doing so they aroused a great volume of discontent in sections of the army disfavored by their policies. When the Wilopo cabinet attempted to go several steps further in the same direction, the antagonism it aroused was implacable.

In the area of civil service rationalization the frustration of goals was less dramatic, but the picture is a similar one. The Hatta cabinet publicly declared, through the President himself, its intention to halve the number of civil servants. Whether it succeeded in reducing the number at all is not clear, but there was certainly no marked reduction. The Natsir cabinet again announced that the number of government servants had to be reduced; indeed, the Prime Minister placed considerable emphasis on this aspect of policy. He spoke to parliament of the need for "ruthless economy in the machinery of government." [6] But Natsir also failed—or achieved only negligible results. His Finance Minister was able to write in May 1951, two months after leaving office, that "at the present time the government absolutely does not know how many public servants it actually has working in its agencies. The estimates range between 300,000 and 500,000." [7] The Sukiman cabinet's proclaimed policy was similar; its Minister for Personnel Affairs declared that a 30 per cent cut in the number of civil servants was necessary.[8] But by the time the Wilopo cabinet came to office the number of public servants, now known as a result of a full survey, was 571,243.[9] The Wilopo cabinet did not commit

[6] Mohammad Natsir, "A Review of Indonesia's Reconstruction," *Indonesian Review*, I, no. 1 (Jan. 1951), 52.

[7] Sjafruddin Prawiranegara, *Indonesia Dipersimpangan Djalan* ("Indonesia at the Crossroads"; Djakarta: Hidup, 1951), p. 22. One explanation of the large divergencies between different estimates lay in the fact that certain categories of employees were included on some counts and excluded from others. This fact contributed to the arithmetical confusion which surrounded the subject of civil service numbers in subsequent years. The most usual basis of computation was to include as civil servants all permanent-status employees both of the central government and of autonomous services of the regional governments and to include police employees but to exclude military personnel, the employees of state enterprises, employees on temporary or day-labor status, and village officials. For a list of the full range of categories of government personnel, with statistics for the end of 1953, see Biro Pusat Statistik, *Statistical Pocketbook of Indonesia, 1957*, p. 220.

[8] Gusti Majur, "Pegawai Negeri Kita" ("Our Civil Servants"), *Mimbar Indonesia*, Feb. 16, 1952.

[9] *Keterangan dan Djawaban Pemerintah atas Program Kabinet Wilopo* ("The Government Statement of the Wilopo Cabinet and Replies to Parliamentary Criticism"; Djakarta: Kementerian Penerangan, 1952), p. 178.

itself publicly to a policy of reducing the number of civil servants, but it sent all its agencies a strongly worded instruction forbidding the acceptance of new employees unless they had special qualifications. Even in this, however, it was not entirely successful.

The attempt to reduce the size of the bureaucracy, or even to maintain it at the existing level, was fraught with enormous political difficulties. To be a civil servant was to have assured employment for a lifetime, to have an established position of high social status, to be able to look forward to a pension, and to be certain of being able to afford education for one's children. Furthermore, it was to be able to see oneself as part of a guardian group in society.[10] Clearly men would not readily allow themselves to be deprived of civil servant status.

Moreover, in resisting the threat of large-scale dismissals, civil servants were asserting a right with deep roots in existing social values. The "right to work"—the employee's right to a "fair share" of whatever employment may be available and the employer's obligation to accord him such employment more or less regardless of efficiency and productivity—is a moral principle prevailing in much of Indonesian enterprise, both agricultural and commercial.[11] In addition, with party-linked trade unions in existence in most government agencies, and most individual civil servants also members of parties, civil service protest could easily find organizational expression. Even disciplinary dismissals were in fact extremely rare in this period.

With white-collar employment outside the government service in short supply, there was indeed little for a high school graduate to do but join the civil service. Thus it was thought that office heads should respond sympathetically when fathers or uncles of such graduates approached them with a request for employment. In fact, many offices had surprisingly large formal schedules of vacancies, which were used to justify employing new persons in these situations. With budgetary organization fluid, it was always possible to find funds for a few more salaries. In Geertz's words, "The bureaucracy and the educational system . . . are locked in a self-perpetuating circle of dis-

[10] Donald Fagg, "Authority and Social Structure; A Study in Javanese Bureaucracy" (doctoral dissertation, Harvard University, 1958), pp. 543 ff.

[11] Clifford Geertz, "Religious Belief and Economic Behavior in a Central Javanese Town: Some Preliminary Considerations," *Economic Development and Cultural Change*, IV, no. 2 (1955–1956), 143; Geertz, *The Development of the Javanese Economy: A Socio-cultural Approach* (Cambridge, Mass.: Center for International Studies, M.I.T., 1956), pp. 71–77.

tention in which the second produces more and more diplomaed graduates which the [first] is forced to absorb." [12]

Finally, all four cabinets of the period under discussion were concerned to establish a mutually beneficial basis of co-operation with foreign investors. They were interested both in attracting new investment and in preventing disinvestment and capital flight from enterprises operating in Indonesia—for instance, such practices as the over-heavy tapping of rubber trees with a view to abandoning them after two or three years of very high earnings. Foreign investors, however, were cautious. The cabinets knew that their ability to attract foreign capital and to prevent disinvestment would depend less on verbal assurances than on observed performance. It would depend on their ability to provide foreign establishments with protection against rebel-bandits and common thieves. It would depend on the stands they took as conciliators and arbitrators between foreign employers and Indonesian labor organizations. And it would depend also—or so most of the leaders of these cabinets thought—on their ability to take certain unpopular measures, such as returning the North Sumatran oil wells to Royal Dutch Shell and evicting peasant squatters from foreign-leased tobacco lands in East Sumatra.

But here again, as already brought out, the cabinets proved to be incapable of taking the actions which were, on their own reckoning, required. In the matter of the North Sumatran oil wells no decision could be taken. The issue was one on which political debate continued throughout the Natsir, Sukiman, and Wilopo cabinets, with proponents of the return of the wells to the Dutch company ranged against advocates of nationalization and with neither course being adopted. On the problem of the tobacco land squatters, action was indeed attempted and the consequences were dramatic: the death of five demonstrators and, as an indirect result, the final tumbling of the Wilopo cabinet. Some new foreign investment was attracted in the period of the four cabinets, but its value was not great, and, on the other hand, disinvestment continued throughout the period.

In all these three areas, where its efforts were to set the country on the path to planned development, the cabinets failed. Where a cabinet had a policy, in the sense that it diverted resources toward the implementation of it, the failure may be seen as one of decision enforcement. Where a cabinet did not have a policy in this sense, as in the case of the Sukiman cabinet's approach to proposals for the return of

[12] Geertz, *The Development of the Javanese Economy*, p. 72.

the North Sumatran oil wells to Royal Dutch Shell, the failure can be described as one of decision making. The difference lies between, on the one hand, attempting a politically hazardous policy and failing and, on the other hand, hesitating to make the attempt (while still believing that it must eventually be made). In both cases the underlying political reality is the same, namely, the incapacity of governments to bring sufficient power to bear to enforce policies with a serious deprivational aspect.

Why then could these governments not bring more power to bear? It was basically because the political elite was divided, because important segments of it were hostile to them. This comes out clearly when one compares the Indonesian political elite with that of India in the early years of its independence—using the term political elite in a similar way to mean the individual political actors who create and resolve major crises. In India the political elite was dominated by the government itself and the leaders of the Congress, which was substantially identified with the government. The "political executive"— in the sense of the cabinet leadership and all political and bureaucratic elements which identified their interests with it—was a preponderant part of the political elite. In Indonesia, on the other hand, the political executive was only a relatively weak segment of the political elite for most of the 1949–1953 period. The power resources held by the cabinet leaders, and by party, military, and civil service figures who identified their political fortunes with those of the cabinet leaders, were small in the context of the political elite as a whole. And if the Indonesian political executive was weak in comparison with that of India, it was very much more so in comparison with the political executives of the two Asian countries other than Indonesia where revolutions had taken or were taking place, China and North Vietnam.

In the Hatta cabinet period Indonesia's political executive was indeed strong. This cabinet was able, particularly in its early months of office, to make and implement important decisions quickly and effectively. This was because of Hatta's great personal prestige, because of Dutch and BFO trust in Hatta (at a time when Dutch troops were still in the country), because of the fact that the parties were still recovering from their eclipse of 1949, because of the great power of the central leaders of the army (who worked closely with the Prime Minister), and not least because of the great abundance of material and prestige resources available to the government as a result of the transfer of power.

But this was an exceptional situation and it passed quickly. Even during Hatta's term of office, his acceptability to the Dutch and the BFO was a quickly dwindling political asset, as Dutch troops departed and the BFO states crumbled. Hatta himself was virtually removed from the political arena in August 1950. At the same time the parties emerged from their eclipse, and with them the party factions. The power of the army leadership began to be offset by that of President Soekarno, with the army leaders and the increasingly influential President tending to support opposing factional groups within the complex of cabinet and party politics.

The subsequent cabinets could bring far less power to bear. Thus the Natsir cabinet was faced by a strong parliamentary opposition, and in the latter part of its period of office, by the hostility of the President. The Sukiman cabinet was internally divided and had the political power of the army leadership ranged against it. The political elite was split along various lines in the period of these two cabinets, and in general there was much less identification with the government among members of the political elite than there had been under Hatta. Both cabinets benefited from the Korean War boom, which helped them to satisfy many of the material and status demands made of them, but even the fruits of the boom did not enable either of them to concentrate power in the face of the fissiparous tendencies operating in the political elite.

The Wilopo cabinet attempted to assert power on a scale greater than either the Natsir or Sukiman cabinet had, and in some areas, such as budgetary reorganization and the creation of the elections law, its efforts were successful. But the costs of its resolute posture, adopted as it was when the post-Korea slump reached its nadir, were high. Its policies and the resentment they aroused were of major importance in fashioning the PNI-NU-PKI alliance—or perhaps it should be called the PNI-Soekarno-NU-PKI alliance—which not only overthrew the cabinet but brought about a denouement in the whole system of government and politics of the period since 1949.

The weakness of the political executive in the 1949–1953 period may be seen, then, in terms of two developments. In the first place, the undoing of the exceptional situation of the Hatta cabinet period allowed elite politics to assume the fluid unstructured character it had had in the early years of the Revolution. Thus play was given to the sharp competition which existed between different "administrator"-led factions in the political elite, factions which did not differ greatly from one another in either their ideological positions or their policy orientations. This fluidity of power relations may be traced in part to the long history of divisions in the Indonesian nationalist leadership, to the fact that the nationalist movement did not develop as a single major organization with established machinery for the settling of disputes. But it should also be seen as following from the political vacuum created by the Revolution and from the stimulus this gave to political ambition. In Geertz's words,

[Under colonialism] as the social system "naturally" grows more complex, the European ruling group takes over each new role of functional importance as it appears, either filling it themselves or permitting certain others, typically non-European immigrants, half-castes, and a few specially chosen native aristocrats, to fill it, thus "sheltering" the native society from the effects of the change. . . . When at length a political revolution occurs, as in Indonesia, the power vacuum revealed as almost all posts of crucial political importance are suddenly left vacant is tremendous and draws almost the whole of social life into it. . . . With the new understanding of what the score really is . . . the scramble for power becomes intense.[13]

In the second place, the political executive grew weaker as the influence of "administrators" generally declined and that of "solidarity makers" rose. This was the trend of almost all major political developments of the period of Wilopo—the NU's secession from the Masjumi, the increasing dominance of Sidik Djojosukarto in the PNI, the new importance of Isa Anshary in the Masjumi, the growth of the Communist Party, and above all two related developments outside parties, the defeat of the "administrator" army leadership of Simatupang and Nasution and the parallel rise in the power of the President. With social unrest continuing to be widespread and with the resources of governments cut sharply by the post-Korea slump, there was a great deal of protest which "solidarity makers" could use against an "administrator"-dominated government. Moreover, as ideological antagonisms of the Pantja Sila versus Islamic State kind came increasingly to the fore, political conflict tended more and more to follow party lines, with the result that the Wilopo cabinet's political support was effectively limited to the Masjumi and PSI.

One additional factor in the weakness of governments in this three-and-a-half-year period was the immobilizing role of the bureaucracy. As the power of the political executive declined, there was a tendency for the military and civil service members of the political elite to lose

[13] *The Religion of Java* (Glencoe, Ill.: Free Press, 1960), p. 363.

their sense of identification with the leadership of the government
and to become politically absorbed instead within the bureaucracy.
Thus nationalist leaders who had been placed in high civil service
posts tended to develop closer ties to particular government departments and particular factional groupings within these departments
than to fellow members of the political executive. Similarly many
members of the revolutionary leadership who were military officers
came to speak more for the army, or a part of it, than for the political
executive.

Thus in implementing a government's policy, the bureaucracy
tended more and more to respond to demands made of it from elsewhere. It frequently vetoed policies which would hurt a significant
portion of its own membership—as in the case of the efforts of successive cabinets to reduce the number of civil servants and the efforts
of the Wilopo cabinet to impose its rationalization scheme on the army.
But it also mirrored the interests of nonbureaucratic groups in society,
both groups with which particular segments of the bureaucracy had
a "client" relationship (for instance, in the case of the Labor Ministry
and the unions or that of the Economic Affairs Ministry and the national importers) and quasi-communal segments of society whose members were represented in particular divisions of the bureaucracy (for
instance, the *santri* community in the Ministry of Religious Affairs
or the Toba Bataks in the education office of the province of North
Sumatra).

It was, in fact, the normal pattern of government for the decisions
of cabinets to be renegotiated frequently in the process of execution.
Bureaucratic leaders, central and local, were expected to be *bidjak-
sana* (discreet, wise in negotiation). As balancers they frequently
played a role of great importance for the preservation of social harmony.[14] But by the same token they were relatively ineffective as instruments for particular policies of the government.

In effect the Indonesian political executive was unable to implement policies with serious deprivational consequences for sections of
the bureaucracy or the army, because it lacked a major basis of nonbureaucratic power to pit against them. The small indigenous propertied groups could provide it with a measure of such power for certain purposes; and it could call on certain of the parties, especially
ones like the Masjumi whose influence within the bureaucracy was
relatively small. But the power which any of these could help it to

[14] See the highly stimulating discussion in Fagg, *op. cit.*, pp. 324 ff., 543 ff.

bring to bear against the bureaucracy was not great. Government leaders could not impose their will on the bureaucracy by virtue of the power resources of a closely knit single party as in Communist or fascist systems (and to some extent in India and Ghana). Nor could they bring to bear the type of power resources possessed by an Ataturk or an Ayub Khan who controls a cohesive military organization. Nor could they fall back on strong propertied elements or strongly organized interest groups as the British, American, and Philippine governments can, and to some extent the Indian one, in order to limit their bureaucracy to an instrumental role.[15]

One might suppose that party and factional division within the bureaucracy and army would have resulted in an increase in the power of the political executive over these. But in fact the opposite was the case, for the divisions within the civil and military services were broadly parallel to the divisions within the political elite itself. Thus, whenever the political executive attempted to use the bureaucracy instrumentally in a way which was strongly opposed by a section of it, this section could appeal to sympathetic groups within the political elite. If the appeal were effective, the political executive might attempt to use an alternative section of the bureaucracy for its policy purposes, the *pamong pradja* corps rather than the police or the Ministry of Information rather than the Ministry of Education; this was often possible because differentiation of functions between these agencies was by no means sharp. But in this event a similar neutralizing mechanism could be brought into play at another level, particularly if the policy to be implemented involved deprivational consequences for a particular group in society. In such a case this group—whether it was a group of squatters, an organization of rebel-bandits, a veterans' league, a commercial enterprise, or an association of cottage industry producers—would endeavor to gain protection from a section of the governmental apparatus which was a political opponent or rival of the section which was to be used against it. The usual result was either inaction or compromise; the particular action with adverse consequences for the group outside the bureaucracy was not taken, or was taken only in a modified form.

The one section of the bureaucracy of which it can be said that it lent itself readily to being an instrument of the political executive

[15] On bureaucratic power as power to frustrate extrabureaucratic policy making, see Fred W. Riggs, "Bureaucracy in Transitional Societies: Politics, Economic Development and Administration" (unpublished paper, Indiana University, 1959).

was the *pamong pradja,* the corps of general territorial administrators which carried over from its prewar past (as the *pangreh pradja* and Binnenlands Bestuur) a fairly high level of professionalization and an aversion to party politics, as well as traditionally based prestige in rural society. In general, the *pamong pradja* remained largely unpoliticized in the 1949–1953 period, despite the efforts of the parties to gain control of its higher levels. But the *pamong pradja* was seen as tainted by colonialism and authoritarianism and therefore suspect in the eyes of a large part of the political public. Moreover, the authority of its officers was often challenged by the leaders of political parties. Thus there were sharp limits to the ability of the political executive to enforce policy through the *pamong pradja* as well.

If one looks at the four cabinets in terms of the resources they possessed, it becomes clear that they were short of both carrots and sticks. Two extraordinary sources of carrots, inducements or rewards, were indeed available to them, as a result of the transfer of sovereignty and because of the Korean War boom. But, on the other hand, social change had raised expectations, by making men aspire to greater status and income and by producing a high level of anxiety. In relation to the existing level of expectations, the rewards which the cabinets of the period could distribute were not great. As for sticks, instruments of coercion or punishment, the cabinets had few of these because the bureaucracy tended to transform their decisions, protecting those against whom it was to enforce deprivational action.

THE MAINTENANCE OF LEGITIMATE AUTHORITY

It would be wrong, however, to confine the focus here to the administrative and economic activities of the four cabinets. The viability of the system of government and politics which these cabinets were operating did not depend only on their success in raising levels of civil security, administrative efficiency, or economic output or only on their capacity to organize power for these purposes. It depended also on their ability to legitimize themselves, that is, to gain voluntary acceptance of the idea that they, these particular cabinets and the regime of which they were part, had a moral right to govern.

To create a general sense of identification with the regime, the cabinets all devoted a great deal of effort to spreading the idea of nationality. The Ministry of Information, with its system of branch offices extending down to the subdistrict level, was responsible for much of this "nation-building" activity. Its representatives spoke to villagers and townsmen in all parts of the country about Indonesia, its geography and history, about the Pantja Sila, about President Soekarno and Vice-President Hatta, and about the tasks of national upbuilding. They told them to wake up to the big things happening all about them, to the new independence, its promise of a better society, and its challenge to men to improve themselves. They urged them to be active, to join in the country's public life, rather than accepting the old local traditions and authorities uncritically. They also spoke to them about specific policies of the government and about important current events in Djakarta, in other parts of the country, and in the world outside Indonesia.

The Information Ministry men spoke directly to the people, especially the villagers. Frequently also they spoke to them through such media as the *wajang* shadow play and popular drama. They reached large groups of people through documentary films shown at each of the three or more daily sessions of Indonesia's approximately 800 cinemas.[16] They reached an increasing number by radio. There was a rapid rise in the number of radio stations, all under the aegis of the Ministry of Information, and the number of licensed radio sets rose from 213,271 to 377,026 between 1951 and 1953.[17]

Schools were a further channel of the highest importance for spreading values, information, and ideas of a similar kind. As brought out earlier, the regular school system was expanded rapidly in these years. In addition, the Mass Education Division of the Education Ministry conducted large numbers of literacy courses in which most of the same themes were stressed. By the middle of 1953, there were 2,711,006 persons who had successfully completed these courses.[18] The same ministry's Culture Division encouraged interregional travel by theater and music groups from particular regional cultures and gave support to various forms of creative work of an all-Indonesian character.

The Ministry of Religious Affairs, based on a you-support-me-and-I'll-support-you relationship between the state and the major religions of the country, gave out considerable quantities of political education materials of a general kind. Various other ministries, such as Agriculture, Health, and the Interior, had information departments of their own, which publicized particular programs and also spread nationalist ideas in general. Last but not least, speech-making tours by President

[16] This was the figure in Sept. 1951. See Roeslan Abdulgani, *Funksi Penerangan di Indonesia* ("The Function of Information Work in Indonesia"; Djakarta: Kementerian Penerangan, 1953), p. 244.

[17] Biro Pusat Statistik, *Statistical Pocketbook of Indonesia, 1957*, p. 163.

[18] *Ibid.*, p. 27.

Soekarno and Vice-President Hatta were a most important nation-building instrument. Both men traveled frequently, going to the remotest parts of the country and giving many addresses daily. In Soekarno's case, this was usually before very large crowds.

These various activities were intended to heighten the sense of Indonesianness, to spread nationalist awareness through all sections of the population and to replace local and ethnic loyalties by national ones. The long-run aim was to create an all-Indonesian political society. It was to do what was done in Western Europe between the sixteenth and nineteenth centuries, when states made nations of themselves by bringing about shared perceptions and values and a capacity for mutual empathy between members of all their various ethnic and social groups.

In addition, such nation-building activities had immediate legitimizing effects; they increased the popularity of the governments and their moral authority. This was in part because most villagers outside the political public responded favorably to the nationalist symbols, especially where these were presented intelligibly, as they were by some of the spokesmen of government agencies and pre-eminently by President Soekarno. Thus emotional bonds were established between the government and the mass of the people, helping to overcome the cultural gap between them and serving as a partial equivalent of the cultural and religious ties which had existed between kings and villagers in precolonial Indonesia. Villagers beginning to step out of their traditional society were provided with a focus for personal orientations.

In addition, village-level nation-building activities added to the authority of governments indirectly, inasmuch as the members of the political public saw the villagers' widening awareness as a cause for satisfaction with the regime. Indeed, many members of the political public expressed the greatest pleasure when they went to a village and saw the many signs of the new awareness—literacy courses, schools, organizations, sports, and the absence of servility, as well as more lighting than before the war, more modern dress, more bicycles, and more varied diets.

However, the four cabinets also acted more directly to create and maintain support in the political public, to persuade persons of potential political effectiveness to have a sense of identification with the governmental leadership, and here they were generally less successful. The problem they faced was the one of transition from Revolution: the chief basis of the regime's legitimacy for the members of the political public was the Revolution itself. Those who governed were seen as having a moral right to do so because they had led the revolutionary movement to victory.

But the Revolution was a thing of the past, and the cabinet leaders of the 1949–1953 period were inclined to stress the fact that it was so. They were concerned to consolidate, to establish control, law, and norms, and to work for the realization of the goals of the Revolution by nonrevolutionary means. Their actions therefore bespoke disagreement with the viewpoint articulated by President Soekarno from November 1952 onward—and with increasing emphasis—that "our national Revolution is not yet completed." [19] It is true that they frequently adduced the experience of the revolutionary past in their exhortations to the people. But this was usually in terms such as these in a Heroes Day message of the Staff of the Combined Armed Forces:

[Let us] redirect the thoughts which for years have been concentrated on heroism in battle. Let us turn them to heroism in other fields which are no less important for the welfare of the state and the nation. . . . National greatness can only be achieved if there are heroes of science, heroes of industry, heroes of shipping, heroes of education, heroes of upbuilding.[20]

Revolution and postrevolutionary upbuilding were treated as sharply discontinuous. Consequently the Revolution could no longer serve as well to legitimize the cabinet's authority. Indeed, as we have seen, there was a tendency for the cabinets to be associated with the alien, humdrum, divisive aspects of government and not with the spirit of the Revolution, the spirit of unity, or the spirit of heroism. When President Soekarno distanced himself from particular cabinets, notably those of Natsir and Wilopo, he was both responding to this tendency and accentuating it.

In addressing themselves to the political public, the cabinet leaders provided a good deal of political education of the least propagandistic type. Their spokesmen gave full and precise accounts and explanations of political occurrences and frequently attempted to turn political debate away from ideological assertion and the preoccupation with undifferentiated clusters of symbols toward concern with specific political and economic issues. One of the Ministry of Information's "Five Prin-

[19] See *Text of the Speech of the President of the Republic of Indonesia on Heroes Day, November 10th, 1952* (Djakarta: Ministry of Information, 1952).

[20] Kementerian Pertahanan Staf Angkatan Perang (Staff of the Combined Armed Forces, Ministry of Defense), "Tjatatan pada Hari Pahlawan 1951" ("Notes on Heroes Day, 1951"), *Mimbar Indonesia*, Nov. 10, 1951.

ciples" was "to deepen the people's political awareness and critical faculties as required for every citizen who values democracy." [21] And the heads of this ministry repeatedly spoke of the need for a critical attitude in political affairs.[22]

At the same time the cabinets did not engage in dramatic foreign policy activities or attempt to evoke excited responses at home to their roles in the international arena. In handling the Irian question, they did their best, within the limits of their relationship to President Soekarno, to discourage agitational support of the claim. Far from establishing external targets for hostility, they condemned expressions of antiforeign sentiment. And, although they organized rallies on certain national holidays, they created no organizational machinery to mobilize the symbol attachments of the ex-revolutionaries on an ongoing basis. In effect they did very little to maintain the nationalist movement as a source of personal values.

This was a consistent set of positions, granted the primary concern of these cabinets with law and order and the pursuit of problem-solving policies in the economic and administrative spheres. But its effectiveness in establishing their own moral authority was small. It was indeed effective for the members of the "generally interested" group of the political public, those who judged government by what it was doing to realize their values and interests, rather than by its capacity to arouse particular states of mind in them. But this was like preaching to the converted; for the members of this group were already sympathetic to the leaders of the four cabinets.

The real problem lay with that large group of the political public whose political participation was primarily expressive, who sought an integrative equivalent of Revolution and expected the national leadership to provide it. For this group the leaders of the four cabinets had little understanding. Being themselves secure in their personal identity as Indonesians, feeling that the idea of "Indonesia" was something almost to be taken for granted, they did not have much sympathy for the state of mind of those in the political public for whom Indonesianness was still a conversion phenomenon, a compelling new perception of sacredness which called for ritual and symbolic action. And thus

[21] *Membangun diantara Tumpukan Puing dan Pembangunan,* p. 50.
[22] See, for instance, the statements of Information Minister Arnold Mononutu, *Aneta,* Sept. 8, 1951, and of the secretary-general of the Information Ministry, Roeslan Abdulgani, *Indonesia Raya,* May 6, 1952.

they declined to play the priestly roles expected of them. In consequence they antagonized the group.

They attempted to cope with the problem of the revolutionary veterans administratively by finding adequate employment for them. In a narrowly economic sense they were fairly successful in this, although some veterans remained in the ranks of the disguised unemployed of the cities. But materially adequate employment was often politically insufficient, because it brought neither the expected status nor a sense of meaning and purpose. Thus many even of those ex-revolutionaries who had found materially adequate employment became alienated from the political system.

In fact, the very success of the cabinets in establishing government on a more routinized basis helped to make their authority less acceptable to the members of the expressive politics group. The effect of routinization was not, as its protagonists had hoped, to lessen the influence of "oppositionism." On the contrary, it contributed to a widespread loss of *élan*, a sense of normlessness, rudderlessness, and "moral crisis," and a feeling of disgust for the selfish, faction-torn, and uninspiring character of public life. The political consequences of this were agitational politics, alternating with passivity. Therefore the propensity of one important section of the political public to look for value coherence in political symbols of the sacred was reinforced, and the power of "solidarity makers" grew. It would seem that the social and psychological upheavals which had been wrought by the Revolution, and by the Japanese occupation before it, had been too great to allow an easy transition to a rule-based system of government and politics. Herein lies a centrally important cause of the failure of the four "administrator"-controlled cabinets to maintain the governmental-political system they had built.

THE FUNCTIONING OF CONSTITUTIONAL DEMOCRACY

This brings us finally to review the operation of constitutional democracy in the period up to the halfway point we have reached. Can this indeed be called a period of constitutional democracy, this period when the existing parliament was not elected and the date of parliamentary elections was repeatedly postponed, when cabinets formally responsible to parliament were frequently prevented from deciding issues in accordance with the wishes of the parliamentary majority because of interference by the army or the President, and when they frequently could not implement their decisions because of bureaucratic dragging of feet?

The answer to this question can only be arbitrary; every observer has the right to his own definition of the minima of constitutional democracy. My own view is that the term may indeed be used—because of the existence of a wide measure of public liberties, because of the respected position of parliament, because governments honored the symbols of constitutional democracy, and because their actions implied that they took constitutionalism seriously. The most important point is the last, that the successive cabinets were *attempting* to establish a parliamentary democracy. Their leaders believed in a strong executive and were prepared to use existing authoritarian relationships for some of their purposes. But they did not attempt to use coercive means to maintain support for themselves—not even the verbal coercion of propaganda and narrow loyalty demands. They took pains to adhere to the forms of government as set forth in the existing constitution. And, actively supported by a distinguished group of top civil servants, especially the secretaries-general and such individuals as Chief Public Prosecutor Suprapto and Police Chief Sukanto Tjokrodiatmodjo, they insisted on maintaining and fostering the rule of law.[23]

This approach comes out in the cabinet's relationships with parliament. Cabinet leaders were meticulous in the attention they gave to parliamentary questions, interpellations, and criticisms.[24] Several months were spent at the beginning of each cabinet's term of office in a general debate on the cabinet's program. On the important question of the budget, parliament was in effect denied its formal rights; only one of the four cabinets of our period submitted a draft budget to parliament before it was due to take effect, and this budget, that of the Wilopo

[23] The model of government they attempted to follow resembles closely both that of contemporary India and the "tutelary democracy" of Edward Shils, which he distinguishes from "political democracy" on the one hand and "modernizing oligarchy," "totalitarian oligarchy," and "traditional oligarchy" on the other. "Tutelary democracy," he writes, "retains all the institutions of political democracy, but it adapts them all in the direction of a preponderance of the executive." See "Political Development in the New States," *Comparative Studies in Society and History*, II, no. 3 (April 1960), 265 ff.

[24] See Miriam S. Budiardjo, "Evolution toward Parliamentary Democracy in Indonesia: Parties and Parliament" (M.A. thesis, Georgetown University, 1955), *passim.* See also Budiardjo, "The Provisional Parliament of Indonesia," *Far Eastern Survey*, XXX, no. 2 (Feb. 1956), 17–23, and J. H. A. Logemann, "The Indonesian Parliament," *Parliamentary Affairs, Journal of the Hansard Society*, VI (Aug. 1953), 346–352.

cabinet for 1953, was not given parliamentary approval until late in 1953, after the cabinet's resignation. Similarly one may point to the fact that all cabinets of this period made heavy use of their power to enact emergency laws. But, in view of the over-all weakness of cabinets—their political weakness, and, on top of that, the constitutional situation in which they could be overthrown by party defections in parliament whereas they could not on their own account dissolve the legislative body—it is hardly surprising that they resorted to such expedients. Wanting to exercise strong executive government but unable to do so, they nevertheless went to some length to attend to the parliamentarians' claims and questions, bothersome and time-consuming as they frequently thought them. Perhaps equally important, it would seem that they made relatively little use of the opportunities they had for secret decision making. The point is not easily demonstrable. The indications are, however, that parliament was told about most of their important decisions, including the financial ones, and that they attempted to keep the gap between formal decision making and effective decision making from becoming too large, and succeeded.

The role which parliament played in the system of politics in this period is difficult to describe in any exact way. It fulfilled legitimizing functions only in small measure, being endowed with little authority. This was in part because it had not been elected, but more particularly because its composition reflected the Round Table Conference compromise between the Republic and the Dutch-sponsored states. Thus it could not come fully under the umbrella of the central agent of legitimation of government, the Revolution. To this extent it was difficult for it to contribute to a gradual transformation whereby the exercise of government power might have come to be justified by a rule-based process of gauging the people's will, rather than by the Revolution. In addition, its authority was the less because there was no place in prevailing Indonesian views of government and politics, views of how these worked or should work, for the process of interests representation.

But parliament did fulfill many of the functions which the operation of constitutional democracy requires. It spread information about the state of feeling in particular groups and regions. It also helped to widen the reading public's understanding of many specific issues of politics. In this way it served to sustain the "generally interested" group of the political public, the group of those whose orientation was to policy rather than ideology. The atmosphere of parliamentary discussion was fairly free. Intense demands for loyalty were made in only a relatively few areas—the unitary state, the West Irian claim, and the "independent foreign policy," but seldom concerning matters of domestic policy —and where they were made it was not by cabinets.

Moreover, parliament was by no means weak. As already seen, it was partly through parliament that three different governments fell in a period of three years. Nor was the power to overthrow a cabinet in the hands of top party leaders only; individual M.P.'s could share in it in some measure, by virtue of their ability to leave one party for another or to switch loyalties from one faction of a party to another.

Thus parliament was an important framework for the process of representation. Although much of parliamentary discussion was about matters of ideology, a good deal of time was spent also on specific grievances, the inept handling of shipping arrangements for pilgrims to Mecca, the Madurese salt industry and its need for protection, poor soldier discipline in South Kalimantan, or the government's slowness to try a particular group of prisoners. On matters like these the cabinets were generally responsive to parliamentary criticism.

On the other hand, the parties were top-heavy, and they articulated the interests of groups in Djakarta much more effectively than those of regional groups. Even more important, it was frequently impossible for cabinets to oblige the civil service or the army to respond to party and parliamentary demands—a fact which led many groups to press their interests directly through the bureaucracy rather than through parties and parliament.

This leads to what is probably the central aspect of parliament's role, the fact that it overlapped at numerous points with the roles of other agencies of government and became locked in an over-all conflict in which parliament, cabinets, the President, the army, and various branches and segments of the civil service were all fully involved. In reality there was little differentiation of functions between these various agencies, with each being used by the particular political groups which controlled it to exercise as wide a range of powers as possible.[25] Relations between parliament, cabinet, and the bureaucracy reflected the over-all power situation, a fluid situation where parties, factions, and cliques jostled for power. In this power struggle the lines of func-

---

[25] For a discussion of this as a general problem of non-Western political systems see S. N. Eisenstadt, "Social Development and Political Stability in Non-Western Societies," in A. Bonné, *The Challenge of Development* (Jerusalem: Eliezer Kaplan School of Economics and Social Sciences, Hebrew University, 1958), pp. 142–144.

tional differentiation dividing the several agencies from one another were heavily blurred. All these agencies served representative functions and all of them attempted to control or influence the making, implementation, and adjudication of decisions. Thus the unresolved party and factional conflict found expression not only in parliamentary division, but also in frequently falling cabinets and in divided and often self-immobilizing administration. With none of the agencies having an area of autonomous power, attention was constantly being directed to the central political tussles, to the ever-vain efforts of major groups and coalitions to come decisively to the top of the whole power heap.

The area in which the conditions of constitutional democracy were most effectively established was the press. In general, the press of these years was lively, informative, and free. On occasion, and especially in the highly popular gossip columns, it was thoroughly irreverent. Although all the papers had informal links with particular parties, very few were direct party organs. Even those which stood closest to particular parties felt free to embellish the specific positions of their parties in their own way. Most of the editors owned their own newspapers, operating with the meagerest financial resources in most cases and dependent on their small circulations—rather than on advertising —for most of their revenues. And it would seem that they believed that neither slavish adherence to party viewpoints nor outright sensationalism would sell their papers. Partly because of the very small circulations, then—no papers had more than 40,000 readers at this time and most less than 10,000—the press was fairly objective. In the case of some of the more prominent Djakarta dailies, notably the Socialist-oriented *Pedoman,* the Chinese-owned and politically independent (but somewhat Socialist-inclined) *Keng Po,* and the Communist Party's *Harian Rakjat,* the standard of editorial comment and analysis was high on any international comparison.

Press freedom was by no means complete. There were occasional arrests of journalists, and sometimes, especially in the smaller towns, an army commander would forbid a paper to continue publication. Dutch, Chinese, and Communist papers were particularly subject to treatment of this kind. Moreover, some half-dozen instances are recorded in this period of attacks by groups of youths on newspaper offices—and here foreign-owned and Communist papers were not the only targets. On the whole, however, the level of freedom was high. The government actively helped the "national press" by subsidies. It gave an outright grant to the news agency *Antara,* and it helped the newspapers owned by ethnic Indonesians by paying a fixed proportion of their newsprint costs.[26] As this proportion was greater for news-papers of smaller circulation—the government, in fact, contributed actively to the existence of a large number of papers—the figure for Indonesian-language dailies rose from 45 in 1949 to 76 in 1953.[27] At the same time it does not appear to have employed the threat to with-draw this financial support in the case of particular groups critical of government policies.[28] Certainly some very strong criticisms were voiced by subsidized journals.

When one considers the high level of public liberties and the positive attitudes of cabinets toward parliamentary institutions, one may judge that constitutional democracy was working in the period under dis-cussion. Clearly, however, it was working limpingly and in a threaten-ing context. And the threat was not diminishing.

In the first place, the level of violence within the society generally was and remained high. The fact that important stretches of the country continued to be held or threatened by rebel-bandit groups was im-portant far outside those areas, not least because of the connections which existed between these groups and legal political parties. Such islands of unredeemed territory illustrated the limits of government authority. Moreover, it was difficult for the government to attempt a strict enforcement of the law against unruly bands of veterans, and persons who described themselves as veterans, as long as rural base areas existed to which bands of such persons could threaten to go. Thus when groups of them demanded free entrance to cinemas, en-gaged in brawling in underworld restaurants, carried guns into ex-amination rooms, or vandalized the premises of newspaper offices, the government's response was frequently no more than a rebuke. There was no clear case of an assassination attempt after that of Sultan Hamid in January 1950, but there were occasions on which ministers received anonymous threats that their houses would be bombed. Although army discipline in general improved markedly in the three and a half years, the unfolding of the October 17 affair of 1952 led to the intimidation of

[26] See Adaham Hasibuan, "Genesis of a Press: Economic Aspects of the National Press in Indonesia," *Gazette, International Journal of the Science of the Press* (Leiden), II, no. 1 (1957), 29 ff.

[27] Biro Pusat Statistik, *Statistical Pocketbook of Indonesia,* 1957, p. 29.

[28] See Mochtar Lubis, "The Press in Indonesia," *Far Eastern Survey,* XXI, no. 9 (Sept. 1952), 90–94. See also Roeslan Abdulgani, *Funksi Penerangan di Indo-nesia,* pp. 237 ff.

both political and military leaders by officers of progressively more junior rank.

The preceding chapters told about the great and rising power of extraparliamentary groups over the month-to-month development of cabinet and party politics. That the President and the army leadership interfered on the political stage, and did so with increasing openness as their sense of identification with the political executive grew weaker, was clearly a threat to the authority of representative institutions. This threat was compounded by the fact that the 1949–1953 period saw a rise to political prominence of parties and party factions having a low degree of commitment to constitutional democracy. With the consolidation of Sidik Djojosukarto's power in the PNI, the secession of the Nahdatul Ulama from the Masjumi, and the rising influence of the Indonesian Communist Party, there was a major decline in the power both of the small group of leaders who held a value commitment to Western-type democratic institutions and of the larger group who were committed on various grounds of current interest.

Moreover, the 1949–1953 period saw the growth of a degree of value conflict in Indonesian society such as posed at least an incipient threat to constitutional democracy. The clearest examples of this were provided in the course of the President's oratorical slogging match with Isa Anshary on the issue of whether the Pantja Sila or Islam should serve as the ideological basis of the state; for it became clear as this debate continued that the Pantja Sila had lost much of its umbrella role and become a partisan symbol. The Pantja Sila–Islamic State argument was intelligible, meaningful, and divisive for very large parts of the village and town *kampong* population. It tended to split the country along the grain of political cultures, setting the Javanese-aristocratic political culture against the Islamic-entrepreneurial. Thus a beginning was made with a process whereby Djakarta-level political conflict and village-level conflict along socioreligious lines would become mutually reinforcing. And a trend was started for the disintegration, or eclipse, of all symbols and institutions which had theretofore provided a minimal basis of consensus for political debate.

Finally, much of what we have noted above of the ineffectiveness of the successive cabinets to implement their administrative and economic policies had direct implications for constitutional democracy. To the extent that the cabinets failed to make rapid progress toward the goals whose importance they themselves stressed, they contributed to the idea that another type of government could perhaps be more effective. This was so particularly because the cabinet leaders often made extremely frank admissions that their policies were not resulting in the improvements they described as essential. This aspect of failure was most effectively dramatized by the frequent cabinet crises. Probably even more important in arousing hostility to constitutional democracy was the fact that these cabinets failed to make their programs appealing in an integrative, value-providing way for a large group of former revolutionaries and that they failed to provide an image of authority which could inspire those who saw sacredness pre-eminently in political leadership.

Throughout this period, indeed, many in the political elite were acutely aware that constitutional democracy was on trial and was presenting no convincing defense. In May 1951 Natsir warned his fellow parliamentarians:

If we want to teach our people to practice parliamentary democracy, let us not make a caricature of democracy. . . . Whoever weakens democracy, whoever for group or personal interests undermines its power to serve as the basis for a strong government, he consciously or unconsciously is quietly arousing a proneness to dictatorship in the hearts of our people.[29]

Roeslan Abdulgani wrote in October 1951 of an "element of public opinion which because of a feeling of disappointment unconsciously falls into the trap of fascism."[30] Six months later he wrote of the forthcoming elections as an opportunity for the people to express their opinion on "whether the present democratic institutions still reflect the will of the great mass of the people."[31] In August 1953 he declared that "in choosing a governmental system which accords with Indonesian personality" there were three choices: "just democracy, which often develops excesses and becomes a caricature of itself," "a system of democracy with 'a certain amount of leadership' or more clearly 'democracy with leadership,'" and "a system of leadership with 'a certain amount of democracy' added where necessary, or more clearly 'a modified Fuehrerprinzip.'"[32] "We have had too much democracy"

---

[29] Dewan Perwakilan Rakjat (People's Representative Council), *Risalah Perundingan* ("Report of Discussions"), X (1951), 4234–4242.

[30] Roeslan Abdulgani, *Kearah Manakah Public Opinion Rakjat Kita Harus Dibimbing Menghadapi Masalah Djepang?* ("In What Direction Should Public Opinion Be Guided in the Japanese Question?"; Djakarta: Jajasan Dharma, 1951).

[31] *Funksi Penerangan di Indonesia,* p. 46.

[32] *Ibid.,* p. 151.

was a common phrase in 1951 and 1952, as was "What we need is discipline and leadership."

Four interrelated themes recurred in discussions of alternatives to the existing system—"dictatorship," "a strong man," "Indonesian democracy" or democracy without its culturally alien elements, and "a second revolution." In November 1951 President Soekarno told a Makassar audience that he had received many letters saying that if the existing situation continued they would prefer a dictatorship.[33] In September 1952 he said in Solo that Indonesia was facing a political crisis "because of our unsettled political views and the parties' jockeying for power—with the result that the situation is seen as a failure of democracy and that the people want a dictatorship." [34] In the same month the PIR leader Abbas Surianataatmadja told a conference of his party that Indonesia needed a "strong man" like Ataturk or Naguib.[35] Talk of a *coup d'état*, "doing a Naguib," and "military dictatorship" was common at the time of the October 17 affair of 1952. Earlier the independent Chinese-Indonesian daily *Keng Po* had argued that Asian experience counseled pessimism about the prospects of Western European-type democracy, particularly because of the absence of a similar tradition and the lack of wide education.[36]

At the same time there were numerous statements criticizing democracy as culturally foreign. Professor Supomo of PIR described Western democracy as abstract, based on numbers and oblivious to matters of quality.[37] Sutardjo Kartohadikusumo, also of PIR, attacked the existing party system for introducing the people to such foreign ideas as individualism, liberalism, and materialism and leading them to fight one another for power and rank and strive against one another to acquire wealth and be big-time corruptors, with anarchy the likely eventual result.[38] A number of PNI leaders spoke in similar terms, decrying "50 per cent plus one democracy" and asserting that democracy could not work in Indonesia because it is rationalistic and ignores factors of feeling.

Finally, there was a group of persons who said, "What we need is a second revolution." Some, including many with no particular sympathies for the PKI or Partai Murba, went on to describe this as a "social revolution."

To these arguments the supporters of the existing parliamentary

[33] *Antara*, Nov. 12, 1951.
[34] *Sin Po*, Sept. 23, 1952.
[35] *Aneta*, Sept. 22, 1952.
[36] *Keng Po*, July 2, 1951.
[37] *Mimbar Indonesia*, May 31, 1952.
[38] *Pedoman*, Sept. 23, 1952.

regime, in broad terms the supporters of the four "administrator"-controlled cabinets, had several replies. Some took the attitude of "Give us time—this is still the period of transition." Others blamed the readiness of particular political groups to circumvent the rules of constitutional democracy when it suited them—President Soekarno and his allies, the army leaders and their allies, groups which overthrew cabinets for no reasons of political principle, and so on. Thus Natsir said of the fall of both his own cabinet and that of Wilopo: "We are trying to establish a Western-type parliamentary system. This system will not work, and will be of no value to the life of the state, if we do not keep to its rules. What we are seeing now is people trying to play tennis without a net or lines." [39]

But the principal answer of the defenders of the existing system was to say: "Is it surprising that parliamentary democracy is not working well when our parliament is a Round Table Conference parliament, not elected and having this Dutch inheritance of a plethora of parties? The way out is to hold elections as soon as possible." On the other hand, there were few who argued that parliamentary democracy, with all its current shortcomings, was better than any existing alternative, few who maintained that without parliamentary democracy there would be no democracy and that without democracy independence would lose half its meaning. There were, in fact, few affirmations of democratic principles.

This brings us back to a question raised in the introductory chapter. Why did the Indonesian leadership of our period attempt to operate parliamentary democracy if only a relatively small number of leaders were committed to the values it embodied and a smaller number to its underlying principles? There is no need here to restate the arguments advanced on this point in the earlier chapter: the various practical considerations arising out of the Round Table Conference situation and the belief that parliamentary institutions had functioned satisfactorily in the Republic in the period of Revolution, the stimulus of national self-respect, the absence of currently available alternatives, and the fact that many in the Hatta half of the nationalist leadership

---

[39] Mohammad Natsir, *Pidato Ketua Umum P.P. Masjumi dalam Pemandangan Umum Babak ke-1 di Dewan Perwakilan Rakjat Sementara pada tanggal 23 Agustus 1953* ("Speech of the Chairman of the Masjumi in the First Reading General Debate in Parliament, August 23, 1953"; Djakarta: Penerangan Sekretariat P.P. Masjumi, 1953), p. 11.

had strong ties of interest to parliamentary forms as *their* forms. But it may be useful to raise two other aspects.

In the first place, Western constitutional forms were well suited to serve the "administrators" because they were concerned with consolidation of the new order that the Revolution had brought in, with the sort of regularization and routinization of the still partly revolutionary social situation which would make possible a systematic tackling of problems of economic development—and would thus enable them to use their modern-state-type skills effectively and with high status rewards. For men with goals like this rules were what was most needed, in every field including the political. As Professor Sumitro was to write in 1959, "It is exactly the virtual absence of accepted mores and of institutionalized rules of political conduct and of constitutional behavior that make it mandatory for responsible leadership to foster the growth of such rules and values and to consider this an essential element of their task." [40] Now it is true that these ends might have been served by an efficient military dictatorship which refrained from arbitrary actions. This did not, however, appear to be possible. Indeed, some "administrator" leaders were hoping for just this sort of solution at the time of the October 17 affair. But when that fizzled out and was defeated, it became clear that the army was so divided that it could not even take power, much less exercise it and remain cohesive. Moreover, the events around October 17, 1952, made it clearer than ever that only a relatively small number of officers were men of "administrator" outlook. It also brought out the fact that a large part of the political public was hostile to the idea of military rule. Under these circumstances a Western-type constitutional system, linked with the legitimizing symbols of democracy on the one hand and with legality on the other, was the best hope of the "administrators."

Secondly, there was a sense in which the operation of a Western-type constitutional system fulfilled functions for the political elite as a whole. This, as we have seen, was an elite united by common cultural attributes, similar social position, common experiences of the past, and frequent face-to-face contact between members. At the same time it was not tied together by political organization. Power was widely dispersed inside the elite, the representation of interests was largely unstructured, and institutional hierarchies were relatively weak. Taken together, these two facts implied that Indonesia was eminently suited

[40] D. Sumitro, *Searchlight on Indonesia* (n.p., 1959), p. 59.

to a system of government based more on consensus than coercion. In fact, it was usually possible to reach compromises on the most bitterly fought issues if only enough time and effort were put into negotiations with a large number of individuals, groups, and cliques—thanks to the cultural homogeneity of the political elite and its sense of common interest. Under these circumstances men were slow to reach for their guns, even where the threat to their political position was great; the October 17 affair is a case in point. On the other hand, with the army divided and no state party in existence—and none ready to become a state party in the manner of the Bolsheviks in 1917 or the Nazis in 1933—no way was in sight whereby an effective dictatorship could be established smoothly. In effect, then, constitutional democracy worked as a set of "club rules" of political behavior, a system of restrained solutions of political issues which was made necessary by the existing distribution of power and possible by personal ties between the politically powerful. The system could be expected to last as long as power remained dispersed and as long as personal ties within the political elite remained strong enough to bridge conflicts of interests and ideology.[41]

[41] I am indebted to Benedict Anderson for this point.

Chapter VIII

The First Cabinet of Ali Sastroamidjojo, July 1953– July 1955:

The Rise of the Parties

WE come now to the most long-lived of all the cabinets of our period. The first of the two cabinets headed by the PNI's Mr. Ali Sastroamidjojo succeeded in maintaining itself in office for a period of two years minus eight days. And it stood in contrast to all its predecessors in many respects other than longevity. The contrasts are closely related to the birth pangs which accompanied its coming into existence, to the fact that the cabinet crisis which preceded its formation was also of record length. It was only after a 58-day period of intense, obscure maneuvering, and after failure of five separate attempts at cabinet formation, that it was possible for the PIR chairman, Wongsonegoro, to assemble a team of mutually acceptable cabinet ministers.

A CABINET CRISIS OF CRYSTALLIZATION

The preliminary skirmishes began immediately after the Wilopo cabinet's resignation, while President Soekarno was deciding who should be *formateur*. Many of the initial comments were guardedly phrased, but it soon became clear that two groups of people knew clearly what they wanted. On the one hand, there was a series of statements in favor of a Hatta cabinet. This proposal had been voiced repeatedly in the preceding years, and especially in periods of cabinet crisis, despite the fact that the constitution makers of 1950 had not included an "escape clause" that might have permitted a Hatta-led presidential cabinet to be formed in emergency conditions as in the period of Revolution. It had most frequently been a cause espoused by Masjumi leaders of the Natsir group (and by Isa Anshary).[1] Now, however, the demand for it had grown wider and was supported by all Masjumi groups as well as by the PSI (which, in 1950, had favored elimination of the "escape clause").[2] Natsir's argument in calling for Hatta as Prime Minister was that "the state is in fact in danger at this time, although this is not evident on the surface." [3]

No one offered direct opposition to this suggestion except Aidit of the PKI. There were, however, a number of statements to the effect that a presidential cabinet was unconstitutional. Sidik Djojosukarto stated that the PNI could not accept a presidential cabinet and that Hatta could form a cabinet only if he first resigned from the vice-presidency. He declared that he did not see any signs that the state was in danger, adding that all countries had their difficulties.[4]

The second alternative advanced forcibly in the early stages of the formation struggle was what the PKI's Aidit called a United Front Government, a government from which the Masjumi and PSI would be excluded—as experience showed that these two parties were "too much concerned to look after foreign interests." [5] Perti and Parindra spokesmen and the PNI's Sidik Djojosukarto advocated such a cabinet in different, more indirect, terms.[6] But to resort to either a Hatta cabinet or a cabinet from which the Masjumi was excluded was widely regarded as undesirable while a possibility remained that a Masjumi-PNI-based cabinet could be formed, a *kabinet perdamaian nasional* (national peace cabinet) as its advocates called it or, in the language of its opponents, a *kabinet inti* (core cabinet).[7]

[1] See the statements of Muhammadijah, *Abadi*, March 31, 1951, and of Isa Anshary and Djuanda, *Keng Po*, March 19, 1952.
[2] See the statements of Sukiman, Jusuf Wibisono, and the PSI's Subadio Sastrosatomo, *Antara*, June 4, 5, 1953, and *Abadi*, June 9, 1953.
[3] *Abadi*, June 9, 1953.   [4] *Antara*, June 9, 1953.   [5] *Abadi*, June 9, 1953.
[6] *Antara*, June 8, 1953; *Sin Po*, June 9, 1953; *Abadi*, June 12, 1953.
[7] These two symbols, each referring with its own set of value connotations to a cabinet in which leadership was shared in roughly equal proportions between the PNI and Masjumi (here presumed to be internally united), were relatively new additions to the political vocabulary. Each of them represented yet another subtle and esoteric way of pointing to the persons one did and did not want in a cabinet, while at the same time leaving oneself free subsequently to deny any

One attempt to form a cabinet of this kind began when Roem of the Masjumi and Sarmidi Mangunsarkoro of the PNI were named *formateurs* on June 15. But press reactions suggested that these two had little hope of success. The PNI-sympathizing *Merdeka* charged that the Masjumi had put forward the controversial Roem as its candidate for the *formateur*-ship because it wanted this attempt to fail so that it could then draw in Hatta. The PSI-oriented *Indonesia Raya* also wrote that the two men could not succeed and added that it seemed that both parties wanted a failure, but predicted that this would be followed by the President's nominating a PNI *formateur*.[8]

The breakdown came quickly as expected. When it did, on June 22, the Masjumi blamed Mangunsarkoro's proposal that consultations should be held with all parties, including the PKI (which had already indicated that it did not want the Masjumi included in the new cabinet). The PNI explained the failure in terms of disagreements on matters of program. In particular it emphasized the obstacle of the various controversial issues whose settlement had been postponed, the "ice chest items" as they were called—the East Sumatra squatter resettlement question, the North Sumatra oil wells, the old issue of ratification of the San Francisco treaty with Japan, and the new conflict over establishment of an Indonesian Embassy in Moscow by the end of the year—on all of which the PNI wanted the new government to take action in accordance with the wishes of parliament.

On June 22 the President named a new *formateur*, the PNI leader and outgoing Foreign Minister, Mukarto Notowidigdo. To this appointment the press reaction was almost universally favorable—until it became clear what course Mukarto proposed to follow. He consulted first with the parties of the Moslem League. Then he went to PIR, the Democratic Fraction, and Parindra. At the same time he received a number of delegations from the PKI-led trade unions, which offered him support in his efforts. It was only on June 25 that he met Masjumi

---

specific intentions which might have been attributed. The two symbols, with the PKI's Kabinet Front Persatuan (United Front Cabinet, or one excluding the Masjumi and PSI and receiving PKI support), now joined the ranks of (and partly displaced) the older symbols of *kabinet presidensiil* (meaning in effect a cabinet of Hatta and his associates), *zakenkabinet* or business cabinet (meaning, at least up to 1953, a cabinet of men of the Natsir group, the Wilopo group, and the PSI and nonparty PSI sympathizers), and *kabinet koalisi nasional* (a cabinet of the Sukiman group of the Masjumi and the Sidik and Sartono groups of the PNI).

[8] See *Antara*, June 16, 17, 1953.

representatives, and then he did so in the presence of his fellow PNI leaders Sidik Djojosukarto and S. Hadikusumo, both men whose relations with the Masjumi leadership were considerably worse than those of Mukarto himself. On the following day the Masjumi executive decided that it would not participate in the cabinet which Mukarto was then forming. For a moment it seemed that a cabinet without the Masjumi would come into being. But two days later Mukarto went to President Soekarno to report that his efforts had met with failure.

If press accounts are to be believed, Mukarto Notowidigdo planned to form a cabinet in which the PNI held three portfolios, including the Prime Ministership (Mukarto himself or Susanto Tirtoprodjo) and the Foreign Ministership, in which the Masjumi received only one portfolio, Finance (Jusuf Wibisono), and in which other major portfolios went to the PSII, the PIR, and the Democratic Fraction.[9] But, after the Masjumi made clear that it would not participate, the Catholics quickly rejected the *formateur*'s offer of a post. The Democratic Fraction followed suit, and then, significantly, the Nahdatul Ulama did the same.[10] Some of the leaders of these parties appear to have been frightened off by the vociferousness of PKI support for Mukarto.[11] Probably more important is the fact that there were many small party leaders (and a number of PNI leaders) who believed a PNI-Masjumi cabinet to be still possible, and preferable.

When Mukarto reported his failure to President Soekarno, the President, surprisingly, offered him a new commission, to form a "business cabinet with sufficient support from parliament." Mukarto then told the press that he wanted to change his approach in order to form a cabinet which would result in national peace. Two days later he added that national peace would be possible only on the basis of co-

[9] For a complete list of the cabinet Mukarto was reportedly planning to bring together see *Aneta*, June 26, 1953.

[10] The Nahdatul Ulama had apparently been offered only the Religious Affairs portfolio. See Deliar Noer, "Masjumi: Its Organization, Ideology and Political Role in Indonesia" (M.A. thesis, Cornell University, 1960).

[11] The PKI linked its pro-Mukarto campaign with demands for the destruction of "Darul Islam fascism." See *Bintang Merah*, IX, no. 7 (July 1953), 320–321. On June 26 railway workers numbering 4,000 demonstrated in Djakarta in favor of guarantees of security. At the same time various PKI-influenced organizations urged President Soekarno to decree that the DI was an enemy of the state and people. PKI leaders apparently concluded later that they had overplayed their hand. Thus Aidit felt it necessary to say that he disagreed with those who thought that the expressions of the people's joy at Mukarto's appointment were what had led to his failure (in the first stage of his formation efforts). See *Merdeka*, July 4, 1953.

operation between the Masjumi, the PNI, and the PSI, and on that day also he began a series of discussions with Roem and Jusuf Wibisono of the Masjumi—with no other PNI person present.

Now, for the first time since the fall of Wilopo, the Masjumi and PNI were negotiating seriously with one another, and on July 4 Mukarto, Roem, and Jusuf reached a compromise on the controversial "ice chest items." [12] Then the bargaining began on seats and their occupants. Mukarto wanted the Masjumi to have two major portfolios, the Deputy Prime Ministership and Finance along with Justice and Information, whereas the PNI was to obtain the Prime Ministership, the two other major portfolios of Foreign Affairs and Economic Affairs, and Agriculture.[13] But the Masjumi, unprepared to concede that its bargaining position was inferior to that of the PNI and hoping that the *formateur*-ship would go next to a Masjumi man or conceivably Hatta, would not accept. After considering a Masjumi counterproposal which was unacceptable to the PNI,[14] Mukarto returned his mandate to the President on July 6.

Then the fourth round started. On July 8 the President called on the parliamentary leader of the Masjumi, Burhanuddin Harahap, to form a cabinet. Burhanuddin's record had earned him no strong hostility from the PNI, and he quickly demonstrated his willingness to come to terms with this party. He accepted the cabinet program formulated by Mukarto and stated that his policy on the "ice chest items" would be similar to that contained in the PNI's most recent note to the Masjumi on the subject. More important, he made a significant concession on the matter of seats and their occupants, requesting only the Prime Ministership (for Jusuf Wibisono) and the three minor posts of Agriculture, Justice, and Social Affairs for the Masjumi, while allowing the PNI to have the Deputy Prime Ministership along with two other major portfolios, Foreign Affairs and Economic Affairs, and the minor one of Information.[15]

For the PNI, however, this was not enough. The party was less antagonistic to the individuals slated for Masjumi posts than it had been to the Masjumi ministerial candidates put up to Mukarto. But

[12] For the terms of the compromise see *Keng Po,* July 4, 1953.

[13] See *Merdeka,* July 17, 1953 (for a draft list of the proposed cabinet); *Keng Po,* July 6, 1953; and *Pedoman,* July 7, 1953.

[14] See *Merdeka,* July 7 and 8, 1953, and *Keng Po,* July 8, 1953. See also Noer, *op. cit.*

[15] See *Abadi,* July 15, 1953, for what purports to be a full list of the projected cabinet.

it did not like Burhanuddin's placement for the Finance Ministry, the PSI's Sumitro Djojohadikusumo. It resented Burhanuddin's veto on Iskaq Tjokroadisurjo, the original PNI candidate for Economic Affairs, whom the Masjumi mistrusted because of his controversial role as Interior Minister of the Sukiman cabinet. Most important of all, the PNI wanted the Prime Ministership for itself.

On this point, however, Burhanuddin refused to budge. The Masjumi leaders felt that they had given large concessions already, and some of them held that PNI responses to these cast doubt on the party's sincerity in wanting a PNI-Masjumi cabinet.[16] So it was that the negotiations broke down. Burhanuddin briefly canvassed the possibility of a cabinet without the PNI. But when it was clear that not even the two Christian parties, otherwise sympathetic to the Masjumi in matters of cabinet politics, would participate in such a cabinet, he abandoned this approach too.[17] On July 18 he returned his mandate to the President.

By this time the cabinet crisis had lasted 46 days, longer than any previous one. There had been three attempts to bring the PNI and Masjumi together, one to establish a cabinet without the Masjumi (or with the Masjumi playing a minor role) and a brief exploration of the possibility of a cabinet without the PNI, and all had proved abortive. Assertions by Masjumi and PSI papers to the effect that the state was in an emergency situation began to carry increased weight. But the President was not pursuaded to name Hatta to form a cabinet. "I still stand on the basis of our constitution and our parliamentary traditions," he said, adding that "so far there is still unanimity between Vice-President Mohammad Hatta and myself."[18]

The President did, however, depart from convention in choosing the next *formateur,* for he did not name a Masjumi or PNI leader but rather the PIR chairman, Wongsonegoro. Wongsonegoro's reception was a mixed one. On the whole, the PNI and PKI press reacted favorably, the Masjumi and PSI press with apprehension. This pattern of responses was confirmed when Wongsonegoro gave the appearance of working very closely with President Soekarno—he conducted many of his hear-

[16] *Abadi,* July 15, 1953. See also Noer, *op. cit.* [17] *Pedoman,* July 31, 1953.
[18] *Antara,* July 18, 1953. Hatta stated at the same time that he would agree to act as *formateur* only if parliament requested this. Shortly thereafter he left Djakarta for Atjeh where he spoke to Teungku Daud Beureueh, chairman of the *PUSA* (Persatuan Ulama Seluruh Atjeh, All-Atjeh Ulama Union), in an effort to dissuade him from rumored plans to initiate an Achinese Islamic rebellion against the central government.

ings with party leaders at the presidential palace. It was confirmed again when he announced a policy that questions which could not be settled by the cabinet would be referred to parliament, with parliament's decision to be taken as binding; this was to accept the original PNI position on the "ice chest items." As the Masjumi and PSI press saw them, these plans signified a second attempt to do what Mukarto had tried in the first phase of his *formateur*-ship, to form a cabinet from which the Masjumi was excluded, or all but excluded. This assessment gained further plausibility after a series of declarations by the PKI and various of its unions in support of Wongsonegoro.[19]

Nevertheless, Wongsonegoro did negotiate seriously with the Masjumi. Indeed, the arrangement of portfolios which he offered it was somewhat more favorable to it than what Burhanuddin had agreed to accept for his party. His final offer called for the Masjumi to receive the First Deputy Prime Ministership and the posts of the Interior, Economic Affairs, and Social Affairs.[20] But on July 28 the offer was rejected. Natsir explained later that his party was unable to accept the Wongsonegoro position on the "ice chest items" and that it was especially opposed to a last-minute demand of the PNI on the matter of the North Sumatra oil wells.[21] In addition, the Masjumi had raised objections to Wongsonegoro's exclusion of the PSI from the cabinet and to the candidacies of Dr. Ong Eng Die (PNI, Finance), Mr. Iwa Kusumasumantri (Progressive Fraction, Justice), Arudji Kartawinata (PSII, Defense), and Dr. F. L. Tobing (SKI, Information).[22] The first three of these were regarded in some Masjumi circles as past or current sympathizers of the PKI. It may be that the Masjumi expected that it could force Wongsonegoro to return the mandate and that the President would thereupon have no alternative but to call on Hatta. Furthermore, it appears to have had assurances from certain Nahdatul Ulama leaders that the NU would not participate in a cabinet from which the Masjumi was excluded.[23]

[19] See *Antara*, July 24, 1953. This time, however, the PKI appears to have been aware of the dangers of too vociferous an assertion of its claims. Jusuf Wibisono's daily, *Mimbar Indonesia*, commented in its gossip columns on Aidit's modesty and politeness in speaking to Wongsonegoro in the course of the meetings of party leaders with the *formateur*. "Comrade Aidit spoke in so soft a voice that the *formateur* was obliged to ask another participant to be his microphone" (*Mimbar Indonesia*, July 24, 1953). Softness of voice is an important part of refinement in Javanese culture, and Wongsonegoro is a prototypical representative of refinement in this culture!

[20] See *Aneta*, July 28, 1953 for the draft list as finally offered.

[21] *Merdeka*, July 30, 1953.   [22] *Antara*, July 29, 1953.   [23] Noer, *op. cit.*

But these Masjumi hopes were not to be realized. After receiving the Masjumi's rejection of his offer, the *formateur* worked speedily toward the formation of a cabinet without the Masjumi. Much concerned to obtain Islamic support, he offered more cabinet posts to the Nahdatul Ulama and PSII. The NU was now offered three seats and thereupon agreed to participate. Wongsonegoro found that the two Christian parties, which were to have been included with a portfolio each, were unprepared to co-operate with him now that the Masjumi would not, but to compensate for this loss he drew in an increased number of minor nationalist parties and two Communist-sympathizing groups.

Thus Wongsonegoro finally succeeded in getting a team together, and in the early hours of July 31 President Soekarno announced that he had given it his endorsement. The names of the new cabinet were announced as follows:

Ministry [24, 25]		*Party*
Prime Minister	Mr. Ali Sastroamidjojo	PNI
First Deputy Prime Minister	Mr. Wongsonegoro	PIR
Second Deputy Prime Minister	Zainul Arifin	NU
Foreign Affairs	Mr. Sunario	PNI
Interior	Prof. Mr. Dr. Hazairin	PIR
Defense [26]	Mr. Iwa Kusumasumantri	Progressive Fraction

[24] A reshuffling of portfolios took place in Sept. and Oct. 1953. Abikusno Tjokrosujoso and Sudibjo resigned from their respective portfolios on Sept. 14 in consequence of an internal conflict in the PSII. Sudibjo's post was taken over by Wongsonegoro on an ad interim basis as of Sept. 29, on which day Roosseno was appointed Minister of Communications ad interim. He was confirmed in his status as Minister of Communications on Oct. 12 and left the post of Minister of Public Works and Power on the same day. This post was assumed on Oct. 12 by Mohammad Hassan of the PSII. On the same day also Dr. Lie Kiat Teng (alias Dr. Mohammad Ali) of the PSII took over the Health portfolio from F. L. Tobing.

[25] A second and major reshuffle became necessary in Oct. and Nov. 1954. On Oct. 23 the three PIR ministers, Wongsonegoro, Hazairin, and Roosseno all resigned, and on Nov. 8 Iskaq Tjokroadisurjo followed suit. On Nov. 6 K. H. Siradjuddin Abbas of Perti entered the cabinet to assume the State Welfare position, which became a full ministry. Iskaq's post as Minister for Economic Affairs was immediately filled on Nov. 8 by Roosseno. On Nov. 19 three new members were added to the cabinet. Dr. A. K. Gani of the PNI became Minister of Communications, Mr. Sunarjo of the NU became Minister of the Interior, and I Gusti Gde Rake of PRN was brought into the Agrarian Affairs position, which was vacated by the NU's Mohammad Hanafiah on the same day and thereupon became a full ministry.

[26] Iwa Kusumasumantri resigned on July 13, 1955.

Ministry		*Party*
Justice	Mr. Djody Gondokusumo	PRN
Information	Dr. F. L. Tobing	SKI
Finance	Dr. Ong Eng Die	PNI
Agriculture	Sadjarwo	BTI
Economic Affairs	Mr. Iskaq Tjokroadisurjo	PNI
Communications	Abikusno Tjokrosujoso	PSII
Public Works	Prof. Ir. Roosseno	PIR
Labor	Prof. S. M. Abidin	Labor
Social Affairs	R. P. Suroso	Parindra
Education	Mr. Muhammad Yamin	Nonparty
Religious Affairs	K. H. Masjkur	NU
Health	Dr. F. L. Tobing (ad interim)	SKI
Minister of State with Responsibility for Agrarian Affairs	Mohammad Hanafiah	NU
Minister of State with Responsibility for State Welfare	Sudibjo	PSII

The result was thus an inversion of the Natsir cabinet situation. The PNI, with its four major portfolios, dominated the new cabinet. The Masjumi was excluded, for the first time in the postrevolutionary period, along with the PSI, the two Christian parties, and the Democratic Fraction—and with the PKI and Murba. The *formateur's* PIR and the rapidly promoted NU became partners with the PNI in cabinet leadership. Four groups not previously included in a cabinet were given portfolios, the PRN (National People's Party) and SKI (Indonesian People's Association) and two under PKI influence, the Progressive Fraction and the BTI (Barisan Tani Indonesia, Indonesian Peasant Front). The Progressive, Iwa Kusumasumantri, was given the important post of Defense, but it was widely believed that his political position was closer to the Murba than PKI.

Here, then, was the culmination of the trends which had brought down the Wilopo cabinet. Victory had come to the alliance of the PNI with the minor nationalist parties and Moslem League parties on the one hand and the Indonesian Communist Party on the other. It was, in fact, a logical extension of the polarizing tendencies which had developed with increasing clarity since October 17 of the previous year.

But the victory had not come easily, as the long history of the formation struggles showed. A number of important groups were manifestly anxious to prevent a situation of outright polarization. The central contest had been inside the PNI. There the Sidik group had pressed for a cabinet like the one which Wongsonegoro eventually formed. The members of this group pointed to the long history of frustrations in the PNI's experience of cabinet partnership with the Masjumi. They argued that the PNI was losing popular support because of its associations with the various recent cabinets, on which the Masjumi and PSI had left the mark of their hesitancy and lack of revolutionary spirit. And they promised extensive electoral advantages from a situation in which the PNI dominated a cabinet.

But there was marked reluctance to accept this line of argument on the part of other groups in the party, both the followers of Wilopo and some of the more conservative and anti-Communist members of the older group of Sartono and Suwirjo. Some of these men argued that a cabinet without the Masjumi would depend on PKI votes in parliament for survival and that a price would have to be paid for these votes. Others asserted that to work with the minor nationalist parties and Moslem League parties in preference to the Masjumi would mean to abandon order and standards further in governmental affairs and to increase the already excessive prevalence of opportunism.

In the Nahdatul Ulama there was a division of a somewhat different kind. This party had only recently dealt what many Moslems saw as an affront to the ideal of Islamic unity when it had left the Masjumi. Could it now go a step further, by joining a cabinet from which the Masjumi was excluded? The choice was complicated by earlier NU commitments to the Masjumi position on several of the "ice chest" issues. It was made still harder by the evident enthusiasm of the PKI for such a cabinet. The Masjumi and PSI press used this enthusiasm to warn the NU against bringing about a repetition of the events of 1947, when the PSII had split off from the Masjumi to accept portfolios in the first cabinet of Amir Sjarifuddin, which had ushered in a series of developments leading to the Madiun revolt.[27]

One factor which may have been of decisive importance for the character of the cabinet was the inability of the Masjumi leaders to make the humiliating withdrawals which the changed circumstances of Djakarta politics demanded. Isolated from the minor nationalist parties and estranged from the parties of the Moslem League, the Masjumi had no allies with sizable parliamentary strength. Therefore it could get into a cabinet only by working with the PNI—except in

[27] See, for instance, *Pedoman,* June 25, 1953.

the event of the President's calling on Hatta. But, seeing their party as by far the largest in the country, the Masjumi leaders could not accept the role of a slightly inferior partner assigned to it in the plans of Mukarto (during his second formation attempt), in the offers of the PNI to Burhanuddin, and in Wongsonegoro's original proposal. If not all of these were submitted in good faith by the PNI, it is almost certain that one or two of them were and that a Masjumi-PNI core cabinet could have been established had the Masjumi been prepared to make more concessions than it did.

Another factor which may have been decisive was the help which Wongsonegoro received from President Soekarno. The President intervened on Wongsonegoro's behalf on a number of occasions—and this time there was no significant counterpressure from the army. Soekarno's actions confirmed the common view that he was strongly against a Hatta cabinet and preferred a cabinet without the Masjumi to one with a basis in PNI-Masjumi co-operation. The confidence with which the President appeared to view the prospect of a cabinet such as the PKI was requesting was trust-inspiring for many. Perhaps most important of all, the President's active support for Wongsonegoro made a number of waverers believe that this *formateur* would succeed and that they had therefore better not be left out.

THE CABINET AND ITS EARLY ACTIONS

Thus the cabinet came into existence. Clearly it was a very different kind of cabinet from any the country had seen in the post-1949 period —and not only because of its party composition. One of the clearest indications of the difference lay in the lack of continuity between the personnel of this cabinet and that of its predecessors. Only four of its twenty members had participated in any of the preceding four cabinets. Some, like the two ministers without portfolio, were little known. Others, like Professor Hazairin, though well known, were new to political life. But the largest group were men who had been prominent in politics before 1949. Six of the most important ministers, Ali himself, Sunario, Iwa, Iskaq, Abikusno, and Yamin, had been prominent leaders of radical sections of the prewar nationalist movement. Most, if not all of these, were prominent again in the period of the Japanese occupation, and three of them were included in the Soekarno cabinet of August to November 1945. At least three were actively involved in the abortive coup of Tan Malaka of July 3, 1946. All of this group of six men had had close personal-*cum*-political associations with Soekarno over a period of two to three decades; none of them had had ties of this kind with Hatta. Thus, to the extent that these were the men whose politics set the position of the cabinet as a whole—and this was largely so—the cabinet may be regarded as marking the return to power of the groups which Sjahrir and Hatta had displaced from top positions in the latter part of 1945 (groups which had made a partial comeback in the Sukiman cabinet).

In terms of the skills to which the individual ministers owed their positions, the cabinet was rather evenly divided between "administrators" and "solidarity makers." For men like Ali, the former ambassador in Washington, Hazairin, a specialist in adat and Islamic law, Roosseno, a former head of the Bandung Technical Faculty, and Ong, a highly trained economist, these modern-type technical skills were an important aspect of their success in obtaining cabinet posts. On the other hand, the cabinet contained men like Zainul Arifin who had headed the Moslem guerrilla force Hizbullah in the Revolution, K. H. Masjkur who had been a top leader of the Hizbullah's sister organization, Sabillilah, Dr. F. L. Tobing who had been military governor of Tapanuli in the Revolution and continued to enjoy a position of paternal authority in that region, and Muhammad Yamin whose stature as a nationalist ideologue was second only to that of the President himself. Compared with the four earlier cabinets, this one contained a larger number of men for whom "solidarity making" skills were an important aspect of their route to political elite status. Moreover, as the subsequent course of the cabinet's term of office showed, the ministers were heavily dependent on the leaders of their parties. Thus the group of men whose influence was most decisive for the Ali cabinet's action included such "solidarity makers" as the Nahdatul Ulama chairman, Kijaji Dahlan, the PSII's Arudji Kartawinata, and the PNI's Sidik Djojosukarto (whose power over the cabinet was believed by many to be as great as that of the Prime Minister himself).

The importance of "solidarity makers" in the composition of the Ali cabinet had its reflection in the ministers' orientations to policy. There was not actually much innovation in the content of policies to be pursued, for the members of the Ali cabinet subscribed in the main to the policies and problem-solving approaches of their predecessors. If there were individuals among them who favored radical economic and political surgery, expropriation of foreign property, expulsion of alien residents and trade nationalization, or dictatorship and forced draft industrialization, they did so as a matter of political instinct rather than of formulated creed. Such views were not expressed by cabinet members, and they found no more than the most indirect expression in cabinet actions.

The chief new factor was that the men of the new cabinet had much less sense of urgency about problem-solving policies than their predecessors. Although they too averred that the country needed planned economic development, and hence fiscal stability, increased production, and an improvement in administrative efficiency, they did not see this need as compelling enough to oblige them to divert major political resources to restrain pressures for patronage, inflationary spending, and the fast Indonesianization of the economy. The intensity with which individual ministers were committed to specific policy goals—as against ideological victory on the one hand and power interests, collective and individual, on the other—was considerably lower for this cabinet than for its predecessors. There is here an important contrast in political personality—quite apart from the fact that the Ali cabinet operated in a situation in which elections were expected and ministers had to devote much of their attention to serving the electoral interests of their parties.

Public responses to the cabinet's formation were very mixed. The Masjumi and PSI press came out with expressions of shock and contempt. Like the PNI at the time of the formation of the Natsir cabinet, it seemed to be saying, "How can they do this to us?" The daily *Mimbar Indonesia,* in its editorial entitled "Our Condolences to the Indonesian People," argued that the cabinet's formation had been forced, that it fell far short of satisfying the ideals of national unity, and that much was to be regretted about its individual ministers, as regards character and *expertise.*[28] *Abadi* declared, "We have moved a step further toward greater chaos in society,"[29] and there were various predictions of exacerbation of hostility between the main parties.

In addition, the opposition dwelt a good deal on the politically heterogeneous character of the group of new ministers. What sort of co-operation could there be, it asked, between the cabinet leaders on the one hand—Ali, who had tried to win PNI support for the San Francisco treaty, Wongsonegoro, an aristocrat regarded as a *pamong pradja* spokesman, and Zainul Arifin, a representative of conservative rural Islam—and the various PKI sympathizers on the other? Arguing that intracabinet conflict would soon prove disruptive and that the cabinet would face strong hostility from particular parts of the coun-

[28] *Mimbar Indonesia,* July 31, 1953.   [29] *Abadi,* July 31, 1953.

try where the Masjumi was strong, many of the critics asserted that the cabinet was unlikely to live long.

The cabinet's supporters spoke in softer tones on the whole. *Merdeka* admitted that "in general the members of this cabinet are not in the category of first-class players," at the same time praising it for its compactness, its unanimous commitment to a program, and the fact that it had the blessing of President Soekarno.[30] Other cabinet supporters predicted that there would now be good cabinet-parliament co-operation. On the other hand, the PKI's Aidit issued a statement entitled "Glorious Victory of Democracy over Fascism," in which he declared that the people were happy because this was the first cabinet to have been formed as a result of the pressures and demands of the people.[31]

When the ballot was taken in parliament on a motion to give the cabinet an "opportunity to work," only two parties, the Masjumi and the Catholics, cast negative votes. The PSI and Partia Murba and a number of nonparty members abstained. The count was 182 to 34 with 26 abstentions.[32] The margin was large enough to allow the cabinet to rebut the opposition critics' charges that it depended on PKI votes.

But the cabinet's early actions showed the critics to be right in their assertions that it was internally divided. Intracabinet conflict gave rise to a number of policy zigzags, as it had in the case of the Sukiman cabinet. Thus the new Finance Minister, Dr. Ong, stated a few days after his installation that foreign investment in Indonesia had henceforth to be channeled through the government, and subsequently had to have his statement explained away by one of his own senior officials. The new Defense Minister, Iwa Kusumasumantri, was more quietly disavowed after he had expressed his agreement "in principle" with a suggestion of the PKI veterans' organization Perbepbsi (Persatuan Bekas Pedjuang Bersendjata Seluruh Indonesia, All-Indonesian Association of Former Armed Fighters) that a "volunteer brigade" be formed to fight the Darul Islam. This was seen as a proposal for the distribution of arms to veterans' groups and reactions to it were strong, from several leaders of the army and of government parties as well as from the opposition.[33]

[30] *Merdeka,* July 31, 1953.

[31] D. N. Aidit, *Pilihan Tulisan* ("Selected Works"), I (Djakarta: Pembaruan, 1959), 155–156.

[32] *Antara,* Sept. 10, 1953.

[33] See *Pedoman,* Aug. 27, 1953, and also Mohammad Natsir, *Capita Selecta,* II ("Selected Works"; Djakarta: Pustaka Pendis, 1957), 287.

However, it was on the matter of hostility to the cabinet in Masjumi stronghold areas of the country that the trend of developments most clearly confirmed the opposition critics' predictions. The Ali cabinet had been in office for only seven weeks when it was faced with the challenge of a full-scale revolt in strongly Moslem Atjeh.

In this area there had been conflict for many generations and especially since the late nineteenth century between the *uleebalang,* a local aristocracy, and the *ulama* or Islamic leaders. In 1946 this flared up into a "social revolution" after some *ulama* leaders had discovered that a part of the *uleebalang* leadership was negotiating with the Dutch for their return to Atjeh. In the course of the "social revolution" a large number of aristocrats and their families were murdered. The *ulama,* organized in PUSA, the All-Atjeh Ulama Union, became the controlling power in Atjeh, and their leader, Teungku Daud Beureueh, was recognized as military governor of Atjeh by the Republic of Indonesia. *Ulama* power was given further endorsement in 1949 when the government of the Republic agreed that Atjeh should have province status.[34]

But with the inauguration of the unitary state in 1950 it was established that there would be only a single province of North Sumatra, one in which Atjeh was joined with Tapanuli and East Sumatra. This step aroused the strongest hostility from the *ulama* group, and it was only after Vice-President Hatta and then Prime Minister Natsir had made personal visits to Atjeh that Daud Beureueh agreed to turn over his authority to the newly installed Governor of North Sumatra.[35] Offended with Djakarta, Daud Beureueh failed to take up his post as a Masjumi parliamentarian and high official of the Ministry of the Interior in the capital, but instead returned to his home village. A number of other PUSA leaders left government posts at the same time.

From 1951 onward the *uleebalang* forces organized on a larger scale than theretofore, enjoying a measure of support from representatives of the central government. At the same time the PUSA leaders capi-

---

[34] Kementerian Penerangan (Ministry of Information), *Republik Indonesia, Propinsi Sumatera Utara* ("The North Sumatra Province of the Republic of Indonesia"; Djakarta: Kementerian Penerangan, 1953), pp. 64–75. See also "Insider," *Atjeh, Sepintas Lalu* ("A Brief Sketch of Atjeh"; Djakarta: Archapada, 1950); Dada Meuraxa, *Atjeh 1000 Tahun dan Peristiwa Teungku Daud Beureueh cs* ("A Thousand Years of Achinese History and the Affair of Teungku Daud Beureueh and His Followers"; Medan: Pustaka Hasmar, n.d. [1954?]; and Tk. Alibasja Talsya, *Sedjarah dan Dokumen-Dokumen Pemberontakan di Atjeh* ("A History and Documents of the Revolt in Atjeh"; Djakarta: Kesuma, n.d. [1955?]).

[35] Kementerian Penerangan, *Republik Indonesia, Propinsi Sumatera Utara,* pp. 400 ff.

talized on dissatisfaction with Djakarta. They charged that gambling and beer drinking had increased greatly in Atjeh since Djakarta had assumed direct control. In particular they condemned the regulations whereby Atjeh was prevented from trading directly with Malaya as had been done in the period of Revolution. They also charged that Atjeh, which had made a major contribution to the struggle for independence—it had been the only large area of Indonesia which the Dutch had never penetrated, and its exports had been important in paying for the Republic's diplomatic activities overseas—was now given stepmotherly treatment with regard to funds for education, road repairs, irrigation, and other regional development.

Moral, political, and economic grievances against the central government were compounded by religious ones in early 1953 after President Soekarno's speech at Amuntai which revived the issue of whether Islam or the Pantja Sila should be the basis of the state. When the President visited Atjeh in March 1953, he was greeted with PUSA banners reading, "We love the President but we love Religion more." In mid-April, Daud Beureueh served as chairman of the All-Indonesian Conference of Ulama at Medan, which outlined a set of constitutional formulations for a "state based on Islam." [36] After the conference PUSA organized on an increased scale, re-establishing youth, women's, and veterans' groups, and Daud Beureueh, a formidable orator, went on a speaking tour through Atjeh. In May the army found evidence of contacts between Daud Beureueh and Kartosuwirjo of the Darul Islam. Rumors began that an Islamic regionalist revolt was imminent in Atjeh. In July, Vice-President Hatta flew there to talk to Daud Beureueh. But his task of persuading the "strong man of Atjeh" to keep faith with the Republic was made harder by the formation of a cabinet from which the Masjumi was excluded.

On the night of September 20 police and army posts at seven widely scattered towns of Atjeh were attacked by black-uniformed men who carried some arms and attempted to capture more. Most of these attacks were repulsed, but it soon became clear that a co-ordinated revolt had begun. Leaflets bearing the signature of Daud Beureueh declared that the Pantja Sila government had disappeared from Atjeh and that Atjeh had become part of the Islamic State of Indonesia first proclaimed by Kartosuwirjo in August 1949. The attacks on towns continued, and government troops were forced to evacuate some fairly

[36] See Boyd R. Compton, "The Medan Ulama Conference," *Newsletter of the Institute of Current World Affairs* (New York), Aug. 20, 1953.

large centers. Railway lines and bridges were destroyed. A considerable number of government servants left the coastal towns to join the rebel forces inland, and a number of army units followed suit. Various members of *uleebalang* families and some non-Achinese civil servants stationed in Atjeh arrived in Medan as refugees.[37]

The government was in a stunningly difficult situation. It had come into office with restoration of security as the first point of its program. It had encouraged the hope that by a new policy of firmness it might succeed against rebel and bandit groups where its predecessors, restrained by their Masjumi members, had failed. But its very accession to office had helped to trigger a revolt which would clearly be difficult to suppress. The Daud Beureueh group included some of the most prominent of Atjeh's leaders in the revolutionary struggle against the Dutch, and it obviously enjoyed considerable popular support. Conversely, to find a basis in Achinese society on which to build power against the PUSA-led revolt would involve the government in relying more heavily on the *uleebalang* leaders, who in many Achinese eyes bore the taint of collaboration with the Dutch. In addition, there were very great military problems. The territory of Atjeh is large and mountainous, roads were poor, and the coastal towns depended for food on inland areas which could not easily be controlled from these towns. Although it would clearly be necessary to rely in large part on soldiers from areas outside Atjeh, this in itself brought many dangers with it, for the government could ill afford to give rebel leaders further cause for inflaming the traditionally strong ethnic pride of the Achinese.

True to its commitment to firmness, the Ali cabinet responded to the revolt in a primarily military fashion. Its troops engaged Daud Beureueh units in scattered battles continuing over a period of more than a month. There was no talk of negotiations or amnesties. On the contrary, troops were rushed to Atjeh from various other parts of Sumatra. The government succeeded in repulsing a series of attacks on the coastal towns, but in Takengon, the capital of the inland regency of Central Atjeh, it was overwhelmed. Takengon was retaken by the government only in December.

---

[37] See *Keterangan dan Djawaban Pemerintah tentang Peristiwa Daud Beureueh* ("Government Statement and Replies to Criticisms on the Daud Beureueh Affair"; Djakarta: Kementerian Penerangan, 1953); S. M. Amin, *Sekitar Peristiwa Berdarah di Atjeh* ("On the Bloody Affair in Atjeh"; Djakarta: Soeroengan, 1956); and Boyd R. Compton, "Daud Beureueh—Lion of Atjeh" and "Revolt in Atjeh!" *Newsletters of the Institute of Current World Affairs* (New York), Sept. 17, Oct. 21, 1953.

By the end of October, however, the character of the war had changed. The rebels no longer spent much of their energies in efforts to seize or hold towns. The struggle had entered the guerrilla stage in which both sides were denied major victories. It was in this stage that it remained for the rest of the term of the Ali cabinet. Minor clashes and occasional raids on towns and communication lines continued throughout this period, but neither side made significant progress. Although the government spent large sums on its military campaign, a great part of the Achinese countryside remained under the effective control of Daud Beureueh. A third and large area of stalemated warfare had been added to the previously existing areas of the kind in West Java and South Sulawesi.

THE EXPECTATION OF ELECTIONS

Perhaps the most important single aspect of political setting for the drama of the Ali cabinet period was the expectation that elections would soon be held. In presenting his cabinet's initial statement to parliament on August 25, 1953, the Prime Minister had set forth a time schedule for the preparations of elections, a schedule which would run for sixteen months beginning with January 1954.[38] The opposition press criticized this, recalling that Roem had said elections could be held within ten months of the creation of the electoral law. But the opposition criticism was not particularly sharp; the time schedule introduced an element of specific commitment which suggested that the government would not readily allow additional delay.

On November 4, 1953, the cabinet announced the membership of a new Central Electoral Committee (Panitia Pemilihan Indonesia) to replace the Wilopo cabinet's stillborn Assaat committee. S. Hadikusumo of the PNI was named chairman, and the eight other members were chosen from Nahdatul Ulama, PSII, PRI, PRN, the Labor Party, and the BTI or Indonesian Peasant Front, all government parties, from Perti, a government-supporting party, and from Parkindo, a party which was not then clearly on the government or the opposition side, but soon afterward became a full-fledged member of the opposition.[39] The Central Electoral Committee, though subject to cabinet authority,

[38] See *Keterangan dan Djawaban Pemerintah atas Progam Kabinet Ali Sastroamidjojo* ("The Government Statement of the Cabinet of Ali Sastroamidjojo and Replies to Criticisms"; Djakarta: Kementerian Penerangan, 1953), pp. 46–47.

[39] For the names of the members see Panitia Pemilihan Indonesia (Central Electoral Committee), *Indonesia Memilih* ("Indonesia Votes"; Djakarta: Panitia Pemilihan Indonesia, 1958 [?]), p. 75.

would have important rule-making and adjudicating functions bearing on the freeness of the elections, as well as being responsible for implementing the technical arrangements,[40] and thus many people felt that this composition was not sufficiently widely representative. Vigorous protests against it came from a number of sources, principally from the Masjumi and PSI, and briefly also from the PKI and SOBSI. Dr. Sukiman, the Masjumi's first deputy chairman, wrote to President Soekarno petitioning for changes, whereupon the President gave a public assurance on November 28 that the Masjumi would be represented on the Electoral Committees of the fifteen electoral districts.

Attention then shifted to these regional Electoral Committees, whose composition was to be determined by the Minister of Justice in consultation with the provincial governors. On these committees, most of them established in the first half of 1954, the government parties were usually given five or six of the seven seats.[41] A similar ratio was common in the composition of the *kabupaten* electoral committees, one level further down, but in the case of the subdistrict level *ketjamatan* ballot committees (and the committees for each polling place, formed much later), the Masjumi was usually better represented, as was the PKI. The various minor parties, mostly having no organizational existence at this level, were given few seats or none. Where there was opposition criticism of the composition of the committees—and there was much of it regarding the Electoral Committees and *kabupaten* electoral committees—government spokesmen replied by asserting that the electoral committees were not representative bodies but executive ones.

In Djakarta the matter of the Electoral Committee's composition became very hotly contested. There the Masjumi mayor, Sjamsuridzal, was replaced in December 1953 by a PNI man, Sudiro, hitherto the Governor of Sulawesi. Before the change-over Sjamsuridzal had all but finalized plans for an Electoral Committee (for the electoral district of Greater Djakarta) and had appointed members of three *kabupaten* electoral committees (for the three *kabupatens* into which this province-status municipality was divided). Then in January 1954 Sudiro changed the composition of the three *kabupaten* committees and went ahead with new plans for the Electoral Committee for the municipality. The responses came in the form of a large Masjumi demon-

[40] On the status and organization of the Central Electoral Committee, see *ibid.*, pp. 8–10, 97.
[41] For full lists of the members see *ibid.*, pp. 511–519.

stration of protest held on February 13, a demonstration at which Kijaji Isa Anshary spoke. To this the government parties replied in kind a week later, when a Sunday crowd which the progovernment paper *Merdeka* estimated to be 300,000 strong heard PNI, PKI, and Perti speakers defend the new mayor and his Electoral Committee.

The denouement of this phase of election preliminaries came a Sunday later, also in the streets and squares of Djakarta. This new demonstration was organized not by the Masjumi itself, but by the Masjumi-dominated Co-ordination Body of Islamic Organizations. The cause was also somewhat different, for the relatively humdrum matter of electoral committees had now been linked to the broader cause of protesting against insults to Islam. In previous weeks there had been mass protests outside Djakarta, particularly in Makassar and Bandjarmasin, against offensive statements about Islam made by Mei Kartawinata of Permai (Persatuan Rakjat Marhaen Indonesia, Union of the Common People of Indonesia) and Mr. Hardi of the PNI.[42] Now these insults, and the lack of any government action to punish those who uttered them, were the subject of fiery speeches by Masjumi leaders to a crowd estimated by several papers to be half a million strong. The atmosphere at this rally reached a high pitch of excitement. Then a group of persons at the periphery made contemptuous remarks about the demonstration and were attacked by a section of the crowd. The subsequent brawling ended in the death of an army captain who had attempted to keep the peace. Electioneering had claimed its first fatal victim, and the shock of the murder reverberated through the whole politically participant community of the nation.[43]

During much of 1954 the opposition found considerable scope for criticism in the cabinet's failure to adhere to its own schedule of electoral preparations. Government regulations for the implementation of the electoral law were promised for November 1953, but they came out only in February of the next year and then included a modification of the original sixteen-month schedule. Although this modified set of

[42] Kartawinata, in speaking to a congress of his mystical-Javanist, Marxist, and decidedly anti-Islamic organization, had declared that Mohammad was a false prophet. Hardi had asserted at a public meeting in Central Sumatra that the Koran was out of date. See *Hikmah,* Jan. 2, 1954, and *Pemandangan,* Jan. 25, 1954. On Permai see Clifford Geertz, "Ritual and Social Change: A Javanese Example," *American Anthropologist,* LIX, no. 1 (1957), 32 ff.

[43] In early 1955, when Colonel Nasution wrote *Tjatatan-Tjatatan Sekitar Politik Militer Indonesia* ("Notes on Indonesian Military Policy"), the most important of the works presenting his formulation of the antipolitician ideology of the army, he dedicated the book to the memory of the army captain.

dates called for voter registration to be completed by mid-April, it was in fact not begun until early May. It was not completed, for the entire country, until October. In all this time the opposition parties hammered hard on the theme that the government parties were delaying elections in order to entrench and enrich themselves so as to be better able to win. They used this argument widely in efforts they made in September, October, and November 1954 to secure the cabinet's overthrow.[44]

The election issue was, however, a two-edged sword. While the government was clearly failing to meet its self-imposed deadlines, the opposition could profitably charge it with bad faith. But the fact was that the government was taking a large number of steps, many of them administratively complex, toward the holding of elections. Thus, whenever an opposition thrust began to threaten the cabinet's position, it could take a new step and then throw the charge of wanting the elections delayed back at the opposition.

This, in fact, is what happened in September and October 1954. At that time the cabinet was in serious political trouble, due in part to a split in PIR and in part to strong dissatisfaction inside the NU and PSII, especially with the policies of Economic Affairs Minister Iskaq. On September 9, therefore, the Central Electoral Committee came out with instructions which closed the period of voters' registration and hastened the beginning of the phase of submission of candidacies. With this the government regained the political initiative. Its supporters thenceforth charged the opposition with trying to bring down the cabinet because it, the opposition, was afraid to face the electorate.[45] Allegations of this kind were an important weapon in the bitterly fought defensive action which enabled the Ali cabinet to maintain itself with only a reshuffling of portfolios at a time when it seemed about to be overthrown or to collapse from within.

The first half of 1955 saw a further series of such waves of charge and countercharge. Late in 1954 Hadikusumo, the chairman of the Central Electoral Committee, had declared that polling for the parliamentary elections would be completed by August 1955. But in February it became apparent that preparations were lagging behind schedule, and several government spokesmen spoke vaguely of elections

[44] See, for instance, the statements of M. Yunan Nasution (Masjumi) and Drs. J. B. A. F. Mayor Polak (PSI), *Antara*, Oct. 22, 1954.

[45] See the statements of Sarwono Sastrosutardjo (PKI), *Pedoman*, Oct. 20, and Sutojo Mertodimuljo, *Suluh Indonesia*, Nov. 12, 1954; see also the *Harian Rakjat* editorial of Dec. 9, 1954.

"before the end of the year." [46] This was a time when the government was directing political attention to the forthcoming Asian-African Conference at Bandung, and the opposition, eager to have an issue of its own, charged repeatedly that the government was again engaged in delaying tactics with regard to the elections.[47]

But eventually the government was again able to answer the charge. On April 16, two days before the Bandung conference was scheduled to begin, Hadikusumo made a detailed statement in which, for the first time, he set actual dates for the elections. The parliamentary elections, he said, would be held on September 29, 1955, and the elections for the Constituent Assembly would follow on December 15. With this announcement the bottom again fell out of the opposition charges. When the cabinet's final struggle to maintain itself came in June and early July 1955, its spokesmen asserted that the opposition was attempting to wreck the orderly development toward elections on the very eve of these elections. On this occasion, however, the argument proved ineffective. New and powerful forces had appeared on the political stage, and the Ali cabinet was eventually forced to resign.

Whether or not the cabinet ever made concerted efforts to delay the holding of elections is not clear. Most of its members presumably enjoyed being in office and viewed the prospect of leaving it with dismay. Furthermore, its member parties were significantly helped in their election chances by the fact of being in office for this two-year period. Certainly the constant pressure exerted by the opposition was of major importance in hurrying the cabinet along in its election preparations.[48]

[46] See *Pedoman,* March 11, 17, 1953.

[47] See, for instance, *Abadi,* Feb. 17, and *Pedoman,* Feb. 22, 1955.

[48] An interesting side light on the long debate is provided by the repeated assertions of opposition leaders to the effect that they did not want to be in office during the period of elections, preferring to campaign on the record of their opposition to the Ali cabinet. See the statements of Sukiman, *Antara,* Nov. 11, 1954; Mayor Polak (PSI), *Berita Minggu* (Djakarta Sunday newspaper), Nov. 21, 1954; and Burhanuddin Harahap, *Antara,* March 7, 1955. In part this represented "sour grapes" sentiment, and the evidence suggests that the opposition group as a whole made vigorous efforts to secure the cabinet's overthrow. But there were apparently some in the opposition camp who believed that popular dislike for the policies of the Ali cabinet would outweigh the electoral advantages accruing to the parties in power. That this sort of overestimation of the modernness of the electorate's behavior had widespread currency within the elite is suggested by press reactions to the actual outcome of the elections. See also the editorial speculation in *Keng Po,* March 27, 1954, as to whether the PNI would withdraw voluntarily from the government before the elections. The actual course of the cabinet's fall does not suggest that the cabinet leadership was at all anxious to step down.

THE ELECTION CAMPAIGN

Even more important than the politics of when, how, and by whom the elections would be held was the politics of actual campaigning. In both length and intensity this was a massive campaign. Such waves of rallies and counterrallies as were occasioned in the first months of 1953 by the President's Amuntai speech and in the beginning of 1954 by the composition of various election committees and the issue of insults to Islam were merely the more dramatic manifestations of a campaign carried on with vigor and determination from early 1953 until the holding of the twin elections almost three years later.

Throughout the period, and particularly in 1954 and 1955, virtually every public event was an occasion for election campaigning. Not only at the many party congresses and party anniversaries, the various meetings and celebrations on national and Islamic holidays, and the protest rallies against particular government actions or against Dutch intransigence in West Irian did the campaigners press their themes, but also at meetings of unions and peasant organizations and of co-operative, educational, and social welfare associations, at student gatherings, and at scout parades. These organizations had always had fairly close ties to particular parties and had seen their own activities as justified by and dependent on the relationship they bore to the ideological position of a particular party. Now the parties had every incentive to make these ties even closer, and the various organizations offered little resistance to the process. Organizational life became more thoroughly political than ever before.

Nor was the campaigning confined to the cities and larger towns—quite the contrary. The most important changes which the campaign wrought were in the small towns and villages, particularly in villages in the more detraditionalized areas, where more than one party could gain a sizable foothold in a single village and where intravillage cleavages were exploited for electioneering purposes. Here a vigorous effort was made by all the major parties to enroll a large number of members. After the Central Electoral Committee had ruled on May 31, 1954, on the applications of the various parties for their ballot paper symbols, replicas of the party symbols appeared in large numbers in villages as well as cities and towns. In all village areas there was active wooing of locally influential persons by party representatives. Some parties, notably the PKI, were active in many areas in providing social welfare services at the village level, in carrying out such "small but effective actions"—this was the PKI slogan—as organizing the sharing of agricultural tools, arranging mutual assistance when feasts were held, building new water channels, and helping the victims of fires and floods.[49]

Much of this village-level campaign activity had a certain autonomy, the appeals employed being often markedly different from those laid down at the parties' Djakarta headquarters. In many village areas, particularly those where detraditionalization had not progressed far and where open conflict was not tolerated, issues had virtually no part in the campaign; there the parties merely extolled the virtues and past services of their leaders and interpreted their respective ideologies and ballot paper symbols in terms of locally held myths, values, and perceptions. Nevertheless, the issues of Djakarta politics were of great importance everywhere; for they set a framework within which village campaigning was contained.

The national campaign issues were principally issues between the government and opposition parties or, more narrowly, between the PNI and the Masjumi. The Great Debate was between the PNI and the Masjumi. The Nahdatul Ulama, PSII, and PIR were of only minor importance in it, and the same may be said of the PSI and the two Christian parties. On the other hand, the Communist Party did in a way constitute a third main party. Thus the debate was in one sense between two protagonists and in another sense between three.

Much of the campaign argument of the Masjumi and its fellow opposition parties consisted of criticism of the cabinet's policies and practices, in particular regarding the economy and placement of government personnel. Inflation, the shortages of essential imports and the abundance of luxury automobiles, "arbitrary" political appointments and dismissals—all of these were subjects of which opposition campaigners made much. And Iskaq's "special licenses" for national importers were a favorite target. Against criticism of this kind, the government parties asserted that with the Ali cabinet a real effort was at last being made to destroy the hold of foreigners over Indonesia's economy. The PKI, supporting the government parties, maintained that the continued poverty of the people was to be laid at the door of imperialism, whose strangle hold over the economy was still great. The Ali cabinet was not to be blamed, the PKI maintained, for this cabinet was relatively progressive, more so than its predecessors. The

[49] For further discussion of the techniques of campaigning see Herbert Feith, *The Indonesian Elections of 1955* (Cornell Modern Indonesia Project, Interim Reports Series; Ithaca, N.Y., 1957), pp. 21 ff.

substance of these charges and rebuttals will be examined further below.

But argument on specific policy charges was a secondary aspect of the campaign. Primary importance attached to issues of a more purely ideological character, and particularly to the Islam versus nationalism issue which had been raised by the President's Amuntai speech and the replies of Isa Anshary.

The main body of the Masjumi's leadership, men of both the Natsir and the Sukiman groups, denied repeatedly that the Masjumi's commitment to the establishment of a "state based on Islam" brought it into conflict with the Pantja Sila.[50] Natsir's position was that the Pantja Sila would not be in conflict with the Koran unless it were given a content which conflicted with the commands of the Koran. "The Pantja Sila will grow and flourish in the soil and climate of Islam," he declared.[51] Correspondingly most PNI leaders were insistent that their strong support of the Pantja Sila as the basis of the state did not imply that they were lukewarm in their attitude to Islam.

However, the extreme positions continued to be of central importance in setting the terms of the debate. In part this was the consequence of electioneering itself; the phenomenon is common enough in Western election campaigns. But if any Western comparison is appropriate, it is not the one with campaigning in Anglo-American political systems, in which agreement exists on basic social and political values and debate centers on a relatively narrow range of issues and personalities, but rather with campaigning in countries like France and Italy, countries with a "fragmented political culture" whose parties represent mutually estranged segments of the community and contest elections by the assertion of separatistic ideological claims.[52]

What was at issue in the Indonesian election campaign was not a mere difference of opinion about the phrasing of constitutional provisions; rather it was a conflict between major symbols representing

[50] For one set of constitutional formulations foreshadowed for an Indonesian "state based on Islam" see Boyd R. Compton, "The Medan Ulama Conference." Other expositions are contained in K. A. Hakim, *Konsepsi Asas Tata Negara Islam* ("The Fundamental Principles of Islamic Constitutional Law"; Djakarta: Sudjas 1953); Isa Anshary, *Ummat Islam Menghadapi Pemilihan Umum* ("The Islamic Community Faces the Elections"; Surabaja: Hasan Aidit, 1953); and Zainal Abidin Ahmad, *Membentuk Negara Islam* ("Forming an Islamic State"; Djakarta: Widjaja, 1956).

[51] *Abadi*, May 22, 24, 1954.

[52] Cf. Gabriel A. Almond, "Comparative Political Systems," *Journal of Politics*, XVIII, no. 3 (Aug. 1956), 400–409.

alternative ideologies, alternative bodies of meaning-creating ideas, alternative categories of personal identification. For those whose whole system of values and perceptions centered on nationalism the Pantja Sila was an intensely meaningful symbol. Such men were not only outraged by the attacks of Isa Anshary upon the Pantja Sila; they were also deeply dissatisfied with a simple acknowledgment like that of Natsir. Conversely, strongly convinced Moslems were not only disgusted by frontal attacks on their symbols, like that of Hardi who called the Koran out of date; they were also annoyed by what they saw as equivocation in the nationalists who called themselves Moslems but refused to put Islam in the center of their social and political creed.

Nor was it merely within the political public that the ideological formulations demanded allegiance. These formulations were able to be related rapidly to existing social cleavages—facilitated in this by the fact that many of these cleavages were, in almost every area of Indonesia, religious in character. Many outside the political public, lower-class townsmen and villagers in relatively detraditionalized areas, were drawn to an active commitment to the ideological positions of particular parties.[53]

The potential for sharp conflict in this superimposition of political ideology on existing social division is clear from Geertz's description (of the situation in an East Java town in 1953–1954):

Because the same symbols are used in both political and religious contexts, people often regard party struggle as involving not merely the usual ebb and flow of party manoeuvre, the necessary factional give and take of democratic government, but involving as well decisions on basic values and ultimates. *Kampong* people in particular [lower-class city and town dwellers—small traders, lower-grade officials, artisans, laborers, and so on] tend to see the open struggle for power explicitly institutionalized in the new republican forms of government as a struggle for the right to establish different brands of essentially religious principles as official: "if the *abangans* get in, the koranic teachers will be forbidden to hold classes;" "if the *santris* get in we shall all have to pray five times a day." The normal conflict involved in electoral striving for office is heightened by the idea that literally everything is at stake: the "if we win it is our country" idea that the group which gains

---

[53] For stimulating discussions of different relationships established between party ideologies and pre-existing social cleavages, see G. William Skinner, ed., *Local, Ethnic and National Loyalties in Village Indonesia* (Yale University, Southeast Asia Studies, Cultural Reports Series; New Haven, Conn., 1959). See also Feith, *The Indonesian Elections of 1955*, pp. 72 ff.

power has a right, as one man said, "to put his own foundation under the state." Politics thus takes on a kind of sacralized bitterness.[54]

But if there were powerful forces at work making for sharp conflict between ideologies, there existed at the same time a strong desire, one with deep roots in the prevailing Indonesian culture, to avoid intense conflict of any kind. All parties therefore attempted, at least when they addressed themselves to persons outside the group of their committed supporters, to appear to be moderate and harmony-seeking while their opponents were extremists and fanatics. One of the most important strategic tasks of the parties was to present their ideologies so that they would accord with existing values and perceptions in particular communal and quasi-communal groups of the population and at the same time not seem to produce conflict between these groups.

In this the Masjumi was relatively unsuccessful. The main body of the Masjumi leadership made numerous efforts to prevent the emergence of too extreme an image of the party. The party leaders repeatedly sought to woo the co-operation of the Moslem parties represented in the cabinet. At the same time they stressed the tolerance of the Islamic religion and its commitment to uphold the freedom of non-Moslems to practice their respective faiths. They also placed much emphasis on affirmations of loyalty to the nation and the ideals for which the Revolution had been fought.[55] When it became clear that the activities of the party's "Anti-Communist Front" (a quasi-autonomous body headed by Isa Anshary) were making the Masjumi appear in some areas as a party of narrow Islamic intolerance, the party decided, at its congress of December 1954, to stop the activities of the Front.

The fact was, however, that a minority of the Masjumi leaders were able to defy the appeals emphasis laid down by the majority. The Isa Anshary group continued to speak in the tones of Moslem radicalism, making free use of the term *kafir* (heathen) for their political enemies.[56] And the community of West Java religious scholars associated with this group went so far as to issue a *fatwa* ordering local religious leaders to refuse a Muslim burial to Communists.[57]

---

[54] Geertz, "Ritual and Social Change," p. 51.

[55] See, for instance, *Masjumi Pendukung Proklamasi* ("The Masjumi, A Supporter of the Proclamation of Independence"; Djakarta: Masjumi, 1954).

[56] Cf. Boyd R. Compton, "Muslim Radicalism: The Anti-Communist Front," *Newsletter of the Institute of Current World Affairs* (New York), March 5, 1955.

[57] For the text see *Abadi*, Feb. 28, 1954.

The PNI was much more successful in arousing the enthusiasm of its adherents while avoiding the impression of being extremist. In part this was because its ideology, built as it was on Hindu-Javanese religious foundations, had a diffuse, syncretistic, and all-enveloping character—in contrast with the specific, doctrinal, and antithesis-oriented ideology of the Masjumi. In part too it was because the PNI was the leading government party in this period of the first Ali cabinet. This fact and the party's close relationship with the President helped the PNI (as it helped the other government parties) to depict itself as a party of unity and harmony.

In addition, the government parties were able to describe themselves as representing the middle ground between the Masjumi extreme on the one hand and the Communist extreme on the other. Not infrequently too this theme was projected internationally. Thus the PNI, the NU, and most of the other government parties claimed to be the true upholders of an independent Indonesian foreign policy, as against the Washington pulls represented by the Masjumi on the one hand and the Moscow pulls represented by the PKI on the other.

All the government parties made anticolonialism a major part of their campaign armory. They spoke frequently of the cabinet's firmness against the remnants of Dutch colonial power in Indonesia and its active efforts to achieve the return of West Irian. They gained a powerful argument with the successful holding of the Bandung Asian-African Conference in April 1955, five months before the parliamentary election.

The PKI, as a government-supporting party, shared some of the situational advantages of the PNI and the other government parties. For the PKI it was a matter of the greatest importance to establish itself as a moderate, tolerant, and genuinely national party. Thus it did its utmost to minimize public awareness of the tensions which existed between itself and the cabinet—tensions over labor policy, over squatters on estate and forest lands, over PKI proposals for the arming of veterans' groups, and over the designation of the PKI's election symbol as the "symbol of the PKI and nonparty people." [58] And as the cabinet

[58] The PKI's proposal to have this designation for its symbol was initially endorsed by the Central Electoral Committee. Subsequently, in January 1955, as a result particularly of pressure from the Nahdatul Ulama, the decision was reversed. The PKI finally agreed to change the wording on its placards and billboards so that the hammer and sickle picture was designated simply as the "election symbol of the PKI." See *Antara*, June 12, 1954, Sept. 17, 1954, and *Pedoman*, Dec. 18, 1954, Jan. 28, 1955.

parties also had an interest in keeping these issues out of view, they were given fairly little publicity. Instead both the government parties and the PKI attacked the Masjumi and PSI as extremist, alien, and inimical to the shared central core of nationalist attitudes. The Communists were vociferous in support of all the attempts of the government parties to depict the opposition as disloyal. In addition, they were the forerunners of the campaign to associate the Masjumi with the Darul Islam on the one hand and with foreign plantation and mining interests on the other. After the PKI's decision of November 1954 to "accept the Pantja Sila as the political basis of the Republic, while suggesting improvements," its leaders contrasted this acceptance with various Masjumi leaders' criticism of the Pantja Sila.

Indeed, so far did the PKI carry the National United Front policy that its appeals included very few specifically socialist ideas—at least at the national level of campaigning. In a number of areas, it is true, the party's workers made promises of the distribution of land if the PKI won the elections—forest land, estate land, land belonging to village officials, and in some areas the land of Indonesian landlords.[59] But at the national level this emphasis was conspicuously absent. In June 1955 the party went so far as to rewrite its election platform. Thenceforth its election efforts were no longer directed toward the establishment of a "People's Democratic Government," but rather toward a "National Coalition Government."[60]

The PKI was particularly anxious not to appear to be antireligious. Thus in April 1955 it signed a formal declaration with the Moslem PSII to the effect that neither party would attack the other.[61] In areas where social divisions were paralleled by a division between specifically Islamic groups and groups basing themselves on the Hindu and pre-Hindu elements of the traditional cultural-religious synthesis —this was the case particularly in the area of East and Central Java, but also elsewhere—the PKI offered itself as a spokesman for the tolerant syncretistic and "originally Indonesian" elements of the cultural-religious tradition. And to a considerable extent it was accepted as that. Its hostility to the Masjumi's Islam did not make it appear as an antireligious party. On the contrary, it tended to create an image of the party as standing with the PNI (and to a much lesser extent the

---

[59] See *Abadi*, Nov. 11, 1954; *Antara*, Dec. 10, 1954; and *Pedoman*, Oct. 24, 1955, Jan. 11, 1956.

[60] *Java Post* (Surabaja), June 27, 1955; *Harian Rakjat*, Aug. 8, 9, 1955.

[61] *Suara Merdeka* (Semarang), April 7, 1955.

NU) in common defense of the oldest and most truly indigenous of religious beliefs and practices.

The Masjumi for its part tried hard to establish the idea of a dividing line between the Communists and all other parties. Its speakers alluded to the subservience of the PKI to Moscow; they frequently recalled the Communists' role in the Madiun rebellion and attempted to institute a Day of National Mourning to mark the anniversary of its outbreak. Again they stressed the antireligious aspects of communism, using to good effect Chou En-lai's statement at the Bandung conference, "We Communists are atheists."

In all this, however, the Masjumi labored under disadvantages which arose directly from its being in the opposition for the greater part of the campaign period and from the PKI's being a government-supporting party for that time. It was the Masjumi alone which attacked the PKI; the government parties remained silent, at least at the national level of campaigning. This situation meant that there was a risk of backfiring involved in any Masjumi attempt to isolate the Communists or brand them as extremists. The fact was that, in terms of cabinet politics, the Masjumi was largely isolated for the two years of Ali Sastroamidjojo's administration. It had to take great care lest its attacks on the Ali cabinet on the one hand and the Communists on the other should result in a strengthening of ties between these two, and thus intensify its own isolation. The PKI by contrast moved far toward gaining acceptance as a party true to the central core of nationalist values.

Campaigning wrought enormous changes in the party system. In the period between 1949 and 1953 the leaders of the parties had concentrated almost entirely on capital-city politics, having little interest in village-level organization—which could rarely be used to produce effects in national or even regional politics. But in 1953–1955 organization at the village level became their central concern. In the course of organizing in the villages and of collecting the funds which made this possible, the parties developed closer ties to interest groups and local leadership groups than ever before. The party system became a means of channeling a wide range of interests and demands.

Wherever party activity became important in village society—and especially where there was sharp competition between parties in a single village or hamlet, usually in the more detraditionalized village areas—it resulted in a recasting of the power and status relationships existing between various village groups. A party-contested election sponsored by the central government meant that village conflict was encouraged to exist in the open. The result was to weaken the position of the groups which benefited from the traditional avoidance of open conflict, in effect the *status quo* groups and those whose authority was traditional and local in its source. At the same time open conflict tended to strengthen the "outsider" groups in the villages, the younger persons who claimed to exercise authority on the basis of education and national and ideological awareness. In many of the more detraditionalized villages it stimulated the creation of new collective entities, new units of social integration consisting of parties and their associated youth and women's organizations, and religious, cultural, and educational bodies, all based on the ideology of the particular party.

But the election campaign did not merely clothe existing conflict in political garb; it also added to the volume and intensity of this conflict, in village and town alike. It is extremely difficult to make any balanced assessment of the extent to which bitter conflict existed in the country as a whole. The press of these years gives ample evidence of brawls at political meetings, of the tearing up of election posters, of pressure and threats from persons in authority to coerce their subordinates to join and support their parties, of politically caused marital strife, of slander, kidnapings, and a few killings. But the press picture probably exaggerates the volume of conflict. In the first place, press reports of this kind were printed because they were newsworthy. Secondly, it was in the interest of all parties to find and publish instances of extreme behavior for which their political opponents could be blamed.

Yet it cannot be doubted that intergroup conflict was given powerful stimulation. Interestingly enough, interethnic hostility was virtually never aroused. Similarly no party used anti-Chinese appeals on any significant scale. But conflicts between groups of different socioreligious orientation, adat leaders and *ulama,* between landlords and tenants, between creditors and debtors, between one clan or kinship group and another, and between ordinary cliques hostile to one another—all these were sharpened as a result of the "opening" and "ideologizing" effects of the campaign.

Sharp conflict was particularly characteristic of certain areas of society—of urban *kampongs,* of estate and former estate areas, and of certain village areas which had been heavily affected by commercializing, urbanizing, and other detraditionalizing tendencies. It is in these areas that ideological commitments were of greatest importance, functioning to provide a value system, a view of the world, a sense of identity, and a set of guides to action for those for whom these were no longer provided by traditional society. But campaigning also had divisive effects in villages where the ideologies drew little serious commitment. Andrea Wilcox Palmer, an anthropologist who spent the years 1955–1957 in the village of Situradja, near Sumedang, West Java, reports that prominent villagers there were obliged to adopt a variety of party loyalties in conformity with the wishes of officials and others in the nearby town who were their patrons in one or another capacity. Here the party conflicts created in the village did not correspond to pre-existing social divisions. But they were nevertheless important. And they resulted in resentment of the parties as disturbers of village harmony and social solidarity.

Moreover, there is a sense in which extreme campaign conflict cast its shadow across Indonesian society as a whole, for an enormous segment of all social life in Indonesia was centered on organizations, and these were all tied to one or another party. Thus where political conflict was acute, its reverberations were quickly felt in many spheres of life whose relationships to politics were highly indirect. And because campaigning intensified the speed of social change in many areas, it added to the already high general level of anxiety and aggression—anxiety seeking a rationale and aggression a target. Social conflict and the psychological facts of anxiety and aggression together provide an explanation of the widespread fears which prevailed—fears of clashes between the veterans' organizations of the parties, of intervention by the Darul Islam or by foreigners, of defeated parties taking to the jungles to continue their fight, of Masjumi coming to power and persecuting *abangan* nominal Moslems, and of Communists in power murdering *kijajis*.[62]

The government had long been keenly aware of the possibilities of social disruption inherent in electioneering. On June 17, 1953, the chief public prosecutor had issued a circular letter banning political speeches and discussions in mosques, churches, and places of religious instruction.[63] After the rally of the Co-ordination Body of Islamic Organizations on February 28, 1954, the rally which resulted in the

---

[62] Clifford Geertz, *The Religion of Java* (Glencoe, Ill.: Free Press, 1960), pp. 364–365.

[63] For the text see *Keterangan dan Djawaban Pemerintah atas Program Kabinet Burhanuddin Harahap* ("The Government Statement on the Program of the

death of an army captain, a temporary ban was placed on all public demonstrations.

For meetings and rallies anywhere in the country it was necessary to obtain prior authorization from the police or at least to inform the local police authorities. And the press of the campaign period provides numerous instances of the seizure of party literature and of the arrest of minor party workers (and occasional top leaders) for making inflammatory speeches, tearing down placards or election symbols, holding unauthorized meetings, and so on. Steps of this kind usually resulted from co-operation between the army, the police, the *pamong pradja* authorities, and the public prosecutor, as represented on the Security Co-ordination Board (Koordinasi Keamanan Daerah) of a particular region. The same security co-ordination boards, which existed at the provincial and *kabupaten* levels, were also active in exhorting and pressing party leaders in order to prevent the emergence of too high a degree of open hostility.

But serious problems arose regarding the legitimacy of the government's role as campaign referee, for the various restrictions imposed were rarely extended to the government parties. When arrests were made, they were almost always of Masjumi or PKI members. The PKI was under strong restraint not to protest against campaign restrictions; but its daily did contain a number of complaints of this kind.[64] In the Masjumi's case the protests were sustained and vigorous. The Masjumi was particularly resentful of the arrest of its second deputy chairman, Mr. Kasman Singodimedjo, in Ambon in May 1954 —for declaring, on this Christian-Moslem island, that the Islamic ideology had been created by God whereas all other ideologies including the Christian one were man-made. Why, the Masjumi asked, were PNI leaders not even questioned about the provocative statements they made?[65] As many Masjumi leaders saw it, electioneering was essentially a struggle between conflicting parties seeking ideological

---

Burhanuddin Harahap Cabinet and Replies to Parliamentary Criticism"; Djakarta: Kementerian Penerangan, 1955), pp. 207–213. The Masjumi protested against this circular letter, arguing that the chief prosecutor had no right to issue it while the Wilopo cabinet had demissionary status (and was thus not authorized to take major policy actions). Three days later the prosecutor's office declared that it represented merely a warning that existing legislation against those who insulted other groups in society or stirred up feelings of hostility against them would be implemented firmly. See *Pedoman*, June 22, 1953.

[64] E.g., *Harian Rakjat*, Jan. 18, March 3, 1955.

[65] *Abadi*, May 24, 1954; *Aneta*, May 25, 27, 1955. Cf. *Hikmah*, Feb. 9, 1954, on the campaign appeals used by Sidik Djojosukarto.

hegemony over one another. There was no moral justification, they declared, for one of the contending parties to impose its own ideology as the framework of campaigning.

The problem was essentially that the state was not seen to stand above the struggle between the parties. There was no widely established view of the existing government as an entity distinct from the state. And in practice the agencies concerned with the legitimation of state authority and with rule making (the characteristically legislative function) and rule adjudication (the characteristically judicial function) were drawn into a close relationship with the cabinet—and thus into the political vortex. The number of umbrella institutions remaining autonomous and able to mediate and set limits to the party struggle was very small.

This is seen clearly as one looks at the role of Soekarno and Hatta in the campaign. The Dwitunggal or duumvirate of Soekarno and Hatta had long served as a symbol of national unity transcending both regional and ideological divisions. But the word Dwitunggal was ceasing to ring true in the Ali cabinet period, as disagreements between the two men were given increased public attention.[66] Hatta's public role was generally small. When he made a speech, it was often on a noncontroversial matter such as the development of the co-operative movement. But where it was on a current political issue—for instance, on the development of the national importers' group [67]—it usually presented a point of view close to that of the Masjumi-PSI opposition. It was almost always at variance with the emphasis in the speeches of the President.

If the Soekarno-Hatta duumvirate could not function well as an umbrella institution, President Soekarno himself was equally unable to place himself above the key struggles. It was not that he made no attempt to play a supraparty role. Indeed, he was acutely aware of the dangers of ideological conflict and saw his own role as primarily a synthesizing one. But he also actively supported the Ali cabinet and displayed more vigor in maintaining it in office than he had in relation to any of its predecessors. Thus when Sartono, the PNI chairman of parliament and a close associate of the President, warned in December 1953 that parliament might be dissolved if tensions between the cabinet and opposition parties in parliament grew too great, the

[66] E.g., *Merdeka,* Feb. 20, 1954.
[67] E.g., *Pedoman,* Nov. 27, 1954 (Hatta's message to the All-Sumatran Economic Conference at Medan).

opposition parties felt this as a serious threat.[68] It was distinctly possible, they believed, both then and at the period of impending cabinet crisis between September and November 1954, that the President and the Prime Minister would together dissolve parliament if this became necessary to preserve the cabinet's existence. Speaking at Palembang on November 8, 1954, when the threat to the cabinet's existence was at its height, the President declared that a foreign plot existed to overthrow the cabinet and that opposition leaders, selling their country for millions of rupiahs, were involved.[69] Correspondingly the opposition made numerous efforts to blacken the name of the President in order to weaken the cabinet. The classic case here was *Indonesia Raya's* sensational reporting in September 1954 of Soekarno's theretofore secret marriage to the recently divorced Mrs. Hartini.[70]

Playing a partisan role in relation to the cabinet, the President could not mediate the campaign authoritatively. Every syncretist symbol he fashioned lost its conciliatory powers because of his association with it. Therefore when he appealed for unity between the nationalist and religious groups, the opposition suspected that he was merely attempting to draw the NU and PSII into closer association with the PNI. When he spoke of the Pantja Sila as the only possible basis for national unity, they dismissed this as PNI propaganda. To them he seemed to be speaking of a unity from which they were excluded. Natsir summed up their position in a comment on Soekarno's Palembang speech: "The President has in fact abandoned his position as the 'Father of the State' and the final arbiter of things and has chosen to take his place with one of the parties in the conflict." [71]

Mediating the campaign conflict and maintaining a legitimate state authority above it were made all the more difficult by partisanship on the part of some government agencies responsible for preparing the elections and influencing mass attitudes toward them. The Central

---

[68] See *Hikmah*, Feb. 9, 1954.

[69] *Antara*, Nov. 10, 1954. Despite opposition challenges, no judicial action was taken on this alleged plot.

[70] In some respects, however, this particular effort backfired. The initial reaction of the political public to the multiple marriage was negative, but the President's prestige rose soon afterward when it became clear that feelings of shame and resentment were not at all widespread outside this public. In the eyes of the mass of the people Soekarno was evidently not just the foremost of a group of leaders of the successful Revolution, but a man with the attributes of kingship. Awareness of this fact was to be an important factor in the thinking of members of the political public in subsequent years.

[71] Natsir, *Capita Selecta*, II, 261.

Electoral Committee, though dominated by the government parties, did not play a partisan role—except perhaps inasmuch as it worked closely with the cabinet in the matter of decisions bearing on the timing of the elections. Its subordinate bodies, on which the parties outside the cabinet were better represented than on the central committee, were rarely if ever the butt of opposition criticism. But segments of the Ministries of Information and Religion, and to a lesser extent of the *pamong pradja,* did become campaign partisans. This brings us to a discussion of the whole matter of the civil service in the period of the Ali cabinet.

THE PARTIES AND THE GOVERNMENT SERVICE

One important aspect of the Ali cabinet's politics is seen in the large number of personnel changes it made at the higher levels of the government service. These effectively strengthened the government parties in the service and brought about an over-all increase in the dependence of civil servants on party leaders. Moreover, they changed much in the whole pattern of administration by giving criteria of party loyalty a place of much increased importance in the making of decisions about personnel, to the detriment of criteria of performance of work.

On previous occasions in our period the advent of a new cabinet had resulted in only a few politically based appointments, dismissals, or transfers. The party balance established within the top level of the bureaucracy in 1949 and 1950, chiefly by Hatta, had remained substantially unchanged until the middle of 1953. Thus some ministries had become and remained predominantly under PNI influence, others predominantly under Masjumi influence, some predominantly under PSI influence, and a few of the more technical ministries under the influence of nonparty people. Indeed, there was often a similar balance inside particular ministries, especially the ministries having politically significant tasks, with the PNI, Masjumi, PSI, and minor nationalist parties sharing influence and each "controlling" a certain number of Djakarta-level divisions and provincial offices.

But there were limits to the importance of party politics in the ministries. Many of the ministers of this early period actively encouraged the development of nonpolitical administration. Being "administrators" in our sense of the word, and in some cases more loyal to their fellow ministers and fellow "administrators" than their parties, they saw this as an important part of their task. Most of them left a great deal of power to their secretaries-general, a group of men with a strongly professional orientation to their work and often a vigorous determination to have continuity maintained, rules adhered to, and competence rewarded.

Thus it was only rarely that a minister had made a serious attempt to alter the party balance in his ministry; the case of Iskaq's tenure of the Interior portfolio in the Sukiman cabinet was one such instance. The composition of the corps of secretaries-general underwent virtually no change in the whole of the period. Of the 18 persons who were in secretary-general posts or their equivalent (including the director of the President's cabinet, the secretary to the cabinet, and the secretary to the Prime Minister) when the Wilopo cabinet resigned in the middle of 1952, all but three—the secretaries-general of Defense, Foreign Affairs, and Labor—had been in the same positions from the time of inception of the unitary state.[72]

With the onset of the Ali cabinet period the balance underwent major change. At the secretary-general level there were changes in six of the ministries in the two-year period—Foreign Affairs, Economic Affairs, Communications, Education, Information, and Labor. The over-all effect of these was to favor the parties of the Ali cabinet and particularly the PNI. One further effect was to lessen the importance of the secretary-generalship as a relatively nonpolitical institution. Once there had been one or two instances where a minister dismissed his secretary-general or made demands on him of the sort which led to the secretary-general's resignation, the position of all secretaries-general vis-à-vis their ministers was quickly weakened.

At other levels the changes made bore the imprint of party influences still more clearly. In the Foreign Ministry there was a rapid decline in the number of Masjumi and more particularly of PSI persons in high posts. A number of PSI ambassadors and first secretaries were recalled from overseas, and PNI men put in their place. Two directorate heads, Dr. Soedarsono and Hadji Rasjidi, former ministers and members of the PSI and the Masjumi respectively, were dropped from their posts on very short notice, to be replaced by PNI members.[73] And large numbers of nonparty employees of the

[72] See Kementerian Penerangan, *Kami Perkenalkan* ("We Introduce"; Djakarta: Kementerian Penerangan, 1954) *passim*. See also Darius Marpaung, ed., *Almanak Pegawai Negeri, 1956* ("Civil Servants' Almanac for 1956"; Djakarta: Upeni, 1956).

[73] The suddenness and abruptness with which personnel changes of this kind were made were particularly strongly protested by opposition critics of the Ali

ministry, as well as some who had hitherto been in other parties, were enrolled as PNI members.

In the Information Ministry, where the PNI had long had preponderant influence, this was extended markedly in the period of the Ali cabinet. The usual procedure was to transfer Masjumi and PSI officials from line positions where they had had wide responsibilities to staff posts where they had status but no power. Although the changes were made at many levels, they were seen with particular clarity in the party composition of the provincial heads of the ministry. Whereas PNI members and nonparty men with PNI sympathies had held six posts as provincial Information heads at the time of the inception of the Ali cabinet (with one in Masjumi and two in PSI hands), PNI members held ten out of the existing twelve posts by the time the cabinet fell and no Masjumi or PSI member held any.[74]

In the Ministry of Religion it was the Nahdatul Ulama which gained from the cabinet's incumbency. At the time of the Wilopo cabinet's fall most senior officials of this ministry were members of the Masjumi; only a small fraction were Nahdatul Ulama members. The next two years saw an almost complete reversal of the ratio. Much of the change was wrought by quiet pressure on Masjumi members to join the NU. In some cases very little pressure was needed, for many of the Masjumi members who had been appointed heads of the ministry in the period of Kijaji Wachid Hasjim's ministership were NU men by "denominational" viewpoint. In other cases, however, outright political dismissals were resorted to: Masjumi heads had been replaced by NU appointees in three of the ministry's provincial offices before the cabinet had been in office for three months.[75]

Transfers were made with particular speed in the first fourteen

cabinet. They pointed to cases where a high official was put out of his post at one or two days' notice and with no more formality than a telephone call from the minister, then given no alternative work to do, and in some cases no desk to sit at. These were some of the standard ways of inflicting extreme humiliation in the operating code of the Indonesian bureaucracy.

[74] See Amelz in *Risalah Sementara Perundingun Dewan Perwakilan Rakjat* ("Interim Transcript of Parliamentary Discussions"), Nov. 4, 1955.

[75] See Mochtar Naim, "The Nahdatul Ulama as a Political Party, 1952–55: An Enquiry into the Origins of Its Electoral Success" (M.A. thesis, McGill University, 1960). The political importance of this ministry is clear from the fact that 21 of the 45 men elected as NU parliamentarians in the September 1955 elections, as well as 15 of the 57 men elected on the ticket of the Masjumi and one of the 57 PNI men, were employees of the ministry. See statement of R. Mohammad Kafrawi, secretary-general of the Ministry of Religious Affairs, *Abadi*, April 3, 1956.

months of the cabinet's life in the powerful Ministry of the Interior and its *pamong pradja* corps. But the pattern here was more complicated than in most of the other ministries affected by these changes. The fourteen months were the period for which the PIR's Professor Hazairin was minister, and many of his appointees were PIR men. But Hazairin was also responsible for many changes—as regards governorships, residentships, regentships, and so on—from which the PNI gained. The irony here was that the PIR members whom Hazairin installed, particularly a number of residents and regents in South and Central Sumatra, were men who had worked with the Dutch in the BFO period. Hazairin's left hand was therefore strengthening the PNI, a party which had spearheaded the destruction of the BFO states, while his right hand was reinstating men who had been demoted because of this destruction. In the last eight months of the cabinet's life, when the NU's Mr. Sunarjo held the Interior post, few political changes were made.

In July 1953, when the Ali cabinet came into office, there were four PNI members and two PNI sympathizers in gubernatorial posts (or the two posts of equivalent status, as head of the Municipality of Greater Djakarta and the Special Territory of Jogjakarta), as well as three Masjumi members, one PIR member, one sympathizer of the PSI, and one nonparty man (without clear sympathies linking him to a particular party). In July 1955, when the cabinet stepped down, the number of PNI members at this level was six, and there was one Masjumi member, one PIR man, one member of the Sulawesi party PKR (Partai Kedaulatan Rakjat, People's Sovereignty Party), and two men who were neither members nor clear sympathizers of any party. At lower than gubernatorial levels of the *pamong pradja* hierarchy the influence of the parties represented in the cabinet grew at a comparable pace.

The other two ministries which were markedly affected by politically calculated personnel policies were Justice and Economic Affairs. In the Justice Ministry the chief trend of these policies was to induce officials to join the PRN of Justice Minister Djody Gondokusumo. This party gained a large number of members, particularly in the public prosecutor's corps. In the case of the Economic Affairs Ministry the PNI's Iskaq Tjokroadisurjo set the direction of the change very early in his term of office when he dismissed the PSI head of the Directorate for Trade and Industry, replacing him with a PNI man. At the same time he ordered a change in the head of the Central Import Office, an office which was to have four different men as head in the period of the Ali cabinet. He left the mark of his thoroughness equally on the area of government banking. Thus Margono Djojohadikusumo, father of Professor Sumitro Djojohadikusumo and a nonparty parliamentarian of PSI sympathies, was taken out of the posts he had held as president-director of the Bank Negara Indonesia (Indonesian State Bank) and Bank Industri Negara (State Industrial Bank) in October 1953. His place was taken by Mr. Abdul Karim and Suwirjo respectively, the one a member and the other the deputy chairman of the PNI. Both banks, and especially the Bank Industri Negara, came to be dominated by PNI members at various other levels as well.[76] But the Bank Indonesia, the central bank and by far the most important of the government banks, continued to be controlled by the Masjumi leader (and sharp critic of the Ali cabinet's financial and economic policies), Sjafruddin Prawiranegara.

The parliamentary opposition chose the personnel policies of the cabinet for particularly vociferous criticism. When the Masjumi's K. H. Tjikwan moved a motion of no confidence in Iskaq in April 1954, he and his supporters placed great stress on the fact that Iskaq had displaced able public functionaries purely in order to put loyal PNI members in their place. Parallel charges were made against several of the ministers when Jusuf Wibisono moved a motion of no confidence in the cabinet as a whole in November 1954. Opposition speakers alleged that the cabinet had abandoned bureaucratic norms in a way which would have serious long-term consequences for the efficiency of the civil service and the job security of public officials. The cabinet's supporters replied that the transfers were natural consequences of a change in the country's over-all political situation. They had criticized the earlier bureaucratic balance, particularly in the large influence it had accorded to members and supporters of the Socialist Party. Now this party's influence over cabinet politics had disappeared, and therefore, they contended, it was at last possible to rectify a long-perceived lack of proportion in civil service power relations.

Many of the personnel changes that the cabinet introduced were primarily efforts to achieve power entrenchment within the government service. Granted the crucial importance of the civil service as a center of power in Indonesia, a top-level political change would

[76] For a full discussion see John O. Sutter, *Indonesianisasi: Politics in a Changing Economy, 1940–1955* (Southeast Asia Program, Cornell University; Ithaca, N.Y., 1959), pp. 782–786, 973–981.

normally tend to find expression, and consolidation, through changes within it. But some of the controversial transfers affected posts which were important not so much for power leverage as for patronage, for the prestige they bestowed and the financial opportunities to which they gave access.

To execute the difficult task of keeping his cabinet in office until the elections, Ali Sastroamidjojo was obliged to devote great energy and resources to keeping favor with the parties in the cabinet and frequently with the factions in these parties which were not represented in the cabinet. Thus he and the other cabinet leaders and the PNI's Sidik worked systematically to satisfy the various groups. Regular meetings were held of the whole cabinet with the leaders of all its member parties, and here agreements on patronage distribution were hammered out. In addition, individual ministers were given increased latitude to make personnel changes favoring members of their own parties and various factions within them.

Finally, the cabinet's political appointments served to help the government parties raise funds to fight the election. Large amounts of money accrued to these parties as a result of one or another form of bureaucratic advantage—whether through "special licenses" issued by Iskaq personally in exchange for donations to his party, through the depositing of government-controlled funds in party banks, or through the use of a party's representatives within the diplomatic establishment overseas to channel business to Indonesian importers supporting the party.[77] These techniques could be used only to the extent that a party had succeeded in establishing a machinelike network of influence in particular sections of the bureaucracy.

As a result of the cabinet's personnel policies many more civil servants became party members and many who had previously not placed great store by their party membership now took it much more seriously. With parties formally establishing branch organizations in numerous government agencies and with bureaucratic cliques tending to follow party lines more closely than before, one's party membership

[77] The volume of circumstantial evidence on this matter is very large. See, e.g., Sutter, *op. cit.*, pp. 997 ff., 1067 ff., and *passim*. Specific proof was afforded in court cases involving receipt of bribes for party coffers. These led to the conviction of Djody Gondokusumo, Minister of Justice in the Ali cabinet and member of the PRN, of the PNI head of the East Java Trade Inspectorate in the Ali cabinet period, and, much later, of Iskaq himself. See *Duta Masjarakat* (Djakarta), Jan. 3, 1956; *Times of Indonesia*, Oct. 23, 1956; *Pedoman*, Dec. 11, 1956; and *Times of Indonesia*, Oct. 8, 1960.

could be a crucial factor determining both advancement possibilities and security of tenure. Most civil servants, especially in the non-technical ministries, became more dependent on top-level party politics. Any cabinet change, especially one which resulted in a particular minister's being displaced by a minister of a different and hostile party, could be expected to have major consequences for large numbers of higher- and middle-ranking civil servants.

In the political elite as a whole there was a weakening of the relative power of the government service vis-à-vis the political parties, with party leaders whose power base lay within the civil service becoming more dependent on those who controlled the party organization. A member of a government party who rose rapidly in the civil service as a result of his party membership was made aware that the decisions he took in his new post were subject to party approval.

These various changes worked to loosen the hold of administrative norms in much of the civil service. It is not only that the trading of favors was put on a political basis, but also that favor-trading became an increasingly important part of administration. Every instance where political considerations produced decisions violating civil service rules made it easier for civil servants to circumvent the requirement of neutrality in nonpolitical decisions. Departure from rules became more general and more widely accepted as normal.

At the same time "kicking upstairs" developed on a large scale. Numerous highly qualified and experienced civil servants associated with opposition parties were given posts which gave them vestigial status but no power and virtually no work. In this way the government service as a whole and in particular the Ministries of Foreign Affairs and the Interior were deprived of the services of a number of highly competent men, some of them men with a professional and nonpolitical approach to their work. Those who took the displaced men's positions sometimes had equal or greater professional skill, but the service lost resources of skill even then, because of the enforced idleness of those "kicked upstairs."

It is difficult to assess the over-all extent to which party control of particular ministries, and divisions and provincial offices of ministries, helped parties in their electioneering. There is no doubt that the PNI benefited greatly from its influence in the *pamong pradja* corps, the Ministry of Information, and the Mass Education Division of the Ministry of Education or that the Nahdatul Ulama gained considerably from its power within the Ministry of Religious Affairs. And there were parts of the country, for instance, a number of areas of Central Java, where both *pamong pradja* officials and Information officers adopted so strong a PNI posture as to make this party appear as virtually a state party.[78] Where this occurred it naturally weakened the sense of identification felt by opponents of the PNI with the state and the polity as a whole.

Nevertheless rural government maintained much of its nonparty character. The *pamong pradja* officials resented the parties in general even when they belonged to one; they saw the parties' commitment to representative regional government as a major threat to their own position. Most of them therefore preferred to continue in the corps's tradition of fatherly but also highly professionalized administration rather than become party agents. Equally important, the army and police were hostile to all the parties. They themselves were effectively prevented from active participation in the campaign—except in certain areas of Darul Islam activity.[79] Moreover, competition between the government parties, which was usually sharper in the regions than at the center, often served to create a system of mutual checks against too much use of government posts for party purposes.

THE POLITICS OF INDONESIANIZATION

If the Ali cabinet's personnel policies represent a radical departure from previous practice, this is true in even greater measure of many of this cabinet's policies in relation to the economy. Whereas the economic policies of the four earlier cabinets of our period were directed primarily toward restoration and expansion of production and were based on a strong belief in the need for financial stability, the Ali cabinet's policies, and in particular the policies of Iskaq, took the indigenization of economic life as a goal with primacy over both expansion of production and stability of prices.

Indonesianization was not of course new as a policy goal. Almost

[78] Feith, *The Indonesian Elections of 1955*, pp. 45 ff.

[79] The political energies of the police force were in part siphoned off as a result of the formation of the Police Employees Association of the Republic of Indonesia, an organization which presented a list of candidates in the elections (and succeeded in having one of them elected to parliament). In the case of the army the same function was performed to some extent by the IPKI (Ikatan Pendukung Kemerdekaan Indonesia, League of Upholders of the Indonesian Independence), an organization formed in May 1954 by a group of army officers (including the former Army Chief of Staff, Col. A. H. Nasution, and several others who had lost their positions of power as a result of the October 17 affair of 1952), veterans, and *pamong pradja* officials.

all the political leaders who wrote on economic policy in the period of Revolution argued for a transition from a colonial to a genuinely national economy. By this they usually meant three things, firstly, diversification of production (the elimination of the existing extreme dependence on raw-material exports), secondly, economic development and prosperity, and, thirdly, the transfer of control and management of economic enterprises from foreign (Western and Chinese) to Indonesian hands.[80] But when faced with the practical problem of priorities, the leaders of the first four cabinets of the post-1949 period decided, in effect, that the third of the goals was not to be pursued where this would be in conflict with the pursuit of the other two.

Indonesianization was therefore carried out at a relatively slow pace in the 1949–1953 period. Large foreign firms were obliged to give staff training and responsibility to more and more of their Indonesian employees. Several new government enterprises were established. And credit and licensing policies were devised to enable private Indonesian businesses, usually newly formed, to survive against the competition of the older mostly foreign-owned firms. This latter policy, as already shown, resulted in a fairly quick development of Indonesian enterprises, particularly in importing. But the economic dominance of foreigners, both the large Western firms and the large and small Chinese establishments, was left largely untouched.

With the Ali cabinet's assumption of office, de-alienization came to move at an entirely different speed. Iskaq, an energetic and tough-willed PNI leader who had been known for some time as an advocate of stronger measure to make the economy effectively "national," set about forthwith to provide credits, licenses, and a protected position to large numbers of new Indonesian firms. He achieved results with astonishing speed.

Whereas national importers had received 37.9 per cent of all exchange allocations for imports in the first four months of 1953, they were given an estimated 80 to 90 per cent in the fourteen months that Iskaq was in office.[81] The increase in the number of national importers was even more rapid. The number of recognized national firms, "Benteng group" firms—the term indicates that they were given

---

[80] For discussions of the "national economy" as a goal of the political leaders see Sutter, *op. cit.*, pp. 1184 ff., and Nan L. Amstutz, "The Rise of Indigenous Indonesian Importers, 1950–1955" (doctoral dissertation, Fletcher School, 1959), pp. 1–8. See also John Paul Meek, "The Government and Economic Development in Indonesia, 1950–54" (doctoral dissertation, University of Virginia, 1956), pp. 1–12.

[81] This is Mrs. Amstutz's estimate, *op. cit.*, p. 61.

exclusive importing rights to certain categories of goods—was 700 when the cabinet assumed office. It had been 250 in 1950. By the time of Iskaq's resignation in November 1954 it had risen to at least 2,211 and possibly 4,000 to 5,000.[82]

The picture in the field of banking was similar. The Ali cabinet's policy was to encourage the existence of new private banks operated by Indonesians by extending central bank credits to national banking establishments, while doing fairly little to supervise the use to which these credits were put. Thus whereas 20 private national banks were operating in mid-1953—the figure for December 1949 had been four —there were approximately 75 private Indonesian commercial banks in existence at the end of 1955.[83] Similarly a large number of new shipping companies were established by private Indonesian citizens, with most of the capital supplied by government lending institutions. By 1955, there were 65 private national shipping companies in existence, a huge increase over the number before 1953.[84]

With government credits so easily available to those with the right connections, "national" business attracted large numbers of persons without previous commercial experience, among them many former civil servants who felt that they could not live adequately on government salaries. One result was a variety of rackets. In the case of importing the new national companies were frequently "brief-case firms" which existed by reselling licenses to foreign and Chinese establishments. Frequently too they were "Ali-Baba" firms, straw-man Indonesian-Chinese establishments in which "Ali," the Indonesian titular head, secured the licenses and "Baba," his Chinese associate, ran the business. So it was that the head of the Central Import Office estimated in early 1955 that only 50 of the many national importing firms were bona fide establishments, with another 200 concerns on the border line.[85]

In the case of banking too, many of the new firms were get-rich-quick organizations, benefiting from the free availability of credits, the absence of firm controls to prevent arrearages, the lack of government-imposed standards, and the great discrepancy between the interest rates of the government banks and those charged in the countryside. As for the national shipping companies, only five of the

[82] See Amstutz, *op. cit.*, p. 53 and *passim* for a full discussion. Mrs. Amstutz's own estimate is 4,300.
[83] Sutter, *op. cit.*, pp. 992–994.   [84] *Ibid.*, p. 946.
[85] Amstutz, *op. cit.*, p. 144.

65 in existence in 1955 were considered by the governor of the Bank Indonesia to be operating on an economic basis.[86]

Although a number of academic studies have been made of the Ali cabinet's Indonesianization measures, it remains unclear how far these measures went to undermine the economic power of foreigners. Masjumi and PSI critics occasionally alleged that Iskaq's policies actually strengthened the power of foreign interests over the economy, but the evidence to support this contention is meager. Foreign economic power may have been increased where particular government departments became more corrupt. It certainly did not suffer where Indonesian nationals sold their licenses to foreigners or established straw-man firms with them. On the other hand, several of the large foreign banks lost power when government agencies shifted their deposits from them to Indonesian banks. The power of the Dutch interinsular shipping company KPM (Koninklijke Paketvaart Maatschappij) was affected when the government took shipping routes from it to give them to Indonesian shipping firms—to private concerns and especially to the government line Pelni (Pelajaran Nasional Indonesia, National Indonesian Shipping). And a sizable group of Chinese businessmen were hurt by the 1954 regulation which debarred persons without Indonesian citizenship from operating rice mills.[87]

Indigenization policies were immensely costly to the government treasury. The government's debt with the Bank Indonesia increased at an unprecedented pace. Between September 1953 and June 1954 it rose from Rp. 1,051 million to Rp. 3,410 million. In the same nine-month period foreign exchange reserves fell from Rp. 1,145 million to a minus entry of Rp. 20 million. In May 1954 the government introduced a drastic cut in imports. Nevertheless it was obliged in August to use an escape clause in the statutes of the Bank Indonesia in order

[86] Bank Indonesia, *Report for the Year 1954–1955* (Djakarta, 1955), p. 152, quoted in Sutter, *op. cit.*, p. 846. The figure five may be excessively low—a result of the governor's Masjumi political position and his commitment to financial orthodoxy.

[87] In its initial form this rice mills regulation referred to all persons "who are citizens other than citizens of Indonesia"—which in effect meant all ethnic Chinese, as the Peking government continued to claim all of these as citizens of China. Subsequently, this wording was eliminated. See Sutter, *op. cit.*, pp. 805–808. On the ways in which Chinese businessmen adjusted to the Ali cabinet's Indonesianization policies see Donald E. Willmott, *The National Status of the Chinese in Indonesia, 1900–1958* (rev. ed., Cornell Modern Indonesia Project, Monograph Series; Ithaca, N.Y., 1961), pp. 75–76, 140.

to continue borrowing from this central bank (although this meant that the ratio of the bank's assets to its loans fell below the statutory minimum of 20 per cent). It was not only the fostering of national firms which required the government to borrow so heavily from the central bank. The Atjeh war was a second major drain on funds. A third was caused by the fact that the Ali cabinet did not devote great political energies to stringent budgeting as the Wilopo cabinet had.[88] And a fourth resulted from further fairly rapid growth in the size of the civil service. Indonesianization does, however, account for a great deal of the rapid borrowing.

The first major groups to be affected adversely by fast Indonesianization were the manufacturers dependent on regular supplies of raw materials and the workers employed by them. The proliferation of channels of imports made for large irregularities in the flow of imports required for industry; lack of minor spare parts often caused lengthy slowdowns and work stoppages. In May 1954 when the government cut imports radically, the effect was to make small bottlenecks into large ones. The shortages of such items as industrial tools and conveyor belts—and, on the consumer side, commodities like canned milk, for which great demand existed in the white-collar strata—stood in sharp contrast to the entry of increased numbers of luxury cars and refrigerators. These luxury commodities, which the cabinet allowed certain groups to import as part of an incentive system designed to stimulate exports, were bidden for in a way which led to a skyrocketing of their prices. Speculation in such items became rampant.

From mid-1954 onward general inflation began to develop. The total size of the money supply, which had been Rp. 7,218 million in July 1953, reached Rp. 8,692 million in June 1954, thenceforth to rise rapidly till it reached Rp. 12,632 million in July 1955. Free market values of the U.S. dollar reflected the consequences: with the official rate fixed at Rp. 11.40, it was possible to sell the dollar for Rp. 25.50 in June 1953, for Rp. 27.00 in July 1954, and for Rp. 46.40 in July 1955. The index of prices of 44 imported items at Djakarta rose by 59.5 per cent between July 1953 and July 1955, with most of the increase developing in the second year. The rice price index rose by

---

[88] It was characteristic of this lack of emphasis on budgeting that the Wilopo cabinet's system of "For Service Use Only" signs on government cars fell into almost complete disuse. By mid-1954 the painted signs had been washed off from all but the oldest and least attractive of the government cars, and thus senior and middle-level civil servants were again able to use their office vehicles for out-of-office purposes.

52.3 per cent between August 1953 and June 1955 in Djakarta and by 24.7 per cent in rural Java and Madura.[89]

While this inflationary trend hit many groups in some degree, its deprivational effect was most marked for exporters and producers of export goods. It meant that the value of the rupiahs they received in exchange for their products not only was well below the real world value of these products, as it had long been, but also continued to fall.[90] It is true that they did not lose the entire margin of difference between the official and black-market rates, for there existed a variety of regulations designed to stimulate exports. There was a system of exchange certificates for certain products, a "barter system" in which exporters from certain areas were allowed a part of their earnings in foreign exchange, and provisions for certain "parallel transactions" in which *ad hoc* valuating took the place of a generally applicable exchange rate.[91] In addition, it was sometimes possible for a merchant to understate the value of an export consignment and keep the difference in actual proceeds abroad—when once he had made a suitable payment to a civil servant (for the civil servant himself or for his party).

But a large group of exporters derived no benefit from any of these chinks in the wall of exchange rate unreality. Moreover, when overseas prices for Indonesia's exports began to recover from their post-Korean War slump level—as rubber prices did slowly from mid-1954 onward—the government eliminated some of the export inducements. In any event the unreal exchange rate meant that large numbers of export producers were forced to sustain major losses of income, losses which were perceived to be all the more damaging as export producers compared themselves with the importers and other "national businessmen" with bureaucratic connections, especially in Djakarta, who appeared to be living most handsomely on the basis of government largess.

Many exporters and export producers found a way out of the situation through the smuggling trade, which flourished on a large

[89] Benjamin Higgins, *Indonesia's Economic Stabilization and Development* (New York: Institute of Pacific Relations, 1957), pp. 159, 162, 166, 167

[90] For a full, stimulating, and controversial discussion of this exchange rate factor by one who sees it as central to political alignments, see Hans O. Schmitt, "Some Monetary and Fiscal Consequences of Social Conflict in Indonesia, 1950–58" (doctoral dissertation, University of California, Berkeley, 1959), pp. 163–167, 263–267.

[91] See Bank Indonesia, *Report for the Year 1954–1955*, pp. 97–99; also Amstutz, *op. cit.*, pp. 136–142.

and growing scale. Indeed, so strong did the pressures for smuggling become that certain top army commanders came to play an active part in the trade, for what seems to have been the first time in our period. Thus in September 1954 the navy detained two Burmese ships carrying copra out of Minahasa in contravention of government regulations—only to find that their captains had authorizations signed by the army's acting territorial commander for East Indonesia, Lieutenant Colonel Warouw, and the army commander for Minahasa, Major Worang. Warouw defended himself by saying that he had approved such copra sales "in order to be able to finance military operations and resettlement schemes." [92] No government action was taken against him—in part because of realization in Djakarta that there was strong support for his actions in the copra-producing regions of East Indonesia where there was great resentment both of the increasingly fictitious exchange rate and of the government's monopolistic marketing organization.

The opposition was not slow to attack the Ali cabinet for its economic policies. As early as October 20, 1953, a parliamentary interpellation was introduced by the Masjumi member K. H. Tjikwan in which Iskaq as Economic Affairs Minister was asked to account for a number of his actions. Tjikwan asserted that the minister's allocations of foreign exchange to importers appeared to be arbitrary and planless and that the hundreds of new firms which the cabinet had recognized as national importers were receiving special consideration as regards foreign exchange, to the detriment of older national firms. In particular he attacked the action of the minister in stripping the Federation of Batik Co-operatives of its previous exclusive rights to import cambrics and giving these rights (equally exclusively) to certain specified firms of national importers.[93] Discussion on the motion became heated, with government-supporting speakers countering with numerous charges of favoritism and nepotism in the earlier cabinets. Finally, on December 2, 1953, Tjikwan called on the government to provide a precise formulation of its conception of what a national economy was and to present a plan for change from the colonial to the national economy.

Discussion on this motion was postponed till April. Then, however,

[92] *Pedoman*, Sept. 29, 1954. See also the full text of the question asked of the government by Subadio Sastrosatomo (PSI) and three other opposition M.P.'s, *Pedoman*, Oct. 6, 1954.

[93] See Sutter, *op. cit.*, pp. 1055–1060.

the motion was presented in a stronger form, as one of no confidence in Iskaq. In presenting their argument the opposition speakers charged that the various irregularities of Iskaq's policy formed a pattern. The aim, Jusuf Wibisono asserted, was not a "national" but a "Nationalist Party" economy.[94] Various opposition speakers made much of Iskaq's system of "special licenses," licenses issued personally by the minister, to firms which were ready to make a contribution—10 per cent of the value of the licenses according to Jusuf—to the PNI's election fund. They unearthed some conspicuous cases of personal-*cum*-political favoritism like that of the new paper importing firm Inter-kertas, half of whose capital had been contributed by the PNI's chairman, Sidik Djojosukarto. Not only had this firm obtained government recognition very fast, but it had also, the critic reported, been given large orders immediately by the Central Electoral Committee. And the Economic Affairs Minister had requested a foreign bank to provide it with a Rp. 10 million credit.[95]

These disclosures were shocking for a significant part of the political public. Moreover, they caused a number of members of government parties to take up positions against the cabinet. Thus when the Tjikwan motion was put to the vote on April 29 government party leaders had some difficulty in mustering their votes. The motion was eventually defeated 101 to 60, but only after there had been a number of signs of restiveness within the coalition.[96]

Rifts within the group of government parties began to appear seriously threatening in early July, when the Nahdatul Ulama submitted a Political Note calling for changes in the economic, personnel, and security policies of the cabinet. According to later reports the Note included the demand that the PNI Ministers of Economic Affairs and Finance and the PIR Interior Minister should resign and that the specific responsibility for security affairs which had been entrusted to Wongsonegoro as First Deputy Prime Minister should be transferred to the Second Deputy Prime Minister, the NU's Zainul Arifin.[97] On

[94] Kementerian Penerangan, *Ichtisar Parlemen* ("Parliamentary Chronicle"), 1954, p. 341, quoted in Sutter, *op. cit.*, p. 1071.

[95] Sutter, *op. cit.*, pp. 1075–1079.

[96] According to *Abadi* of April 28, 1954 (quoted in Sutter, *op. cit.*, p. 1075), five out of the seven M.P.'s of "a certain government party" insisted that they would back the Tjikwan motion and changed their minds only after the party leaders had made them a variety of promises. Sutter reports that nine members, representing five parties, abstained from voting on the motion and that the chairman of the NU fraction, A. A. Achsien, absented himself from the session.

[97] *Abadi*, Oct. 13, 1954.

July 21 the PIR party council, meeting in a joint session with the parliamentary fraction of the party, discussed the demands of a large group of the party's parliamentary representatives for the withdrawal of the PIR ministers from the cabinet. The meeting finally decided to work toward the cabinet's dissolution under certain conditions, a decision which was not, however, made public till much later.[98]

The situation of impending cabinet crisis dragged on throughout the third quarter of 1954. It was finally brought to a head in October by a split inside PIR. A party conference of PIR held at Solo in the beginning of the month was completely deadlocked on the issue of whether the party should continue in the cabinet.[99] On October 17 the anticabinet faction of the party succeeded in holding a meeting of the party council at which a decision was taken to demand that the cabinet resign by October 25. If the resignation was not forthcoming, the meeting resolved, the three PIR ministers would be withdrawn.[100]

From October 22, PIR was in effect two parties, each with its own set of office bearers, each claiming to be the original PIR and denouncing the other for causing the split, and each endeavoring to capture the party branches which were as yet uncommitted to either side. It soon became clear that the anticabinet party, commonly known as PIR-Hazairin or PIR-Tadjuddin Noor, commanded the support of PIR branches in most parts of the country outside Java. The procabinet party, known as PIR-Wongsonegoro, had the support of most of the Java branches and of a few in Sumatra.

The split had serious consequences for the cabinet because 19 of the 22 PIR parliamentarians—almost all of them were men from the BFO states—associated themselves with the party of Hazairin and Tadjuddin Noor. With its majority cut by 19 members, the cabinet would clearly be in a much weaker position in parliament and correspondingly more dependent on PKI votes.[101] Moreover, the Nahdatul

[98] See the statements of Wongsonegoro, *Abadi,* Oct. 28, 1954, and of Tadjuddin Noor, *Indonesia Raya,* Oct. 29, 1954.

[99] *Pemandangan,* Oct. 14, 1954.

[100] For the full text of the statement see *Abadi,* Oct. 18, 1954.

[101] However, the parliamentary position of the cabinet had been enhanced markedly as a result of a law enacted in Dec. 1953, on parliamentary initiative, for the filling of vacancies in parliament which had resulted from death or resignation. By the terms of this law the vacancies could be filled by the parties or fractions concerned or, in the case of nonparty and nonfraction members, by cabinet appointment. On the basis of this law 23 new members were sworn in between

Ulama was still pressing the demands of its Political Note of July. And on October 14 the PSII had called for the resignation of the Ministers of Economic Affairs, Finance, and the Interior.

On October 22 the three PIR ministers resigned from the cabinet. Hazairin declared he was complying with the decision of the October 17 meeting. Wongsonegoro and Roosseno, who supported the cabinet's continued functioning, said they were resigning "in order to clear the air until a definite viewpoint is expressed by the new PIR party council and in order to give the government-supporting parties an opportunity to review the cabinet's composition." [102]

Reshuffling portfolios to keep the coalition in existence was no easy task. The numerous conflicts between government parties led many opposition members to believe that it could not be accomplished and that a cabinet resignation was in sight. As in most previous situations where a cabinet's position had become shaky, there were a number of opposition calls for a presidential (in this case read Hatta-led) cabinet.[103] But eventually Prime Minister Ali succeeded in bringing about a reshuffle with which the respective parties of the cabinet were satisfied.[104] The reshuffled cabinet was not strong in parliamentary support, but it managed to weather the crisis. On December 14 it succeeded in defeating by 115 to 92 the motion of no confidence in the cabinet moved by Jusuf Wibisono. It was the first time in the history of the Indonesian parliament that an outright no-confidence motion had been moved against the whole cabinet. The government's margin of survival was not great—opposition critics made much of the point that it could not have obtained its majority if PKI members and sympathizers had been instructed to abstain on the ballot—but the fact was that it had survived.

This success was due in the first place to the PNI's willingness to have Mr. Iskaq step down. The public image of the cabinet became more favorable as a result of the early actions of Iskaq's successor, Professor Roosseno, particularly certain reforms in the foreign trade

---

Feb. and Aug. 1954. Two of them were cabinet nominees and all but seven were supporters of the cabinet. See Kementerian Penerangan, *Kepartaian dan Parlementaria di Indonesia* ("Political Parties and Parliamentary Affairs in Indonesia"; Djakarta: Kementerian Penerangan, 1954), pp. 670–673.

[102] *Pedoman*, Oct. 23, 1954.

[103] See the statement of the Gerakan Pemuda Indonesia Angkatan-Proklamasi (Indonesian Youth Movement of the Generation of the Proclamation of Independence), *Abadi*, Oct. 22, 1954, and also the editorial in *Indonesia Raya*, Oct 29, 1954.

[104] For the changes made see p. 338, note 25.

sector.[105] A second important factor in the cabinet's survival was the active support of President Soekarno. This operated partly through public declarations, most notably the Palembang speech of early November in which the President alleged that opposition leaders were involved in a foreign plot to overthrow the cabinet. It was also related to fear of the President's power to dissolve parliament. Many in the government parties who considered supporting the cabinet's resignation as an alternative to a reshuffle edged away from this course because they thought that the President might act as Sartono, the chairman of parliament, had warned in the previous December and join with the Prime Minister to dissolve parliament, maintaining the cabinet on an extraparliamentary basis until elections were held.

Most important perhaps, the coalition partners had worked out minimally satisfactory ways of co-operating with one another. The leaders of the more important parties in the cabinet shared certain values, holding a common hostility to Masjumi Islamic modernism on the one hand and the "administrator" view of government and politics on the other. And all of them had benefited from the cabinet's generous apportioning of patronage. Thus there was a general feeling among them that their grievances against one another should be settled by the *intra muros* method of reshuffling. None of them could feel certain that the alternative power arrangements which would grow out of a cabinet resignation would serve their interests as well.

After the cabinet had survived its test vote of December 14, 1954, it had a number of months of relative political calm. From January 1955 much attention was given to the Asian-African Conference, now due to be held in Bandung in April. Moreover, elections were promised for August 1955. It seemed increasingly likely that the Ali cabinet would stay in power until the elections were over.

But the first six months of 1955 were a time of extraordinarily fast price rises, with speculation becoming more rife than ever in our period. A new Plymouth or Dodge would often sell for Rp. 400,000 ($35,088 at the official rate or approximately $10,000 at current black-market rates). The number of newly imported luxury cars was large,

---

[105] Thus on Dec. 6 Roosseno ordered a new screening of the bank accounts of importers, with the declared aim of reducing the number of national importers by half (Sutter, *op. cit.*, p. 1027). He did not in fact complete the rescreening before the Ali cabinet fell more than seven months later, but he was responsible for a number of measures which went some way toward tightening government controls over national importers and national banks. See Schmitt, *op. cit.*, pp. 176–177, and Amstutz, *op. cit.*, pp. 65–68.

and the much-read wags of the opposition dailies' gossip columns coined epithets like "Kabinet Mercedes-Benz" and "Kabinet Opel." Still more important, textile prices were rising particularly fast, a fact which was to make itself felt especially in April and May, with the approach of the Lebaran holidays when it is customary to buy new clothes. In Djakarta the textile price index for April 1955 was 103.5 per cent higher than it had been a year earlier.[106]

Thus the cabinet was again under political pressure for its economic policies. In May the PSI-oriented trade union federation KBSI (Kesatuan Buruh Seluruh Indonesia, All-Indonesian Unity of Labor) held a one-day demonstration strike against high prices. In June the PNI executive took the unusual step of issuing a statement which implied criticism of the cabinet's economic policies—apparently in an effort to disclaim responsibility for the inflation in the face of the impending elections.[107] At the same time the opposition press made much of scandals and corruption, especially of the "Hong Kong barter scandal" in which it was discovered that the system of allowing selected exporters to retain foreign exchange had opened the way to gross corruption. This was the context in which the cabinet had to fight its last battles. Before a discussion of these, however, the cabinet's actions in the field of foreign relations must be considered.

FOREIGN POLICY AND THE BANDUNG CONFERENCE

With foreign policy, as with so much else, the first Ali cabinet set off on new courses. Several of the previous cabinets had declared that their foreign policy was not only independent, but active. In effect, however, the international posture of all the former cabinets was primarily passive. For them home policy had absolute priority over foreign relations. They saw Indonesia as a country still young and finding its feet in the world, a country whose principal task was to sort out its own pressing problems. In foreign relations their concern was to find the most advantageous ways of channeling international pressures so that they would be of assistance to Indonesia in its internal development and, more important, not stand in the way of such development. They saw themselves as necessarily limited to responding to outside, principally Western, initiatives. They were not concerned—except briefly and in a limited way under Foreign Minister Subardjo of the Sukiman cabinet—with attempting to seize the diplomatic initiative.

The Ali cabinet's view of Indonesia's situation was different. It saw

[106] Higgins, *op. cit.*, p. 166.   [107] *Pedoman,* June 13, 1955.

Indonesia's internal problems as great but not oppressive, and it looked out on the world with a sense of confidence born of faith in Asia resurgent. It was militantly anticolonial and aspired to gain for Indonesia a position of leadership within the anticolonialist movement. Moreover, it was keenly aware of the integrative functions of an active foreign policy and of the consequent internal political advantages. Therefore the cabinet set forth, under the vigorous leadership of its ex-diplomat Prime Minister, to make its foreign policy truly active.

It was some time before the contrast emerged. In presenting his program to parliament, the Prime Minister stressed that continuity would be maintained with the foreign policy positions adopted by previous cabinets.[108] He declared at the same time that his cabinet would implement the Rondonuwu motion (for the establishment of an Indonesian Embassy in Moscow by the end of 1953), but added "after making the best possible preparations and provisions." [109] An Indonesian Embassy was not actually established in Moscow until March 1954.

It was in the area of Sino-American relations that the Ali cabinet found its opportunities for an active foreign policy. The cabinet's term of office began shortly after two important events, Stalin's death in March 1953 and the Korean War armistice of July 27. From this time the Chinese People's Republic began to adopt increasingly conciliatory external positions, both ideologically—the change from the left-wing "join the Revolutionaries" line to the right-wing line of "Union with All"—and in diplomatic relations. The earlier attacks on Asian nationalist and neutralist leaders as functionaries of imperialism were halted, and there were signs that China sought to develop more regular relations with the states of non-Communist Asia.

To the uncommitted powers of Asia, particularly India, Burma, and Indonesia, these seemed to be tendencies worthy of the strongest encouragement. Those in authority in these countries viewed Communist China as a great power whose existence and internal stability were not to be denied, and some of them sympathized with its leaders, whom they saw as honest and dedicated men pushing ahead with great determination toward social and economic goals which were

[108] *Keterangan dan Djawaban Pemerintah atas Program Kabinet Ali Sastroamidjojo* ("The Government's Statement on the Program of the Ali Sastroamidjojo Cabinet and Its Replies to Parliamentary Criticism"; Djakarta: Kementerian Penerangan, 1953), pp. 28–32.
[109] *Ibid.*, pp. 32–33.

basically similar to their own. All of them believed that the aggressive tendencies which China had shown were due in large part to its exclusion from the community of nations.

This was of course in complete contrast with the United States view of China. The United States did not accept the Peking government as legitimate; indeed, it was in some measure committed to its overthrow. It regarded the C.P.R. as an inherently aggressive regime, whose expansionist tendencies could be held in check only by the application of superior force from outside. Thus it saw the C.P.R.'s conciliatory behavior of 1953 and 1954 as representing merely a temporary change of tactics.

The position of the uncommitted states of Asia came into particularly sharp conflict with the American position when the Indochina crisis began in early 1954. At this time the Communist-led Vietminh was winning major military victories against the French—thanks in some part to military assistance from Peking. One hope of reaching an over-all settlement in Indochina lay in the projected Geneva conference, at which both China and the United States were to be represented. But in late March 1954, as the Geneva conference was about to begin, France requested direct U.S. military intervention in the area, believing this the one way to save its position, and for several weeks there seemed a possibility that the United States might accede to the request. At the same time the United States was both skeptical and apprehensive about what the Geneva conference might achieve and was concentrating its own efforts on the fashioning of a Southeast Asian military alliance to prevent the Vietminh success from spilling over into other countries of the area.[110]

United States intervention and the possibility of a second Korea were averted as a result of several factors. Most important probably was British pressure to restrain the United States. But this was not a situation in which the uncommitted states of Asia (or indeed other Asian states which were not so uncommitted) were prepared to have their views left out of account. The governments of the uncommitted states in the main regarded the Vietminh with a good deal of sympathy, seeing its struggle as primarily a nationalist one against an intransigent colonialism. All of them were concerned that an effort be made to create peace in Indochina and prevent the development of a major Sino-American war in this part of Southeast Asia. As they saw

[110] See Miriam Farley, *The United States and Southeast Asia 1950–55* (New York: Institute of Pacific Relations, 1956), pp. 9–18.

it, such an effort required in the first place the restraining of America.

This situation of March and April 1954 gave rise to the first of the Prime Ministers' meetings of what were thenceforth to be known as the Colombo Powers. In response to Nehru's initiative, the Prime Ministers of India, Pakistan, Ceylon, Burma, and Indonesia conferred at Colombo between April 28 and May 2—during the first week of the Geneva conference—in an effort to exert pressure in favor of the conciliatory elements at Geneva, a peaceful solution in Indochina, and the negotiated settlement of Asian Cold War issues in general.

At this first Colombo Powers meeting Indonesia's Ali Sastroamidjojo proposed the idea which was to make him world-famous. He suggested to the other four Prime Ministers that they should jointly sponsor a large and high-level conference of the independent states of Asia and Africa, to be held in Indonesia. The conference, he declared, not only would contribute to the relaxation of Cold War tensions in the two continents, but would also serve as a rallying point for the continuing struggle of Asians and Africans against colonialism.

Initial responses to Ali's idea were cool. The predominant Indian view of Indonesia was one of a country with very great internal problems which it ought to be solving before it embarked on bold international ventures.[111] Nehru and Burma's U Nu told their Indonesian counterpart that they did not think the large conference a useful or feasible project.[112] The meeting finally resolved that the proposal should be given "further study."

But a series of developments in the middle of 1954 made Nehru change his mind. In June, Chou En-lai went to New Delhi, and Nehru became more convinced than ever of the need to encourage the trends in Chinese policy which were working to make the C.P.R. come to terms with its neighbors. Thus the two men announced the Panch Shila, or Five Principles of Peaceful Coexistence. Chou En-lai's actions in the last and crucial stages of the Geneva conference in July served to strengthen Indian faith in the genuineness of the Chinese wish for peace.

In September, Ali went to Delhi. To the surprise of many, and to the great disappointment of Ali's domestic critics, particularly those of the India-philic PSI, the Indian reception was one of warm accla-

[111] See Phyllis Rolnick, "Indian Attitudes towards Indonesia, Fall 1950–Spring 1955" (unpublished paper, Cornell Modern Indonesia Project, 1959).
[112] George McT. Kahin, *The Asian-African Conference, Bandung, Indonesia, April 1955* (Ithaca, N.Y.: Cornell University Press, 1956), p. 2.

mation.[113] At this meeting Nehru gave his blessing to the Asian-African Conference project, provided that China were invited to attend. Ali's original proposal had been for a conference of UN members only, but he agreed to the change. Although the Indonesian Prime Minister continued to see the conference more in terms of its symbolization of Asian-African resurgence and solidarity than in the light of the world-level diplomatic tasks which were primary for his Indian colleague, there was a broad area of agreement between the two men. Both hoped that the conference would succeed in drawing China into closer association with its fellow Asian powers and thus perhaps loosen its ties to the Soviet Union. Ali shared much of Nehru's strong conviction that it was possible and desirable for the conference to formulate general principles which China and all other states of the area could accept and which would be all the more difficult to violate because they had been imposed by Asians upon themselves.[114]

With Nehru's blessing secured, it was not long before the conference was actually scheduled. The Prime Ministers of the five Colombo Powers met at Bogor, Indonesia, in late December 1954 and there came to a series of agreements on a conference to be held at Bandung for a week beginning April 18. At the same time they established a Joint Secretariat for the conference, on which the five sponsoring powers had representation, with Indonesia entrusted with the chairmanship. Invitations were thereupon sent to 30 independent or almost independent states of Asia and Africa—including China and North Vietnam (as well as South Vietnam). The two Koreas, Outer Mongolia, Israel, and South Africa were the independent states of the two continents not invited; the white-governed Central African Federation was the one invitee which declined. Twenty-nine states agreed to attend and to be represented at a ministerial level.

Meanwhile the cabinet had been active in improving Indonesia's relations with China. We have noted how Sino-Indonesian relations were strained for much of the period before the Ali cabinet took office. The strain was greatest when the Sukiman cabinet was in office, but it extended over almost the whole of this earlier period. No Indonesian ambassador to Peking was appointed until May 1953.

But by mid-1953 China had shown a desire for more cordial relations with Indonesia. From 1951 onward invitations had been extended for Indonesian leaders of an increasingly wide range of political views to visit the People's Republic, and by 1952 wholesale attacks

[113] Rolnick, *op. cit.*   [114] Kahin, *The Asian-African Conference,* pp. 4–5.

on the Indonesian leadership were beginning to disappear from the Chinese press.[115] China also gave indications of wanting to trade with Indonesia.

Accordingly in December 1953 the Ali cabinet concluded Indonesia's first trade agreement with Peking. The total value of the trade provided for under the treaty was only $2 million (for the year 1954).[116] And the goods which Indonesia was to sell would not include strategic commodities covered under the UN embargo resolution of 1951. But it was a significant beginning. In August 1954 the trade agreement was renewed for 1955, and the value of goods to be traded was raised to $16.8 million. In the same month a Chinese pavilion was opened at an international trade fair in Djakarta, alongside Russian and American pavilions.

In May 1954 the Ali cabinet proposed a nonaggression pact in which China, India, Burma, and Indonesia would become partners, in effect a pact to counterbalance the Southeast Asia pact which America's Dulles was preparing. Although the idea came to nothing, it cannot but have pleased the C.P.R. Then in December 1954 and February 1955 the government deported two resident Chinese who had been active political workers for the Kuomintang in Indonesia. Indonesian spokesmen made a number of fairly pro-Peking statements in the course of the January 1955 crisis over the offshore islands in the Formosa Straits.

Indonesian government leaders had been dissatisfied for some time with the existing legal position of their country's Chinese minority. They were concerned about the fact that China continued to claim as its citizens persons who had acquired Indonesian citizenship under the passive choice system established under the Round Table Conference Agreement. Some of them felt that this passive system had made it too easy for Chinese persons born in Indonesia to become Indonesian citizens. Thus when the C.P.R. government announced in April 1954 that it was willing to negotiate with Southeast Asian countries on the citizenship of their resident Chinese,[117] the Ali cabinet quickly accepted the offer. Talks between Indonesian and Chinese representatives were held intermittently for almost a year, and Prime Minister Nehru appears to have assisted Indonesia in pressing Chou

[115] See David P. Mozingo, "Sino-Indonesian Relations" (unpublished paper, Cornell Modern Indonesia Project, 1960).
[116] See *Antara*, Jan. 16, 18, 1954.
[117] *Antara*, April 7, 1954, quoted in Mozingo, "Sino-Indonesian Relations."

En-İai to make concessions to the Indonesian point of view.[118] The matter was finally settled at the Bandung conference, when Chou and Indonesia's Foreign Minister, Sunario, joined to sign a Dual Nationality Agreement.[119]

This was an important agreement. Under it, persons with dual nationality—who these were was left unstated—would be asked to make an active choice and become either Indonesian or Chinese nationals; both states would recognize the exclusive validity of these persons' citizenship once the decision had been made. The citizenship of those failing to choose either way would be determined by paternal ancestry. One significance of this lay in the fact that it incorporated an unprecedented concession to the effect that China would in certain circumstances waive her traditional claim that all ethnic Chinese were her nationals. In addition, Indonesia persuaded China to agree to a treaty whereby it would be relatively difficult for Chinese residents to become Indonesian nationals. The agreement represented an important diplomatic victory for Prime Minister Ali.[120]

Sino-Indonesian relations were becoming progressively more cordial. The zenith was reached when the two countries' Prime Ministers exchanged visits of good will. Between April 25 and 28, immediately after the conclusion of the Bandung conference, Chou En-lai was an official guest of the Indonesian government. Ali was in China between May 26 and June 7, returning with certain further concessions to the Indonesian point of view on the citizenship question and going on to make a particularly strong statement of support for the Peking position on Taiwan.[121] A great deal had changed since the time only a little

[118] Willmott, *op. cit.*, p. 44. See also V. Hanssens, "The Campaign against the Nationalist Chinese in Indonesia," in B. H. M. Vlekke, ed., *Indonesia's Struggle, 1957–58* (The Hague: Netherlands Institute of International Affairs, 1959), p. 62.

[119] For the text of the treaty and a full discussion of its provisions see Willmott, *op. cit.*, pp. 44–66, 130–134. See also Mozingo, "Sino-Indonesian Relations," and Mary F. Somers, "Questions concerning the Chinese in Indonesia since the Chou-Sunario Treaty" (unpublished paper, Cornell Modern Indonesia Project, 1960).

[120] There was hostility toward it from many Chinese persons of Indonesian citizenship who resented the idea that they should have to make their choice once more. In addition, several parties opposed the agreement. The Indonesian parliament ratified the treaty on Dec. 17, 1957. But, for a complicated series of reasons, the instruments of ratification were not exchanged until Jan. 20, 1960. The two-year option period began as of that date. See Somers, *op. cit.*; also David Mozingo, "The Sino-Indonesian Dual Nationality Treaty," *Asian Survey*, I, no. 10 (Dec. 1961), 25–31.

[121] In a statement of elucidation of an earlier less specific Indonesian endorsement of the C.P.R. stand, the Indonesian Prime Minister declared that "China's exercise of its own sovereignty over Taiwan is purely a matter of internal affairs." See *PIA News Bulletin* (hereafter cited as *PIA;* formerly *Aneta*), June 11, 1955.

more than two years earlier when Indonesia had preferred to stall on the sending of an ambassador to Peking. As the U.S. government saw it, Indonesia had moved fast from a friendly neutralism to one which was pregnant with hostility.

But perhaps even more important than the change in Indonesia's posture toward China was the different way in which Indonesian nationalism was projected into international affairs in the Ali cabinet period. This can be seen as one looks at the what the cabinet attempted in relation to West Irian.

The year 1954 saw the first, or first major, series of experiments with infiltration into Irian. After two minor attempts made early in the year, a group of 48 infantrymen landed on the Irianese south coast in late October. Some of these were taken by the Dutch and subsequently tried (and in part repatriated), while another group left the territory again, taking a Dutch police officer with them. Whatever the precise purpose of these forays, for which the government did not admit responsibility, they indicated a willingness to go outside the field of diplomacy in pursuit of the West Irian goal.[122]

Diplomatic efforts were not abandoned, however. Between June and early August 1954 an Indonesian delegation under Foreign Minister Sunarjo negotiated with the Netherlands in an effort to annul the Netherlands-Indonesian Union and modify the Round Table Conference agreements. The result was the Sunario-Luns Protocol, an agreement which dissolved the all but fictitious Union and canceled certain cultural and military clauses of the Round Table Conference settlement, along with small portions of the financial and economic clauses.[123] From the Indonesian nationalist position the agreement was a minor success, if not a failure, for it left the major guarantees of Dutch investment untouched. Most important of all, the cabinet had won no concessions on the claim to West Irian. Its own prior declarations of intent notwithstanding, the Indonesian delegation had conducted negotiations with the Dutch despite steadfast refusal by the Dutch to discuss the subject of West Irian in any formal way.

The government's next step was something new. On August 17, 1954, a day chosen with appropriate concern for nationalist symbolism, the Indonesian representative to the United Nations requested the

[122] F. J. F. M. Duynstee, *Nieuw Guinea als Schakel tussen Nederland en Indonesië* (Amsterdam: De Bezige Bij, 1961), pp. 221–222; Justus M. van der Kroef, *The West New Guinea Dispute* (New York: Institute of Pacific Relations, 1958), p. 21.

[123] *Antara*, Aug. 11, 1954. See also van der Kroef, *The West New Guinea Dispute*, p. 19, and Duynstee, *op. cit.*, pp. 214–217.

UN Secretary-General to place the West Irian question on the agenda of that year's regular session of the General Assembly. The item was included on the agenda on September 24. Then came the struggle for votes. When debate was begun on the issue, Indonesia came forth with ringing declarations of the case against colonial rule. But the draft resolution which Indonesia finally submitted was in fact very mild. It merely expressed the hope that the two governments would "pursue their endeavours in respect to the dispute that now exists between them to find a solution in conformity with the principles of the Charter of the United Nations." [124] Nevertheless, Indonesia failed by 7 votes to obtain the necessary two-thirds majority. When voting was held on December 10 the division was 34 to 23, with 10 abstentions.

This was a second rebuff, but it did not leave the cabinet off base. In the first place, this cabinet, in contrast with its predecessors, associated itself with the groups which expressed radical nationalist sentiment on the Iran issue. The mass meetings which took place in Indonesia while the General Assembly was discussing the issue were organized principally by the PNI, the Moslem League parties, and the PKI, and thus the cabinet could indirectly exercise control over them. The small Murba party excepted, there was no opposition group in a position to outdo the cabinet with radical nationalist appeals. In addition, plans were in hand for a series of next steps. On December 18 President Soekarno called for an All-Indonesian Congress by which it would be possible to overcome internal divisions and create power to carry on the struggle for West Irian. At the Bogor conference later in the month Prime Minister Ali succeeded in persuading the other four Prime Ministers of the Colombo Powers group to include a strong statement of support for the Indonesian position on Irian in their final communiqué.[125] And after Bogor would come Bandung.

The Bandung conference was clearly the Ali cabinet's big triumph. It is impossible here to assess the conference as an event in diplomatic history or as an instrument of the China policy of Nehru and those who thought like him. But there can be little doubt that it was highly successful in establishing and demonstrating a sense of unity and solidarity among leaders of the ex-colonial world. In spite of the many serious political disputes which arose in the conference's committees,

[124] Robert C. Bone, Jr., *The Dynamics of the Western New Guinea (Irian Barat) Problem* (Cornell Modern Indonesia Project, Interim Reports Series; Ithaca, N.Y., 1958), p. 130.
[125] *Antara,* Dec. 30, 1954.

the conference did succeed in fashioning a minimal consensus. The final communiqué, for which unanimous assent was obtained from the 29 powers, was a general but by no means a purely platitudinous document.[126]

For Indonesia the triumph was particularly great. It was not only that the conference was an Indonesian idea or that Bandung was an Indonesian city. In addition, administrative arrangements went very much better than most observers had expected. And security arrangements were effective and fairly inconspicuous—a major achievement in view of the size of the conference, its location not far from Darul Islam fastnesses, and the fact that Chou En-lai for one was expected to attract would-be assassins among the (Chinese) residents of Indonesia. Furthermore, Indonesia gained two specific diplomatic victories in the course of the conference, the signing of the Dual Nationality Agreement and the inclusion of an affirmation of support for the West Irian claim in the final communiqué.[127]

In addition, the actual procedures of the conference were studded with honors for Indonesia. Its Prime Minister Ali was elected president of the Conference. The secretary-general of its Foreign Affairs Ministry, Roeslan Abdulgani, who had headed the Joint Secretariat which prepared the conference, was chosen secretary-general. Ministers Roosseno and Yamin were elected to chair the Economic Committee and the Cultural Committee respectively. Most important of all, granted the central importance of symbolism for the conference as a whole, Indonesia supplied the only two speakers of the opening session, President Soekarno and Prime Minister Ali Sastroamidjojo.

It goes without saying that the glory of Bandung was important for domestic politics. Whereas opposition critics had been inclined up to the end of March 1955 to belittle and ridicule the planned conference and decry it as a gimmick designed to distract attention from pressing problems at home,[128] they could no longer afford to do this when the

---

[126] For the text see Kahin, *The Asian-African Conference*, pp. 76–85.

[127] The relevant sections read: "The Asian-African Conference, in the context of its expressed attitude on the abolition of colonialism, supported the position of Indonesia in the case of West Irian based on the relevant agreements between Indonesia and the Netherlands.

"The Asian-African Conference urged the Netherlands Government to reopen negotiations as soon as possible, to implement their obligations under the above-mentioned agreements and expressed the earnest hope that the United Nations would assist the parties concerned in finding a peaceful solution to the dispute" (quoted in *ibid.*, p. 82).

[128] See, for instance, *Indonesia Raya*, Dec. 3, 1954, and *Pedoman*, Feb. 22, 1955.

conference came closer. The conference's appeal was too great. The Information Ministry spread knowledge of plans for it far and wide, and when the conference actually began, it made much of the important role which President Soekarno and Prime Minister Ali were playing there. Immediately after the conference the opposition press was able to strip the government of a little of its newly won prestige by publicizing a discovery that the conference's Joint Secretariat had organized a "Hospitality Committee" to provide for the sexual diversion of the delegates. But the sense of national pride which the conference had aroused in the political public in general, as well as beyond it, was not easily dispelled.

The Ali cabinet's foreign policy was vigorous, and if a foreign policy's effectiveness is judged by its ability to put a country "on the map," to make it a factor to be reckoned with in the foreign ministries of the world, it was certainly effective. If it lacked the militancy and flamboyancy which came to characterize Indonesia's approach to the outside world in later years, it was much more active and spirited than had been the foreign policy of the previous four cabinets. Diplomatic professionalism and the symbols of anticolonialism proved to be a powerful combination.

THE ARMY AND THE TOPPLING OF THE CABINET

If there is any one factor which can be considered of key importance in giving the Ali cabinet its longevity, it is the army. In the case of the three previous cabinets, the army and President Soekarno were always in some measure balanced off against one another. The Natsir and Wilopo cabinets could work better with the army leadership than with the President; the Sukiman cabinet by contrast leaned more on the President and was frequently in conflict with the army. And there were significant differences in the degree to which different cabinets acted in independence of each of these extraparliamentary centers of power. But all three cabinets, and in a somewhat different sense the Hatta cabinet before them, were limited in the actions they could take by the existence of these two major power centers, one the rival of the other, each endowed with strong claims to pronounce on the meaning of independence and each inclined to view itself as the ultimate guardian of the state's welfare. None of the three cabinets could go too far in defiance of either Soekarno or the leaders of the army without courting the possibility of its overthrow.

The maintenance of this balance depended, however, on a minimal army unity. The army leaders could act as a counterpoise to the President only as long as their authority to represent the army in the over-all politics of the country was not challenged inside their own force. Yet their ability to do this was ended by the crisis of October 17, 1952. As we have seen, the October 17 affair ended with a number of the army's top leaders removed from their posts, with the officer corps far more deeply divided than theretofore, and with hierarchical authority in the army greatly weakened. Thus from November 1952 four territorial commands were controlled by the "pro-October 17 group," the other three by the "anti-October 17 group." Not only was there a strengthening of the pro-Soekarno and radically nationalist elements in the army. In addition, the over-all bargaining strength of the army vis-à-vis everyone else in the political arena was seriously impaired.

These two related changes were central aspects of the new power situation which made possible the Wilopo cabinet's downfall and its replacement by the cabinet of Ali. Further, the ability of the Ali cabinet to survive was largely a function of the maintenance of this new constellation of power. Having the fullest support of the President, the cabinet could effectively meet such challenges as were proffered— but only so long as there was no restoration of the counterpoise situation in which the President's influence was matched and in some measure offset by the influence of the army. Thus the cabinet had to fear two eventualities, firstly, a possible weakening of the pro-Soekarno "anti-October 17 group" within the army and, secondly, a healing of the October 17 divisions such as would enable the army once more to bargain with a single voice in the marketplace of national politics.

For a long time the cabinet succeeded in maintaining the army *status quo*. It continued to view the matter of the October 17 affair as unresolved, encouraging the expectation that its chief public prosecutor might at any time lodge charges against the leaders of the "pro-October 17 group." Its Defense Minister, Iwa Kusumasumantri, devised personnel policies to encourage the "anti-October 17 group" and in that way maintain the cleavage. On November 4, 1953, reportedly in implementation of an agreement reached between the President and Wongsonegoro at the time of the cabinet's formation, the cabinet produced a regulation abolishing the post of Armed Forces Chief of Staff.[129] The regulation was an indirect way of ousting Major

[129] See *Abadi*, Nov. 5, 1953.

General Simatupang, the last survivor of the quadrumvirate (the Sultan of Jogjakarta, Ali Budiardjo, Simatupang, and Nasution) which had held power in the Defense Ministry before October 17, 1952.[130]

In early December 1953 Iwa took a very much bolder step. Without prior consultation with the Acting Chief of Staff of the Army, Colonel Bambang Sugeng, he appointed Colonel Zulkifli Lubis, the intelligence officer and prominent leader of the "anti-October 17 group" to be Deputy Chief of Staff. At the same time he moved two other members of this group, Lieutenant Colonels Sapari and Abimanju, into high positions in the General Staff. This was a direct affront not only to Bambang Sugeng's authority, but also to the principle on which he had insisted earlier that no actions involving the October 17 affair cleavages would be taken from outside the army, at least not until there had been a judicial settlement of the affair. The Acting Chief of Staff therefore called a conference of the seven territorial commanders, telling them that he had asked to be relieved of his duties. Four of the seven commanders, the four of the "pro-October 17 group," gave vigorous support to Bambang Sugeng and urged various steps to force the minister's resignation. For a brief period it seemed that either Iwa or Bambang Sugeng would have to resign. But the cleavages of 1952 were still working to the government's advantage. The four "pro-October 17 group" commanders were eventually persuaded to forego their demands for Iwa's resignation, and Bambang Sugeng withdrew his resignation, accepting Lubis and Iwa's other controversial nominees in their new posts.

For most of 1954 the situation remained largely unchanged. There were numerous instances of conflict between the cabinet and particular sections of the army. North Sumatra's Colonel Simbolon was frequently at odds with the cabinet on matters related to military action against the Daud Beureueh revolt in Atjeh. West Java's Colonel Kawilarang made a number of arrests which antagonized the government, including in May 1954 the arrest of Sidik Kertapati, a parliamentarian of the Defense Minister's own Progressive Fraction. More significantly, East Indonesia's Warouw, who had been in the "anti-October 17" camp, was in conflict with the central government on numerous occasions in 1954 over copra smuggling and several other

[130] The Masjumi's Burhanuddin Harahap, moving a parliamentary motion for the regulation to be revoked, argued that the government was basing its personnel policy on the October 17 cleavage and charged Defense Minister Iwa Kusumasumantri with attempting excessive interference in the work of the armed forces. The motion was defeated by 101 votes to 69 on Feb. 19, 1954.

issues. These commanders and other officers with them were antagonized by Iwa's placement policies in the army. Furthermore, almost
all officers were convinced that the army's budget was grossly inadequate. But when conflicts came to the fore on these matters, they were
nearly always between the cabinet or the Minister of Defense and
particular commanders. The army as such remained too divided to
act concertedly in advancing its interests.

By the beginning of 1955, however, the situation had changed. Indeed, the beginning of the change can be traced to mid-1954. Then a
group of prominent officers representing the two chief factions in the
army came together to plan an over-all reconciliation.[131] The source
of the initiative here remains unclear, but the actions taken appear to
have had the active support of Bambang Sugeng as Chief of Staff.
Among the active participants in the reconciliation moves were Zulkifli
Lubis and Sapari from the side of the "anti-October 17 group" as
well as Colonel Suprapto and Lieutenant Colonels Sutoko and S. Parman of the "pro-October 17 group." These officers toured the various
commands to spread their ideas, which were subsequently discussed
at a meeting of territorial commanders and headquarters officers held
in Djakarta on December 3, 1954. Not long after this plans were in
hand for a large conference devoted principally to achieving and for-
malizing reconciliation between the factions formed on the October 17
issue.

This larger meeting took place in Jogjakarta from February 17 to
25, 1955. Two hundred and seventy officers, including almost every
leading figure in the army, attended, and both pro- and anti-October
17 factions were fully represented. After several days of speeches, a
working committee of 50 officers was elected to draft a resolution and
a charter of unity. On February 24 the resolution and the charter were
accepted by the conference as a whole, and on the final day the
charter was signed by the Chief of Staff, Bambang Sugeng, in an
atmosphere of awesome ritual.[132]

The fact of the conference and the wording of its resolutions were

[131] See Sumantri, "Langkah Penjelesaian Peristiwa 17 Oktober 1952" ("Steps
toward a Settlement of the Affair of October 17, 1952"), in *Yudhagama* (monthly
journal of the Defense Ministry), May 1954, pp. 2351–2358.

[132] For an account of the proceedings of the conference, as well as the text of the
final resolution and charter of unity, see Darius Marpaung, ed., *Almanak Angkatan
Perang, Tahun 1956* ("Armed Forces Almanac for 1956"; Djakarta: Upeni, 1955
[?]), pp. 56–69. See also Sumantri, *loc. cit.*, and J. R. W. Smail, "The June 27th
Affair" (unpublished paper, Cornell Modern Indonesia Project, 1957), pp. 4–8.

such as to give the cabinet pause. There were indeed cabinet supporters who argued that the unity achieved at the conference was
more ceremonial than political. Numerous conflicts of interest and
orientation clearly continued to exist in the officer corps, to say nothing of personal rivalries. But the degree of cohesion achieved was impressive on a number of counts.

The conference declared that it regarded the October 17 affair as
"wiped out," and it asked the government to give formal endorsement
to this view before August 17, 1955. Its resolutions also included a
request for "clarification of the limits of political influence on the
army." It stressed that technical ability should be the sole criterion for
military appointments. Moreover, the conference resolution did not
refer to the Panglima Tertinggi or Supreme Commander (Soekarno),
but consistently to the Dwitunggal or Duumvirate (Soekarno-Hatta).
It included the ominous injunction: "[Be it decided] to obey all decisions taken by the Government together with the Dwitunggal."
When all this is considered in connection with the fact that "pro-
October 17 group" persons were strikingly prominent in the organization of the conference and the further fact that the Presidium of the
conference's Working Committee was headed by a leading figure of
the "pro-October 17 group," Colonel Simbolon, it becomes clear that
this was a resounding declaration of defiance of Iwa and the cabinet.
The conference showed the army determined to close its ranks in the
face of outsiders, so determined indeed that the "anti-October 17
group" was prepared to go along with a return of the "pro-October 17
group" to a position of dominance.[133] The President and cabinet might
participate in the ceremonials of the conference's closing day, but they
knew that a major blow had been dealt to the basis of their power
position.

The implications of the change were made clear soon after the
Bandung conference. On May 2 Bambang Sugeng, a supporter of the
Jogjakarta conference resolutions who felt that he could not himself
implement them, submitted his resignation as Chief of Staff. The government accepted it nine days later. Immediately the question of a
successor arose. The cabinet was determined to appoint an officer of
the "anti-October 17 group" and submitted the names of Colonels
Zulkifli Lubis, Sudirman (of East Java), and Bambang Utojo (of
South Sumatra) to Soekarno and Hatta. But when the 50-man Work-

---

[133] The interpretation here is based largely on that of Smail, "The June 27th
Affair," *passim.*

ing Committee of the Jogjakarta conference met on May 9, it made clear that it had different ideas, declaring that the vacancy should not be the occasion for competition between factions, but should be filled on the basis of the best interests of the army.[134] The point was more than re-emphasized a little later by the Working Committee's chairman, Simbolon of North Sumatra, when he asserted that "I am sure that if the government gives full attention . . . to the results of the recent officers' meeting at Jogjakarta the new appointment will be made in such a way that no disturbing consequences will ensue." [135] A meeting of the territorial commanders at the end of the month declared that the appointment should be based on seniority. This pointed in the first place to Simbolon, the most senior active officer, and possibly also toward Colonels Nasution and Gatot Subroto, both then on nonactive status as a result of October 17.

On June 10 the cabinet decided to appoint Colonel Bambang Utojo, a man of PNI sympathies and fairly low in seniority as an officer. The appointment was clearly in defiance of the leaders of the Jogjakarta conference, and Bambang Utojo initially refused it. But a little later he agreed.

Bambang Utojo was formally installed as Chief of Staff on the morning of June 27, 1955. At the same time he was made a major general. But the army was not there to see it, except for some five or six officers. The ceremony was boycotted by virtually every officer invited. So effective was the boycott, carried out on the orders of Acting Chief of Staff Zulkifli Lubis, that no military band could be found to play the national anthem. In a society where ceremonial occasions were always handled with meticulous attention to every ritual detail, the army's highest officer was sworn in to the strains of a fire brigade band!

On the same morning Lubis told the cabinet that he would refuse to surrender his authority to Bambang Utojo. The government immediately responded by suspending Lubis from office. Lubis countered by holding a press conference on the same day. There he de-

---

[134] *Merdeka*, May 11, 1955, quoted in Smail, "The June 27th Affair," p. 14.

[135] *Pedoman*, May 20, 1955, quoted in Smail, "The June 27th Affair," p. 15. Perhaps even more significant was a similar threat made three days later by a spokesman for the East Indonesia command speaking on behalf of Warouw of the "anti-October 17 group" (Smail, *loc. cit.*). The terms "pro-October 17 group" and "anti-October 17 group" are being used here with reference to the 1952 situation, with no account taken of the alignment changes which had occurred since then.

fended his actions on grounds of conscience. He had committed an act of insubordination, he confessed. It was legally indefensible, he agreed. But he had acted on the dictates of his innermost heart. He went on to a richly rhetorical denunciation of the politicians who had worked to split the army. The hitherto shadowy figure of the 31-year-old intelligence officer had suddenly emerged commandingly at the center of the political stage.

The whole of the cabinet's position was immediately threatened. It was clearly the cabinet's turn to act, but there was nothing it could do. The boycott had demonstrated the high degree of unity in the army. Yet the cabinet's prestige was committed to Bambang Utojo. Before long there were echoes of the boycott in parliament. On June 29 Zainul Baharuddin, the Defense section chairman (and a relative of Lubis), moved a motion of no confidence in Iwa, and the motion was signed also by a member of a government party, Hadjarati of Parindra.[136]

What the government did was to stall. It affirmed that it stood by the constitution and the principles of parliamentary government, but beyond that it kept silence and hoped that the army's unity would break in a little time.

The following days brought few signs of encouragement for the cabinet. A meeting of territorial commanders and headquarters officers held from June 29 to July 2 stood firmly by Lubis. A conference of the officers' association ending on July 3 was equally strong in its support. More significant still, the efforts of the President and the cabinet to win the support of the "anti-October 17 group," territorial commanders on whom it had previously relied, were largely unsuccessful. Warouw of East Indonesia was firmly with Lubis. Sudirman of East Java was ambivalent in his support, but refused to come out against the dominant army position. Colonel Ibnu Sutowo, who had succeeded Bambang Utojo in South Sumatra, was the one most strongly for the cabinet, but in this the officers of the territory were not with him, and as a newly installed commander his position was weak.

Nor could the cabinet find much support from the political public. While the PKI press and some of the PNI papers were warning of the danger of a military dictatorship, Lubis and the army were careful to avoid giving the impression that this was their goal. They advanced no further than the position they had taken on June 27, with frequent affirmations, made in tones of high moral seriousness, that

[136] For the text see *Pedoman*, June 30, 1955.

the army as the "backbone of the national potential" would not allow
the intrusion of political influence.[137] To this claim the newspaper-
reading public responded. Much of the public, including many of the
members of all parties, had by now developed a thorough distaste for
party politics; the bitter electioneering had gone on for too long.
Furthermore, the cabinet was unpopular on other counts, including
inflation, conspicuous luxury, and scandals. Now the public was being
offered a way of being against all this—and a way which was deeply
appealing to nationalist sentiment. No longer could the cabinet, with
its reliance on the President, appear as the only true custodian of the
heritage of the Revolution. Indeed, the challenge of the army under
Lubis was that it represented the nation as a whole and did so in a
way more unsullied by partisan politics than President Soekarno himself. Symbolic integrators of the nation were in great demand. Moreover, Lubis, intense, sharp-eyed, exuding personal authority and possessed of an almost Soekarnolike sense of drama, was an attractive
spokesman.

In the lengthy negotiations between the army and the cabinet held
in the first half of July, the army refused to retreat an inch, and Hatta,
the one man who might have brought about a compromise to save the
cabinet, stayed aloof from the negotiations.[138] The onus was on the
cabinet to make the next move, but the cabinet had nothing to bargain
with. At the same time it showed itself weak before parliament. Twice
on July 5 it failed to gain a quorum for discussion of its bill for ratification of the Sunario-Luns Protocol dissolving the Netherlands-Indonesian Union. More seriously, the government coalition itself showed
signs of falling apart. On July 12 the Parindra group in parliament
called on the party council to recall its minister from the cabinet. On
July 13 the PSII reportedly decided to urge the cabinet to resign.[139]

On July 13 also Iwa resigned. On the same day the cabinet proposed
a compromise solution to the army. The government would withdraw
its suspension of Lubis, it would retire Bambang Utojo, and it would
choose a new Chief of Staff from a list submitted by the army; the
army would merely have to make a formal acknowledgment of Bambang Utojo's authority. But the army leaders felt strong enough to

[137] Compare the ideologically packed orders of the day issued by Lubis on July
8 and 17. See *Pedoman*, July 9, 1955, and *Indonesia Raya*, July 18, 1955.

[138] See *Indonesia Raya*, July 8, and *Pedoman*, July 9, 1955, for interesting discussions of Hatta's role.

[139] *Indonesia Raya*, July 15, 1955.

turn down even this. On July 18 the President left the country for a pilgrimage to Mecca and a state visit to Cairo. He had once, on July 10, postponed his departure to help save the cabinet. Now apparently he thought that unattainable.

On July 20 the Nahdatul Ulama decided to urge the cabinet to resign. The next day the PRN and the Labor Party did the same. On July 24 Ali returned the cabinet's mandate to Vice-President Hatta.

More clearly than any of the previous cabinets of this period, the Ali cabinet was toppled by a single power group. The mechanisms by which it fell were those of parties and parliament, but the momentum for the overthrow came from the army and no one else. It was the new defiance of the army which changed the whole power situation. As the army cleavages of October 17 had made possible the cabinet's emergence and its relatively long period in office, so the healing of these cleavages led to its being forced to step down.

What, then, had made possible the re-establishment of the army's ability to act as a cohesive force? The rifts of October 17, 1952, were deep. They involved not only rivalry for top posts, but the personal fortunes of a large part of the officer corps. Arising in large part from skill group conflicts, they were also tinged with value disagreements. How was it possible for these wounds to be healed? If, as was charged, the cabinet, and Iwa in particular, had infiltrated the army, why did the infiltrants show no loyalty to their backers? And how indeed was it possible for the army to close ranks at a time of such great political polarization, granted that so often previously the army's internal politics had tended to parallel the politics of society at large? The mere effluxion of time since 1952 is clearly insufficient explanation.

There is evidence that the cabinet, the President, and Iwa in particular gave political considerations a high priority in implementing policies with regard to the army. A basis existed for the numerous charges made that they had raised ranks arbitrarily to strengthen the position of their own factional supporters in the army, that they had distributed supplies to favor these supporters and disfavor others, and that in general they had upset professional and bureaucratic norms and brought considerable confusion into the army. Practices of this kind were likely to arouse the strongest hostility from members of the "pro-October 17 group," both because these were the strongest advocates of military professionalization and because they were the cabinet's clearest enemies. Thus Simbolon of North Sumatra was acutely resentful of what he saw as the cabinet's policy of placing men hostile to him in the officer corps of his command, denying him adequate supplies for barracks and soldier health and for use against the Daud Beureueh rebels, and at the same time playing the heavily armed mobile brigade of the police force off against him in the Achinese theater of operations. Kawilarang of West Java had a number of similar grievances; he was particularly hostile to an announced plan of the minister to establish the area of Greater Djakarta as an eighth territorial command and thus in effect cut out the heart of Kawilarang's own area of authority.[140]

But grievances of this type cannot have been enough to arouse so many officers of the old "anti-October 17 group" to take sides against the cabinet, for the men of this group were the usual beneficiaries of whatever discriminatory treatment there was. Why, then, did so many of them support the course of action which led from the Jogjakarta conference to the fall of the cabinet?

The answer would seem to lie in actions of the cabinet which affronted the army as such. In the first place, every army officer felt that the budget allocation for defense was entirely inadequate, and the contrast was frequently drawn between the smallness of this allocation and the apparent generosity of the cabinet with funds for a number of other purposes. Nasution published an article concerning the defense budget on the day before the Jogjakarta conference began.[141] In it he criticized the fact that only 20 to 25 per cent of the total budget was normally set aside for defense in Indonesia. He was particularly critical of the situation in 1954 when the army had, as he asserted, received virtually no foreign exchange funds at all. New supplies of weapons and ammunition, maintenance of equipment, and soldier health—all these, he said, were being neglected for lack of funds. Nasution's analysis, presented in expanded form in his book on military policy published in May 1955,[142] was a fitting complement to the continuing cry of large numbers of commanding officers at this time that their soldiers were badly fed, provided with inadequate medical care, and living in ever more dilapidated barracks.

There was yet a further consequence of small military budgets, which was given less attention in public statements than the shortage of up-to-date military equipment and the bad living conditions of soldiers, but was probably no less important in shaping the course of

[140] *Pedoman*, Oct. 23, 1954.   [141] *Pedoman*, Feb. 17, 1955.
[142] Nasution, *Tjatatan-Tjatatan Sekitar Politik Militer*

officer political action. This was a relative decline in the status position of officers, as they compared themselves with people of comparable rank in civilian hierarchies such as the *pamong pradja* corps, the police, and particular parties. Thus a regimental commander who had previously had second highest status in a residency capital, with only the resident or local *pamong pradja* head driving a newer car, might now have fallen to a No. 5 place, defeated in the status competition by one or another senior civil servant and, as was almost always the case, by powerful local leaders of parties. From an officer point of view, it was not hard to see that something could be done to rectify this and the various other consequences of small military budgets if only the army as a whole could swing more weight at the highest political levels.

In the second place, the officer corps in general was resentful of what it saw as efforts of the Defense Minister to give arms to irregular organizations outside the army. We have seen how this issue was raised in the very first days of the Ali cabinet's existence when Iwa made a favorable comment on such a proposal by the pro-Communist veterans' organization, Perbepbsi. The cabinet as a whole then vetoed the plan, but that was not the end. In September 1954 support was widely sought on a Perbepbsi proposal for a large "Congress for the Security of the People in the Elections," which was to strengthen village guard units and weld them into an over-all national organization. The army, knowing the influence of the Communists within village guard groups in many parts of the country and remembering the troubles it had had with "private" and political armed units in the period of the Revolution, was deeply suspicious. Eventually the proposal was rejected by the cabinet, but this was not until after four cabinet ministers, including Iwa, had given it their formal support.[143] In February 1955 a West Irian Liberators' Front was established with headquarters in Semarang and indirect government support, and some of its members received quasi-military training in the following months.[144] A number of officers maintained in early 1955 that Iwa was channeling both money and arms to the Perbepbsi (but little evidence was provided in support of this assertion). Some officers regarded Iwa as a PKI supporter, others thought him still a supporter of the Partai

---

[143] *Suluh Indonesia,* Sept. 27, 1954; *Abadi,* Oct. 5, 11, 1954.

[144] See *Nieuw Surabaiasch Handelsblad* (Surabaja), June 21, 1955. For evidence of army hostility to the organization see *ibid.,* July 20, 1955, and *Pikiran Rakjat* (Menado), Oct. 4, 1955.

Murba, and others again thought he was both.[145] In any event he aroused their suspicions, both because he seemed to want to strengthen Communist organizations and because he threatened to undermine the army's monopoly of the means of violence.

Another important bone of contention between the army and the cabinet was the matter of the army's rights in the elections and the position of IPKI, the League of Upholders of Indonesian Independence, established in May 1954 as a sort of army front organization. Army members were permitted to stand as candidates in the elections and 73 of them submitted their names, mostly for inclusion on IPKI lists, the understanding being that the army would place them on nonactive status for a period of six months before and between the (double) elections. They were initially informed that this latter provision would enable them to campaign for the parties or organizations they belonged to. Later, however, in September 1954, the cabinet issued an absolute ban on campaigning by army members.[146] This was seen as a direct hit at IPKI, which seemed to many officers to have a chance of emerging as a major force in the elections, thanks to the esteem and affection enjoyed locally by army members (and by various *pamong pradja* officials with clean revolutionary records who were also among the League's candidates).[147] For that majority of army officers who accepted the IPKI depiction of itself as representing the interests of all factions of the army, the "anti-October 17 group" included, a blow against IPKI was a blow against the army. As a number of army offi-

---

[145] In the June 27 crisis, charges were frequently made, particularly perhaps to Westerners, that Iwa had attempted to nurture PKI and Murba influence in the army itself. But there were probably no more than two or three senior officers with PKI sympathies in the whole army when the Ali cabinet fell. The number with Murba sympathies was greater. However, the Partai Murba had lost most of its organizational cohesion by 1955, and thus Murba sympathizers were not seen as infiltrators acting obediently in response to directions given from outside the army.

[146] Government Regulation no. 47 of 1954, issued Sept. 22, 1954. See Penerangan Angkatan Darat (Army Information Division), *Brosur Pemilihan Umum untuk Angkatan Darat* ("Elections Brochure for the Army"; Djakarta, 1954); Penerangan Angkatan Darat, *Brosur Tambahan tentang Pemilihan Umum untuk Anggauta Angkatan Perang* ("Additional Brochure on Elections for Members of the Armed Forces"; Djakarta, 1954); A. H. Nasution, "Tentara dan Politik" ("The Army and Politics"), *Pedoman*, June 29, 1955; S. Parman, "Dapat Goalkah?" ("Can We Succeed?"), *Duta Tamtama* (periodical of the Ikatan Perwira Republik Indonesia, Officers' Association of the Republic of Indonesia), I, no. 1 (Jan. 1956), 20–26.

[147] Most officers and many others expected that IPKI would gain much more than the 1.4 per cent of the total vote (and four parliamentary seats) it actually obtained.

cers saw it, the ban on campaigning showed that the politicians were so determined to prevent the army from exercising due influence that they would not even let it compete for power on the politicians' home ground.

There was yet a further powerful stimulus to cohesion in the army. Army officers of every faction shared an image of the army as the founder of the nation, and most of them saw it as a powerful force for the maintenance of national unity and the authority of the state. They saw themselves pre-eminently in a guardian role. If matters were to go seriously awry as a result of the mistakes and wrongdoings of civilian politicians, if the whole content of the independence for which the army had fought were to be imperiled, then it would be incumbent on the army to step in to save the body politic—so ran the common army view.

What the army witnessed in the period of the Ali cabinet made many of its members believe that the need and opportunity for their saving intervention would soon come. The volume of corruption among civilian politicians and bureaucrats had grown markedly in the two years of this cabinet, as inflation had reduced civil servants' real income and as the government parties' machine politics practices had undermined civil service norms and morale. On the one hand, there had been a marked rise in the spectacular corruption which was symbolized by the resort bungalow and satirized bitterly in various of the short stories of Achdiat K. Mihardja [148] and in Usmar Ismael's immensely popular film "Krisis." On the other hand, petty corruption had become general and largely accepted. The latter situation was summed up in an open letter to President Soekarno written by Dr. A. Halim, who in 1950 had been Prime Minister of the Republic of Indonesia, which was a member of RUSI. Writing on May 27, Halim said: "In general the wages of government servants are only sufficient for subsistence for two weeks or, at the most, twenty days. . . . The majority . . . eventually fall into the chasm of dishonor and start to indulge in minor corruption." And, speaking as head of Djakarta's Central Public Hospital and its approximately 1,800 employees, he added that "there has been a general trend towards petty theft—once or twice a week . . . to increase their income." [149] And between the

[148] Achdiat K. Mihardja, *Keretakan dan Ketegangan* ("Rupture and Tension"; Djakarta: Balai Pustaka, 1956). See especially "Kisah Martini," "Ketjewa," and "Keluarga Raden Sastro."

[149] Quoted in Boyd R. Compton, "Dr. Halim's Open Letter," *Newsletter of the Institute of Current World Affairs* (New York), June 30, 1955.

bungalow buyers and the petty thieves there was a growing middle group of civil servants who operated normally on the basis of exchanges of favors.

At the same time the army leaders saw the instruments of state as no longer having authority in the eyes of the people. The government parties' electoral interests seemed to have become of primary importance in shaping the activity of almost every agency of state which had political significance, the Ministries of Information and Religious Affairs, the government-owned radio authority, the *pamong pradja* corps, the judiciary, and President Soekarno himself. Pitted against one another by party conflict, the country's civilian leaders were no longer able to offer authoritative leadership to the nation as a whole, so many officers believed. Only the army itself had successfully evaded embroilment in the struggles of the parties, and therefore it alone, they declared, could restore the authority of the state.

One further development which led officers to think in terms of army intervention in politics was the rising power of the Communist Party. The PKI had made the fullest use of the opportunities given to it in the Ali cabinet period to organize freely on a large scale. According to the PKI's own figures, which were usually treated with more respect than those of any other Indonesian party, Communist Party membership rose from 7,910 to 100,000 between March and September 1952 [150] and from 165,206 to 500,000 between March and November 1954.[151] In February 1956 Aidit was to speak to the twentieth congress of the Communist Party of the Soviet Union "in the name of one million Indonesian Communists." [152] The three PKI-led peasant organizations existing in mid-1953 were fused in the Ali cabinet period into the BTI or Indonesian Peasant Front, with total claimed membership rising from something over 400,000 to about two and a quarter million.[153] And the PKI and BTI between them appeared to be ahead of all others in the volume of their village-level campaign activity, at least in Java.

[150] See D. N. Aidit, "Djalan ke Demokrasi Rakjat bagi Indonesia" ("The Way to People's Democracy for Indonesia"), *Bintang Merah*, IX, no. 9–10 (Sept.–Oct. 1953), 460–461, 464–465. These figures include members and candidate-members together.

[151] *Bintang Merah*, X, no. 4–5 (April–May 1954), 146; *Harian Rakjat*, Dec. 2, 1954.

[152] *Bintang Merah*, XII, no. 2–3 (Feb.–March 1956), 112.

[153] Donald Hindley, "The Communist Party of Indonesia, 1951–1961: A Decade of the Aidit Leadership" (doctoral dissertation, Australian National University, 1961), pp. 344–345.

In addition, the stigma of Madiun was being erased rapidly, despite the Masjumi's efforts to maintain it. When several cabinet ministers attended the opening of the party's congress in March 1954 and President Soekarno sent the congress his good wishes, the PKI was well on the way to being accepted as a full-fledged part of the nationalist political framework.[154]

In the view of the officer corps, most of whose members were decidedly anti-Communist in orientation, these were alarming signs. But they also represented an opportunity. Both aspects were related to the possibility, which was privately discussed by many throughout the Ali period, that parliamentary democracy would not last much longer. We have noted how the desirability of a "military dictatorship," a "strong man," a "truly Indonesian democracy," or a "second revolution" was discussed before 1953. This discussion continued throughout the period of the first Ali cabinet. Now it was often in tones of cynicism, as if constitutional democracy were something one wanted to be rid of but could not. The events around October 17, 1952, had led political elite members to a fuller awareness of the difficulties involved in bringing together enough power to establish and maintain a new, more authoritarian regime. But there continued to be a desire for some sort of change in the system. One common sentiment among members of the political elite was, "Well, elections are supposed to put an end to this mess, and perhaps they will. But if they don't, there will have to be a radical change somehow."

As far as officers were concerned, this sentiment was important in

[154] *Harian Rakjat*, Dec. 20, 1954. However, while President Soekarno spoke of the PKI in tones of increasing warmth in the latter part of the Ali cabinet period, the PNI became more and more apprehensive about Communist strength. The PNI's regional leaders in East and Central Java were most emphatically anti-Communist, but the same feeling grew in the Djakarta leadership also, resulting in early 1955 in several conciliatory approaches to leaders of the opposition parties. It was partly fear of this PNI hostility which led the Communist Party's Politbureau to decide on June 24, 1955, to change the party's election aim from a "People's Democratic Government" to a "National Coalition Government." See *Harian Rakjat*, Aug. 8, 9, 1955. The anti-Communist trend in PNI actions reached its culmination when the PNI decided in July 1955 to withdraw from participation in the All-Indonesian People's Congress, which had been proposed by President Soekarno in the previous December (at a PNI congress) and was due to be held in August. The Masjumi, PSI, and Christian parties had refused to participate in the Congress from the beginning, and PKI influence was strong in the preparatory committee. The PNI decision represented marked defiance of President Soekarno, who eventually addressed a PKI-Murba-PSII-led Congress at which all-Indonesian unity was conspicuously absent. For the resolutions of the Congress and a report on the President's speech see *Harian Rakjat*, Aug. 17, 1955.

loosening the inhibitions of constitutional democracy. If the parliamentary regime was indeed nearing its end, it was pointless, they thought, for them to be bound too strongly by the constitutional morality which confined the army to a nonpolitical role. Indeed, it was worse than pointless, for excessive reticence on the army's part could result in transference of the initiative to other potential heirs of the parliamentary regime, the PKI and possibly President Soekarno. To officers with this expectation the need that the army be ready for united action was obvious. All in all, it seemed to the officer corps that the times were such that neither the state nor the army could afford to let the army remain divided.

Some senior army officers took this logic one step further and argued at the time of the June 27th affair in favor of going on from that day's achievements to the enactment of a military coup. The form and precise purposes of this proposal are not clear, nor is it known how much support it received at the meetings of commanders at which it was discussed. But evidently the support was insufficient. The decision reached was to postpone action for a year and to reconsider the matter then if no improvement in civilian-run government and politics had occurred.

Although the officers' disgust with existing parliamentary democracy was great, they were not prepared as a group to act directly against it at that particular time, with the long-promised elections about to be held. In Pauker's words, "Their guiding consideration in postponing the coup was the fear that they might stand accused of destroying the chances of constitutional democracy in Indonesia." [155] Their attitude here reflects the high hopes of the political public that elections would restore the country's political health. Put another way, it reflects the fact that the army lacked suitable means of making a military take-over legitimate. It presumably also reflects the shakiness of the army's new-found unity.

TRENDS IN SOME POLICY AREAS

Mounting inflation notwithstanding, production figures were rising in most sectors while the first Ali cabinet was in office. The smallest increases were in the estate sector; there production of certain products was falling, partly because foreigners were gradually liquidating their assets (though sometimes this liquidation resulted initially in

[155] See Guy J. Pauker, *The Role of the Military in Indonesia* (research memorandum; Santa Monica, Calif.: Rand Corporation, 1960), p. 40.

high output, as in the case where rubber trees were slaughter-tapped).[156] In other export sectors production rose fairly fast. This was notably the case with small holders' rubber (presumably even more so than the statistics show, if it is true that smuggling was increasing). It was also very clear in the field of oil, the one area in which large quantities of new foreign capital were being invested. Industrial capacity rose somewhat in this period, despite irregularities in the flow of imports.[157] Bigger advances took place in the field of food production. In 1954 and 1955 Indonesia came closer than at any other time since before the war to being self-sufficient in rice; self-sufficiency might have been reached in 1955 had not widespread floods occurred in that year.[158] The fact that the price rises of the period were confined mainly to urban areas was in large part the result of this expansion.

In the controversial areas of economic policy few of the conflicts were resolved. With regard to the land conflict in East Sumatra which had come to a head in the Tandjong Morawa affair, the Ali cabinet adopted a somewhat new policy when it first entered office. On August 27, 1953, it cabled Medan to halt the bulldozing of squatters' plots, which till then had been proceeding in continuation of the Wilopo cabinet's policy of land reallocation—and had claimed two more peasant lives on August 25.[159] In March 1954 it installed a State Commission on East Sumatra Estate Lands Distribution Affairs. In the same month the new Governor of North Sumatra, Mr. S. M. Amin, issued a "stand fast" order stating that all squatters who had settled since August 27, 1953, would have to move within a week and that the fate of those who had settled earlier would be decided by the new State Commission.[160] But in practice the cabinet was forced to make a series of further modifications as it attempted to implement these decisions and the recommendations of the commission. In June of 1954 it passed an emergency law establishing a new "stand fast" date for squatters on foreign-leased estate lands throughout the country. All who had settled before June 12 would be countenanced, but there would be evictions and fines or jail sentences for all who had settled after this date. And throughout the period of the cabinet, local army, police, and *pamong pradja* authorities in a number of areas made ar-

[156] See Higgins, *op. cit.*, p. 149.
[158] *Ibid.*, pp. 165, 168.
[160] Sutter, *op. cit.*, pp. 762–768.

[157] *Ibid.*, pp. 161, 171, 172.
[159] *Harian Rakjat*, Aug. 28, 1953.

rests of peasants, sometimes by the hundreds.[161] In most of the areas, however, they failed to stop a continuing inflow of the land-hungry. As in the matter of squatting on state forest lands (and the illegal cutting of forest wood) in Java, the government's decision-enforcing capacity appeared to be even smaller than during the tenure of the earlier cabinets. A new area of weakness was opened up when it became clear that the government could not or would not prevent army-organized smuggling in Sulawesi.

A similar situation of continued deadlock and frustration of policy goals existed in the matter of the North Sumatran oil wells. Here the government made a number of efforts at reorganization and several important personnel changes, but, if anything, these merely aggravated the conflict, with union groups of different political affiliations taking opposite sides on the issue of the new appointments and the over-all issue of whether or not the wells should be returned to Royal Dutch Shell. When the cabinet fell, the output of the wells was still a tiny trickle, and their limbolike status remained unchanged, no decision having been taken for either nationalization or return to the Dutch company.[162]

Equally important, the government had done nothing to break the existing deadlock on the granting of new exploring rights and leases to foreign oil companies. However, they reached important agreements with the Standard Vacuum and California-Texas oil companies under which these companies would make large new investments in their plants over a period of a number of years ($70 to $80 million over three years in the case of Stanvac, $100 million over four years in the case of Caltex). Furthermore, by making it more difficult for foreign estate companies to transfer their profits abroad, they forced a rise in the previously very low rate of replanting of rubber.

In implementing policy to restore security in rebel- and bandit-torn areas, the first plank of its program, the cabinet had little success. It was able to split off a number of lieutenants of Kahar Muzakar in South Sulawesi, and it settled a minor rebel-bandit problem in Minahasa by negotiation. But these successes were small when it is noted that most of rural Atjeh was taken away from effective government authority in the Ali cabinet period.

[161] For examples of arrests of estate squatters in the Kediri area of East Java and the Subang area of West Java see *Harian Rakjat*, April 12, 1954, Jan. 22, 1955.
[162] Sutter, *op. cit.*, pp. 837–846.

By 1954 there were three major areas of conflict, in West Java, South Sulawesi, and Atjeh, where the characteristic situation was one of deadlock between the army and the rebels. Far from being able to break through with the tough, resolute action many expected when the cabinet first assumed office, the cabinet found itself forced more and more to accept stalemate. In large part this reflected the state of cabinet-army relations; the cabinet was in conflict particularly with the territorial commanders in the three areas of large-scale rebel and bandit activity, Colonels Simbolon, Kawilarang, and Warouw. Most openly in Sulawesi, but to a large extent also in West Java and North Sumatra, the army units concerned avoided major drives against the rebels. The number of casualties inflicted by the Darul Islam in West Java increased in the period of the Ali cabinet as did the volume of reported damage and destruction.[163]

One significant achievement of the cabinet was a speeding up of the legislative process.[164] Thanks to the relatively secure parliamentary majority it enjoyed, the Ali cabinet was able to dispose of much of the backlog of bills existing when it came into office. There was a significant shift in this period away from the earlier very extensive use by cabinets of emergency laws. However, many of the most important pieces of legislation, including the long-planned bill on decentralization and regional autonomy which was discussed in the time of this cabinet, were not finalized.

As a cabinet which was under far greater "solidarity maker" influence than any of its predecessors, the Ali cabinet devoted considerable effort to the manipulation of nationalist symbols. We have seen the great emphasis it placed on the pursuit of an active foreign policy. In addition, it spent larger sums than its predecessors on celebrations of Independence Day and other national days, on the building of statues and memorials, and on the restoration of ancient temples and monuments. Moreover, it held a series of extended trials of Dutch persons charged with involvement in subversive activities.[165] Pro-

[163] Nasution, *Tjatatan-Tjatatan Sekitar Politik Militer*, pp. 91–92.
[164] Miriam S. Budiardjo, "The Provisional Parliament of Indonesia," *Far Eastern Survey*, XXV, no. 2 (Feb. 1956), 18.
[165] See Ministry of Foreign Affairs, Republic of Indonesia, *Subversive Activities in Indonesia: The Jungschlaeger and Schmidt Affair* (Djakarta: Government Printing Office, 1957); R. Soenarjo, *Proses L. N. H. Jungschlaeger* ("The Case of L. N. H. Jungschlaeger"; Djakarta: Gunung Agung, 1956); Justus M. van der Kroef, "The Jungschlaeger Case in Indonesia," *Pacific Affairs*, XXX, no. 3 (Sept. 1957), 254–260; and Leslie H. Palmier, *Indonesia and the Dutch* (London: Oxford University Press, 1962), pp. 85–93.

tracted press discussion on these trials and the lack of government effort to discourage expressions of antiforeign feeling contributed to an atmosphere in which men felt that they were expected to be uncritical in their national loyalty. Indeed, government-channeled nationalism became notably more radical and strident in this period and was frequently used as an instrument against opposition groups.

Chapter IX

The Burhanuddin Harahap Cabinet, August 1955–March 1956:

The Elections and After

ACTING President Hatta's very first meeting after hearing from Mr. Ali of his cabinet's resignation was with Colonel Zulkifli Lubis. This fact epitomizes what had happened to cabinet politics. It is a fact which gave a new stamp to the cabinet crisis which followed.

THE SWING OF THE PENDULUM

At the time of Ali's resignation the army held a great preponderance of power. By maintaining its unity in the face of four weeks of effort to divide it, it had achieved a political triumph without precedent in its postrevolutionary history. It had done so by a sparing use of power which had gained and kept a large measure of sympathy for it in the political public. Would it now go further and expand its bridgehead into a major invasion of the sphere of civilian politics? Some senior officers may still have been considering the possibility of a military dictatorship, but the majority of officers had decided they were opposed to any over-all take-over action at a time when elections were about to be held. However, this majority wanted to do something. None of those who had led the army from the Jogjakarta conference via the June 27 affair to the day of the Ali cabinet's resignation wanted to let the initiative slip out of their hands. Their point of view found its rationalization in the words of *Indonesia Raya,* which came closer than any other daily at the time to being a spokesman for the army: "If the Army's challenge to the Government should show results devoid of anything positively constructive, this would be a staggering psychological blow to the many who are hoping for a change for the better, for justice and honesty. And the army would then be regarded with utter disappointment." [1] Lubis and the army leaders for whom he spoke were determined to leave an impressive testimonial of their incursion into civilian politics.

It was in the shadow of this kind of attitude in the army—and in the conspicuous absence of President Soekarno overseas—that the first steps were taken toward forming a new cabinet. Two days after Ali's resignation, the army's official spokesman denied that the army had suggested a particular composition for the new cabinet. He added, however, that the army felt that formation of the new cabinet on the basis of a struggle for ministers' seats would be improper; the basis should be the safety of the state and the welfare of the people.[2] The army leaders apparently believed that they should not point openly to particular political figures whom they wanted elevated to cabinet office. But, granted the fact that they had consciously overthrown the Ali cabinet, their moral exhortations served to strengthen the groups which had been most hostile to this cabinet.

Further, the army leaders helped the Masjumi and PSI by repeatedly injecting an emphasis on urgency and crisis into the atmosphere of politics. If indeed the situation was one of crisis, if it was as Hatta himself said "explosive," [3] then extraordinary measures were clearly required. This in turn justified the Masjumi and PSI position that a national business cabinet or presidential cabinet would be needed—as against the view of the PNI and PKI which feared that this meant a Hatta cabinet and proposed instead a parliamentary or coalition cabinet. The army leaders themselves did not come out in favor of a Hatta cabinet. But the declaration of IPKI, the officer-led League of Upholders of Indonesian Independence, that only a government headed by the Dwitunggal (Soekarno and Hatta) could save the country from the danger of collapse was taken as representing the view of at least a section of the dominant army leadership.

---

[1] *Indonesia Raya,* quoted in *PIA,* July 24, 1955, from Smail, "The June 27th Affair" (unpublished paper, Cornell Modern Indonesia Project, 1957), p. 44.

[2] *Pedoman,* July 27, 1955.   [3] *Ibid.,* July 28, 1955.

Thus the Masjumi and PSI rose quickly to an entirely new position of strength and self-confidence. Their press began to adopt a tone of militant opposition to the PNI and the parties of the Ali cabinet, allowing itself a much greater degree of freedom than theretofore. *Indonesia Raya,* the most sensational of the Masjumi and PSI-sympathizing dailies, ran a series of "Now the Story Can Be Told" articles on the alleged misdoings of the former cabinet.

On July 29 Hatta as acting President announced the names of three *formateurs,* Sukiman of the Masjumi, Wilopo of the PNI, and Assaat, the nonparty parliamentarian who had been Acting President of the (member-state) Republic of Indonesia in 1950. He did not specify that they should form a parliamentary or business cabinet, but instructed them to form "a cabinet which will obtain sufficient parliamentary support and will include men who are honest and have authority [*orang-orang jang djudjur dan disegani*]." [4] The foremost tasks of the cabinet, Hatta went on to specify, would be:

1. to restore the moral authority of the government, specifically the trust of the army and of society;
2. to hold elections according to the plans already made and to hasten the formation of a new parliament.[5]

The efforts of Sukiman, Wilopo, and Assaat to form a cabinet are interesting chiefly because the three men came close to establishing a cabinet in which Hatta held the posts of Prime Minister and Minister of Defense. The idea of a new Hatta cabinet, which had been advanced so often before and was to be advanced so often in subsequent years, always unsuccessfully, was almost realized at this time. Within the PNI, now greatly weakened, the Wilopo group had re-emerged to a position of influence. Some members of this group now argued strongly that the party's only hope of returning to government office —and thus its only hope of preventing a wholesale undoing of the power position which the party had built for itself in the two previous years—lay in waiving its long-held objections to a Hatta-led cabinet. The three *formateurs* succeeded within a few days in reaching agreement on the holders of the major portfolios in such a cabinet, but then the question arose of the terms of Hatta's serving as Prime Minister.

Hatta himself insisted that a parliamentary resolution be passed requesting him to serve in the cabinet, and the *formateurs* prepared

[4] *Abadi,* July 28, 1955.   [5] *Ibid.,* Aug. 1, 1955.

a draft resolution of this kind (which could easily gain support if both of the two large parties endorsed it). The formula they proposed was that Hatta be declared nonactive as Vice-President, the implication being that he would return to the vice-presidency at the end of his period as Prime Minister. But the PNI refused to accept the resolution in this form. In replying to the *formateurs* it stated that it would support a "parliamentary resolution to make it possible for Bung Hatta as a citizen to lead a parliamentary cabinet" and that it was prepared to co-operate in a PNI-Masjumi joint committee to draft such a resolution. In the Masjumi view this was a rejection of the *formateurs'* formula and an attempt to keep Hatta from subsequently returning to the vice-presidency in the event of his now assuming the prime ministership. Thereupon the Masjumi instructed Dr. Sukiman to join with his two colleagues in returning the *formateur*-ship. The three men did this on August 3 (two days before the expiry of their mandate) amid sharp accusations between the Masjumi and the PNI, each charging the other with insincerity in its efforts to bring a Hatta cabinet into being.[6]

Hatta's second commission, again with the same terms set, went, as expected, to a single *formateur* from the Masjumi. The man he named was Mr. Burhanuddin Harahap, a relative and friend of Zulkifli Lubis. Burhanuddin was helped as he started his work as *formateur* by the action of the army in arresting Jan Dulken, a PNI member of Dutch origin and deputy head of the Foreign Exchange Institute, whom the army alleged to be involved in corruption. This was the first of a number of arrests of supposed corrupters in high places, made by the army on its own initiative. The supporters of the former cabinet were tersely reminded that the army was still in the political arena.

Burhanuddin negotiated first with the PNI, and again the PNI made important concessions. It was prepared to accept a Masjumi Prime Minister. For itself it would be content with the three posts Burhanuddin offered it, the Deputy Prime Ministership, Foreign Affairs, and Public Works. But it could not agree with the *formateur*

[6] For a PNI account of this episode see D.P.P. P.N.I. Departemen Pen. Prop. (Information and Propaganda Department of the PNI Party Executive), *Pendirian dan Sikap P.N.I. dalam Situasi Baru* ("The Position and Viewpoint of the PNI in the New Situation"; Djakarta, Aug. 18, 1955). For another view see Deliar Noer, "Masjumi: Its Organization, Ideology and Political Role in Indonesia" (M.A. thesis, Cornell University, 1960), and *Indonesia Raya*, Aug. 3, 4, 5, 1955. See also the account of Wilopo in *Abadi*, Aug. 8, 1955.

on the matter of the individual persons to fill these posts. The PNI submitted two series of three candidates,[7] but Burhanuddin, confident that the PNI had much greater need of co-operation with him than he had of co-operation with it, rejected men of both. The PNI for its part did not accept the *formateur*'s own choices and was opposed particularly to having a Masjumi man as Minister of Defense. Thus on August 9 a new deadlock was reached. Burhanuddin stopped negotiating with the PNI and turned his attention to the Moslem League and minor nationalist parties.

Here, however, there were many more difficulties than he had expected. Within the Nahdatul Ulama there were some who opposed participation in the cabinet, hoping that if Burhanuddin failed the NU would be next in line for the *formateur*-ship, particularly now that President Soekarno had returned from his pilgrimage. (The President had arrived back on August 4, but immediately left Djakarta for Bogor, stating that he would be occupied with preparation of his address for Independence Day, August 17.) Eventually the NU agreed to participate in Burhanuddin's cabinet, in part as a result of direct pressure from officers. But there remained the problem of the small parties' claims to portfolios. The parties which were faced with virtual extinction in the impending elections were particularly effective in raising the price of their parliamentary support. Burhanuddin was finally obliged to give two seats each to four of these, the PIR of Hazairin, the PRN, the Labor Party, and Parindra. (None of these except PIR had ever before had more than one seat in a cabinet.) On August 11 he took a virtually final list of his cabinet to Hatta, and on the following day the cabinet was sworn in. Its membership was as follows:

Ministry [8, 9]		Party
Prime Minister	Mr. Burhanuddin Harahap	Masjumi
First Deputy Prime Minister	Djanu Ismadi	PIR-Hazairin

[7] Noer, *op. cit.*

[8] Initial disagreements within Parindra and the opposition of Hatta to one of the Parindra candidates named made it impossible for the ministers of this party to be sworn in with the rest of the cabinet. The posts of Education and Public Works were filled on Aug. 26 by Prof. Ir. Suwandi and R. P. Suroso respectively.

[9] The NU and PSII ministers resigned on Jan. 19, 1956. The Minister of Public Works and Power, R. P. Suroso, became also Minister of the Interior ad interim on that date. Minister of State Sutomo was made Minister of Social Affairs ad interim in addition to his previous post, and Minister of Agriculture Sardjan became also Minister of Religious Affairs ad interim. The post of Second Deputy Prime Minister was abolished.

Ministry		Party
Second Deputy Prime Minister	Harsono Tjokroaminoto	PSII
Foreign Affairs	Mr. Ide Anak Agung Gde Agung	Democratic Fraction
Interior	Mr. Sunarjo	NU
Defense	Mr. Burhanuddin Harahap	Masjumi
Justice	Mr. Lukman Wiriadinata	PSI
Information	Sjamsuddin Sutan Makmur	PIR
Finance	Prof. Dr. Sumitro Djojo-hadikusumo	PSI
Agriculture	Mohammad Sardjan	Masjumi
Economic Affairs	I. J. Kasimo	Catholic
Communications	F. Laoh	PRN
Communications (Junior Minister)	Asrarudin	Labor
Public Works and Power	——	Parindra
Labor	I. Tedjasukmana	Labor
Social Affairs	Sudibjo	PSII
Education	——	Parindra
Religious Affairs	K. H. Iljas	NU
Health	Dr. Johannes Leimena	Parkindo
Agrarian Affairs	Mr. Gunawan	PRN
Minister of State	Abdul Hakim	Masjumi
Minister of State	Sutomo (alias Bung Tomo)	Indonesian People's Party
Minister of State	Drs. Coomala Noor	PIR-Hazairin

This list disappointed many. Those who had expected that a cabinet formed by the Masjumi under Hatta's aegis, and in an army-created atmosphere of moral renewal, would indeed bring new authority to government were left with a sense of anticlimax. The cabinet's very size, 23 posts, suggested that there had been a good deal of "cow trading." Moreover, the small parties, in particular the small nationalist parties to whom the stigma of opportunism had long clung, had obtained extraordinary concessions. And along with men who enjoyed great respect within the political public, the cabinet included a number who were regarded as second-rate and some suspected of involvement in corruption. Eleven of the 22, including the Prime Minister and the First Deputy Prime Minister, had had no previous cabinet experience.

For the Masjumi there was some satisfaction in the fact that all three of the major Islamic parties were represented in the new cabinet; it had gone some way toward drawing the NU and PSII away from the PNI. In addition, the very fact that the cabinet excluded the PNI was a cause of gratification to those in the Masjumi and PSI who had been hoping for a cabinet which could settle scores with the PNI and bring Masjumi and PSI men back to the positions of power from which the Ali cabinet had dislodged them. The PSI drew satisfaction from Professor Sumitro's position. In a "bottom-heavy" cabinet headed by relatively inexperienced men, Sumitro, as a man of high intellectual attainments and notable political skill, would be able, some PSI persons believed, to assume wide powers of general leadership. Many who were favorably disposed to the cabinet were pleased with the inclusion of Sutomo, a revolutionary hero, who would be able to contribute noteworthy "solidarity making" skills and radical nationalist appeal. But in general the reaction of those who had led opposition to the Ali cabinet was one of disappointment. "Half of our right to make a moral case against the Ali cabinet has been forfeited" was a characteristic response of this group.

One clear implication was that army support would now be harder for the Masjumi and PSI to obtain. Indeed, some sections of the army had given indications of their displeasure as the cabinet was in the final stages of being formed.[10] And IPKI had refused the *formateur*'s offer of a ministership without portfolio.[11] Although Lubis had played a major role throughout the period of Burhanuddin's *formateur*-ship —one report has it that he personally scrutinized the names of all candidates for ministerial posts, eliminating those whom he averred were suspected of past corruption—there would undoubtedly be internal army opposition if he gave too much direct political support to the new cabinet. Claiming for itself the right to speak for the nation as a whole, the army would in any case have to exercise care lest it be too closely linked with a partisan group of politicians. But the problem was aggravated by the fact that this particular group of politicians did not measure up to the standards of moral authority for which the army claimed to be fighting.

In many ways the Burhanuddin Harahap cabinet was the polar opposite of the cabinet it replaced. Unlike any earlier cabinet of our period, it based itself explicitly on a platform of hostility to much of what its predecessor had done.[12] Only three of the 22 new min-

---

[10] See *Indonesia Raya*, Aug. 10, 1955, for the views of "army circles" on a draft list of cabinet personnel.

[11] *Ibid.*, Aug. 11, 1955.

[12] See *Keterangan dan Djawaban Pemerintah tentang Program Kabinet Burhanuddin Harahap* ("The Government Statement on the Program of the Bur-

isters had held portfolios in the Ali cabinet, and one of these, Sudibjo, only very briefly. If there had been a major swing of the pendulum of power when the Wilopo cabinet gave way to the cabinet of Ali, this new swing was sharper and broader.

But in another sense there were important similarities between the two cabinets. One was the counterpart of the other. Both of them were products of the pre-election situation with its polarizing effects and its tendency to limit government policy to a matter of *ad hoc* decisions made with an eye on their consequences for party fortunes.

The leaders of the cabinet, such as Burhanuddin Harahap himself, Sumitro, Foreign Minister Anak Agung Gde Agung, and Economic Affairs Minister Kasimo, were men with a strong concern with problem-solving policy and a common approach to it. "Administrators" all, their view of their governmental tasks was similar to that which the Wilopo cabinet had held, or for that matter the Natsir or Hatta cabinet. Thus they saw the control of inflation as a necessity of the highest importance. They believed that economic stabilization was required and that expanding production would have to take precedence over indigenization of ownership. They held that Indonesia needed foreign capital. And they favored stringent budgetary economies and a rationalization of the bureaucracy.

But their ideas of long-term policy were of relatively little importance with regard to their actions in the period of this cabinet. In the first place, the cabinet was necessarily to be short-lived. When the elections for parliament and the Constituent Assembly had been completed, it would be required to return its mandate. It might expect to last six months or nine—the timetable set down by the previous cabinet provided for a two and a half months' period between the parliamentary elections and the elections for the Constituent Assembly and a further period after the Constituent Assembly elections before parliament could assemble—but with a new parliament established it would have to make way for a new cabinet. In one sense it was merely a caretaker ministry.

Secondly, as the cabinet's leaders saw the situation, nothing of long-term importance could be achieved until certain immediate wrongs resulting from their predecessors' actions were righted. In their view, Indonesia had lost the confidence of the outside world, its governments and its business leaders, and would have to regain this quickly.

hanuddin Harahap Cabinet and Replies to Parliamentary Criticism"; Djakarta: Kementerian Penerangan, 1955 [?]), *passim.*

The cabinet also had to act fast to keep inflation from getting out of control, and an immediate overhaul of foreign trade machinery would therefore be necessary. Above all, the government service would have to be purged of the effects of the Ali cabinet's personnel policies.

Thirdly, the cabinet was under immediate political pressures. The government parties wanted it to help them as they faced the elections. They wanted it to produce dramatic price drops in its first weeks in office; what happened to price levels later was a matter of lower priority. Some of them wanted changes in the timing of elections and in the personnel of the electoral committee. Before everything else, the government parties wanted jobs. For many in the Masjumi and the PSI this was a matter of turning the tables on the PNI. They felt that their parties' members of the civil service had for two years been victimized and evicted from positions of power. Now they wanted a redressing of grievances and a change in the balance of power in the bureaucracy, even if this went beyond and contrary to the "restoration of administrative norms" to which the cabinet was committed.

As for the Nahdatul Ulama and PSII, they were against too much settling of scores. As parties which had benefited from the Ali cabinet's personnel and patronage policies, they tended to support the *status quo* of bureaucratic power. But they had no strong commitment to problem-solving policies. The small nationalist parties for their part were largely unconcerned with both power and policy. Most of them were not strong partisans in the intrabureaucratic struggle between the PNI on the one hand and the Masjumi and PSI on the other. On the whole their ministers did not share the emphasis of the Burhan-uddin cabinet's leaders on problem-solving policies. Even where they did have a strong personal commitment to policy, their actions were often more affected by patronage pressures, particularly in the case of the parties which knew that their chances of gaining inclusion in a postelection cabinet were slight.

Within a few hours of the cabinet's formal installation the military police took a step of unusual boldness. It arrested Djody Gondokusumo —who till that day had been (demissionary) Minister of Justice—on suspicion of corruption. The deputy chief public prosecutor stated later that the action had been taken without the knowledge of the new cabinet.[13] Whether this was true or not, it greatly strengthened the cabinet's position. The army's power to intervene in civilian affairs was manifestly not spent, and every attack on the previous cabinet

[13] *Pedoman*, July 22, 1955.

helped the leaders of the one now assuming office. The arrest of an ex-minister for presumed corruption was without precedent in post-revolutionary Indonesia, but the action seemed to gain approval from a large part of the political public.

Similar arrests followed, with the cabinet and the army now collaborating closely. On August 14 Iskaq Tjokroadisurjo left Djakarta for the Netherlands—with a son who was to be placed in a school there for the deaf and dumb. He failed to heed a subsequent summons for questioning by the chief public prosecutor.[14] Among those who were arrested in August were several employees of the Central Import Office, a vice-consul in Singapore, and a number of persons employed in agencies of the Ministry of Justice.[15] Although the government made repeated declarations that its cleanup was not directed against members of particular parties, it was a fact that PNI men were prominent among those arrested and that no person identified as Masjumi or PSI was detained. (The PKI was also conspicuously unrepresented, but this was not interpreted as indicating army support for the PKI!) Meanwhile the government-supporting press came forth with voluminous charges of corruption against other members and appointees of the Ali cabinet. At least eight of the outgoing ministers were subjected to repeated press assertions that they had enriched themselves by irregular means.

The anticorruption drive gave the Burhanuddin cabinet a great deal of political initiative. But the opposition was by no means paralyzed, and it was not long before it became vociferous in its criticisms of the new government. The whole crisis from June 27 onward had aroused intense bitterness, but up to the time of the Burhanuddin cabinet's emergence the humiliated and angry supporters of the Ali cabinet had hesitated to express their feelings in strong language. The PNI had hoped to be able to win inclusion in a new cabinet. The PKI had felt itself becoming isolated from the PNI. Both had been afraid of the army, and the PKI reckoned with the possibility of a major

[14] On the Iskaq case see *Keterangan dan Djawaban Pemerintah tentang Program Kabinet Burhanuddin Harahap*, pp. 106–107. Iskaq returned to Indonesia on April 23, 1956, by which time much had changed in cabinet and army politics. Thus he was not then subjected to legal action. He was brought to trial in 1959 and again in 1960 on charges related to his tenure of office in 1953–1954 and subsequently convicted. See *Duta Masjarakat*, Jan. 5, 1960, and *Times of Indonesia*, Oct. 8, 1960.

[15] For a list of those arrested in the cabinet's first ten days in office see *Abadi*, Aug. 22, 1955.

crackdown like that of the Sukiman cabinet in August 1951.[16] But now that the cabinet was formed and the President had returned home, the reasons for hesitancy lost much of their weight.

Thus the press of these two parties adopted a tone of increasingly intense hostility to the cabinet. As it was principally for lack of honesty that the ministers of the Ali cabinet were being arraigned, so it was the personal integrity of the new ministers which was the principal target of opposition charges. Indeed, in the seven weeks between the cabinet's formation and the parliamentary elections the PNI and PKI press so often referred to the cabinet cynically as one composed of "men who are honest and have authority" (Hatta's phrase in the commission he gave the *formateurs*) that the cabinet's supporters were obliged to drop the phrase from their vocabulary. Of the many epithets with which the cabinet was endowed by the opposition, the one which stuck longest was "Kabinet B.H." (the initials of the Prime Minister, but also a Dutch and Indonesian euphemism for *buste houder* or brassière)!

THE LONG-AWAITED ELECTIONS

One particular focus of the opposition's criticisms of the cabinet was the charge that it was planning to postpone the holding of elections. Officially, according to the timetable announced by the Central Electoral Committee in April, the parliamentary elections were to be held on September 29. But election preparations had fallen behind schedule in July and early August. According to the existing timetable the appointment of members of polling station committees (*panitia penjelenggara pemungutan suara*) was to have begun on August 1 throughout the country, but in many areas this was not begun till early September. The Masjumi and PSI press made much of reports that election supplies had not been received in a number of areas, and opposition newspapers construed this as preparing the ground for a government decision changing the election date to some time later than September 29.

On August 15 the chairman of the Central Electoral Committee, S. Hadikusumo (of the PNI), stated that the parliamentary elections could definitely still be held on September 29. Two days later the President used his Independence Day message to declare that elections would have to be held "without a day's delay. . . . Let there

---

[16] At the time of the cabinet crisis there were reports that PKI leaders were leaving the capital for undisclosed destinations.

not be anyone who would betray the elections or try to delay their holding. . . . Whoever tries to put obstacles in the ways of holding them . . . is a traitor to the Revolution." [17] But cabinet spokesmen were mostly vague in their references to the date. On August 22 the Prime Minister declared that "the cabinet has absolutely no intention of postponing the elections," but went on to add that "whether or not polling takes place precisely on September 29 will depend on the completion of the preparations." [18]

While the opposition press made repeated charges that the cabinet was bent on delaying the elections, the cabinet itself was divided on the issue. On the one hand, the ministers of the Nahdatul Ulama were strongly in favor of adhering to the September 29 date; on the other hand, several ministers, reportedly of the PSI and PIR, argued for delay and linked this with demands for early changes in the composition of the Central Electoral Committee and its subordinate committees. Finally, on September 8, the Information Minister announced the decision: elections would be held on September 29 except in a certain small number of areas where preparations were not sufficiently advanced. They would be held everywhere by November 29.[19]

In the three weeks that remained at the time of this decision, an immense amount of work had to be done. Ballot papers, candidate lists, and a variety of other papers had to be transported long distances from the electoral district committees to the *ketjamatans* or subdistrict offices, from where they would be carried to the polling stations on election eve. In many areas membership of the polling station committees had still to be finalized, and in almost all of them training had yet to be given to the appointed members. The copying out of separate registers of voters for each polling station, the delivery to the voters of their letters of notification, and the erection of cubicles, fences, and sometimes roofs, which went to make a polling station— all these had to be done with great speed. The task was complicated by last-minute new technical regulations, some of them made by the Central Electoral Committee after the appointment to it, on September 26, of five new members from parties hitherto unrepresented on it (the Masjumi, PSI, Catholic Party, Parindra, and Indonesian People's Party). But as is often the case with Indonesian administra-

[17] *Fly on, Radjawali* ("Speech of His Excellency the President of the Republic of Indonesia"; Djakarta: Ministry of Information, 1955).

[18] *Antara*, Aug. 22, 1955.

[19] In actual fact voting was held in Sept. 29 at 85 per cent or more of the country's approximately 93,532 polling stations.

tion, the crisis of feverish last-minute activity produced a high level of efficiency. Where it was impossible to adhere rigidly to the complicated and technically worded regulations of the Central Electoral Committee, a variety of adaptations and modifications were made by electoral authorities at various lower levels. But local improvisation appears to have been generally faithful to the spirit of the central instruction. When election day came, the polling station committees were ready.

During the last few weeks before the elections, the cabinet made a number of decisions expected to increase its popularity with the voters. As of September 1 the price of gasoline was brought down from Rp. 1.80 per liter to Rp. 1.04. On the same day the cabinet announced that it was "freezing" the Central Import Office, reputedly a nest of corruption, and replacing it by a new office, the Badan Perdagangan Devisen (Foreign Exchange Trading Body). With this went a series of new measures aimed at "natural screening" of national importers. National importers were now required when applying for licenses for particular commodities to deposit beforehand the rupiah equivalent of their landed import price (plus the import surcharge). Among national importers so qualifying, foreign exchange permits would be issued to those offering the most favorable bids. In addition, the government liquidated various other means of restraining trade, including the Jajasan Perbekalan dan Persediaan (Supplies and Equipment Foundation), a government body with monopoly controls over certain imports.[20] And it abolished various special regulations for imports and exports—parallel transactions, barter arrangements, and so on. One result of these steps was a dramatic fall in the prices of a number of imported goods, particularly textiles, and indeed of the urban price level in general.[21] The free market value of the rupiah rose markedly, and the gold price fell. On the other hand, the PNI and Communist opposition was able to point to shortages of rice, sugar, and salt in various urban centers occurring in the last weeks before September 29, and although the cabinet explained

[20] See John O. Sutter, *Indonesianisasi: Politics in a Changing Economy, 1940–1955* (Southeast Asia Program, Cornell University; Ithaca, N.Y., 1959), pp. 1028–1029, and Hans O. Schmitt, "Some Monetary and Fiscal Consequences of Social Conflict in Indonesia, 1950–58" (doctoral dissertation, University of California, Berkeley, 1959), pp. 192–194.

[21] In Djakarta the gold price, a widely accepted index of the value of money, fell by 12.9 per cent between June 30 and Sept. 26. See also Bank Indonesia, *Report for the Year 1955–1956*, pp. 56 ff.

these as resulting from floods and in part from the mistakes of its predecessors, their effect was to give the opposition a campaign issue.

Throughout September, party leaders were traveling almost incessantly. Party dailies were printed in much-increased quantities and distributed free of charge on a large scale. Their contents included ever more bitter attacks on their enemies. The PKI's *Harian Rakjat* ran a special daily feature carrying personal attacks on leaders of the Masjumi, pointing particularly to instances of collaboration with the Japanese during the occupation (a subject which was otherwise scarcely ever referred to in the political invective of our period) and with the Dutch during the revolutionary struggle. The PNI's *Suluh Indonesia* predicted that PNI and NU leaders would be arrested immediately before polling day.[22] The PSI's *Pedoman* published a letter to the editor in which the President was referred to as a lackey of the "Co-operative Organization for Corruption," the Masjumi-PSI name for the Ali cabinet's supporters.[23] *Indonesia Raya* went into detail on the business interests of its opponents (another subject which was normally out of bounds in the polemics of the period).[24] At the same time all these papers carried reports of meetings and "political feasts" on the one hand and rumors, threats, brawls, and intimidations on the other.

In many areas this bitterness existed at the village level. Here the emphasis shifted in the last few weeks and days from large public meetings to small meetings and house-to-house canvassing. In particular the parties went to considerable effort to instruct their supporters in the techniques of voting. But in many village areas the process of winning over voters believed not to have made up their minds went on. In certain areas village heads, religious leaders, and village guard members applied pressure actively to win the votes of those whom they thought were intending to vote for their opponents. More than at any previous stage of the long campaign, the social harmony of villages and their hamlet subdivisions was under strain.

In the last days before September 29 the atmosphere was one of tense and anxious anticipation. Alarmist rumors about the elections

---

[22] *Suluh Indonesia*, Sept. 9, 1955.

[23] *Pedoman*, Sept. 3, 1955. See also *ibid.*, Sept. 5, 1955.

[24] For an excellent brief analysis of the contents of party appeals in *Suluh Indonesia, Abadi, Harian Rakjat*, and *Pedoman* between Sept. 1 and Sept. 29 see Irsjaf Sjarif and Batara Simatupang, "Pers Indonesia dan Pemilihan Umum" ("The Indonesian Press and the General Elections"), *Warta dan Massa*, I, no. 2 (Nov. 1955), 19–28.

had been abroad in village communities in many parts of the archipelago for some months. In certain areas there were detailed stories of forthcoming submarine landings, of white men about to descend from mountains, and of impending attacks from yellow-clad ghost armies. Invulnerability dealers were reported from several parts of Java to be selling special election potions, many storekeepers hoarded goods, and in a few isolated places there was a rush to the pawnshop. The poisoning scare which spread through many parts of Java immediately before and immediately after the parliamentary elections is to be seen as an expression of the same abnormal sociopsychological conditions.[25]

Such rumors as were abroad in the final days before the elections were checked but little by the government's frequent radio appeals for calm. The movements of troops to be seen in cities and towns and on every major road just before September 29 served only to heighten fears that awesome and calamitous happenings might occur on that day. In many parts of the country an unproclaimed curfew was observed for two or three nights before election day. Accounts from every part of the archipelago tell of the spontaneous closing down of all shop and market trade in town and village areas alike after midday on September 28. In some areas the quiet was described as comparable to that after an air raid.

On election day itself the atmosphere was striking. Voters arrived at their polling stations early. By seven in the morning large numbers were gathered at every center, and everyone had arrived by eight. The number of those assembled occasioned great surprise. Women in advanced stages of pregnancy came—and in a number of cases their babies were born at the polling station. In many cases too villagers were there who had long been absent from the village. All were in their best clothes. Almost everywhere solemnity prevailed and at many places tension, a clear indication of the far-reaching effects of the long campaign on the whole population of the country. An un-

---

[25] This scare led to beatings of foodsellers in many parts of the island and was even discussed at some length in the cabinet. The Eyckmann bacteriological institute of the Central Public Hospital in Djakarta received more than 600 samples of supposedly poisoned food within a period of four days, but it found that none of this was actually poisoned. Nor was there evidence elsewhere of any foundation for the rumors. Charges were leveled against several parties for instigating the poisoning and, later, for spreading the false rumors, but the evidence suggests that the tensions of the social situation were the primary cause of the scare, that specific fears spread because of their function of providing a rationale for intensely felt anxiety (and in some cases also outlets for aggression).

natural, uncanny quietness, broken only by whispering, was reported from a large number of polling stations.[26]

But in many of these there was a remarkable release from tension as soon as polling got under way. The first voters were confused, and ashamed to be so. Some pierced a symbol on the candidate list on the wall of the cubicle instead of on the ballot paper; others could not fold the paper properly. Frequently, however, they were corrected by the spectators, with the children joining in lustily. After some time everyone understood the procedure. It continued to be awesome, but, like a religious rite repeated a number of times, it ceased to inspire disquiet. At the same time everything was peaceful. Except in insecure areas there were no soldiers or policemen to be seen at the polls. Nothing remained to sustain the earlier vague fears. The widespread feeling that something bad would happen on this day was gradually disappearing.

Thus a new atmosphere came to prevail at numerous polling stations, an atmosphere like that of a national celebration, serious but no longer tense. The dominant reaction of the voters was one of relief, pride, and satisfaction. Many villagers, as well as townsmen, were abundantly happy after casting their vote, proud to have been able to participate in this important national ceremonial activity.

The turnout of voters was extremely high. On September 29 or shortly thereafter more than 39 million Indonesians went to the polls. Of all who had been registered 87.65 per cent cast a valid vote; approximately 91.54 per cent voted.[27] About 2.5 per cent more would have died in the 12 to 17 months since registration. Thus only about 6 per cent of the registered voters failed to use the franchise. This included many from areas directly threatened by rebel and bandit groups. It included some of the very old and the very ill and some

---

[26] Cf. Boyd R. Compton, "The Silent Election," *Newsletter of the Institute of Current World Affairs* (New York), Sept. 29, 1955. For a selection of press comment see *Indonesia Memilih*, pp. 19–32. The evidence on which my reconstruction here and on the following pages is based includes press accounts, personal observation, a large number of *post factum* interviews, and information provided by personal friends living in widely scattered parts of the country who were kind enough to make observations on the basis of lists of questions I had previously sent them.

[27] Feith, *The Indonesian Elections of 1955* (Cornell Modern Indonesia Project, Interim Reports Series; Ithaca, N.Y., 1957), p. 50. This figure assumes that the valid vote was 95.75 per cent of the total vote. Figures for invalid voting are available to me for only 11 of the 15 electoral districts, but it is a reasonable estimate that 4.25 per cent of all votes cast were not valid.

who could not travel to where they were registered and were ignorant of the procedure for absentee voting. It included a very small group of city dwellers unaffected by the social pressure for participating in the elections. Finally, it included several tiny groups, most of them mystical, who had conscientious objections to voting. In almost every area of the country the total number of nonvoters was significantly smaller than in the elections of village heads.

As a number of observers of efforts to operate Western-type democratic institutions in Asia have explained the difficulties encountered by reference to the village voters' apathy, ignorance, fear, and gullibility, it may be useful to look briefly here at the nature of villagers' participation in the 1955 elections. Was it voluntarily that Indonesian villagers went to the polls in such large numbers? Did they make a free choice? Did they understand what they were voting for?

It was plainly not concern about political issues which brought such large numbers to the polls. Fear is undoubtedly part of the explanation. Villagers in many areas believed that voting was compulsory and that those not voting would be severely punished. Even where no rumors of this kind circulated, voters were afraid of the wrath of their *lurah* and other village councilors if they did not go to the polls. Again they were afraid of the anger of the party leaders who had canvassed for their votes.

More important than specific fears of this kind, however, was the powerful community obligation which villagers felt. Elections had been accepted by whole communities, in that the leaders of a village or hamlet accepted the new moral notion and spread it quickly to other members of the community. Indeed, there is an important sense in which the elections were accepted voluntarily by both village leaders and ordinary villagers.

In the political thinking of the nationalist leadership two main arguments had long been put forward in favor of the holding of elections. The first was that of democratic ideology: Because Indonesia was now a democratic country elections must be held. Frequently associated with this was an argument of nationalist pride: Ability to conduct elections had to be proved before the eyes of the world as a demonstration that Indonesia was indeed ripe for nationhood. A second major argument was the more pragmatic one that elections were necessary for the attainment of political stability or, as some said, that they would create political stability. Since before the October 17 affair of 1952, much current dissatisfaction with the country's political condition, with squabbling and faction on the one hand and ineffectiveness of policy action on the other, had been channeled into feeling against the existing temporary and unrepresentative parliament and the multiplicity of parties in it. These facts, so ran the widely accepted argument, resulted in frequent cabinet crises, and thus in political instability. Elections would create a representative parliament and one with moral authority and at the same time lessen the number of political parties.[28] They would put an end to political instability and thereby undo most of the current political wrongs.

In a mass publicity campaign lasting almost three years the Indonesian voter had repeatedly been given these ideas in one form or another—by the parties as they explained the idea of elections, by the local agents of the Ministry of Information, by his *lurah*, by the literacy teacher who came to his village, and by his own children who were at school. At this level, of course, the arguments were put in less complicated terms. The villager was told two simple things about elections, that they were part of independence and that they would make independence better. But both of these he understood clearly.

His understanding was not perception of a cause-effect relationship; it was perception and acknowledgment of a moral (and in most cases also religious) duty.[29] However much they might seem like discord, which was sharply opposed to the traditional values of his society, elections, he had been taught to believe, were something good, a noble national activity. When he actually came to vote, it gave him a sense of participation in greatness. It was not the feeling that he was taking part in governing the nation, but rather that he had a part in its nationhood in a symbolic ceremonial sense, the same feeling a new communicant has of participation in a Christian church. Moreover, to the extent that the elections were free—and to the extent

[28] For a summary of the arguments for holding elections see "Problems of Elections," *Indonesian Affairs*, vol. II, no. 2 (April–May 1952). See also *Mendjelang 29 September* ("Anticipating September 29"; Djakarta: Kementerian Penerangan, 1955), a collection of pre-election radio addresses given by Vice-President Hatta, Prime Minister Burhanuddin Harahap, Information Minister Sjamsuddin Sutan Makmur, Religious Affairs Minister K. H. Iljas, and Chairman of the Central Electoral Committee S. Hadikusumo.

[29] Several *fatwas*, Moslem religious edicts issued by councils of *ulamas* (scholars), stressed that voting was obligatory for a Moslem. The most important *fatwa*, often quoted particularly in Sumatra, was the one issued by the All-Indonesian Conference of Ulama held at Medan in April 1953.

that more than one party existed within his village—he could see that they gave him a right to choose freely between the rival groups of his social superiors in the village.

But to what extent were the elections free? The electoral machinery was operated by village leaders, and the effectiveness of the controls which were formally built into it—multiparty committees, public counting of votes, and so on—depended on the internal power relationships of particular villages and hamlets. Controls were unnecessary and of little meaning in those villages (a sizable minority) where only one party had organized support. And they were ineffective in those villages (a very small part of the total number) where several parties were in existence but a single power group, and one with strong commitments to a particular party, supplied all members of the polling station committees. It is probably villages like these, and towns as well, which account for the reported cases of fraud and for the several scores of polling stations where a second poll had to be held because of suspected irregularities in the first.[30] But at most polling stations a plurality of parties existed and were represented on the committees, and there the control machinery worked well.

Even at these stations, however, existing social organization imposed important limits on the extent to which the ballot was effectively secret. In fact, large numbers of villagers were not convinced at the time of the September elections that no one would know which way they had voted. Not only were there many who did not understand the electoral technique well enough to appreciate the guarantee it created. In addition, many voters in sharply divided villages expected to be questioned by their social superiors after the poll about how they had cast their ballots.

Intimidation was certainly widespread in the last stages of campaigning. Sizable numbers of voters felt pressed to vote Masjumi in areas of Atjeh and West Java where Darul Islam strength had to be reckoned with. And the newspaper record makes it clear that intimidation was practiced fairly widely by PNI *lurahs* and their assistants, and to a lesser extent by PKI village guards, in parts of East and Central Java.

Some of this was direct intimidation. In some Javanese villages *lurahs* threatened voters with jail sentences and fines if they did not vote PNI. In others they threatened to withhold supplies of salt and

[30] For examples of the types of fraud discovered see Feith, *The Indonesian Elections of 1955,* pp. 42–43.

other goods normally distributed through them. In still others *djagos* (village bullies) employed by *lurahs* suggested that villagers might be compelled to leave their villages unless they followed voting instructions. And there were instances where Communist youths, equipped with knives and truncheons for guard duty, went from house to house at night collecting signatures and thumbprints of membership of PKI front organizations.

More frequently intimidation was subtle. A *lurah* would make it known that the *tjamat* would be angry with him if his village did not produce a PNI majority or would say he had been told that "Pak Karno" (President Soekarno) wanted at least 20 PNI votes in every village. Because most village voters saw no distinction between the office of a person in authority and that person as a citizen with political views, it is difficult to determine the point at which exhortation became intimidation.

Undoubtedly there was a sizable minority of voters in different parts of the country who were subject to the pressure of one or more threats as they made their final voting decisions. Most frequently, however, pressures to vote for a particular party were felt as social obligations rather than threats. In general, villagers felt themselves obliged to vote for the party of those to whom they were or would be indebted, their *kijaji*, their *lurah*, their landowner if they were tenants or their creditor if they were owners or sharecroppers, their local head of the village guard, or their senior kinsman. Where these were competing obligations, as they were in that large majority of villages where more than one party had organized strength, individual voters had a significant degree of freedom of choice. Only by the application of perfectionist standards, of a kind which political theorists have generally abandoned in the case of the voter in the West, could it be said that they were not casting free ballots.[31]

Moreover, the choices which this group of voters made were most frequently perceived as bearing some relation to wider ideological

[31] Bernard Berelson, an American authority on voting behavior writes: "Perhaps the main impact of realistic research on contemporary politics has been to temper some of the requirements set by our traditional normative theory for the typical citizen." Speaking from observation of the American scene, he goes on to say that "voters do not ratiocinate about voting as they do about the purchase of a house or car. They do not attach efficient means to explicit ends. . . . Voting preferences are more like cultural tastes. . . . Individual voters cannot satisfy the requirements of classical democratic theory. But the [American political] system meets certain requirements" (B. R. Berelson, P. F. Lazarsfeld, and W. N. McPhee, *Voting* [Chicago: University of Chicago Press, 1954], pp. 306–312).

issues. Some sort of connection had been established in all except very remote villages between the local and traditional loyalties of the villager and the ideological currents of the nation. A probable majority of the village voters were thus able to register meaningful choices—meaningful not as judgments on the performance of particular governments but as ideological identifications.

The Indonesian experience cannot therefore be regarded as confirming the notion that voting by Asian villagers makes a farce of democracy. It would certainly be wrong to attach much importance to the village voter's behavior as a causal factor in the malfunctioning of parliamentary institutions—except in the sense that the appeal to the village voter was of great importance in aggravating ideological cleavage, and so undermining consensus on the ends of the state.

It should be added, however, that many members of the political elite and of the political public judged the village voter by the very high standards of traditional democratic theory and concluded from what they saw of village attitudes to voting, and of the effectiveness of money and the power of government officials, that Western-type democracy could only be a mockery under prevailing conditions in Indonesia. This conclusion was most important in preparing these men to accept an abandonment of constitutional democracy.

As it became possible about October 8 to see a picture emerging of the over-all results of the elections, the number of surprises was great. (The final results are shown in Table 2.) Outstanding was the success

Table 2. The results of the parliamentary elections

	No. of valid votes	Percentage of total valid votes	No. of seats	No. of seats in provisional parliament (at time of its dissolution)
PNI	8,434,653	22.3	57	42
Masjumi	7,903,886	20.9	57	44
Nahdatul Ulama	6,955,141	18.4	45	8
PKI	6,176,914	16.4	39	17
PSII	1,091,160	2.9	8	4
Parkindo	1,003,325	2.6	8	5
Partai Katholik	770,740	2.0	6	8
PSI	753,191	2.0	5	14
IPKI	541,306	1.4	4	—

	No. of valid votes	Percentage of total valid votes	No. of seats	No. of seats in provisional parliament (at time of its dissolution)
Perti	483,014	1.3	4	1
PRN	242,125	0.6	2	13
Partai Buruh	224,167	0.6	2	6
GPPS (Movement to Defend the Pantja Sila)	219,985	0.6	2	—
PRI	206,261	0.5	2	—
PPPRI (Police Employees' Association of the Republic of Indonesia)	200,419	0.5	2	—
Partai Murba	199,588	0.5	2	4
Baperki (Consultative Council on Indonesian Citizenship)	178,887	0.5	1	—
PIR-Wongsonegoro	178,481	0.5	1	3
Gerinda (Indonesian Movement)	154,792	0.4	1	—
Permai	149,287	0.4	1	—
Partai Persatuan Daya (*Dayak* Unity Party)	146,054	0.4	1	—
PIR-Hazairin	114,644	0.3	1	18
PPTI (*Tharikah* Unity Party)	85,131	0.2	1	—
AKUI (Islamic Victory Force)	81,454	0.2	1	—
PRD (Village People's Party)	77,919	0.2	1	—
PRIM (Party of the People of Free Indonesia)	72,523	0.2	1	—
Acoma (Younger Generation Communists)	64,514	0.2	1	—
R. Soejono Prawirosoedarso and Associates	53,305	0.1	1	—
Other parties, organizations, and individual candidates	1,022,433	2.7	—	46
Total	37,785,299	100.0	257	233

Source: A. van Marle, "The First Indonesian Parliamentary Elections," *Indonesië*, IX (1956), 258.

of the Nahdatul Ulama which was to raise its parliamentary representation from 8 to 45, and another was the unexpectedly small vote received by the Masjumi. PNI and Communist strength also caused surprise. A great deal of comment was devoted to the low vote of the Socialist Party, and some to the even lower vote of the national-communist Partai Murba and the virtual disappearance of the minor nationalist parties—PRN, the two PIR's, of Wongsonegoro and Hazairin respectively, Parindra, SKI, and the Labor Party, which had had such important roles in the cabinets responsible to the temporary parliament in the preceding five years. Although some observers had predicted the emergence of the PNI, Masjumi, NU, and PKI as the "big four," none expected as sharp a delineation as evolved, with the smallest of the four major parties, the PKI, receiving more than five times as many votes as the largest of the other parties, the PSII.

Interestingly enough, persons of different political allegiances were surprised by substantially the same aspects of the result. Few had been confident that they could predict the outcome; all had expected surprises. But their expectations appear to have had a great deal in common. No PNI, NU, or PKI politician or editor, for example, thought it necessary to explain why the PNI or PKI or NU vote was so low or why the Masjumi vote was so high. On the contrary, all sought to offer explanations of why the PNI, PKI, and particularly NU had done as well as they had and why the Masjumi and PSI had polled so much more poorly than had been expected.[32]

One feature of the result which drew particular attention was the regional distribution of votes. The specifically regional and ethnic parties had clearly not done well, and even the parties which obtained a large part of their vote from one or a few electoral districts did not account for a large part of the vote.[33] But some highly important lessons of political geography were contained in the distribution of votes of the four main parties. Thus the PNI obtained 85.97 per cent of its parliamentary vote in Java, the NU 85.6 per cent and the PKI 88.6 per cent, whereas the population of Java—51,637,552 persons of Indo-

[32] For a discussion of these explanations and of the election results see Feith, *The Indonesian Elections of 1955*, pp. 57 ff.

[33] The PSII obtained 62.4 per cent of its total vote in West Java and Sulawesi, and the Parkindo 86.3 per cent of its vote in North Sumatra, Sulawesi, Maluku, and East Nusa Tenggara. Of the Catholic vote 59.6 per cent came from the one district of East Nusa Tenggara; 60.2 per cent of the Socialist vote came from West Java and West Nusa Tenggara (Bali and Lombok), 72.8 per cent of the Perti vote from Central Sumatra, and 81.7 per cent of the IPKI vote from West Java.

nesian citizenship out of an all-Indonesian total of 77,987,879 according to Central Electoral Committee statistics of 1954 [34]—was no more than 66.2 per cent of that of Indonesia. More particularly the strength of these three parties was concentrated in the two electoral districts of East and Central Java. In this area, where 45.6 per cent of Indonesia's population lived, the PNI got 65.5 per cent of its total vote, the NU 73.9 per cent, and the Communists 74.9 per cent. On the other hand, the Masjumi obtained only 51.3 per cent of its total vote in Java (only 25.4 per cent in East and Central Java) and 48.7 per cent outside Java. It thus emerged as the leading party by far among that third of Indonesia's population living outside the main island. Although a number of observers had foreseen that the PNI, PKI, and NU would be particularly strong in Java and that the Masjumi would obtain a high vote in Sumatra, few if any of the party leaders and commentators had anticipated the sharp delineation of strengths which the election results disclosed. The new perceptions of interregional politics resulting from the outcome of the elections were of the greatest importance in the developments of the next few years.

A RECAST PICTURE OF POLITICS

For the Burhanuddin Harahap cabinet the election results were a shattering blow. It is true that the parties of the cabinet had together polled a majority of the votes cast, but it was a narrow majority, much narrower than had been expected. Moreover, a very large part of the voting strength of the cabinet parties had been contributed by the Nahdatul Ulama and to a lesser extent the PSII. These two parties had entered the cabinet reluctantly and continued to have common interests and affinities of feeling with the PNI with which they had cooperated in the period of the Ali cabinet. Their power within the cabinet was markedly inferior as compared with the Masjumi and PSI, which provided the leadership of the team. But once the election results were known, it was evident that they would not be satisfied to remain in this weak position. Thus the cabinet leaders were soon to be faced with a devil-and-deep-sea choice—between making major concessions to the NU and PSII on the one hand and on the other hand courting the real possibility that these two parties would leave the

[34] This figure was dated Oct. 30, 1954. In a joint statement of the Indonesian delegation to the UN Seminar on Population in Asia and the Far East, held in Nov. to Dec. 1955, the population in 1955 was estimated as 82.3 million (including foreign nationals). It was further estimated that 54.2 million of these lived in Java. See *Ekonomi dan Keuangan Indonesia*, IX, no. 2 (Feb. 1956), pp. 90–115.

coalition and thus create the situation where a cabinet based on one of the country's four main parties was ranged against an opposition composed of the other three.

As soon as a general picture of election strengths emerged, political leaders began to make plans and calculations as regards the composition of the new cabinet which would be formed as soon as the elected parliament had assembled. The electorate had given no clear "verdict," and therefore the leadership and composition of the new cabinet would depend in large measure on bargaining between the four main parties. Indeed bargaining began forthwith.

In practice, it soon became apparent, two major possibilities existed. The three large non-Communist parties could form a cabinet together, or, alternatively, the PNI and NU could together form a cabinet like that of Ali Sastroamidjojo which had recently been toppled, with PKI support (and perhaps one or two PKI members or sympathizers included) and with the Masjumi in the opposition. Whereas the first of these two possibilities was generally considered the one more likely to be realized—because of growing anticommunism in the PNI and NU, and especially because of army pressure—the second could not be ruled out. From the point of view of both the Masjumi and the PSI it was vitally important that the cabinet should be in line with the first possibility. As they saw it, great efforts had to be made to bring this about, which meant working for closer relations with both the NU and the PNI. Masjumi-PSI concern on this score had important moderating and restrictive effects on the actions of the Burhanuddin cabinet.

The power relationships of the new situation became evident soon after the elections. In September the cabinet had found itself working under major legal limitations in its efforts to marshal evidence against those it had arrested for corruption. Government prosecutors who were personally certain of the guilt of the arrested persons had found it impossible to establish a case which would convince a judge. The persons concerned, these prosecutors maintained, had been careful enough to destroy the evidence of their malfeasance. To cope with this situation the cabinet had drafted a bill which would make it possible to establish separate tribunals to hear corruption cases and which would oblige accused persons to answer questions put to them in the course of the proceedings of these courts.[35]

[35] See *Keterangan dan Djawaban Pemerintah tentang Program Kabinet Burhanuddin Harahap*, pp. 93–98, 192–194. Opposition spokesmen maintained, and government leaders denied, that this would in effect reverse the onus of proof.

On September 30, the day after the elections, the cabinet decided after lengthy debate that it would enact these changes in the form of an emergency law, thus one which required only *post factum* parliamentary approval. The decision was taken against the strong opposition of the Nahdatul Ulama, several of whose members had been mentioned in press accusations of corruption.

The bill went next to President Soekarno for his signature. The President first delayed his signing and then gave the cabinet a refusal. There had been intermittent conflict between the President and the cabinet's leaders from the very inception of the cabinet. On August 17 the President had made a speech whose whole emphasis was at odds with the political position of the cabinet. Not only had he said that there was not to be a day's delay in the holding of elections; he had also made no reference to the drive against corruption. Immediately before election day, conflict had arisen over the President's pro-Pantja Sila speeches before large mass rallies and the cabinet had ordered the cancellation of a rally the President was to address in Bandung on September 26. But the vetoing of a major piece of legislation and one which was in line with the popular drive against corruption—this was to take the conflict one step further.

The cabinet was confronted with a most difficult situation. It could accept the President's suggestion that it take the anticorruption bill to parliament. But this would mean to lose time and allow the momentum of the drive against corruption to flag. Moreover, there would be difficulties in marshaling the necessary parliamentary votes. In any case the cabinet would suffer a loss of prestige. Alternatively it could take the bold and risky course of defying the President and take the bill to Vice-President Hatta, who, it was believed, would if he were asked sign it while the President was outside the capital. For this there might be sufficient support from the army, whose leaders continued to feel strongly on the issue of the Ali cabinet's corruption. But, on the other hand, the cabinet leaders could not expect the army to give them the sort of support which would seem to range it openly against the electoral voice of the people, as shown in the emergence of the PNI, NU, and PKI as three of the country's four major parties.

The Masjumi, on which the burden of this decision fell more than on any party, was sharply divided on what was to be done. Eventually the voices of caution prevailed. Granted the cabinet's dependence on the Nahdatul Ulama and granted the dangerous implications for the composition of the future cabinet in a policy of antagonizing the President, the PNI, and the NU all at once, it was agreed that the cabinet should back down. On November 8 the cabinet took the anticorruption bill to the agenda committee of parliament. The bill never reached the parliamentary floor.

THE REAPPOINTMENT OF COLONEL NASUTION

The month of October saw one further development which served to slow down the cabinet's political momentum. This was the appointment of a new Chief of Staff of the Army. The matter had been pending since the time of the June 27 affair. In August the cabinet had formally retired Major General Bambang Utojo and rescinded the earlier suspension of Colonel Zulkifli Lubis. At the same time it had formally declared the October 17 affair of 1952 closed, an action which brought with it the possibility of a return to active service of the officers who had been suspended as a result of the affair. But Lubis remained Deputy Chief of Staff; he was not formally installed as Acting Chief of Staff.

During all this time there was much discussion and negotiation inside the army on the matter of the officer to whom the highest post would eventually go, and early in October the General Staff submitted three names to the cabinet. They were, in order of seniority, Colonels Simbolon, Gatot Subroto, and Zulkifli Lubis.[36] For most of the rest of the month the government parties considered the three candidates, but they clearly found difficulty in making a decision.

In line with the Jogjakarta conference's emphasis on seniority, Simbolon appeared to be the strongest candidate. He had considerable experience as a field commander, and although he had not had military training other than that provided by the Japanese to the officers of their auxiliary corps Gyu Gun (the Sumatran Peta), he was accepted as a thoroughly professional officer. At the same time his political ideas were in line with those of the cabinet leadership. A leader of the "pro-October 17 group," he was a sympathizer of the Socialist Party and in his five years as territorial commander in North Sumatra had earned the fear and strong dislike of the PKI. He had the support of Vice-President Hatta for his candidacy.

But certain factors stood in the way of his obtaining the coveted post. He was a Protestant, and there was a feeling in NU, PSII, and certain Masjumi circles that it was enough that a Christian should have been the country's highest military commander between 1950 and 1953—this was the Armed Forces Chief of Staff, Colonel (later Major

[36] *Indonesia Raya,* Oct. 7, 1955.

General) T. B. Simatupang. Secondly, Simbolon had for some time been a personal rival of Zulkifli Lubis and as such had earned the enmity of a sizable number of officers who supported Lubis. A complicating argument against him was that Simbolon and Lubis were both Bataks and that it would be wrong for the Chief of Staff and Deputy Chief of Staff to be men from the same region. Finally, Simbolon was disliked by President Soekarno.

The second strongest candidate was Lubis. He had distinguished himself notably in the previous months, demonstrating not a little political skill. Thus his prestige in the army had risen, and at the same time the cabinet owed him a political debt. It was rumored that he had support from certain leading members of the Masjumi. On the other hand, he had earned the lasting hatred of the President. In addition, the seniority emphasis of the Jogjakarta conference spoke against him. His training was considerable, as high as that which any Indonesian had obtained from the Japanese. But he was young and had never been a field commander. As most of his experience had been in intelligence work, the cloak-and-dagger image continued to cling to him, despite his period of almost two years as Deputy Chief of Staff. Moreover, his history in military politics was zigzaggish. He had been regarded as a Soekarno man during and after the Revolution and had been a principal assistant to the President in the October 17 affair. His promotion to the No. 2 post in the General Staff had been initiated by Iwa Kusumasumantri. Sometime in 1954, he had begun to cooperate with the pro-October 17 group of officers whom he helped to lead over the June 27 affair.

All these factors were eventually enough to rule him out in the cabinet's mind as a serious candidate for the Chief of Staff post. Consideration continued, however, to be given to a "way out" formula whereby Lubis would be formally made Acting Chief of Staff, with the appointment of a permanent chief postponed.

The General Staff's third nominee, Gatot Subroto, was a compromise candidate. He was not seriously mistrusted by the supporters of either Simbolon or Lubis. Indeed, Lubis switched at one point to supporting the candidacy of Gatot Subroto, apparently in the hope that, with Gatot in the Chief of Staff's chair, he, Lubis, would be able to dominate the General Staff from the no. 2 position. Gatot was a former soldier of the KNIL, and he had been an active member of the "pro-October 17 group" in 1952, suffering the consequences in the form of an ouster from the East Indonesia command and a subsequent two-

and-a-half-year absence from active service. But he was not a man of strong political views, nor was he the head of a large officer faction. He was, in fact, a far more passive candidate than the other two. And there was general agreement that he would be a weaker and less professionally able Chief of Staff than either of them.

At some point fairly late in the negotiations the name of Colonel A. H. Nasution, the man who had been Chief of Staff on October 17, 1952, was brought into the cabinet's discussions, as a result of pressure from the Nahdatul Ulama and of a letter from Colonel Sudirman, the commander in East Java. For a number of reasons Nasution had not been considered earlier. After his retirement from the Chief of Staff's post in December 1952 he had stated that he was leaving military service. He retained his rank as a colonel on nonactive status and was a frequent writer on military subjects. But he did not participate in the Jogjakarta conference. When the Burhanuddin Harahap cabinet reopened the possibility that those who had lost their positions over the October 17 crisis might return to active service, he did not move to take advantage of this offer. In some people's minds he was no longer really an officer. Moreover, his role in the October 17 affair had been so important that many assumed that his candidacy would be even more difficult for President Soekarno to accept than those of Lubis and Simbolon. An additional factor of importance was that Nasution had personal-*cum*-political disagreements with both Lubis, who was a relative, and Simbolon.

Nevertheless, there was considerable support for Nasution as soon as the possibility of his taking the coveted post came under discussion. Like Gatot Subroto he was a compromise candidate, a man chosen as a way out of the difficulties created by the rivalry between the two front runners, Simbolon and Lubis (and between their respective supporters). Like Gatot too, Nasution was a man with little organized factional support. At the same time he was a man of great political and administrative ability. He had had prewar officer training and had served with distinction both as a field commander and as Chief of Staff in the 1950–1952 period. Since then he had given his attention to military matters of a more theoretical character, had thought through the basic problems of military policy, and had written on them extensively. From any professional point of view he was extremely well equipped to take back his old post.

On October 25 Nasution formally agreed to be a candidate. On the next day his name was added to the list of those supported by the

General Staff. On October 27 the cabinet decided, on the last of three evenings of discussion of the issue, to appoint Nasution to the post. Four days later the President signed the decree.

Much of the significance of the appointment became clear within a short time of the announcement. There was a curious absence of negative comment from any side except the PKI.[37] It was not surprising that the government-supporting press was uncritical of the new appointee. But why was there no criticism from the side of the PNI, when virtually every other personnel change of any importance which the Burhanuddin cabinet made was the subject of vociferous PNI criticism? Why should *Merdeka*, the paper which had been so prominent in demanding Nasution's ouster in October 1952, now praise him? [38] There was something very unusual about a last-minute candidate whose appointment was criticized by almost nobody, at a time of political bitterness when virtually every decision of the cabinet was condemned by the opposition.

The explanation was to emerge in the course of the following months. Colonel (now Major General) Nasution, it became evident, had reconsidered his whole political position in his three years out of office. He had come to the conclusion that he had made serious mistakes in his earlier period as Chief of Staff. He had attempted to move too rapidly against the officers without professional training, the *bapakist* leaders who had become officers largely on the basis of their influence as manipulators of nationalist symbols. He had gone too far in ignoring civilian politics, underrating the political importance for the army of maintaining good relations with the politicians. Above all, he had not appreciated the power and central importance of President Soekarno.

This change in Nasution's ideas, it now appeared, had made possible a reconciliation with the President. There had been certain signs of this reconciliation in the weeks before the appointment.[39] But the cabinet's leaders had not considered it a factor of importance. Thus they were greatly disappointed when it became clear, as it did before

[37] See *Merdeka,* Nov. 8, 1955. For one example of PKI criticism see the statement of Sarwono Sastrosutardjo in *Times of Indonesia,* Nov. 4, 1955.

[38] *Merdeka,* Nov. 11, 1955.

[39] See, for instance, *Nieuwsgier,* Aug. 25, 1955. Here Nasution was reported to have told an IPKI meeting in Makassar that it was impossible for Indonesia to solve the West Irian problem along the political path pursued up to that time. He was reported also as saying that the Revolution was not completed and should be brought back to its original lines and that young veterans should maintain their fighting attitude.

the year was out, that the new Chief of Staff was in general closer to the President than to the cabinet on issues where the two were in conflict. The Masjumi leaders in particular were soon regretting that they had supported Nasution's candidacy.

The appointment of Nasution (and the consequent eclipse of Lubis) was a major factor in weakening the cabinet. But it had wider significance as well. If the President and the Army Chief of Staff could indeed co-operate harmoniously (and if the new Chief of Staff could succeed in building his formal position into a real center of the army's power), this would create a major change in the general constellation of power. It would mean an undoing of the situation which had prevailed between February and October 1955, and earlier between 1950 and 1952, whereby the President and the army leadership were political opponents, standing at each side of the arena of cabinet and parliamentary politics. If it were indeed possible for the President and the army to work together politically—and not merely on the basis of army division and weakness as in the period of the first Ali cabinet—the combination would certainly be powerful. And it would have major consequences for civilian party politics.

FIGHTING FROM POSITIONS OF WEAKNESS

From the time of the elections the Burhanuddin cabinet was the target of more and more strongly worded attacks from the PNI and PKI press. The PNI seemed to want to settle scores with those who had humiliated it over the June 27 affair, while the PKI, grateful to be standing with the PNI again, was making up for the restraints which fear had imposed on it in July and August. There were repeated demands that the cabinet should confine itself to a caretaker role, eschewing major policy decisions, and occasional demands that it immediately resign. Within the cabinet, the NU and PSII were more and more strongly inclined toward the view that the cabinet should act merely as a caretaker. They had always been hesitant in their support of corrective and balance-restoring measures, and the election results had served to turn their reluctant support into hostility. There were also strong Masjumi pressures for the cabinet to adopt a conciliatory posture such as would prevent the party's exclusion from the next cabinet.

But the cabinet leaders had an intense commitment to various measures they had planned before the elections, measures which, as they saw them, would undo the bad effects of two years of PNI domination of government and enable the next cabinet to start with a clean slate. And they continued to enjoy the support of important sections of the army leadership and of Vice-President Hatta. In addition, they felt that their prestige would fall away entirely if they did not now fight to implement the measures they had long advocated. Therefore the leaders of the cabinet, Burhanuddin himself, Sumitro, and Anak Agung (and the Masjumi chairman, Natsir, who was sometimes described as the "Super-Premier" because of Burhanuddin's heavy reliance on his judgment), went ahead to carry out as many as possible of the measures they had planned.

On November 12 the cabinet issued an instruction preparatory to the Constituent Assembly elections in December in which it forbade any party to use the name or picture of the President or Vice-President in its campaigning. At the same time it placed a general ban on the abuse by government servants of their official influence, position, or power for the benefit of a particular party. This was directed specifically toward heads of areas, from governors to *lurahs*. The Minister of Information issued a regulation of his own at the same time, banning his employees from using their position for party advantages.

Most important and most controversial were the actions of the cabinet in the field of personnel policy. Here the general pattern was one of taking PNI men out of line positions and "kicking them upstairs" into positions as advisers and members of policy staffs, with members of government parties, mainly Masjumi and PSI persons, replacing them in their line positions. It was very much a repetition of what had been done in the Ali cabinet period with a simple reversal of roles. On the whole it was the same ministries which were affected—Information, Foreign Affairs, and to a lesser extent Economic Affairs and the Interior. One principal difference lay in the fact that the Masjumi and PSI were little concerned with patronage as such. Their interest was almost exclusively in positions of power. This cannot, however, be said of the small parties within the Burhanuddin cabinet, which demanded patronage positions and managed to get them. The other important contrast was that the Burhanuddin cabinet encountered much stronger internal bureaucratic resistance to its policies than had its predecessor. The Ali cabinet's policy of placing PNI men in more and more top-level posts meant that ministries were run increasingly by men whose social background and outlook were similar to those of most ordinary civil servants. The Burhanuddin cabinet's policy of favoring Masjumi and PSI men for high posts often had the opposite effect.

The Minister of Information, Sjamsuddin Sutan Makmur of the PIR of Hazairin, was most spectacular in his personnel policies. A former chairman of the Information section of parliament, he was on record as favoring the abolition of the ministry, and many of his critics believed that this was indeed the long-run aim of the personnel policies he pursued as minister. In less than seven months he succeeded (amid blazing press and parliamentary publicity, both favorable and hostile) in replacing PNI men by Masjumi or PSI members in six of the twelve province-level officers of the ministry, as well as making numerous changes of a similar sort in the ministry's central offices. To overcome the strong resistance of the predominantly PNI-led trade union of the ministry to his policies, he helped Masjumi, PSI, and PIR-Hazairin members to establish a rival union.[40] Supporters of his policies maintained that he had restored a political balance in the ministry. Opponents argued that the balance was one between two political armed camps and that Sjamsuddin had brought the actual work of the ministry to a standstill.

The personnel policies of Anak Agung Gde Agung as Foreign Minister were less widely publicized, but almost equally far-reaching. Here, as in the Information Ministry, the minister side-stepped a PNI secretary-general and went ahead to decree a great number of transfers. Orders were issued for the recall of all diplomats, from attaché up to counselor rank, who had been overseas for longer than two and a half years.[41] At the same time extensive changes were made in the Foreign Ministry's offices in Djakarta. Again the effect was to re-establish a political balance, but at the expense of a further weakening of administrative norms and internal co-operation in the ministry.

The Ministry of the Interior was far less seriously affected by the change-over, its minister being still Mr. Sunarjo, who had held the post in the last eight months of the Ali cabinet period. But here too there was political drama. Particular interest focused on the case of the mayor of Semarang, Hadisubeno Sosrowerdojo, who was concurrently chairman of the PNI of Central Java. The Minister of the Interior attempted over a period of six months to transfer Hadisubeno to a staff position under the mayor of Djakarta, but Hadisubeno re-

---

[40] *Abadi*, Aug. 30, 1955; *Suluh Indonesia*, Sept. 5, 1955, and Aug.–Sept. *passim.*
[41] *Keng Po*, Nov. 10, 1955.

sisted in a variety of ways.[42] He finally succeeded in having the minister delay the transfer until the time that the cabinet itself resigned.

The Burhanuddin cabinet's personnel policies in the air force were particularly controversial and brought the cabinet to one of its most important defeats.[43] In fact, there had been little internal peace in the air force since the time in early 1953 when a factional struggle between the Chief of Staff, Commodore Suryadarma, and the current head of the education division, Vice-Commodore H. Sujono, had come to a climax with the suspension and house arrest of Sujono and a number of his associates and the resignation en bloc of a number of their supporters from the force. The Ali cabinet had thrown its full support to Chief of Staff Suryadarma, and Sujono and his associates were kept under city arrest. However, no charges were laid against them.

With the Burhanuddin cabinet's accession to office the suspension of Sujono and four senior officers supporting him was lifted. The action bore similarities to the official closing of the October 17 affair in the army, but it had been preceded by no reconciliation such as the two army factions had managed to achieve through the Jogjakarta conference.[44] Then on December 5 a decree was issued, signed by the Prime Minister and Vice-President Hatta, appointing Vice-Commodore Sujono as Deputy Chief of Staff of the Air Force.

The appointment had been made without the official knowledge of Chief of Staff Suryadarma and immediately aroused great hostility among Suryadarma's supporters. *Merdeka* reported that approximately 50 officers had threatened to leave the air force if the appointment were not rescinded.[45] On December 13 Suryadarma submitted his resignation to the President in protest.

Sujono was to be sworn in on December 14 in a formal ceremony at the air force base at Tjililitan outside Djakarta. But just as the ceremony was about to begin, a group of noncommissioned officers ran shouting onto the parade ground. One seized the air force standard and carried it away, while another delivered physical blows to Sujono and three other high officers who were his supporters. The Prime Minister himself rose to his feet to demand that the standard be fetched back, but the Acting Chief of Staff of the Air Force declared

[42] *Keng Po*, Jan. 25, Feb. 17, 1956; *Suluh Indonesia*, April 4, 1956.
[43] For a general discussion of the air force see Willard A. Hanna, "AURI: The Biography of the Indonesian Air Force," *Newsletter of the American Universities Field Staff* (New York), May 3, 1957.
[44] Cf. *Keng Po*, Aug. 16, 1955; *Indonesia Raya*, Aug. 31, 1955.
[45] *Merdeka*, Dec. 13, 1955.

that this could not be done. The ceremony had to be stopped; Sujono was not sworn in.[46] The humiliation was all the more jarring because of the presence of an array of high dignitaries, including foreign military attachés.

It was immediately evident that Air Vice-Marshal Suryadarma must have known of plans for this action, and Burhanuddin as Minister of Defense signed a warrant for his house arrest. But because Suryadarma had just submitted his resignation to President Soekarno, who had not yet agreed to accept it, the President was immediately brought into the whole matter. Since Soekarno supported Suryadarma, the air force leader was not put under arrest. The entire incident then became the subject of protracted negotiations between the cabinet, the President and Vice-President, Major General Nasution, and the various air force officers immediately involved.

The outcome was a victory for the President and Suryadarma and a virtually complete defeat for the Vice-President, the cabinet, and Sujono. Suryadarma's resignation was not accepted. No disciplinary action was taken against any of those who had organized the wrecking of the ceremony, although a sergeant who had personally participated was brought before a military tribunal in March 1956. Sujono was not installed.[47]

Late in November of 1955 active campaigning had begun for the elections for the Constituent Assembly due to be held on December 15. Campaigning was much less intense on this occasion than before September 29. Various declarations to the contrary notwithstanding, it seems that the party leaders did not believe that the Constituent Assembly would have an importance comparable to that of the normal legislative body. In general, these leaders expected that no constitution radically different from the interim one would be adopted; they thought that this would be prevented by the interim constitution's requirement of a two-thirds majority for acceptance of a new constitution. In addition, it was frequently said that the parties had almost exhausted their financial resources. And many of the smaller parties and organizations virtually gave up hope after receiving only an insignificant number of votes at the parliamentary elections. Most important, many political leaders thought the results of the second poll would probably be similar to those of the first regardless of what they

[46] See *Merdeka, Indonesia Raya, Pemandangan,* and *Pedoman,* Dec. 16, 1955.
[47] For the text of Burhanuddin Harahap's announcement of the terms of the settlement see *Indonesia Raya,* Dec. 27, 1955.

did. On the other hand, very great issues were at stake in the current Djakarta political struggles; for these would determine the composition of the next cabinet. The attention of the top party leaders was directed more to these struggles, fought out with the methods characteristic of Djakarta-level politics, than it was to electioneering.

When election day came on December 15, the atmosphere was very different from that of September 29. At this second election there were next to no alarmist rumors and little tense anticipation. Many voters traveled long distances to be able to vote where they had been registered. But many others who had done so on September 29 did not do it a second time. On election day there was again little trade or public transport, but not the virtually complete standstill of September 29. With many voters leaving the polls as soon as they had cast their vote, balloting was a less communal and more individual affair. It still had a ceremonial aspect, but much less markedly than on September 29. Nevertheless, the level of participation was again very high, only slightly lower than for the parliamentary elections. If my estimate of 1.75 per cent for invalid voting is correct, the number who voted was approximately 89.33 per cent of the total number of registered voters, only 2.21 per cent less than in the first election.

The available evidence suggests that the volume of intimidation was markedly smaller than in the parliamentary elections. This was partly due to the lesser intensity of campaigning and partly to steps which the Burhanuddin Harahap cabinet had taken between the two elections to prevent the abuse of government authority for party purposes and to make voting cubicles more fully enclosed. But perhaps the most important factor was the new understanding of the secrecy of the ballot which voters had acquired in September (in areas where there had been no electoral abuses then). These voters now really believed that if they could evade or refuse interrogation on the point, their voting choices would remain a secret.

But however effective the Burhanuddin cabinet's conduct of these second elections, they also detracted from its power and prestige. In part this was because the President had defied the cabinet with great openness in the ten days before the elections by going on a series of speech-making tours through Sumatra, Kalimantan, and Sulawesi, tours in which his constant theme was the existence of a threat to the Pantja Sila. More particularly the cabinet suffered because of the election results. In general, these showed great similarity with the results of the parliamentary elections, with an over-all trend for all medium- and small-sized parties to lose votes and for the four largest parties to gain them. But one major difference of another kind emerged: the PNI gained 635,565 more votes than in September, a gain of 7.5 per cent, while the Masjumi, the sole exception to the general trend for the four large parties to add to their appeal, lost 114,267 votes.[48]

NEGOTIATIONS WITH THE NETHERLANDS

The final drama of the Burhanuddin Harahap cabinet developed as a result of negotiations with the Netherlands. From the very beginning of its term of office, the cabinet pursued an active foreign policy and one aimed at re-establishing fairly close relations with the Western world. In October it sent Mr. Roem to Australia as the head of a six-man good-will mission and in November entertained the Australian Minister of External Affairs, R. G. Casey, when he paid a state visit to Indonesia.[49] At the same time there were similar exchanges with the United Kingdom, Singapore, and Malaya and a visit by Pakistani and United States warships which subsequently held a naval exercise in the Java Sea. All these appear to have modified the image of Indonesia which had developed in Western and Western-oriented countries in the period of the Ali cabinet, the image of a militant and Communist-befriending neutralist. More specifically they helped prepare the ground for the major negotiations with the Netherlands which were to follow.

The Burhanuddin cabinet was confident that by launching an "offensive of reasonableness"[50] it could persuade the Dutch to concede important modifications in the terms of the Round Table Conference Agreement, in addition to those they had agreed to in the mid-1954

[48] Feith, *The Indonesian Elections of 1955*, p. 65.

[49] The effectiveness of this exchange was somewhat marred by the PNI's refusal to let Mr. Wilopo accept an invitation to join the Roem delegation and by the fact that President Soekarno was not prepared to receive Casey. Both actions were reflections of hostility to the cabinet's pro-Western turn in foreign policy. At the same time they were responses to the Australian government's actions in Feb. 1955 in revoking an invitation extended to an Indonesian parliamentary delegation. The revocation had come after M. H. Lukman of the PKI and Silas Papare, an Irianese or Papuan and former leader of Indonesian nationalism in West Irian, were included in the delegation.

[50] The phrase was used in the Dutch Labor Party-oriented weekly *Vrij Nederland*, Sept. 10, 1954, cited in Robert C. Bone, Jr., *The Dynamics of the Western New Guinea (Irian Barat) Problem* (Cornell Modern Indonesia Project, Interim Reports Series; Ithaca, N.Y., 1958), p. 134.

negotiations. (The results of these had been condemned by the Masjumi and PSI and remained unratified by the Indonesian parliament.) Furthermore, the cabinet leaders believed that if progress were achieved in discussions of the Round Table Conference agreements, the Netherlands government might be persuaded to negotiate on the issue of West Irian. Cabinet supporters declared that the time was propitious for negotiations, pointing to business pressure on the Dutch government to act conciliatorily toward Indonesia. And after the elections Masjumi and PSI leaders saw negotiating with the Dutch as one way whereby their parties' poor electoral showing might possibly be turned to advantage. Would the Netherlands leaders not see that the cabinet which succeeded the existing one would almost certainly be more radically anti-Dutch? Would they not realize that to refuse concessions to Burhanuddin would be to court unilateral actions by subsequent Indonesian cabinets against the still immense Dutch interests in the archipelago?

Preparations for the projected top-level talks were made over a period of three months. From September onward a special ambassador of the cabinet, Mr. Utojo Ramelan, was in The Hague for this purpose, and on October 10 Anak Agung himself began to negotiate in the Dutch capital. But in Indonesia hostility to the cabinet's plans was great and was growing. The leaders of the PNI were apprehensive lest Burhanuddin and Anak Agung should prove capable of drawing greater concessions from the Dutch than Ali and Sunario had obtained in August of the previous year. They were also resentful when the cabinet decided not to press for discussion of the Irian issue at the UN General Assembly in November. That the cabinet should, in this year of the Bandung conference, have contented itself with a unanimously adopted resolution of the Assembly, expressing the hope that "the problem will be peacefully solved" and that the forthcoming bilateral negotiations would be "fruitful" [51]—this was indeed galling to all whose names were linked to the triumphant conference of the previous April. Thus PNI and other opposition organs denounced the cabinet for begging from the West, at a point when Asian-African solidarity, and support for Indonesia on West Irian, had made this entirely unnecessary.

Opposition to the Burhanuddin cabinet's policy of negotiations with the Netherlands became threateningly vociferous just as ministerial-

[51] Quoted in Bone, *The Dynamics of the Western New Guinea (Irian Barat) Problem*, pp. 141–142.

level discussions between the two countries were about to start. On December 6, four days before the beginning of the ministers' conference at The Hague, the Nahdatul Ulama announced that it would not be represented in the delegation. On December 13 President Soekarno made his hostility to the talks very clear when he told a mass rally that the battle for Irian would be won not in The Hague or in New York but in Indonesia.[52] Then came the Sujono installation incident in the air force, which affected both the domestic and the overseas prestige of the government. A day later Arudji Kartawinata, who was to have been the PSII representative in the delegation (and to have obtained the title of Minister of State for the purposes of the conference), canceled his plans to leave Djakarta. Later in December there were numerous rumors of an impending withdrawal of the NU ministers from the cabinet.

It was against this domestic background that the negotiations went on, first in The Hague and then in Geneva.[53] One central focus of discussion was the Indonesians' proposal to have the Netherlands-Indonesian Union abrogated on terms which would free them from the financial and economic clauses appended to it at the time of the Round Table Conference Agreement, clauses dealing with investment guarantees, profit transfers, trade co-operation, debt payments, and so on. Another was West Irian, about which the Netherlands eventually agreed to talk, "with the understanding that each party maintains its point of view on the matter of sovereignty."[54] Here Indonesia sought to induce the Dutch to accept some kind of "unfreezing" of the situation, perhaps to agree to Indonesian participation in various activities in the disputed area—literacy campaigning was one—perhaps to promise to relinquish the colony within a fixed number of years, after which its people would decide by plebiscite whether or not to join Indonesia.

The Dutch for their part wanted the informal settlement of a number of specific claims and grievances of Dutch business establishments in Indonesia. In addition, they were concerned about the then current and pending trials of L. N. Jungschlaeger and Captain H. C. J. G. Schmidt, Dutch nationals arraigned on subversive activities charges in Indonesia; they wanted Indonesia to admit a defense counsel and

---

[52] See *Abadi*, Dec. 31, 1955.

[53] For a full discussion see F. J. F. M. Duynstee, *Nieuw Guinea als Schakel tussen Nederland en Indonesië* (Amsterdam: De Bezige Bij, 1961).

[54] *Ibid.*, p. 229.

witnesses for the defense from outside the country. They hoped too to negotiate the repatriation of some of the 12,000 or so Ambonese persons, former KNIL soldiers and their dependants, who had been in the Netherlands since 1950–1951 and were mostly still in camps and without work.

For several weeks the Indonesian delegation made very little headway. Domestic criticism of the Burhanuddin Harahap cabinet seemed only to strengthen the disinclination of the Dutch delegation head, Foreign Minister J. M. A. H. Luns, to make the concessions which his Indonesian counterpart, Anak Agung, was demanding. But Indonesia had considerable sympathy from the United States and Great Britain.[55] When the Geneva negotiations went into high gear in the first week of January 1956, American, British, and also Indian diplomatic pressure was brought on the Netherlands to make it accept a number of the Indonesian formulations.[56] Finally, it was possible on January 7 to arrive at an interim agreement on certain of the most important issues. The two delegations were to take this agreement to their respective governments and, if these advanced no objections, there would be further talks a little later.[57]

This was the high point of the Indonesian delegation's success. The delegation had prevailed upon the Dutch to agree to the dissolution of the Netherlands-Indonesian Union with the appended financial and economic agreements and had successfully insisted that the agreements to replace these would not be subject to third-party arbitration. It had obtained significantly greater concessions than had the Sunario delegation in August 1954, although like the Sunario delegation it had failed to exact any concessions on the politically all-important matter of West Irian. But the members of the delegation hoped that when the negotiations were resumed they would be able to extract a Dutch promise to negotiate about Irian at a later stage. On January 9 Anak Agung left for Great Britain on a four-day state visit.

In Indonesia, however, hostility to Anak Agung's efforts was growing stronger. On January 9 the NU and PSII demanded the abroga-

[55] See the analysis by the editor of *Abadi*, S. Tasrif, in *Abadi*, Dec. 31, 1955.

[56] On this phase of the negotiations see *Pedoman*, Jan. 4, 5; *Suluh Indonesia*, Jan. 7; and *Abadi*, Jan. 7, 1956.

[57] The specific provisions of the Jan. 7 settlement have not to my knowledge been made public, but what seem to be fairly full accounts are contained in *Abadi*, Feb. 14 (reprinting an article from the *Nieuwe Rotterdamse Courant* of Jan. 17), and *Abadi*, Jan. 21, 1956. For comparisons with the contents of the Sunario-Luns Protocol of Aug. 1954 see *Pedoman*, Feb. 22, 23, 24, 1956.

tion of the talks. A week later the cabinet, responding to the NU-PSII pressure, called the whole delegation home to explain its actions. At this point the three ministers left at Geneva—Anak Agung, Sumitro, and Leimena—reportedly resolved to submit their resignations, feeling "like a fisherman who has caught something and is told to throw it back into the water."[58] Three days later the NU and PSII decided to withdraw their ministers from the cabinet without waiting for the delegation to return. Thereupon the cabinet instructed the delegation, which was still in Europe, to stay there. At the same time the cabinet also gave it instructions to initial the January 7 agreement as soon as the Dutch were prepared to do likewise.

Then, however, the Dutch government stalled. Its provisional acceptance of the January 7 formulation had brought it under strong attack from unconciliatory groups inside the government parties.[59] Further, it interpreted the most recent developments in Indonesian domestic politics as improving its own bargaining position. Thus it switched from its earlier reluctant acceptance of the January 7 agreement to a position of refusing to initial it. For several weeks the Indonesian delegation was kept waiting in Europe, and the domestic prestige of the cabinet fell further. A statement by Dr. Sukiman calling the Geneva talks a "national tragedy" showed the Masjumi itself to be divided on the issue.[60] On January 26 the PNI party executive demanded a cessation of the talks, declaring that if the cabinet attempted to force a parliamentary ratification of the results of the Geneva talks the PNI would reserve its right to undo such a ratification (presumably when a new parliament and a new cabinet were in existence).[61]

The beginning of February saw the delegation still waiting for the Dutch to resume talks on the basis of the January 7 interim agreement. Meanwhile government-supporting papers in Djakarta were threatening the Dutch with grave consequences in the event that the conference collapsed without any positive results.[62] On February 4 the Indonesian delegation decided to leave Europe and notified Foreign Minister Luns accordingly. On the same evening, just as the Indonesian delegation was about to tell the press that the talks had failed,

---

[58] This phrase was attributed to Health Minister Leimena, *Abadi,* Jan. 21, 1956.

[59] On the strong anti-Indonesian sentiment which existed in the Netherlands at the time see Duynstee, *op. cit.,* pp. 189 ff., and Justus M. van der Kroef, *The West New Guinea Dispute* (New York: Institute of Pacific Relations, 1958), pp. 18–25.

[60] *Indonesia Raya,* Jan. 24, 1956.   [61] *Suluh Indonesia,* Jan. 27, 1956.

[62] See, e.g., *Abadi,* Jan. 30, 1956.

the Dutch Foreign Minister notified it that he would agree to resume negotiations on terms Anak Agung could accept.[63]

Thus a final series of talks began on February 7. It soon became clear that the most Indonesia could now expect was a confirmation of the results set down on January 7. The Dutch, on the other hand, remained unprepared to go as far as this. In particular they again demanded a form of third-party arbitration which would make it possible for the proposed new financial and economic agreements between the two countries to be enforceable where they conflicted with national legislation in Indonesia. This, however, the Indonesian delegation refused to accept.

As the talks went on, government-supporting papers in Djakarta were speaking increasingly of the possibility of unilateral Indonesian abrogation of the Union.[64] At the same time the Prime Minister sent Agriculture Minister Sardjan to the Dutch High Commissioner in Djakarta, informing him that Indonesia would indeed abrogate the Union unilaterally unless the Netherlands agreed to the tentative settlement of January 7. But the Dutch assessment was that this threat would very probably not be implemented. And within both the major Dutch government parties, the Catholic People's Party and the Labor Party, there were large factions maintaining pressure against the concessions which the January 7 agreement embodied. On February 11 negotiations broke down.

On February 13 the Indonesian cabinet announced the unilateral abrogation of the Union. At the same time it declared that it was considering further steps in connection with the related agreements made at the Round Table Conference.

The step was in one sense meaningless. The Dutch had long agreed to bury the stillborn Union, and the economic and financial agreements linked with it were not in any automatic way voided; all would depend on how the unilateral Indonesian review of them was implemented.[65]

[63] See *Abadi*, Feb. 9, 1956, for a full account of these developments.

[64] E.g., *Keng Po*, Feb. 6, 1956, and *Abadi*, Feb. 6, 1956.

[65] Among those interested in the technical aspects there was considerable discussion of what attitude Indonesia would take on the debts and pension obligations it had assumed at the Round Table Conference and what changes would be made in Indonesia's pattern of trade and payments. But on these matters no immediate decisions were made, except for an instruction issued by Finance Minister Sumitro, halting interest payments on one debt which Indonesia had assumed at the Round Table Conference. See E. P. M. Tervooren, *Statenopvolging en de*

But in another sense the abrogation decision was of the greatest importance. Now, for the first time since the days of the Revolution, Indonesia had broken through legality to act in defiance of the Dutch. A complicated and humiliating series of negotiations and compromises had ended in a clear and intelligible solution of which an Indonesian nationalist could be proud. Indonesia had stopped playing the game on the Dutch home ground of agreements and formal regulations. It had seized the initiative in a symbolic assertion of national self-reliance.

For the Burhanuddin cabinet's political position the action was a boon of the highest importance. The cabinet had been on the defensive for three months because of its policies in negotiations with the Dutch. Indeed, it had seemed to lose virtually all initiative, becoming the victim of a vicious circle of domestic political hostility and Dutch unwillingness to make concessions. But now all this had changed. Burhanuddin and his associates had dared to act symbolically in a way which their predecessors had considered and rejected. Who, then, could say that this was a cabinet which readily gave in to the Dutch?

No party opposed the abrogation. Most of the opposition parties denied the right of the Burhanuddin cabinet to take the action, declaring that it was unconstitutional or that it was meaningless unless accompanied by implementing action, which in any event could only be effected by the next cabinet. But this was widely regarded as no more than "sour grapes" sentiment. When the national flag was flown for the three days of February 22, 23, and 24 to celebrate the abrogation, there was a general sense of satisfaction within broad layers of the population throughout the country—despite the fact that several opposition parties ordered their followers to desist from flying the flag.

Meanwhile there had arisen the issue of when and in what circumstances the cabinet was to resign to make way for its successor, the cabinet formed to be responsible to the elected parliament. Under the existing provisions the allocation of parliamentary seats would be by a lengthy and complicated procedure, which would make it impossible for parliament to assemble before the end of April 1956. Thus the Burhanuddin cabinet would presumably stay in office until that time. However, faced with frequent demands for its immediate resignation, the cabinet decided in January to speed up the procedure by a month,

Financiële Verplichtingen van Indonesië ("The Succession of States and Indonesia's Financial Obligations"; The Hague: Nijhoff, 1957), p. 324.

enacting an emergency law for the purpose.[66] Several days later President Soekarno refused to sign this as an emergency law, but on February 10 parliament accepted it as an ordinary law.

The opposition, however, still hoped that the cabinet's resignation would come in response to criticism of its policies. Further, it wanted the cabinet to step down before it could name the appointed members of the new parliament, the thirteen or so persons who would bring minority representation up to the constitutionally required minima of nine, six, and three for the minorities of Chinese, European, and Arab descent respectively and the three who would represent Irian. (The election law was not specific about which cabinet was to appoint these nominated members or about the criteria by which their choice was to be made.) On February 15 Sutardjo Kartohadikusumo of the PIR of Wongsonegoro, along with SKI and Progressive parliamentarians, moved a motion urging the cabinet to return its mandate immediately and requesting the President to form a caretaker cabinet of experts to hold office until the elected parliament had come into session. On the following day A. A. Achsien, the parliamentary leader of the Nahdatul Ulama, joined with leaders of the PNI, PSII, Perti, and SKI in moving an outright motion of no confidence in the cabinet.

The next two weeks were a period of sharp intracabinet conflict. The Masjumi continued to press for conciliatory policies toward the opposition. Anxious for their party to gain inclusion in the next cabinet, Masjumi leaders did not want to antagonize the PNI, NU, or President Soekarno too greatly. But most of the other parties of the coalition were under no such restraint. This was true particularly of PIR-Hazairin, Parindra, PRN, the Labor Party, and the Democratic Fraction, groups which would have only one or two members in the new parliament, or none at all, and were thus enjoying the fruits of office for what would probably be the last time.

On the matter of when the cabinet would resign Masjumi conciliatoriness seemed to prevail: on February 21 the Prime Minister declared that he would return his mandate as soon as the Central Electoral Committee had announced the names of the newly elected parliamentarians (announcement was scheduled for March 1). But some of the smaller parties endeavored to undo this decision. In addition, the Masjumi was willing to accede to opposition demands on the matter of the parliamentary appointees for the minorities and West Irian

[66] *Duta Masjarakat*, Jan. 22, 1956.

and leave this matter for the next cabinet to handle. The smaller parties, however, were most reluctant to let it out of their hands.

Most important was the question of last-minute appointments, transfers, and disbursals of credit. Here the Masjumi failed to exercise much restraining influence against the strong pressures of the smaller parties. Indeed, the Masjumi was by no means entirely opposed to the measures which were taken. Thus the last weeks of February saw Finance Minister Sumitro extending credits for a variety of causes which suggested political patronage—credits to particular national banks and trading and industrial firms and to agencies promoting the tourist trade.[67] The same period saw a rapid series of personnel changes, notably in the Ministry of the Interior (controlled by Parindra since the resignation of the NU and PSII ministers), the Catholic-controlled Economic Affairs Ministry, and, most spectacularly, the Foreign Ministry under Anak Agung of the Democratic Fraction.[68] Needless to say, these measures angered the opposition and strengthened its resolve to force the cabinet to an immediate resignation.

On February 28 the government and the opposition had their showdown. In parliament that evening the opposition attempted to have the Achsien no-confidence motion discussed forthwith. The government, on the other hand, wanted priority for a discussion of its bill for the abrogation of the Netherlands-Indonesian Union and its appended agreements. In a dramatic series of parliamentary moves the government defeated the opposition. By a vote of 108 to 80 it was decided that the government's bill would be discussed first. Thereupon the chairman of parliament, Sartono of the PNI, and the second deputy chairman, Arudji Kartawinata of the PSII, resigned their posts, and the entire opposition membership left the floor of the House. But a quorum remained, as a result of the small parties' many votes, and the

[67] *Suluh Indonesia,* Jan. 31, Feb. 2, 24, 28, March 15, 1956; *Harian Rakjat,* Feb. 23, March 16, 27, 1956.

[68] The Interior Minister appointed new men as Governor of North Sumatra and resident of Djambi, as well as a number of *bupatis.* See S. M. Amin, *Peristiwa Berdarah di Atjeh* ("The Bloody Affair in Atjeh"; Djakarta: Soeroengan, 1956), pp. 240 ff., and *Pedoman,* March 3, 1956. The Economic Affairs Minister appointed a new co-ordinator of the North Sumatran oil wells and carried through an overall change in the organizational structure of his ministry. See *Indonesia Raya,* Feb. 11, 1956; *Suluh Indonesia,* Feb. 13, 14, 1956; and Sutter, *op. cit.,* p. 846. The Foreign Minister on Feb. 24 obtained the agreement of the cabinet for a series of diplomatic transfers, involving 22 heads of mission and including those placed in Washington, London, Moscow, Peking, New Delhi, and New York (the United Nations). President Soekarno, however, refused to sign approval of any of these appointments. See *Harian Rakjat,* March 1, 6, 1956, and *Pedoman,* March 7, 1956.

first deputy chairman, the Parkindo's Tambunan, immediately assumed the chairmanship. On the same evening, the government's bill for the abrogation of the Union was accepted by unanimous vote.

Thanks in part to the bonds of patronage, the government parties had stayed together, and as a result they had scored a triumph. The no-confidence motion was never discussed in parliament. Now, however, the Masjumi leaders of the cabinet no longer had need of the smaller parties. In the next few days, therefore, it was they who were able to get their way. Thus on March 2 the cabinet decided to return its mandate forthwith. It also decided to desist from nominating the minority representatives for the new parliament and declared that the new parliament would assemble on March 26. By capping off its parliamentary victory with this act of political self-denial the cabinet regained some of the prestige which it had lost by its spoilsmanship of the previous weeks. On March 3, Burhanuddin returned his mandate to the President.

So this highly controversial cabinet came to an end—or, more precisely, to a three-week period of demissionary status. In its seven stormy months of office it had achieved a few of its goals, but had been defeated as regards many others. It had succeeded in undoing some of the power which the PNI had built for itself in the government service in the two years of the Ali cabinet, although it had certainly not lessened the importance of political criteria in administrative affairs. It had brought about a decline in corruption in high places, in part by its army-backed drive against corruption in August and September and in part by simplifying the foreign trade structure and thus lessening the scope of bureaucratic discretion. But it had changed little in regard to the volume of patronage dispensed. And, whereas the party conflict had greatly diminished in most village areas once the elections were over, there had been no decline in the bitterness of conflict at the level of the political public. On the other hand, the political atmosphere of the Burhanuddin period was a relaxed one as far as nationalism was concerned. Far fewer demands were made for uncritical nationalist loyalty than under the first Ali cabinet.

The Burhanuddin cabinet had been thwarted in several of the most important of its political activities. On the matter of the emergency law to make it easier to prosecute corruptors, it was stopped by a combination of the Nahdatul Ulama and the President; subsequently the flow of its anticorruption activities slowed down markedly. Its efforts to change the power balance in the air force were defeated.

Nor did it succeed in the bold efforts it made to develop a "different approach" (*djalan lain*) to the problem of the Darul Islam rebellion. Its envoys negotiated with rebel leaders in both West Java and Atjeh in this effort to reach a political settlement, and in the case of Atjeh they apparently almost succeeded. Finally, however, the effort failed, partly because of lack of support from particular army leaders; its failure was advertised by the arrest of the cabinet's couriers by local military authorities in both areas.[69]

The field of foreign policy was the one political area where the cabinet succeeded in turning defeat into victory, but even this success was in some ways unsatisfying. Some of the cabinet's leading supporters regretted its decision to abrogate the Netherlands-Indonesian Union. Others, who accepted the decision as being politically necessary at the time it was made, were critical of the cabinet for negotiating with the Dutch in the first place. Indeed, it was probably not in the long-term interests of the parties represented in this cabinet to create a breach in relations with the Netherlands and set an example of repudiating an international agreement. In this long-term sense one may doubt whether the cabinet's foreign policy was successful.

But the positive response to the abrogation action brought a great amount of immediate political credit to the cabinet and the parties composing it. Furthermore, there was an element of immediate success in the responses evoked outside the country. Thus on March 2, 1956, the cabinet's last full day in office and little more than two weeks after the abrogation of the Union, Foreign Minister Anak Agung formally accepted American surplus foodstuffs to the value of $96,700,000 to be delivered over a two-year period.[70] Ten days later U.S. Secretary of State Dulles arrived in Djakarta for a one-day visit and extended a first invitation to President Soekarno to visit the United States. The act of treaty repudiation had clearly not turned the United States against Indonesia.

As far as problem-solving policies were concerned, the cabinet also achieved fairly little on the whole, but it did effect a number of im-

[69] See *Suluh Indonesia,* Aug. 26, 27, 1955; *Sin Po,* Dec. 5, 1955; and the statement of the Prime Minister in *Pemandangan,* Feb. 1, 1956. See also *Suluh Indonesia,* Feb. 4, 14, 17, 1956; *Berita Minggu,* Feb. 12, 1956; and *Pedoman,* Feb. 14, 1956.

[70] This agreement was based on U.S. Public Law 480 of 1954. Under the agreement 20 per cent of the rupiah proceeds of sales of the agricultural commodities in Indonesia would be given to U.S. establishments in the country, with the other 80 per cent being set aside as a loan to Indonesia for agreed-upon development purposes.

portant changes in the economy. Most important of these was a general overhaul of foreign trade machinery which was begun in September and continued after the elections and which contributed to a major fall in the price of imported goods.[71] In addition, the cabinet straightened out a large number of budgetary matters, re-establishing a fairly powerful control position for the Finance Ministry within the bureaucracy. And in part because of economizing measures and a rise in the volume of exports, but especially because of a considerable increase in the overseas prices of rubber and certain other Indonesian export commodities, the budget deficit was reduced markedly.[72]

On the other hand, the cabinet could do only relatively little to allay the very serious shortages of rice which followed the 1955 floods.[73] Despite large extra shipments of rice from overseas, the rice price rose steeply throughout the country for virtually the whole period of the cabinet's incumbency. Between June 1955 and March 1956 the price index for Djakarta rose by 84.4 per cent and the one for rural Java and Madura by 68.8 per cent.[74] Outside Java and Madura rice prices generally rose even more steeply. It was only in March when the Burhanuddin Harahap cabinet's status was demissionary that prices began to fall significantly, this as a result both of an alleviation of congestion in the ports and of the beginning of the new harvest.

[71] See Sutter, *op. cit.*, pp. 1028–1029.

[72] See Sumitro Djojohadikusumo, "Stabilization Policies in 1955," *Ekonomi dan Keuangan Indonesia*, vol. IX, no. 1 (Jan. 1956). See also Bank Indonesia, *Report for the Year 1955–1956*, pp. 101–111.

[73] Boyd R. Compton, "Indonesia, 1955," *Newsletter of the Institute of Current World Affairs* (New York), Feb. 4, 1956, pp. 17–18.

[74] Benjamin Higgins, *Indonesia's Economic Stabilization and Development* (New York: Institute of Pacific Relations, 1957), p. 167.

Chapter X

The Second Cabinet of Ali Sastroamidjojo, March 1956–March 1957:

The Eclipse of the Parties and the Rise of Their Heirs

BORN AMID HIGH EXPECTATIONS

WHEN elections were held in September 1955, they were heralded as promising to bring in a new era of political stability, of upbuilding, of a purposeful pursuit of national goals. The claim that they would bring all these good things with them had been made repeatedly for a number of years. Indeed, this claim and the expectations to which it had given rise had been an important part of the political public's vision of Indonesia in the whole postrevolutionary period.

The years between 1950 and 1955 had brought disappointment to a large part of the country's population. The members of the political public, who had on the whole the highest expectations of independence, were those most bitterly disappointed. There were, it is true, a number of developments which had a positive value for them. In the villages there were many more schools in 1955 than in 1950 or 1942, many more bicycles, more brick houses, better lighting, more reading, more traveling, more sports, more people belonging to organizations, more national awareness, and more national pride. In the cities and towns they saw large numbers of new schools and of new buildings of every kind and an extraordinary increase in motor and bicycle traffic. The national, modern style of life which was theirs and which they hoped would become general for society as a whole— the white-shirt style of life of the government official and the student —was gaining adherents very rapidly throughout society. Foreigners were more and more losing the positions of leadership they had held, and Indonesians were fitting with increasing poise and sense of ease into what were once foreign roles.

But the members of the political public saw much which disappointed and shamed them. They saw a snobbish aloofness in the ranks of the elite, an immoral ostentation among the newly rich, laziness and corruption among government servants, and everywhere self-seeking and conflict—the conspicuous absence of a sense of national unity and national purpose. At the same time they saw a lack of advance in the tackling of particular problems. Large parts of the country were still insecure; there were beggars in the cities and large numbers of unemployed and underemployed. Many government plans for economic progress were being implemented at a snail's pace or not at all.

How were these serious shortcomings to be explained? How could they be squared with the fact that this was now the period of independence of which so much had been expected? Many found consolation in the frequently expressed idea that "we are still a young state," that "these are children's diseases," and that "this is still the period of transition." But this was only part of the explanation for most. Only those with a low degree of personal involvement in the revolutionary cause (as well as a small group who imposed intellectual detachment upon themselves) were inclined to tell themselves that the expectations had been too high. Other explanations were required.

For many the principal explanation lay in the continuing hold of imperialism over the country. Indonesia was not really free, it was believed, so long as Dutch and Chinese capital continued to dominate the country, so long as huge profits flowed out of the country, and so long as West Irian was still under Dutch domination. Some linked this with the new cultural imperialism of Hollywood films, Cadillacs, and Coca-Cola. Some linked it with the continuing hold of Dutch thinking over a large part of those who had had higher education.

Another broad line of explanation of existing shortcomings was in terms of a failure of leadership. The Indonesian leaders had failed to rise to their tasks, it was said. Or as Hatta frequently put it, quoting Schiller:

> Eine grosse Epoche hat das Jahrhundert geboren,
> Aber der grosse Moment findet ein kleines Geschlecht.
> (The century has given birth to a time of greatness,
> But the great moment finds man small.)

The failure was attributed variously to Soekarno, to Soekarno and Hatta, to "the ruling clique," to "the older generation," to "those who were trained by the Dutch," to "the half-intellectuals," to "those whose only education has been in political tactics," to "those who came to power by the grace of the Round Table Conference," to "those who have grown rich through 'national business.'" In every case the assumption was that the tasks were essentially capable of being tackled satisfactorily and this would require only a change in top personnel.

But there was yet another line of explanation, which had extremely wide currency and usually served to buttress all others. This focused on politics and the weakness of the political system. The basic cause of the existing difficulties, it was said, lay in the fact that there were too many parties. This led to weak and short-lived coalition governments, and hence to the lack of achievement in the making of policy. In addition, it resulted in the creation of political bottlenecks in the administrative machinery by which decisions were being implemented. Moreover, it was producing an exacerbation of all conflict in society and a politicization of all social life. (The word usually employed, the Dutch *verpolitiseering*, has strong negative connotations.) To make matters worse, most of this conflict was not about principles at all but was part of a selfish scramble for jobs and favors.

For those who saw the party system as the central cause of the shortcomings of independence, elections assumed very great importance. There were indeed those who felt from the beginning that elections would not get to the root of the trouble. Some believed that that could be achieved only by the complete abolition of parties or by a return to the single-party system which had been formally established in the first two weeks after the proclamation of independence. Others thought that only a "strong man" or a military dictatorship would solve the problems which had come to a head in the party system. But there were many who hesitated before such radical solutions, whether for reasons of democratic principle or because of a stake in the *status quo* of civilian, party, parliamentary, and cabinet government—and for them elections provided the answer. Elections would reduce the number of parties, eliminating the small ones which were the most opportunistic of all. They would tap new leadership talents. And perhaps in this way the parties would return to their real task of working for the establishment of political principles.

Elections were thus seen as a way of saving democracy and as an important step toward the broader goals for which the Revolution had been fought. They seemed a panacea. They permitted nationalists of the political public to maintain most of the same high, inchoate expectations of independence which they had held in the period of the Revolution and still be able to explain why these expectations had as yet remained unrealized.

Nor was it only within the political public that these perceptions existed. As the campaign progressed, the party leaders, in speaking to all sorts of audiences, made much of the regenerative powers of elections. In offering reassurance to rural leaders concerned about the socially divisive effects of campaigning, they made extensive promises of political and socioeconomic improvements which would follow from the elections. Similarly, when government functionaries, at the central or the local level, were presented with grievances with which they felt incapable of coping, one of their most frequent answers was: "Just wait till after the elections. It will be possible to settle these various things then."

Now the elections had come and gone. The actual experience of election day, especially the day of the first election of September 29, was memorable. Millions had had a sense of participation in a national celebration of great scope. But what now? What of all the promised amelioration? It was not thought that there had been significant improvements in the five months between the September elections and the Burhanuddin cabinet's resignation; these had been months of politicking very much in the old style. Now, however, there would be a new parliament and a new cabinet responsible to it. Surely things would be better now? These expectations were usually inchoate. Those who attempted to give them specific political formulations averred that this would probably be a longer-lived cabinet than those which had gone before it, that co-operation between the parties composing it would probably be more harmonious, and that the state's authority would be restored. But inchoate or formulated, the expectations were high.

This was one aspect of the context in which the postelection cabinet was formed. But another aspect was the bitterness and extreme polarization of forces which characterized politics in the last months of the Burhanuddin Harahap cabinet's term of office. In much of the countryside, it is true, the acuteness of party antagonisms declined rather rapidly after the elections. But in the urban centers tensions remained high. Large parts of the bureaucracy, particularly such ministries as Information and Foreign Affairs, which had been PNI-ized and de-PNI-ized in turn, were rent with party conflict. And virtually every newspaper in the country was fully on either the Masjumi or the PNI side. Moreover, hostility between Soekarno and Hatta was more manifest than at any previous time in our period. These circumstances promised to make it extremely difficult to establish a cabinet with enough cohesion and capacity for resolute action to meet existing expectations even in a minimally satisfactory way.

This, however, is what Mr. Ali Sastroamidjojo set himself to do when President Soekarno on March 8, 1956, named him as *formateur*.[1] When Ali began his work, the biggest decision had already been made for him by the PNI: the cabinet was to be based on a PNI-Masjumi-NU coalition—rather than a PNI-NU combination supported by the Communist Party. Although there were PNI leaders who were against any cabinet co-operation with the Masjumi and others who thought the PNI-Masjumi breach too sharp to make a cabinet partnership practicable, the more widely held view was that healing this breach was both possible and necessary, particularly in view of the PKI threat, of which regional PNI leaders spoke ever more frequently. At least the attempt had to be made. The PNI party executive made it particularly clear that this was its view by instructing Wilopo to assist Ali in the tasks of cabinet formation.

It was apparent from the beginning of Ali's *formateur*-ship that he would succeed. The PNI and NU had worked out a basis of co-operation in the previous weeks. The Masjumi very definitely wanted to be included in the cabinet and recognized that its bargaining power was (therefore) not great. As to all the other parties, they would have to take what they could get. The *formateur* had little need to include them since a coalition of the three largest parties provided him with a sizable parliamentary majority. Thus it was possible to

---

[1] The President had decided soon after the Burhanuddin cabinet's resignation on March 3 not to ask for the formation of a caretaker cabinet, as had been suggested by the sponsors of the Sutardjo Kartohadikusumo motion. Instead Ali was asked to form a cabinet which would be able to take office at the same time that the new parliament was installed on March 26.

agree quickly on the essence of Ali's plan, a cabinet of which the PNI was unambiguously the leader, with the Masjumi and NU placed at parity with one another, both definitely with less influence than the PNI.

But a number of conflicts had to be resolved before agreement on the cabinet's composition could be reached. Thus Ali wanted to include no one who had been a member of the Burhanuddin Harahap cabinet for the whole length of that cabinet's term of office, and eventually no one in this category was included. (Burhanuddin himself, Sumitro, Leimena, and Abdul Hakim had all been discussed in the course of the negotiations preliminary to the formation of the cabinet.) He also initially expressed opposition to the candidacy of Roem, who had been given honorary ministerial status as a member of the Anak Agung delegation that had negotiated with the Netherlands, but subsequently Roem was accepted as First Deputy Prime Minister. In addition, the *formateur* stood by his decision not to allow a PSI representative in the cabinet.

The Masjumi for its part raised objections to certain of the PNI's candidates. It was, in fact, dissatisfied with the choice of Ali as *formateur,* but could do little either about this or about Ali's intention to hold both the Prime Ministership and the Defense portfolio. It did, however, prevent the return of the Nahdatul Ulama's Zainul Arifin to the Second Deputy Prime Ministership which he had held in the first Ali cabinet. (The NU man who eventually took the post, Idham Chalid, was more sympathetic to the Masjumi.) And it succeeded, with the support of the Nahdatul Ulama, in excluding Sadjarwo, of the Communist-line BTI, who had been Minister of Agriculture in the first Ali cabinet and continued to enjoy Ali's confidence.

By March 16 Ali Sastroamidjojo had succeeded in ironing out the remaining differences as regards the candidacy of particular individuals, and on that date he presented a cabinet list to the President. But the list was not immediately accepted as it stood. As at the time of the Wilopo cabinet's formation, the President asked for time to consider the draft composition. There followed four days of fast political pressuring that centered on the question of whether or not a PKI-sympathizer would be included in the cabinet.

The PKI attitude toward plans for this postelection cabinet had undergone a number of changes. Initially in October the party's leader, D. N. Aidit, had asked for the establishment of "a National Coalition Government carrying out the anticolonial policies of the Ali-Arifin cabinet, a cabinet led by the PNI and NU, with the participation also of the PKI, the Masjumi, the PSII, the Parkindo, and other groups and parties." [2] Subsequently, however, the party had stressed that it was not particularly concerned about its own inclusion in the cabinet, as long as the Masjumi was not included. Its principal demand then had been for a cabinet without the Masjumi.[3] But, when Ali had begun his work and it was clear that the Masjumi would indeed be included, the party changed its position again and pressed hard for the inclusion of certain PKI sympathizers. In particular it urged Ali to accept one or more men such as Sadjarwo of the BTI as Minister of State for Transmigration Affairs, A. M. Hanafi, the secretary-general of the All-Indonesian People's Congress, as Junior Minister of Labor, and Professor Ir. Purbodiningrat, a Jogjakarta aristocrat, veteran leader of PKI-line peace committees and PKI candidate in the parliamentary elections, as Minister of State for Parliamentary Relations.[4]

Ali had rejected all these candidates before he took his draft list of cabinet members to President Soekarno. But the President asked him to reconsider his decision. Would it not be possible, he asked, to go some way toward meeting the modest requests of the PKI by inclusion of one PKI-sympathizing minister, giving him a minor portfolio? He mentioned the names of Sadjarwo, Hanafi, Purbodiningrat, and a fourth man of less marked PKI sympathies, the Bandung newspaper editor (and husband of an adopted daughter of President Soekarno) Asmara Hadi. Since early 1955, Soekarno had demonstrated sympathy with the PKI at points of PNI-PKI disagreement. He had been disappointed in the PNI because of its failure to support him in the organization of the All-Indonesian People's Congress, and grateful for PKI support. In a number of speeches made after the parliamentary elections, he had urged the inclusion of all four large parties in the post-

[2] D. N. Aidit, *Pilihan Tulisan* ("Selected Works"), I (Djakarta: Pembaruan, 1959), 470.

[3] See the New Year's message of the PKI central committee in *Harian Rakjat*, Dec. 31, 1955.

[4] See *Harian Rakjat*, March 16, 20, 1956; *Keng Po*, March 20, 1956; and *Pedoman*, March 21, 1956. The basis of the PKI's desire to be represented in the cabinet in this small and indirect way was given various interpretations. Some argued that the PKI was anxious to have a reconnaissance man in the cabinet, to guard against the possibility of sudden repressive action against the party. (In the draft program suggested to the *formateur* by the party's Politbureau the point placed first was "guarantees of the broadest democratic rights for the people and the people's organizations" [*Harian Rakjat*, March 7, 1956]). Others stressed the importance for the PKI of symbolic identification with the leaders of nationalism.

election cabinet as a necessity for national unity. It was quite illogical, he repeatedly asserted, for that 20 per cent of the Indonesian electorate which had voted Communist to be isolated and excluded from the national unity.[5] It would thus be a blow to the prestige of the President if no Communist or Communist sympathizer were included in the cabinet.

Ali took the President's request to the parties which he had decided to include in the cabinet. Meanwhile Soekarno went for a trip to Surabaja and Malang, centers of PKI strength, where large demonstrations reminded both him and the press of the "20 per cent of the Indonesian people" whose exclusion from the cabinet the President had frequently opposed. It was clearly a showdown situation, with one side bound to lose.

Eventually it was the President who gave way. A conference of regional leaders of the Nahdatul Ulama voted overwhelmingly against acceptance of a PKI-supported candidate. The Masjumi was naturally strongly opposed, as was Ali himself. He finally told the President that he could not accept any of the four PKI-supported candidates. It was then agreed that Ir. Djuanda, the nonparty former Minister of Economic Affairs and Communications, would be included in the cabinet as Minister of State for Planning Affairs. Djuanda was not a PKI-supported candidate, but he was a man in whom the President placed great personal trust, and therefore this was in one sense a face-saving solution.

On March 20 the cabinet list was announced as follows:

Ministry [6, 7]		Party
Prime Minister	Mr. Ali Sastroamidjojo	PNI
First Deputy Prime Minister	Mr. Mohammad Roem	Masjumi
Second Deputy Prime Minister	Idham Chalid	NU

[5] E.g., *Harian Rakjat*, Dec. 9, 1955.

[6] The cabinet was reshuffled by stages in Dec. 1956 and Jan. 1957. Dahlan Ibrahim resigned on Dec. 26, 1956, and his portfolio was taken by Deputy Prime Minister Idham Chalid. The five Masjumi ministers resigned on Jan. 9, 1957. The First Deputy Prime Ministership was thereupon taken by Idham Chalid. Sunarjo became Minister of Justice ad interim, Djuanda Minister of Finance ad interim, and Soehardi Minister of Public Works and Power ad interim (each keeping his earlier portfolio as well). A. B. de Rozario moved up to become Minister of Communications ad interim. Rusli Abdul Wahid resigned on Jan. 15, 1957, and was not replaced.

[7] The two PSII ministers, Sudibjo and Sjech Marhaban, resigned on March 13, 1957. Sudibjo's Information portfolio was taken by Idham Chalid on an interim basis, whereas Sjech Marhaban was not replaced.

Ministry		Party
Foreign Affairs [8]	Roeslan Abdulgani	PNI
Interior	Mr. Sunarjo	NU
Defense (ad interim)	Mr. Ali Sastroamidjojo	PNI
Justice	Prof. Mr. Muljatno	Masjumi
Information	Sudibjo	PSII
Finance	Mr. Jusuf Wibisono	Masjumi
Agriculture	Eni Karim	PNI
Deputy Minister of Agriculture	Sjech Marhaban	PSII
Economic Affairs	Mr. Burhanuddin	NU
Deputy Minister of Economic Affairs	N. F. Umbas	Parkindo
Communications	Suchjar Tedjasukmana	Masjumi
Deputy Minister of Communications	A. B. de Rozario	Catholic
Public Works and Power	Ir. Pangeran Noor	Masjumi
Labor	Sabilal Rasjad	PNI
Social Affairs	K. H. Fatah Jasin	NU
Education	Sarino Mangunpranoto	PNI
Religious Affairs	K. H. Iljas	NU
Health	Dr. H. Sinaga	Parkindo
Agrarian Affairs	Prof. Mr. Soehardi	Catholic
Minister of State for Veterans' Affairs	Dahlan Ibrahim	IPKI
Minister of State for Parliamentary Relations	H. Rusli Abdul Wahid	Perti
Minister of State for Planning Affairs	Ir. Djuanda	Nonparty

The general reaction to the publication of these names was one of suspended judgment. The PNI came out with a cautiously worded statement of approbation for the *formateur*,[9] and in general the papers of the government parties were guardedly hopeful. The press of the excluded PSI was critical, but not severely so. Only the PKI took a firmly negative stand, with Deputy Secretary-General M. H. Lukman expressing regret that the demands of the people and the efforts of the President to improve the cabinet's composition had failed and declaring that although the cabinet's program was rather progressive this was not matched by its personnel.[10]

[8] Roeslan Abdulgani was placed on nonactive status as a minister on Jan. 28, 1957, and returned to active status on March 14, 1957.
[9] *Antara*, March 21, 1956.　　　　[10] *Harian Rakjat*, March 22, 1956.

Within the political public at large, few were filled with enthusiasm by reading the cabinet list. There was indeed satisfaction with the ability of most of the men chosen for the major portfolios. Most of these were men of prestige. They were also "administrators," men whose power rested largely on skills related to the running of a modern state and who placed high priority on the solving of practical economic and administrative problems. Those who hoped for effective PNI-Masjumi co-operation were pleased about the ministers of these two parties; most of the more strongly anti-Masjumi leaders of the PNI had been left out of the cabinet, as had the intransigently anti-PNI leaders of the Masjumi. The cabinet list included no one reputed to be corrupt.

On the other hand, the cabinet's very size, as well as the inclusion of deputy ministers, was seen as a sign of "cow trading." The fact that 17 of the 24 new ministers were without previous cabinet experience suggested that the *formateur* and the parties had been influenced by the sentiment of "I have never yet had a turn at being minister." Of a number of individual new ministers it was said that they were no more than loyal party hacks, and of insufficient stature to merit a cabinet post. All in all, this seemed to be "just another cabinet." It did not evoke trust or confidence commensurate with the hopes which had been pinned on the elections.

Similarly the installation of the new parliament failed to stir enthusiasm. President Soekarno, in opening the parliament on March 26, sounded a note which was in line with the "new start" expectations that the elections had aroused. He told the country that as the years between August 17, 1945, and December 27, 1949, had been the period of Indonesia's armed struggle and as the following six years could be characterized as the period of survival, so the country was now entering a third and new period, the period of planning and investment.[11] But the new parliament itself was not such as to promise any dramatic change for the better. In the first place, the actual number of parties and other groups was even larger than in the provisional parliament: 28 as compared with 20, a fact which was sometimes cited as showing that the elections had made things actually worse.[12] Secondly, the be-

[11] Kementerian Penerangan (Ministry of Information), *Ichtisar Parlemen* ("Parliamentary Chronicle"), no. 31 (1956), pp. 257–259.

[12] The small parties were on the whole so small as to be virtually incapable of affecting the stability of government. But the Indonesian political public's hostility to them resulted not only from the belief that they undermined governmental stability, but also from the view that parties should represent principles and that

ginning of March had seen a number of undignified scrambles for parliamentary seats, where party executives had attempted to persuade
elected members to decline parliamentary membership in order that
another person, lower on the party list in a particular electoral district,
could represent the party there.[13]

When the names of the elected members were announced, it became evident that the variety of proportional representation used in the
Indonesian electoral system had been such as to favor densely populated areas, and thus Java. The way in which the remainder votes
were allocated resulted in the election of 170 persons from the four
electoral districts in Java, which on a population basis had been
allocated the right to choose only 168. Therefore Java with 66.2 per
cent of the population received 69.65 per cent of the total number of
parliamentary seats. The thinly populated electoral district of East
Kalimantan elected no members at all. The areas outside Java thus
not only lacked the guarantees which a second chamber might have
provided, but also were underrepresented in terms of population.[14]
Certainly they were much less strongly represented than they had

---

only parties with distinctive principles had a right to exist. Most of the very small
parties banded together in fractions soon after the opening of parliament. Seven
persons who had been elected on the PKI ticket but were not declared members
of the PKI formed themselves into the Fraksi Pembangunan (Upbuilding Fraction). A group of ten members of Marxist, quasi-Marxist, nationalist, and mystically
oriented groups, all from Javanese electoral districts (Murba, Younger Generation
Communists, Permai, Baperki, PRN, PIR-Wongsonegoro, Gerinda, and the one
successful individual candidate, the octogenerian mystical teacher from Madiun,
R. Soedjono Prawirosudarso), formed the National Progressive Fraction. The
Fraction of Upholders of the Proclamation was formed by ten representatives of
a heterogeneous but somewhat pro-Masjumi-PSI-oriented group of parties: IPKI,
the Labor Party, PRI, PRIM, and PRD. Thus the total number of fractions was 17.
See Parlaungan, *Tokoh-Tokoh Parlemen* ("Parliamentary Figures"; Djakarta:
Gita, 1956), for complete listings of the M.P.'s, with biographical information.

[13] This was frequently done in order to secure an ethnic balance within the
group of a party's parliamentary representatives from a particular area. Thus, for
instance, the Masjumi executive asked a man elected on its ticket in South Sumatra
to step aside, because unless he did so, the Lampong people, one of the main
ethnic groups of South Sumatra, would have no Masjumi representative in parliament. See *Pedoman*, March 9, 1956, and *Abadi*, March 15, 1956.

[14] In ethnic terms the peoples of the areas outside Java (if they may be taken
together) were not underrepresented. The number of persons belonging to one of
Java's three ethnic groups who were elected from an electoral district outside Java
was smaller than the number of persons of ethnic groups centered outside Java
who were elected in electoral districts in Java. In part this was a result of the
marked underrepresentation of the Sundanese of West Java; less than half of this
area's parliamentary representatives were persons usually considered Sundanese.

been in the provisional parliament. This fact was to provide a focus for expressions of dissatisfaction with Djakarta in these areas.

Finally, there was some disappointment about the actual members of the new parliament. There was indeed a great deal of new blood. Only 63 of the 257 elected members had been members of the previous parliament. Only 88 of the 257 were residents of Djakarta at the time of candidacy, and 88 lived neither in Djakarta nor in the capital of any electoral district.[15] Fifteen women were elected, as compared with 8 in the provisional parliament. But it was a common opinion that most of the new men and women were merely loyal party workers, persons chosen for their acceptability to the Djakarta executives of their parties, rather than "real leaders" who had the full confidence of the people in the regions where they had been elected and were capable of inspiring such confidence at the national level. For all these reasons there was a growing feeling that elections had failed to satisfy the hopes which had been placed in them and that the body politic continued to suffer from most of the same afflictions it had had theretofore.

A NEW BEGINNING WITH PROBLEM-SOLVING POLICY

When the second cabinet of Ali Sastroamidjojo assumed office, it was committed to long-term-oriented policy on "administrator" lines. By no means all of the individual members of this cabinet were intensely concerned with problem-solving policy, but several of the holders of the major portfolios were. Because of the expectations with which the cabinet was viewed some degree of policy commitment was essential. Moreover, with the PNI and the Masjumi both included in the cabinet, there would be less need than before, it was thought, for cabinet members to spend time battling to stay in power. Many hoped that this cabinet would last the full four-year period for which the parliament had been elected.

Thus the official cabinet program announced by the *formateur*, a longer and somewhat more detailed document than those which had served as the formal bases of policy making for earlier cabinets, was specific in promising action on a large number of long-term problems that had been shelved by earlier cabinets because of their politically controversial character or because of the pressure of more imme-

[15] These figures are based on the names announced on March 1, 1956, by the Central Electoral Committee and do not take account of the changes of personnel made by the parties in the following 25 days before parliament assembled. See *Antara*, March 1, 1956.

diately urgent business.[16] The program called for the legal enactment and implementation of the long-prepared Five-Year Plan, for changes in land ownership legislation, for regional autonomy and a law regulating the financial relations between the center and the regions, and for the establishment of compulsory military training for all citizens. It promised the creation of a marriage law. Not since the time of Wilopo had a cabinet set itself so broad a range of difficult policy tasks.

But it became clear in the first five months of the cabinet's term of office that few agreements had been reached between the coalition partners of the new cabinet on the politically contentious aspects of long-termed-oriented policy. These months were in fact a period of deadlock and inaction.

On certain issues the cabinet did act with speed. One of its first acts was connected with the Burhanuddin cabinet's abrogation of the Netherlands-Indonesian Union and related agreements. Responding to the President's unwillingness to sign the Burhanuddin cabinet's abrogation bill (which had been passed by parliament in its stormy and legally controversial session on February 28), the Ali cabinet drafted a new bill abrogating the Round Table Conference accords as a whole. In most legal respects this was similar to the earlier bill. It also referred to no specific aspects of the large body of agreements made at The Hague in 1949. But its symbolism was notably more radical. The bill was signed by the President on May 3, 1956.

In July the cabinet was able to gain parliamentary approval for a bill establishing new regional legislative assemblies for a transitional period. These assemblies were to replace the interim legislative bodies established in various provinces and regencies on the basis of the controversial Government Regulation 39 of 1950, and they were to function for a year until the planned regional elections had been held. Their composition would be determined on the basis of the votes received by the respective parties in each region in the parliamentary elections of September 1955. Meanwhile preparations were begun for the regional elections (for assemblies to replace the one-year transitional ones) which were scheduled for the first half of 1957.[17]

---

[16] See *Keterangan dan Djawaban Pemerintah tentang Program Kabinet Ali Sastroamidjojo (kedua)* ("The Government Statement on the Program of the Second Cabinet of Ali Sastroamidjojo and Replies to Criticisms"; Djakarta: Kementerian Penerangan, 1956), pp. 4–8.

[17] The first regional elections were held in Greater Djakarta in June 1957. By Dec. 1957 elections had been held for all provinces and regencies of Java and South Sumatra, and they were held throughout Kalimantan in the course of the following year.

One of the most significant political achievements of the cabinet in its first months of office lay in restoring a fairly stable balance of bureaucratic power in the ministries which had been rent by political appointments, transfers, and dismissals in the previous months and years. There was some undoing of political appointments made by the Burhanuddin Harahap cabinet, notably its appointment of the Masjumi man Djohan as co-ordinator of the North Sumatran oil wells and its appointment of Sutanto of the PSI as head of the Foreign Exchange Trading Body. But in both these cases the men who replaced the dismissees were relatively uncontroversial compromise figures. In the Ministry of Information where the pendulum of bureaucratic power had been jerked sharply to one side in the period of the Burhanuddin cabinet, it was swung back somewhat in the first months of the second Ali cabinet. However, when this trend seemed to be threatening the whole body of changes which the Burhanuddin cabinet had introduced in this ministry, the normal *quid pro quo* mechanisms of PNI-Masjumi coalitions were brought into play. Mr. Roem, as Deputy Prime Minister, wrote a letter of complaint to Sudibjo, the PSII Minister of Information.[18] At the same time the PNI, which was the chief beneficiary of Sudibjo's changes, was given hints that the Masjumi Minister of Communications would retaliate against PNI men in government agencies and government concerns in the field of railways, airways, and shipping unless the dismissals of Masjumi and PSI heads in the Information Ministry were stopped.

But as far as economic problem solving was concerned, the impression the cabinet conveyed in its first few months in office was one of weakness and indecision. On the matter of implementing abrogation of the economic agreements of the Round Table Conference, there was a signal slowness to move. The cabinet was divided from the beginning on whether or not to repudiate the debts it had assumed from the Netherlands Indies government at the Round Table Conference. Several months went by before a decision could be made. On August 4 the cabinet announced that it would repudiate 3,661 million Dutch guilders of its debt to the Netherlands, the sum which it saw as representing the costs of the Dutch military campaigns of 1945–1949 against the Republic.[19]

[18] *Abadi*, May 4, 1956. See also *Suluh Indonesia*, April 30, 1956.

[19] The decision was interpreted as prompted by President Nasser's decision of July 26 to nationalize the Suez Canal and as timed to follow the Aug. 1 decision of the International Monetary Fund to grant Indonesia credit to the amount of $55 million. For discussions of the debt abrogation see Alastair M. Taylor, *Indonesian Independence and the United Nations* (Ithaca, N.Y.: Cornell University Press,

Even then, however, a number of the most important matters raised by the repudiation of the Hague agreements were left unresolved. In particular, what would Indonesian policy now be toward Dutch capital? Most members of the cabinet were opposed to early nationalization, but the issue remained a live one as it became apparent that the Dutch firms were liquidating their assets with accelerated speed, or selling them, mainly to Chinese buyers. The consequent uncertainty, along with the government's inability to agree on a solution of the old problem of the North Sumatran oil wells, served to make almost meaningless the bill on foreign investment which the cabinet approved on June 26, 1956, and subsequently sent to parliament.[20]

The same slowness of action was characteristic of the government's handling of the matter of the Five-Year Plan. This plan, which was actually no more than an attempt to co-ordinate the separate, already existing plans of the various government agencies (with some systematic allocation of priorities), had been prepared over a period of more than two years before the second Ali cabinet took office. Although the plan was officially scheduled to come into effect at the beginning of 1956, it was October 1956 before the government had submitted it to parliament.[21]

In part these delays sprang from the natural slowness of a new group of men finding their feet in cabinet policy making. In part they were a result of the absences of the President, who took large delegations of top political figures with him on trips to the United States and Western Europe (May 14 to July 3) and the U.S.S.R. and the Chinese People's Republic (August 28 to October 16). Most important of all, they were a reflection of the continuing conflicts of power and interest between a PNI-led majority group of the cabinet and a Masjumi-led minority. The government parties as a group had yet to work out clear

1960), pp. 437–439, and E. P. M. Tervooren, *Statenopvolging en de Financiële Verplichtingen van Indonesië* ("The Succession of States and Indonesia's Financial Obligations"; The Hague: Nijhoff, 1957), pp. 330–334.

[20] This was a redrafted version of a bill originally prepared in the period of the Wilopo cabinet. It was not passed in the lifetime of the Ali cabinet. For the text see Benjamin Higgins, *Indonesia's Economic Stabilization and Development* (New York: Institute of Pacific Relations, 1957), pp. 127–132. For a discussion of various possible solutions which the cabinet considered in dealing with the problem of the oil wells, see *Keng Po*, July 16, Dec. 4, 1956, and *PIA*, Oct. 23, 1956.

[21] See National Planning Bureau, "Some Explanations of Indonesia's 1956–60 Five-Year Development Plan," *Ekonomi dan Keuangan Indonesia*, IX, no. 11 (Nov. 1956), 661 ff. See also Douglas S. Paauw, *Financing Economic Development: The Indonesian Case* (Glencoe, Ill.: Free Press, 1960), pp. 363–392.

compromise positions on many of the central matters at issue in any discussion of the country's economic future—on such matters as the role of foreign capital, the distribution of developmental energies between Java as a net consumer of imported goods and the Outer Islands as net producers of exports, and the incipient conflict between Java's bureaucratic patterns of social and economic organization and the entrepreneurial patterns more common in the Outer Islands.

If there were many in the political public who thought that the cabinet should be more actively playing a developmental role in the economy, there were also many who were against it for being soft on corruption and too much concerned with distributing spoils to the top party leaders and their friends. It is a fact that the cabinet did not follow up its predecessor's efforts to tighten up existing legislation against corruption. When Iskaq, who had been Economic Affairs Minister in the first Ali cabinet, returned from his eight-month overseas trip on April 23, he was called to the chief public prosecutor's office for investigation, but no charges were pressed against him. And on July 20 it was announced that the President had decided to grant a partial reprieve to Mr. Djody Gondokusumo, the Justice Minister of the first Ali cabinet, whom the Supreme Court had convicted on a corruption charge in January 1956 and sentenced to a year's imprisonment.

These early months also provided no evidence that the second Ali cabinet was more capable than its predecessors of making policies with deprivational consequences for the bureaucracy as a social group. Early in June the Masjumi Finance Minister, Jusuf Wibisono, declared that there would have to be a 30 per cent cut in the number of government servants. This, he said, would be implemented by stages over a number of years and combined with the introduction of premiums for *expertise* which would attract and keep in the government service more people with higher training. Whether this plan was ever given cabinet endorsement is not clear. It definitely had Masjumi support and was more or less sympathetically received by the PNI's daily, *Suluh Indonesia.*[22] But nothing was done in the whole of the period of this cabinet to begin its implementation.

Patronage allocation demanded a great part of the cabinet's time and effort. The cabinet started its work with a sizable store of distributable patronage: the minority and West Irian representatives in the new parliament and Constituent Assembly, whom it would have

[22] *Pedoman,* June 7, 1956; *Suluh Indonesia,* June 4, 1956.

the right to appoint, and in addition the large number of high diplomatic vacancies which the Burhanuddin cabinet had created or prepared and then had been unable to fill. On the other hand, it faced a situation where many individuals and groups were demanding rewards from the cabinet parties for the political and financial assistance they had provided in the course of the long election campaign. Thus the cabinet expanded the diplomatic establishment.[23] It also allowed a large number of persons to travel overseas as members of presidential, parliamentary, and other delegations.[24] One indication of the intensity and openness of the pressures exerted on cabinet leaders for rewards of this kind was a Perti statement issued in August to the effect that it was reconsidering its membership of both the cabinet and the Moslem League (in which it was federated with the NU and PSII) because of "unfairness inside the cabinet as regards the appointment of overseas functionaries, members of the party of the President traveling overseas, minority members of parliament, and so on." [25]

The parties, moreover, pressed for economic rewards as well as prestige ones. Some effects of this were seen in the way the cabinet implemented the Indonesianization of harbor and warehousing facilities, an area of business which had theretofore been dominated by Dutch and Chinese companies. A measure which had originally been planned by Economic Affairs Minister Iskaq of the first Ali cabinet, and promulgated as Government Regulation 61 of 1954, made it impossible to give licenses for the handling of sea cargo to enterprises controlled by "persons who are citizens other than citizens of Indonesia." [26] The measure was implemented in the first few months of the second Ali cabinet's incumbency, and in practice it was this cabinet that determined which national Indonesian firms would take over the facilities of the existing Dutch and Chinese harbor enterprises (and obtained the necessary government credits). The procedure was a classic example of spoilsmanship. Each of the main government parties had its own association of warehousing firms, many of the mem-

[23] See *Kabinet Ali-Roem-Idham, Program Dan Pelaksanaan* ("The Ali-Roem-Idham Cabinet, Its Program and Execution"; Djakarta: Kementerian Penerangan, 1956), pp. 672–673.

[24] See *Pedoman*, June 19, 1956.   [25] *Pedoman*, Aug. 23, 1956.

[26] This wording, taken from the Elucidation to the Regulation, made it possible to act against Chinese of Indonesian citizenship on the grounds that they were also citizens of China. See John O. Sutter, *Indonesianisasi: Politics in a Changing Economy, 1940–1955* (Southeast Asia Program, Cornell University; Ithaca, N.Y., 1959), pp. 953–957.

bers' firms being fledgling units established after the promulgation of Regulation 61, and the government simply divided up the existing warehouses and stevedoring and harbor transport plants among the warehousing associations of the different major parties!

Indeed, the same pattern of party channeling developed to some extent in the whole field of government credit to national trading and industrial establishments, with the Finance Minister, Jusuf Wibisono, allocating a reported Rp. 325 million (in less than 10 months) as credits to firms named by particular government parties.[27] Party members in government banks and licensing offices dealt increasingly with clients who presented them with *kaart belletjes,* letters of recommendation from top party leaders. At the same time several instances were uncovered where commercial groups with access to party chiefs in Djakarta had special regulations made favoring them in ways which rendered consistent economic policy impossible.[28] There was a renewal of comments on "Kuomintang phenomena" in the politico-economic system.[29]

In these various respects, government seemed to be fraught with almost all the same problems which had beset it in the pre-election period. Little seemed to have changed, except that there was now a spoken commitment to long-term policy—and that more large parties drew on the advantages of cabinet office. But there were major changes in the political responses which government practices evoked.

No party formally opposed the Ali cabinet. Nearly all the parties which had gained electoral strength had won inclusion in it. Among those outside the cabinet, the PKI, the PSI, and the various small parties, there was little direct criticism of what the government was doing. The PSI had not yet recovered from the sharp blow which the election results had dealt to its prestige or from the subsequent attempt by Sumitro to challenge the leadership of Sjahrir. On the whole its posture was one of waiting on the side lines to see what would now develop. The small parties were mostly in a state of disarray, with a number of their leaders looking for ways of attaching themselves to other political organizations. As for the PKI, it became markedly conciliatory in its attitudes toward the cabinet following its initial hostile comments, made when the President's efforts to gain inclusion for

---

[27] *Antara,* Feb. 22, 1957.　　[28] *Pedoman,* June 8, 21, July 13, 1956.
[29] See the statement of Hamid Algadrie of the PSI in *Pedoman,* June 21, 1956. Cf. the *Keng Po* editorial of March 6, 1956.

PKI-supported candidates had just been rebuffed.[30] Thus on April 20 it was possible for the Ali cabinet to win the unprecedented victory of an "opportunity to work" vote granted by acclamation, 229 votes to none.

But the lack of party criticism of the government was by no means a sign of general satisfaction with the state of affairs. It signified rather that parties had begun to lose their importance as channels of political articulation.

In the years 1953, 1954, and 1955, the parties had developed into probably the most important set of instruments for the expression of political demands. Through parties, all sorts of groups in society had been able to make their ideas and material claims felt—to the extent that these groups were believed able to contribute to the parties' electoral success. The parties had become less oligarchical. There had been a lessening of the volume of political demands made through other channels, particularly the bureaucracy. There had also been relatively little political protest of the more "spontaneous" and less highly institutionalized type, such as usually characterizes political movements, or of the still more transient and "anomic" type of collective behavior, such as where a group of youths smashes the offices of a newspaper or stones a house where Western-style dancing is in progress. Those who

[30] See, for instance, the editorial in *Harian Rakjat*, April 10, 1956, commenting on Prime Minister Ali's initial statement to parliament. See also M. H. Lukman's statement in *Harian Rakjat*, April 19, 1956. The PKI was also then suffering from internal conflict. In January, as Aidit left Indonesia to attend the twentieth congress of the Communist Party of the Soviet Union, he had issued a warning about the efforts of the foreign imperialists to split the PKI (*Harian Rakjat*, Jan. 31, 1956). On March 25, while the secretary-general was still outside the country, the veteran PKI leader Alimin, who had been displaced from the central committee of the party in 1954, sent a letter to the committee in which he attacked the whole of the PKI's strategy since 1950, describing it as a "class collaboration policy" that had allowed "opportunists and moderates" to enter the party and made the PKI into an "ordinary bourgeois party." Alimin specifically opposed co-operation with the PNI and charged that internal democracy in the PKI had been destroyed. Two months later *Indonesia Raya* published extracts from this frontal attack, whereupon the PKI felt obliged to publish the text in its own daily, along with a full refutation by the central committee. See *Harian Rakjat*, July 4, 1956. There followed a personal attack by Alimin, who called Aidit "no more than a petty bourgeois of the type of Mangunsarkoro" (*Pedoman*, Aug. 11, 1956), and various reports in the anti-Communist press of splits in the PKI's branches in different parts of Java (*Abadi*, July 25; *Pedoman*, July 9, Aug. 13, 15). But it is probable that these reports were exaggerated. For a full discussion of splits and fictitious splits in the party see Donald Hindley, "The Communist Party of Indonesia, 1951–1961: A Decade of the Aidit Leadership" (doctoral dissertation, Australian National University, 1961), pp. 195–215.

might otherwise have led political protest of the "movement" or "anomic" type were actively involved in the campaign activities of particular parties.

With the elections over, much of this changed. Many groups which had earlier been able to make their members' views and interests felt through the party system, because of the party leaders' need for their money or influence, now found themselves unneeded and unheeded. Similarly a large number of individuals who had actively worked for a party in the period of campaigning found themselves politically unemployed. The parties could no longer provide them with meaningful and prestigeful roles or ways of channeling protest.

This, then, was a time when the over-all level of political expectations and demands was very high, in large part because the elections had functioned as a device for the postponement of expectations. But the government could not even approach meeting all the strongly pressed demands, and the parties, being identified with the government, could not serve as channels of political protest.

So it was that protest found alternative channels of expression. If 1953, 1954, and 1955 had been party years, 1956 was a year of political movements and "spontaneous" mob actions—and of military coups. The first major series of developments of this kind had anti-Chinese sentiment as its basis.

A WAVE OF ANTI-CHINESE FEELING

On March 19, 1956, a convention of the All-Indonesian Congress of National Importers was opened at Surabaja. The keynote speaker was Assaat, a businessman who had earlier enjoyed great prestige as the nonparty chairman of the Inner Parliament of the revolutionary Republic, Acting President of the (member-state) Republic of Indonesia in 1950, and Minister of the Interior in the cabinet of Natsir. Assaat made a speech which expressed with shattering directness feelings which many Indonesians had long had, but hesitated to express in public.

Assaat called for a specifically racial policy in government regulation of the economy, a policy which directly favored ethnic Indonesians in their competition with all others, Chinese of Indonesian citizenship included. In the course of his address he accused the Chinese of responsibility for a great many of the difficulties of Indonesia's economy. He also called them a group of opportunists, who had helped the Dutch in the Dutch period and Chiang Kai-shek in China in the period of Kuomintang rule and were now supporting the government of Mao Tse-tung. He maintained that it was difficult to distinguish Chinese of Indonesian citizenship from foreign Chinese. Included too were remarks that Chinese have beautiful cars while Indonesians must walk, that Chinese sit in *betjaks* (bicycle trishaws) while Indonesians drive them, and that all the best places in trains and all the most beautiful places of public entertainment are occupied by Chinese.[31]

The effect of Assaat's speech was immediate. Once a man of his authority had defied the prevailing restraints on public expression of racialist feeling, these restraints quickly lost their power. Within a few weeks committees created in support of Assaat's ideas were in existence in many parts of the country. Now there were repeated demands for governmental recognition of the principle of preference for ethnic Indonesians and for governmental action to prevent Chinese from circumventing regulations designed to help others overcome their competition. Thus was born the "Assaat movement," which was to grow and acquire organizational cohesion in the course of the following year.

The Assaat movement drew sympathetic responses from most groups of Indonesians who knew of it, but active participation was confined largely to businessmen. Branches were in the main established in strongly Moslem areas of the Outer Islands—in South Sulawesi, Lombok, and various parts of Kalimantan and Sumatra. In addition, there were a number of branches in Java, with membership drawn largely from Sundanese, Madurese, and *santri* Javanese. Significantly, there was little active support from the Javanese *prijaji* community or from this community's businessmen, the "new capitalists" who had entered business from politics and civil service employment in the postrevolutionary period (and frequently worked together with Chinese businessmen in straw-man or other arrangements).

It was not long before the anti-Chinese wave which Assaat had touched off took new forms. On June 23 a rich young businessman of Chinese descent and Indonesian citizenship, Ir. Han Swie Tik, became involved in a traffic argument with an army officer, Captain Dr. Harjono. Harjono used insulting language to Han, whereupon the latter began using his fists. There were exchanges of spitting and then more fighting. Han, a trained boxer, then quickly got the better of the cap-

[31] Badan Pekerdja Kensi Pusat (Central Working Committee of the All-Indonesian National Economic Congress), *Kensi Berdjuang* ("The All-Indonesian National Economic Congress Fights On"; Djakarta: Djambatan, 1957), pp. 51–62.

tain. Harjono was not seriously hurt, but he had been publicly humiliated, and he threatened to take legal action.

Han thereupon got in touch with Major General Bambang Sugeng, the former Chief of Staff of the Army, who apparently gave him a letter for the public prosecutor of the Djakarta High Court, R. Soenario, in an effort to forestall a lawsuit. Reports that approaches of this kind had been made were carried by the sensation-loving *Indonesia Raya* and stirred strong reactions. Then one night in mid-July some scores of army members, along with civilians who had been members of student army units during the Revolution, staged a raid on a motor firm owned by Han (and situated on one of the main thoroughfares of Djakarta). They broke windows, painted threatening slogans, and fired a few bullets. No action was taken against them by the police or military police, and they (or a similar group) made another such raid a few nights later, and then another. Still there was no disciplinary action, and many sections of the press expressed approval. *Indonesia Raya* led the press in playing on the incident, using it to criticize not only the Chinese but also Indonesian high officials who were accepting Chinese bribes. Most papers (other than Chinese-owned papers or those of the PKI) joined in issuing warnings to Han and the Chinese in general not to think that they could have Indonesian leaders "in their pockets." [32] At the same time threatening anti-Chinese leaflets appeared on lampposts in Djakarta, Bandung, Semarang, and Solo.[33] Han had gone into hiding and become the object of a search by police.

Meanwhile a variety of other developments occurred. There had been occasional newspaper reports for several months indicating that the employees of the State Printery resented the influence of a certain Lie Hok Thay, a Chinese businessman of Indonesian citizenship who had recently been made deputy director of the printery. The circumstances of Lie's appointment were said to have been most irregular, and it was alleged that he was able to dominate the printery's Director Piet de Queljoe. Lie, like Han, was young, rich, and able. As Han was reputed to have been a member of the Pao An Tui (a Chinese Defense Corps established in Dutch-controlled areas in the period of Revolution),[34] so Lie was said to have been an officer of the Dutch in-

[32] See, for instance, *Suluh Indonesia*, July 16, 1956.
[33] *Ibid.*, July 27, 1956.
[34] See Victor Purcell, *The Chinese in Southeast Asia* (London: Royal Institute of International Affairs, 1951), p. 564.

telligence agency, NEFIS. In addition, there were rumors that Lie was a high-powered blackmailer with influence in many sections of the political elite. On July 17 Lie was suddenly kidnaped by a group of youths, who at the same time left anti-Han Swie Tik leaflets. For three days the government took no action on the kidnaping. Then it found Lie and arrested him. Several days later Han himself was found and jailed.

With the Han and Lie cases the outburst of feeling triggered by Assaat assumed new proportions. Alongside the fairly well controlled and clear-targeted Assaat movement there had arisen a phenomenon of collective behavior which was less well organized, but possessed of greater explosive power. The initiative had passed from businessmen who advanced economic claims with racialist arguments to army groups, veterans, youth bands, and a sensational daily, groups which shared no clear goals but a powerful inchoate anti-Sinicism. Although the proposals of Assaat had drawn criticism from large sections of the political leadership,[35] there was scarcely any political leader or editor who stood strongly for legal and constitutional guarantees in the cases of Han and Lie.[36]

On the contrary, the July phrase led a number of political leaders to make demands extending Assaat's ideas beyond the sphere of economics. For example, the Masjumi leader and head of the Education section of parliament, Dr. Ali Akbar, called for educational quotas for Chinese, declaring at the same time that there would be fewer difficulties in the matter of school buildings if the rich Chinese helped in this regard instead of merely looking after themselves.[37] At the same time Djadja Wiriasumita, an NU parliamentarian reporting an investigation he had made of army-organized smuggling in East Sumatra, declared that whereas the army leaders' actions there were morally defensible, though not legally so, the Chinese involved in the smuggling operations should be deported.

The government's response to these developments was essentially passive. No charges were laid against any of those who had taken the law into their own hands in the cases of Han and Lie. Han and Lie

[35] See the views of Wilopo, Jusuf Wibisono, Sumitro, Leimena, and Kasimo in *Star Weekly* (Djakarta), April 7, 1956.

[36] For a discussion of positions taken by various political parties see Donald E. Willmott, *The National Status of the Chinese in Indonesia, 1900–1958* (rev. ed., Cornell Modern Indonesia Project, Monograph Series; Ithaca, N.Y., 1961), pp. 92–95.

[37] *Abadi*, July 13, 24, 1956.

themselves were later tried and convicted.[38] But it should not be concluded from this that the cabinet witnessed the anti-Chinese campaign with satisfaction. Although some of the leaders of the cabinet had anti-Chinese feelings personally, many if not most were apprehensive about such political explosions as developed from the cases of Han and Lie. In addition, the PNI leaders of the cabinet had strong suspicions regarding the role of *Indonesia Raya* in these cases, for Major General Bambang Sugeng, Public Prosecutor Soenario, and State Printery Head de Queljoe were all members or sympathizers of the PNI. To many in the PNI, whose leaders were on the whole freer from anti-Chinese feelings than the leaders of the Moslem parties, the Han-Lie episode appeared as a devilishly clever move of the PSI, with some second-echelon leaders of the Masjumi and their friends in the army, to channel anti-Chinese feeling against the PNI and the Ali cabinet.

On the other hand, there was considerable support in the cabinet for the demands of the Assaat movement. In October, Economic Affairs Minister Burhanuddin of the NU issued a general statement on the government's position concerning the questions which Assaat had raised. Although this did not go nearly as far as Assaat had demanded, it went a considerable way by stating that the highest degree of government support would be given to enterprises which were controlled 100 per cent by ethnic Indonesians.

There remains the complex question of why this wave of anti-Sinicism swept the country when it did. It is, of course, a fact of central importance that Chinese business power was very great. Although Chinese businesses had been subjected to a variety of discriminatory restrictions in the postrevolutionary period, their over-all power had not declined. If anything it had risen, as Dutch businesses had withdrawn from the field, with Indonesian entrepreneurs unable to fill the gaps at the same pace. Moreover, anti-Chinese feeling had existed for decades—and in certain areas for centuries. It had given rise to pogroms in some places in the course of the Revolution. And it continued to be very great, particularly in the groups we have characterized as sharing in the Islamic-entrepreneurial political culture. Although the community of *peranakan* Chinese (those born in Indonesia and usually having Indonesian blood) was culturally Indonesian

---

[38] Han was sentenced to one and a half years' imprisonment on Nov. 12, 1956, and Lie to seven years on July 30, 1958 (*Keng Po*, Nov. 12, 1956; *Sin Po*, July 30, 1958).

as much as it was Chinese, the social distance between ethnic Indonesians and *peranakans* was enormous in most parts of the country, especially in the larger towns and cities.[39] Indeed, it was so great that many urban Indonesians were unaware of the social and cultural distinctiveness of the *peranakans* which set them apart from the community of *totoks* (those born in China, or in some cases in Indonesia but of parents recently arrived from China).

But why did these long-harbored anti-Chinese sentiments find political expression at this particular time? The question actually deserves to be reversed—what calls for explanation is the absence of political anti-Sinicism between 1949 and 1955. If anti-Chinese feeling was strong at this earlier time—and the evidence is overwhelming that it was—why did it find no political expression? In particular, why was there no employment of this potentially powerful political appeal in the three years of election campaigning? One part of the answer would seem to be that the political elite felt a greater commitment to uphold legal norms in the early postrevolutionary period. As far as the years of election campaigning are concerned, much of the explanation lies in the channeling and restraining role of the party system. Some of the major parties did not want to use anti-Chinese appeals because they were accepting Chinese money or because they felt that such appeals could be turned against them by their enemies with equal or greater facility. Others, like the Masjumi, were restrained by a group of their top leaders who saw anti-Sinicism as threatening the legal order which they were working to strengthen. Once such emphases had been laid down at the top level of leadership, they were not violated by party chiefs at lower levels.

With the end of the period of elections and the subsequent eclipse of the parties as channels for political activity, these restraints ceased to be effective. Moreover, within parties like the Masjumi and PSI, whose support came from towns and communities where anti-Chinese sentiment was particularly strong, there was a feeling that the leaders of these parties had been generally "too clean and too good" in the way they had organized campaigning and that this had lost them electoral appeal. In addition, two particular developments had aroused the spe-

[39] See Donald E. Willmott, *The Chinese of Semarang: A Changing Minority Community in Indonesia* (Ithaca, N.Y.: Cornell University Press, 1960), pp. 81 ff.; Leslie H. Palmier, *Social Status and Power in Java* (London: Athlone Press, 1960), pp. 108 ff.; Clifford Geertz, *The Religion of Java* (Glencoe, Ill.: Free Press, 1960), pp. 370 ff.; and G. William Skinner, "Java's Chinese Minority: Continuity and Change," *Journal of Asian Studies*, XX, no. 3 (May 1961), 353–362.

cial resentment of Indonesian businessmen. Firstly, the foreign trade regulations made by Finance Minister Sumitro of the Burhanuddin Harahap cabinet had restored some of the competitive advantages of foreign importers over national firms.[40] Secondly, the repudiation of the Round Table Conference agreements had led many Dutch companies to sell their establishments in Indonesia, and the buyers, those able to pay in foreign currency, were in very many cases Chinese. Finally, the general level of political dissatisfaction was high in the post-election period, and there were many who wanted to express hostility toward the government and society, toward people in places of power or privilege, but found no channels for this in the parties. Those who sought to use anti-Chinese sentiment to discredit particular government leaders of PNI persuasion were certainly working in a highly favorable political climate.[41]

REGIONAL PROTEST: THE PHASE OF ARMY-SUPPORTED SMUGGLING

The same inchoate political dissatisfaction and the same search for new channels through which interest demands could be pressed and general protest expressed provided the background for another more important development in the period of the second Ali cabinet, the rise of ethnic and regional movements. Here again is a case where a complex of problems which had been mounting over a period of years came to a head in the period of the postelection cabinet.

Over the whole of the period which followed the formation of the unitary state there was a crescendo of demands from the provinces and regions. Provincial spokesmen denounced "Djakarta" for not giving them enough autonomy. They castigated it for its cumbersome administrative procedures, for the fact that governmental leaders in the regions had often to fly to Djakarta for approval of quite minor decisions of policy. They criticized the central government for the supervision which it exercised over their affairs through its *pamong pradja*

[40] Sutter, *op. cit.*, pp. 1028–1029; see also Nan L. Amstutz, "The Rise of Indigenous Indonesian Importers, 1950–1955" (doctoral dissertation, Fletcher School, 1959), pp. 68–72.

[41] The anti-Chinese appeals made at this time were not usually combined with anti-Communist appeals, but their anti-Communist potentialities were quite clear, granted the fact that the most strongly anti-Chinese sections of the community were also those supporting the most strongly anti-Communist parties. By May 1957 Assaat was speaking of the Indonesian Chinese as a potential fifth column (Assaat, *Usaha Nasional Harus Diperlindungi oleh Pemerintah* ["National Enterprises Must Be Protected by the Government"; Medan: Pertjetakan Indonesia, 1957], p. 17).

representatives, governors, residents, regents, and so on. Sometimes they censured it for sending *pamong pradja* heads of a particular out-side ethnic group; in the case of the regions outside East and Central Java the complaint was most frequently against Javanese *pamong pradja* officials. Above all, they reproached the center for not giving them enough money.[42]

These criticisms were voiced during the whole of the 1949–1957 period. But their vociferousness was mounting as the period wore on. In part the aggravation reflected the cumulative growth of disappoint-ment with the fruits of independence. In part it resulted from a gradual fading of the stigma "Dutch," previously attached so strongly to all ethnically based political demands and demands for a federal con-stitutional order as a result of the Dutch effort to use federalism and ethnicity against the nationalism of the revolutionary Republic of Indonesia. In part too it must be related to the new situation created by the sudden diminution in the importance of parties in channeling the articulation of political protest.

Economically much of the protest had its roots in rising inflation and the existence of a major discrepancy between the official value of the rupiah and its much lower real value on the international free market. With the rupiah overvalued, exporters and export producers were in effect deprived of a part of their earnings; importers and im-port consumers were being correspondingly subsidized. But with Indonesia's foreign-exchange-earning assets regionally distributed as they were, the artificial exchange rate penalized certain parts of the country outside Java. It definitely penalized the dominant social groups of the Outer Islands. In one sense it disfavored the general population of these islands, inasmuch as it drew away from them funds available for developmental investment. On the other hand, it worked in favor of the dominant social interests of Java, that is to say, of the importers, the bureaucracy (inasmuch as its members were consumers of im-ported goods), and the small group of industrial producers depend-ent on imported raw materials.[43]

---

[42] For a full discussion see Gerald S. Maryanov, *Decentralization in Indonesia as a Political Problem* (Cornell Modern Indonesia Project, Interim Reports Series; Ithaca, N.Y., 1958), pp. 38–47.

[43] This argument is taken in large part from Hans O. Schmitt, "Some Monetary and Fiscal Consequences of Social Conflict in Indonesia, 1950–58" (doctoral dis-sertation, University of California, Berkeley, 1959), *passim*. See also J. A. C. Mackie, "The Political Economy of Guided Democracy," *Australian Outlook*, XIII, no. 4 (Dec. 1959), 285–292; D. W. Fryer, "Economic Aspects of Indonesian Disunity," *Pacific Affairs*, XXX, no. 3 (Sept. 1957), 195–208; and Leslie H.

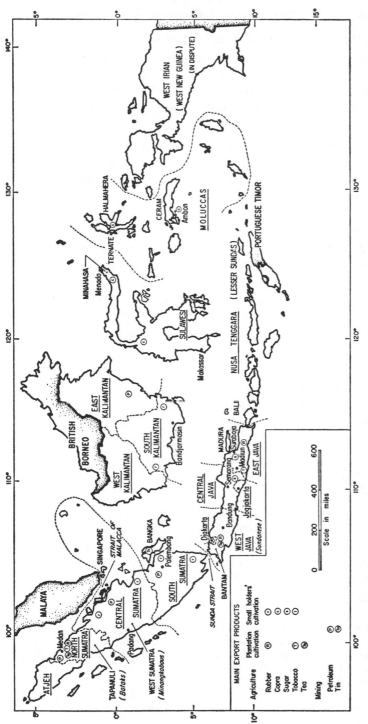

Map 2. Indonesia in early 1957. All the province boundaries here are as they were drawn in August 1950 except that Atjeh was then part of North Sumatra and Kalimantan a single province. Not marked on this map is the province of West in the Northern Moluccas and jurisdiction over a small area of what was previously included in the Moluccas province. (From George McTurnan Kahin, editor, *Governments and Politics of Southeast Asia*, Map 3; reproduced by permission, Cornell University Press.) Irian, established in August 1956, with its capital at Soa-Siu

The fact that the rupiah was kept overvalued for the whole of the 1949–1957 period was a reflection principally of the political weakness of the exporting interests, a weakness which followed largely from the fact that foreign concerns formed so large a part of the export sector. The basic sociopolitical reason why the rupiah was not devalued was that this would have raised the real cost of imports, thus the real cost of living for Java; and the beneficiaries, the export producers, would have been in large part foreigners. Therefore, although the central government devised various measures to give exporters incentives to produce—and some of these, like the foreign exchange certificate system of the period of the Hatta, Natsir, and Sukiman cabinets and the various import surcharges, made an important difference, functioning as a system of multiple exchange rates [44]—it never did so to the extent of giving them real income returns commensurate with their contribution to the gross national product.

The exchange rate discrepancy grew in importance in the years after 1953, especially in the period of the first cabinet of Ali Sastroamidjojo. This cabinet took inflationary financing much further than any of its predecessors. As already pointed out, it used currency expansion to finance a large increase in the number of national businesses, most of them in Djakarta, and to dispense patronage generously, again with an extremely high proportion of the beneficiaries in Djakarta. It also enabled the bureaucracy to grow further. In real income terms the costs of this were borne mostly by the exporting interests outside Java. Whereas a large part of these were foreign and thus capable of little effective political protest, the other part, which was Indonesian, could and did express its resentment.

The first Ali cabinet also encouraged a centralization of licensing procedures which hurt the remoter regions because it meant that foreign trade firms had to have offices in Djakarta.[45] Finally, the cabinet initiated a number of Indonesianization measures in the field of shipping, which seriously disrupted the flow of interinsular commerce in certain areas, particularly copra areas in East Indonesia.[46]

Palmier, *Indonesia and the Dutch* (London: Oxford University Press, 1962), pp. 153–159. For a chart showing the pattern of insular trade in Indonesia in 1955, see Biro Pusat Statistik (Central Bureau of Statistics), *Statistical Pocketbook of Indonesia, 1957* (Djakarta: Biro Pusat Statistik, 1957), p. 136.

[44] Schmitt, *op. cit.*

[45] See *Pedoman*, Nov. 11, 1954, Aug. 22, 1955. See also Sutter, *op. cit.*, p. 1104.

[46] See Boyd R. Compton, "Indonesia, 1955," *Newsletter of the Institute of Current World Affairs* (New York), Feb. 4, 1956.

Thus the years from 1953 were a time of rising regional protest. September 1953 saw the beginning of the revolt in Atjeh. September 1954 saw the emergence of large-scale army-organized smuggling in Sulawesi. In February 1955 a sort of economic coup took place in the copra region of Minahasa. The Coconut Foundation of Minahasa, a new army-backed organization of copra growers and leading citizens, seized the local assets of the Copra Foundation, the large Djakarta-run marketing organization for this commodity, and forced the Djakarta Foundation to give these to them as a "gift." [47] The same period saw an increasing amount of discussion of federalism and the establishment of various small federalist movements in various parts of the Outer Islands. [48]

This was also a period in which internal party cleavages showed an increasing tendency to follow a Java versus non-Java line. Thus when the PIR split in October 1954, it was into a predominantly Javanese faction, that of Wongsonegoro, and another which was influential principally outside Java, that of Hazairin and Tadjuddin Noor. When the PRN split in January 1956, at the time of the Supreme Court conviction of its chairman, Djody Gondokusumo, it was into a faction of mainly Javanese leadership, that of Djody, and one with predominantly non-Javanese leaders, that of Bebasa Daeng Lalo (and the PRN ministers in the Burhanuddin Harahap cabinet, F. Laoh and Gunawan). [49] There were incipient tendencies in the same direction in several of the larger parties.

One important new development of 1956 which affected the whole cast of the regional problem was a large increase in the volume of specifically ethnic demands. The year saw the birth of new ethnically based organizations among the Sundanese, the Lampongese, the Minangkabaus, the Achinese, the people of East Sumatra, and a number of other groups. Most of these were avowedly cultural in aim, but they engaged in a great amount of specifically political activity,

[47] See Bank Indonesia, *Report for the Year 1954–1955* (Djakarta, 1955), p. 125; Sutter, *op. cit.*, pp. 1103 ff.; and also John D. Legge, *Problems of Regional Autonomy in Contemporary Indonesia* (Cornell Modern Indonesia Project, Interim Reports Series; Ithaca, N.Y., 1957), pp. 68–69.

[48] See, for instance, the reports on the Gerakan Federalisme (Federalist Movement) established in Padang (*Penerangan* [Padang], Aug. 8, 1953), the Gerakan Pemuda Federasi Republik Indonesia (Federal Youth Movement of the Republic of Indonesia) established at Bandjarmasin (*Antara*, April 12, 1954), and the Partai Federal Indonesia established at Makassar (*Suluh Indonesia*, Aug. 1, 1955).

[49] See *Abadi*, Jan. 5, 1956; *Harian Rakjat*, Jan. 10, 1956; and *Times of Indonesia*, Jan. 12, 1956.

which was usually directed against a particular ethnic group. All of this was done with unprecedented openness.

The development went particularly fast among the Sundanese of West Java. Many Sundanese urbanites had long-harbored resentments against the Javanese in their area. Some of this group felt that the central government was dominated by Javanese who wanted to maintain the positions of their fellow Javanese as governmental heads in West Java. Now, from about March 1956 onward, feelings of this kind found political outlets. The existing Sundanese ethnic organizations became increasingly active, not only in Bandung and Djakarta but in a number of smaller towns of West Java as well, and they added a sizable dose of politics to the cultural activities which had hitherto been their principal *raison d'être*.[50] Further, they drew to themselves a considerable number of persons who had participated actively in the Revolution—in addition to those whom they had attracted earlier, persons who had been passive in the struggle for independence or had supported the Dutch-built state of Pasundan. In June 1956 the Front Pemuda Sunda (Sundanese Youth Front) was established to co-ordinate and further politicize the various existing organizations. With this development and with the subsequent arrest of two leaders of the Front for issuing pamphlets titled "Destroy the PNI and Javanese Imperialism," Sundanese ethnic politics acquired some of the militancy and dynamism of a political movement.[51]

At the same time anti-Javanese feeling found expression in other areas also, and not least in Djakarta. Minangkabaus in the capital were infusing an increasing amount of anti-Javanese politics into the activities of their mutual assistance organization, the Minang Sajo (of which all Minangkabaus were *ipso facto* members). One Masjumi parliamentarian of Minangkabau origin, Dr. Ali Akbar, charged publicly that Javanese applicants were being favored for entrance into the police academy.[52] The Masjumi and PSI press in Djakarta gave full play to the development of ethnic and regional protest and was charged

[50] See *Pedoman*, March 14, May 17, 29, June 12, Aug. 23, 1956, and *Keng Po*, Oct. 20, 1956. See also Andrea Wilcox Palmer, "The Sundanese Village," in G. William Skinner, ed., *Local Ethnic and National Loyalties in Village Indonesia* (Yale University, Southeast Asia Studies, Cultural Reports Series; New Haven, Conn., 1959), pp. 42–51.

[51] See Soelaeman Soemardi, "Regional Politicians and Administrators in West Java (1956): Social Backgrounds and Career Patterns" (M.A. thesis, Cornell University, 1960).

[52] *Abadi*, July 31, 1956.

by the papers of the PNI and PKI with stirring up anti-Javanese feeling.[53]

But the ethnic group political activity which developed in this period was by no means merely anti-Javanese. It was directed against a variety of groups and appeared in several areas of ethnic tension. It was particularly important in East Sumatra, near Medan, where ethnic group conflicts had long been acute and where one group, the Toba Bataks, were especially strongly disliked.[54] Early in 1956 these conflicts were given an open political character with the establishment of an Action Committee for the Demand for a Province of East Sumatra. The sponsors of the committee were East Sumatra residents of a number of ethnic groups. They included East Coast Malays, Karo Bataks, and Simelungun Bataks (the three main groups for whom East Sumatra is home), and in addition Achinese, Minangkabaus, Javanese, and Bataks from South Tapanuli (the predominantly Moslem Angkola and Mandailing peoples). Uniting these various groups was their common hostility to the Toba Bataks, whom they saw as growing dominant in East Sumatra, both because of the prominent positions they held in the army, in education, and in commerce and because of the rapid influx of large numbers of Toba Batak villagers who were leaving their impoverished home area on the Tapanuli plateau to become squatters in the estate lands of East Sumatra. The supporters of the East Sumatra autonomy idea asserted that the Toba Bataks could be stopped from becoming completely dominant in East Sumatra only if the region were administratively cut off from Tapanuli, where the Tobanese formed the majority group. Many of them argued further that such a redrawing of provincial borders would allow East Sumatra to receive greater benefits in exchange for its large contribution to Indonesia's export earnings.

The widespread activity in favor of East Sumatra autonomy soon evoked a response from the Toba Bataks, and the Committee for the Unity of the Province of North Sumatra was established. In February 1956 there was a large brawl in Medan between groups of Toba Batak youths and Achinese youths—following on a similar fight between groups of Toba Bataks and Bangkanese in Bangka in the previous month. In both cases there were persons killed, and in both the

[53] See, for instance, *Suluh Indonesia*, March 8, 1956.

[54] For a discussion of the position of the Bataks in Medan see Edward M. Bruner, "Urbanization and Ethnic Identity in North Sumatra," *American Anthropologist*, LXIII, no. 3 (June 1961), 508–521.

implications for interethnic relations in general were serious enough to require that the conflict be settled by conciliation committees composed of persons of very high status and political position from each of the ethnic groups involved.[55]

But more important than the specifically ethnic protest organizations was the growth of new forms of political action, engaged in by the military and civilian leaders of particular exporting regions who demanded greater returns for these regions for the goods they were exporting. This development led to a series of massive challenges to the cabinet's authority, challenges which were to keep the cabinet off balance for the rest of its term of office and to contribute heavily to its final downfall and the disintegration of constitutional democracy.

The first story of the series came out in the Djakarta press in early May 1956.[56] Between February and April not less than six foreign ships of sizable tonnage had put in at Bitung, the newly opened deep-sea port of Minahasa. They had loaded large quantities of copra, reportedly more than a quarter of Minahasa's annual production of approximately 100,000 tons, and they had unloaded a variety of foreign goods, rice, cars, jeeps, and machinery of various kinds. An overwhelming presumption existed that this was an action illegal in the eyes of the government at Djakarta. Nevertheless, the loading and unloading had been done in the full light of day, clearly with the cooperation of local government authorities, including military authorities, in Minahasa. However, the matter was not mentioned in the Minahasa press. The *Antara* correspondent who sent Djakarta its first reports was beaten up.

Djakarta reacted slowly and hesitantly at first. It had had ample evidence before of the intensity with which Minahasans resented its copra policies. On the other hand, to do nothing now was to let its own meager authority in the area dwindle further. It had already allowed one major smuggling action to go unpunished, in September 1954, and acquiesced in the coup in which the assets of the Copra Foundation in Minahasa were seized. But the smuggling of 1956 represented a further degree of challenge, if only because of the

[55] See *Indonesia Raya*, Feb. 15, 1956; *Pedoman*, Feb. 9, 1956; and *Indonesia Raya*, Feb. 27, 1956.

[56] *Pedoman*, May 8, 16, 1956; *Times of Indonesia*, May 22, 1956. See also Boyd R. Compton, "The Fall of the Copra Foundation" and "Bhinekka Tunggal Ika," *Newsletters of the Institute of Current World Affairs* (New York), June 16, July 28, 1956.

great quantity of copra involved. Djakarta's problem was all the greater because Minahasa is an area of high ethnic and social homogeneity and because Minahasans living in parts of East Indonesia outside their own small area were well placed to give expression to the very widespread resentments of Djakarta which existed in the various copra-producing areas.

Eventually the government did attempt action. Early in June it ordered the closing of Bitung harbor to ocean shipping. But to this there was immediate reaction. On June 3 a joint meeting of twenty organizations at Menado issued a statement denouncing the harbor-closing order and demanding its revocation by June 10. Several days later First Deputy Prime Minister Roem and Information Minister Sudibjo arrived in Menado, the capital of Minahasa, on tour from Djakarta. The two ministers are reported to have been forcibly held and threatened by a meeting-hall crowd. The banners they were shown included two reading, "To close Bitung as a deep-sea port is to invite us to be naughty" and "Let there be no repetition of Atjeh, of the South Moluccas Republic, and of South Sulawesi on account of Bitung Harbor." [57] The army commander in Minahasa, Lieutenant Colonel Worang, himself a Minahasan, appeared to have a considerable degree of sympathy for those who issued these threats.

The situation was explosive indeed. The Minahasan leadership seemed strongly united in support of the smuggling, and public backing for it was overwhelming after smuggled rice and cloth had brought down the prices of these commodities sharply. Moreover, it was privately reported that a large body of troops stood ready to support any move to rebellion.[58]

The central government hesitated for several days. Then it backed down, its surrender clothed in legalities. On June 10, Communications Minister Suchjar Tedjasukmana declared that the closing of the harbor was a temporary measure which had been resorted to only because certain legal preliminaries had been neglected when the harbor was opened in the period of the Burhanuddin Harahap cabinet. Several days later Prime Minister Ali declared that the cabinet had in fact had no intention of closing the harbor.

The army leadership too had some face restoring to do, especially after Lucas Kustarjo, the IPKI leader of a parliamentary mission sent

[57] *Pedoman*, June 9, 1956.
[58] Compton, "The Fall of the Copra Foundation," *loc. cit.*

to Minahasa, reported that the smuggling had been army-organized and that leadership for it had come from Worang, who had acted upon suggestions made by the territorial commander for East Indonesia, Colonel Warouw. In mid-July, Major General Nasution went personally to Minahasa. There he took part in a ceremony at which a large part of the smuggling proceeds were handed over to him—65 jeeps, 15 Land Rovers, three trucks, an ambulance, 63 cases of spare parts, 15 cases of building material, 119 cases of shoes, and 38 rolls of textiles.[59] These were promptly allocated to various public agencies, both in Minahasa itself and in various other copra-producing areas of Sulawesi. It was announced a little later that Worang would be transferred to a regimental commander in South Sumatra. But the successor who was named, Major J. D. Somba, was another man of Minahasan origin.

The government had succeeded in creating a legal façade to suggest that its authority in Minahasa was unimpaired, and it had persuaded the leaders of the smuggling action to halt their activities. On the other hand, it had allowed them to retain the fruits of their smuggling and had taken next to no punitive action against them. The over-all effect was to suggest that Minahasa had formidable advantages when it came to measuring strengths with Djakarta and that Djakarta's ability to apply sanctions against a united Minahasan leadership was slight in the extreme. It also threw new light on the significance of one important aspect of the transfers policy on which Nasution had recently embarked, the fact that most of the men who had been or were to be appointed as new territorial or regimental commanders were "native sons" of their areas of command.[60]

The implications of what had happened in Minahasa appeared even more serious in the light of certain parallel developments arising from East Indonesian resentments of the central government's copra-marketing organization, the Copra Foundation. This organization had been paying extremely low prices for the copra its agents bought from the growers throughout the postrevolutionary period. In 1955–1956 the figure was Rp. 130 to Rp. 140 per quintal (220 pounds)—at a time when soap manufacturers in Java paid up to Rp. 225 per quintal for the copra they bought from the Foundation and when the Amsterdam price was 60 to 70 Dutch guilders (or Rp. 180 to Rp. 210 at the official, and highly fictitious, exchange rate).[61] The copra growers were thus

[59] *Suluh Indonesia,* July 20, 1956.   [60] See *Pedoman,* April 20, 1956.
[61] Compton, "The Fall of the Copra Foundation," *loc. cit.*

under a double handicap—not only the exchange rate but high marketing costs as well.

But despite its large margin of profit, the Copra Foundation was rapidly sinking into debt by 1955. It had spent large sums on port projects, the development of coconut growers' co-operatives, and the displacement of Chinese middlemen by Indonesians. It had lost some important overseas markets and therefore sold more copra to factories in Java for a much smaller real income price—indeed, the ratio of overseas purchases to Java purchases had changed from 5:1 to 6:7 between 1950 and 1955.[62] It had used some of its funds to build Foundation directors' houses in Djakarta. And, if the regional charges are to be believed, it had become a nest of corruption.

In the month of March the Foundation's payments to growers were suddenly stopped. Soon thereafter it became known that the Bank Indonesia had refused to give it more credit. The result was a sharp intensification of the demands which had been made for some time (and especially since February 1955 when Minahasa had effectively "seceded" from the Copra Foundation) for the abolition of the Foundation. At the same time smuggling grew apace.

On April 27 there was a dramatic proclamation in Makassar.[63] An Action Committee for the Decentralization of the Copra Foundation declared that it had taken over the leadership, properties, and functions of the Copra Foundation in all of East Indonesia exclusive of Minahasa and Sangir-Talaud (which had also already "seceded"). The Action Committee was composed principally of veterans who had gone into business; it had the fullest support of Lieutenant Colonel Andi Mattalata, the military commander of Makassar. Its power in South Sulawesi was clear when the Acting Governor of Sulawesi and the Copra Foundation's director for all of East Indonesia signed an agreement on the day of the proclamation acceding to all the demands of the committee.

The central government was better placed to meet this particular challenge, in that Makassar was not itself a major depot for copra. Thus, while not denouncing the Action Committee, it instructed ships from other ports in Sulawesi to sail directly to Java without calling at Makasar. The Action Committee countered by unloading a copra-laden ship which was to make a delivery overseas—and it issued

[62] *Ibid.*
[63] Boyd R. Compton, "Macassar, June 14th," *Newsletter of the Institute of Current World Affairs* (New York), June 25, 1956.

strongly worded demands that the Copra Foundation should immediately pay its debts to growers in East Indonesia.[64]

By the middle of May the government had decided that radical concessions were required. Administratively and financially something had to be done about the now-insolvent Foundation. More important still, the government had been convinced by the events of Bitung and Makassar and by insistent demands from various other parts of the Copra Foundation area that its political authority was under serious challenge. On May 25 a government-called conference of various copra growers' representatives and regional leaders in the copra-growing areas accepted a formula for settlement of the conflict. The Copra Foundation would be dissolved by July 12, 1956. It would be replaced a year later by a Central Copra Co-operative and in the meantime by a series of preparatory committees. Subsequently, in mid-July, the government allocated Rp. 125 million [65] for payment of the Foundation's debts to growers. With the inflow of large debt payments over the next few months, the sting of East Indonesian hostility was temporarily drawn.[66] Before long Java-bound copra ships could again pass through Makassar. So ended this phase of the regional conflict, although a sharp tug of war continued as preparations were being made for the new Central Copra Co-operative. Again the solution was clearly a victory for the regions, though not as completely as in the case of the Bitung affair.

Finally, the months of May to July saw a major challenge to the government's authority in Sumatra. For one to two months from the middle of May the North Sumatra military command under Colonel Simbolon was organizing a large-scale smuggling operation through the small out-of-the-way port of Teluk Nibung in East Sumatra. The story came out gradually from the time of the first reports in the Medan press in early June.[67]

The heads of the North Sumatra command had been vociferous for some time about the deteriorating state of welfare among their soldiers. Housing and health conditions had become so bad, they asserted, that soldier morale was seriously threatened. And the funds that Djakarta

[64] *Abadi,* May 26, 1956.

[65] See Bank Indonesia, *Report for the Year, 1956–1957* (Djakarta, 1957), pp. 145–146.

[66] *Times of Indonesia,* July 13, 1956.

[67] *Suluh Indonesia,* June 20, 1956. See also Boyd R. Compton, "Army Smuggling, North Sumatra," *Newsletter of the Institute of Current World Affairs,* July 13, 1956.

was supplying were entirely inadequate in their eyes. At the same time they saw smuggling activities going on around them and yielding handsome profits.

They decided, therefore, to join in. They made arrangements with a Chinese firm in Medan and with the navy and gave notice of their intentions to a number of high officials in Djakarta. Between May 15 and June 5 seven foreign ships called at Teluk Nibung and carried away some 5,000 tons of rubber and coffee under army protection.[68] The proceeds, reportedly Rp. 50 million, were put to use for various army purposes, including the building of barracks.

On June 30 the cabinet instructed Simbolon to stop the Teluk Nibung action. Early in July, Simbolon came to Djakarta. There he assumed personal responsibility for the action and then went to work out a settlement with the civil and military authorities of the central government. On July 8 a further order was issued to the North Sumatra command to stop the Teluk Nibung smuggling, and after that date there was no more smuggling of this kind. At the same time it was made clear that no punitive action would be taken against Simbolon.

The significance of Simbolon's "official smuggling" stems in part from its context of large-scale ordinary smuggling. Smuggling in small craft had long been taking place on a sizable scale, the efforts of the small Indonesian navy notwithstanding, and the Straits of Malacca had been its area of greatest activity. Up to a certain point, indeed, it served useful political functions for the central government, in a way which helped to make up for its effects on government revenues. It was principally small holders' products which were smuggled out, as well as the products of Chinese estates and of thefts from estates of all nationalities. The large Western estates were not able to sell in this way. Thus smuggling made it possible for the anti-Djakarta resentments of Indonesian small holders to be relieved in some measure, without extending commensurate benefits to the foreign establishments, as would have been done in a devaluation.

But by 1955–1956 the scale of smuggling had become such as to detract seriously from the government's authority. The chief public prosecutor may have given an exaggerated impression of this when he cited an "official estimate" that one-third of Indonesia's annual rubber crop was being exported by smugglers,[69] but certainly smug-

---

[68] *Times of Indonesia*, July 17, 1956; *Pedoman*, July 11, 19, 1956.

[69] *Pedoman*, July 7, 1956. Cf. the statement of the PNI parliamentarian Selamat Ginting who said that the value of Malaya's registered imports from Indonesia

gling had grown rapidly. Needless to say, the successes of Simbolon, and of Worang and Warouw, gave further stimulus both to smuggling and to the loss of governmental authority which was at once its cause and its further effect.

Perhaps the most important aspect of the Teluk Nibung action was its meaning in terms of military politics. The North Sumatran smuggling was an army affair. Its leaders did not claim, as their counterparts in Sulawesi did (and with some justification), to be leading a popular movement. Their grievances were certainly genuine; soldier conditions were undeniably bad in North Sumatra. It is also a fact that the North Sumatra command had suffered material shortages over a lengthy period, partly as a result of mistrust of Simbolon by the leaders of the first Ali cabinet. But these were not the only factors in the North Sumatran army situation. An additional fact of crucial importance was the conflict between Simbolon and Nasution.

Simbolon had been a major rival of Nasution for the Chief of Staff's post. The two men had had a number of disagreements in previous years. More important, when Nasution obtained the much-coveted post, it was clear to his rivals that he did so on terms which favored the President; and Simbolon knew that Soekarno had long wanted to move him out of North Sumatra. Soon after Nasution's installation it became known that he would try to shift Simbolon to a staff position in Djakarta. But Simbolon, it soon appeared, was reluctant to leave. The Teluk Nibung action seems to have strengthened Simbolon's position within his own division and therefore to make it more difficult to transfer him. In Djakarta the word "warlordism" came to be used more and more.

MANEUVERS, COUPS, AND COLONEL ZULKIFLI LUBIS

In August 1956 the focus of political attention shifted from Sulawesi and Sumatra to West Java and Djakarta. Whereas smuggling, regionalism, and the position of regional military leaders had been the central problems between May and July, the following four months were a period of power maneuverings in and near the capital. Military leaders were again the principal actors, and the period was another one of diminishing government authority.

The events which came to a head in the months of August to November 1956 were in one sense a direct consequence of the appoint-

---

had been 93 per cent higher in 1955 than that of Indonesia's registered exports to Malaya (*ibid.*, July 22, 1956).

ment of Nasution as Chief of Staff in October 1955. On assuming his post in November the new army head had declared that there would be a comprehensive set of transfers of officers, as had been asked for by the Jogjakarta conference. By February 1956 he had completed an over-all plan of reassignments involving all territorial commanders—there had been no change in these since November 1952—all territorial chiefs of staff, inspectors general, and General Staff officers. The plan was approved by the Burhanuddin Harahap cabinet.[70]

But it soon became apparent that strong resistance existed to Nasution's plans. Many announcements were made in the first half of 1956 of transfer of officers, but there was little progress in realizing scheduled transfers of territorial commanders. There were repeated reports in the Masjumi and PSI press of dissatisfaction inside the officer corps. Major General Simatupang, the former Armed Forces Chief of Staff, gave a newspaper interview in July criticizing the large number of officers who were in Djakarta with no work to do. The term "tour of duty," he said, was coming to be interpreted as "tour of *tjuti* [holiday tour]." [71] At the same time the PNI press criticized officers who were refusing to obey transfer orders, calling them traitors to the Jogjakarta charter, and it charged that certain politicians were attempting to sabotage the Chief of Staff's transfers plan.[72]

The resistance which Nasution found came in part from individual commanders long entrenched in powerful positions and reluctant to leave them for staff posts. But it also had broader political implications. The transfer plans hit at the power of the very officers who had been most prominent in organizing the army's resistance to the first Ali cabinet. The Chief of Staff seemed to be concerned on the one hand with undermining the power of Simbolon and his associates of the old "pro-October 17 group" (including Kawilarang, of the key command of West Java) and on the other hand with weakening the Deputy Chief of Staff, Zulkifli Lubis, and his immediate supporters.

In fact, it was clear by mid-1956 that the army unity of June 1955 had been shattered, that the army was again split into two blocs, as it had been by the events of October 1952. On the one side was the group of Nasution and his principal assistant (later Deputy Chief of

[70] See the statement of Captain Harsono, deputy head of army information, in *Abadi,* July 11, 1956. For a complete listing of senior army functionaries in early 1956 see Darius Marpaung, ed., *Almanak Angkatan Perang 1956* ("Armed Forces Almanac 1956"; Djakarta: Upeni, 1956), pp. 51 ff.

[71] *Pedoman,* July 9, 1956.   [72] *Suluh Indonesia,* June 8, July 27, 1956.

Staff), Colonel Gatot Subroto, supported by a large number of the officers who had been on the "anti-October 17" side in 1952. On the other were Simbolon and Zulkifli Lubis, now brought to increasingly close co-operation with one another. This division moreover corresponded roughly with political antagonisms outside the army. Nasution had clearly defined and fairly smooth relationships with both President Soekarno and Prime Minister Ali. (He had gained his fellow officers' approval for Ali's accession to the Defense portfolio in exchange for a promise that he, the Chief of Staff, and his associates, would have a free hand in army affairs.) The Simbolon-Lubis group had the support of the press of the Masjumi and particularly of the PSI.

Significantly, the cleavage tended to parallel two other lines of conflict as well. On the one hand, it paralleled the conflict between Djakarta and the islands outside Java; the Simbolon and Lubis groups were extremely well placed to use the rising tide of regionalist resentment against Djakarta. On the other hand, it approximated the cleavage which was created by the rise and open voicing of feeling against the ethnic Javanese. The anti-Nasution and anti-Soekarno-Ali group of officers were mostly non-Javanese and, by fostering an image of the Sumatran Nasution as a tool of the Javanese Soekarno and Ali, they could identify themselves with anti-Javanese feeling, both in the Outer Islands and in West Java.

By July it was clear that a showdown between the two groups was approaching.[73] A beginning had been made with the transfers of territorial commanders. Before long the remaining commanders would be instructed to leave their posts. At an all-Indonesian military conference in early August dates were set for a number of the transfer ceremonies. Kawilarang would have to surrender the crucial West Java command on August 14 (to a General Staff man, Lieutenant Colonel Suprajogi). Warouw would have to leave his East Indonesian command between August 23 and 26 (to a man who had recently been installed as his Chief of Staff, Lieutenant Colonel Sumual). On September 17 Simbolon would be obliged to leave his North Sumatra post to Zulkifli Lubis (who was to have transferred his duties as Deputy Chief of Staff to Gatot Subroto between August 14 and 20).[74]

[73] See *Pedoman*, June 28, 1956; *Abadi*, July 11, 1956; and *Suluh Indonesia*, July 14, 27, 1956.
[74] *Pedoman*, Aug. 3, 1956.

If these transfers could now finally be realized, the Chief of Staff's power would be vastly enhanced; those who had been fighting his personnel policies would have few important command posts left from which to carry on their resistance. August, then, was a crucial month. The anti-Nasution forces were challenged to act immediately or accept relegation to a position of markedly inferior power.

On the morning of August 13 the Foreign Minister, Roeslan Abdulgani, was to leave Djakarta for London to join in the conference on Egypt's seizure of the Suez Canal. At six that morning two uniformed men arrived at Roeslan's home with a warrant to arrest the Foreign Minister. The signature was that of Kawilarang, and the legal basis Kawilarang's authority as administrator of the State of War and Siege in West Java. Roeslan, the men said, was wanted for questioning in connection with the case of Lie Hok Thay, the deputy director of the State Printery, who was under arrest. But while Roeslan was dressing, his wife succeeded in phoning the Prime Minister. Then, just as the minister was about to be taken from his house, the Djakarta military commander arrived to tell him that the arrest order had been revoked by Chief of Staff Nasution. Several hours later Roeslan Abdulgani left Djakarta for London.[75]

In the course of the day *Indonesia Raya* came out with a special edition. Its blazing headlines declared that Roeslan had been involved in corrupt activities with Lie Hok Thay of the State Printery. Lie had told his police interrogators—indeed, he had provided them with proofs, *Indonesia Raya* asserted—that the Foreign Minister had accepted favors from him. Now the West Java division, which had committed itself at a 1955 conference to the fighting of corruption, had acted to arrest the Foreign Minister. *Indonesia Raya* went on to urge that Nasution be stopped from ousting Kawilarang from his post.[76]

For a day acute tension prevailed in Djakarta. The *Indonesia Raya* of August 14 carried a statement of Zulkifli Lubis charging that the Prime Minister and the Chief of Staff had defended evil by releasing Roeslan from the hands of his would-be arresters. Warouw of East Indonesia issued a statement on the same day threatening not to leave

[75] This account is based on the statements of Mrs. Roeslan (*Suluh Indonesia,* Aug. 15, 1956), of Prime Minister Ali Sastroamidjojo (*Suluh Indonesia,* Aug. 16, 1956), and of the official spokesman of the army (*Suluh Indonesia,* Aug. 16, 1956).

[76] Quoted in *Pedoman,* Aug. 14, 1956.

his own command unless a settlement of the Roeslan case were reached by the joint efforts of the Chief of Staff, the Deputy Chief of Staff (Zulkifli Lubis), and the West Java commander.[77]

But the same day saw conclusive evidence that Kawilarang's move had failed. The ceremony in which he transferred his duties to Suprajogi was held on that day as scheduled. Nasution was quickly able to take control of the situation in the capital. On August 15 the Prime Minister gave parliament a full report on the incident, declaring that an attempt had been made to overthrow the cabinet by extraparliamentary means. It was true, Ali said, that the Foreign Minister's name had been mentioned in the Lie Hok Thay interrogations, but no reason existed for preventing his departure for London.[78] It was not long before the implications of Kawilarang's defeat became clear. Lubis, reportedly the planner of Kawilarang's action, gave up his post as Deputy Chief of Staff on August 20. Warouw was obliged to leave his post in East Indonesia two days later.

Indonesia Raya and *Pedoman,* however, continued to feature stories of alleged corruption in which Lie and Roeslan had been involved.[79] Thus it became apparent that Roeslan's name would have to be cleared —or he would have to resign—if he was not to do serious damage to the cabinet's prestige. Later in the month, after Roeslan had returned from London, the cabinet decided to establish a small committee of ministers and others (including Chief Public Prosecutor Suprapto) to hear evidence on his alleged corruption. This committee, of which the Masjumi's Roem was made chairman, considered the evidence upon which Kawilarang had justified his attempt to arrest Roeslan and came to the unanimous conclusion that no grounds existed for a charge against the Foreign Minister.

Meanwhile the power struggle inside the army continued. The Lubis-Simbolon coalition had lost a major battle, but they had by no means lost the war. There was still considerable support for them in different parts of the army. Further, they had succeeded once more, as in June 1955, in making the anticorruption issue their own.

In September the conflict shifted to the regimental commands of West Java. Kawilarang had built up strong support inside the West Java division before his transfer, and Suprajogi, his Nasution-backed successor, was still in a weak position. Therefore Lubis, now an ordinary General Staff officer, found considerable support when he

[77] *Suluh Indonesia,* Aug. 16, 1956.　　[78] *Suluh Indonesia,* Aug. 16, 1956.
[79] *Pedoman,* Aug. 21, 22, 1956.

approached a number of West Java regimental commanders with a plan for a military coup. His aim, it seems, was to oust Nasution, to overthrow the cabinet, and to replace it by a new one, which would function under the supervision of a military council. Suprajogi held a roll-call meeting of his battalion commanders in the middle of September in order to combat Lubis' influence and then a conference of regimental commanders at the end of the month for the same purpose. Subsequently he issued an order forbidding his officers to hold meetings bearing on political activities. But these measures did not stop Lubis and his supporters from continuing to organize.

The tension mounted in October, with repeated reports that pro-Lubis units would attempt some sort of coup. On October 4 the Chief of Staff established an *ad hoc* committee of officers to assist him in investigating suspected political activities of army members and in taking administrative and disciplinary action against those found to be engaged in them. The pro-Lubis officers, fearing that Nasution would soon start to order their dismissal or arrest, felt they had to move fast. They wanted also to act before President Soekarno's return from Russia and China, scheduled for October 16.

Their first act came on October 11. That morning a convoy of military transports carrying nine pro-Lubis battalions from the Tjirebon and East Priangan commands was sent on its way to Djakarta. But they were stopped in the Bogor residency, on the instruction of the regimental commander for Bogor and Banten, Major Achmad Wiranatakusumah. There was no shooting, but the move was effectively thwarted. A number of arrests of pro-Lubis officers followed, and the regimental commanders in Tjirebon and East Priangan were suspended and obliged to leave their posts.[80]

The final phase of the crisis came in November. On November 7 Nasution issued a summons to Lubis and two of his leading supporters in Bandung, Colonels Sukanda Bratamenggala and Sapari. The latter two responded and were questioned and then suspended from their posts and placed under surveillance. Lubis promised to heed the summons on the following day. But when the morning of November 8 came, he phoned to say that he would be late since he would have to take his sick wife to a doctor. Later in the morning, when Lubis had still not arrived, Colonels Gatot Subroto and Kretarto were sent

---

[80] *Pedoman*, Oct. 17, 1956. See also the Prime Minister's full statement to parliament on the October and November developments in West Java, in *Times of Indonesia*, Dec. 14, 1956.

to call on him, and a heated discussion ensued. Lubis protested against the restrictions placed on Sukanda and Sapari, and he threatened that the territorial commands of North Sumatra (Simbolon) and Kalimantan (Colonel Abimanju, a new appointee, but a Lubis supporter) would dissociate themselves from the Chief of Staff unless the two staff colonels were allowed their freedom. Soon after the meeting Lubis left his house.

On the morning of November 16 the army's commando training unit under its pro-Lubis commander, Major Djaelani, moved from its base near Bandung to Krandji near Djakarta. There it waited for other troops from Tjirebon. Together these two groups were to back up a number of Djakarta units which were to arrest the Chief of Staff and seize control of the capital that morning. But this attempt too was a failure. The Tjirebon units never reached Krandji, and nothing happened in Djakarta that morning. At noon all troops in the capital were confined to their barracks for a four-day period. Djaelani's men returned to Bandung.[81]

For several days tension continued to be high, and new attempts at a coup were expected in Djakarta. Djaelani continued to refuse a Nasution summons of November 13. Lubis' whereabouts was unknown. At the same time reports reached Djakarta of an order issued on November 14 by Abimanju, the pro-Lubis commander in Kalimantan, to arrest all civil and military officials of the central government arriving in Kalimantan and in addition all members of parliament and of the Constituent Assembly.

Within a few days, however, it became apparent that the Lubis forces in West Java had been weakened too much to attempt a further coup. On November 21 Djaelani was arrested. Nine days later the Lubis-sympathizing military commander for Djakarta, Major Djuhro Sumitradilaga, formally gave up his post to a Nasution man, Major Endang Dachjar. By the end of the month the Chief of Staff seemed to be in fairly full control of the situation in and near the capital. On November 28 the cabinet issued a statement declaring that Lubis had led the preparations and implementing actions of an attempted *coup d'état*. At the same time it suspended the colonel from all his duties.

Lubis continued to be at large, however. A warrant for his arrest had been issued for some time, and many claimed to know where

[81] See the Prime Minister's statement in *Times of Indonesia*, Dec. 14, 1956, and the statement of the army information division in *Pedoman*, Dec. 8, 1956. See also *Pedoman*, Nov. 23, Dec. 8, 1956.

he was. But no one arrested him. Moreover, he issued a series of open letters and press statements. In them he denied that he had been attempting to enact a *coup d'état* or change the basis of the state and declared that he would willingly report to the authorities when a business cabinet had been established under the leadership of Hatta and the Sultan of Jogjakarta.[82]

Lubis had been thwarted repeatedly in his efforts to overturn the political balance in the capital. Indeed, there is some doubt about whether he had come close to success in any of these efforts. But he had not been defeated. The central conflict remained unresolved.

THE ALTERNATIVE FORMS OF GOVERNMENT DEBATED

In the discussion thus far we have emphasized internal conflict in the army as central to the Lubis maneuvers. But there was another equally important aspect to the Lubis challenge, the fact that the rebellious colonels gave expression to the demand for greater army power within the government.

In earlier chapters we saw the long development of army hostility to civilian politicians. We saw how a temporarily cohesive army leadership overthrew a cabinet in June 1955 and came close to attempting some sort of take-over of state power. It desisted from this then, largely because of the impending elections and because no means appeared to be at hand whereby a military take-over could be made legitimate in the eyes of the political public. It decided to wait a year to see what changes resulted from the elections.

The period since the elections had increased the opportunities for army action. The moral authority of party and parliamentary government had declined sharply, and it had become evident in the development of the regionalist movements (and on a much smaller scale in the way in which the ethnic and anti-Chinese movements unfolded) that army men could now gain acceptance as legitimate political leaders, at least in some situations.

But the central leaders of the army were not now in a position to speak for the army's claims against the civilians. Chief of Staff Nasution had earlier been a principal spokesman for the anti-civilian-

[82] See *Pedoman*, Nov. 25, 1956, and *Keng Po*, Dec. 14, 16, 1956. The Sultan had played no part in Djakarta politics since his resignation from the Wilopo cabinet in Jan. 1953. Instead he had devoted his efforts to developing the Special Territory of Jogjakarta, where he was both the reigning Sultan and the regional head, governing and representing Djakarta.

politician ideology of the army. But in the 1956 situation he depended on the President and the Prime Minister to buttress his still unconsolidated position inside the army. He therefore could not lead the cry against civilians. Obliged by their weak position to defend the *status quo* in army-civilian relations, Nasution and his associates were necessarily disppointing to many of their fellow officers. They were in effect offering a vegetarian diet to a tiger which had tasted blood. Lubis, on the other hand, was qualified by both his past role and his current political position to act as a principal leader of the "anti-civilianist" sentiment. Whether or not he hoped to establish a military dictatorship on Egyptian lines as the Prime Minister alleged,[83] he definitely stood for much-increased military power over civilian affairs.

The weak moral position of parties and parliamentary government was evident in much of what was happening on the political stage in the four months of Lubis' maneuvering in West Java—and particularly in much of what was being said. If the months of May to July 1956 were a period in which parties were increasingly being bypassed in the flow of political events, the following four months were ones of open challenge to the ideology which legitimized the parties' power.

The general social and political unrest described for the earlier months of the cabinet's incumbency continued in this middle period. Although there were no anti-Chinese mob phenomena in the months of August to November, there was violence in two cases of demonstrations against Western actions.

On September 17 a minor riot occurred in Djakarta as members of the Communist youth organization Pemuda Rakjat (People's Youth) were demonstrating outside the courthouse where the Dutch Captain Schmidt was standing trial on a charge of involvement in subversive activities. After one of the demonstrators had been injured by a blow from a policeman's rifle butt, the demonstration became angry. In consequence the Dutch woman lawyer defending Schmidt was beaten on the back and considerable damage was done to the body of her car. A Dutch journalist was attacked by a group of youths and suffered minor injuries.[84]

The second case of rioting followed the Anglo-French-Israeli invasion of Suez. A large rally was held in Djakarta on November 7 to protest the invasion, and after the rally one part of the crowd proceeded to the British Embassy. The police guard there was weak, and so the crowd attacked the embassy's library building and then threw the

[83] *Times of Indonesia*, Dec. 14, 1956.   [84] *Keng Po*, Sept. 18, 1956.

tiles off its roof and burned books, films, and furniture on the street. Parts of the same crowd went on to do minor damage to the French Embassy building and the residences of the British and French ambassadors.[85] Several individual Westerners who crossed its path were attacked in the streets.

In early December a *Keng Po* editorial pointed to the increasing trend for people to act as their own policeman and judge. It discussed recent instances of raids on newspaper offices, interethnic brawls, and the beating up of people alleged to have poisoned others or acted as firebugs. According to this editorial there had been a growth in the number of protective organizations, a direct response to the rising level of insecurity and violence.[86] At the same time the press reported demonstrations against pornographic literature and rock-and-roll dancing. On December 19 some 40 persons, aroused by a prophet who predicted the end of the world in nine days and told his followers to sell all their belongings, demonstrated in a *kampong* area of Djakarta.[87]

The same period saw frequent expressions of radical dissatisfaction and disgust with the general political situation. Many of the criticisms centered on corruption. The case of the Foreign Minister, Roeslan Abdulgani, was a particularly important focus here. When the cabinet declared, on the Roem committee's recommendation, that no grounds existed for trying the Foreign Minister, a number of newspaper editors were vociferously indignant. Some argued that the Roem committee should have made its findings public, others said the minister ought to have resigned at the time of the first press charges against him. In October the corruption issue was kept alive by reports on the investigation of Lie Hok Thay and of Indonesian officials who had been arrested for questionable associations with him. Furthermore, that month saw reporting of division in the cabinet on an anticorruption bill prepared by the Masjumi Minister of Justice, Professor Muljatno. Only after Muljatno had threatened to resign over the issue did the cabinet accept the relatively tough bill which he had drafted. The high-status Auditing Board (Dewan Pengawas Keuangan) added to the general impression that the state was rotten when it issued a statement to the effect that a number of ministries had not given it explanations of their expenditures up to tens of millions of rupiahs.[88]

---

[85] *Ibid.*, Nov. 7, 1956.   [86] *Ibid.*, Dec. 3, 1956.   [87] *Ibid.*, Dec. 19, 1956.
[88] *Java Bode*, Oct. 27, 1956, quoted in J. M. van der Kroef, "Instability in Indonesia," *Far Eastern Survey*, XXVI, no. 4 (April 1957), 56.

In December, Mochtar Lubis, the editor of *Indonesia Raya*, stood trial on a government-brought libel charge for reports his paper had carried of corrupt dealings between Roeslan Abdulgani and Lie Hok Thay. Dramatically the editor presented the court with photostats of documents showing Roeslan to have accepted a house and car from Lie and to have carried dollars overseas for him in violation of foreign exchange regulations.[89] This brought the whole cabinet into disrepute. The sums of money which Roeslan had apparently received were not great, compared with what certain ministers in other cabinets were believed to have received in irregular ways. But the case of the Foreign Minister had become something of a *cause célèbre*. On the basis of the Roem committee's findings, the cabinet had committed the whole of its prestige to the declaration that Roeslan was innocent. Now its case seemed to have been exploded. The cabinet leaders maintained that the Roem committee had made its decision without knowing of the existence of Mochtar Lubis's evidence, and this appears to have been the case. But the fact was that they were politically cornered. They remained so on this account until January 28, 1957, when the chief public prosecutor's office announced that Roeslan's case had been submitted to the Supreme Court for action.[90]

Thus, throughout the period of August to November 1956 and, in fact, until January 1957, the cabinet was under constant criticism for protecting corruptors. This period saw a great number of demands, many of them coming significantly from particular army commanders, for a tougher policy against corruption.[91] Granted the political situation of the time, these were all thrusts at the cabinet, in function if not in intent.

There was also a new wave of charges against the way in which political leaders had isolated themselves from the people and profiteered at their expense. Thus the regimental commander for Bogor and Banten, Achmad Wiranatakusumah, issued pamphlets in early October in which he attacked the "power drunkenness and rank drunkenness" existing among government and political leaders and the fact that "the patriotism and heroism which existed at the beginning of the

---

[89] See *Indonesia Raya*, Dec. 3, 1956.

[90] *Times of Indonesia*, Jan. 30, 1957. Roeslan Abdulgani was charged before the Supreme Court of violating foreign exchange regulations by carrying U.S. dollars in an envelope from Lie Hok Thay in Djakarta to Lieut. Col. M. J. Prajogo of the military police who was then in Washington. On April 16, 1957, he was found guilty of an unintentional violation of these regulations and fined Rp. 5,000.

[91] See, for instance, the statement of Lieut. Col. Suprajogi, the territorial commander of West Java, in *Keng Po*, Sept. 28, 1956.

Revolution has given way to a feeling of egoism and a pursuit simply of material satisfactions for oneself." The greater part of the people, the regimental commander declared, had experienced no improvement in their fortunes. Those who had benefited had been a small group, politicians, intellectuals, profiteers, foreigners, and those who had been traitors and agents of the enemy during the Revolution.[92] Paralleling statements like these were general warnings that the condition of the country was one of emergency.[93]

Condemnations of politicians and parties became particularly frequent. The PSI-sympathizing weekly *Siasat,* commenting in August on the way in which the government and the party bosses dominated parliament, spoke of a "politicians' plot." [94] In November 1956 Mohammad Hatta touched on a similar theme in his last address before resigning the vice-presidency: "Parties . . . have been made into an end in themselves, the state being their tool. . . . The standing of the government has become that of a messenger boy of the political parties." [95] In March 1957 when the publishing house "Pembangunan" conducted an essay contest and induced 355 readers of different Djakarta newspapers to write on "What are we as a nation and as a country?" only eight of the writers were relatively favorable in what they said of the political parties whereas at least twenty were strongly critical of the parties.[96]

It is true that statements, allegations, warnings, and appeals of these kinds had been made very frequently before. This was the largest wave of them but there had been others, in the first half of 1953, for instance, which were almost as large. In the case of many of the diagnoses the medication offered in 1956 followed lines familiar from earlier years. Thus there were repeated calls by various groups for a presidential or business cabinet, led by Hatta or by Soekarno and Hatta.[97]

But there was a new element in the case of this particular series

[92] *Keng Po,* Oct. 9, 1956. It is significant that this appeal came not from a pro-Zulkifli Lubis commander, but in fact from a man who, only a few days after the issuing of these pamphlets, helped to forestall one of Lubis' attempted coups.

[93] See, for instance, the statements of Masjumi parliamentarians Sjarif Usman and Dr. Ali Akbar, *Keng Po,* Nov. 12, 1956, and *Suluh Indonesia,* Nov. 29, 1956; also the Masjumi's note to the cabinet of late November, *Pedoman,* Nov. 29, 1956.

[94] *Siasat,* Aug. 8, 1956.

[95] Mohammad Hatta, *Past and Future* (Cornell Modern Indonesia Project, Translation Series; Ithaca, N.Y., 1960), pp. 12, 16.

[96] Guy J. Pauker, "Indonesian Images of Their National Self," *Public Opinion Quarterly,* XXII, no. 3 (Fall 1958), 320.

[97] See the statements of the IPKI leader Sumitro Kolopaking (*Keng Po,* Nov. 10, 1956) and of Parindra (*Suluh Indonesia,* Nov. 20, 1956).

of statements, because many of the general complaints made were now joined with criticism of basic political machinery. On October 5 Nasution gave the stamp of official recognition to the discussion ot nondemocratic alternatives to the existing political system. In an Armed Forces Day message, he spoke of the selfishness of the political leaders and the sense of disappointment existing among the people, and then referred specifically to the existence of proposals for a "military junta" and a "youth junta." [98] When Achmad Wiranatakusu-mah issued his pamphlets three days later, he included in them a dec-laration that the multiparty system "has not demonstrated a usefulness which can be directly felt by the people. On the contrary, the parties are competing with one another to get and keep power and material gain for themselves, thinking little or not at all about the interests of the state or the public." [99]

The point was made in a particularly threatening form by the IPKI parliamentarian and former army major Lucas Kustarjo. Speaking on October 24, Kustarjo declared that the military no longer had any respect for the politicians and that there was therefore a desire to make radical changes in the system of parliamentary democracy. He added that two main lines of thought currently existed in the army. One group wanted the abolition of parties and parliament and the taking over of the government by a military council. The other group merely demanded that the politicians be honest and sincere in facing the problems bearing on the interests of the people or, if this proved to be impossible, then the formation, by Soekarno, Hatta, and the army together, of a government of really sincere and responsible men. Kustarjo concluded: "If the politicians still want the system of parlia-mentary democracy, their only chance is to change their characteristics and their ways of thinking so as to become politicians of patriotic spirit, forgetting their own groups and parties and attending to the interests of the state and the people." [100] One counterpart to this was presented in the Masjumi note to the cabinet mentioned above. "What is at stake now," the Masjumi told the cabinet, "is not only this cabinet but democracy itself." [101]

Which, then, were the groups which threatened constitutional de-mocracy? The question is not easy to answer. The PNI press averred that the threat came essentially from "the groups that had lost the elections." [102] As PNI men saw it, the Masjumi and PSI had never

[98] *Mimbar Indonesia,* Oct. 13, 1956.   [99] *Keng Po,* Oct. 8, 1956.
[100] *Keng Po,* Oct. 24, 1956.   [101] *Pedoman,* Nov. 29, 1956.
[102] *Suluh Indonesia* and *Merdeka,* quoted in *Pedoman,* Nov. 20, 1956.

been able to reconcile themselves to their electoral defeat. Therefore they were trying everything to deprecate, side-step, and finally over-throw the parliament in which they were a small minority. Hence they were sponsoring anti-Sinicism, anti-Javanism, smuggling, and regionalist demands, a campaign to victimize certain public officials by charges of corruption, and now the ambitions of a group of rebel-lious would-be-Nasser colonels. And the Masjumi was doing these things while a member of the cabinet. The threat, as these PNI leaders saw it, came not so much from the army as such as from an officer group with a political party "riding on its back." [103]

From a Masjumi viewpoint the origins of the antiparliamentary drive seemed different. Masjumi men admitted that they shared many politi-cal goals with such army leaders as Zulkifli Lubis. And the Masjumi ministers in the cabinet showed great reluctance to join their cabinet colleagues in condemning the actions of Lubis.[104] But they denied that they, as a group of civilian politicians, had control over Lubis' group or any other part of the officers' corps. As many of them saw it, the actions of Lubis were but one manifestation of a drive by the army as a whole for greater power in the state, a drive which would soon hurt the interests of the Masjumi as much of those of the PNI. In the eyes of the Masjumi it was the PNI which had done most to encourage this drive because it was under two PNI-led cabinets, the two cabinets of Ali Sastroamidjojo, that the government had most rapidly lost its moral authority. On this view the Masjumi was about to become a

[103] *Suluh Indonesia,* Oct. 6, 1956. This *Suluh Indonesia* editorial contains four interesting reasons why a military coup was successful in Egypt and would not be so in Indonesia. The Egyptian army, it stated, was clean, united, possessed of members with ability in statecraft, and not ridden upon by a particular party current.

[104] This was only one of a series of occasions in this period on which PNI-Masjumi relations within the cabinet were strained almost to the breaking point. They were greatly strained on Sept. 10, when Foreign Minister Roeslan Abdulgani, who was in Moscow with President Soekarno, signed a Joint statement with the Soviet Union. Natsir thereupon declared that there were sections of his party in "the regions" demanding that its ministers be withdrawn from the cabinet (*Keng Po,* Sept. 12, 1956). The demand grew stronger after the cabinet decision to suspend Zulkifli Lubis and again when Mochtar Lubis produced his photostat evidence on Roeslan Abdulgani. The Natsir leadership of the party stood up against the pressure for some time, fearing the rise of PKI influence in government in the event that a rump PNI–NU coalition continued in office with PKI support. But by early December this had become extremely difficult, with such men as Sjarif Usman and Isa Anshary openly urging the resignation of the cabinet (*Pedoman,* Dec. 4, 8, 1956). For a full discussion see Deliar Noer, "Masjumi: Its Organization, Ideology and Political Role in Indonesia" (M.A. thesis, Cornell University, 1960).

victim of a decline in civilian power to which the PNI had been the chief contributor.

Both the parties had a part of the truth. The issue was indeed one of the army versus civilians, as Masjumi leaders said. In the words of Lucas Kustarjo, "The present stir in the army turns on dissatisfaction caused by what is seen as too great a contrast between the politicians and the military." [105] The officer group as a whole, and not merely the Lubis group, was concerned to dislodge the civilian politicians from a part of the power and privileges they had had over the previous seven years. On the other hand,—and here the PNI argument was the strong one—the immediate challenge was from Lubis and those who in one or another degree followed him into opposition to the Chief of Staff. Not only were this group of officers against politicians as a whole; they were particularly against politicians of the PNI and its allies.

Up to this point our discussion has focused exclusively on the army, and particular army groups, as threatening parliamentary democracy and bidding to supplant it. In fact, however, a political force of an entirely different kind was making similar efforts at the same time. This was President Soekarno.

For the whole of this second Ali cabinet President Soekarno had been noticeably independent of the cabinet. He had disagreed with Prime Minister Ali at the time of the cabinet's formation. He had subsequently differed with him over economic policy; the Prime Minister, playing an "administrator" role, favored a number of measures against strikers and squatters and was in favor of foreign investment, whereas the President opposed these measures, on the grounds that they would make the government hated by the people. The two men had come into serious conflict over the President's two marathon overseas trips of May to July and August to October. The striking success of Soekarno's flamboyant and intensely personal diplomacy posed a threat to Ali's control of an area of policy making in which he had particular interest. This came out with great clarity in Soekarno's readiness to support the signing in Moscow of the Indonesian-Soviet Joint Statement, which subsequently became a highly controversial document in Indonesia. At the President's suggestion Foreign Minister Roeslan Abdulgani signed the Joint Statement without consulting the Prime Minister or the cabinet.[106]

---

[105] *Keng Po,* Oct. 24, 1956.

[106] The most controversial clause of the Joint Statement reads: "The Soviet Union and Indonesia have declared that the existence of military pacts does not

But the independent role which President Soekarno played in the period after March 1956 was not merely a consequence of disagreements between him and Prime Minister Ali. It would seem to have resulted also from the President's sensing that the Ali cabinet would inevitably become a target for the mounting feelings of disappointment and frustration and from the belief that he as President should therefore avoid too close an identification with the cabinet. It is impossible to say at what point the President saw party and parliamentary government as disintegrating. But it is a fact that he was active from about March 1956 both in staking an ideological claim to the heirship of the party and parliamentary regime and in drawing to himself a group of nonparty men who could conceivably assist him in making good this claim.

When the President opened the newly elected parliament on March 26, 1956, he urged it to work on the basis of "real Indonesian democracy" and not on the basis of "50 per cent plus one are always right." That indeed was the method in the West, the President said, but in the West people's thinking was individualistic and thus a 50 per cent plus one majority system was necessary. But Indonesian society was not individualistic. Rather it was a familylike society, a society of brotherhood, a society of *gotong rojong* or mutual help. The President hoped, therefore, that the new parliament would work in the spirit of being part of the great family of the Indonesian people.[107]

This was not a new theme for the President, but it was one he was to emphasize with increasing frequency as 1956 wore on. More and more he spoke of the need for a form of democracy which accorded with Indonesia's own identity and characteristics—a "guided democracy" (*demokrasi terpimpin*) which was not a "democracy of just voting" (*demokrasi stem-steman*).[108] Similarly he spoke on occasion

---

promote the efforts to reduce international tensions which are sorely needed for the attainment of world peace." Also severely criticized was the fact that no mention was made in the statement of Indonesia's claim to West Irian. The statement, dated Sept. 10, 1956, referred also to a program of Soviet aid valued at $100 million and given without strings. See Willard A. Hanna, "Moscow Comes to Bung Karno—and So Does Peking," *Newsletter of the American Universities Field Staff*, Nov. 30, 1956 (New York: A.U.F.S., 1956).

[107] Kementerian Penerangan, *Ichtisar Parlemen*, no. 31 (1956), pp. 258–259.

[108] See, for instance, *Abadi*, April 3, 1956. The President began using the term *demokrasi terpimpin* in 1954. The term *demokratie met leiderschap* (democracy with leadership), as we have noted, appeared in his address of acceptance of the presidency of the Republic of the United States of Indonesia, Dec. 17, 1949: *Amanat Presiden Pertama Republik Indonesia Serikat* ("Address by the First

against the political parties, chiding them for their "sectarianism." [109] And he spoke a great deal in praise of the political role of youth.

At the same time the President worked to build up a new group of political leaders who would be able to help him realize the goals which these symbols reflected. Increasingly he co-operated with a group which came to be known as "the youth" or "the 1945 generation." [110] The most prominent of the members of this group was Chaerul Saleh, the Tan Malaka follower, who had led the People's Army rebellion in West Java in 1949–1950, had then been arrested, and spent 1952–1955 in Europe on a study assignment. In 1956 he appeared to be anxious for a political comeback, but he joined no party. On the contrary, he declared in August that "the parties have lost their authority because they have failed over the six years past to bring about growth in the national potential or to exploit the working capacity or creative capacity of the Indonesian people." [111]

A second prominent leader of the new Soekarno group was Achmadi, who had led the Student Army in Central Java during the Revolution and subsequently been active in Indonesian student politics in Europe, and a third was Major Isman, a one-time commander of the Student Army in East Java. The group also included A. M. Hanafi, the secretary-general of the All-Indonesian People's Congress, and Major Pamurahardjo.

Apart from the fact that they enjoyed the President's favor, the members of this cluster of men had two important things in common. Firstly, they had little stake in the existing political system, dominated as it was by the leaders of a handful of large parties. All of the group were nonparty men, at least in a formal sense. Certainly none were connected with any of the "old," "established," and patronage-blessed parties which became the focus of antiparty and antipolitician feeling, the PNI, Masjumi, NU, PSI, and smaller nationalist and Moslem parties. To the extent that the men of the new Soekarno group had party connections, they were with the Partai Murba and, to a lesser extent, the PKI.

Secondly, all were persons with a history of active participation in the Revolution. All were radical nationalists and all, or almost all, had

President of the United States of Indonesia"; Jogjakarta: Kementerian Penerangan, 1949), p. 7.

[109] *Suluh Indonesia,* Aug. 14, 1956.

[110] Both these terms were also used in a wider sense, and each had been used earlier by other political groups.

[111] *Suluh Indonesia,* Aug. 18, 1956.

a high degree of "solidarity-making" skill, being effective as political organizers and communicators of political symbols. Several of them had a large personal following among veteran and youth groups.

When Nasution spoke on October 5 of efforts to establish a "youth junta," he was referring to the efforts of the President to organize this group of revolutionary leaders as a possible instrument with which to oust and supplant the now-unpopular parties. But for the greatest part of the political public this implication became clear only a little later, after the President's return from the Soviet Union and China on October 16. By this time army leaders had made a number of sharp criticisms of parties and parliamentary institutions, staking out claims for increased power for the army and their groups within it, and it was widely believed that any drive to curtail the influence of parties and parliament would benefit the army or particular sections of it. The initiative seemed to lie with the army.

Then on October 28 Soekarno made a speech by which the initiative, or a great part of it, passed to him. Addressing an audience of delegates from youth organizations, the President spoke of the "disease of parties."

Let us be frank about it, brothers and sisters. We made a very great mistake in 1945 when we urged the establishment of parties, parties, parties. . . . Now that mistake is wreaking its vengeance upon us. . . . Do you know, brothers and sisters, what my dream is as I speak to you now? . . . My dream is that the leaders of the parties would meet, would consult together with one another, and then come together to the decision of "Let us now join together to bury all parties." . . . I know that the young people who are politically aware do indeed want a nation that is not split by parties and more parties. I know that they don't support the youth groups which just follow their father parties obediently. . . . Exercise the sovereignty of youth! Don't just parrot the parties.[112]

Two days later the President followed up this blast with a second. Speaking this time to a congress of the teachers' union, he said he had long been dissatisfied with the way in which the parties had become just vehicles of the personal interests of their leaders. But he had said nothing. Now, after seeing the Soviet Union and China and the way they were building up their countries, he could no longer keep his thoughts to himself. He had to speak out, and he did. This time he

[112] Soekarno, *Indonesia, Pilihlah Demokrasimu jang Sedjati* ("Indonesia, Choose Your Own True Democracy"; Djakarta: Kementerian Penerangan, 1956), pp. 11–12.

said that he not only dreamed that the leaders of the parties would meet together and bury the parties—he urged this upon them. He went on:

I do not want to become a dictator, brothers and sisters. . . . That is against my spirit. I am a democrat. I am really a democrat. But my democracy is not liberal democracy. . . . What I would like to see in this Indonesia of ours is guided democracy [*demokrasi terpimpin, geleide democratie*], democracy with leadership, but still democracy.[113]

As for what forms this would take, what would be done after the parties had been buried, the President added:

That is up to the leaders. Bung Karno certainly has his own opinion, but Bung Karno is no director-proprietor or dictator. It is up to the leaders whether they will then set up a single party, or have no party but a mass movement, or set up a few parties on a rational basis. Yes, that is up to the leaders, brothers and sisters, not up to me. But of course I have my own plan [*konsepsi*], and if I am asked I will, God willing, present it.[114]

The two speeches drew a great variety of reactions. The Partai Murba was the one group which gave the President outright support immediately. It called for the formation of a broad organization supported by all political currents existing in Indonesia, an organization based on the minimum program which had already been set down by the All-Indonesian People's Congress.[115] There was outright hostility from sections of the Masjumi and others who opposed the President's influence. Natsir declared that "if the parties are buried, democracy will be buried automatically." [116]

Most other groups were far less clear in their reactions to this radically new proposal. The PNI leaders were hesitant and divided. Some spoke in favor of the *konsepsi*; others were guardedly opposed to it. One characteristic reaction was to evade the central issue and merely stress the need for self-correction on the part of all parties.[117] The NU reaction was similarly ambiguous. The PKI announced enthusiastic support for guided democracy and the President's *konsepsi*, but declared itself opposed "to an outright doing away with the parties." [118]

In effect the two Soekarno speeches had opened up a whole range of new possibilities and uncertainties. Was the President merely

[113] *Ibid.*, p. 24.   [114] *Ibid.*, p. 27.   [115] *Antara*, Nov. 3, 1956.
[116] *Abadi*, Oct. 30, 1956, quoted in Noer, *op. cit.*
[117] See the statements of Mangunsarkoro and Sajuti Melik ("Juti") in *Suluh Indonesia*, Dec. 8, 1956.
[118] See the statement of D. N. Aidit in *Harian Rakjat*, Oct. 30, 1956.

"dreaming" and "urging"? Was he merely popularizing new slogans? Or was he beginning a drive to restructure the whole constellation of power? If the latter was the case, how did he propose to go about making the change? Thus Major General Simatupang wondered what constitutional basis could be found for a dissolution of the parties and whether this would perhaps be attempted by a "coup from above." In Simatupang's words, "If parties are to be dissolved, the question arises, what if they do not want to bury themselves? Are they then to be forcibly dissolved?" [119] The President had frequently announced his hostility to military dictatorship, and he did so again in November.[120] Thus it seemed that he wanted to establish himself as a rival of the army rather than its ally. But in that event how could he muster the power with which to force the parties to dissolve themselves?

The basic question which the President's addresses posed was whether or not the parties and parliament could survive. Coming as they did at a time when military dictatorship was being discussed publicly by leading army and parliamentary figures and when one faction of the army was attempting to organize a military coup, the addresses suggested that the President thought the days of parliamentary democracy were over. The President was known as a sensitive barometer of political change; his political intuition was widely admired by others in the political elite. But had things indeed gone so far? Had the authority of parties and parliament really dwindled away so completely that no alternative remained except to support either Soekarno and Chaerul Saleh on the one hand or Zulkifli Lubis (or perhaps Lubis and Hatta) on the other? Was this the meaning of the President's tendency of the previous eighteen months, ever since the beginnings of the All-Indonesian Congress in early 1955, to edge away from support of the PNI and look for links with the PKI, the Partai Murba, and particularly the "youth" of Chaerul Saleh, Achmadi, and Isman?

These were all unanswered questions, but the fact was that the President had now gone further than ever before in dissociating himself from the PNI, the party which had theretofore relied so heavily upon him and which was now under fire from several directions at once. At the same time he had made it clear to the Masjumi that if the cabinet fell it would not necessarily be succeeded by a government

[119] *Keng Po,* Nov. 5, 6, 1956.
[120] Arguing against imitation of Egypt with its military junta, the President declared that "in Indonesia the people are already too mature in their education for democracy" (*Pedoman,* Nov. 22, 1956).

of Hatta and/or Lubis elements, that an entirely different range of alternatives existed.

Thus the Masjumi leadership now attacked the President's ideas of burying the parties, while watching with apprehension the moves of the Lubis elements in the army. The PNI leaders condemned Lubis and all ideas of military dictatorship while keeping an embarrassed and fearful eye on the President. Both of the main parties had lost the initiative. A minority group of PNI leaders switched loyalties from the PNI to the President, and a minority of Masjumi leaders became actively associated with Lubis elements in the army. But the two parties as such were left helpless and almost too demoralized to protest. As for the cabinet in which they worked uneasily together, it had been side-stepped in the onrush of political forces bigger than itself.

Throughout November and December the President made speeches criticizing "liberal democracy." But he did not disclose his own plan or *konsepsi* of what exactly he wanted to supersede it. He would make it public in due course, he said, after it had been discussed with the appropriate authorities. Meanwhile there were all sorts of rumors. Zulkifli Lubis, writing to the press from his undisclosed place of hiding, claimed that the President had chosen China as his model of political organization.[121] One report to which the parliamentarian Sutomo (Bung Tomo) gave currency said that the President wanted to oust Nasution and put Isman in his place so that he could use the army to impose his reorganization.[122] Another rumor ran that he intended to proclaim a State of War and Siege for the whole country.[123]

But the promised disclosure was to be made only later, after a new wave of challenges had come crashing in upon government and politics.

REGIONAL PROTEST: THE PHASE OF THE COUPS

The period of August to November 1956 was fairly uneventful as far as regionalist politics was concerned. What with the maneuvers of Zulkifli Lubis and the debates on military dictatorship and burying of parties, Djakarta dominated the political stage for these months. But this does not mean that the regional pressures which had caused the central government such acute embarrassment in May, June, and July had abated. The situation was quite the contrary.

---

[121] *Keng Po*, Dec. 14, 1956.
[122] *Ibid.*, Dec. 5, 1956. Cf. *Suluh Indonesia*, Dec. 7, 1956.
[123] *Keng Po*, Dec. 20, 1956.

The success of army commanders and army-led regionalist movements in forcing Djakarta to accept their *faits accomplis* in the matter
of smuggling and the ill-fated Copra Foundation had had profound
effects on the way in which regional leaders, and particularly regional
military leaders, looked on their relations with the capital. A number
of important grievances had long had currency within the leadership
groups of the regions, particularly those of certain regions of Sumatra
and Sulawesi. First of all, there had long been strong resentment of
the unreal exchange rate in the leadership groups of all exporting
areas. Secondly, there were long-standing grievances, in exporting
areas and virtually all others, about the state of communications and
public works in particular regions and the amount of industrial activity.
Thirdly, there had long been hostility to the slow and complicated
bureaucratic procedures in Djakarta, which the regional leaders saw
as encumbrances on their freedom to make even small decisions within
their own bailiwicks. The annoyance here was particularly great in
the case of the outlying regions whose leaders could not easily go to
the capital and cut through the red tape by dint of personal pressure.
All these grievances were given political expression through demands
for "regional autonomy," although there were few signs of an actual
desire for regional autonomy in the usual sense of this term.[124]

With the events of May to July before them, regional leadership
groups, and particularly the ones outside Java, came to look at all
these grievances in a new way. These events had shown that Djakarta
was virtually powerless when it came into conflict with a determined
and cohesive group of regional leaders who had the active support of
army commanders in their area. They had shown that the capacity of
the Djakarta government to compete with civilian leadership groups
in the regions for the support of military commanders, had greatly declined. In effect, then, a vacuum of power had appeared, and this afforded strong incentives for many of the regional leaders to bid
actively for the redressing of their long-standing grievances. It was
not so much that leaders in regions like West Sumatra or Minahasa had
grown desperate after repeated unsuccessful efforts to have Djakarta
attend to their grievances, but rather that these leaders now perceived
opportunities for action which had not existed theretofore.

The same perception of an existing power vacuum served as a
stimulus to ethnic self-consciousness in many of the regions. Ethnic

[124] Maryanov, *Decentralization in Indonesia as a Political Problem,* p. 52; Legge,
Problems of Regional Autonomy in Contemporary Indonesia, pp. 65–70.

feeling had existed under the political surface for much of the post-revolutionary period, and it had been growing in importance and rising to the political surface as the Revolution and the Dutch use of ethnicity against Indonesian nationalism receded into the past. Moreover, it had risen in early 1956 as the political energies which had previously been absorbed in the electioneering activities of the parties sought alternative channels. Now from mid-1956 onward it gained greatly increased prominence in a number of areas for reasons of political strategy. A power vacuum having been perceived, it was clear that a period of increasingly active power contest with Djakarta was beginning. In this situation a regional leadership group stood to gain if its region was ethnically homogeneous, that is to say, if province borders, and the borders of military districts, coincided roughly with lines of ethnic distribution. Similarly it was to the advantage of such a group if the civilian and military agencies of the central government in its area were headed by men of the same ethnic background as themselves. So it was that ethnic feeling was given a great deal of political expression, principally in demands for changes in boundaries of provinces and military districts and for the removal of civil and military functionaries who were ethnically alien to their area.

But the power vacuum existed not only in relations between the central government and particular regions; it involved also civilian-military relations. Just as the regions had long-standing resentments against the capital, so the officers of the army had long-standing grievances against the civilian politicians. And now, with the legitimacy of the civilian central government visibly diminishing, an opportunity to right these grievances became manifest. For officers stationed in areas where regional leadership groups were cohesive and in a strong position to lodge claims against the central government, close association with these groups was the simplest means of obtaining greater power. The civilian politicians of these regions were prepared to let the officers take the lead in anti-Djakarta protest activity and to accord them great power, prestige, and material rewards, for they needed army backing above all else. Indeed, it has been argued that the most important function which the regionalist movements fulfilled was not to press regional demands but to expand the political role of the army.

The combination of rising regional demands and mounting protest from the military (against both civilian politicians and the officers allied with them) resulted in December in a series of events which changed the whole political balance of the country. In mid-November the initiative appeared to lie with Djakarta. Major General Nasution had succeeded in transferring several of his most powerful opponents from positions as territorial commanders, he had thwarted three attempted coups in and near the capital, and he had arrested a dozen or so of the officers who had worked with Colonel Lubis to make these coups. At the same time President Soekarno had cut some ground from under the regionalists' feet by presenting himself as a leading spokesman for feeling against the political parties. But this initiative was not to last.

From November 20 to November 24 there was a reunion meeting in Padang, West Sumatra, of former officers of the Banteng (Wild Buffalo) Division, a unit which had fought in Central Sumatra in the Revolution (and subsequently been dissolved, by the then Colonel Nasution). The opening session was attended by 746 persons, including a large part of the officer corps of the regiment stationed in West Sumatra and also including Lieutenant Colonel Barlian, the acting territorial commander in South Sumatra. Shortly after the opening, the participants proceeded to Bukittinggi, where they took part in a solemn midnight ceremony at the military cemetery.

The reunion made decisions as regards invalids, widows, orphans, and the writing of the revolutionary history of the region. But it also issued a demand for the filling of important government posts in Central Sumatra by "persons who are able, honest, creative, and consistently revolutionary and as far as possible come originally from the region itself." [125] Most important of all, it made a general statement on national problems: "[The reunion meeting] demands the immediate implementation of progressive and radical improvements in all fields, especially in the leadership of the Army and also in the leadership of the State, with safeguards for the unity of the State of the Republic of Indonesia." [126] At the same time it elected a Banteng Council of seventeen men to press for implementation of the meeting's demands. As chairman of the council it elected Lieutenant Colonel Ahmad Husein, the commander of the West Sumatra regiment.

A few days after the Padang reunion meeting there was a "Special Meeting" of the Army Staff and Command School in Bandung with

[125] For the full text of the resolution see *Keterangan Pemerintah tentang Kedjadian-Kedjadian di Sumatera dalam Bulan Desember 1956* ("Government Statement on the Developments in Sumatra in December 1956"; Djakarta: Kementerian Penerangan, 1957), pp. 39–42.

[126] *Ibid.*, p. 40.

some of its graduates, where unanimous agreement was reached on a manifestolike announcement calling for "over-all change in the composition of functionaries in the leadership of the army." [127] Early in December the Officers' League of the Republic of Indonesia (Ikatan Perwira Republik Indonesia, IPRI) was to take the step of writing to Nasution and the fugitive Lubis asking each of them in similar terms for written statements of their plans for "improvements in the state and the army according to the Jogjakarta Charter." [128] Nasution had become the overt target of officer resentments, just after his success in warding off the challenge of the Lubis attempted coups.

On December 1 Hatta left the vice-presidency. He had submitted his resignation on July 20, 1956 (the day of the announcement of President Soekarno's partial reprieve of Djody Gondokusumo, the first Ali cabinet's Justice Minister who had been convicted for corruption). His plan was to leave office after the opening of the Constituent Assembly. This finally took place on November 10, 1956, and three weeks later he moved from the vice-presidential residence. The reason he gave for his resignation was the formal one that he had originally accepted the office on the understanding that it would be for a period of one to two years.[129] He issued no ringing statement as he left public office. But in his last address as Vice-President, one made in acceptance of an honorary doctorate from the Gadjah Mada University in Jogjakarta, he made it clear again that basic differences of political approach separated him from President Soekarno.[130]

The effect of the resignation was to heighten resentment of President Soekarno in particular and "Djakarta" in general in all the areas outside Java, especially in Sumatra. The political differences between the President and the Vice-President were in no sense new to the political public. But now even the symbol of Soekarno-Hatta unity was no more. Its loss was not easy to accept, particularly for non-Javanese. Many non-Javanese, and especially Sumatrans, had tended to regard Vice-President Hatta as their representative in a two-man partnership in which President Soekarno was seen as representing the Javanese. This was all the more widespread a view in 1956 because of the prominence of regional and ethnic factors in political perceptions in that year. It was in this light that the resignation was viewed. As many in Sumatra saw it, the situation in official Djakarta

---

[127] For the full text see *Keng Po*, Dec. 17, 1956. See also *ibid.*, Dec. 13, 1956.
[128] *Ibid.*, Dec. 12, 1956.   [129] See *Times of Indonesia*, July 24, 1956.
[130] See Hatta, *Past and Future, passim.*

had become so bad, and Hatta so powerless to exercise his potentially beneficent influence upon it, that he had chosen to wash his hands of it, even though he knew that to do so was to destroy the symbol of the Duumvirate, a cardinal symbol of the unity of Indonesia.

The wave of protest became manifest next in North Sumatra. North Sumatra's commander, Colonel Simbolon, arrived in Djakarta on November 25 to discuss his long-postponed transfer out of his command. Pressed by Chief of Staff Nasution, Simbolon agreed to surrender his authority about the middle of December and to accept as his successor his Chief of Staff, Lieutenant Colonel Djamin Gintings (whom the Chief of Staff had named as the new commander after revocation of the appointment of Zulkifli Lubis). But he avoided commitment to a particular date, declaring that he would need time to convince certain of his regimental commanders to accept Gintings as their superior.

It seems that, as early as the middle of November, Simbolon had been urged by Zulkifli Lubis to sever all ties between his command and the central government and take over civilian authority in North and Central Sumatra.[131] Then on his way to Djakarta he had attended the closing ceremony of the Banteng Division's reunion. In Djakarta he had witnessed a great deal of officer hostility to Nasution, as well as the anti-government reactions which followed the Hatta resignation. Returning to Medan, he found much of the same radical discontent among groups of his own officers, in particular those who had attended the "Special Meeting" of the corps of the Staff and Command School.

Faced with the transfer order on the one hand and these various signs of incipient revolt on the other, Simbolon decided to attempt a new effort to defy Djakarta. He did so knowing clearly that he could not count on the support of all of his subordinate officers, for the officer corps in North Sumatra reflected most of the political divisions of this ethnically and socially heterogeneous area. As a Toba Batak, Simbolon attracted intense loyalties from the most powerful single ethnic group in North Sumatra. On the other hand, he was at least potentially a target for the widespread anti-Toba feeling of other groups in the area.

On December 4 a large meeting of officers of Simbolon's command was held in Medan. After hearing a report from the officers who had returned from the Staff and Command School's "Special Meeting," the assemblage discussed various types of action which could be taken against the central government. Although there was considerable

[131] *Merdeka*, Nov. 16, 1956.

disagreement, the majority of those present favored radical steps, such as Simbolon himself was known to favor, including if necessary the severing of connections between the North Sumatra command and Djakarta. The "December 4 idea" was then turned over to a committee for further study.

On December 16 a meeting of the 48 top officers of the North Sumatra command was held to hear the committee's report. Accepting a now more fully formulated version of the "December 4 idea," this meeting agreed to entrust the implementation of the idea to Simbolon. On the evening of December 16 the 48 officers took an oath together "to take firm and revolutionary measures to realize the ideals [of the Independence Proclamation of 1945] in the shortest possible time" [132] —then drank a toast and smashed their glasses as a symbol of their break with the past.

The next in this chain of events was a major new departure. On December 20 a ceremony was held in Bukittinggi in which the regimental commander in West Sumatra, Ahmad Husein, acting in his capacity as chairman of the Banteng Council, formally took charge "for the time being" of government in Central Sumatra. The Djakarta-appointed governor Roeslan Moeljohardjo, a Javanese but a member of the Masjumi, leading party of the province, transferred his powers to Husein without offering any apparent resistance. At the same time a Banteng Council leader was placed in charge of the Central Sumatra police. Husein declared that the take-over action had been in implementation of the decision of the reunion meeting of the Banteng Division and that it was not motivated by feelings of provincialism.[133] The ex-Governor declared that it was not aimed at creating a state within a state.[134] It was a coup, albeit an entirely peaceful one. That it was a carefully prepared one, for which support existed in many sections of society in Central Sumatra, or at least in the populous West Sumatra residency, the area of the Minangkabaus, was clear from the names of the more than 50 men who would serve in "assistance teams" to help the Banteng Council in the affairs of government.[135]

---

[132] For the full text of the oath see *PIA*, Jan. 24, 1957.

[133] For the text of the Document of Transfer as well as a statement and an announcement signed by Husein and dated Dec. 20 see *Keterangan Pemerintah tentang Kedjadian-Kedjadian di Sumatera dalam Bulan Desember 1956*, pp. 44–48. See also *Madjalah Penerangan Sumatera Tengah* ("Central Sumatra Information Magazine"), Nomor Istimewa, "Peristiwa 20 Desember" ("Special Issue on the 'December 20 Affair,'"), no. 159 (Feb. 15, 1957).

[134] *Keng Po*, Dec. 22, 1956.   [135] See *ibid.*

On the following day Husein held a press conference in Padang at which he declared that the products of the Central Sumatra region would not thenceforth be sent to the central government. An announcement made in his name at the same time said that cash funds could not be disbursed by banks in the province without approval from his office. According to Husein the right of the Banteng Council to exercise governmental functions over the whole Central Sumatra province (thus over the residencies of Riau and Djambi, as well as West Sumatra, the area of Husein's own regiment) had been accepted in a "gentlemen's agreement" reached with the naval commander in authority in Riau and with Barlian of South Sumatra, whose authority extended over Djambi.[136] On the same day, Ismael Lengah, a Banteng Council member, went to Djakarta as an emissary of the council. On his arrival in the capital he declared that Central Sumatra had no intention of cutting itself off from the central government.

Djakarta had less than 36 hours in which to consider all this before a second coup was enacted, in Medan. Early in the morning of December 22 the Medan radio announced that connections between the military district of North Sumatra and the central government had been temporarily severed and that a State of War and Siege had been proclaimed in this military district. The North Sumatra command did not wish to establish a separate state, Simbolon told his listeners, but it no longer recognized the existing cabinet. It took its action, he said, "to improve the situation of the nation and of the Indonesian people by turning over the reins of government to those national leaders who, with honesty and integrity, can develop the nation, free from a lust for power and self-seeking." [137] When a new cabinet of such leaders had been formed, the North Sumatra command would restore its relations with the central government.[138] At a press conference later in the day Simbolon denied that his action was connected with the "Zulkifli Lubis Movement" in Djakarta.

Djakarta reacted quickly to both coups, apparently having prior

---

[136] *Haluan* (Padang), Dec. 22, 1956.

[137] *Keng Po*, Dec. 22, 1956. See also *Keterangan Pemerintah*, pp. 59–61.

[138] Who these leaders would be was made specific on Dec. 24. On that date Simbolon declared: "We urgently seek the restoration of the unity of the Duumvirate of Soekarno-Hatta as a basis of national peace. It is our conviction . . . that the Duumvirate may no longer serve merely as a symbol, but must function as a moving force, with a careful division of duties" (*Keterangan Pemerintah tentang Kedjadian-Kedjadian di Sumatera dalam Bulan Desember 1956*, pp. 62–63). Translated into the terms of political reality, this was a demand for a Hatta-led cabinet.

knowledge of plans for them. But it reacted in quite different ways. In Central Sumatra its approach was at least partially conciliatory. It cut off air links with Padang immediately, but at the same time dispatched an investigating committee to Padang, choosing a former Banteng Division officer, Colonel Dahlan Djambek, as its head. Only a little later, after this mission had been sent back to the capital—the Banteng Council had decided that it would not receive a mission sent in the name of the cabinet, but only one authorized by the President—did it resort to such measures as stopping rice ships from sailing to Padang, instructing the resident of Riau to deal directly with Djakarta in all governmental matters (rather than going via the provincial capital of Padang), and transferring the pro-Banteng Council resident of Djambi to Djakarta.

In the case of North Sumatra, Djakarta acted both speedily and dramatically. On the very day of Simbolon's proclamation the cabinet announced that Simbolon had been suspended from office and that authority over the North Sumatra command was vested in the man who had been scheduled to succeed him, Djamin Gintings. In addition, it instructed the regimental commander in East Sumatra, Lieutenant Colonel A. Wahab Macmour, to assume authority over the command in the event that Gintings was unable to do so. At the same time the cabinet declared that two of the four regiments of the North Sumatra command, those of Atjeh and West Sumatra, had been temporarily placed under the direct authority of the Chief of Staff. It also set up a navy blockade against Medan and instructed the air force to be ready for action.

The events of the next few days showed the cabinet's action in the case of North Sumatra to have been extraordinarily shrewd. It wanted to have Gintings overthrow Simbolon. It knew that many of those on whom Gintings' support rested, both inside and outside the army, would favor an action of this kind; for Simbolon was a Toba Batak and an opponent of the East Sumatra autonomy movement, and Gintings a Karo Batak and a supporter of this anti-Toba movement. On the other hand, it knew that Gintings was in sympathy with some of the demands which Simbolon was making on the central government. It expected therefore that he might be reluctant to carry out a Djakarta instruction to overthrow his chief. Thus it named Wahab Macmour, who represented a third corner in a triangle of power relationships in East Sumatra, giving him a rival claim to the commander's post in order that he might spur Gintings on. It knew that Macmour, as a man with pro-Communist officers in his regiment, could be expected to urge implacable hostility to Simbolon. It was aware that his strongest extramilitary support came from Communist-run labor, peasant, and village guard organizations in and near the estate town of Pematang Siantar, which was his regimental headquarters. And it also realized that many of the groups which backed Gintings would go to great lengths to keep Macmour out of power, not only because Macmour had Communist sympathies, but also because he and his Communist supporters were opposed to East Sumatran autonomy. The Djakarta calculation was that if the ethnic hostility of Gintings' group to Simbolon proved insufficient to secure his overthrow, use would have to be made of the sociopolitical hostility of the group of Wahab Macmour (and, a step further removed, of the Gintings group's fears, ethnic as well as sociopolitical, of Macmour).

The story of the hectic days which followed the government's decision is immensely complex.[139] But in broad lines it appears to have followed the government's expectations. Simbolon made great efforts to keep Gintings loyal to him, making him military governor under the State of War and Siege and head of a Gadjah (Elephant) Command which would deal with problems arising from the transfer of authority.[140] For several days Gintings remained loyal to Simbolon, and Macmour did nothing. In the course of these days regulations were announced permitting duty-free imports, forbidding cash remittances outside North Sumatra, establishing heavy penalties for smuggling, and banning strikes and further squatting on unoccupied land.

But on December 24 the tide began to change. On that day a joint resolution was taken by a group of 27 captains and lieutenants in Macmour's regiment, including several with strong PKI sympathies. The resolution noted that Gintings was taking no action against Simbolon and urged Macmour to act, adding that "if he does not want to execute the government decree, we are united in our determination to execute it." [141] Two days later Wahab Macmour, in a public statement made in Pematang Siantar, declared himself commander of North Sumatra. He stated that Gintings had shown that he did not want to

[139] One major effort to unravel it has been made by John R. W. Smail in "The Military Politics of North Sumatra, December 1956–October 1957" (unpublished paper, Cornell Modern Indonesia Project, 1958).

[140] For details of Simbolon's governmental organization see *Waspada*, Dec. 26, 1956, quoted in Smail, "The Military Politics of North Sumatra," p. 7.

[141] For the text see *Keterangan Pemerintah tentang Kedjadian-Kedjadian di Sumatera dalam Bulan Desember 1956*, pp. 68–69.

carry out the government's order. On the same day he distributed arms to a sizable number of his civilian supporters—one figure was 2,000 [142]—chiefly men of the labor and estate unions of the PKI.

For those who wanted to see Gintings rather than Macmour as commander and for others who saw Simbolon's defeat as impending and wanted to have a part in it, this was the cue for immediate action. Thus in the night of December 26 to 27 a military operation was launched in both Medan and the Karo regency to wrest the provincial capital from Simbolon's control. The initiative for the operation came from the army commander in the city of Medan, Lieutenant-Colonel Sugiharto, a Javanese, from a group of Karo officers, from the influential PNI parliamentarian and ex-major of Karo origin, Selamat Gintings, and from several smaller factions. Between them these groups prevailed on Gintings to throw his weight against Simbolon, and then in the early morning of December 27 they moved troops and armored cars into the streets of Medan. At 3 A.M. Simbolon fled the city with a battalion of troops in the direction of Tapanuli. By 6 A.M. Gintings had formally taken over the North Sumatra command.

This did not mean that the tension in East Sumatra was at an end. Shooting almost broke out between Simbolon's men and those of Macmour before Macmour allowed Simbolon's group to pass through Pematang Siantar on their way to Tapanuli. For several days after that it seemed that fighting might start between Macmour's East Sumatra regiment and the Tapanuli regiment under Major Junus Samosir, who was a supporter of Simbolon as well as his host and who had also, like Macmour, distributed arms to his civilian supporters.

The struggle between Gintings and Macmour and the various groups standing behind each of them was even more explosive. In Smail's words, the reports of the week after December 26 give an impression of

the scattering of power into small units all over the map and all through a wide range of political positions, and then of the clumping together once more of these units, reforming into larger and more coherent shapes. All around the [East Sumatra] area in that week, officers were being arrested, civilians were being armed and disarmed, small units of troops marched by night and made announcements by day, committees met and candidates for power sought support. And underneath it all was the fear on all sides that the situation would slide from military politics to *suku* [ethnic group] war.[143]

---

[142] This figure was given by Lieut. Col. Sugiharto, the Medan City commander. See *Waspada*, Jan. 3, 1957, quoted in Smail, "The Military Politics of North Sumatra," p. 11.

[143] "The Military Politics of North Sumatra," pp. 13–14.

Macmour did not formally surrender his claims to the North Sumatra command until January 3. And the Macmour challenge to Gintings' position was not broken until October 1957, when the civilians whom Macmour had armed were finally forced to surrender their weapons, and Macmour himself was transferred out of his regimental command.[144]

But as far as the central government was concerned, the events of December 27 represented a signal triumph. Simbolon's influence had been confined to the poor plateau residency of Tapanuli. The rich exporting lowlands of East Sumatra and the key port of Medan were safely in loyal hands again. With the Djakarta-Medan axis re-established, the threat to Indonesia's territorial cohesion was greatly lessened. Furthermore, all this had been achieved without bloodshed.

Meanwhile, however, there had been disturbing events in South Sumatra, the province of largest export riches. The acting commander of the South Sumatra military command, Barlian, had been in fairly close contact with Husein and Simbolon before December 20. Like them he was a Hatta sympathizer. And although he was a recent Nasution appointee, he actively supported the demand for increased power for the army in political affairs. Like Husein and Simbolon too, he was a native of the area over which he exercised command and a patron of regionalist political aspirations. In the South Sumatra situation this meant an association with anti-Javanese feelings; for South Sumatran regionalism found its targets of hostility in the Javanese, who had long been influential in civil service and military posts in the province and who were entering the Lampang area of the province in rather large numbers on government resettlement schemes.

Barlian did not attempt a take-over action himself in December. But he applied strong pressure on the Governor of the province, Winarno Danuatmodjo, a Javanese and a member of the PNI, to do as he and his supporters wished. On December 24 the Security Co-ordinating Body of the province (Koordinasi Keamanan Daerah), meeting under the Governor's chairmanship, but with Barlian and his supporters in political control, decided to take radical measures on behalf of the province. In particular it decided to begin forthwith the execution of a draft law which had been approved by parliament eleven days earlier and regulated relations between the central government and the province with autonomy status. It thus acted in anticipation both of the promulgation of the law and, more important, of the issuing of

[144] *Ibid.*, pp. 19–24.

government regulations for its implementation. Taking a cue from the clause in the new draft law which provided for a regional government to obtain 90 per cent of the proceeds of taxes and customs receipts in its region, the Security Co-ordinating Body decided to appropriate these tax and customs revenues immediately and to use them to build barracks for the army and police as well as student hostels, roads, and a bridge across the River Musi at Palembang. At the same time it banned the outflow of money from the province unless specific permission had been given by the Governor. Two days later it announced that no person could leave the province with more than Rp. 2,500 in cash.

From this time the chief center of power in South Sumatra was Barlian and the group of officers, veterans, and others, all close to Barlian, who were united in the Badan Penjalur Kehendak Masjarakat Sumatera Selatan (Channeling Body for the Wishes of the Community of South Sumatra).[145] On December 27 Governor Winarno announced that he had decided to ask for the Interior Minister to transfer him. But he was not transferred and remained a target of regionalist hostility for another two months.

The last ten days of 1956 thus placed momentous questions before the central government. What lay behind this storm of anti-central-government activity in the country's richest island? Was it principally the demand for greater regional powers and less bureaucratic stifling from Djakarta, or for more money for the regions, or for more functionaries of local origin? Or was it primarily a move of officers against a civilian government, a move in a militarist or warlordist direction? Or was its aim not regional at all, but a matter of changing the balance of power in Djakarta? Was it a continuation of the same politico-military maneuvering against the cabinet, Soekarno and Nasution, which Zulkifli Lubis had led in West Java and Djakarta a month earlier?

More important, what could and should be done to cope with the outburst? Some measures had already been taken, and they had been partly successful. But the bulk of the problem remained. Central Sumatra appeared to be under the effective control of Husein. Tapanuli was under the pro-Simbolon regimental commander, Junus Samo-

[145] After Jan. 15, 1957, when the Dewan Revolusi Garuda (Revolutionary Council of the Garuda Bird) was formed, with many of the same members as the Channeling Body, it was this Revolutionary Council which acted as the *de facto* governing council.

sir. There were doubts about the loyalty to Djakarta of Lieutenant Colonel Sjamaun Gaharu, the regimental commander in Atjeh. And in South Sumatra, Barlian had all but taken over power in association with a group whose political composition resembled that of the Banteng Council. In Central Sumatra and South Sumatra efforts were being made to deny the central government the rupiah revenues from local taxation and customs. The possibility existed that these two provinces would attempt to organize barter trade with the outside world and thus deprive the central government of large quantities of foreign exchange. Should the government then attempt to solve the problem by negotiating and giving concessions? Or should it take a tough line and endeavor to re-establish its authority by using the existing divisions in Sumatran society and in Sumatran leadership groups, military and civil, as it had done so effectively in the case of North Sumatra?

The outbreak of the coups immediately led many in Djakarta to a position of more active hostility toward the Ali cabinet and provided its opponents with a major new argument against it. In the words of *Pedoman,* the Banteng Council's seizure of power rang a death knell for the Ali cabinet, because this cabinet would be unable to solve the regional problem.[146] Thus on December 26 IPKI, the League of Upholders of Indonesian Independence, withdrew its one minister from the cabinet. The minister, Dahlan Ibrahim, was himself a former officer of the Banteng Division in Central Sumatra. The League had come to sympathize more with the anti-Nasution groups in the army than with the Chief of Staff, who had been one of its founders in the days before his reappointment. As it withdrew its minister, IPKI called for the cabinet's resignation and its replacement by a business cabinet under Hatta.[147]

At the very same time an appeal for a Hatta-led business cabinet was issued by the Masjumi's chairman, Natsir. Hatta, Natsir said, was the only man who could solve the Sumatran problem. On the following day the Masjumi party congress, which was then in session, decided that the party's representatives in the cabinet should endeavor to persuade their fellow ministers to dissolve the cabinet and that if the latter were unprepared to do this the Masjumi ministers should resign.

But the PNI, as the leading party of the cabinet, was decidedly opposed to resigning at this critical point, and in this it had the sup-

---

[146] *Pedoman,* Dec. 22, 1956.   [147] *Keng Po,* Dec. 27, 1956.

port of the Nahdatul Ulama. Both parties asserted that to resign would be to allow a dangerous vacuum of authority to develop. Indeed, with the regional coups coming on top of the public debates on military dictatorship and the President's advocacy of the burial of the parties, it was entirely unclear what sort of a cabinet could be formed in the Ali cabinet's stead. Thus the PNI and NU leaders argued that the cabinet should continue in office at least until the situation crystallized further. This was apparently a convincing argument also for the PSII and the two Christian parties in the cabinet, for they did not join the Masjumi and Perti in urging the cabinet's immediate resignation, although each of the three was at one point close to the point of doing so. On January 9 the five Masjumi ministers, weary after repeated efforts to persuade the cabinet as a whole to return its mandate, resigned. Six days later the one Perti minister followed suit.

By this time it was the belief of most, both participants and observers, that the Ali cabinet could not survive long. The real question was not how long this cabinet would last, but what sort of cabinet would succeed it—and, more important still, what sort of constitutional order and pattern of territorial integration. What answers were eventually to be given to these questions would depend principally on developments on two political fronts. It would depend firstly on the way in which power relationships unfolded between the rebellious regions and the central government (meaning here President Soekarno and Major General Nasution as well as the rump cabinet) and secondly on the support that the President would be able to gain for the *konsepsi* or plan for a new guided democracy which he was expected to reveal shortly.

Between December and March relations between Djakarta and the rebellious regions of Sumatra were characterized by a slow and involved series of probes, maneuvers, and multiple negotiations. The central government was both flexible and tough. On the one hand, it declared that there were legitimate grounds for dissatisfaction in the regions, particularly with regard to the lack of effective regional autonomy. It promised speedy action in implementation of two recent laws, one a general law on regional government and the other a law on financial relations between the central government and the autonomous regions. And it established a State Commission to make recommendations on the division of the country into autonomous regions. At the same time it acted generously in remitting funds to the rebellious regions. The missions it sent to Central and South Sumatra in January took with them Rp. 150 million and Rp. 370 million respectively.

In addition, the government was prepared to close its eyes to a number of politically challenging aspects of government in the rebellious and semirebellious areas. In South Sumatra it acted as if Governor Winarno continued to exercise real power, though this was patently not the case. In Central Sumatra it dealt with Lieutenant Colonel Husein, although it recognized him only as commander of the West Sumatra regiment, and accorded no recognition to the Banteng Council.

On the other hand, the central government also took actions of a much less conciliatory character, at least in the case of Central Sumatra. Thus it carried out a policy of partial blockade against West Sumatran ports for much of January, stopping the entry of such commodities as newsprint. (The earlier food blockades had been lifted by the beginning of the month.) More important, it made vigorous efforts to destroy the influence of Husein and the Banteng Council in the residencies of Djambi and Riau. It did this not only by a series of personnel transfers, but also by a decision made on January 9 that a bill should be introduced in parliament giving each of these areas province status. When air communications with Central Sumatra were restored, a ban was maintained on services between Padang and the Riau town of Pakan Baru. If Husein's account is to be believed, the government also instructed the air force to prepare the airport of Pakan Baru for use as a base in the event of hostilities.[148]

But in fact Djakarta did not act as a cohesive government in its response to the regional challenge. The policies described here were those of the cabinet, acting in what seemed to be close association with the President and the head of the air force. But there was in addition another set of policy makers, namely, Major General Nasution and his associates, and their approach to the problem of Sumatra was markedly more conciliatory. Thus one of the earliest actions of Nasution after the coups broke out was to appoint the former Banteng Division officer, Colonel Dahlan Djambek, as one of his deputies. In January the Chief of Staff traveled in all Sumatra, visiting Husein in Padang and holding meetings with the officially execrated Colonel

[148] See Djawatan Penerangan Propinsi Sumatera Tengah (Information Department of the Province of Central Sumatra), *Perundingan antara Delegasi Pemerintah Pusat dan Delegasi Dewan Banteng* ("Negotiations between the Delegation of the Central Government and the Delegation of the Banteng Council"; Padang: Djapenste, 1957).

Simbolon. He wound up his visit with a conference in Palembang of the territorial and regimental commanders of all Sumatra and there laid down terms for an over-all military settlement on the island, terms which were distinctly favorable to the regionalist commanders. Thus he formalized the effective autonomy of the pro-Simbolon regimental commander in Tapanuli, freeing him of formal subordination to the North Sumatra commander, Djamin Gintings (and placing him instead under a Liaison Staff in Medan, whose first head was Dahlan Djambek). Most significant of all, the Chief of Staff agreed to appoint Husein as commander of a new military command of Central Sumatra. This in effect meant giving him authority (in formal terms only over military affairs) in Djambi and Riau—at a time when the Ali cabinet was doing its utmost to win Riau and Djambi away from him and the Banteng Council.[149]

The over-all effect of these various Djakarta policies was to leave the regionalists in a very strong position. The central government did have success in weakening the position of the Banteng Council somewhat in Djambi and Riau, but the Council maintained a great deal of its power in those areas. In West Sumatra it remained completely in control; it was able to continue to hold high officials of the central government under house arrest and to prevent the circulation of a number of Djakarta dailies, including the official organ of the PNI. (The PKI fared notably worse, having several of its leaders arrested and the office of its provincial committee seized.) Economically the Council was not hurting the central government as much as many had expected. It made no major inroads on the government's supplies of foreign exchange, although it did obtain funds from foreign companies [150] and although it contributed to inflation by extracting large

----

[149] For the results of the Palembang conference see *Djawaban Pemerintah atas Pemandangan Umum Babak ke-1 D.P.R. tentang Kedjadian-Kedjadian di Sumatera dalam Bulan Desember 1956* ("Government Reply to the First Round of Debates on the Developments in Sumatra in December 1956"; Djakarta: Kementerian Penerangan, 1957), pp. 51–53. These results were by no means entirely satisfactory to the regionalists in Sumatra. But that they represented major concessions to them is clear from the strongly critical reaction of a number of pro-Soekarno officers in the army. See *PIA*, Feb. 8, 1957, for an account of an officers' meeting held at the home of Lieut. Col. Pamurahardjo to protest against the Palembang decisions. For a regionalist comment on the contrast between the Prime Minister's approach and that of the Chief of Staff, see the statement of Jazid Abidin, chairman of the People's Action Body of Central Sumatra, in *Keng Po*, Feb. 23, 1957.

[150] Formally these were advances on tax payments which these companies were to make to the central government. See the statement of Major Sofjan Ibrahim,

rupiah allocations from the government. But politically its challenge remained formidable. To some extent, indeed, it was able to turn the central government's activities in Djambi and Riau to its own advantage; for in political warfare it made much of the charge that Djakarta was using the old Dutch methods of divide and rule by fanning the ethnic hostility of the Malays of Riau and Djambi against the Minangkabaus of West Sumatra.

Indeed, as far as political warfare was concerned, the initiative remained entirely with the regionalists, and particularly the Banteng Council, which used its radio stations for strong attacks on "the center" and "the Djakarta politicians." Nor was the Banteng Council's appeal entirely negative. As far as its local governmental policies were concerned, the Council functioned as a genuine reform administration, attracting enthusiasm from the political public for its strong measures against hoarding, black-marketeering, and gambling and for its crash programs to build roads and schools.[151] It was also quick to exploit its local popularity for its political battles against Djakarta.[152]

The fact that the Banteng Council was able not only to maintain itself and continue to attack the central government, but also to receive money from the central government, was bound to have its effects in other parts of Indonesia before long. Thus in January and February officer-*cum*-veteran-led councils sprang up all over the country (outside East and Central Java); each one demanded money, autonomy, and radical political change in Djakarta and threatened to take over government in its own region. In mid-February, Husein spoke of six regionalist councils other than his own—in South Sumatra, Tapanuli, Kalimantan, North Sulawesi, South Sulawesi, and the Moluccas—and said that these would soon hold a meeting "to confront the central government and demonstrate its weaknesses, if the central government is unable to bring about an over-all settlement."[153] Apart from

---

head of the Civilian Affairs Staff of the Banteng Council, in *Keng Po*, Jan. 25, 1957. The matter of relations between the Banteng Council and large foreign firms which operated in Central Sumatra, particularly the two U.S. oil companies California-Texas and Standard Vacuum, was shrouded in secrecy. But it is clear that the foreign companies did provide the Council with facilities of various kinds.

[151] This judgment rests in part on my personal observations, although it was July 1957 before I visited West Sumatra.

[152] Its most important efforts in this direction came in mid-March when it acted as host to two all-Sumatran conferences, one of Moslem scholars and the other of leaders in the field of adat or customary law. Both were attended by large numbers of prominent persons with regionalist political sympathies.

[153] *Keng Po*, Feb. 12, 1957.

these councils there were new regionalist youth movements, reconstruction movements, channeling bodies for the wishes of the people, and committees demanding separate province status for what were then parts of provinces. Moreover, a large number of former military units, guerrilla units, and military academies of the period of the Revolution held reunion meetings—until these were banned by the Chief of Staff in early March. At the same time the Masjumi, PSI, and IPKI and notably also the Nahdatul Ulama advocated that the Constituent Assembly should establish a bicameral parliament to assure adequate representation for the regions outside Java. The Constituent Assembly itself had barely begun to discuss the substantive issues on which it was required to make decisions.

THE PRESIDENT'S *KONSEPSI* AND THE CONFLICTS BETWEEN THE PARTIES' HEIRS

With the regionalist leaders continuing their successful challenge to the authority of Djakarta, the groups in the capital pressing for a Hatta-led cabinet as a way out of a crisis situation were able to present a strong front. It was as if the onus lay on Hatta's opponents to produce a convincing alternative, one which the regionalists too might be persuaded to accept.

But neither the regionalists nor their political party backers, Masjumi, PSI, and IPKI, had a monopoly of political pacemaking in these first two months of 1957. Some initiative lay with President Soekarno, because he had promised the country a *konsepsi* of his own, a formula which would afford a way out of the failures of party government. The President was at an advantage in that he agreed in many of the regionalists' targets of hostility. He too was against the party politicians and had attacked them earlier than had most of the current regionalist leaders. Secondly, he had distanced himself for some time from the Ali cabinet, which was now the target par excellence for all political dissatisfaction. Thirdly, he had received a number of declarations of trust in him personally from rebellious regionalist leaders, who, although they disliked his politics, wanted to emphasize their basic loyalty to the Republic. Probably most important of all, Soekarno seemed to have broader, more comprehensive, and more ideologically satisfying solutions than most of the regionalists had; this was an immense asset at a time when the bottom seemed to have been knocked out of the whole constitutional structure and new over-all solutions were in demand. Vague as his formulations of "guided democracy" were so far, they appeared to many to promise solutions more fundamental than those which the regionalists and their allies were advocating, a Hatta cabinet, regional autonomy, and (in some instances) bicameralism. At the same time they represented no abandonment of the still powerful symbolism of democracy, as did formulations which suggested steps toward military dictatorship. Finally, the President had tactical advantages, in that he was able to choose his own time to announce the contents of the long-awaited *konsepsi*.

For much of January and the first half of February, Soekarno discussed his plans privately with a number of top political leaders but disclosed them only by fragments. It was thought that he himself had not come to definite decisions as to the institutional forms in which his ideas of guided democracy should be cast, or at least that he was still in the process of probing current political realities to see how far he could go in introducing the changes he wanted. At any rate no clear statement was provided at this time as to the precise contents of the *konsepsi*. At least from mid-January, however, there were full, frequent, and much-discussed rumors on the innovations which Soekarno was hoping to introduce.

At this stage the President was clearly no longer concerned to dissolve the parties. He maintained his hostility to the idea of an institutionalized opposition and continued to advocate that decisions be made by consensus rather than voting. Moreover, he spoke repeatedly of the need for a more dynamic society; evidently he hoped to fashion institutional forms through which to combat mass apathy and political indifference and keep the revolutionary spirit alive. Several times he advocated establishment of an appointed advisory council of high status which would not be established on a party basis and would reach its decisions on the basis of consensus. Most important, he spoke of the need for a cabinet of all large parties, including the PKI.

But the President kept the country guessing on many details of these ideas. The political public had no way of knowing whether he would propose a constitutional change, whether the Constituent Assembly would be left to continue its work or not, or whether cabinet responsibility to parliament would continue to exist. More important still, the public could only hazard guesses on such questions as whether Soekarno would give real power to the PKI, whether he would bring non-party men like Chaerul Saleh to the center of the political stage, whether he would invite Hatta to participate in the new structure (and offer him a position of sufficient power to attract him), whether he would give major inducements to the army leaders in a bid for their support, how he would endeavor to solve the problem of Sumatra, and, not least important, how much power and responsibility he would allocate to himself. So the situation remained until February 21.

Meanwhile the cabinet tottered on the brink of self-dissolution. Various spokesmen of its constituent parties proposed reshuffle schemes in a last-ditch effort to save it, but none of these held much promise of being accepted. Indeed, they were not advanced with great determination. Most party leaders saw that the conditions no longer existed for the type of politics to which they were accustomed. Many of them therefore concerned themselves not with saving their parties' influence, but rather with finding ways for themselves and their associates and followers to work with some of the new actors entering the political stage. Indeed, most party leaders were seriously demoralized, and this was particularly true in parties like the PNI and NU (and to some extent the Masjumi) which could not identify themselves unequivocally with either the new regionalism or the President's *konsepsi*.

But one large party was palpably confident and vigorous. This was the PKI. In fact, the Communist Party had become increasingly active in national politics since the onset of the regional coups. It was the one major party which did not have either its prestige or its internal *élan* damaged by the general mood of antiparty sentiment, for it had neither participated in the much-cursed party cabinets, nor tied itself ideologically to constitutional democracy. Furthermore it knew where it stood in the current political situation, having an enemy manifestly before it in the form of the regionalist movement with its Masjumi-PSI-IPKI links and its associations with the old-time anti-Communist, Hatta. In addition, the PKI's value as an ally had increased with the development of the regional conflict. From the role of pro-PKI officers in the overthrow of Colonel Simbolon and from the anti-Communist actions of the Banteng Council, it was clear that implacable hostility existed between the Communists and the regionalists. The PKI could therefore be regarded as a reliable ally of all groups in Djakarta who wanted to stand up to the regionalists' demands.

This situation provided the party with new opportunities in capital-city politics. In the first place, the PKI was the most vociferous spokesman for the continued existence of the Ali cabinet. On February 10 it acted as chief sponsor of a Djakarta "Mass Meeting against Subversive Movements" at which a reported 150,000 persons expressed their support for the cabinet, as well as denouncing the regionalist councils.

More important, the party made active efforts to support President Soekarno in all that he did. In fact, the Communists succeeded in January and February 1957 in presenting themselves as even more ardent supporters of the President and his *konsepsi* than the "youth" or "1945 generation" group of Chaerul Saleh, Achmadi, and Isman, who had been his most articulate supporters when he presented his party-burial ideas in October 1956. Whereas the PKI had responded in "Yes . . . if . . ." terms to the October phase of the President's guided democracy ideas, it demonstrated sustained and enthusiastic acclamation in January and February, when the President no longer spoke of burying the parties and when it had been made clear to the PKI that the *konsepsi* would constitute no threat to its freedom to maintain an independent political organization. In return the party appeared to be earning rewards in terms of the President's confidence. In the words of a *Keng Po* editorial, "The way in which PKI people are coming and going at the palace has attracted general attention, so that the impression has arisen that Bung Karno is now closer to the PKI than to the PNI which he has occasionally been criticizing for the liberalistic-capitalistic current visible in it." [154]

But, valuable as his link with the Communists was to the President, it also made him susceptible to criticism from groups whose help he needed. Opposition to his "guided democracy" ideas was in large part focused on the proposal that the Communists be represented in the cabinet. And on this matter the Nahdatul Ulama was aligned with the Masjumi and PSI.

On February 21 the President finally unveiled the *konsepsi*. He spoke before a gathering of 900 palace guests. At the same time tens of thousands of pro-*konsepsi* demonstrators, many of them with hammer and sickle flags and banners, were listening to him at the front of the palace. In addition, the Information Ministry had asked radio owners throughout the country to listen to the address and make it possible for others to do so from their sets.

President Soekarno began by reiterating the need for an entirely new system of government, one which accorded with Indonesia's own personality. The proclamation of independence which was to have brought peace and harmony, happiness and welfare, had led instead to eleven years of disturbance. The underlying reason for this was that

[154] *Keng Po,* Feb. 15, 1957.

"the democracy which we have been applying is not in harmony with the spirit of the Indonesian people." [155] The trouble lay basically with "what I call Western democracy, call it parliamentary democracy if you like, but what is clear is that . . . it is an imported democracy, a democracy which is not the democracy of Indonesia." Then he made his specific proposals. Firstly, he advocated the formation of a "*gotong rojong* cabinet," literally a cabinet of mutual assistance, based on the principle that "all members of the family should eat at a single table and work at a single workbench." This would be a cabinet in which all parties and other groupings which had a defined minimum number of seats in parliament would be included. The PKI would be included, for "can we continue to ignore a group which received the votes of six million human beings in the elections?" [156]

Secondly, he advocated the establishment of a "National Council" composed principally of functional groups in society. This council would stand alongside the cabinet and give it advice, both solicited and unsolicited. It would serve as a "reflection of society in the same way as the cabinet will be a reflection of parliament." It would, God willing, be led by the President himself. Its membership would include representatives of workers, peasants, intellectuals, national entrepreneurs, Protestants and Catholics, Moslem scholars, women, youth and the 1945 generation, and also "representatives or members of groups who can present the problems of the regions." Presumably all these would be appointed representatives, but this was not stated specifically, nor was there any clear indication as to who would choose them. The chiefs of the three armed forces would sit on the councils, as would the police chief, the chief public prosecutor, and several key ministers. There was no suggestion that the President thought that a constitutional change would be required for the establishment of the National Council.

This was the long-awaited *konsepsi*. The party leaders were asked to return in a week's time and give the President their considered views of it. In its institutional aspects the plan was less radically new and less ideologically satisfying than many had expected. At the same time it raised many questions of constitutional dynamics which it left unanswered. But politically it was a clear enough statement of intent. The

[155] *Dewan Nasional* ("The National Council"; Djakarta: Kementerian Penerangan, 1957), p. 25.
[156] *Ibid.*

conclusion was general that Soekarno would not make concessions to the demands of the regionalist movements, or invite Hatta to accept any position of major power, or go any part of the way toward bicameralism and federalism. On the other hand, it was clear that the President himself was not intending to make a "coup from above," that he had found no dramatically new solution to the problem of widely dispersed power. Instead he would fall back on the PNI for the power resources he needed, conceivably also on the Nahdatul Ulama, and definitely on the PKI. And he would give the central leaders of the armed forces an increased formal claim to political power. On this last aspect great uncertainty remained. How much power would the President give the military leaders? This was closely connected with the biggest question of all: what would he do if the parties, or a great part of them, refused to accept his *konsepsi?*

The February 21 address was followed by a week of heavy political pressuring. From the side of those who opposed the *konsepsi* there were a few statements but little organizational activity. But the supporters of the President's ideas were very active. In cities and towns in most parts of the country, committees arose, representing dozens of parties and organizations, united in support of the *konsepsi* and often sending delegations to Djakarta. In several cities there were large mass rallies in support of the President's new formula. Although most of this activity was based on associations between PNI-related groups and those under PKI leadership, the PKI-led groups provided by far the greatest amount of energy. It was as a result of PKI activity that painted slogans appeared in the streets of Djakarta and several other cities and on the walls of public and private buildings, to an extent without precedent in the whole postrevolutionary period. As the week drew to a close, goon-squad-like groups of youths roamed the streets of the capital. Leaders of the Nahdatul Ulama as well as the Masjumi declared that they were being subjected to intimidation.[157] It seemed to many that Communist power had become a central political issue.

But if the aim of this activity was to bring the leaders of the parties to accept the President's *konsepsi,* it failed. On February 28 delegations from each of the parties went to the President to give him their decision, while a large pro-*konsepsi* crowd waited outside the palace. The parties responded very much as had been expected. The PNI and PKI gave the *konsepsi* their approval, as did the Partai Murba,

[157] *Keng Po,* Feb. 28, 1957.

the PRN, the Baperki organization of Indonesian citizens of Chinese origin, and the Police Employees' Association. Beyond that there was no group which supported the President. Only the Masjumi and the Catholic Party gave him directly negative answers, but all the vague, ambiguous, noncommittal, or conditionally positive answers given by the NU, PSII, Parkindo, IPKI, and PSI were tantamount to rejections.[158] Of particular importance was the fact that the Nahdatul Ulama, highly influential because of its balance position, had stuck by the position it had announced earlier of opposing the inclusion of the PKI in a cabinet. Thus not only had Soekarno failed to receive a consensus in favor of his formula; he had failed to obtain even majority support. And this was despite the use of such new techniques as government-ordered radio listening and capital-city goon squads.

After hearing the various parties' views, the President stated that he thought it only natural that there should be differences of opinion on his *konsepsi*. He added that he would think about the whole matter further and "boil up" the various views together, that he would travel to Surabaja for several days, and that on March 4 he would announce what additional steps he would take. Meanwhile there continued to be a great amount of pro-*konsepsi* activity. There were more mass meetings and more delegations arriving in Djakarta. On March 1 a group of top leaders of the Masjumi, NU, PSII, Parkindo, and the Catholic Party visited the chief public prosecutor to complain of intimidation of party leaders.

On March 2 came the countermove. In Makassar at seven that morning, a proclamation was read by Lieutenant Colonel H. N. V. Sumual, the territorial commander in East Indonesia. Sumual, a Minahasan, declared before a gathering of 51 top military, government, and political leaders of many ethnic groups in Makassar that the whole of the area under his command would thenceforth be under a State of War and Siege. At the same time he announced the names of four military governors who would exercise authority on his behalf in the different areas of East Indonesia. In the case of North Sulawesi, Nusa Tenggara (the Lesser Sunda Islands), and the Moluccas and West Irian province, he named the local regimental commander as military governor. In the case of South Sulawesi, where the situation was complicated by the existence of a Battle Area Command with nine battalions of East Java troops (under the former East Java territorial commander Colonel Sudirman), he named the Governor of all Sulawesi, Andi

[158] For a statement of the views of each of these parties, see *ibid.*

Pangerang Petta Rani, as military governor.[159] He also immediately blocked transfers out of the East Indonesia area of cash sums larger than Rp. 5,000.

At the same time, Sumual's Chief of Staff, Lieutenant Colonel Saleh Lahade, from South Sulawesi, read out the text of a lengthy Piagam Perdjuangan Permesta (Charter of Common Struggle) of the East Indonesian military command. This charter, which gave the name "Permesta" to the East Indonesian regionalist movement, was a remarkable document, following the lines of regionalist declarations in Sumatra, but going further to make more specific demands. It called for each province to have a five-year plan of its own, for "surplus areas" to be allowed to keep 70 per cent of their own earnings and "minus areas" 100 per cent of theirs with additional subsidies. It asked that East Indonesia be given a set quota of all scholarships for study in and outside the country. It requested that the various regions should obtain allocations of foreign exchange, domestic and overseas credits, and Japanese reparation commodities, on a basis proportionate to surface area and not population. It contained various requests for benefits for veterans, and it asked that the 70:30 barter system should immediately be extended to East Indonesia.[160]

More important still, however, were the directly political clauses of the charter. One of these called for 70 per cent of the members of the National Council of the Soekarno *konsepsi* to be representative of province-status regions, "in order that the Council might ultimately obtain the status of a Senate." Another said that the *gotong rojong* cabinet must be presidential in character and be given a minimum life span of five years by parliament. Finally, the charter said that both the National Council and the cabinet would have to be led by Soekarno and Hatta. The formulation was a masterpiece of political semantics, for, while using the language of Soekarno, it succeeded in conveying all the principal demands of Hatta. If it was true, as soon became appar-

---

[159] The Battle Area Command had been established in July 1956 shortly before Col. Warouw had transferred his authority as East Indonesian territorial commander to Lieut. Col. Sumual. Its commander, whose status was that of *panglima*, thus equivalent to that of one of the seven territorial commanders, exercised military authority over seven regencies of South and Southeast Sulawesi, where security was disturbed by Kahar Muzakar's forces and other rebel-bandit groups (*Indonesia Raya*, July 17, 1956).

[160] This was a system of export inducements introduced for several Sumatran ports, notably Kutaradja in Atjeh and Pakan Baru and Rengat in Riau, in Oct. 1956. Under it, exporters were allowed to keep 30 per cent of their foreign exchange earnings for overseas purchases.

ent, that the military heads of the large and ethnically heterogeneous area of East Indonesia had been able to agree on so far-reaching a set of demands, this reflected very widespread hostility to Djakarta. And this time there could be no doubt (for anyone trained to decode political messages) that the challenge extended to President Soekarno as well as the Ali cabinet.

The question immediately arose whether Sudirman's nine battalions of Javanese troops could be used to overthrow Sumual. It was quickly given a negative answer. By March 4 the Army General Staff in Djakarta had sent instructions to Sudirman to take no action which could lead to bloodshed.[161]

But if there was not to be a new countercoup on the Gintings-Macmour model, how was Djakarta to cope with the new challenge? More particularly, how was the President to deal with it? Coming on top of the hostility of so many parties to the President's *konsepsi*, the East Indonesia coup was a very damaging blow. Hard upon it came others. For days there were threatening declarations from military leaders in Atjeh and Kalimantan, foreshadowing possible coup-like actions there. Then on March 8 the regional legislative council of South Sumatra voted no confidence in the Governor, Winarno Danuatmodjo. On the following day Winarno left the province and Lieutenant Colonel Barlian took over direct control. At the same time there was a rising chorus of demands for Hatta's return to the government. On March 11 the Nahdatul Ulama added its voice to the demands for a restoration of Hatta to a position in the government.[162] With the Communists and the regionalists each apparently in a mood for toughness, the situation was tense indeed. Again the press spoke of the possibility of civil war.[163] The cabinet continued to exist, its member parties waiting for the moment when a resignation was not likely to leave them too powerless. It was the President who had to act, but what could he do? Could he now force through the *konsepsi*? Would he be obliged to make a complete *volte-face* and yield to the demand that Hatta return with real power? What were the possibilities of a course midway between these two?

It was at this point that initiative came to be exercised by Major General Nasution and his group of General Staff officers in Djakarta. The months since the regional coups began had seen Nasution and his associates gain considerable independence of the civil branch of

[161] *Keng Po,* March 4, 1957.   [162] *Ibid.,* March 11, 1957.
[163] *Ibid.,* March 5, 1957.

government, both of Prime Minister Ali, whose power was declining throughout this period, and of President Soekarno. In the months of August to November 1956 Nasution had been a target for great hostility within the army and forced by the challenge of Zulkifli Lubis to fall back heavily on the power of the cabinet and the President. But with the Lubis challenge defeated, Nasution was able himself to speak for an increased political role for the army, and thus internal army hostility toward him lessened. In addition, the Chief of Staff, as a Sumatran, was able to play something of a mediator role between the civilian government in Djakarta and the Sumatran regionalists. Indeed, as we have seen, he was playing this role with considerable independence of the Djakarta civilian authorities at the Palembang conference in late January. Finally, Nasution was known as a man of anti-Communist convictions from the days of the Madiun rebellion, and his deputy and close associate, Gatot Subroto, had a similar reputation. Therefore with the Communist issue now more important as an aspect of tension between the President and the regionalists, the Chief of Staff's power as an arbiter was all the stronger.

In early March, Nasution and Gatot Subroto figured prominently in most political news. Immediately after the Permesta proclamation of March 2 they appeared to throw their weight on the side of those working for a Hatta solution. This was the interpretation placed on efforts they made then to persuade Soekarno to meet the former Vice-President—although it is by no means certain that Nasution and his deputy wanted Hatta to return to the government on the terms on which Hatta himself was informally insisting, as a Prime Minister with full powers. Certainly there was heavy pressure on them from inside the army not to give way too far to the regionalists' demands.[164] In any event their efforts failed. The President was finally not prepared to meet Hatta.

Thereupon Nasution and Gatot Subroto turned their efforts in another direction, toward what might become a genuine compromise between Soekarno and the regionalists. They had their own formula for this, one which would serve at the same time to strengthen their own position. This was the proclamation of a nationwide State of War and Siege. Such a proclamation would legalize the power of military

[164] See *Suluh Indonesia,* March 13, 1957, for a report on the abortive attempt by a group of staff officers in Djakarta to proclaim a Dewan Merah Putih (Council of the Red-and-White, the national colors) in protest against the Chief of Staff's "lack of firmness" in the face of the Banteng Council, Simbolon, and Sumual.

leaders over civilian affairs in such areas as Central and South Sumatra and East Indonesia. At the same time it would provide a legal framework and over-all face-saving formula within which the central government, particularly the central military leadership, could tackle the regional problem. It would give new power and status to military leaders in other areas of the country. In effect it would help the officers who had not risen in power and status through association with regionalist movements to catch up with the others who had. Additionally it would strengthen the position of the central military leadership by vesting it with authority to issue decrees in a wide range of fields.

Such was the solution which finally emerged. At 10 A.M. on March 14 Ali Sastroamidjojo formally returned his cabinet's mandate to the President. At 10:30 the President proclaimed a nationwide State of War and Siege. The Ali cabinet came to an end with both a whimper and a bang.

The one year of the cabinet's life had brought far-reaching changes in the country's political constellation. When the Ali cabinet began its work, the dominant conflict was one between political parties, notably between the PNI and the Masjumi. The army was still outside the main political arena, powerful but content to use its power only sporadically. Similarly the President was still at the edge of the arena, exercising a great deal of influence, but indirectly and subject to a variety of restrictions of constitutional propriety. The PKI was powerful, but isolated. As for the regionalist movement, it existed only in embryo.

By the time of the cabinet's resignation a completely new pattern had emerged. Parties had lost very much of their importance, with the crucial exception of the PKI. The Masjumi had become a subordinate ally of the regionalist movement. The PNI had linked itself to the President's cause, reluctantly agreeing to leave the center of the political stage. The Nahdatul Ulama continued to be in the midway balance position. But none of these three had retained any large measure of initiative. They had to accommodate themselves to a situation to which they were peripheral. Four main power concentrations had emerged to prominence, and it was with these that the political initiative was to lie in the years which followed. The four were the Communist Party, President Soekarno, the central leadership of the army, and the military-civilian regionalist movement.

How could the parties' power decline so rapidly? How could they be so easily pushed from the center of the political arena just after an elected parliament had come into existence? How could they become so quickly an object of general hatred and disdain? And why was it that they appeared to be so incapable of defending themselves against the attacks to which they were subjected from all directions, being able to say little more than Mangunsarkoro's "We will carry out a self-correction in the party," or Natsir's "There are still some honest and idealistic people among the party leadership," or the sad affirmation of Sajuti Melik of the PNI that it was certainly no worse than the other parties? [165]

The answer is not one that can be given in terms of parties only. Parties had indeed reaped widespread hatred. But what collapsed in the twelve-month period of the second cabinet was more than the power and prestige of parties. What collapsed, although its collapse was by no means complete, was parliamentary democracy. Indeed, it was more; it was constitutional government.

As far as the twelve-month period of the Ali cabinet is concerned, the collapse was principally a collapse of a system of legitimacy. Constitutional government was side-stepped because the particular form of it which existed, namely, parliamentary democracy, no longer commanded acceptance. The hectic events of this year were basically a response to a power vacuum, to a discrepancy between claimed authority and actual power, a discrepancy which arose because those who claimed to exercise authority no longer had legitimacy in the eyes of those who had power. Thus the basic question of all political systems presented itself: "Why should I do as the man in the government tells me? Why should I obey this politician when it is against my interests and my moral predispositions and when I have power resources of my own?" The power vacuum appeared at points all over the political map. It appeared where the authority which the central government claimed over a defiant region exceeded the power the center could effectively exert over it. It appeared where the authority which civilian political leaders claimed to exercise over the army was greater than they could effectively exert over it. In a third sense it appeared where the authority which the party-based cabinet claimed over Soekarno was greater than the control it could exert over him when the issue was joined at the level of simple power. Again, the power vacuum appeared where a discrepancy existed between the

[165] *Suluh Indonesia,* Dec. 8, 1956; *Keng Po,* Jan. 19, 1957; *Suluh Indonesia,* Dec. 8, 1956.

universalistic claims of law on the one hand and on the other the political support available for judicial practice of a universalistic kind —this particularly where foreign or out-grouped minorities were involved and universalism came into conflict with nationalism.

At all of these points direct power asserted itself, expanding into a rapidly shrinking field of legality and constitutionality. Legality ceased to be commanding in a number of political areas because those who made and enforced the legally binding rules were no longer regarded as having a right to do so. They were regarded as mere politicians, as selfish politicians, as leaders who had become estranged from the people. And, to the extent that the pattern of defiance of them had already been set, they were regarded as leaders who had failed. Once there had been a sequence of violations of authority, their effect began to be cumulative, for the legitimacy of government was closely related to its success in making good its claims.

Thus for Prime Minister Ali to attempt to assert authority by pointing to the constitution and the rules of parliamentary government led to allegations that he was being "legalistic." Indeed, charges of "legalism" and "formalistic thinking" were frequently thrown at the leaders of the second Ali cabinet.[166] Further, Chief of Staff Nasution was warned by the Staff and Command School corps not to talk so much about military norms (*main norma-norma militer*, literally play with military norms).[167] The implication was that legal claims to authority were hollow where they did not rest on moral claims. Political authority would thenceforth be vested with "real leaders," with men who were "close to the people" or "still close to the people" (as in the days of the Revolution) and thus had a moral right to power.[168] These men were not Ali Sastroamidjojo, Mohammad Roem, or Idham Chalid, but Soekarno on the one hand and Lubis, Husein, and Barlian on the other.

Underneath these new moral claims lay the fact that certain key groups, with direct power of which the system of parliamentary democracy had not allowed them full use, were asserting it and tearing themselves loose from the restraints of a constitutional propriety which was no longer believed in. One result of this was a major reshuffling

[166] See van der Kroef, "Instability in Indonesia," p. 51.

[167] *Keng Po*, Dec. 17, 1956.

[168] For a penetrating analysis of being "close to the people" as an aspect of legitimate leadership see Donald Fagg, "Authority and Social Structure: A Study in Javanese Bureaucracy" (doctoral dissertation, Harvard University, 1958), pp. 236–237, 243.

of the pattern of interest representation. Groups of all kinds, which had theretofore pressed their interests through the parties or particular groups of party leaders, now switched to the support of the regionalist movement, the President, the central leadership of the army, or the PKI.

Why, then, did party and parliamentary government lose its legitimacy so rapidly in this particular twelve-month period? The transformation does not appear to be connected with particular events which happened outside the political system at this time. There were no international events or crucial world price movements which contributed to it in any important way.

The change was often related to the failure of the second Ali cabinet to solve administrative and economic problems. Critics frequently pointed to the cabinet's slowness in making decisions implementing the abrogation of the Round Table Conference agreements. They condemned it for inaction on the Five-Year Plan. They pointed to the fact that it was obliged twice, in July 1956 and in February 1957, to make use of an escape clause provision which allowed it to borrow from the central bank, even where this meant that the bank's ratio of reserves to loans fell below the legally stipulated level of 20 per cent.[169] Some deplored its failure to take action to reduce the number of civil servants. Many spoke about the deteriorating condition of roads, of interinsular shipping facilities, and of irrigation and flood control installations.[170]

But in fact the cabinet was not particularly ineffective in problem-solving policy. In the economic field it could point to the opening of several large governmental or semigovernmental factories, spinning mills, and a sodium and chloride factory and to the forthcoming opening of a large cement plant at Gresik in East Java, which would produce an annual 250,000 tons, half of the country's needs.[171] It could point to the fact that it had been able to keep prices fairly stable —thanks largely to a high volume of imports, as well as to the cheap purchase of U.S. goods under the Surplus Agricultural Commodities

[169] Cf. Bank Indonesia, *Report for the Year 1956–1957*, pp. 71–75.

[170] Deterioration in these areas of maintenance was something on which Mohammad Hatta dwelt repeatedly in 1956. See *Pedoman*, March 3, 9, June 6, 1956, and also *Past and Future*, p. 13. See also the editorial "Are Floods a Small Matter?" in *Keng Po*, Dec. 10, 1956.

[171] *Kabinet Ali-Roem-Idham, Program dan Pelaksanaan* ("The Program of the Ali-Roem-Idham Cabinet and Its Execution"; Djakarta: Kementerian Penerangan, 1956), pp. 84–85.

agreement. It certainly allowed its reserves to dwindle alarmingly.[172] But this was due in the first place to falling export prices. With the end of the short-lived boom of late 1955, overseas prices for Indonesia's rubber and other goods fell again, rising only briefly at the time of the Suez crisis in late 1956.[173]

The cabinet could and did point to the fact that it had succeeded in pushing through long-delayed and highly controversial legislation on regional government. Thus it was responsible for Law no. 1 of 1957, a new basic law which greatly increased the power of elected legislative councils in the provinces, regencies, and municipalities and provided for the gradual elimination of the *pamong pradja* from territorial jurisdiction.[174] It also established a legal framework for financial relations between the central government and autonomous regional governments. And it made changes in provincial boundaries, the first since 1950, gaining parliamentary approval for bills which divided Kalimantan into West, South, and East Kalimantan and separated Atjeh from North Sumatra.

On the matter of squatting, the second Ali cabinet acted with considerable resolution. In the early months of its period in office it forced petty traders and *kampong* dwellers to vacate a number of illegally occupied areas in the cities of Djakarta and Surabaja. The toughness of its police representatives in the Pakis area of Surabaja resulted in four deaths.[175] This was, in fact, another Tandjong Morawa affair, but one which produced no broad political challenge to the government's actions. In October the cabinet enacted an emergency law which greatly increased its powers to cope with squatting on estates. With the abrogation of the Round Table Conference agreements, it seems, squatting on Dutch-owned estates was given a fresh stimulus.[176] To cope with this and the situation generally the cabinet now provided speedier procedures of eviction than had existed theretofore and raised the penalties for persons convicted for illegal occupation of estate land. Moreover, it extended these penal provisions to persons squatting on government estates and on state forest land.[177]

[172] Bank Indonesia, *Report for the Year 1957–1958* (Djakarta, 1958), p. 113.

[173] Bank Indonesia, *Report for the Year 1956–1957*, pp. 11–12, 114–115, 141.

[174] For full discussions see Gerald S. Maryanov, *Decentralization in Indonesia: Legislative Aspects* (Cornell Modern Indonesia Project, Interim Reports Series; Ithaca, N.Y., 1957), pp. 71–75, and Legge, *Problems of Regional Autonomy in Contemporary Indonesia*, pp. 50–62.

[175] *Abadi*, May 8, 1956; cf. *Indonesia Raya*, June 12, 1956.

[176] *Pedoman*, April 20, 1956.

[177] *Kabinet Ali-Roem-Idham, Program dan Pelaksanaan*, p. 204.

Again, the cabinet appears to have had some modest successes in its efforts to eliminate rebel-bandit activity. In Sulawesi it split off several of Kahar Muzakar's battalions. In Atjeh it laid most of the groundwork for the cease-fire agreement which was reached in June 1957—by allowing Kutaradja exporters to keep 70 per cent of their foreign exchange, by giving Atjeh province status and an Achinese governor, and by placing its military commander, also an Achinese, directly under the authority of the Army Chief of Staff. By comparison with what the two previous cabinets had achieved—and the comparison must necessarily be so rough as to be almost meaningless—the cabinet was moderately successful in solving its practical problems.

But it was not viewed as moderately successful. On the contrary, it was seen by most in the political public as an utter and complete failure. Most of those who assessed its problem-solving performance, like most of those who judged it for its "leadership," for the moral attributes which its image conveyed, were deeply disillusioned about the cabinet.

In large part it was the elections which had made the difference. The elections, as already noted, were regarded as a panacea and served as a device for the postponement and accumulation of expectations. A level of policy-making effectiveness which was regarded as temporarily tolerable in the pre-elections period now became the object of active resentment.

Moreover, the elections had wrought major changes in the way in which the political system dealt with ferment and unrest. For the virtually three years of campaigning the parties had provided roles to those who participated in politics, especially protest politics, in order to make their personal lives meaningful. Now, with electioneering finished, the parties no longer had satisfying work for the many who wanted to participate politically for reasons of personal integration. The cabinet itself could give these men no political work to do. Thus they were released to be active in other, less institutionalized, agencies of politics, particularly various political movements. And these movements had to attack parties, and the system which conferred authority on those who had gained electoral success, in order to establish their own claims to influence.

In addition, the elections helped weaken the authority of parties and parliamentary institutions because they produced an increasingly active disrespect on the part of members of the political elite for the electoral verdict. Stories of blind and idiosyncratic behavior by village and urban lower-class voters had widespread currency in the elite and the political public, and there was general agreement on one "lesson" of the elections, that it was effective electioneering to rely heavily on money and bureaucratic influence. That government should be in the hands of those whom the ballot box singles out had never been a strongly held view for more than a tiny minority of the political public—although belief in the sacrosanct nature of the "will of the people" was widespread and had contributed to the great hope with which the forthcoming elections were viewed. Most members of this public had always seen good government and democracy in terms more of building a just and prosperous society in the future, in terms of the people's "real will," than in relation to achieving accountability in the present. They had seen it as a matter of good leadership and active response, of leaders having a feeling for the people and the people having a feeling for the state, rather than as fair regulation of conflicts of interest. Thus there was only tentative support for either the effort to keep to the rules of constitutional democracy or the idea of the ballot box as the sanction behind these rules. Once the elections had been held, this tentative support fell away. It had become clear that the ballot box could not be the bearer of the sacredness attaching to the "will of the people." There was a correspondingly greater emphasis on the source of legitimacy which had been more compelling than any other for the whole of the period of this study—and which was the antithesis of rules—the Revolution. The right to wield governmental power, it was now asserted with increasing vociferousness, lay with those who had led the Revolution—and who had not forfeited their claims by losing their revolutionary spirit and growing estranged from the people.

But there is also another sense in which the end of the long period of electioneering was important in producing challenges to the parliamentary creed. The protracted and bitter election campaign had sharpened tensions in many sections of society and given great prominence to ideological conflict. Thus it had destroyed virtually all the previously existing consensus on the purposes and ideological character of the state. It had split or made uninfluential virtually all the institutions of government which might otherwise have been stretched umbrellalike above the party struggle. The result was to aggravate the general uneasiness which existed within the political public, an uneasiness which was expressed in support of those who promised to restore order and harmony in government and solidarity in society, to do away with the purposeless bickering of the parties, and to make possible a recapturing of the unity, the dedication, and the commitment to clear goals which had prevailed in the days of the Revolution.

But while the election campaign was still on, no major attack on the parties could be launched. Firstly, too many interests had associated themselves with the parties. There was also the inhibiting effect of the panacea view of elections. But when the elections were over and when it became clear that they had not brought about any major improvements—that government seemed to be no more harmonious or purposeful and no more effective in the making and enforcement of administrative and economic decisions—these restraints fell away.

Thus the elections had served both to undermine faith in parliamentary democracy and to stay the hand of those who had an interest in its overthrow. Once the elections were over, the long-term factors working against the parliamentary system and its creed asserted themselves, and they did so with the force of several years of accumulated energy.

In the period of the second Ali cabinet, belief in party and parliamentary government collapsed. This resulted in a major power shift, favoring groups which had been restrained in the use of their power in the 1949–1957 period. But the assertion of power by these groups was not direct. They too advanced claims to legitimacy. By calling for a return to the spirit of the Revolution, they were claiming that they themselves were imbued with this element of sacredness. By charging parties, politicians, and "Djakarta" with having swerved from the goals of the Revolution and having grown apart from the people, they were asserting that they themselves had not lost these essential attributes of authority.

One central question facing the country at the time the second Ali cabinet fell was whether the legitimacy claims of these various political forces, especially of President Soekarno and the regionalists, could be honored together within a single polity. That a major rebellion or civil war broke out within a year of this cabinet's fall reflects the fact that it proved impossible to make the rival claims to legitimacy mutually compatible.

Chapter XI

Conclusion

IN bringing this study to a conclusion, March 1957 will be taken as a dividing point. First the period from mid-1953 when the Wilopo cabinet fell will be reviewed. Following this will be an examination of politics since 1957, especially of the further abandonment of constitutional democracy. Finally, the findings on the central questions under consideration will be summed up.

ECONOMIC AND ADMINISTRATIVE POLICY, 1953–1957

In an earlier chapter we looked at the system of government and politics as it existed in the period from December 1949 to June 1953, the period of the Hatta, Natsir, Sukiman, and Wilopo cabinets. We saw these cabinets intensely concerned with solving administrative and economic problems, with the strengthening of law and order, administrative regularization and consolidation, the maximization of production, and planned economic development. We noted that they had some success in implementing their policies, but failed to deal adequately with particular policy tasks which called for strong government. When we examined the four cabinets' legitimizing activities we saw their efforts to establish a ruled-based legitimacy alongside the basis which existed in current perceptions of the Revolution. We saw too how this led them to run afoul of those sections of the political public, an important part of the ex-revolutionary group, who sought to participate in radical nationalist politics in order to achieve personal integration such as they had experienced in the Revolution itself. We noted strong efforts made by these cabinets to maintain a functioning

556

system of constitutional democracy. And we saw that this attempt was partially successful, although operating under conditions of permanent threat from the side of a number of groups which accepted its terms reluctantly or not at all.

What, then, are the generalizations to be made about the way in which the over-all system functioned in the period of the next three cabinets, the two cabinets of Ali Sastroamidjojo and the Burhanuddin Harahap cabinet? These cabinets do not form a unity in the same sense. Particularly as regards policy approaches there was no basic continuity in the 1953–1957 period, as there was in the earlier period. But the fact that the cabinets of the later period all differed so markedly from the cabinets of the earlier one, in their approaches to policy and especially with regard to the context in which they were working, justifies an attempt to make generalizations.

On the basic questions of economic policy, the three later cabinets had fewer strong commitments to particular positions. In general, they were all less intensely concerned with maximization of production, fiscal stability, and administrative rationalization than their predecessors and more concerned with restructuring the economy in such a way that Indonesian nationals held positions of advantage within it. But they pursued no consistent policies in this regard. On the whole, their measures of Indonesianization failed to bring about any major increase in the *power* of Indonesian nationals within the economy, a fact which suggests that the patronage function of these measures may have been more important than their policy aspect. Moreover, they were inconsistent in their policies toward foreign investment. By and large, they were hostile to foreign capital, at least the two Ali cabinets. They abrogated the Round Table Conference agreements protecting Dutch capital, and they repudiated a large part of the debt which Indonesia had accepted from the Netherlands at that conference. But here again they were not consistent. All three cabinets issued formal declarations designed to attract new foreign investors; foreign capital was assigned an important role in the Five-Year (1956–1960) Plan which the second Ali cabinet approved; and all the cabinets made politically costly efforts to stop squatting on estate land. Furthermore, it appears that none of them planned any large-scale nationalization of Dutch or other foreign business.

In point of fact these cabinets had no distinctive set of policies for solving problems in the economy, or for that matter in administration. Their approach was essentially one of working from the policy framework set by their predecessors, while having fewer value commitments to this framework—this is true particularly of the first cabinet of Ali Sastroamidjojo—and being concerned more with power as such, both for themselves as cabinets and for their parties. It is therefore extremely difficult to make any assessment of their performance without running the risk of attributing to them policy goals which they did not actually hold. Our concern here will thus be not to assess the three cabinets' effectiveness in moving toward their policy goals, but rather to describe developments in economic and administrative policy in their period and relate them to the changing political situation of those years.

The period of their incumbency was one in which major difficulties came to the fore in the economy. In the first place, the production of food commodities for local consumption rose only slightly between 1953 and 1956, in contrast to the rapid rises which had taken place in the previous three years. The figures for rice are a clear indication of the pattern. Whereas rice production had jumped from 5.8 to 7 million tons between 1950 and 1953, it rose only to 7.3 million tons in the following three years.[1] The effort to make Indonesia self-sufficient in rice, which came close to success in 1954 and 1955, was abandoned in 1956 when 779,000 tons were imported.[2] A similar flattening out of a rising curve is evident if one looks at production of the other principal food crops, maize, cassava, sweet potatoes, peanuts, and soybeans, and the pattern is little different with regard to fish production.[3]

In the field of manufacturing there was no period of rapid expansion in the early 1950's, and the gradual increases in output of the 1950–1953 period continued in the following three years. The establishment of the large-scale industries which had been planned since the time of the Natsir cabinet (and in some cases since before the war) proceeded very slowly indeed. It was only in June 1957, with the coming into operation of the large cement plant at Gresik in East Java, that a major success was achieved. On the other hand, smaller-scale industrial enterprise maintained itself and grew—in such fields as weaving, knitting, food, cigarette, soft-drink, and ice production, the production of leather goods and furniture, and printing. Most of these industries benefited from tariff barriers, and in some cases they ex-

[1] Biro Pusat Statistik (Central Bureau of Statistics), *Statistical Pocketbook of Indonesia, 1957* (Djakarta: Biro Pusat Statistik, 1957), p. 51.

[2] Biro Pusat Statistik, *Statistical Pocketbook of Indonesia, 1959* (Djakarta: Biro Pusat Statistik, 1960), p. 119.

[3] Biro Pusat Statistik, *Statistical Pocketbook of Indonesia, 1957*, pp. 51, 78.

panded as Chinese entrepreneurs, obliged to leave trading as a result of Indonesianization, turned to manufacturing activities.[4]

The area of greatest difficulties was exporting. The problem here was in large measure one of low overseas prices. But it was also one of low production—a consequence of the disadvantageous exchange rate, of rising labor costs, of squatting, thefts, and rebel-bandit activity.[5] The double difficulty can be seen clearly in the case of rubber, which contributed 50.8 per cent of the total value of Indonesia's exports in 1951, 33 per cent in 1953, and 40.2 per cent in 1956. One pound of rubber (No. 1 ribbed smoked sheets) fetched an average of 169.55 Straits-dollar cents on the Singapore market in 1951, the year in which the Korean War boom was at its height, 67.30 cents in 1953, the trough year of the post-Korea slump, and 96.76 cents in 1956. Production figures for these three years were 791,000, 692,000, and 687,000 long tons respectively. Examining the figures for 1953 to 1956, one finds that prices were rather consistently low and that production was generally declining.[6] This may have been only an apparent decline, a result of the increased scale of smuggling in these years. But it is clear that there was no significant rise in production in these years. Foreign currency earnings from rubber were thus much lower in the second half of our period than the first.

The picture was a more encouraging one in the case of oil and oil products, which was the country's second largest earner of foreign exchange throughout the period—the range of its contribution to total foreign exchange was between 13.5 per cent in 1951 and 26.4 per cent in 1954. Oil production was rising fairly rapidly in the 1953–1956

[4] See Bank Indonesia, *Report for the Year 1956–1957* (Djakarta, 1957), pp. 173–174; Biro Pusat Statistik, *Statistical Pocketbook of Indonesia, 1957*, p. 93; and Benjamin Higgins, *Indonesia's Economic Stabilization and Development* (New York: Institute of Pacific Relations, 1957), pp. 68–81, 161. See also A. Kraal, "Enige Aspecten van de Ontwikkeling der Industrie in Indonesië," *Ekonomi dan Keuangan Indonesia*, X (1957), 253–261, and J. M. van der Kroef's review of H. J. van Oorschot, *De Ontwikkeling van de Nijverheid in Indonesië* (The Hague and Bandung: van Hoeve, 1956), in *Pacific Affairs*, XXXI, no. 2 (June 1958), 204–206.

[5] Most of these difficulties were felt more acutely by the large foreign establishments, plantations, and, to some extent also, mines than by Indonesian smallholder producers. Hence there was a tendency for small holders to account for increasing proportions of the total production of certain commodities produced by both estates and small holders, such as rubber, sugar, tobacco, and coffee.

[6] The Java Bank, *Report for the Financial Year 1951–1952* (Djakarta, 1952), pp. 121, 160; Bank Indonesia, *Report for the Year 1954–1955* (Djakarta, 1955), pp. 97, 119–120, *Report for the Year 1956–1957*, pp. 117, 140, and *Report for the Year 1958–1959* (Djakarta, 1959), p. 182.

period as it had in the previous three years. But the rise in exports was not as large, because increases in the production of oil products (gasoline, kerosene, and so on), as distinct from crude oil, were offset by the rapid growth of domestic consumption of these fluids.[7] In the case of the No. 3 export commodity, tin, there was a marked drop in foreign exchange earnings between 1953 and 1956, resulting from falling production.[8] Copra, fourth largest export commodity, was produced on a rising scale, but a large and growing proportion of production was used domestically. The marked fall in recorded foreign exchange earnings from copra between 1953 and 1956 can perhaps be accounted for by increased smuggling, but certainly there was no rise in over-all (legal and smuggled) exports of this commodity.[9] In the case of sugar and tobacco there were also important rises in production, but the expansion in domestic consumption proceeded at almost the same pace in each case.[10] The total figure for recorded export earnings (including revenue from export duties) was Rp. 10,055 million in 1956, whereas it had been Rp. 9,344 million in 1953 and Rp. 4,908 million in 1951 —which latter was the equivalent in foreign currency values of Rp. 14,724 million.[11]

On the other hand, domestic demand was high and growing rapidly. This resulted in part from the growth of population, estimated officially to have risen from 76.6 million in 1950 to 84.4 million in 1956.[12] But, more important still, domestic demand was a consequence of social change, particularly of expansion in the number of those who had stepped out of their traditional society and developed modern behavior

[7] Bank Indonesia, *Report for the Year 1954–1955*, pp. 142–143, and *Report for the Year 1956–1957*, pp. 166–167.

[8] Bank Indonesia, *Report for the Year 1954–1955*, p. 143, and *Report for the Year 1956–1957*, p. 168.

[9] Bank Indonesia, *Report for the Year 1954–1955*, p. 124, and *Report for the Year 1956–1957*, pp. 145–146.

[10] Bank Indonesia, *Report for the Year 1954–1955*, pp. 131, 138–140, and *Report for the Year 1956–1957*, pp. 155, 162–164.

[11] See Higgins, *op. cit.*, p. 155, and Bank Indonesia, *Report for the Year 1958–1959*, p. 146.

[12] These are the figures given in Biro Pusat Statistik, *Statistical Pocketbook of Indonesia, 1960* (Djakarta: Biro Pusat Statistik, 1961), p. 11. The 1957 edition of the same publication gives the figure 85 million for 1956 (p. 11). All figures later than those for 1940 are given with the qualification "preliminary data." An annual net increase of 1.5 per cent to 2 per cent was assumed by those who drew up the Five-Year Development Plan made in 1955–1956, but the creators of the Eight-Year Development Plan drawn up in 1959 assumed a net increase of 2.3 per cent per annum. See Guy J. Pauker, "Indonesia's Eight-Year Development Plan," *Pacific Affairs*, XXXIV, no. 2 (July 1961), 115–130.

and aspirations. The size of this group grew rapidly in the years of this study, notably through urbanization, schooling, expansion of the mass media, and increases in the membership of parties and organizations. The population of the thirteen principal towns listed in the Statistical Pocketbooks rose from 5.04 million at the end of 1952 to 5.9 million four years later.[13] The school population went from 5.45 million in 1952–1953 to 6.62 million in 1956–1957.[14] The total circulation of the daily press rose from 413,700 at the end of 1949 to 933,810 at the end of 1956, and the total circulation of periodicals from 1,096,600 at the end of 1950 to 3,366,200 at the end of 1956, while the number of licensed radio sets increased from 213,271 at the end of 1951 to 539,043 at the end of 1956.[15] Film viewing was on the increase at the same time. An important additional factor raising consumer expectations was the rapidly growing amount of overseas traveling.[16]

With population growing and with more and more persons aspiring to a modern style of life, consumption levels rose quickly. Total consumption of rice rose from 5,954,000 tons in 1950 to 7,900,000 tons in 1956, and per capita consumption from 78.6 kilograms to 94.5 kilograms in the same period.[17] The number of passenger cars rose from 22,164 in January 1950 to 73,219 in January 1957, and the number of motorcycles and scooters from 5,546 to 99,079 in the same period, while the number of bicycles imported over this seven-year period was 1,020,369.[18] Gasoline consumption increased by 64.5 per cent between 1950 and 1956, and kerosene consumption by 200.5 per cent.[19] As already noted, there were major increases also in the domestic consumption of copra (for margarine and soap production), sugar, and tobacco. Douglas Paauw estimates that aggregate demand grew by an average of 10 per cent per year in the five years prior to 1957. He links this firstly with a heavy preference for consumption rather than saving—his estimate is that the marginal propensity to consume was "perhaps four-fifths"—and secondly with the fact that the taxation system was fairly insensitive to changes in income.[20]

[13] Biro Pusat Statistik, *Statistical Pocketbook of Indonesia, 1957*, p. 11.
[14] Biro Pusat Statistik, *Statistical Pocketbook of Indonesia, 1960*, p. 24.
[15] Biro Pusat Statistik, *Statistical Pocketbook of Indonesia, 1957*, pp. 29, 163.
[16] *Ibid.*, pp. 14–15.   [17] *Ibid.*, p. 200.
[18] *Ibid.*, p. 151; *Statistical Pocketbook of Indonesia, 1959*, p. 167.
[19] Bank Indonesia, *Report for the Year 1954–1955*, p. 143, and *Report for the Year 1956–1957*, p. 167.
[20] Douglas S. Paauw, "The High Cost of Political Instability in Indonesia, 1957–1958" in B. H. M. Vlekke, *Indonesia's Struggle, 1957–1958* (The Hague: Netherlands Institute of International Affairs, 1959), p. 30. For a full discussion of the

Throughout our period then, and especially in its second half, aggregate demand and aggregate supply were out of equilibrium. The demand for imports, for locally produced goods and services, and for government expenditures and credits exceeded the supply of goods and services produced and taxes raised. And there was little foreign aid to help close the gap.[21] Indeed, the inflow from aid was not much larger than the outflow in interest and amortization payments on external debts taken over from the Netherlands Indies government through the Round Table Conference Agreement.[22] Therefore inflationary pressures were strong. One immediate cause of these lay in import restrictions, but the most important mechanism was deficit financing. Except in 1951, when the Korean War boom was at its peak, there were deficits for every year of the period between 1950 and 1956, and they ranged from Rp. 3,602 million or 30.5 per cent of current receipts in 1954 to Rp. 1,563 or 8.5 per cent of current receipts in 1956.[23] The money supply rose from Rp. 7,204 million in June 1953 to Rp. 13,361 million in March 1957, as it had risen earlier from Rp.

---

problems of the taxation system in this period see Douglas S. Paauw, *Financing Economic Development: The Indonesian Case* (Glencoe, Ill.: Free Press, 1960).

[21] Most aid came from the United States. This included the $100 million loan extended by the Export-Import Bank in 1950 and not finally used up until after the end of our period. It also included the $40 million of Marshall Aid grants made available in 1950 and $46.93 million of grants, "project aid," appropriated in the following six years by the International Cooperation Administration (under its various successive names). Finally, it included the Surplus Agricultural Commodities arrangement whereby agricultural products worth $96.7 million would be sold (between 1956 and 1958) on the Indonesian market, with 80 per cent of its rupiah earnings being available to the Indonesian government for developmental projects approved by the United States. In addition to the Netherlands loan of 280 million guilders, Indonesia received short-term commercial-interest-bearing loans from several countries of Western Europe. Grant aid received from various United Nations agencies and through the Colombo plan—for scholarship programs, the services of specialists, and capital and other goods—involved fairly small sums of money. No Soviet aid funds were actually appropriated in our period. Nor had the flow of Japanese reparations funds started, although Indonesia had incurred trade debts to Japan in anticipation of a reparations agreement. See Donald H. Pond, "Foreign Sources of Indonesian Government Revenue" (unpublished paper, Cornell Modern Indonesia Project, 1960); Paauw, *Financing Economic Development*, pp. 423–424; and Willard A. Hanna, *Bung Karno's Indonesia* (New York: American Universities Field Staff, 1960), xxiv, 3–14.

[22] See Alastair M. Taylor, *Indonesian Independence and the United Nations* (Ithaca, N.Y.: Cornell University Press, 1960), pp. 479–484, for detailed specifications of the obligations which Indonesia assumed through this agreement.

[23] Biro Pusat Statistik, *Statistical Pocketbook of Indonesia, 1957*, p. 169.

3,309 million (3,309 million Dutch guilders) in December 1949.[24]

Successive governments used various devices of foreign trade policy to hold inflationary pressures in check, particularly prepayments for imports and import surcharges. Relatively easy to institute and administer, these devices succeeded in keeping prices from rising at extreme speeds.[25] Galloping inflation appeared close at hand by the middle of 1955. But it was prevented from developing by the Burhanuddin Harahap cabinet's liberalization of imports, effected as this was in the context of a short-lived rubber boom.

But the various stabilization devices did not go to the root of the problem, the disequilibrium between aggregate demand and aggregate supply. The prepayment schemes had only a once-over effect. The import surcharges were actually harmful to price stability in the long run. In Douglas Paauw's words, "the danger of open inflation was always just around the corner" in the years after 1952.[26] The corner was to be reached in 1957.

Nor were inflationary pressures the only cost of operating a disequilibrium economy. One other important cost was deterioration in such key areas of government maintenance activity as road making and road repairing, shipping, forestry, irrigation, and flood control. Pressed to provide funds for a large variety of causes on the basis of relatively small revenue, governments found it difficult to make sizable allocations for work in fields where needs had something of a long-term character—and where few strong political demands were being made, thanks to the weakness of Indonesian business groups. Thus not only was little done to build new roads, irrigation dams, and water-control schemes; in addition, a number of existing facilities were allowed to remain unrepaired—after seven and a half years of neglect,

[24] The Java Bank, *Report for the Financial Year 1951–1952*, p. 71; Bank Indonesia, *Report for the Year 1953–1954* (Djakarta, 1954), p. 51, and *Report for the Year 1956–1957*, p. 67.

[25] For full discussions see Higgins, *op. cit.*, pp. 27–39, and Paauw, "The High Cost of Political Instability," pp. 25–32; see also Hans O. Schmitt, "Some Monetary and Fiscal Consequences of Social Conflict in Indonesia, 1950–58" (doctoral dissertation, University of California, Berkeley, 1959), pp. 121 ff. and *passim*. Weighted index numbers for Djakarta suggest that the cost of living rose by 137 per cent for a characteristic civil servant and his family between 1950 and 1956 and by 182 per cent for a (blue-collar) municipal worker and his family. In rural Java food prices trebled in the same period, while textile prices, which were notably high in 1950, rose by only approximately 20 per cent (Biro Pusat Statistik, *Statistical Pocketbook of Indonesia, 1957*, pp. 218, 214–216).

[26] "The High Cost of Political Instability," p. 25.

deforestation, and scorched-earth policies before 1949—and in some cases to come into worse disrepair.

The state of roads in Sumatra and Sulawesi had become so bad by 1956 that some established trade patterns were seriously threatened.[27] For instance, Kerintji in Central Sumatra, previously a "rice bowl" area, was now producing only a little more rice than it needed, because only small amounts could be transported to outside markets along the bad roads and still be sold profitably. Shipping services had become notably less reliable in a number of areas where previously KPM-operated routes had been allocated to national shipping firms; an estimated 30 per cent of the total number of ships were lying idle in the first half of 1956.[28] The major floods of 1955, which defeated the attempt to achieve self-sufficiency in rice, resulted both from deforestation and erosion and from the lack of new flood control projects.[29]

One cannot, of course, account for this series of difficulties by a single explanation. The problem was partly one of shortage of technical skills. It was partly one of administrative and entrepreneurial ineffectiveness. A further important factor was the government's lack of coercive capacity, for instance, in the matter of forests, where a great deal of the damage resulted from squatting, the illegal grazing of livestock, and illegal woodcutting.[30] But one most important aspect was the financial-political one: meager funds and clamorous claimants.

One final point to be made about economic functioning concerns Indonesianization. As already brought out, the cabinets of the 1953–1957 period were very much more active than their predecessors in efforts to expand the role of Indonesian nationals, in practice usually ethnic Indonesians, within the economy. Thanks to government credits, licensing policy, and policy in the allocation of materials, private "national businessmen" came to play a much larger role than before 1953 in importing, banking, interinsular shipping, stevedoring, and some sections of manufacturing and processing. Moreover, their role in handicraft and cottage industry appears to have grown, and the share

[27] Bank Indonesia, *Report for the Year 1956–1957*, pp. 175–176.

[28] Bank Indonesia, *Report for the Year 1955–1956* (Djakarta, 1956), p. 157; cf. the statement of P. M. Tangkilisan, chairman of the Communications section of parliament, in *Keng Po,* Jan. 21, 1956.

[29] Cf. the statement of Vice-President Hatta in *Pedoman,* March 8, 1956; see also Boyd R. Compton, "Indonesia, 1955," *Newsletter of the Institute of Current World Affairs,* Feb. 4, 1956.

[30] See *Merdeka,* Dec. 3, 1954, and Compton, "Indonesia, 1955," *loc. cit.*

taken by Indonesian small holders in the production of such export commodities as rubber, sugar, tobacco, and coffee expanded at the expense of the share of the foreign estates. There was nationalization of electric power and of the theretofore semigovernmental airline, Garuda, in this period,[31] and many of the larger new industrial plants were government enterprises. But by far the greatest amount of Indonesianization consisted of an expansion of private Indonesian business activity.

Economically, the costs of Indonesianization were high. Many of the new private firms, in the field of importing particularly, were bogus units, either license-reselling "brief-case firms" or "Ali-Baba" establishments, Chinese-run with Indonesian front men, which were effective enough as businesses but "national" only in name. Similarly many of the new national banks were get-rich-quick organizations, benefiting from the discrepancy between the low interest rates of the government banks and the very high ones set by the market. Where a new national firm obtained its credits by means of political influence, its incentive to develop commercial viability was slight, and much of the money was often spent in prestige-creating consumption, on furniture, cars, and mountain bungalows "for the staff." If one failed to make profits, there were established Dutch and Chinese competitors on whom the blame could be put. Furthermore, it was sometimes possible to evade repayment to government lending institutions. Frequent cabinet changes were generally a salutary influence in these respects, in that many of the firms founded on political favors could not expect the flow to continue in the event of a cabinet change. But others were able to fortify themselves financially against this contingency or to exact subsidies from successive cabinets of different political color, either by virtue of political agility or in some cases because no government could afford politically to have them close down. The latter factor operated with particular force in the case of enterprises owned by the government itself, some of which showed losses consistently.[32]

What was achieved at such a high economic cost, moreover, resulted in only a minor diminution in the role of foreign capital. There was certainly an increase in the power of Indonesians within the economy

[31] John O. Sutter, *Indonesianisasi: Politics in a Changing Economy, 1940–1955* (Southeast Asia Program, Cornell University; Ithaca, N.Y., 1959), pp. 885–900.

[32] See, for instance, the catalogue of losses by Pelni, the government shipping line, in G. van Zuiden, "A Brief Survey of the Economic and Financial Position of Indonesia," in B. H. M. Vlekke, ed., *Indonesia in 1956* (The Hague: Netherlands Institute for International Affairs, 1957), p. 70.

between 1953 and 1956. But the Dutch KPM was still providing most interinsular shipping services. Dutch, British, and Chinese firms continued to dominate big banking, and Chinese capital remained of the greatest importance in the provision of credit in rural areas. Dutch and Chinese firms continued to control most of the country's internal distributive trade. In the all-important field of export production the foreign role was still larger than the Indonesian, despite the increases in small-holder production of rubber, copra, sugar, and other commodities. There was indeed the tendency of foreign plantation companies to sell their assets. This grew markedly after the Round Table Conference Agreement was abrogated and subsequently when the second Ali cabinet repudiated a large sum of debts assumed under the agreement. But the result of these sales was rarely Indonesianization, because most of the buyers were Chinese. On the matter of the North Sumatran oil wells, whose status had long been an outstanding illustration of the government's ambivalence and division on the issue of the role of foreign capital, indecision continued to the end of our period, with production at little more than a trickle.

Administration as such continued to be beset by many problems. In some respects time was producing improved levels of administrative competence, as a result of the increase in trained men and the greater experience and self-confidence of those who had been in responsible posts for some years. But other factors were working in the opposite direction. One such was the growing number of civil servants, which meant that more and more effort had to be devoted to spreading the work load, lest morale suffer too greatly as a result of idleness. Another factor was the increasing importance of party conflict, particularly in the period of the first Ali cabinet and the cabinet of Burhanuddin Harahap, when a fully fledged system developed by which trained people who were unacceptable to a currently dominant party were "kicked upstairs." A third similar factor was increasing corruption and trading of favors, which resulted partly from accelerating inflation, partly from examples set at the level of cabinet, and partly from the effects of machine politics in undermining the norms of impersonal administration. Finally, it has been argued that the very effluxion of time had negative effects on administrative efficiency in that the rules and standards of performance set by the Dutch and adopted by many of the Indonesians who had worked under them were adhered to less and less as 1949 receded into the past.

In broad terms, however, administration was carried out reasonably effectively in the 1953–1957 period. It was relatively ineffective where it was launching into fresh fields, establishing new factories or licensing schemes, or adapting taxation practices to new conditions. But routine administration, with which the greatest part of government activity was concerned, in general ran fairly well.

There was one notable source of danger, and this lay in the government's heavy reliance on the politically exposed *pamong pradja* corps. It was the *pamong pradja,* this corps of general territorial administrators which had been highly professionalized in the prewar period, that provided the country's most efficient administrative service. It played a role of major importance in knitting together the otherwise ramshackle structure of government in the regions. And it was certainly an effective instrument of central government control and policy implementation in regional and local situations.[33] But the *pamong pradja* was under more or less constant political attack in our period, as a colonial-type instrument and as a major obstacle in the path of regional autonomy and a more democratic pattern of regional and local government. Most of the parties and many in the regionalist movements were opposed to its influence. Indeed, it was clear that any important stride toward regional autonomy, whether at the provincial or regency level and whether in Java or outside Java, would involve reducing the *pamong pradja's* influence. This in fact is a major reason why little was done about regional autonomy before the fall of the second Ali cabinet. Successive cabinets were loath to lessen the influence of this efficient and politically unambitious administrative service.

There was little development of regional autonomy in the whole of the 1949–1957 period. The existing province, *kabupaten,* and municipality councils were very weak indeed, because of the meager powers formally transferred to them, their tiny budget allocations, and the close financial controls which the *pamong pradja* corps exercised over them. Thus neither the interim legislative and executive councils established (in some provinces, *kabupatens,* and municipalities) on the basis of the controversial Regulation 39 of 1950 nor the "transitional" councils established in 1956 on the basis of the 1955 election results enjoyed an important degree of power—despite the fact that

[33] For a full discussion see Donald Fagg, "Authority and Social Structure: A Study in Javanese Bureaucracy" (doctoral dissertation, Harvard University, 1958), pp. 210 ff. A brief and most interesting description of the *pamong pradja's* work is contained in Compton, "Indonesia, 1955."

many important local party leaders were represented on these various councils.[34] This absence of autonomy had important administrative advantages. But it also meant that regions far from Djakarta, and some not so far, had long periods of waiting before they could get authorizations for their projects. Most important were the political risks involved: with the *pamong pradja* under fire from so many parties and powerful regional interests, it was in danger of being legislated out of existence, the administrative consequences notwithstanding. This, in fact, is what was attempted in Law no. 1 of 1957, the basic law on regional government enacted in the last months of the second Ali cabinet.[35]

As far as internal security was concerned, the 1953–1957 period was one of near-stalemate. The volume of active banditry in a region like West Java or South Sulawesi would sometimes rise for several months and then fall again for a similar length of time. The army would occasionally succeed in driving bands out of a particular area, with the usual consequence that they established themselves elsewhere. Now and again a large number of band members would surrender on amnesty terms or on the basis of an agreement for their incorporation into the army or its reserve organizations. But the terms of these agreements were usually risky for the government. It was frequently obliged to allow the surrendering leaders to keep their followings organizationally intact, and therefore the possibility of renewed rebellion remained. This was sometimes realized, with groups of "rehabilitated" guerrillas returning to the mountains. It was a case of "plus ça change, plus c'est la même chose." Although several attempts were made to recapture the momentum which the government and army had had in their security drives of 1950 and 1951, none were markedly successful. As far as one can see from the large volume of contradictory evidence on the subject, there were no major increases or decreases either in the over-all volume of rebel and bandit activity or in the amount of territory effectively controlled by the government.[36]

[34] See Gerald S. Maryanov, *Decentralization in Indonesia: Legislative Aspects* (Cornell Modern Indonesia Project, Interim Reports Series; Ithaca, N.Y., 1957), pp. 20–22, and John D. Legge, *Central Authority and Regional Autonomy in Indonesia* (Ithaca, N.Y.: Cornell University Press, 1961), pp. 21–52, 154 ff.

[35] This law had been only partly implemented when its effects were undone by Presidential Decree no. 6 of 1959, which re-established the *pamong pradja's* strength.

[36] This picture of near-stalemate is confirmed by the available statistics for West Java. The figures collected by *Antara* without attribution to any particular government agency, and possibly very inaccurate, are as follows:

In most areas of problem-solving policy where immediate deprivational consequences were involved for particular social groups, the cabinets of the 1953–1957 period were cautious almost to the point of paralysis. Thus little was done to reduce the size of the bureaucracy or even "hold the line." The first Ali cabinet decreed a compulsory retiring age of 55 for all civil servants other than those declared "indispensable." The second Ali cabinet began to make plans for a large-scale reduction in civil service numbers, but it did not implement them. Although the available statistics are scrappy, it seems that the service grew at roughly the same speed between 1953 and 1957 as it had in the previous years, something like 10 per cent per year.[37]

In the field of army reorganization there was a similar avoidance of tasks whose implementation would arouse intense hostility in one or another group. Thus there were no mass retirements and few further moves toward creating a younger army or preparing for compulsory military training. Where men were retired from the army, they were given generous pensions. Therefore only a small part of the military budget was devoted to the acquisition of capital goods and weapons supplies. There was probably some decline in the power of *bapakist* commanders at the lower levels, but at the territorial level personal ties to particular commanders remained strong. No changes were made at this level between late 1952 and the middle of 1956, and when Major General Nasution made his comprehensive series of transfers in 1956, he was obliged to make greater concessions to demands for "native sons" than he had in 1949–1952.

Moreover, the three cabinets were generally unsuccessful in dealing with squatting, whether on estate lands, in forests, or in cities. Each of the cabinets acted at times to evict squatters and sometimes to arrest

	Killings	Kidnapings	Torturings	Houses burned down	Estimated damage
1953	2,473	1,114	465	15,175	Rp. 41,718,438
1956	2,212	712	185	63,084	Rp. 62,285,348

See *Antara*, Jan. 21, 1959 (which gives full statistics for 1953 to 1957 and provisional statistics for 1958); cf. *Antara*, April, 1953 (which gives comparable statistics for 1952 and also for West Java only), and *Antara*, Oct. 5, 1954 (which gives comparable statistics for the years 1950 to 1953 for the residency of Priangan in West Java). See also A. H. Nasution, *Tjatatan-Tjatatan Sekitar Politik Militer Indonesia* ("Notes on Indonesian Military Policy"; Djakarta: Pembimbing, 1955), pp. 91–92.

[37] See Biro Pusat Statistik, *Statistical Pocketbook of Indonesia*, 1960, p. 237; *Nieuwsgier*, July 27, 1954, quoted in *Cultureel Nieuws* ("Cultural News"; Amsterdam), no. 40 (1955), p. 102; and *Pos Indonesia* (Djakarta), Oct. 2, 1958.

them. But none of them was capable of bringing sustained pressure to bear on this problem on a scale sufficient to halt the flow. A commission of inquiry established by the Estates Division of the Ministry of Agriculture in mid-1957 found squatters occupying 220,000 hectares of estate land in Java and Sumatra, or 31.4 per cent of the total cultivated estate area of these two islands.[38]

Thus in a number of fields where their policies called for strong measures, the cabinets of the 1953–1957 period were demonstrably weaker than their predecessors. It is not only that they were less concerned to solve problems of administrative and economic maintenance and development, but also that they were forced to stop short of consistent policy making and enforcement in the face of strong sectional resistance.

These three cabinets were therefore more and more inclined to adopt the posture of *menampong*, literally of accommodation, incorporation, and channeling off, the posture of meeting challenges by buying off the hostility of the challengers. The clearest instance of this came in the unfolding of the regionalist challenge, where one act of governmental tolerance led to a larger act of regional defiance, bringing about a spiraling effect. Thus Djakarta's authority vis-à-vis the exporting regions suffered a progressive decline—from Colonel Warouw's unpunished smuggling of September 1954 to the seizure of the Copra Foundation's assets in Minahasa in February 1955, the wave of army-organized smuggling in Sulawesi and Sumatra in May, June, and July 1956, and the seizure of power by the various regional councils in December 1956 and March 1957.

The underlying causes of cabinet weakness were for the most part the same as in the first half of our period, but with several additional factors aggravating the problem. Governments were again caught in a scramble for power from which no aspect of governmental functioning could gain autonomy. The bureaucracy was again a mediating instrument, and by the same token a force for immobilization of active government.

One major new factor was the greater importance of ideological antagonisms, a result of the election campaign. Electioneering, in fact, gave rise to a circular effect: party leaders had to emphasize their ideological positions to appeal to communal segments of the electorate. But by doing so they aggravated the divisions between these segments.

[38] See *Warta Ekonomi* (periodical of the Ministry of Economic Affairs), vol. II, no. 47–48 (Nov. 29, 1958).

And these ideologically reinforced divisions in society at large then sustained the newly sharpened cleavages in the political elite. Members of this elite became more and more closely bound to their party and ideological supporters and thus felt less sense of common fate with their fellow members of the political elite who were of other parties. Leaders of the government and opposition behaved with less restraint in their relations with one another.

Opposition leaders were thus prepared to be more active in foiling the execution of controversial government policies. Some of them provided the resisters to these policies with protection. Others achieved a similar effect by providing ideological ammunition such as undermined the government's authority. One common pattern was: "We are Masjumi, and we don't like Prime Minister Ali because he is against Islam. So we won't help the government on this scheme for low-price purchasing of rice." Or alternatively: "I am PNI. Why should I carry out Prime Minister Burhanuddin Harahap's instruction about not employing new people in government offices? He only makes a rule like that to hit the PNI as the party of most of the civil servants."

Secondly, cabinets were weaker in this second period than in the first because certain interests became more organized than theretofore. This is especially clear in the case of the exporting interests in particular areas, notably the areas of East Indonesia and certain of the small holders' rubber areas of Sumatra, notably those with ethnic cohesion. Using organization, these interests became increasingly active in the 1953–1957 period in protest against the current governments' distribution of economic rewards. Some members of the political elite therefore attached themselves more to these protesting groups than to the cabinet of the day (or, after the elections, their parties).

Thirdly, cabinets were in some respects weakened by changes in the pattern of military-civilian relations. The earlier cabinets, as we noted, worked rather closely with the central leaders of the army, the "administrator" group of Simatupang and Nasution. Thus the central army leaders supported these cabinets in their effort to rid the army of localist power and incipient warlordism, while the cabinets accepted the right of these central army leaders to an extensive informal say in political matters in Djakarta—and also gave them an important share of the then fairly abundant supplies of material resources.

But this pattern of co-operation was destroyed by the crisis of October 17, 1952. As a result of this crisis, "administrator" influence in the army's central leadership was sharply reduced, the central leadership as such was much weakened, and the locus of power shifted to two rival groups of territorial commanders. With the army thus deeply divided, the civilian politicians of the capital gained a new ascendancy over their military counterparts, and the volume of material resources accruing to the army was reduced—at a time when material resources were generally in short supply. But the army did not readily accept its position of diminished power. On the contrary, an increasingly active sense of grievance developed within the officer corps. By the time the army had restored its own cohesion in 1955 its leaders were more actively hostile to civilian politicians than ever before, and some were determined to take action to destroy their dominance. According to our earlier terminology, it may be said that the army was less fully a part of the political executive in the 1953–1957 period than it had been before October 1952. It was thus more difficult for the cabinets of this later period to use army power to impose deprivational policies.

Finally, and perhaps most fundamentally, the weakness of these later cabinets stemmed from their shortage of disposable rewards. In this respect the cabinets of the 1953–1957 period were particularly handicapped, because they had no large supply of partonage to distribute, such as the earlier cabinets had had because of an initial inheritance of both material goods and prestige positions in December 1949 and later because of the Korean War boom. Moreover, the number of material rewards and prestige roles which government was expected to provide did not decrease. The earlier cabinets had borne the brunt of the problem of absorbing those uprooted by the Revolution, but the later cabinets had to cope with the constantly expanding number of persons demanding the opportunity to live life in a modern "national" way, to go to high school and then to the university, to become a civil servant or an organizational leader, to own a bicycle or a car, a wrist watch or a camera, or a shelfful of books. In sum, then, these cabinets were almost as poorly equipped to reward as to punish.

LEGITIMACY AND CONSTITUTIONAL DEMOCRACY, 1953–1957

The development of an impasse in various aspects of problem-solving policy, along with the growing immobilization of cabinets in the face of various political pressures, represents one aspect of the malfunctioning of the political system which led eventually to its disintegration and transformation. But equally important was the system's inadequacy with regard to legitimacy and social cohesion.

When one comes to review the legitimizing activities of the cabinets of the 1953–1957 period, comparing them with those of the previous years, the contrasts appear more significant than the similarities. What these later cabinets did to heighten the sense of Indonesian nationality in the population at large was not greatly different from what their predecessors had done. Many of the same themes were stressed when the Information Ministry's representatives spoke to the village population. But in relation to the members of the political public, and some at the perimeter of this public, the approach of the later cabinets was very different from that of the earlier ones.

Whereas the Hatta, Natsir, Sukiman, and Wilopo cabinets had been concerned to legitimize a whole regime, this was less true of the later cabinets—with the partial exception of the second cabinet of Ali, which took the brunt of the attack on parliamentary democracy and thus had to defend this system in order to defend itself. In general, the legitimizing activities of these later three cabinets were direct attempts to establish the moral validity of rule by themselves as cabinets. To the extent that they attempted to gain authority for a regime as such, their claims were for a nationalist rather than a constitutional democratic regime. They certainly made few attempts to identify the existing constitutional system with democracy and the goals for which the Revolution had been fought. And whereas the earlier cabinets had made sustained efforts to have rules adhered to in political competition, occasionally handicapping themselves as a result, their successors were relatively unconcerned about this. Nor did they devote resources to developing the critical interest of the political public in specific political and economic issues, to countering the disposition of this public to accept panacea solutions in politics, or to combating the antiforeign feeling which existed in its ranks.

In fact, these cabinets, with the partial exception of the Burhanuddin Harahap cabinet, did little to encourage the influence of the "generally interested," those in the political public who participated in politics but did not depend on it for the security of their personal values. Consequently some who had previously been members of this "generally interested" group, and as such had supported the "administrators," now felt themselves debarred from political life and became apathetic, or more frequently cynical, about it. In this way a number of former Republicans came to join the old BFO supporters as alienated members of the political public.

The later cabinets were generally more concerned with those whose political participation was expressive, whose responses were to symbols and images rather than to assessed performance. They concerned themselves more actively than their predecessors with foreign policy activities and adopted a more militant and assertive attitude in relation to the world outside. At the same time they associated themselves prominently with radical positions in the struggle for West Irian. But they could not compete with the parties, or in the case of the second Ali cabinet with the various new political movements, in attracting those who sought to participate in a personally integrative form of politics. Indeed, they scarcely tried to compete. Thus the amount of governmental manipulation of expressive political activities was much smaller than it became after 1957. It was nevertheless markedly greater than it had been before 1953.

It was not, however, what cabinets did that was of greatest importance in changing the legitimacy system in the years between 1953 and 1957. The most important influence was the long campaign which preceded the 1955 election.

This was indeed no ordinary election. It was rather a climactic effort to resolve the hitherto insoluble political conflicts, to arrive definitively at an over-all top-level settlement of the many rival claims which for so long had given politics the characteristics of a scramble. An over-all settlement was of crucial importance because government as such was so important in Indonesia, as both the chief disburser of rewards and values for groups and the foremost means of social mobility for individuals. It was important too because so much of governmental activity had become dependent on the shifting tides of top-level politics, with virtually no government agency being specific and autonomous enough in its functions to enable it to work undisturbed. Thus enormous resources were thrown into the electoral cauldron.

Electioneering, as pointed out earlier, increased the amount of value conflict in society. Particular parties became the primary objects of loyalty, because they succeeded in devising ideological formulations which accorded with existing value and cognitive notions in communal segments of the population. Moreover, the pattern of party alignments corresponded increasingly with the deepest of communal cleavages in Indonesian society, that between the "Javanese-aristocratic political culture" and the "Islamic-entrepreneurial political culture."

Hence value attachment to the state as such lost much of its intensity. The Pantja Sila and almost every other symbol of state became in some measure partisan property. The Dwitunggal or Duumvirate was split, with Soekarno and Hatta taking sharply opposing stands on a number of important issues. The volume of shared values declined, and the arbiters of political competition themselves became involved in it. Thus the readiness to accept a common set of political rules grew less. The fact was highlighted by the two jarring ceremonial fiascos of 1955, the boycotted installation of Colonel Bambang Utojo as Army Chief of Staff and the disrupted attempt to install Vice-Commodore Sujono as Deputy Chief of Staff of the Air Force.

By the time the three-year election period ended the problem of consensus and legitimacy had reached a critical stage. For many, state authority was now little more than the will of particular parties. A great number of persons in the political public and outside it no longer saw validity in government by leaders of parties and party blocs to which they were opposed.

Into this situation there now came an onrush of people who sought to participate in a personally integrative form of politics; these were the people who had been active in the political parties and for whom the parties now no longer had satisfying roles. Released from the institutional channeling which had previously been provided by the parties, these persons now created a series of political explosions. Movement-type politics and moblike collective behavior appeared in many areas of social tension. Political unrest seemed to be rising, just when government authority was at an ebb. To many in the political elite civil order and the cohesion of the state seemed threatened. Anarchy, territorial disintegration, civil war, foreign intervention—each of these appeared on the horizon of possibility for some members of the political elite, and so did Communist take-over. It was in these circumstances that different groups of the army were emboldened to step directly into the political arena and that President Soekarno came forward with his *konsepsi*.

Looking at the functioning of constitutional democracy in the 1953–1957 period, one sees further aspects of the crumbling of the prevailing system of government and politics. It was not that there were major changes in the operation of parliament or the breadth of civil liberties as compared with the period before 1953; the situation in these respects was in fact largely the same as then. Parliament continued to be an important forum and channel for the communication of ideas and a secondary but nevertheless important instrument for the articulation of demands. Its freedom was unimpaired, and it remained a central part of the machinery of political authority. There were more governmental demands for uncritical loyalty than in the earlier years, but little direct coercion. Only on one or two occasions at the very end of the 1953–1957 period were goon squads allowed to intimidate opposition leaders. Moreover, there was no increase in the over-all volume of violence in urban society as compared with the earlier period, and perhaps some decline.

Similarly there was no major change in freedom of the press. The dichotomization of politics was indeed reflected in the press; and newspapers generally became party organs to a greater extent than before. Furthermore, there was an increase in the degree to which cabinets assisted the dailies supporting them and placed obstacles in the way of those opposing them. Papers that supported a particular cabinet would usually receive bulk orders from government offices. They might obtain credit with which to buy their own presses. And they were favored when it came to distributing invitations for journalists to travel overseas with government delegations. Opposition dailies, on the other hand, might have their journalists called to the office of the Attorney General for frequent interrogations. Or they might, very occasionally, be forced to cease publication for a few days. One result of all this was that numerous new papers which were started during the period of the Ali and Burhanuddin cabinets did not long survive the fall of the respective cabinets. At the same time there continued to be unpunished cases of vandalism directed against newspaper offices and of mistreatment of journalists. But none of this stopped opposition groups from making themselves heard. Financially strong papers could survive being part of the opposition, and there was no diminution in the sharpness or irreverence with which they criticized governments or indeed the President. The associations of journalists and newspaper publishers were very vigilant in this period, protesting vigorously whenever press rights were infringed.

Numerous public liberties continued to exist, but forces were at work removing the conditions which made their enjoyment possible. The cabinets of 1953–1957 were led by men who had less strong value commitments to constitutional democracy than those in power in the earlier years. Moreover, these men, unlike their predecessors, placed little store by the notion that the outside world expected Indonesia to be a Western-style democracy. The leaders of the earlier cabinets had tended to see Indonesia as a young country with formidable internal problems to solve, a country which had to prove itself before the world—and by this they meant the Western world and India. Those who led the later cabinets saw Indonesia more as a leader of the Asian renascence, a country which had no need to keep up with the standards that others set for themselves and thus no need to follow Western political models.

In part this change reflected the diminution of "administrator" power. In an earlier chapter we noted how constitutional democracy was able to serve the interests of the "administrator" group as such, in that it helped to legitimize a program of consolidation and regularization of the postrevolutionary situation—and thus a regime in which modern-type economic and administrative skills could be employed in effective and prestige-conferring ways. "Administrators" continued to hold important cabinet posts after 1953, but many of them were heavily dependent on "solidarity makers" within their respective parties. The "administrator" group as a whole was far less influential than before 1953. "Solidarity maker" influence grew correspondingly.

The years after 1953 also saw further growth in the influence of forces which could either initiate an abandonment of constitutional democracy or provoke others to do the same in order to forestall them. Thus the army grew more independent of civilian leadership in these years and more determined to play an open political role itself. One important factor contributing to this determination was the rising power of the PKI and the PKI's evident organizational superiority over all other parties. And signs that the officers were growing impatient with the existing order stimulated the President to prepare himself to participate in effecting a change. There was in fact a widespread expectation that the system of parties and parliament would have to be abandoned or changed in important ways, and this strengthened a number of groups with prospects of surviving and becoming influential in the new or changed system that would follow.

Finally, this 1953–1957 period saw an important deepening of divisions within the political elite. Owing in part to electioneering, in part to a rising volume of unsatisfied demands from various segments of society, and in part to the simple passage of time which made the common struggle of the Jogjakarta years recede further into the past, political leaders grew increasingly embittered with one another. Moreover, cleavages were more rigid than before 1953; there was little variation after that year in the situation in which Soekarno was one of two principal magnets of civilian politics and Natsir the other. With political antagonisms increasingly personal, little remained of the earlier situation where even the most sharply exacerbated political conflicts could often be compromised, because of the personal ties and sense of common interest which existed in the political elite. Constitutional democracy, operating as a set of "club rules" of reciprocal restraint in political behavior, was increasingly resented as leaders grew less and less prepared to be restrained in their actions toward their foes.

In fact, then, the years between 1953 and 1957 saw both a decline in the influence of those who supported constitutional democracy and an attenuation of the functions which constitutional democracy was able to fulfill for the political system as a whole.

EPILOGUE: ONWARD TO "GUIDED DEMOCRACY"

The fall of the second cabinet of Mr. Ali Sastroamidjojo was only one in a series of developments marking the abandonment of the 1949–1957 system of government and politics. One may describe it as a midway point in a period of rapid political change which lasted roughly from the middle of 1956 to the middle of 1958. Before mid-1956 and again after mid-1958 political events formed a pattern; the participants and close observers could predict the immediate future with some degree of accuracy. But this was not the case in the intervening two years. This was a period of structural transition; the feeling that "anything could happen now" pervaded the minds of even the most centrally placed political figures. Let us then look briefly first at the rapids through which politics passed in the fifteen months after March 1957 and then at the bed in which the stream subsequently flowed.

The cabinet crisis of March to April 1957 bore several new features, most of them connected with the role of the army. With the proclamation of a nationwide State of War and Siege, a legal basis was given to the exercise of civil powers by the regionalist regimes, or at least by their chairmen, the respective commanders of military districts; in this way some of the immediacy was taken out of the challenge to Djakarta. At the same time the power of the central army leaders was increased, as was that of the three territorial commanders in Java. There followed a regional commanders' conference which concerned itself directly with the character of the new cabinet to be formed, and here again Major General Nasution and his associates were able to play a crucial mediating role. As it was this group which had provided the formula for the old cabinet's dissolution, so they were able now to mute the regionalist commanders' demands in exchange for equivalent concessions from President Soekarno. They were in fact highly influential in setting the terms on which a successor cabinet would be established, terms which lay midway between the regionalists' solution of a Hatta-led presidential cabinet and President Soekarno's *konsepsi* of February 21.

One further new feature of this cabinet crisis was a statement by the Communist-led labor federation SOBSI threatening a general strike if a cabinet took office in which the Masjumi was represented and the PKI was not. This threat was accompanied by an actual 24-hour general strike of SOBSI unionists in South Sumatra which protested the freezing of the provincial legislative council by Lieutenant Colonel Barlian. The two actions stand in strong contrast to the PKI's usual disinclination to put its political strength to the test.[39]

But in other ways this was just another cabinet crisis, the preceding political thunder notwithstanding. Thus President Soekarno's first nominee for the *formateur*-ship was Suwirjo, the newly elected chairman of the PNI. (Sidik Djojosukarto had died in September 1955, a victim of the hectic last weeks of campaigning which had preceded the parliamentary elections.) Suwirjo negotiated with party leaders in much the old way, failed to form a cabinet, was given a renewed mandate to form a business cabinet, again failed, largely because the NU refused to work in a team from which the Masjumi was excluded, and finally returned his mandate on April 2.

The cabinet crisis entered its final stage two days later when President Soekarno appointed himself, as "Citizen Soekarno," to form an "emergency, extraparliamentary business cabinet." On April 8 he was able to announce the names of a new cabinet, to be headed by the widely respected nonparty leader and veteran cabinet minister, Djuanda.[40] The members of this new cabinet were specifically chosen as individuals and not as party representatives, and the list included a number of men with high technical and professional qualifications. Most, however, were members of parties, four being from the PNI, four from the NU (which initially expressed misgivings about the

[39] Donald Hindley, "The Communist Party of Indonesia, 1951–1961: A Decade of the Aidit Leadership" (doctoral dissertation, Australian National University, 1961), p. 560.

[40] For a list of the cabinet's membership see *Antara*, April 9, 1957.

cabinet but did not punish those of its members who accepted seats in it), one from the Christian Party, Parkindo, and one from the PSII. The one Masjumi member included was expelled from his party immediately after being sworn in. Among those belonging to no party were two sympathizers of the Partai Murba and two of the PKI. In political color this resembled the first cabinet of Ali Sastroamidjojo. It was also not very different from the second Ali cabinet in its last two months, after Masjumi, IPKI, and Perti had withdrawn their representatives—apart from the inclusion of the PKI- and Murba-sympathizing ministers.

One of the cabinet's earliest actions was to set up the National Council called for by the President's *konsepsi*. The Council was established by emergency law in May, and on July 11 the President named 42 men and women who would sit on it under his chairmanship: one Deputy Prime Minister, the three service chiefs, the police head, and the chief public prosecutor, as well as various men appointed to represent workers, peasants, youth, veterans, national entrepreneurs, artists, journalists, women, the 1945 generation, Indonesian citizens of foreign origin, the various religious groups, and the various regions.[41] As the Djuanda cabinet saw it, the Council was no more than a body empowered to give it advice. The Prime Minister affirmed that there had been no basic change in constitutional dynamics when he told parliament that the cabinet continued to be responsible to it. But the National Council's prestige was high. And as it had been established on the advice of the President (who had argued for it as part of an over-all transformation of the liberal parliamentary system), many believed it weakened the constitutional status of cabinet and parliament.

Although a variety of political positions were represented in the Council, it was effectively dominated by the President.[42] It therefore legitimized his greatly increased powers and formed a new vehicle for their exercise. In this sense the National Council served functions for President Soekarno somewhat similar to those which the State of War and Siege proclamation served for the army leaders around Major General Nasution. Each in its own way marked the end of cabinet government in the usual sense. Not only was the cabinet no longer the domi-

[41] For the membership of the Council see *Dewan Nasional* ("The National Council"; Djakarta: Kementerian Penerangan, 1957), pp. 15–17.

[42] For a full discussion of the operation of the Council by its deputy chairman and secretary-general see Roeslan Abdulgani, "Indonesia's National Council: The First Year," *Far Eastern Survey*, XXVII (July 1958), 97–104.

nant center of governmental power—indeed, it was little more than a broker of governmental forces, standing between the President, the central army leadership, and, a few paces away, the regionalist military commanders. In addition, its claims to a *formal* monopoly of governmental power were no longer accepted.

The period between April and November 1957 was marked by a long and many-faceted tug of war between Djakarta and the regionalist-controlled areas. In some respects relations between Djakarta on the one hand and Padang, Palembang, and Makassar remained normal; much of government business in the areas under regionalist control stayed unaffected by the political rupture. But the sense of tension and uneasiness was widespread in the political public of all areas, and the possibilities of ethnic strife, separatism, civil war, and "another Spain" were frequently discussed.

Djakarta's approach to the dissident regional councils was sometimes hostile, as when it arrested civilian members of the councils, when it tried in March and April to "do a Gintings" in South Sumatra, instigating an abortive ouster of Lieutenant Colonel Barlian by an officer of his own command, and when it succeeded in June in dismissing Lieutenant Colonel Sumual from his East Indonesia command and splitting this command into four separate military districts. At other times, however, it was distinctly conciliatory, for instance, when it provided the dissident-controlled areas with large sums of money for their developmental projects, when it increased exporters' earnings by a new system of foreign exchange certificates—this was virtually devaluation to a floating rate of exchange [43]—and in July when it sent a high-level mission of four Minahasans to negotiate with Sumual (who had established a new Permesta council headquarters in Menado after he had been ousted from his command in Makassar). Occasionally its approach was hostile and conciliatory at the same time, this largely because of the many hands at the wheel, most prominently those of Soekarno, Nasution, and Djuanda.

For some weeks it would appear that Djakarta was gaining the upper hand in this struggle, that the councils could be split from one another or toppled one by one. Then the pendulum would swing the other way, with increasing co-operation between the councils and

[43] On this system, introduced in June 1957, see Bank Indonesia, *Report for the Year 1957–1958* (Djakarta, 1958), pp. 135–138, 254–257. See also Schmitt, *op. cit.*, pp. 241–249, and J. A. C. Mackie, "Indonesia: The Search for Stability," *Australia's Neighbours* (Australian Institute of International Affairs, Melbourne), 3d ser., nos. 87 and 88 (July and Aug. 1958).

with the likelihood that Djakarta would have to accept their demands for an over-all settlement on Hatta lines. But these were relatively small swings. There was no major change in relative strengths throughout the period.

There was, however, an over-all hardening of relationships. Each side thought that the stalemate would probably break down soon, and each was becoming increasingly attentive to those in its ranks who demanded that it reach for its ultimate weapons. Within the regionalist camp there was more and more pressure to deny Djakarta the foreign exchange earnings from locally produced rubber, tin, and oil; a great part of the foreign exchange concerned was in fact still at Djakarta's disposal.[44] There was pressure for more seeking of overseas support and for an open ideological confrontation with Djakarta on the issue of the Communist threat. In the capital there were demands for an all-out effort to bring the rebellious regional leaders to their knees, demands for denying them rupiah currency, for blockading their areas, and for military action against them if that proved necessary. Repeated instances of hand-grenade throwing in Djakarta—with Communists and other antiregionalists the chief targets—served to raise the general political temperature.

On the other hand, the prospects of a negotiated settlement grew somewhat as a result of the regional elections held in Java in June, July, and August. The Communist Party emerged from these elections as the island's strongest party, with 27.4 per cent of the total vote as compared with 20.6 per cent in September 1955, a rise of over two million votes, and with an increased vote in every single one of the 100 *kabupatens* and municipalities.[45] The immediate result was a drawing together of the three main non-Communist parties. To the leaders of the NU and most of the leaders of the PNI, the party which had lost the most votes in the regional elections, the Communists seemed a greater threat than the regionalists.

A major attempt to arrive at an over-all settlement between Djakarta and the dissident regions was made in September, when the results of the regional elections were still fresh in people's minds. Apparently as a result of Prime Minister Djuanda's initiative, a National Consultative Conference (Musjawarah Nasional) was held in Djakarta in

[44] Large-scale "barter trade" was conducted by several of the rebellious regions from May and June onward, but this still affected only a fraction of the total exports of these regions. For an estimate of its cost to the central government see Bank Indonesia, *Report for the Year 1957–1958*, p. 14.

[45] For further statistics and a full discussion see Hindley, *op. cit.*, pp. 469–478.

that month, with top-level representation from military and civilian leaders of every region, including those of the council regimes. The attempt was momentarily successful; for some weeks it seemed that the conciliatory elements in each camp had gained the upper hand and that some sort of compromise could be reached. There was hope particularly that the army-command-positions aspect of the conflict might be settled by a seven-man committee on military affairs established by the conference, a committee of which Hatta and the Sultan of Jogjakarta were members as well as Soekarno, Nasution, and Djuanda. Indeed, there might have been a settlement if there had not been a series of dramatic developments in late November and early December.

In November the UN General Assembly was due to discuss West Irian once more, and a group of pro-Indonesian states had tabled a motion which called for the Netherlands and Indonesia to negotiate a settlement of this issue. In October and November the Indonesian government launched a major nationwide campaign in favor of the Irian demand, and nationalist fervor reached a high pitch of intensity, spilling over into numerous acts of vandalism and intimidation of Dutch residents. At the same time government leaders made threatening declarations about the likely consequences of a further defeat of the Indonesian claim on this issue. In that event, the President declared on November 8, "we will use a new way in our struggle which will surprise the nations of the world."

The ballot was taken on November 29, and the pro-Indonesian motion failed to obtain a two-thirds majority. On the following day there was an attempt to assassinate President Soekarno. A group of youths, apparently followers of Colonel Zulkifli Lubis, threw hand grenades into a school bazaar crowd in which the President was standing. Eleven persons lost their lives in this fully organized affair. The President himself escaped narrowly.[46]

With this the political crisis reached a climax, and the initiative lay with President Soekarno. On December 2 there was a nationwide 24-hour strike, ordered by the cabinet as a demonstration against the Dutch position in West Irian. But matters did not stop there. On the following day workers of the central office of the Dutch shipping line KPM read a proclamation "taking over" the company, and the same thing happened at the offices of the Dutch trading company Geo.

[46] See R. Surjo Sediono (Major), *Peristiwa Tjikini* ("The Tjikini Affair"; Djakarta: Soeroengan, 1958), for the proceedings of the subsequent trial.

Wehry. The government responded with many voices. Djuanda declared that all actions in the West Irian struggle required prior authorization from the military. But the cabinet decided on December 5 that enterprises already taken over would thenceforth be controlled by the government. Justice Minister Maengkom declared that all Dutchmen who were not in employment must leave Indonesia and suggested that the departure of all except experts would be welcomed.

Thereupon the take-overs began to snowball, spreading into many parts of the country, with the government in less and less control of the situation until December 13, when Major General Nasution forbade any further take-over actions and decreed military control over all the enterprises seized. The Dutch government had earlier offered immediate repatriation to all of its approximately 46,000 citizens remaining in Indonesia, and these began to leave the country in large numbers in the second half of December. By this stage virtually all Dutch enterprises had been taken over. Prime Minister Djuanda declared that they would be returned as soon as the Netherlands agreed to a transfer of West Irian to Indonesia, but they were subsequently nationalized in February 1959.[47]

So the Gordian knot of Dutch capital was cut. The huge Dutch business establishment was no more. As often before when a radical symbolic action had been taken after frequent hesitations, the political public responded enthusiastically. Whatever the source of initiative for the take-over actions—the evidence is obscure here, although it is clear that a major role was played by Lieutenant Colonel Pamurahardjo, a Murba-oriented associate of President Soekarno—their effect was to strengthen the position of the President in Djakarta and the position of Djakarta vis-à-vis the regional councils.

Economically, the take-overs resulted in chaos. The banking system was severely jolted because of seizure of the Dutch banks, as was much of trading by the take-over of the large Dutch commercial establishments. Estate production fell markedly. But the biggest effect came in the field of shipping, for the captains of KPM ships on the seas were instructed to take their vessels to non-Indonesian ports. Indonesia was eventually obliged to allow all KPM vessels out of its ports, and the

[47] For a general discussion of the take-overs see Justus M. van der Kroef, "Disunited Indonesia," *Far Eastern Survey*, XXVII, no. 4 (April 1958), 49–63. The various decrees involved are discussed in Bank Indonesia, *Report for the Year 1957–1958*, pp. 203–204. See also Louis Fischer, *The Story of Indonesia* (New York: Harper, 1959), pp. 227–230, 300; also Leslie H. Palmier, *Indonesia and the Dutch* (London: Oxford University Press, 1962), pp. 99–108.

result was a loss of no less than 78 per cent of total tonnage for inter-insular shipping.[48]

As far as the regional contest was concerned, the take-overs seem to have had an exacerbating effect. To the leaders of the regional councils the shipping crisis was an additional stimulus to direct barter with the outside world. But the central government, its foreign exchange position increasingly precarious, intensified its efforts to stop all barter trading. A further aggravation of the conflict came from the departure from Djakarta of a number of prominent leaders of the Masjumi. These men, notably Natsir, Sjafruddin Prawiranegara, and Burhanuddin Harahap, left for Sumatra virtually as political refugees. All had been subjected to the sharpest of attacks in the government-supporting press, and some to insinuations that they had been involved in the attempted assassination. In several instances there had been goon-squad intimidation. With these three, two of them ex-prime ministers, and with Professor Sumitro Djojohadikusmo (who had fled Djakarta and a corruption investigation in the previous May) on the regionalist side, this cause now had the active support of a sizable segment of the country's political leadership as well as of the officer corps. Regionalist hostility to Djakarta grew more bitter late in the year when an arms-buying mission left Djakarta for Yugoslavia, Czechoslovakia, and Poland. (The central government had met with repeated delays in efforts it had been making since July to get Washington approval for a $420 million purchase of arms in the United States.[49])

On January 6, 1958, President Soekarno left the country for a six-week rest trip overseas, and his absence served as an incentive to the regionalist leaders to play their cards fast toward an over-all political transformation. In addition, there were rumors in Sumatra that Djakarta was planning military action against the regions, just as there were rumors in Djakarta that the regionalist leaders were treating with Western powers to get political, diplomatic, and military support from them for their struggle against Djakarta.

In January numerous meetings were held in Sumatra, with Lieutenant Colonels Husein, Barlian, and Sumual all attending as well as the more senior but commandless Colonels Lubis and Simbolon and, from the side of the civilian politicians, Sjafruddin, Natsir, Burhanuddin Harahap, and Sumitro. The meetings brought out sharp differences of political strategy, but eventually it was possible to arrive at

[48] Bank Indonesia, *Report for the Year 1957–1958*, p. 195.
[49] *PIA*, April 11, 1958.

agreement. On February 10, six days before the President was due to return home, Husein issued an ultimatum to the central government: unless there were a new cabinet in five days, a cabinet led by Hatta and/or the Sultan of Jogjakarta, a new government would be formed in Sumatra.

Djakarta's immediate response was to deal out dishonorable discharges to four of the officers involved. In other respects there were signs of a more conciliatory attitude, but Husein and his associates were not deterred. On February 15 the Revolutionary Government of the Republic of Indonesia (Pemerintah Revolusioner Republik Indonesia, PRRI) was proclaimed in Padang. Sjafruddin Prawiranegara was named Prime Minister, with a cabinet including men from various parts of Sumatra and Sulawesi as well as two from Java.[50] The counter-government's radio transmitters came out with resounding denunciations of Soekarno, guided democracy, and communism, but their positive appeals, for regional autonomy and a state truly based on faith in God, had a weaker ring.

Three related questions immediately dominated all political thinking: How large an area of Indonesia could this new government control? How much foreign support would it receive? And how would Djakarta respond to the challenge of its existence? It was immediately clear that the military commanders of Central Sumatra and North Sulawesi were fully behind the proclamation, and there were signs of support from Tapanuli. But no declarations of support came from the commanders in South Sulawesi, the Moluccas, or the Lesser Sunda Islands, none from those in Kalimantan or Atjeh, and, most important, only equivocal indications from Barlian in South Sumatra. Among those living outside PRRI-controlled areas only isolated individuals left to throw in their lot with the new government.

As for foreign support, there was some of this, but most of it was either covert or tentative. United States Secretary of State Dulles had implied a degree of sympathy with the Padang group when he had suggested to a press conference on February 11 that guided democracy might be unconstitutional and unsatisfactory to large segments of the population of Indonesia; and subsequent statements by U.S. government spokesmen struck a similar note. Equally important, PRRI army commanders were receiving very modern American arms, which could not have been bought without some measure of approval by the U.S. government. But no state, Western or otherwise, recog-

[50] For membership of the cabinet see van der Kroef, "Disunited Indonesia," p. 63.

nized the PRRI, even to the extent of according it belligerent status. No response came to Padang's appeal to overseas banks to freeze the funds of the central government. And Caltex oil, with its wells in Central Sumatra, continued to pay dollars to Djakarta.

The central government was clearly divided on how to respond. Many in Djakarta, thinking of the costly and long-deadlocked conflict with Darul Islam, believed a military solution to the challenge of Padang would require resources which the government could simply not muster. Some expected that many of Djakarta's officers and men would be unwilling to fight against their fellow Indonesians in Sumatra or Sulawesi. On the other hand, there was pressure for a radical and clear-cut solution; to many it seemed that there had been too much temporizing already.

When President Soekarno returned from overseas on February 16, he almost immediately conferred with Hatta. Then, however, the air force bombed towns in Central Sumatra and North Sulawesi, and Nasution declared that there could be no compromise with the rebels. But a certain amount of hope for a negotiated settlement remained, and when the President met Hatta for a second time on March 3, it seemed briefly that a Soekarno-Hatta government would be formed. Four days later, however, the army staged a landing at Bengkalis on the east coast of Central Sumatra, and therewith all hope of reconciliation disappeared. It was at this point that an aircraft carrier of the U.S. Seventh Fleet was sent to Singapore, and, with U.S. statements indicating that a threat was seen to American persons and property at the Caltex oil wells near Bengkalis, it appeared for some days that the United States might itself intervene in Sumatra.

This did not happen, however. On March 12 the important oil town of Pakan Baru was taken in a parachute action which met no resistance from PRRI soldiers on the spot, and the conclusion was drawn that the rebel leaders' men would not fight. Padang's fortunes rose on March 16 when the Medan airport and part of the city were taken by a force under the pro-PRRI officer, Major W. F. Nainggolan, siding against his commander, Lieutenant Colonel Djamin Gintings. But a day later Nainggolan was driven far out of the city. By the second half of March, Barlian and many others in and outside the country who had been watching which way the wind would blow were drawing closer to the central government's side.

On April 17 the government effected a landing at Padang itself, and two days later the city was taken, after virtually no fighting.

There was more resistance further north as the government's troops drove into the rebel-held area of Tapanuli, but none of it stopped the advance. The rebels were able to take the initiative briefly later in the month when their units from North Sulawesi staged landings in the Northern Moluccas, and unidentified planes started bombing raids on government troops and installations in various parts of Kalimantan and East Indonesia. But these were only short-lived setbacks for Djakarta. On May 4 its troops took Bukittinggi, the last large rebel-held town in Sumatra.

In the second week of June a landing was staged in North Sulawesi. There the rebel resistance was more determined than anywhere else, but by June 26 Menado had fallen to the government's troops. By the end of July the PRRI no longer controlled any major town, and the war had become one of guerrilla attrition. Some small towns remained in the countergovernment's hands, as did large rural areas in Sumatra and Northern Sulawesi, and there were occasional raids on other small towns and on villages and estates. Moreover, no major leader of the PRRI had either surrendered or been captured. The rebel radio continued its broadcasting, and its overseas representatives their publicity activities. But the challenge to Djakarta was henceforth scarcely greater than that of the Darul Islam. The government and its army had won a major victory, and done so in quicker time than most observers in or outside the country had predicted.[51]

With this victory, the picture of politics assumed an entirely new shape. In the first place, all who had associated themselves with the regionalist cause were discredited. This was true of the Masjumi, which refused to condemn those of its members who were active on the PRRI side, and of the PSI, which did condemn its members who had taken the part of the countergovernment. It was true of Hatta. And it applied to a sizable group of officers. Not only had the core group of regionalist leaders been removed from the political arena;

---

[51] The fullest account of these events is given in James Mossman, *Rebels in Paradise: Indonesia's Civil War* (London: Cape, 1961). See also Rudy Pirngadie, *Peristiwa P.R.R.I. Ditindjau dari Sedjarah TNI* ("The PRRI Affair in the Light of the History of the Indonesian Army"; Djakarta: Endang, 1958), and *Rebels without a Cause: The Permesta Affair* (Djakarta: New Nusantara Publishing Company, n.d. [1958?]); van der Kroef, "Disunited Indonesia," *loc. cit.*, and "Disunited Indonesia II," *Far Eastern Survey*, XXVII, no. 5 (May 1958), 73–80; Vishal Singh, "The Revolt in Indonesia in Retrospect," *Foreign Affairs Reports* (New Delhi), VIII, no. 1 (Jan. 1959), 1–11; and F. J. van Rootselaar, "Een Ontvoering in Noord-Celebes" ("A Kidnaping in North Sulawesi"), *De Groene Amsterdammer*, Jan. 10, 1960.

in addition, a sympathizer group had been virtually debarred from legitimate political participation.

Secondly, there had been rapid growth in the power of the army and its central leadership around Major General Nasution. This group of leaders had assumed an increasing number of political functions throughout 1957. It had initiated arrests of numerous allegedly corrupt politicians. Through a Veterans Legion and a Youth-Military Co-operation Body, it had begun to supervise the activities of veterans' and youth organizations of all political colors.[52] And it had issued decrees on a wide range of subjects—from Chinese schools to the investigation of dubiously acquired property—all on the basis of its martial law authority. With its intervention at the time of the take-over actions, it had acquired an immense amount of patronage, in the form of both prestige positions and opportunities for profit, and its power continued to grow as it distributed this. Then came the victory over the PRRI, which not only enhanced the army leadership's prestige greatly but also increased the power of the General Staff over the regional commanders. Once these commanders could no longer threaten to give their allegiance to Padang, they immediately became far more dependent on Djakarta. But the struggle with the PRRI was by no means over, and thus martial law was maintained. When the Djuanda cabinet was reshuffled in May 1958, Colonel Suprajogi became Minister of State for Economic Stabilization and the first regular army officer to sit in an Indonesian cabinet.[53]

Until about April 1958 the PKI had enjoyed a position of particular favor. For over a year there had been a number of signs of presidential indulgence toward the party. It had maintained a high rate of activity while other parties had become much more passive. It had been a vigorous ally of the central government in the struggle against the dissident councils and then against the PRRI. Its prestige had been raised by the willingness of Poland and Czechoslovakia to sell Indonesia arms after the United States had refused to sell these. (Agreements with these two Eastern European countries and Yugoslavia were announced in early April.) Its confidence grew when Western military support for the rebels came to light and top government leaders denounced Western powers, especially the United States, and

[52] See Rudy Pirngadie, "The Problems of the Government and the Army in Indonesia" (unpublished paper, Harvard University Center for International Affairs, 1960), pp. 89–97, and Guy J. Pauker, "The Role of Political Organizations in Indonesia," *Far Eastern Survey,* XXVII (Sept. 1958), 129–142.

[53] For the changes in the cabinet's composition see *Antara,* May 22, 1958.

Nationalist China. For a time, indeed, these leaders' statements suggested that the government might accept the offers of "volunteers" and similar help made from Peking and Moscow.

But with the PRRI challenge receding, the Communists lost much of their position of advantage. Djakarta no longer had need of their help against the rebels; it would clearly not need to invite Russian or Chinese volunteers. Moreover, the United States made vigorous attempts in mid-May to regain sympathy in the Indonesian capital. Presented with an Indonesian government request that he condemn outside intervention in the rebellion, Secretary Dulles on May 20 responded as requested. On the following day Washington agreed to release a small supply of arms for sale to Djakarta, as well as large new supplies of rice.

Coming when it did, the U.S. attempt at *rapprochement* drew an immediate favorable response, primarily in the form of words and actions directed against the PKI. On May 13 the PNI had declared that it would not join in a PKI-sponsored rally against foreign intervention because it was against foreign intervention "in whatever manifestation and from whatever side." On May 22 Soekarno went to lunch at the home of the U.S. ambassador, an action almost without precedent. Earlier the army had issued a warning against molestation of foreigners and threats to their property. It had placed restrictions on May Day celebrations and prevented the departure of a youth delegation to see May Day in Peking. Its increasingly active policy of press control, its arrests of journalists and temporary bans on their papers, had been applied to Communist-sympathizing publications as well as to those supporting the Masjumi and PSI. Indeed, so strong was the new determination of governmental groups to draw away from Communist positions that the new atmosphere was not greatly disturbed even by the announcement on May 27 that Indonesia had shot down an American and former U.S. air force officer, A. L. Pope, who was piloting a B-25 bomber in a PRRI raid on Ambon. On August 13 the United States agreed to sell large quantities of arms to the government, for rupiahs.

Clearly, however, there were groups with government influence which saw themselves threatened by too strong a policy of anticommunism. It was the army groups around Nasution which led in implementing the anti-Communist policy, and others soon came to feel that its further prosecution would result in an excessively great concentration of power in the hands of these groups. Fears of military dictatorship were frequently expressed, and large numbers of civilians resented the new power, prestige, and wealth which had accrued to both officers and men in the previous six months. The army's new position was a threat particularly to President Soekarno. Thus, while the President had associated himself with the "forgive America" policies of May and June 1958, he exerted vigorous and largely effective pressure in the subsequent months to prevent the pendulum from swinging too far in a pro-American and anti-Communist direction.

This, in fact, was a principal mechanism of politics in the three years after mid-1958: President Soekarno and the army leadership under Major General (subsequently Lieutenant General and later General) Nasution were the principal power elements in government. There was close co-operation between them on a large number of matters, a good deal of complementarity of functions, and some division of governmental areas into spheres of influence of one or another partner. But the two remained fairly sharply distinct, and there was considerable competition and conflict between them. It was in many ways a tug-of-war relationship, and central to the whole pattern of political alignments in this three-year period.

President Soekarno had power as the chief legitimator of government. His importance in this respect had grown as rules and order had been upset, as parties and parliament had lost their legitimacy, and as the claim of the regionalist leaders to political authority had been destroyed through military defeat. Furthermore, the President succeeded in maintaining himself as the nation's chief seeker for and discerner of ideological truth. But this was not much to pit against the army's resources of organization and the means of violence.

Soekarno continued to lack a political organization of his own. In order to maximize his influence vis-à-vis the army, therefore, he needed to find support from political groups hostile to the army. He found some of this from the political parties, particularly the PNI. But, with the ideological themes of guided democracy receiving more and more stress and with condemnations of the old "liberal" democracy issuing from almost every organ of mass communications, most of the parties lacked both prestige and *élan*. There was support for the President from groups and individuals of radical nationalist orientation, some of them within the Murba circle, and a certain amount of backing from the civilian bureaucracy, which resented the army's intrusions into its spheres of operation. Furthermore, some top leaders of the air force supported the President against the Army Chief of Staff.

But it was the PKI which provided Soekarno with his best organized, most vociferous, and most reliable body of support against the army leaders. Hence it was that the President repeatedly shielded the PKI against efforts of Nasution and his associates to reduce its power. Soekarno needed Aidit to bolster his position against Nasution, just as Aidit needed Soekarno to protect his party against the ever-present possibility of army repression. Thus for the three years to mid-1961 the Communists were a principal focus of conflict between the President and the army leaders. Turbulent and eventful as these three years were, they brought little or no change in this basic pattern of political alignments established in mid-1958.

It was not only in the matter of alignments, however, that mid-1958 was a watershed. It was that also as regards political functioning. By then the system of politics we have discussed in this book was no more; the principal features of the 1949–1957 system had been undone. Moreover, the stage of structural transition was at an end. The extreme unpredictability of the two years since mid-1956 had given way to more clearly patterned interaction, to what may be called a system.

What, then, were the determinants of the post-mid-1958 system? For the sake of convenience we shall refer to this new system as guided democracy, using the name of its dominant governmental symbol. But the question is one of description, not merely of naming. What are the characteristics of this political system which grew out of the disintegration and abandonment of the one with which this study has been concerned?

One notable new feature was that parliamentary institutions were largely peripheral to politics, not only to the making of decisions, but also to their legitimation. The parliament elected in 1955 was deprived of much of its authority and many of its functions, partly by martial law conferences of army commanders and partly by such large new consultative bodies as the National Council (subsequently transformed into the Supreme Advisory Council), the National Planning Council, and the Interim People's Consultative Council. The elected Constituent Assembly was dissolved in July 1959 after it had failed to give a two-thirds majority to a government proposal to reintroduce the constitution of 1945, and this constitution was then re-enacted by presidential decree. As this was a permanent constitution and embodied the Pantja Sila, an end was put, by fiat as it were, to the long-debated issues of Pantja Sila versus Islamic State. Under the new constitution President Soekarno assumed the Prime Minister-ship, with Ir. Djuanda the First Minister and Nasution the Minister of National Security. In March 1960 the elected parliament was dissolved by decree, to be replaced some months later by a new, appointed *gotong rojong* (mutual help) parliament. Elections, though still prom-ised, were repeatedly postponed.

Parties were severely restricted in their activities and were subjected to a great variety of army-implemented controls. Party-sponsored pub-lic meetings became rare. Senior civil servants were debarred from the holding of party membership from 1959, and every party was obliged to submit a list of its members in the following year. In that year a National Front was established which took over some of the parties' functions. The Masjumi and PSI were banned in August 1960, and in April 1961 dissolution was ordered of all except ten parties (PNI, Nahdatul Ulama, PKI, Murba, the two Christian parties, PSII, Perti, IPKI, and Partai Indonesia or Partindo, which had splintered off from the PNI in 1958). Subsequently disbandment orders went out to a number of internationally linked organizations said to be out of con-formity with the Indonesian national personality (including the Free-masons, the Rosicrucians, and Moral Rearmament), and Boy Scout groups were unified under government control.

The effects of the change were great, too, in the field of civil liber-ties. Political arrests were made more frequently and more arbitrarily, though still not in large numbers, and legal guarantees carried much less weight than before. The press was subjected to severe controls— arrests of journalists, temporary bans of papers and in some cases permanent bans, and the seizure of printing establishments. Although implemented differently in different military commands, these con-trols usually hit the Masjumi and PSI-sympathizing press hardest, with the Communist-sympathizing press dealt occasional blows. At the same time narrow loyalty demands were made of civil servants and the employees of government enterprises, with "retooling"—demotion or pensioning off—as the penalty for suspected disloyalty.

But the regime of 1958–1961 was by no means monolithic. Although there was now virtually no legal opposition, power continued to be dispersed. Power competition between the President and the Nasution-led group of army leaders was particularly important in giving the system flexibility, for several other groups could exercise influence by virtue of their ability to throw support to either side. Authoritarian measures which would work to the advantage of the army were frequently countermanded by the President, and those which would tilt the balance far in favor of the President were often forestalled or whittled down by the army. Moreover, an active contest existed throughout this period for the succession to Soekarno. Political articulation had certainly lost its earlier open character; much existing dissatisfaction could not be expressed; and a number of groups had their channels of influence closed off. But most groups could still press demands with a measure of effectiveness—through party or other politicians associated with one of the new councils, through army officers, or through the civilian bureaucracy. And there was no attempt to resort to extreme forms of coercion, concentration camps, elaborate secret police organization, or isolation from the outside world.

Just as important as coercion for the government's maintenance of power under the new system was the distribution of rewards. The takeovers of Dutch enterprises provided one source of rewards, and another came as a result of the emigration of over 120,000 Chinese in 1960 and 1961, following upon the government's ban on foreigners' engaging in retail trade in rural areas. A somewhat similar effect was achieved by a general relaxation of legal restraints on powerful military and civilian officials. Regional military commanders in particular were given a very free rein—subject to political and ideological loyalty to the government in Djakarta.

Finally, legitimizing activities were accorded great importance. But whereas the earlier governments, particularly those of 1949–1953, had sought to establish a rule-based system of legitimacy, the whole emphasis of government ideology in the years after mid-1958 was on that antithesis of rules, the Revolution. Returning to the Way of the Revolution became a dominant ideological theme, and the Revolution was repeatedly declared to be still unfinished. What was now repeatedly urged was not adhering to rules or maintaining standards, but keeping the revolutionary spirit, the spirit of dynamism.

Throughout this period the President repeatedly fashioned new symbols of state, new formulations of the meaning of the present and of the goals to be sought in the future, and these immediately dominated virtually all mass communication. His central ideological theme from 1959 onward was Manipol-USDEK, Manipol standing for the Political Manifesto (President Soekarno's speech of August 17, 1959) and USDEK being an acronym summarizing the five essential points of this Manifesto: the 1945 constitution, Indonesian Socialism, Guided Democracy, Guided Economy, and Indonesian Personality or Identity.

Among his other slogans were Gotong Rojong (Mutual Help), NASAKOM (the Unity of Nationalists, Religious People, and Communists), Building the World Anew, and the Message of the Suffering of the People. Their negative counterparts were "free fight liberalism," "Dutch thinking," "textbook thinking," individualism, cosmopolitanism, conservatism, and reformism. Through these symbols and slogans emotional links were forged between the President and various segments of the people, chiefly some men of the "expressive politics" group of the political public, who responded to the radical and revolutionary symbols and often the nativistic ones, but also some outside the political public, who were attracted especially by the symbols of traditional culture.[54]

One other way in which the governments of the 1958–1961 period legitimized themselves was by acquiring the insignia of national power and prestige. They began the building of a steel plant. They acquired an atomic reactor. They bought a cruiser and destroyers and TU-16 long-range bombers. They devoted great resources to building the stadia and hotels which would enable them to be host to the Asian Games of 1962. Their foreign policy was intensely and flamboyantly active, the President making frequent trips abroad and receiving large numbers of foreign heads of state in Indonesia. Moreover, they pressed the issue of West Irian with the greatest vigor, breaking off diplomatic relations with the Netherlands in August 1960 and subsequently refusing to accept the U.K. ambassador as a representative of the Dutch crown.

Whereas the governments of the earlier period had spoken a great deal of their efforts to solve practical problems, attempting to justify themselves on the basis of their performance in these areas, the stress after mid-1958 was not on assessed performance, but on perceived image. In particular it was on identification with a person and his values and with symbols of national culture and national prestige. Whereas the earlier governments had sought to base their power primarily on the "generally interested" segment of the political public, this segment was subsequently paid little attention. Conversely,

[54] For stimulating discussions see J. M. van der Kroef, "Javanese Messianic Expectations: Their Origin and Cultural Context," *Comparative Studies in Society and History*, I, no. 4 (June 1959), 299–323, and Moehammad Slamet, *Kembali Kepribadian Bangsa Indonesia* ("Returning to the Indonesian National Identity") and (with Bushar Muhammad) *Sekali Lagi Mengenai Kepribadian Bangsa Indonesia* ("More on the Indonesian National Identity"; both Bandung: Social Research Centre, Padjadjaran State University, 1960).

whereas the governments of 1949–1957 had tended to ignore expressive politics, allowing it to frustrate them or to devour itself in ideological conflict between parties, the later governments were able firstly to deny it outlets and secondly to manipulate and channel it themselves, providing targets for aggression—the Dutch, the Chinese, the PRRI, and occasionally the Americans—and crisis situations affording a rationale for anxiety.

Thus the political system of 1958–1961 solved a number of the problems of malfunctioning of the system of 1949–1957. Political unrest was no longer a threat to governments. The consensus problem had been made manageable by the incapacitation of the Masjumi and the decreed ending of argument about the constitution. Centrifugalism was checked by an unacknowledged *de facto* federalism operating through the regional military commanders. And there was a good deal of stability in top-level political relationships, despite recurring rumors of impending drastic change.

On the other hand, there was little achievement in the years between 1958 and 1961 in administrative and economic policy. It is true that stronger government made it possible to push through certain policies which had theretofore been countermanded by sectional pressures. Thus strike activity was reduced to insignificant proportions. Squatters were evicted from estate, forest, and urban land in significant numbers. And, with the *pamong pradja* restored to some of its earlier influence, much of rural administration appeared to have become more efficient. In addition, party conflict was no longer an important obstacle to effective administration.

But these advantages were outweighed by other effects of the political transformation. Administrative and economic efficiency suffered particularly from the immense importance attached to state ideology in this period and from the fact that the ideology seemed to minimize the importance of routine activity and the solving of practical problems. This was a period of "solidarity maker" dominance of government, and so administrative and economic efficiency was poorly rewarded. Many of the country's most efficient people were excluded from positions of influence and others had to work with the greatest caution, lest their decisions should appear to be in conflict with the state ideology.

Export production fell rapidly in these years, as did the production of some other goods, and inflation progressed at a far more rapid rate than in the earlier period, bringing speculation, bottlenecks, and corruption with it. The problem of proliferating controls became a much-increased source of inefficiency and prevented success in the government's efforts to regulate the distribution of various goods. Most of the immediate administrative and economic problems arising from the take-overs of Dutch enterprises and the PRRI rebellion were adequately overcome, and a start was made with a number of new developmental projects forming part of the Eight-Year Overall Development Plan (1961–1968). But arbitrariness and the absence of fixed rules remained a major barrier to effective performance of tasks in a large area of administration and the economy.

THE ABANDONMENT OF CONSTITUTIONAL DEMOCRACY

Why, then, did the political system change from what had existed up to the middle of 1956 to what had been brought into being by the middle of 1958? What were the factors which produced a transformation of the earlier system of government and politics? What was it that led to the abandonment of constitutional democracy, its abandonment or overthrow, abdication or disintegration—it was in some measure all of these—in short, its failure?

The question can perhaps be answered most readily in terms of political dissatisfaction and its use and manipulation by those interested in structural change. The 1949–1957 period was one of high and rising political unrest. This unrest could be blamed on the existing party and parliamentary system. And forces existed which could present themselves to certain crucially important groups as capable of constructing a preferable alternative system. Each of these three statements will now be examined further.

Political dissatisfaction was indeed widespread and intense throughout the period of this study. It was particularly manifest in 1956, when it became apparent that the expectations of improvement after the elections were not to be realized and when parties lost much of their earlier role of channeling the energies of political protesters. But the volume of unrest was high from 1949 onward and showed an over-all tendency to rise. Its effects could be seen in urban mob politics, in denunciations of "Djakarta" and of selfishness, corruption, faction, falsehood, temporizing, and weakness in "the leaders," and in the ready responses accruing to radical appeals of most kinds, especially radical nationalist ones.

This general dissatisfaction can be seen as reflecting a discrepancy between what government and society were expected to provide and

what they did. In the Indonesia of our period three types of expectations were high, in each case a result both of the social change of the
past (particularly of the Japanese occupation and the Revolution, although the history of the preparatory hollowing out of social structures goes back very much further) and of the ongoing change of the
present.

Material expectations comprise the first type. As we saw in our
earlier discussion of domestic demand, Indonesia's economic system
was expected to produce a rapidly expanding volume of goods and
services throughout the 1949–1957 period—this as a result partly of
population growth but more particularly of increases in the number of
the "mobilized," those who have stepped out of their traditional society
as a result of schooling, urbanization, travel, associational membership,
newspaper reading, or, usually, a combination of these. Rice and fish,
margarine and corned beef, bicycles, kerosene lamps, pencils, automobiles, cameras, and radios, all of these were being demanded in
quickly growing quantities. Similarly the economy was expected to
provide satisfactory work for a rapidly increasing number of persons
whose training had led them to seek modern employment.

This leads immediately to the second type of expectation, that of
increased social status. Those who sought modern employment were
insistent that this should also be prestigeful; they wanted to be white-
collar workers, not mechanics. Moreover, the whole phenomenon of
expanding consumer demand was in large part social; the welfare
effects which followed from increased consumption were usually
valued less than its effects in raising prestige. What had happened to
Indonesian society in the years after 1942 had destroyed a great variety
of social barriers, spreading the idea that the peaks of social status were
scalable by the able and stimulating vast new status ambitions. After
1949 the same process went on, furthered by the egalitarian nationalist
ideology and by the absence of much governmental effort to shore up
what remained of the older status barriers. Thus more and more men
of humble origin now wanted to be part of the white-collar strata of
society. And of those who had gained their white collars large numbers aspired to be "leaders," men of influence, but above all of status,
in politics, administration, or social life generally. As nineteenth-century
Englishmen read popular tracts on *Self Help* and *Money* and twentieth-
century Americans books like *How to Make Friends and Influence
People*, so Indonesians of our period read booklets on How to Become a Leader. Indonesian society was expected to create a great

number of white-collar positions and many "leadership" roles as well.

Finally, there was a psychological dimension to expectations. With society changing so rapidly values were thrown into confusion. With old status barriers destroyed or in process of crumbling, many became uncertain of their place in society, and thus uncertain about the moral norms to which they should adhere. Should a man adopt the values of his father in the village from which he came or those of his brother in the student and journalist world of the city? Should he accept the *abangan* values of his own background or the *santri* values of the family into which free-choice marriage had thrown him? The dilemmas were not easily resolved or disposed of. They were all the more painful by contrast with the days of the Revolution, when one's goals had been clearer and one's moral commitment more intense.

Many of those whose lives had been most strongly affected by social change were actively looking for an authority from which moral imperatives would come clearly and meaningfully. Since most of these men had perceived sacredness in political authority in the years of Revolution, it was to political leadership that most of them looked for the meaning and certainty they sought in the postrevolutionary situation. Some of them found this through active membership in a political party. But this could be only a partial solution while the parties were fighting one another, for none had succeeded in imposing its values on society as a whole. Hence many of those who sought to have authoritative sanctions for their values demanded these from government.

Thus the governments of the period were not only expected to provide expanding income and rising social status for many. They were also expected to provide a large number with the integrative leadership which is usually characteristic of an organic state (or a pluralistic one in times of war).

The fact that there was so much political unrest throughout the period makes it clear that they failed to come up to the level of expectations. It is not that they failed in any absolute sense, that their performance was in some objective sense poor with regard to the creation of wealth, the distribution of prestige, or the provision of meaningful images of leadership. It was rather that the effectiveness of their performance in these three areas taken as a whole was low in relation to the existing level of expectations.

This is one important aspect of the failure of the governments of 1949–1957, and its affords a partial explanation of the abandonment of the political system of those years. With the volume of unrest persistently great, there was always potential support for those who sought radical political change.

But political unrest alone does not explain enough. In particular it fails to explain why the system was abandoned, or overthrown, when it was rather than earlier—why indeed could constitutional democracy survive for as long as it did? It also fails to account for the character and direction of the change—why was it that "liberal democracy" could be made the chief focus of condemnation and guided democracy, as symbol and system, the accepted alternative?

When it is asked why constitutional democracy was able to last as long as it did, one comes immediately to the difficulties which faced any attempt to bring about structural change. The problem was partly one of inertia. Once the 1949–1957 system had been in operation for some time, most groups in society had worked out ways of furthering their interests with at least minimal satisfaction within it, and the prospect of a radical structural change, a change in the whole political order, was fraught with imponderabilities, some of them severely threatening to each group. Moreover, power was widely dispersed, with no state party in existence, no candidate state party apart from the PKI, and an army which generally lacked cohesion. Therefore a very large number of groups and individuals had to be persuaded of the desirability of political changes before they could be effected.

In addition, there was active rivalry between the forces which were in a position to effect major changes in the political order, principally the army and segments of it and President Soekarno. Thus any move by one group that could lead to a type of structural change from which this group would benefit tended to unite other groups in defense of the existing arrangements.

Perhaps the most important reason why the system was abandoned when it was, is related to consensus on the purposes of government. The very fact that the struggle for independence was over meant that attention would in our period become focused on internal differences of political values. Moreover, history has left Indonesia with a "mixed political culture"; views of what government should be and should do are markedly different in different ethnic groups and different social segments of these groups. For large parts of the groups concerned, these orientations to politics were latent in 1949, but the rapid expansion of mass communications of subsequent years was likely to make them much less so by heightening group consciousness in each of the potentially distinct communities.

In circumstances like these, free competition between ideologically based parties was fraught with danger. The possibility was always there that intensified ideological conflict would threaten the basic consensus which is required for a pluralistic and largely coercion-free politics, that leaders of one major ideological party would come to feel incapable of either sharing power or alternating in power with leaders of another major ideological party without betraying their own values and their own supporters. Thus divisions might grow to be so deep, in both the political elite and society at large, as to make it impossible for the government to keep effective control over the whole country.

As a result of the long election campaign, and of the high level of unsatisfied demands fed into this campaign, the disruption of consensus approached this point. Latent value conflicts between different social and ethnic groups became open ideological battles. The civil service became torn by many of the same antagonisms, and particularly by the central antagonism between the PNI-led group of parties and the Masjumi-led group. The army was divided along parallel lines. And by the time that the two campaign-period cabinets had done their work there was virtually no agency of state which stood above the partisan conflict. Furthermore, when the attempt was made after the elections to compose the central conflict by bringing the chief protagonists into a coalition cabinet, the result was hamstrung government, buffeted about by recurring explosions of political unrest.

To many elite persons, men who had theretofore seen their interests as adequately safeguarded by the current system of politics, the 1956 situation appeared threatening. And the threat seemed all the greater as these men looked at the results of the elections; for they could not but note that the PNI-led group of parties appealed chiefly to Java and the Javanese and the Masjumi-led group of parties to the people of the Outer Islands and West Java. Thus not only did chaos and communism come into their field of vision but also secession and civil war. The result was to make many of them see the unrestricted propagation of sectional demands and symbols as posing a real danger to their positions. These men thus became active supporters of moves toward a more coercive and restrictive form of government, seeing such government as the only possible means by which the newly sharpened divisions in the polity could be held in check.

One further factor important for the timing of the big change was the reappointment of Colonel Nasution as Army Chief of Staff. Rivalry between the President and the leaders of the army was an important factor buttressing constitutional democracy for most of the period of this study. But after the reappointment of Colonel Nasution to the post of Army Chief of Staff in October 1955, the central army leadership was prepared to co-operate with the President. Here existed an alignment of forces which could conceivably change the whole political order. The army leaders could contribute organized power and the prestige which the army enjoyed as a founder of the state. The President could contribute legitimacy. His status as the Czar and Lenin in one person, the fact that he had proclaimed the Republic and been its head of state ever since, surviving all changes of cabinet—this gave him enormous power in a situation in which a major change of the political order was being attempted. And his power was all the greater because of his personal skills of political perception and communication. His formula of guided democracy, or democracy with leadership, would appear to have been a particularly sensitive clustering of symbols, linking as it did the most desired element of the existing order, democracy, with what was most acutely missed in it, leadership.

But precisely because this alliance was so formidable, it evoked the strongest hostility from other groups, especially from the officers and civilian politicians who came to lead the regionalist movement. Thus for eighteen months there was deadlock between a new pair of rivals for the heirship to the existing political order, the Soekarno-Nasution alliance on the one hand (supported by the PKI) and the regionalist movement on the other. This was, however, an uneven balance, and the deadlock was eventually resolved when the core of the regionalist movement was destroyed by military action. By the time that the PRRI revolt had been crushed, the old problem of amassing enough power to establish an alternative to constitutional democracy had worked itself out.

But why was it that the trend away from constitutional democracy took the direction that it did? The question is partly answered in the foregoing discussion of alignments in the crucial years of structural transition between 1956 and 1958. The political system which was established by the middle of 1958 was thus a product of interaction between the President and the Nasution-led group of army officers, with the President providing the ideology and the army the machinery of coercive authority.

But in another sense the direction of change must be seen as a reflection of prevailing values in the political public, and to some extent of values outside it. In this sense the question to be answered is, why was it that President Soekarno's condemnation of "liberal democracy" and the existing party system fell on such fertile ground? One should be careful not to exaggerate the importance of this aspect of the change. For it is a fact that the regionalists' negative symbols of "Djakarta" and "the center" were for some time serious rivals of the President's "liberal democracy" and "the party system" as magnets for existing political dissatisfaction, the issue being finally settled by force of arms. Nevertheless, it is undeniable that the President's appeals had very widespread support. Indeed, they were to some extent taken over by the regionalists themselves. And there were very few passionate defenses of the institutions or principles of constitutional democracy in reply.[55]

The power of "liberal democracy" as a focus for dissatisfactions reflected the fact that there had never been widespread commitment to the basic ideas of constitutional democracy. It reflected the feeling of many in the political elite that parliamentary procedures and elections were sham and pretense. In addition, it reflected a sense of accumulated frustration, the feeling which was widespread in the political elite that "we have tried hard to work by these rules, but it just won't work." It reflected the perception which existed in a wider group that the political world was changing and that one should adapt oneself to new situations as they appeared, in order to be "attuned to the Cosmos."[56] It reflected traditional values, in that the importance of social harmony is strongly stressed in virtually all the traditional societies of Indonesia. And it also reflected the effects of social change, in that this had contributed to the craving of many in the political public for an organic meaning-providing state.

Finally, the great appeal of opposition to "liberal democracy" was a reflection of the political public's deep hostility toward the Netherlands in particular and the West generally. Expression of this hostility had been restrained in earlier years by the fact that pro-Western leaders

[55] The most important of the defenses were made by Natsir and Hatta. For Natsir's views see *Keng Po*, Jan. 19, 1957, and *Abadi*, March 1, 4, 8, 1957. See also Deliar Noer, "Masjumi: Its Organization, Ideology and Political Role in Indonesia" (M.A. thesis, Cornell University, 1960). Hatta's position is presented in his "Membahas Konsepsi Bung Karno" ("A Consideration of Bung Karno's Conception"), *Indonesia Raya*, March 5, 1957.

[56] "Attuned to the Cosmos" was the title of President Soekarno's Independence Day address of 1954. The idea is one of great importance in the Javanese religious tradition.

had been in control of government (particularly in the years before 1953).[57] But its importance as a focus for political dissatisfaction and unrest was very great, as result of the whole of the colonial relationship of the past, of the power which Dutch business continued to wield after 1949, of the continuing sense of shame at the country's "backwardness," and of the feeling that Indonesia was failing in its efforts to overcome this "backwardness" rapidly. One aspect of this anti-Westernism was a sense of revolt against a political morality felt to have been imposed by the West (and India). Another aspect was hostility to leaders regarded as pro-Western, including men like Hatta, Natsir, and Sjahrir who were closely identified with "liberal democracy."[58]

Having separated out the four main parts of the process by which constitutional democracy was abandoned—the high and rising level of political unrest, the effects of this in disrupting consensus on the purposes of government, the realignment of would-be heirs to the existing system, and the fact that political unrest could readily be channeled against "liberal democracy"—we may now recapitulate the argument of the study as a whole. It may be said that the history of the period is the story of the political failure of the Hatta group of leaders, a generally Western-oriented group who were in power in 1949 partly because Indonesia had needed to seek Western diplomatic support in order to win its independence at the minimum cost and who subsequently fell from power. Among this group there were some with value commitments to constitutional democracy, and most had commitments of interest. The group had preponderant influence on government in the three and a half years after December 1949. As an "administrator" group and one with ties to nonbureaucratic business, they wanted to conserve most of what colonialism had left in the way of a modern administrative and economic structure. And thus they attempted in those years to solve basic problems of administrative and military reorganization and of economic restoration, stimulation, and develop-

---

[57] For a discussion of this type of restraining factor see W. Howard Wriggins, *Ceylon: Dilemmas of a New Nation* (Princeton, N.J.: Princeton University Press, 1960), pp. 463–465.

[58] The President and his supporters frequently said in 1956 and 1957 that the root of Indonesia's political ills lay in the decision of Nov. 1945 to abandon the 1945 constitution, to change from a presidential to a parliamentary cabinet, and to call political parties into existence. Hatta and Sjahrir were the persons most prominently involved in the introduction of these changes. See George McT. Kahin, *Nationalism and Revolution in Indonesia* (Ithaca, N.Y.: Cornell University Press, 1952), pp. 153–155.

ment. Had they solved these problems and succeeded at the same time in keeping the support of predominant segments of the political public, they might have fashioned a new rule-based politics of which they themselves would have been the principal beneficiaries. They might have stabilized the postrevolutionary situation, establishing order on the basis of firm controls and transforming the legitimacy system by gradually developing rule-based popular choice as a major part of the process by which power holders acquire moral authority. And they might have succeeded in establishing and maintaining a basis of elite consensus within which party competition could operate without damaging effects on social cohesion.

But they failed. The property basis of their power was always weak. And the military basis of it, the fact that their supporters had preponderant control over the army, was to be proved destructible. Yet they attempted to implement policies which aroused strong hostility against them. Concerned for legality, for maximum production and fiscal stability, they defended the continued prominence of Dutch capital in the country. In so doing they ran afoul of general nationalist sentiment, and specifically of the powerful drive of a large part of the political elite for control of the means of producing wealth. Moreover, their efforts at routinization were widely resented. By insisting that administrative and economic affairs be managed on the basis of autonomous norms of each of these spheres, rather than of overriding political norms, they antagonized a powerful group of former revolutionaries, the men who stood to lose wherever appointments were made or credits dispensed on the basis of training or ability to perform specified tasks, rather than on the basis of services to the cause of the Revolution. And they antagonized many of the same men by their effort to make the whole process of government rule-based; for the ex-revolutionaries demanded that the state should have momentum and *mystique*. For all of these reasons the Hatta group were eventually overwhelmed by opposition. In the middle of 1953 they were forced out of government power.

They were replaced by a group of men who were not only far less fully committed to parliamentary democracy but also less inclined to grapple with the manifestly difficult tasks of strengthening controls, order, rules, and functional differentiation in a situation dominated by political unrest, exhortation, messianic ferment, and expressive politics. The earlier effort to lay down basic conditions for constitutional government was relaxed, alongside the earlier effort to maximize production and ward off inflation. Thenceforth cabinets concerned themselves less with the control of political ferment and more with its manipulation, less with the enforcement of law and more with the fashioning of ideology. In one sense a stop had already been put to the effort to operate parliamentary government, although more than three years were to elapse before there would be an ideological abandonment of the system. The developments of these three years, and in particular the course of electioneering, which projected sharp ideological conflict onto large areas of society, were an important cause of the system's decline and abandonment. But the severest blows had been dealt it as early as 1953, when the control-oriented and resolutely problem-solving Wilopo cabinet was overthrown. The group of leaders who had held power before 1953 could not make more than a momentary political comeback in the subsequent years. And most of them were politically incapacitated by 1958.

If any single set of factors can account for the failure of the Indonesian effort to operate constitutional democracy, it is the factors related to political unrest. The revolutionary transition to independence had created a great deal of political unrest. This was of major importance in thwarting the group of leaders who were in power before 1953 and again in producing the final abandonment of constitutional democracy in 1956–1957.

Thus the central issue of our period, both for the general power struggle and for constitutional democracy, was how this unrest would be handled. Would governments attempt to control unrest, and ultimately to draw its sting by increases in production? Or would they attempt rather to channel and manipulate it, using it to reorganize society along more "national" and "revolutionary" lines? The former was the course of action compatible with constitutional democracy. It was the logical course of action for "administrators," for nonbureaucratic business groups, and for all others with an interest in maintaining and developing the modern and differentiated administrative and economic structures which were part of the colonial legacy. But "solidarity makers" would benefit more by the latter course of action, and so would many others, notably those favorably placed politicians, officers, and civil servants who stood to gain from a more complete political domination of the economy and the rest of society.

On the one hand were men like Roeslan Abdulgani who wrote of "the necessity of deliberately allowing and encouraging the instability of society. . . . We welcome this social instability because it provides the opportunity for progress. Progress positively demands an element of instability and even of risk." [59]

On the other hand, there were men like Professor Sumitro Djojohadi-kusumo who wrote that "under the particular conditions of social change in a newly emerging nation, where the cultural values are going through a process of *Umwertung aller Werte* a prime task of the . . . political leadership is the establishment of a climate conducive to the application of generally accepted standards." [60]

The issue was usually summed up in terms of the question, is the Revolution to be considered completed? In the words of the editor of *Pedoman:* "One side has been saying that our Revolution is not yet completed and therefore we do not need to bother sticking too closely to formalism and legalism. But there is also another side saying that it is now more than time that we started thinking about affairs of state in terms of concepts like law and order, so that our ideals for the people's livelihood can be quickly realized." [61]

But the foremost speakers in this Great Debate were Soekarno and Hatta. In the words of Soekarno in 1960:

The activities of the Revolution go on. . . . "For a fighting nation there is no journey's end." . . . I am one of the people who is in love with the Romanticism of Revolution, I am inspired by it, I am fascinated by it. . . . The Logic of Revolution is that, having once sparked off the Revolution, we must go through with it until all of its ideals have been realized. . . . There are people who ask "Do we have to keep stirring up the spirit of Revolution? . . . Can't we work a bit more patiently, slowly but surely?" Heavens! Slowly but surely is impossible. Impossible unless we want to be crushed by the People. . . . The People's Awareness demands that every unjust situation or relationship be torn down and changed . . . changed fast and in a revolutionary way. If it is not the new Awareness will produce an explosion. . . . The world of today is a tinderbox of Revolution.[62]

Hatta presented the opposite point of view in an address he gave on November 27, 1956, immediately before his resignation from the vice-presidency:

[59] Roeslan Abdulgani, "Indonesia's National Council: The First Year," pp. 98, 103.

[60] D. Sumitro, *Searchlight on Indonesia* (n.p., 1959), p. 59.

[61] *Pedoman*, Dec. 31, 1955.

[62] Departemen Penerangan, *Haluan Politik dan Pembangunan Negara* ("The Course of the State in Politics and Upbuilding"; Djakarta: Departemen Peneran-gan, 1961), pp. 98–99.

A thorough-going social analysis would show that all our rebellions and our splits, our political anarchy and adventurism, and all the steps taken in the economic field which have created chaos, are the result of the fact that our national Revolution was not dammed up at the appropriate time. Those who say that our national Revolution is not completed are wrong indeed. A Revolution is a sudden explosion of society. . . . A Revolution shakes the floor and the foundations and loosens all hinges and boards. Therefore a Revolution should not last too long, not more than a few weeks or a few months. It should then be checked; the time will then have arrived for a consolidation which will realize the results produced by the Revolution. What is left unfinished is not the Revolution itself, but the efforts to carry its ideals into effect over a period of time after the foundations have been laid.[63]

In the last analysis constitutional democracy was defeated by the way in which the contest between these two views was resolved. The effort to establish constitutional democracy was made by one segment of the political elite, by those who wanted to "dam up the Revolution." The men who attempted to build a rule-based politics were the same group who sought to deal with political unrest by controls, who wanted to develop an efficient and somewhat nonpolitical administration and army, to raise production fast, and to ensure the continued autonomy of nonbureaucratic business. But this group lost out in the battle for power. Their power resources were always relatively small, and much of what they attempted to achieve aroused strong hostility against them. Thus their rivals were able to use and fan political unrest against them. Both the battle itself and its outcome were important in bringing about an end to constitutional democracy. Neither a rule-based politics nor a largely coercion-free government could be maintained for long in the face of persistent, and persistently restimulated, revolutionary ferment.

---

[63] Mohammad Hatta, *Past and Future* (Cornell Modern Indonesia Project, Translation Series; Ithaca, N.Y., 1960), p. 15.

INDEX